OCR Classical Civilisation

GCSE

ROUTE 1

ALSO AVAILABLE FROM BLOOMSBURY

OCR Classical Civilisation GCSE Route 2: Women in the Ancient World,
Robert Hancock-Jones, Dan Menashe and James Renshaw

OCR Classical Civilisation AS and A Level Component 11: The World of the Hero, Sally Knights

OCR Classical Civilisation AS and A Level Components 21 and 22: Greek Theatre and Imperial Image,
Robert Hancock-Jones, James Renshaw and Laura Swift

OCR Classical Civilisation A Level Components 23 and 24: Invention of the Barbarian and Greek Art,
Athina Mitropoulos, Laura Snook and Alastair Thorley

OCR Classical Civilisation A Level Components 31 and 34: Greek Religion and Democracy and the Athenians,
Athina Mitropoulos, Tim Morrison, James Renshaw and Julietta Steinhauer

*OCR Classical Civilisation A Level Components 32 and 33:
Love and Relationships and Politics of the Late Republic*,
Matthew Barr, Lucy Cresswell and Alastair Thorley

OCR Ancient History GCSE Component 1: Greece and Persia,
Sam Baddeley, Paul Fowler, Lucy Nicholas and James Renshaw

OCR Ancient History GCSE Component 2: Rome,
Paul Fowler, Christopher Grocock and James Melville

OCR Ancient History AS and A Level Component 1: Greece,
Charlie Cottam, David L. S. Hodgkinson, Steve Matthews, Lucy Nicholas and James Renshaw

OCR Ancient History AS and A Level Component 2: Rome,
Robert Cromarty, James Harrison and Steve Matthews

Books published for the OCR specifications in GCSE and AS / A Level Latin and Classical Greek are
also available, including editions of every set text for A Level. Please see our website
www.bloomsbury.com/uk/education/secondary/classics

OCR Classical Civilisation

GCSE

ROUTE 1:
Myth and Religion

BEN GREENLEY
DAN MENASHE
JAMES RENSHAW

GENERAL EDITOR:
JAMES RENSHAW

BLOOMSBURY ACADEMIC
LONDON · NEW YORK · OXFORD · NEW DELHI · SYDNEY

BLOOMSBURY ACADEMIC
Bloomsbury Publishing Plc
50 Bedford Square, London, WC1B 3DP, UK
1385 Broadway, New York, NY 10018, USA
29 Earlsfort Terrace, Dublin 2, Ireland

BLOOMSBURY, BLOOMSBURY ACADEMIC and the Diana logo are trademarks
of Bloomsbury Publishing Plc
First published in Great Britain 2017
Reprinted 2017, 2018 (twice), 2019 (twice), 2021, 2022, 2023, 2024

Cover design by Terry Woodley and Olivia D'Cruz
Cover image © Getty/Universal History Archive

A catalogue record for this book is available from the British Library.

A catalogue record for this book is available from the Library of Congress.

ISBN: PB: 978-1-3500-1487-9
       ePDF: 978-1-3500-1489-3
       ePub: 978-1-3500-1488-6

Typeset by RefineCatch Limited, Bungay, Suffolk
Printed and bound in India

To find out more about our authors and books visit www.bloomsbury.com
and sign up for our newsletters

ACKNOWLEDGEMENTS

The authors divided the text between them as follows:

'Myth and Religion' by Ben Greenley
'The Homeric World' by Dan Menashe
'Roman City Life' and 'War and Warfare' by James Renshaw.

The authors would like to thank the many anonymous reviewers at universities, schools
and OCR who read and commented on drafts of this text. All errors remain their own.

CONTENTS

INTRODUCTION

Welcome to your textbook for OCR GCSE Classical Civilisation.

This book has been created to support the new OCR GCSE (9–1) specification with the Thematic Study option 'Myth and Religion'. You will study this section followed by a choice of one out of the three Literature and Culture sections, 'The Homeric World', 'Roman City Life' and 'War and Warfare'.

Through your reading of this textbook and your wider study in class, you will be able to gain a broad knowledge and understanding of a range of literary and cultural materials from the classical world. As well as learning about the culture, history and ideas of the ancient Greeks and Romans, you will read ancient texts in translation and study ancient art and objects from the classical world, together with the surviving remains of religious and domestic architecture.

The specification requires you to respond to the prescribed source material and assess content through analysis and evaluation. The box features (see pp. x–xi) are designed to build up your skills and knowledge, while exam tips, practice questions, and chapters on assessment will prepare you for taking your final examinations.

A Companion Website, available at www.bloomsbury.com/class-civ-gcse, supports this textbook with further information, resources and updates. If you have any suggestions for improvement and additional resources please get in touch by writing to contact@bloomsbury.com.

We hope you will enjoy this wide-ranging and fascinating GCSE course, and that it will inspire you to go on to further study of the ancient world.

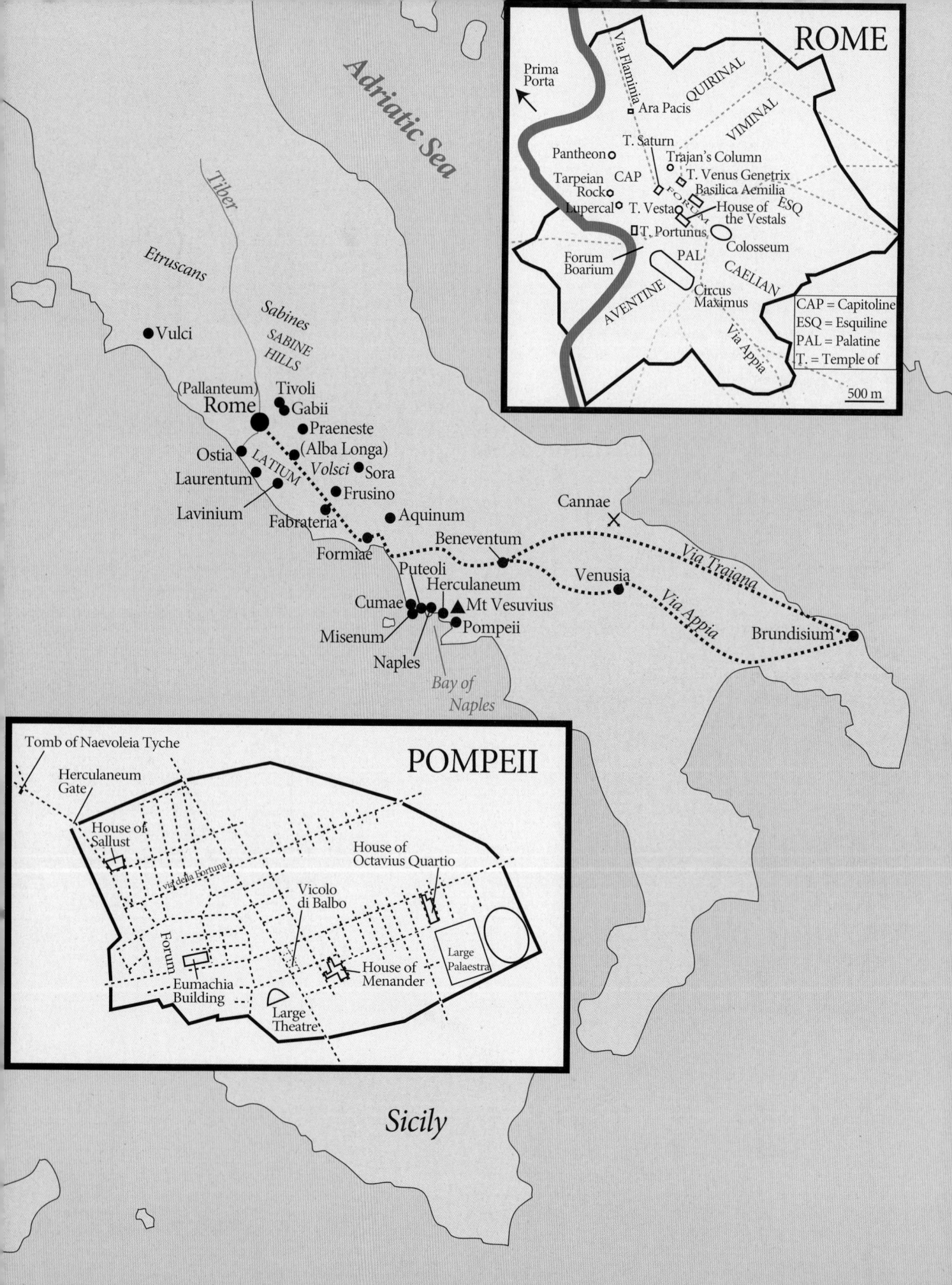

ROME

Prima Porta

Via Flaminia

QUIRINAL

VIMINAL

Ara Pacis

T. Saturn

Pantheon

Trajan's Column

Tarpeian Rock

CAP

T. Venus Genetrix

Basilica Aemilia

Lupercal

T. Vesta

House of the Vestals

ESQ

T. Portunus

Colosseum

Forum Boarium

PAL

CAELIAN

AVENTINE

Circus Maximus

Via Appia

CAP = Capitoline
ESQ = Esquiline
PAL = Palatine
T. = Temple of

500 m

Adriatic Sea

Tiber

Etruscans

• Vulci

Sabines

SABINE HILLS

(Pallanteum)

Tivoli

Rome

Gabii

Praeneste

Ostia

LATIUM

(Alba Longa)

Laurentum

Volsci

Sora

Lavinium

Frusino

Fabrateria

Aquinum

Cannae ✕

Formiae

Beneventum

Via Traiana

Puteoli

Herculaneum

Venusia

Via Appia

Cumae

▲ Mt Vesuvius

Misenum

Pompeii

Brundisium

Naples

Bay of Naples

POMPEII

Tomb of Naevoleia Tyche

Herculaneum Gate

House of Sallust

via della Fortuna

House of Octavius Quartio

Vicolo di Balbo

Forum

Large Palaestra

Eumachia Building

House of Menander

Large Theatre

Sicily

GAUL

Comum
Padua
Forum Iulii

Dacians

Danube

Black Sea

(Colchis)

THRACE

(Amazons)

BITHYNIA
PONTUS

ASIA   Persians   PARTHIA
MINOR   Hittites   Tarsus

MAGNA
GRAECIA

Carthage

Knossos   Ulu Burun

Crete

Mediterranean Sea

Alexandria

Nile

EGYPT

ATHENS

Kerameikos

Panathenaic Way

Bouleuterion   Agora

Areopagus   Erechtheion

Pnyx   Parthenon

Acropolis   Theatre of
Dionysus

Long Walls   Sanctuary of
Dionysus

Temple of
Athena Nike

Philippi ✕

Hellespont

MACEDON

Hisarlik (Troy)

▲ Mt Olympus

THESSALY

Cape
Artemisium

(Lapiths)

Aegean Sea

Actium ✕

Thermopylae ✕

Delphi

Thebes   Eleusis

Plataea   ATTICA ✕ Marathon

Ithaca   Patras   Megara   Brauron

ELIS   Corinth   *Salamis*   Athens

Olympia   Argos   Mycenae

Pisa   Mantinea   Dendra

✕   Tiryns   Troezen

Bassae   Epidauros

Pylos   MESSENIA   Sparta

Naxos

LACONIA

Miletus

Akrotiri

Santorini

(Taenarus)

PELOPONNESE

HOW TO USE THIS BOOK

The layout design and box features of this book are designed to aid your learning.

COLOUR

Box features that focus on assessment preparation and exam skills are coloured in blue.

Box features with Stretch and Challenge material are coloured in yellow.

All other box features are coloured in red.

ICONS

The Prescribed Source icon **PS** flags a quotation or image that is a source prescribed in the specification.

The Stretch and Challenge icon **S&C** indicates that an exercise extends beyond the core content of the specification.

The Companion Website icon **CW** highlights where extra material can be found on the Bloomsbury Companion Website www.bloomsbury.com/class-civ-gcse.

BOX FEATURES

In the margins you will find feature boxes giving short factfiles of key events, individuals and places.

Other features either **recommend** teaching material or highlight **prescribed** content and **assessment** tips and information.

Recommended teaching material is found in the following box features:

Activities
Debates
Explore Further
Further Reading
Modern Parallels
Study Questions
Topic Reviews

Prescribed content and assessment-focused tips and information are found in the following box features:

Exam Overviews
Exam Tips
Practice Questions
Prescribed Sources

Material that extends beyond the specification is found in the Stretch and Challenge box features. Remember that the specification requires students to study extra sources and material not listed in the specification, so S&C information and exercises will provide a good place for you to start.

A NOTE ON QUESTIONS

Discussion prompts found in Topic Review boxes and Study Question boxes are not worded in the form you will find on the exam papers. They are intended to encourage investigation and revision of the material, but do not reflect the questions you will answer in the exam. Practice Questions at the end of each topic, and the questions found in the 'What to Expect in the Exam' sections do mirror the format and wording you will encounter in the exam.

GLOSSARY

At the back of the book you will find a full glossary of key words. These words are also defined on pages in margin features.

Spellings of names and texts are formatted in line with the OCR specification.

On the Companion Website you will find a colour-coded glossary that highlights which components the words come from.

IMAGES

Illustrations give you the opportunity to see the ancient visual material you are required to study. Images of the prescribed visual/material sources are flagged with the **PS** icon, but other images illustrate other relevant aspects of the ancient world. Often what survives from the ancient world does not provide us with ways to illustrate what we study. Thus, art, drawings and reconstructions from later periods and the modern day may be used to illustrate this book. Don't forget that these are not sources like your prescribed texts and visual material – they are later interpretations of aspects of antiquity and do not represent evidence for analysis.

TRANSLATIONS

If not otherwise specified, translations are copyright OCR. Documents of translations covering the prescribed sources for each component are available from the OCR website and include OCR and other translations of the texts.

COMPANION WEBSITE

Resources will include:

- links to the text of Prescribed Literary Sources
- further images and information on Prescribed Visual/Material Sources
- annotated further reading
- links to websites that give useful contextual material for study
- quizzes on key topics and themes
- worksheets to supplement Activity box features in the book

DON'T FORGET

Look out for cross references to other pages in the book – this is where you will find further information and be able to link concepts or themes.

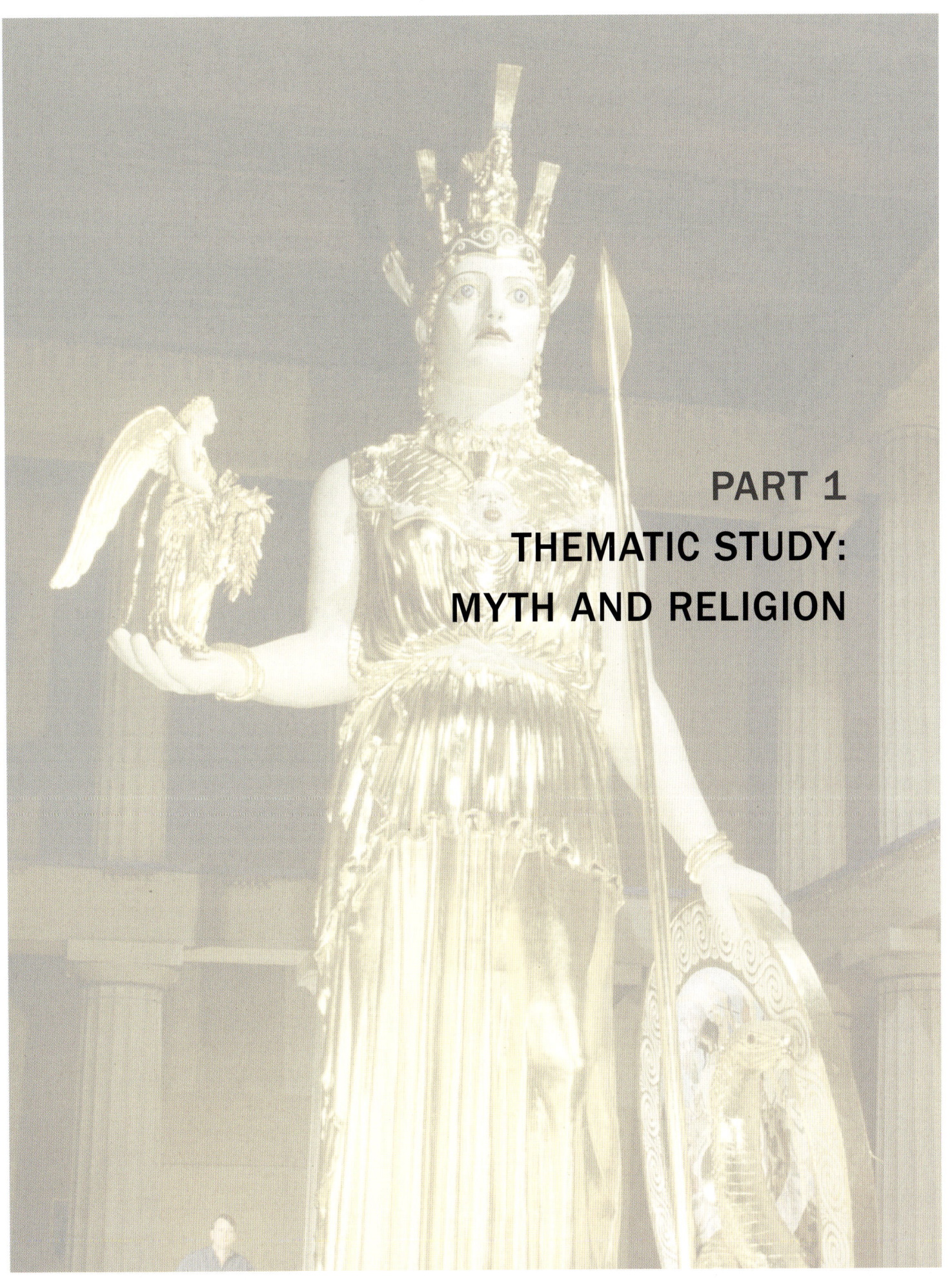

PART 1
THEMATIC STUDY:
MYTH AND RELIGION

Introduction to Myth and Religion

Half of your GCSE in Classical Civilisation involves a Thematic Study. This component provides the opportunity to study both Greece and Rome, looking at literature and visual/material culture. You will also be expected to draw informed comparisons between Roman and Greek ideas, including the characteristics of the different societies, and the impact of the different cultural contexts on the theme studied.

OCR offers the choice between two options:

Myth and Religion   J199/11
Women in the Ancient World   J199/12

This textbook includes the content for the option Myth and Religion.

EXAM OVERVIEW   **J199/11**

Your assessment for the Thematic Study option will be:

      50% of the GCSE   1 hr 30 mins   90 marks

58 marks will test AO1: demonstrate knowledge and understanding of:

- literature and visual/material culture from the classical world
- how sources reflect their cultural contexts, and
- possible interpretations of sources by different audiences and individuals.

32 marks will test AO2: analyse, interpret and evaluate literature and visual/material culture from the classical world, using evidence and producing coherent and reasoned arguments.

The Thematic paper is divided into three sections:

Section A	Greece	30 marks
Section B	Rome	30 marks
Section C	Greece and Rome	30 marks

In Section C you will be expected to draw comparisons between the two cultures.

Myth and religion have always been areas of study popular with learners, and so this exploration of religion and mythology in the ancient Greek and Roman world will surely prove to be engaging and appealing. 'Rome' here is primarily taken to mean the city of Rome, although reference may be made to other towns and cities which betray typical 'Roman' characteristics, e.g. Pompeii.

Many learners come to Classical Civilisation with a love of the mythology of the ancient world, and so this forms a central part of this thematic component. Learners will study myths regarding the role of the gods and heroes in the founding of Athens and Rome and the importance of Heracles/Hercules to both the Greek and Roman world. These are well-known stories that learners will enjoy engaging with and studying in increased depth. Myth as a symbol of power will also be explored, as will ever-popular myths about the underworld.

Learners will also look at the role of religion in the everyday lives of ancient Greeks and Romans. The study of temples, sacrifice, festivals, death and beliefs in the afterlife will give a broad overview of religion in the ancient world, and provides opportunity for the study of a wide variety of material that remains, including awe-inspiring temples and art works.

1.1 The Gods

Greek and Roman gods, their responsibilities and symbols and how they are typically represented in ancient Greek and Roman art.

Greece

- Zeus, Hera, Demeter, Poseidon, Hephaistos, Apollo, Artemis, Athena, Aphrodite, Ares, Dionysos, Hestia, Hermes and Hades

Rome

- Jupiter, Neptune, Vulcan, Mercury, Mars, Pluto, Apollo, Juno, Venus, Minerva, Diana, Bacchus, Vesta and Ceres

The prescribed source for this topic is:

- *Homeric Hymn to Demeter*, 1–104, 301–474

Don't forget that you will be given credit in the exam if you study extra sources and make relevant use of them in your answers.

---

pantheon the term given to the gods when we speak of them collectively, not to be confused with the Pantheon in Rome, which was a temple built by the Romans and dedicated to all the gods (see also p. 63)

iconography the symbols attached to a particular character when represented in an image

This topic will examine the **pantheon** of gods, focusing on the twelve Olympian gods, as well as Dionysus*/Bacchus and Hades/Pluto. The topic will explain what unique skills each of them had, and how the Greeks and Romans typically represented them in their art and literature. This can be referred to as the **iconography** of the gods.

For the comparative element of the topic you will be expected to compare and contrast the Greek and Roman gods and why certain gods would appeal to each civilisation.

* The Latinised spelling is used in this book although the specification refers to Dionysos.

INTRODUCTION TO GREEK AND ROMAN RELIGION

To the modern reader the relationship between the Greeks and Romans and their gods may seem a strange one. There are several key features to understand:

- *hiera* and *religio*
- **polytheism**
- **anthropomorphism**
- **epithets**

hiera and *religio*

While it is fully acceptable for students to use the term 'religion', the Greeks and Romans did not actually have a word for religion. Instead the Greeks used the word *hiera* 'holy affairs' and the Romans *religio* 'the correct worship of the state gods', when referring to religious acts. This is important as we should not think of Greek and Roman religion as purely based on faith. It was not enough to just believe in the gods; Greek and Roman religion was about action. They had to physically worship the gods by performing sacrifices and making offerings, either in private or public.

Polytheism

Greek and Roman religion was polytheistic (from the Greek *poly* meaning many, and *theos* meaning god) with hundreds of gods and goddesses, each with their own unique skills. In this topic we will focus on the twelve Olympians.

Anthropomorphism

The gods were anthropomorphic (from the Greek *anthrōpos* meaning human, and *morphē* meaning form). By looking and acting like humans the gods were more relatable to the Greeks and Romans, who wove the gods into stories that explained the nature of things in the world. Furthermore, it explained the relationship between the Greeks and Romans and their gods; the gods were to be honoured and revered as they could be happy or sad, generous or selfish, merciful or vengeful.

Epithets

An epithet was a word or phrase applied to the gods to describe a quality or skill they had. For example, an athlete at Olympia may swear an oath to Zeus Horkios, 'keeper of oaths', or a sailor about to embark on a journey may sacrifice to Poseidon Enosichthon, 'earth-shaker'.

> **polytheism** the belief in many gods
>
> **anthropomorphism** giving human form or attributes to something that is otherwise not human
>
> **epithet** an adjectival word or phrase regularly added to a name to denote a personal or physical quality

GREECE

There were hundreds of gods. However, the chief gods were known as the Olympians, who were believed to live on Mount Olympus. Mount Olympus was a mountain in north-eastern Greece, but it was also believed to be in the clouds above the mountain itself. An exception to this was the god Hades, who lived in the underworld. Figure 1.1 shows the gods' family tree, in which the gods in black are prescribed gods for the GCSE.

FIGURE 1.1
Greek gods' family tree.

Zeus

After defeating his father Cronos during the war with the Titans, Zeus took control of the earth and became unquestionable king of the gods with power over all others. He divided

FIGURE 1.2
Zeus (with Hermes).

the earth between himself and his brothers. Zeus took the skies and heavens, Poseidon acquired the seas and Hades the underworld. Despite being married to his sister Hera, Zeus had a rather promiscuous personal life, bearing children with several women, both human and divine. Zeus was often seen as the keeper of justice, god of the skies and the fate of men. These roles are seen in the *Iliad* and *Odyssey*, Greek epics composed by Homer. As ruler of the skies, Zeus was typically represented as a bearded man wielding a lightning bolt. In addition to this he could be shown holding an eagle or seated on a throne with a sceptre.

Titans

The Titans were gods that came before the Olympians. The youngest of the Titans, Cronus, castrated his father Uranus to become king of the Titans. Uranus prophesied that Cronus' children would rise against him and so Cronos swallowed them. His wife Rhea hid Zeus and brought him up in secret. When Zeus grew up he managed to free his siblings and in revenge they waged war against Cronus and the Titans for control of the cosmos. The Olympians won and Zeus imprisoned some of the other hostile Titans in Tartarus. Two Titans avoided this punishment due to their co-operation with the gods. These were Atlas, who instead was tasked with holding up the heavens for eternity, and Prometheus (see p. 29).

Homer's *Iliad* and *Odyssey*

The *Iliad* and the *Odyssey* are the two oldest epics attributed to the bard Homer and were possibly first put in writing around 700 BC, although this date is debated. The *Iliad* takes place in the tenth year of the war raging between the Greeks and Trojans and centres around the wrath of the Greek hero Achilles. The story ends with an epic battle between Achilles and the Trojan Prince Hector. The *Odyssey* is named after its protagonist Odysseus, king of Ithaca. After the Greeks defeated the Trojans, Odysseus set sail for home. However, after incurring the wrath of Poseidon, he was blown off course and endured a ten-year epic journey back home. On his journey, Odysseus' will and leadership were tested as he and his men faced monsters, witches, giants and gods.

Poseidon

Brother of Zeus and god of the seas, Poseidon was a very important god for sailors and those taking sea journeys. Poseidon features prominently in Greek literature, siding with the Greeks in the *Iliad* due to the fact that the Trojans never paid him for helping to build their city. However, in the *Odyssey* Poseidon relentlessly pursues the Greek Odysseus after he blinded the Cyclops Polyphemus, Poseidon's son. Poseidon was also a key god in the contest for Athens against Athena, which he lost (see also p. 68). In art Poseidon was typically represented as a bearded man holding a trident.

FIGURE 1.3
Poseidon.

FIGURE 1.4
Hades.

---

chthonic relating to the gods that were connected with the earth and the underworld

cornucopia a horn shell that contained an endless supply of food and drink

diadem a crown often associated with gods or kings

Hades

Hades was a **chthonic** deity and ruler of the underworld. Despite being brother to Zeus, Hades does not enjoy extensive mention in Greek literature. An exception to this is his role in the abduction of Persephone, described at length in the *Homeric Hymn to Demeter* (see also p. 125). This episode led to Hades acquiring the young goddess Persephone as a wife, the daughter of goddess Demeter. In art Hades is typically represented with a **cornucopia** showing the links with his wife and mother-in-law. In addition to the cornucopia he is also often depicted with his wife Persephone.

Hera

As wife of Zeus, Hera was the queen of the gods and responsible for marriage, women, childbirth and the family. Despite being Zeus' wife, Hera is often represented as a powerful independent goddess who is not to be crossed. In Homer's *Iliad*, Hera opposes the Trojans due to Paris not choosing her in the story of the Golden Apple. Additionally, she spent much of her time taking revenge on the many women who bore children by her husband Zeus, and taking revenge on the children themselves. A prime example of this is the myth of Heracles (see also p. 22). In art Hera is typically represented wearing a **diadem** (see Figure 1.5).

EXPLORE FURTHER

The Golden Apple

Read the story at www.theoi.com/Olympios/JudgementParis.html
What led to Hera's hatred of the Trojans?

FIGURE 1.5
The Judgement of Paris. Paris sits between Hera (left) crowned with a diadem and Athena (right) wearing a helmet. Behind Athena, you can just make out Aphrodite.

Athena

Athena (also known as Athene) was the goddess of war and wisdom. Athena's birth was one of obscurity. Zeus impregnated the goddess Metis who later gave him the prophecy that the next child born by him would be the new leader of the gods. To avoid this Zeus tricked Metis into turning into a fly which he then swallowed. Zeus then developed a very bad headache. To fix this Zeus called on Hephaistos. Hephaistos decided that the best fix for Zeus' headache was to strike him on the head with his hammer. As he did this Athena sprang from Zeus' head. When she arose she was not a baby but an adult woman. As goddess of wisdom Athena was frequently depicted with an owl; as goddess of war and military intelligence she is depicted with a helmet, spear and the **aegis**, a breastplate or shield engraved with the head of a gorgon (see Figures 1.5 and 1.30). Athena was also often depicted with Nike, the winged goddess of victory. Later in life Athena was victorious against Poseidon in a contest to win possession of Athens (see also p. 68). One common epithet for her was *Parthenos* 'the virgin', and it is from this that the Parthenon on the Athenian **Acropolis** took its name.

Demeter

As sister of Zeus, Demeter was the goddess of agriculture and the harvest. This made her incredibly important to the Greeks as their society was built on agriculture and they depended on the harvest for survival. One of the best insights to Demeter comes from the *Homeric Hymn to Demeter*, in which she loses her daughter Persephone to Hades (see also p. 125). Demeter was held in particularly high regard by the Greeks at Eleusis, where she had a Mystery Cult dedicated to her known as the Eleusinian Mysteries. In art Demeter is depicted wearing a diadem and holding a bundle of wheat, grain or flowers.

aegis the breastplate or shield of Athena that contained an image of a gorgon in the centre

acropolis the highest point in a Greek city, usually reserved for religious buildings

KEY PLACE

Parthenon the temple to Athena built on the Athenian Acropolis (see also p. 48)

PRESCRIBED SOURCE

Homeric Hymn to Demeter, 1–104, 301–474

Date: uncertain, 7th–6th century BC (debated, see p. 125)

Author: attributed to Homer

Genre: poetry

Protagonists: Demeter, Persephone and Hades

Significance: provides an insight into what the Greeks thought the relationships between the gods and men was like

CW

Read it here: OCR sources booklet

S & C

Hesiod

Hesiod was a Greek who is believed to have lived during the eighth century BC. Throughout his life he wrote poetry about the family of the gods, from their birth to Hesiod's time. This was called the *Theogony*. Read the *Theogony* lines 886–962 to learn about Hesiod's account of the birth of the gods.

FIGURE 1.6
Hestia.

Eleusinian Mysteries

The Eleusinian Mysteries were a set of secret rituals that took place in the town of Eleusis near Athens. The fact that they were called mysteries means that we do not actually have much information about them as initiates were not allowed to speak about their experiences. The mysteries were linked to Demeter and her daughter Persephone, and are discussed in the *Homeric Hymn to Demeter* (lines 470–479). Mystery cults were popular as they offered salvation after death, something that traditional Greek religion did not. With this in mind, Persephone as Queen of the underworld and Demeter as goddess of regeneration and the harvest would be appealing gods for those who sought a happy afterlife.

Hestia

Hestia was the goddess of the home and hearth, the fireplace kept in the home. As the Greeks were a civilisation without electricity and central heating, Hestia was vital to their survival and every sacrifice that took place in the home started with an offering to her. Hestia's importance extended outside the home, as her fire came to be a symbol of the security of the city. A city would often have a fire lit and maintained by officials as a symbol of its power. Although rarely depicted in art, Hestia is shown with a veiled head.

FIGURE 1.7
Hephaistos.

Hephaistos

Hephaistos was the god of metalworking, fire and craftsmen. According to the *Iliad*, Hephaistos was the son of Zeus and Hera. However, the poet Hesiod states that he was the son of Hera who bore him alone in revenge for Zeus giving birth to Athena alone. Hephaistos also walked with a limp which, like his birth, was explained in two varying stories; the first relates that Hephaistos was born with a limp, the second notes that Hephaistos suffered his foot injury when Zeus threw him from Olympus. After falling for a whole day he landed on the island of Lemnos, where the local people looked after him. In art Hephaistos is often depicted with a hammer.

Aphrodite

Aphrodite was the goddess of love and beauty. Unlike many of the other gods she was not the daughter of Zeus or Hera, instead she was born from the sea. According to the *Homeric Hymn to Aphrodite*, with the exception of Athena, Hestia and Artemis, no human or god could resist the influence of Aphrodite (*Homeric Hymns*, 5, 9–44). Aphrodite's beauty had powerful effects on more than one occasion. First, as the winning goddess in the story of the Golden Apple, Aphrodite gave Helen of Sparta to the Trojan prince Paris, which resulted in the Trojan War. Second, Aphrodite was caught by her husband Hephaistos having an affair with the god of war Ares. Catching them in bed, Hephaistos ensnared them in an unbreakable net and called all the gods to witness their humiliation (Homer, *Odyssey*, 8.266–366). In art Aphrodite can be depicted in various ways, one of which shows her rising from a sea shell. In sculpture she is usually depicted naked.

Artemis

Artemis was the goddess of hunting, wildlife and childbirth. As twin sister of Apollo she came to be associated with the moon, while Apollo was associated with the sun. In the same vein she was also referred to as *Phoebe* and Apollo as *Phoebus*, 'shining'. In art she was depicted with a bow and arrow, and with wild animals.

Apollo

Apollo was the god of music and the arts, education, archery and prophecies. As twin brother to Artemis he was associated with the sun, while she was associated with the moon. He was given the epithet *Phoebus*, meaning 'shining'. The wide range of responsibilities this god had shows how important he was to the Greeks. While he was widely worshipped across the Greek world, he had cult centres in Delos, where he was said to have been born, and Delphi, the site of the biggest **oracle** in the Greek world. In art Apollo was depicted with his bow and arrow, and **lyre**. Unlike the other gods, Apollo was depicted in eternal youth.

Hermes

Hermes was the god of travel and trade, and messenger of the gods. Hermes was also given the honour of being the only god, other than Dionysus, who could travel to the underworld and consort with Hades. As a traveller god, Hermes is depicted in art with his traveller's cap, **caduceus** and winged sandals (see Figure 1.2).

Ares

Ares was the god of war. In the *Homeric Hymns* Ares is seen as a god who gives men the courage to stand their ground in order to uphold peace, and to stand up against hostilities in order to avoid a violent death. However, in the *Iliad* he is described as a merciless killer when Zeus attacked him by saying, 'always your delight is in strife and war and fighting'. (Homer, *Iliad*, 5.891). With this in mind, Ares should be considered as the opposite to Athena in that she represented tactics and control in battle, whereas Ares represented the raw violence of the fight. Like Athena, Ares is depicted in art wearing his armour.

Dionysus

Dionysus was the god of wine and theatre. As son of Zeus and the **Theban** mortal Semele, Dionysus attracted the wrath of Hera, which forced Zeus to hide him from her. As Dionysus was the son of both a god and a mortal he was seen as an outsider and therefore not one of the original Olympians. Dionysus received a great following from the Greeks and as god of wine and theatre he was pivotal to public and private celebrations. Additionally, as god of the theatre he enjoyed his own festival in Athens, the Dionysia (see also

FIGURE 1.8
Artemis and Apollo.

oracle an utterance, often ambiguous or obscure, given by a priest or priestess said to be speaking the words of a god

lyre a small Greek harp consisting of a sound box with two curved arms connected by a crossbar from which strings are attached.

caduceus a traveller's staff most closely associated with the god Hermes (Mercury)

Thebes an ancient city in Greece that is the focus of many mythological stories See map, Figure 1.10

FIGURE 1.9
Dionysus holding a wine cup and **thyrsus**.

thyrsus a staff associated with the god Dionysus, which was tipped with a pine cone; it could also be intertwined with ivy

maenads female followers of Dionysus

satyrs in myth, half man, half goat attendants of Dionysus, known for their promiscuous nature

p. 88). In art Dionysus is depicted with a **thyrsus**, vines and an animal skin. In addition, he is often depicted with his companions, the **maenads** and **satyrs**.

EXPLORE FURTHER

The *Homeric Hymns*
Choose one of the *Homeric Hymns*.

1. What do we learn about the personality and powers of the god/goddess from the poem you chose?
2. Explain why the god/goddess is so important to the lives of the Greeks.

Homer's *Iliad*
Read Homer's *Iliad* Book 1.

1. What gods are involved and what powers do they use?
2. Explain why the gods are so important to the progression of the plot in Book 1 of the *Iliad*.

Homer's *Odyssey*
Read Book 5 of the *Odyssey*.

1. How do the gods demonstrate their anthropomorphic qualities?
2. How does the meeting between the gods highlight the relationship between gods and men?

ACTIVITY

Create top trump cards for each of the Greek gods and goddesses. When creating the cards, you must decide:

● what criteria you will include for your gods' powers
● what score you will assign each god on a scale from 1–5 with 5 being the strongest.

EXAM TIP

You may be given any image of a god mentioned in the specification. It is important that you are able to recognise them in many different situations. For any non-prescribed sources, you will be told the medium the god has been drawn on, for example an amphora, relief sculpture or statue.

PRACTICE QUESTIONS: GREECE

Source A: A Greek vase

Study **Source A**.

1. a. Who is the god labelled **A** and how do you know? [2]
   b. Specifically why would the Greeks have worshipped this god? [1]
2. a. Who is the god labelled **B** and how do you know? [2]
   b. Specifically why would the Greeks have worshipped this god? [1]

ROME

Before Rome was founded, Italy was inhabited by lots of tribes. Some of these were indigenous, while others had their origins in the wider Mediterranean world; some engaged in friendly trade, others had more aggressive militaristic intensions. When Rome was believed to have been founded in 753 BC, one of the biggest and most influential of these tribes were the **Etruscans**. Although based to the north of Rome in Etruria, they colonised much of Italy. As Roman influence grew and Rome expanded, the Etruscans were slowly brought under Roman control. This prolonged exposure to the Etruscans led to the Romans adopting and adapting several aspects of Etruscan culture, namely temple design and divination (see also p. 56).

An influence on the Etruscans and Romans were the Greeks. The Greeks, or **Hellenes**, were not only living in what we now know as Greece, but also migrated to other areas including southern Italy and Sicily from as early as the ninth century BC (see Figure 1.10). The large quantities of Greeks that inhabited these areas led to it being known as **Magna Graecia** (Great Greece). Much like the Etruscans before them, Rome was in contact with the Greeks from its foundation. When Rome looked to expand throughout Italy, especially south, they had further contact with the Greeks. Again, much like with the Etruscans, Rome borrowed and adapted the religious ideas of the Greeks. By 270 BC, when the whole of Magna Graecia came under Roman control, Greek religion and mythology were having a major influence on Roman religious ideology.

> **Etruscans** the exact origins of the Etruscans are not known, although it is believed that they inhabited Italy from at least the ninth/eighth century BC. By the time Rome was founded they were well established in Italy
>
> **Hellenes** a collective name for the Greeks, a group of peoples who shared the same social and religious customs and language
>
> **Magna Graecia** 'Great Greece', the term used to describe the region of southern Italy and Sicily where there were many independent Greek cities

FIGURE 1.10
Map of the Mediterranean showing Greek settlements.

FIGURE 1.11
Roman gods' family tree.

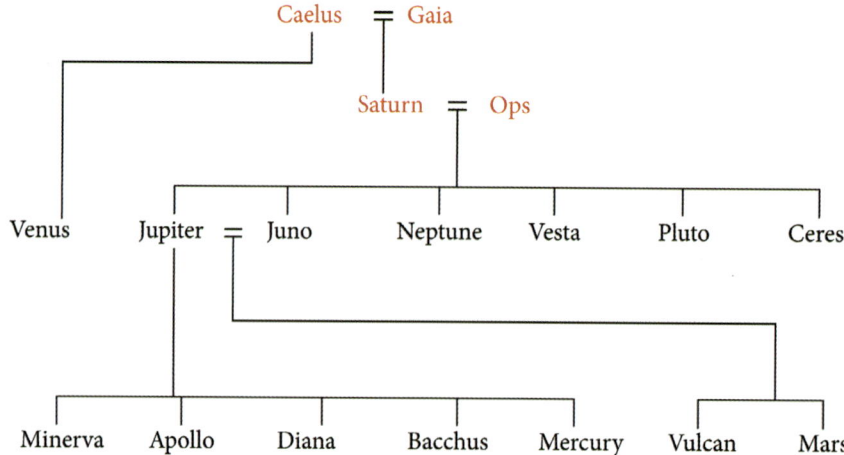

Figure 1.11 shows the gods' family tree, in which the gods in black are prescribed gods for the GCSE.

Jupiter

As the king of the gods and controller of the skies, Jupiter was equated with the Greek Zeus. The name Jupiter comes from *Iov pater* 'Father Jove', showing the Roman links with the Etruscans, who worshipped Jove as a sky god. Jupiter's major temple was the Temple of Jupiter Optimus Maximus, 'Jupiter the Best and Greatest', which stood on the Capitoline Hill, one of the most important hills in Rome. Although the Temple of Jupiter Optimus Maximus has now been destroyed, you can still see its foundations in the Capitoline Museum in Rome, which was built over the site of the temple. Like the Greek god Zeus (see Figure 1.2), Jupiter was typically represented as a bearded man wielding a lightning bolt. In addition to this he could be shown holding an eagle or seated on a throne with a sceptre.

Neptune

Neptune was the brother of Jupiter and god of the seas, earthquakes and storms. Like the Greek Poseidon, Neptune was also linked with horses. With the Romans always looking to expand throughout the Mediterranean, Neptune became an increasingly important god to Roman sailors, traders and travellers. In art, like Poseidon (see Figure 1.3), he was typically represented as a bearded man holding a trident.

Pluto

Pluto was the brother of Jupiter and Neptune, and god of the underworld. In literature Pluto makes a brief appearance in the story of Orpheus and Eurydice in Ovid's *Metamorphoses*, which makes reference to his abduction of Proserpina (Persephone) (see also p. 131). Due to his position beneath the earth he was not often represented in Roman art. However, the myth of Proserpina's abduction at the hands of Pluto was a popular decoration for Roman **sarcophagi**.

Juno

Juno was the wife of Jupiter, queen of the gods and responsible for marriage, women, childbirth and the family. Juno was equated with the Greek goddess Hera. Like Hera, Juno was a powerful and wrathful goddess. In the opening of Virgil's *Aeneid* Juno takes revenge on the Trojan Aeneas, destroying his ships and killing many of his men. In art Juno is typically represented wearing a diadem (like Hera, see Figure 1.5), holding a sceptre or accompanied by a peacock.

Ceres

Ceres was the goddess of the harvest and grain. Ceres was incredibly important to the Roman **plebs** as they relied on grain, and by extension bread, for their survival. Her importance was reflected in the fact that she had both a temple on the Aventine Hill and an annual festival in Rome called the **Cerealia**. In art, Ceres is depicted wearing a diadem and holding a bundle of wheat, grain or flowers.

> **plebs** the lowest social class of Romans, making up the majority of the Roman population
>
> **Cerealia** a major festival in honour of Ceres held in Rome every year between 12th and 19th April

Vesta

Vesta was the goddess of the hearth and fire. For this reason she was one of the most important goddesses to both the family and the state. For the family, the hearth or fire was the central part of the home as it provided light and heat for cooking and warming the family. As a state goddess Vesta had her own priesthood and temple complex (see also p. 59). Vesta's flame was believed to have been brought to Italy by Aeneas and symbolised the security of the state. The Romans believed that if the flame went out,

---

S & C **The *Aeneid***

The *Aeneid* was a Roman epic poem composed by the poet Virgil who died in 19 BC. Virgil's epic was heavily influenced by Homer's *Iliad* and *Odyssey* and continued the story from a Trojan perspective. Ultimately, Virgil sought to tell the story of how the Roman race was founded. The epic starts at the end of the Trojan War, after the walls had been breached and the city captured by the Greeks. The hero Aeneas and his fellow Trojans fled Troy and sought to establish a new home elsewhere. While many of the gods make an appearance in the *Aeneid*, the two main gods are Juno and Venus. Juno's hatred of the Trojans meant she was constantly trying to kill Aeneas. On the other hand, Venus, the mother of Aeneas, helps him along the way. After landing on the west coast of Italy, Aeneas went to war with a native tribe. After fighting a long and bloody war, Aeneas married Lavinia, daughter of King Latinus, and became king of Latium. Aeneas' son Ascanius founded the kingdom of Alba Longa and from this line Romulus and Remus were born. Aeneas is therefore seen as the founder of the Roman race, while Romulus is seen as the founder of Rome itself (see also p. 79).

FIGURE 1.12
Ceres.

Rome would be destroyed. Although rarely depicted in art, Vesta is shown with a veiled head (like Hestia, see Figure 1.6).

Vulcan

Vulcanalia a festival held in Rome each year on 23rd August in honour of the god Vulcan

Vulcan was the god of metalworking, fire and craftsmen. Industry and warfare were essential to the Roman way of life and therefore as god of craftsmen Vulcan was vital to the Romans. He had a festival called the **Vulcanalia** each year in Rome. He also had an important role in Virgil's *Aeneid* as he crafted the shield that Aeneas used in battle. In art Vulcan is depicted with a hammer (like Hephaistos, see Figure 1.7).

Venus

Venus was the goddess of love and beauty. She was particularly important to the Romans as she was the mother of their ancestral founder Aeneas. The Roman emperor Augustus linked his own family to Venus, and utilised her symbols in his art. In art Venus can be depicted in various ways, but in sculpture she is usually depicted naked or accompanied by her son Cupid.

Minerva

Minerva was the goddess of war and wisdom. Although Minerva was a goddess of war, it appears that the Romans more closely associated war with Mars. As goddess of wisdom, Minerva was frequently depicted with an owl, whereas as goddess of war and military intelligence she was depicted with a helmet, spear and the **aegis** (like Athena, see Figure 1.5).

FIGURE 1.13
Venus.

Diana

Diana was the goddess of hunting, childbirth and the moon. She could also be referred to as Phoebe. Diana had a temple and shrine on the Aventine Hill. The temple was dedicated by the sixth king of Rome Servius Tullius who, according to legend, was born a slave. Diana's cult therefore gained a large following from the urban poor and slaves. As a goddess of hunting, in art she was depicted with a bow and arrow (like Artemis, see Figure 1.8).

> **S & C**
>
> **Servius Tullius**
>
> According to the Roman historian Livy, one of the sixth-century Roman kings Servius Tullius was born into a slave family. When he became king he made a treaty with the neighbouring Latins, which recognised Rome as the head of Latium. In order to honour the treaty, he built a temple to Diana who was universally worshipped in Latium.

Apollo

Apollo was the god of music and the arts, education, archery and prophecies. The Roman gods usually stemmed from those of the Etruscans who came before them, and were then equated with Greek gods. Unlike the other Roman gods, Apollo had no Etruscan alternative, hence he was taken straight from the Greek **pantheon**. As god of the arts, Apollo was popular among sculptors and poets. Apollo was also important to the Roman leaders. After the battle of **Actium**, Apollo was a god favoured by the Roman emperor Augustus, who built him a temple in Rome and honoured him with festivals, prayers and sacrifices. Apollo was often depicted with his lyre (see Figure 1.8), in eternal youth.

> **Actium** port on the west coast of Greece, it is now called Preveza

> **S & C** **Actium**
>
> In 31 BC Octavian (later known as Augustus) fought Mark Antony and Cleopatra at the harbour of **Actium** in a final civil war that cemented Augustus' power over the Roman Empire. Apollo had a sanctuary at Actium and after Augustus was victorious he accepted that he was under the protection of Apollo. To honour him he extended Apollo's sanctuary at **Actium** and built him a temple on the Palatine Hill in Rome. You can read more about the battle on page 385.

> **votive** an offering to the gods
> **lararium** a small shrine to the household gods (Lares) that was found in Roman homes

Mercury

Mercury was the god of travel and trade, and messenger of the gods. Since the Roman Empire extended from Britain to Syria and from Germany to Egypt, Mercury was very important for the protection of travellers. On a more personal level, Mercury was a popular household god due to his role as god of trade and wealth, and there are many examples of small **votive** statuettes to Mercury that would have been kept in the home's **lararium**. In art Mercury is depicted with his traveller's cap, caduceus and winged sandals (like Hermes, see Figure 1.2).

Mars

Mars was the god of war. However, in early Roman history he was also associated with agriculture. Rome was an expansionist civilisation and often did this through military conquest. With this in mind, Mars was very important to the Romans. The area just outside Rome was known as the Campus Martius, 'Field of Mars', and was traditionally where the army would assemble to train and before going to war. Mars was also the father of Romulus, the founder of Rome (see also p. 79) and so enjoyed great favour among the Romans. In art Mars is depicted wearing his armour.

FIGURE 1.14
Mars.

S & C **Mars**

Like Apollo, Mars was an important god to the emperor Augustus. After the assassination of his adopted father Julius Caesar, Augustus vowed to avenge his death. In 42 BC Augustus fought Caesar's murderers Brutus and Cassius at Philippi in Greece. While in battle Augustus vowed to build a temple to Mars if he were successful, which he was. In 27 BC he began building his new forum and, at its centre, a temple to Mars Ultor (Mars the Avenger). From that point the senate met there when discussing war, generals conducted a ceremony before leaving for war, and a victorious general would dedicate a portion of booty to Mars at the altar just outside the temple.

Bacchus

Bacchanalia a Roman festival in honour of Bacchus

Bacchus was the god of wine and theatre. The Romans equated him with the Greek god Dionysus. Around 200 BC the **Bacchanalia** was introduced to Rome from Greece. As a mystery cult what happened in it was meant to be kept secret. Therefore we are not completely sure what happened. However, the fact that cult members met in private was met by fierce opposition from the Roman state, which feared rebellion, and around 186 BC the cult was banned. Despite this, Bacchus continued to be popular among the Roman lower classes. In art Bacchus is depicted with a **thyrsus**, vines and an animal skin. In addition, like Dionysus (see Figure 1.9) he is often depicted with his companions, the maenads and satyrs.

Study questions

1 Choose the three most important gods for the following Roman occupations and justify your choice:
   a. A soldier
   b. A merchant
   c. A slave
   d. A magistrate
2 Explain why it was beneficial for the Romans to integrate the gods/goddesses of the Greek pantheon into their own rather than to omit them.

EXPLORE FURTHER

Read Book 1 of Virgil's *Aeneid*.

1. How do the gods demonstrate their anthropomorphic qualities?
2. How do the actions of Aeneas and his men demonstrate the relationship between gods and men?

ACTIVITY Which god or goddess are you?

Construct a table like the one below and fill the categories with as much information about yourself as possible. An example has been done for you. Be careful not to include information that is specific to the modern world, i.e computer games.

Skill	Personal trait	Interests
Creative	Short tempered	Travelling

Once you have filled the table you must decide which Roman god you most resemble. You must justify your decision by drawing comparisons with the god or goddess you have chosen.

PRACTICE QUESTIONS: ROME

Source A: *Virgil*, Aeneid, *1.8–11*

Muse, tell me the cause: how was she offended in her divinity, how was she grieved, the Queen of Heaven, to drive a man, noted for virtue, to endure such dangers, to face so many trials? Can there be such anger in the minds of the gods?

1. **a.** Who is the goddess described in **Source A** and how do you know? [2]
   b. Specifically why would the Romans have worshipped this goddess? [1]
2. Why were the gods important to the everyday lives of the Romans? [8]

TOPIC REVIEW

You should be able to:

1. Describe:
   - the key responsibilities of each of the Olympian gods
   - the symbols used to identify the Olympians, as well as Hades/Pluto
   - any differences between the Greek and Roman versions of the Olympian gods
   - the storyline of the *Homeric Hymn to Demeter*.

2. Explain:
   - the character of Greek and Roman religion, including polytheism and anthropomorphism
   - the importance of epithets to describe the gods
   - what the relationship between men and gods was like
   - the importance of the *Homeric Hymn to Demeter* for the Greek understanding of the cycle of the seasons.

PRACTICE QUESTIONS: COMPARING GREECE AND ROME

Source A: *Relief from a stone coffin (sarcophagus) showing the abduction of Persephone/Proserpina.*

Source B: *Homeric Hymn to Demeter, lines 267–277; 292–315; 399–406.*

"I am Demeter, the honoured one, who for mortals and immortals alike has been made the greatest blessing and source of joy. But come, let all the people build me a great temple and an altar beneath it, below the steep walls of the city above Kallichoron, upon the rising hill. And I myself will inaugurate my mysteries, so that from now on you may perform them in all purity and be reconciled to my heart." As the goddess said this, she changed her stature and form, throwing away old age . . . But as soon as dawn appeared they told powerful Keleos exactly what had happened, just as the goddess had commanded, Demeter with her lovely crown. So he called to assembly his innumerable people, and he ordered them to build for Demeter with the lovely hair a sumptuous temple and an altar upon the rising hill. They heard his voice and hurriedly obeyed him, building it as he commanded. And it grew as the goddess decreed.

Now when they were finished and done with their labour, each man went back to his house. But golden-haired Demeter sat there, far away from all the blessed gods, she stayed there, wasting with longing for her deep-breasted daughter. And she made the most terrible and cruel year for human beings on the deeply nourishing earth. The earth did not send up seed, for rich-crowned Demeter kept it hidden. Many times the oxen dragged the curved plough across the fields in vain, and many times the white barley fell upon the earth fruitlessly. So she would have destroyed utterly the mortal race of human beings, starving them to death, and depriving those who lived on Olympus of the glorious honour of gifts and sacrifices, if Zeus had not noticed it and reflected upon it in his heart.

After Hermes' intervention at the request of Zeus, Hades agreed to free Persephone but tricks her before she leaves. Demeter explains the result of the trick . . .

. . . But if you did eat anything you will have to go back again to the secret depths of the earth and live there for a third part of the seasons of the year, but for the other two parts you will be with me and the other immortals. But whenever in spring the earth blossoms with sweet flowers of every kind, then you will rise again from the realm of dusk and darkness and be a source of great wonder for mortals and for gods.

Study **Sources A** and **B**.
1. Explain why Homer and the deceased's family may have chosen to use this myth in these contexts. [3]
2. Explain a benefit of having gods with human forms and qualities. [3]

1.2 The Universal Hero: Heracles/Hercules

TOPIC OVERVIEW

The myths associated with Heracles (known to the Romans as Hercules) and how he is typically represented.

Greece

Heracles and Olympia:

- Heracles as founder of the Olympic games
- The 12 Labours of Heracles as represented on the Temple of Zeus at Olympia
- *Homeric Hymn to Heracles the Lion Hearted*

Rome

Hercules in Ovid and Virgil:

- The myth of Hercules and Cacus, and Hercules as protector of Rome
- Battles with Achelous and Nessus, and the death of Hercules

The prescribed sources for this topic are:

- *Homeric Hymn to Heracles the Lion Hearted*
- The Temple of Zeus at Olympia (metopes)
- Virgil, *Aeneid*, 8.154–279
- Ovid, *Metamorphoses*, 9.1–272

Don't forget that you will be given credit in the exam if you study extra sources and make relevant use of them in your answers.

For the Greek element of the topic we will examine the twelve labours of Heracles and his importance to the site of Olympia. For the Rome element of the topic we will study Hercules' victories against Achelous and Nessus as told by the poet Ovid. We will also learn about Hercules' victory over Cacus and why this was important to the Romans by reading a section from Virgil's *Aeneid*. For the comparative part of the topic we will compare and contrast the importance of Hercules to the Greeks and Romans.

GREECE

The birth of Heracles

KEY INDIVIDUALS

Alcmene wife of Amphitryon, descendant of Perseus

Amphitryon husband of Alcmene and nephew of Sthenelus

The story of Heracles' birth is set in mythical times when Alcmene and Amphitryon lived in Thebes. At this time, Creon was king of Thebes. When Creon was on a campaign with Amphitryon, Zeus visited Alcmene. As is explained in the *Homeric Hymn to Heracles the Lion Hearted*, Heracles was born to a human mother and a divine father. In order to avoid suspicion, Zeus took the form of Amphitryon and therefore Alcmene thought she was sharing a bed with her husband:

> Heracles, Zeus' son, I will celebrate, who, greatest and best of those on earth, was born in Thebes' beautiful places, Alcmene having slept with the black-clouded son of Cronus.

Homeric Hymn 15, lines 1–3

seer a person who is reputed to be able to see the future

Upon his return Amphitryon slept with Alcmene, but then he found out from a **seer** that Alcmene had slept with another man. Although initially fuming at this, when he discovered that the other man was in fact a god, Amphitryon was surprisingly relieved.

Thus, Alcmene was now pregnant with two children, one was Zeus', the other Amphitryon's. When the boys were about to be born, Zeus boasted that he would now have a son that could match him on earth: while he ruled the skies, his son would rule the earth. Enraged by his promiscuities, Hera made Zeus vow that the first son of the House of Perseus born that night would indeed rule.

FIGURE 1.15
Roman copy of a Greek statue of Heracles. On his right he leans on his club and in his left hand he holds his lion-skin cloak.

PRESCRIBED SOURCE

Homeric Hymn to Heracles the Lion Hearted

Date: around 700 BC

Author: attributed to Homer (see also p. 125)

Genre: poetry

Protagonist(s): Heracles

What we learn from the poem: the birth and labours of Heracles

Significance: the poem outlines some of the key aspects of Heracles' life

Read it here: OCR sources booklet

Once he did this, Hera asked her daughter Eileithyia to prolong Alcmene's labour until Sthenelus' son Eurystheus was born. Having succeeded in this, Hera hoped the prolonged labour would kill both Alcmene and the unborn Heracles. However, due to the help of Alcmene's midwife, this plan failed and Heracles was born. This meant that Eurystheus became king of Mycenae while Heracles and his brother Iphicles held no official power.

Unhappy that her plot to kill Heracles was unsuccessful, Hera sent two snakes to poison Heracles. Again this plot failed when Heracles strangled the snakes. Frightened by Hera's wrath, Alcmene abandoned Heracles in the woods where he was recovered by Athena. Athena took Heracles to Mount Olympus in the hope that he would be accepted there, but Hera rejected him and ordered that he be returned to Alcmene to raise him. From this point, Athena was Heracles' protector.

The early life of Heracles

Many things he did that were reckless, many things he suffered.

Homeric Hymn 14, lines 6–7

Here the *Homeric Hymn* is making reference to Heracles' early life. When he came of age, Heracles married Creon's daughter Megara. The marriage did not last long. Still enraged by Zeus' affair, Hera sent the goddess Madness to infect Heracles. Driven insane, Heracles killed his children and wife.

In his depression Heracles exiled himself from Thebes and went to consult the oracle at Delphi as to what he should do. Again, unbeknown to him, Hera was in control of the oracle and advised Heracles that he should serve King Eurystheus for twelve years. It was from this time that Heracles started his twelve labours.

KEY INDIVIDUALS

Eileithyia daughter of Zeus and Hera, goddess of midwives and childbirth

Eurystheus son of Sthenelus

Iphicles son of Alcmene and Amphitryon, brother of Heracles

Sthenelus uncle of Amphitryon and King of Mycenae, descendent of Perseus

EXAM TIP

Either spelling of Heracles/ Hercules will be accepted in the examination. However, students should try to use Heracles when referring to Greece and Hercules when referring to Rome.

FIGURE 1.16
Heracles strangling the snakes sent by Hera. Athena stands to the left.

Study questions

Examine the story of Heracles' birth.

1 What does this story reveal about the relationship between:
   a. gods and men
   b. gods and gods?
2 To what extent were the gods responsible for the lives of men?

EXPLORE FURTHER   S&C

In 416 BC the Greek tragic playwright Euripides wrote the play *Heracles*. The play focuses on the tragedy of Heracles' family.
   Read Euripides, *Heracles*, 815–1177

1. How responsible was Heracles for the death of his family?
2. Does Euripides expect the audience to feel pity or hatred for Heracles? Explain your answer.

EXPLORE FURTHER   S&C

The Roman comic writer Plautus wrote a comedy on the birth of Heracles.
   Read Plautus, *Amphytro*, 1–152.

To what extent does Mercury's speech suggest that the gods are no better than men in their behaviour?

The twelve labours of Heracles

As punishment for killing his family, Eurystheus initially challenged Heracles to complete ten labours, which he believed would be impossible. During two of the labours Heracles either received help or payment so when he returned successful, Eurystheus demanded he complete a further two labours.

The Labours of Hercules

1. Nemean Lion
2. Lernaean Hydra
3. Golden Hind
4. Erymanthian Boar
5. Augean Stables
6. Stymphalian Birds
7. Cretan Bull
8. Mares of Diomedes
9. Belt of Hippolyte
10. Cattle of Geryon
11. Apples of the Hesperides
12. Cerberus

FIGURE 1.17
Map showing the location of Heracles' labours.

DEBATE Labours of Heracles

The stories of Heracles were an oral tradition. This means that originally stories about Heracles were told verbally between friends and families. It was not until the mid-sixth century BC that his labours were recorded in writing.

Discuss

Why might sources vary with regards to the precise details about the order and events of Heracles' labours?

ACTIVITY

Read the description of Heracles' labours on the following pages and identify the labours depicted in the pictures on the Companion Website.

The Nemean Lion

> The Nemean Lion whom Hera, the queenly wife of Zeus, trained up and settled among the hills of Nemea, to be a plague to mankind . . . Nevertheless, the force of strong Heracles subdued him.
>
> Hesiod, *Theogony*, 327

This was the first of Heracles' labours, and so in art he is sometimes depicted more youthful than in his later labours. After attacking the lion with his bow and arrows and his sword, Heracles realised that the skin of the lion was impregnable to weapons, therefore he strangled it to death. Even dead the lion still posed problems for Heracles, because he needed to present a prize to King Eurystheus as proof of his victory. But he could not skin the lion with his knife. Finally, Athena told Heracles to use one of the lion's own claws to skin it. He was successful and took the prize back to the king. From this point Heracles was often depicted wearing the lion skin as a cloak with the lion's head as a helmet.

The Lernaean Hydra

> The grisly-minded Lernaean Hydra, whom the white-armed Hera nourished because of her quenchless grudge against the strong Heracles. Yet he, Heracles, son of Zeus, of the line of Amphityron, by design of Athena the spoiler and Iolaus killed the beast with the pitiless bronze sword.
>
> Hesiod, *Theogony*, 313

DEBATE Hydra

Sources vary as to the number of heads the hydra had with the number ranging from a few to a hundred. Several versions of the myth mention an immortal head that could not be killed.

hydra a many-headed serpent monster

As the second of the labours, Eurystheus tasked Heracles with killing the Lernaean Hydra. The **hydra** had many heads and venom for blood. The main problem that Heracles faced was that when one head was removed from the hydra, two more would grow back in its place. So Heracles got help from his cousin Iolaus. After Heracles removed one of the heads, Iolaus would seal the neck with a flaming torch. Enraged at Heracles' progress, Hera sent a giant crab to attack him. After it bit Heracles on the foot, he crushed it and continued his attack on the hydra. Once all the heads were removed, Heracles detached the immortal head and buried it under a pile of rocks. When the hydra was defeated, Heracles used its venom as poison for his arrows.

Upon returning to Eurystheus, he was told by the king that the labour did not count as he had been helped by his cousin.

The Golden Hind

> **hind** a deer

The Golden **Hind** was also known as the Ceryneian Hind as it was from Mount Ceryneia in Arcadia. This hind was special as it was said to be larger than a bull and golden from horns to hooves. It was also sacred to Artemis. As Heracles' third labour, the Golden Hind did not pose the same level of danger as the previous two. However, the task was

---

DEBATE Snaring it

Two ancient writers wrote differing accounts of how Heracles caught the Golden Hind. Writing in the first century BC, Diodorus Siculus wrote:

> Some say that he captured it by the use of nets, others that he tracked it down and mastered it while it was asleep, and some say that he wore it out by running it down. One thing is certain, that he accomplished this Labour by his sagacity of mind, without use of force and without running any perils.
>
> Diodorus Siculus, *Library of History*, 4.12.13

However, writing in the second century AD (*c.* 200 years later), Pseudo-Apollodorus wrote:

> Heracles shot it (the Hind) just as it was about to cross the stream, and catching it put it on his shoulders and hastened through Arcadia.
>
> Pseudo-Apollodorus, *Bibliotheca*, 2.5.4

Based on your knowledge of Heracles so far, which do you believe to be the more likely account?

S & C

Diodorus Siculus

Diodorus Siculus was a Greek historian who lived in the first century BC. He wrote the *Bibliotheca Historia* (Library of History) and his work covered the period from the mythic beginnings of both Greek and non-Greek civilisations around the Mediterranean to the Greek and Roman world around 60 BC.

Pseudo-Apollodorus

The *Bibliotheca* was originally believed to have been written by a man called Apollodorus of Athens who lived in the second century BC. However, a reference made to a man who lived around 100 years later in one of the chapters made it impossible for this Apollodorus to have been the author. For this reason, pseudo is added before the name Apollodorus (from the Greek word pseudes, meaning false). The *Bibliotheca* is considered one of the best collections of mythology ever compiled.

difficult owing to the swiftness of the animal. Heracles tracked the hind for a whole year before he was finally able to catch it by snaring it. He then bound its legs and carried it back to Mycenae.

On his journey back to Mycenae, Heracles was met by Apollo and his sister Artemis who was angry that Heracles had caught her sacred hind. Fortunately, when he told her that he had been forced into it by King Eurystheus, and that he only intended to borrow the animal, her anger subsided and she allowed him to continue on his way.

The Erymanthian Boar

As his fourth labour, Heracles was ordered by Eurystheus to bring the Erymanthian Boar back to him alive. Like the Golden Hind, the boar was much larger than normal boars and was terrorising the countryside of Arcadia. Heracles wore the boar down by chasing it through the thick winter snow. When the boar was tired, Heracles caught it, bound its legs and carried it back to Mycenae. On Heracles' arrival, the king was so scared that he hid in a sunken **pithos** jar.

> **pithos** (pl. **pithoi**) a large clay storage jar

The Augean Stables

As his fifth labour Heracles was tasked with cleaning the stables of Augeas, King of Elis, in one day. Augeas was famed for having a herd of enormous cattle that produced an extremely large amount of dung and so Eurystheus thought the task impossible. Heracles once again rose to the challenge and with a combination of brains and brawn diverted the rivers Alpheios and Peneios through the stables, cleaning them instantly. Initially, Augeas promised Heracles payment. However, once the task was complete, he refused. Enraged at this, Heracles returned with an army and defeated the king. To commemorate his victory Heracles founded the Olympic Games for his father Zeus (see also p. 31).

The Stymphalian Birds

The sixth of Heracles' labours was to defeat the Stymphalian Birds. The birds had been ravaging the farm lands of Stymphalos, some accounts even suggesting that they ate the residents too. This task took Heracles deep into the Arcadian forests where the Stymphalian Marsh was. Unsure of how to rouse the birds, Heracles received help from Athena who gave him a rattle made by the god Hephaistos. After shaking it the birds flew into the sky, and Heracles then shot them down either with his arrows or a sling shot.

The Cretan Bull

For his seventh labour Heracles had to bring Eurystheus the Cretan Bull to Mycenae. The bull had been destroying Cretan homes and farmland, and so when Heracles arrived, King

S & C **The Stymphalian Birds**

We have already seen that the writers Diodorus Sicilus and Pseudo-Apollodorus differed in their accounts of Heracles' labours. Again in this labour their writing differs, this time regarding how Heracles defeated the birds:

> Now it was not possible to master the animals by force because of the exceptional multitude of them, and so the deed called for ingenuity in cleverly discovering some device. Consequently, he fashioned a bronze rattle whereby he made a terrible noise and frightened the animals away.
>
> Diodorus Siculus, *Library of History*, 4.13.2

> Heracles was stumped by the problem of driving the birds out of the woods, but Athena got some bronze noise-makers from Hephaistos and gave them to him, and by shaking these from a mountain adjacent to the lake frightened the birds. Not enduring the racket, they flew up in fear, and in this manner Heracles reached them with his arrows.
>
> Pseudo-Apollodorus, *Bibliotheca*, 2.90

The writer of the *Bibliotheca* was a mythographer, Diodorus Siculus was a historian. Given this information why may their accounts of Heracles differ? Support your answer with evidence from the text.

Minos was happy to let him remove it. To do this Heracles crept up behind the bull and strangled it, but importantly he released his grip before the bull passed out. He then rode the bull across the sea to Greece. Upon returning to Mycenae, King Eurystheus was once again terrified of the animal brought before him and hid in his pithos. Heracles let the bull loose and it wandered to Marathon, where it was later defeated by Theseus (see also p. 72).

The Mares of Diomedes

Diomedes was the King of the Bistones in Thrace. The king owned a set of horses that he kept tethered in a bronze manger with iron chains. The horses were crazed as their master fed them on the limbs of defeated enemies and passing strangers. Upon arriving Heracles defeated the stablemen looking after the horses. When he discovered the loss of his horses, Diomedes set out with his men to overcome Heracles. Heracles left the horses with his companion Abderos while he went to fight Diomedes. While he was away the horses overpowered Abderos and ate him. In retaliation Heracles fed Diomedes to his own horses after defeating him. With their appetites calmed Heracles took the horses back to Eurystheus. At this point the story varies, one account suggests the horses, now eternally calm, were freed to roam the plains of Argos. Apollodorus stated that they were set free and when they arrived at Olympus they were killed by wild animals.

The Belt of Hippolyte

Hippolyte was the queen of the Amazons, a race of female warriors who lived near the Black Sea. Hippolyte was given a magical belt by her father Ares. Eurystheus' daughter wanted the belt for herself and so the king sent Heracles to retrieve it as his ninth labour. Like his journey to Diomedes, Heracles once again took an army because he expected trouble. Unbeknown to Heracles, Hippolyte greatly admired the deeds Heracles had performed, so when she greeted him she freely offered her belt to him. Unhappy with the ease of this task, the goddess Hera took the form of an Amazonian. She then spread rumours that Heracles actually planned to steal the queen, not her belt. Enraged by Heracles' apparent scheming the Amazons rode out to kill Heracles and his men. Seeing the Amazons arriving from a distance Heracles now thought that the queen had been scheming all along and had never planned to hand him the belt. A bloody battle followed in which Heracles killed Hippolyte and took the belt.

The Cattle of Geryon

Unlike his previous nine tasks the cattle of Geryon took Heracles beyond the Greek world to the edge of the earth. Eurystheus tasked Heracles with fetching Geryon's cattle who were famed for their red hides. To steal the cattle, Heracles first had to defeat the herdsman Eurytion and his dog Orthrus. After beating them with his club, Heracles began to leave with the cattle. Another shepherd had warned Geryon of Heracles' actions and so Geryon quickly rushed after Heracles. Geryon was no normal man, he had three heads and three sets of arms and legs. Eventually Heracles was successful, using his club and bow to defeat Geryon. The journey back took Heracles through southern Italy and it was here that the Romans forged their link with Heracles in their version of the story (see also p. 35). Upon his return to Mycenae, Eurystheus sacrificed the bulls from the herd to Hera.

Although Eurystheus only originally gave Heracles ten tasks, he did not count the Lernaean Hydra owing to the help he had received, nor did he count the Augean Stables as he was offered money for the task. He therefore gave Heracles two more tasks.

The Apples of the Hesperides

In the garden of the Hesperides grew the golden apples which Gaia (Earth) presented as a wedding gift to Zeus and Hera. The apples were guarded by the Hesperides, who were Nymphs, daughters of Atlas, and were associated with the light of the world. Heracles' eleventh task was to collect the golden apples. This turned out to be one of Heracles' longest tasks as he was initially unaware of where the garden was. His journey took him from Northern Africa to the Near East, then to Illyria. It was in Illyria that he fought the river Achelous (see also p. 39). His final stop was on Mount Caucasus. It was here that the Titan Prometheus was chained. For defying the gods, Zeus chained him to the mountain and each day an eagle would come and peck out his liver. Each night his liver grew back and the process started again (see also p. 48). When Heracles arrived, he killed the eagle. As a reward, Prometheus told Heracles how to acquire the apples. Heracles travelled to Atlas who had been tasked with holding up the skies by Zeus. Heracles offered to hold the sky if Atlas would get the apples, Atlas accepted. When he returned, Atlas offered to deliver the apples himself so that he would not have to take back the skies. Heracles now showed his cleverness. He accepted but asked that Atlas take them back for one moment while he got some pillows to cushion his shoulders. When Atlas took them back, Heracles picked up the apples and ran off with them. As the apples were the property of Zeus they were not allowed to stay with King Eurystheus. Once Heracles presented them to him, Athena took them back to the garden.

Cerberus

Heracles' final task was the retrieval of Cerberus from the underworld. In Homer's *Odyssey*, Odysseus travelled to the underworld and met the ghost of Heracles who stated:

> He [Eurystheus] sent me down here (to Hades) to bring back the Hound of Hell. And under the guiding hands of Hermes and bright-eyed Athena, I did succeed in capturing him and leading him out of Hades' realm.
>
> Homer, *Odyssey*, 11.623–626

In order to gain the favour of Persephone, Heracles was initiated in the Eleusinian Mysteries (see also p. 10). Upon arriving in the underworld, he was greeted by both Persephone and Hades who presented Heracles with a challenge. If he could capture Cerberus without any weapons, he would be allowed to take him to Eurystheus. Heracles accepted and used the stranglehold that had proved so successful against the Nemean Lion and Cretan Bull. After presenting Cerberus to Eurystheus he was returned to Hades to guard the entrance to the underworld.

Study questions

1 What heroic qualities did Heracles display while completing his labours?
2 Use the heroic traits you devised in question 1 to identify which of Heracles' labours was his most heroic. Ensure you justify your answer with evidence from the stories.
3 'Heracles always used brute force over brains during his labours.' To what extent do you agree with this statement? Make sure you support your answer with evidence from the stories.

ACTIVITY

Create a newspaper article on one of Heracles' victories. In the article, you should include:

- an eye catching headline and sub headings
- artist impressions of what happened during the labour
- statements from Heracles and various eye-witnesses.

HERACLES AND OLYMPIA

Olympia was in Elis, a kingdom in the west of the Peloponnese. The traditional date for the founding of the Olympic Games was 776 BC, although it is clear that some form of festival had taken place since long before this. As was usual for the Greeks, they devised stories to explain the origins of the games.

Pelops and Hippodamia

This story was shown on the eastern pediment of Zeus' temple at Olympia (see also p. 52). Hippodamia was the daughter of Oinomaos, King of a town near Olympia called **Pisa**. Oinomaos had received an oracle that he was going to die once his daughter married. In order to avoid his daughter ever marrying, he set up a chariot competition as he was a very skilled rider. He challenged any suitors of his daughter to a race. If they won they would wed his daughter, if they lost they would be killed. By the time Pelops arrived many suitors had lost and died. Pelops challenged Oinomaos to a race. To ensure victory, Pelops bribed Oinomaos' charioteer to replace his bronze **linchpins** with ones made of wax. While racing, the heat from the wheel melted the wax and threw Oinomaos from the chariot killing him. Pelops married Hippodamia and set up the Olympics as funerary games in honour of Oinomaos.

> **Pisa** a town near Olympia in the Greek Peloponnese
>
> **linchpin** (pl. **linchpins**) a fastener used to stop a wheel from coming off its axis

Heracles and the Augean Stables

As we saw in the previous section, Eurystheus ordered Heracles to clean the stables owned by Augeas, the King of Elis (see also p. 27). On completion of his fifth labour, Augeas refused to pay Heracles the promised money and so Heracles promised revenge. As Pseudo-Apollodorus wrote:

> Not long after (he completed the twelve labours) Heracles collected an Arcadian army, and being joined by volunteers from the first men in Greece he marched against Augeas . . . and marching on Elis took the city . . . He also celebrated the Olympian Games and founded an altar of Pelops, and built six altars of the twelve gods.
>
> Pseudo-Apollodorus, *Bibliotheca*, 2.7.3

Which then was the correct version of the founding of the Games? In truth, the ancient Greeks could pick and choose which stories they believed and there is no evidence that conflict ever arose from these competing stories. This mythic equality is best exemplified in the architecture of the Temple of Zeus.

Heracles and the Temple of Zeus

The story of Pelops is represented on the eastern **pediment** of the temple of Zeus at Olympia. The labours of Heracles are represented on twelve **metopes**, six are above the front entrance and six over the back entrance.

> **pediment** triangular area at the top of each end of a temple, which could contain sculpture
>
> **metope** (pl. **metopes**) square decorative spaces that ran around a Doric temple and could contain sculpture

---

PRESCRIBED SOURCE

The Temple of Zeus at Olympia (metopes)

Date: started 472 BC

Material: local marble

Original location: Temple of Zeus, Olympia

Current location: Olympia Museum

Significance: the metopes were included on a temple dedicated to Zeus, emphasising Heracles' importance to the site and games.

FIGURE 1.18
A plan of Olympia.

The sculptor had several objectives to fulfil when sculpting the metopes. These were to:

- create a scene that could be easily recognisable
- create realism in his scene
- fill the space so as not to leave big blank areas.

We will use Figure 1.20 for our analysis.

Create a scene that could be easily recognisable

The context in which the metope is placed makes this instantly easier for the viewer as all the metopes on the temple are of Heracles. To assist the viewer Heracles holds his club even though the myth suggests that he strangled the bull.

Create realism in his scene

Heracles' body is well sculpted; the abdominals follow the correct line as they bend away from the bull. Heracles' right pectoral correctly reacts to the movement of his right arm. The rearing bull's head and legs suggest movement away from Heracles. Both figures are in the correct proportion.

Fill the space so as not to leave big blank spaces

The sculptor has been very clever with his execution of the scene. He has formed a cross between the two characters using diagonals to fill the space. The space left by the rearing bull's front legs is taken up by Heracles legs. Although, according to the myth, the club was not used in the labour, the sculptor has used Heracles' raised club arm to fill the top left hand space.

FIGURE 1.19
Diagram showing where the Heracles metopes and pediment are found on the Temple of Zeus at Olympia.

PS

ACTIVITY

The Thebans have decided to build a statue to commemorate Heracles' greatest achievement. You must choose what that achievement was and then design a statue to honour the great hero.

FIGURE 1.20
Metope from the temple of Zeus at Olympia showing Heracles wrestling the Cretan Bull (left) and a modern interpretation of the same metope (right).

PS

Study questions

1 Why may the architect have chosen the internal metopes to display the twelve labours of Heracles?
2 Examine the metopes on the Companion Website.
   a. Identify which of Heracles' labours is depicted.
   b. Comment on how effectively the sculptor has filled the space of metopes A, B, E, F, H and I.

PRACTICE QUESTIONS: GREECE

Source A: *Sculpture of a labour of Heracles*

1. Who were Heracles' parents and why did this make him a demi-god? [3]
2. Study **Source A.**
   a. Where was this sculpture originally displayed? [1]
   b. Which of Heracles' twelve labours is depicted in Source A and who asked Heracles to do it? [2]
   c. Why was this myth significant to Olympia? [1]

ROME

The Romans inherited their ideas about Hercules from the Greeks. The following stories formed some of Hercules' other adventures. The battle with Cacus formed part of the Roman Epic the *Aeneid*, written by Virgil. It explained why Hercules' cult in Rome was founded. The battle between Hercules and Achelous, and between Hercules and Nessus were known to both Greeks and Romans and were recorded by the Roman poet Ovid in his *Metamorphoses*. The final myth is of Hercules' death, again this was known to both Greeks and Romans and told by Ovid.

Hercules and Cacus

The context of the story

The story between Hercules and Cacus took place during Hercules' tenth labour, the cattle of Geryon. Although the myth of Geryon was originally Greek, the Romans wove their own history into the story, which they believed took place about 500 years before Romulus founded Rome. Once Hercules had captured the cattle and killed Geryon, he had to get them back to Eurystheus. To do this he had to travel up through southern Spain, into France and down through Italy. As Rome had not yet been founded, the area around the **Tiber** was inhabited by others. As Virgil wrote:

> Arcadians have chosen a site on this coast, a race descended from **Pallas**, friends of King Evander, who followed his banner, and located their city in the hills, named, from their ancestor Pallas, Pallantium.
>
> Virgil, *Aeneid*, 8.53–56

The cult of Hercules in Rome stemmed from the story of Hercules and Cacus. The story took place by the Aventine Hill next to the Tiber (see Figure 1.14). According to Evander, Cacus terrorised the city of Pallantium. When the people had almost lost hope, Hercules arrived.

Cacus and his lair: lines 190–199

Evander began his story by characterising Cacus through description of his lair and physique.

> Now look first at this rocky overhanging cliff (the Aventine Hill), how its bulk is widely shattered, and the mountain lair stands deserted, and the crags have been pulled down in mighty ruin. There was a cave here, receding to vast depths, untouched by the sun's rays, inhabited by the fell shape of Cacus, the half-human, and the ground was always warm with fresh blood, and the heads of men, insolently nailed to the doors, hung there pallid with sad decay. Vulcan was father to this monster: and, as he moved his massive bulk, he belched out his dark fires.
>
> Virgil, *Aeneid*, 8.193–199

PRESCRIBED SOURCE

The *Aeneid*, Book 8, lines 175–279

Date: 19 BC

Author: Publius Vergilius Maro (Virgil)

Genre: epic poetry

Protagonist(s): Hercules

Significance: the poem outlines some of the key aspects of Heracles' life

Read it here: OCR sources booklet

Tiber the main river running through Rome

Pallas a Giant who fought against the gods, not to be confused with Evander's son, also called Pallas, or with Athena when called Pallas Athena

ACTIVITY

Read Virgil's *Aeneid*, 8.190–199.

Draw a picture of Cacus and his home using only Virgil's description. Annotate your image with quotes from the *Aeneid* to support your drawing.

FIGURE 1.21
Roman sarcophagus showing the twelve labours of Heracles, around AD 240.

Hercules arrives in Pallantium: lines 200–212

When Hercules arrived in Pallantium he was welcomed as a god. It is important to remember that this adventure took place during his original twelve labours; therefore, he is not yet a god, Evander is, however, telling the story after Hercules was deified:

> Now at last time brought what we wished, the presence and assistance of a god. Hercules, the greatest of avengers, appeared, proud of the killing and the spoils of three-fold Geryon, driving his great bulls along as victor, and his cattle occupied the valley and the river.
>
> Virgil, *Aeneid*, 8.200–204

While Hercules slept, Cacus stole eight of his cattle and took them back to his cave. In order to fool Hercules, he led the cattle into his cave backwards. This meant that the hoof marks led away from where they were being held.

Hercules chases Cacus: lines 213–249

While preparing to leave, Cacus' plan was thwarted by a single trapped cow whose moos were heard by Hercules:

> At this Hercules' indignation truly blazed, with a venomous dark rage: he seized weapons in his hand, and his heavy knotted club, and quickly sought the slopes of the high mountain. Then for the first time my people saw Cacus afraid, confusion in his eyes: he fled at once, swifter than the East Wind, heading for his cave: fear lent wings to his feet.
>
> Virgil, *Aeneid*, 8.219–224

Having fled to his cave, Cacus blocked the entrance with a huge boulder. Despite his best efforts, Hercules was unable to move the rock.

> Hot with rage, three times he circled the whole Aventine Hill, three times he tried the stony doorway in vain, three times he sank down, exhausted, in the valley.
>
> Virgil, *Aeneid*, 8.230–233

Study questions

1 Did Hercules use brain or brawn in his pursuit of Cacus? Justify your answer with evidence from Virgil's *Aeneid*.
2 How does Virgil create a vivid scene in lines 213–249?

Study questions

1 How successfully does Virgil create a vivid image of Cacus' home?
2 How does Cacus' home add to the heroic feat of Hercules?
3 How successfully does Virgil create a fearsome monster in Cacus?
4 Where would you rank Cacus when compared to the other monsters faced by Hercules during his twelve labours? Justify your answer with detail from the *Aeneid* and the other labours you have studied.

Study questions

1 How heroic was Hercules when he fought Cacus? Support your answer with details from the *Aeneid*.
2 Where would you rank Hercules' battle with Cacus when compared to Hercules' twelve labours? Justify your answer with detail from the *Aeneid* and the other labours you have studied.

It may have been at this point that a lesser man would have given up. However, Hercules noticed a huge flint peak on the top of the mountain and, using his body weight and strength, lifted the top of the mountain clean off, exposing Cacus in his lair.

Hercules kills Cacus: lines 250–268

Exposing his lair Hercules bombarded Cacus with whatever he could find including trees, stones and boulders. In defence, Cacus breathed huge plumes of black smoke to conceal his whereabouts. Enraged by Cacus' actions, Hercules:

> . . . threw himself, with a headlong leap, through the flames, where the smoke gave out its densest billows, and black mist heaved in the great cavern. Here, as Cacus belched out useless flame in the darkness, Hercules seized him in a knot-like clasp, and, clinging, choked him the eyes squeezed, and the throat drained of blood.
>
> Virgil, *Aeneid*, 8.256–262

Hercules then brought the body out to show Evander and his people.

The cult of Hercules in Rome

As Evander was originally Greek, the cult of Hercules followed the Greek tradition rather than Roman. In Virgil's epic, the hero Aeneas travelled to Evander's city to seek friendship. When he arrived at Pallanteum:

> By chance that day the Arcadian king was making solemn offering to Hercules, Amphitryon's mighty son, and other gods in a grove in front of the city.
>
> Virgil, *Aeneid*, 8.104–107

Only men were allowed to take part in the ritual, which involved the sacrificing of an animal and burning of incense. Evander and his son Pallas attended the sacrifice with:

> all the leading young men, and his impoverished senate offering incense, and the warm blood smoked on the altars.
>
> Virgil, *Aeneid*, 8.106–108

The sacrifice was an annual one that took place at the Great Altar of Hercules. The Great Altar was located between the river Tiber and the Palatine Hill in a place that was later known as the Forum Boarium:

Because of that this rite is celebrated, and happy posterity remembers the day: and Potitius, the first, the founder, with the Pinarian House as guardians of the worship of Hercules, set up this altar in the grove, which shall be spoken of for ever by us as 'The Mightiest', and the mightiest it shall be for ever. Come now, O you young men, wreathe your hair with leaves, hold out wine-cups in your right hands, in honour of such great glory, and call on the god we know, and pour out the wine with a will. He spoke, while grey-green poplar veiled his hair with Hercules's own shade, hanging down in a knot of leaves, and the sacred cup filled his hand. Quickly they all poured a joyful libation on the table, and prayed to the gods.

Virgil, *Aeneid*, 8.268–279

In the second century BC the Temple to Hercules the Victor was constructed in the same area.

FIGURE 1.22
The temple of Hercules the Victor in the Forum Boarium.

PRESCRIBED SOURCE

***Metamorphoses*, Book 9**

Lines: 1–272

Date: AD 8

Author: Publius Ovidius Naso (Ovid)

Genre: poetry

Protagonist(s): Hercules

Significance: Hercules' battle with Cacus explains why the Romans worshipped Hercules

Read it here: OCR **CW** sources booklet

Study question
Who has the more convincing argument for the hand of the princess? Make reference to the text opposite in your answer.

EXPLORE FURTHER

In *The Early History of Rome* the Roman historian Livy also wrote an account of the encounter between Cacus and Hercules.
   Read Livy, *The Early History of Rome*, 1.7.

1. How heroic is Hercules in Livy's account?
2. From which account can we learn more about:
   a. Hercules as a hero
   b. Hercules' cult in Rome?

Justify your answer with evidence from both Livy and Virgil.

The cult was initially run by the Potitii and Pinarii families who, according to tradition, were instructed by Hercules himself how to correctly worship him. In 312 BC this responsibility was transferred to a selected group of slaves. As slaves made up a large amount of Rome's population, Hercules would have been very popular with the masses. In addition to slaves, gladiators also worshipped Hercules. When a gladiator was freed, he was presented with a wooden sword that was hung in the Temple of Hercules the Victor.

THE LESSER ADVENTURES OF HERCULES

Hercules and Achelous

The context of the story

The story of Hercules and Achelous was told to the hero Theseus by the river god himself while he waited for the river waters to recede after a flood.

> Theseus, having played his part in the united effort, turned back towards Athens, Tritonia's city, where Erechtheus once ruled. But the River Acheloüs, swollen with rain, blocked his immediate path, and stalled his journey.
>
> Ovid, *Metamorphoses*, 8.547–549

After telling Theseus and his men several stories, Theseus asked the river god why his horn was broken off his head.

The plot of the story

The story describes the contest between Hercules and Achelous for the hand of the princess Deianira of Aitolia. Both Hercules and Achelous refused to back down over who should wed the princess, so they decided that whoever won a fight would marry her. The greatness of Hercules was explained to Theseus by Achelous:

> I will tell it as it happened: since the shame of being beaten is no less than the honour of having fought. It is a great consolation to me that the victor was so famous.
>
> Ovid, *Metamorphoses*, 9.5–7

The argument: lines 11–26

After the other suitors backed out of the contest, both Achelous and Hercules put forward their argument as to why they should be allowed to wed Deianira. Hercules made reference to his divine parentage and labours. Achelous claimed that his status as a god was superior to Hercules' status as a man. He also attacked Hercules' argument suggesting that the labours were his own fault and that the story of his birth was either a lie or a scandal.

Study questions

1 How would you characterise Hercules and Achelous from their words and actions?
2 Who had the greatest fighting skill?
3 How does Ovid create a vivid and entertaining battle scene?
4 Where do you think Hercules would rank this battle when compared with his twelve labours?
5 'More brawn than brains.' How accurate is this description of Hercules, based on this battle with Achelous?

FIGURE 1.23
Greek krater showing Hercules and the single-horned Achelous.

The fight: lines 27–86

Enraged by Achelous' counter argument, Hercules reverted to his fighting skill rather than his words to defeat him. Unable to back down through fear of shame Achelous accepted the challenge and both engaged in a fight. The first battle was an intense contest with both showing great skill and strength, finally Hercules was victorious. Far from over, Achelous used his powers as a river god to change his form into a snake. Hercules made fun of this new appearance and reminded Achelous that he had defeated the hydra, which had posed a much greater threat than a single snake. Hercules easily won the bout. Changing again, Achelous took the form of a single horned bull. Although Hercules makes no reference to previous labours here, the audience would have had in their minds Hercules' fight with the Cretan Bull and Erymanthian Boar. Hercules quickly won this final battle with Achelous, breaking his single horn, which was then filled with fruit and used as a cornucopia.

Hercules and Nessus

Nevertheless he only had the loss of that adornment, which had been taken from him, to lament: he was otherwise unhurt . . . But you, fierce Nessus, the centaur, a passion for that same virgin girl destroyed you, hit in the back by a flying arrow.

> Ovid, *Metamorphoses*, 9.98–102

Plot of the story

Having wed Deianira, Hercules sought to return home to Tiryns. The couple arrived at the river Evenus, which was too deep to walk across. While Hercules was able to swim across, Deianira could not. The **centaur** Nessus offered to assist but while Hercules was crossing the river Nessus decided to run off with Deianira. Hercules acted quickly:

> **centaur** a mythical creature with the upper body of a man and lower body of a horse (see also p. 100 for more information on centaurs)

shooting the arrow he fired, across, at the fleeing back. The barbed tip jutted from the centaur's chest. When the shaft was pulled out, blood, mixed with the deadly arrow-poison of the Lernean Hydra, gushed out simultaneously from the entry and exit wounds.

> Ovid, *Metamorphoses*, 9.127–130

Study questions

Read Ovid's *Metamorphoses*, 9.97–133. Answer the questions that follow ensuring all your answers are supported with examples from the text.

1 How would you characterise both Hercules and Nessus in this episode?
2 How effectively does Ovid create tension in this episode?
3 How heroic is Hercules in this episode?
4 Consider what Nessus said to Hercules before he died and his gift to Deianira. What do you think is going to happen?

Nessus' final act would prove to be the downfall of Hercules:

> Nessus trapped this (poison), and murmured, to himself of course: 'I will not die without revenge' and gave his tunic soaked with warm blood to Deianira, whom he had abducted, presenting it to her as if it were a gift for reviving a waning love.
>
> Ovid, *Metamorphoses*, 9.130–132

The death of Hercules

Plot of the story

The death of Hercules is set several years after the episode with Nessus. Ovid returned to the jealousy of Juno: this time she had the help of the goddess Rumor to spread lies about Hercules to his wife. The lies made her think that Hercules was in love with Iole, a princess from Oechalia in Thessaly. After much deliberation with herself, Deianira decided to give Hercules the cloak of Nessus in the hope that it would make Hercules fall in love with her again. Ignorant of what it would actually do, her slave gave it to Hercules to put on. While giving sacrifice to the gods, the heat from the altar caused the cloak to catch light and stick to his skin. While dying, Hercules built himself a funeral **pyre**, laid on it and died. On seeing his son dying, Jupiter gave a speech to the gods asking that Hercules be allowed onto Olympus because of his heroic deeds on earth. The gods agreed, including Juno, and Hercules shed his human form and entered Olympus.

> **pyre** a funeral mound made of wood on which to cremate a body

Study questions

Read Ovid's *Metamorphoses*, 9.133–272. Answer the questions that follow, ensuring all your answers are supported with examples from the text.

1 Were Deianira's actions rational or irrational?
2 'It was the gods that were to blame for the death of Hercules, no one else.' To what extent do you agree with this statement?
3 How successfully does Ovid create a vivid image of Hercules' death?
4 How do the actions of Hercules support his claim that he was both human and god?
5 What do we learn about the relationship between the gods in Jupiter's speech?
6 How successfully does Ovid describe Hercules' transition from man to god?

ACTIVITY

You are Theseus, a close friend of Heracles. You have been asked by Amphitryon to write an obituary for Heracles.
In it you must include Heracles' greatest achievements and why you, the Greeks and the Romans have admired him.

PRACTICE QUESTIONS: ROME

1. In the myth of Hercules and Cacus:
   a. What did Evander do to thank Hercules for his help? [2]
   b. Why was this significant to the Romans? [2]
2. Why do you think Hercules deserved to become a god? Use the source as a starting point **and** use your own knowledge in the answer. [8]

TOPIC REVIEW

You should be able to:

1. Describe:
   - how Heracles was born
   - the key events of each of Heracles' twelve labours
   - Hercules' battle with Cacus, Achelous and Nessus
   - how Hercules died.

2. Explain:
   - why Heracles' birth made him a demi-god
   - why Heracles was sent on his ten labours, and why he was given two more
   - why Heracles was important to the site of Olympia and how the Greeks honoured him
   - why Hercules was important to Rome and how the Romans honoured him.

PRACTICE QUESTIONS: COMPARING GREECE AND ROME

1. Who honoured Hercules more, the people of Olympia or Rome? [15]

1.3 Religion and the City: Temples

TOPIC OVERVIEW

Temples and their use, including the position of the altar; temple layout; the cult statue; use by worshippers; the roles and responsibilities of priests in worship and sacrifice; the purpose of sacrifice; officials; animals.

Greece

- The Parthenon and Temple of Zeus at Olympia
- The *hiereus* and *hiereia* (priest and priestess); the *mantis* (prophet)
- Animal sacrifice

Rome

- The Temple of Portunus (Fortuna Virilis) and the Pantheon
- The Pontiffs and Pontifex Maximus; the Augurs/Augures; the Vestal Virgins.
- Animal Sacrifice; the Haruspex

The prescribed sources for this topic are:

- The Parthenon
- The Temple of Zeus at Olympia
- The Temple of Portunus (Fortuna Virilis)
- Tho Pantheon

Don't forget that you will be given credit in the exam if you study extra sources and make relevant use of them in your answers.

In this topic we will study the design, function and importance of temples in Greece and Rome. In order to do this we will be using the Parthenon and Temple of Zeus in Greece, and the Pantheon and Temple of Portunus (Fortuna Virilis) in Rome as case studies. We will also examine the various religious officials that existed in the Greek and Roman world and their roles and responsibilities. Finally, we will examine the procedure and importance of animal sacrifices to those who conducted them. For the comparative element of the topic you will need to be able to compare and contrast each of these elements and draw conclusions on the importance of each.

GREECE

The sanctuary

sanctuary an area of holy land dedicated to a god or gods that contained the temple and altar

pollution when a person has done something to make them impure in the eyes of the gods

The **sanctuary** was a holy area in a city or town that contained a temple and an altar to a god. The sanctuary was usually separated from the rest of the city with a wall. Importantly a sanctuary could have temples and altars to many gods, it did not have to be specific to one god or goddess. The sanctuary often also had a fresh water source at its entrance for people to wash their hands and feet. This was because it was important to the Greeks that their holy sites were not **polluted** as this could discourage the favour of the gods. A person could be polluted for a number of reasons; anyone who had come into contact with a dead person or new-born or had committed homicide was polluted. Pollution could last a number of days or be immediately removed with a wash.

The function of a Greek temple

A temple was a building dedicated to a god and was used to house the cult statue of that god. It may be more easily understood as a house that gave the gods a residence on earth for when they left Mount Olympus. As Demeter demanded:

> Let all the people build for me a great temple and an altar beneath it . . . But when they had finished they rushed from their toil and each man went home. Golden-haired Demeter, however, sat there, staying far away from all the blessed immortals, reduced to yearning for her deep-bosomed daughter.
>
> *Homeric Hymn to Demeter*, 270–271, 301–304

EXPLORE FURTHER
Discuss

Why do you think the altar and temple were orientated east to west?

Importantly only the priests were allowed into the temple itself, therefore the majority of the population would never set foot inside the building.

As stated above, Demeter also demanded an altar to be built outside her temple. The altar was a very important part of the sanctuary as this was where the sacrifice and offering to the god took place. The sacrifice also was the most communal part of the god's worship and could involve the whole city if it took place during a festival.

colonnade an open-air covered walkway supported by columns

cella (Greek: naos) meant *small room* in Latin and was the room of the temple that contained the cult statue

opisthodomos the rear room in a temple that contained the city or town's treasures.

THE TEMPLE BUILDING

The temple building came in many sizes but often conformed to the same rectangular shape. The temple was usually orientated on the same axis as the altar it served, the most common was east to west.

Figure 1.24 shows the plan of a typical Greek temple. The temple was built on a solid foundation plinth (1) that also provided steps up to the temple. This raised it above the ground level to increase the sense of grandeur. The **colonnade** (2) stood on the foundation plinth and ran around the temple, which provided support for the temple roof. The room that housed the god's cult statue was the **cella** or **naos** (3). Finally, at the rear of the temple was an **opisthodomos** (4). This held all the treasure acquired in warfare and offerings to the gods.

FIGURE 1.24
Plan of a typical Greek temple: 1 steps; 2 colonnade; 3 cella/naos; 4 opisthodomos.

Temple decoration

The two areas that were decorated in a Greek temple were the pediments and friezes. These sculptures could be related to the city in which the temple was built or they could relate to the Greeks as a whole civilisation (see also pp. 49 and 52).

- **Pediment** The triangular space at the either end of a temple was called the pediment. This could contain sculpture or be left blank.
- **Ionic frieze** A continuous strip of stone or marble that runs around a temple. It was a good frieze to use if the sculptor wanted to tell a continuous story or use many characters. This is exemplified on the Parthenon.
- **Doric frieze** A continuous strip of stone or marble divided into square spaces called **metopes**. The Doric frieze was good to use if the sculptor wanted to tell several stories or several scenes from one story. This is exemplified on the Parthenon and the Temple of Zeus at Olympia.

> **Ionic frieze** an unbroken strip of marble that goes all the way around a temple
>
> **Doric frieze** a continuous strip of stone or marble divided into square spaces called metopes

Priests

The Greeks had both priests called a **hiereus** and priestesses called a **hiereia**; their name highlighted their chief role as *one who sacrifices to a god*. Usually the gods were attended by priests, while the goddesses were attended by priestesses. However, on occasion there were exceptions, notably the temple of Apollo at Delphi, which had both.

The role of a Greek priest highlights the difference between modern religious leaders and the ancient. In modern times a priest is usually a full-time position in which the person involved undergoes religious training to ensure they are suited to the role. This was not the case for the Greeks. A priesthood was a temporary role that required no special training. Some could last for just one festival, some for a year, while others could be for life. In order to show commitment to their city, a good citizen would hope to become priest of their local god at least once in their lifetime. A Greek priest would also not be expected to hold regular services, spread the message of their god nor act as a pastoral carer for the community. The priest simply had to undertake and oversee the correct ritual at the correct time and assist in the upkeep of their temple. There were

> **hiereus** (pl. **hiereis**) 'one who sacrifices to a god', a Greek priest
>
> **hiereia** (pl. **hiereiai**) 'one who sacrifices to a god', a Greek priestess

many gods and goddesses all with their own priests. Depending on who the god was and where their temple was, the importance of the priest varied. A priest of Dionysus in Athens sat on a throne in the front row at the City Dionysia (see p. 88). In Olympia, the Priestess of Demeter was the only female allowed to watch the Olympic Games, all other women were banned from the games.

The Greeks also used soothsayers called **manteis** in order to predict the outcome of future events. The mantis may loosely be compared to a modern fortune teller. Anyone could claim to tell the future, but some Greeks made careers out of the role. Those who predicted correctly were more closely followed than less accurate manteis. Omens would be read by looking at the entrails of sacrificed animals. If any blemishes or imperfections were seen, then the signs would be bad. The Greeks also read the flight of birds; this was called an **augury**. The mantis was so important that one would accompany the army and make a reading before the battle.

> **mantis** (pl. **manteis**) a Greek soothsayer who read entrails of animals or bird signs to predict the outcome of future events
>
> **augur** a person who reads the flight of birds to predict the outcome of future events

Sacrifice

In order to honour the gods the Greeks would give them offerings. These could include gifts of money, dedications of songs and war booty. The gift of food was a popular offering to the gods and the main way this was done was through the killing of an animal as a **blood sacrifice**.

> **blood sacrifice** the killing of an animal as offering to a god

The sacrifice was not merely killing the animal, but a carefully planned ritual that had several stages to it before it could be correctly completed. First, the correct animal would have to be chosen for the sacrifice. Usually the animal chosen would be a domestic animal belonging to the person undertaking the sacrifice. Different gods required different sacrifices and some animals were cheaper than others. A household may restrict their sacrifice to animals such as chickens and piglets. Cities, as part of a festival, would spare no expense. The most expensive of sacrifices would be the **hecatomb**, that took place in festivals such as the Great Panathenaia and Olympic Games, in which one hundred oxen would be killed. At an approximate cost of 8,000 drachmae (34 kilograms of silver) this would be no small expense.

> **hecatomb** the sacrifice in honour of a god of at least 100 oxen during large festivals

The sacrifice can be divided into three parts:

- the preparation
- the kill
- the sharing of the sacrifice.

> **S & C**
>
> ### Apollo and Cassandra
>
> The Trojan princess Cassandra was a priestess of Apollo at Troy. Apollo offered her the gift of prophecy if she would sleep with him. She agreed, but once she received her gift she went back on her word and rejected Apollo. To punish her, Apollo made sure that no one would believe the prophecies Cassandra gave. The fifth-century tragedian Aeschylus uses this in his play *Agamemnon*. Throughout the play, Cassandra screams her warnings that Agamemnon's wife is dangerous and a threat to him, but everyone ignores her.

The preparation

First all the participants would ensure they were clean and well in order not to pollute the sacrifice. Participants would wear their best clothes and garlands of leaves or twigs, dependent on the type of sacrifice. Next the animal was prepared by **gilding** the horns if it had any. Attendants would then lead the animals to the altar. These attendants included a maiden, who would carry a basket full of barley grains or cakes. This basket also hid the sacrificial knife that would be used for the kill. The number of attendants that joined the procession could vary. As can be seen from the Panathenaic procession, the whole city could take part. However, if it was a smaller sacrifice it would, at a minimum, include musicians and water bearers. The musicians were important as their playing would reduce the chance of the animal taking fright at the noise of the crowd. If the animal did become scared, the whole sacrifice would have to be started again as a frightened animal symbolised a negative sign from the gods.

Once the procession arrived at the sanctuary the participants would cleanse themselves with water again and gather around the altar. At this point the fire was lit. Note here the importance of the altar in the worship of the god rather than the temple building itself. The participants would take a handful of grain and the sacrificer would pour water on the head of the animal, causing it to nod. This was important as the animal had to be seen to agree to the sacrifice. The chief sacrificer would utter a prayer to the god and the other participants would then throw their grain into the fire to confirm their participation.

> **gilding** the covering of a surface in a thin layer of gold

The kill

Once the preparations were complete, the chief sacrificer would take the knife from the basket and remove some of the animal's hairs, throwing them into the fire. When this was done the animal's throat was cut. If the sacrificial animal was large, a bowl would be used to collect the blood; if it was a smaller animal it would be held above the altar. It was key that the animal's blood be poured over the altar. As at funerals, women would then let out a high-pitched scream to mark the animal's passage from life to death.

The sharing of the sacrifice

After the animal was killed the feast began and the Greeks ensured that none of the animal went to waste. The most important recipient of the sacrificial meat was the god for whom the sacrifice was intended, so they received their portion first. The god's portion was prepared by removing the animals thigh bones and wrapping them in fat. This was then burned on the altar while wine was poured on the fire. The reason the gods received the bones and fat, and not the meat was explained by the myth of Prometheus. Once the god had been satisfied, the entrails of the animal were read for omens. When this was completed they were cooked and shared amongst the immediate participants. The remaining meat was then cut up, cooked and shared with the wider community. Meat was not a normal part of the Greek diet, so sacrifices offered a rare opportunity for it to be eaten. This element of the sacrifice stresses the communal spirit and benefits of sacrifice to those who participated. Once the feasting had finished, the animal skin was given to the sanctuary.

S & C

Prometheus

Prometheus was a Titan who was a great supporter of humans, this is attested in several of his myths. One myth explains why the Greeks divided their sacrificial meat as they did. Once Prometheus took a sacrificial animal and divided it into two portions; one portion was made of a thigh bone wrapped in glistening fat, the other was the best cuts of meat wrapped in the animal's entrails. He gave Zeus the choice of which portion he wanted to receive. Zeus was tricked and chose the visually appealing bones wrapped in fat. For this reason the Greeks offered the sacrificial animal's bones wrapped in fat to the gods and kept the meat for their own consumption. Prometheus enraged Zeus further when he stole fire from Olympus and taught men how to create it on their own. For this he was chained to Mount Caucasus. An eagle was then sent to peck out his liver, which grew back each night. This cycle continued until Heracles freed him (see also p. 29).

EXAM TIP

You are expected to understand the context of the Parthenon and its location on the Acropolis. However, you do not need to know about the other buildings. You do not need to know all the epithets of Athena.

The Parthenon

Pericles and the Parthenon

When the Persians sacked Athens in 480 BC, they burnt the city to the ground, including notably the main religious buildings on the Athenian **Acropolis**. Despite this, the Athenians, allied with other Greeks, saw off the Persian threat, and Athens then became the head of a naval alliance known today as the Delian League. By the 450s, the League had effectively become an Athenian Empire. As a statement of Athens' power, the leading politician Pericles moved the treasury of the Delian League from the neutral island of Delos to Athens.

Athens used vast quantities of the money from the treasury to pay for an extensive and remarkable building programme to decorate the city again. The focal point of this programme was the Acropolis, which was already a sanctuary dedicated to Athena. A

FIGURE 1.25
Reconstruction of the Acropolis in Athens.

complex of buildings was now constructed on the Acropolis that was designed to honour the city's patron goddess (and other divine figures too). Pericles hoped to turn Athens into the architectural centre of the known world, and the Parthenon was one of the most prominent buildings in this programme. The opisthodomos of the Parthenon then became the location of the Athenian Empire's treasury.

Although Pericles approved the plans, the lead architect was a man called Phidias, who was in charge of the general design and sculpture, including the statue of Athena in the naos. In addition to Phidias, Iktinos and Kallikrates were also two of the lead architects on the project.

Location

The Parthenon was part of the sanctuary of Athena on the Acropolis (see Figure 1.25 opposite). The complex had several buildings and sculptures that focused their worship on Athena. On entering the Acropolis, visitors would see a huge statue to Athena Promachos (in Greek *pro* means 'to go before' and *machos* means 'battle'). In the south-eastern corner was the small temple of Athena Nike (*Victory*); to the north was the Erechtheion (see also p. 69); the Parthenon on the south-east side was dedicated to Athena Parthenos (*the Virgin*). All these temples sought to worship Athena Polias (*of the City*) and an altar to Athena Polias stood on the eastern side of the Acropolis between the Erechtheion and Parthenon.

Plan

The Parthenon is huge in size, measuring 69.5 metres in length and 30.9 metres wide. The Parthenon had many similarities with standard Greek temples:

- It was orientated east to west.
- It stood on a three-stepped base.
- It was surrounded by a colonnade.
- It had a naos and opisthodomos.

The Parthenon also had a unique feature to its design. Behind the external façade stood another row of columns that supported an Ionic frieze (see Figure 1.27 and p. 87).

Study questions
Compare the plan of the Parthenon in Figure 1.26 with the typical plan of a Greek temple in Figure 1.24.

1 What are the differences between the two?

2 Why do you think these differences exist?

PRESCRIBED SOURCE

The Parthenon

Date: 447–432 BC

Commissioned by: Pericles

Architect: notably Phidias, Iktinos and Kallikrates

Dedicated to: Athena

Material: marble

Style: Doric and Ionic

Location: Athens

Function: temple and treasury

Significance: the building and its decoration symbolised the power of Athens

FIGURE 1.26
Plan of the Parthenon.

FIGURE 1.27
A cross section showing the outer and inner colonnade.

PS

This frieze was 165 metres in length and went around the whole of the Parthenon. Again, the inclusion of the Ionic frieze was intended to increase the grandeur of the building by providing another surface for sculpture.

Athena and the Parthenon

The Acropolis focused on the worship of Athena and the main temple for this was the Erechtheion, which housed a small wooden statue of Athena. Just outside the temple stood the Altar of Athena Polias where the sacrifices took place. The Parthenon was an offshoot of this cult and, therefore, did not have its own altar or priesthood. As a temple to Athena Parthenos, the Parthenon housed the city's treasury, and its sculpture honoured Athena through its stories about the goddess. It also stood as a monument to Athens' greatness and accordingly the Athenians decorated the Parthenon to reflect this.

The pediments of the Parthenon are heavily fragmented and so we rely on Pausanias, writing in the second century AD, for information on them:

As you enter the temple that they name the Parthenon, all the sculptures you see on what is called the pediment refer to the birth of Athena, those on the rear pediment represent the contest for the land between Athena and Poseidon.

Pausanias, *Description of Greece*, 1.24.5

On the eastern pediment above the entrance the Athenians depicted Athena's birth. The western pediment shows the contest for the naming of Athens. As Apollodorus wrote:

In his time, they say, the gods resolved to take possession of cities in which each of them should receive his own peculiar worship. So Poseidon was the first that came to Attica, and with a blow of his trident on the middle of the acropolis, he produced a sea . . . After him came Athena . . . she planted an olive tree . . . But when the two strove for

FIGURE 1.28
Reconstruction of the birth of Athena on the eastern pediment of the Parthenon.

FIGURE 1.29
Reconstruction of the central scene of the western Pediment of the Parthenon showing the battle between Athena and Poseidon.

possession of the country, Zeus parted them and appointed judges . . . and in accordance with their verdict the country was adjudged to Athena . . . Athena, therefore, called the city Athens after herself, and Poseidon in hot anger flooded the Thriasian plain and laid Attica under the sea.

Pseudo-Apollodorus, *Bibliotheca*, 3.14.1

FIGURE 1.30
Reconstruction of the gold and ivory statue of Athena.

EXAM TIP

You will not be shown a picture of the original Parthenon pediments as they are so fragmented, but you are expected to understand the stories told on them and why they were important to the Athenians.

The cult statue of Athena

In the naos of the Parthenon stood a 13-metre statue of Athena. It was designed by the architect Phidias and was added to the Parthenon around 438 BC. The statue caught the attention of the ancient geographer Pausanias when he visited Athens:

> The statue itself is made of ivory and gold. On the middle of her helmet is placed a likeness of the Sphinx . . . and on either side of the helmet are griffins in relief . . . The statue of Athena is upright, with a tunic reaching her feet, and on her breast the head of Medusa is worked in ivory. She holds a statue of Victory . . . and in the other hand a spear; at her feet lies a shield and near the spear is a serpent.

Pausanias, *Description of Greece*, 1.24.5–7

S & C Statues made from gold and ivory were called chryselephantine statues (in Greek *chrysos* means gold and *elephantine* means ivory). They were made from attaching gold and ivory to a wooden statue. The ivory represented the skin of the god while the gold represented their clothes. The statues were made in parts so that they could be melted down and replaced if the city needed extra money. There are pieces of evidence that suggest the statue of Victory was made from solid gold and melted down when needed. At approximately 172 cm, the height of a man, this would be incredibly expensive. In times of prosperity this was then replaced. It is for this reason that both this and the statue of Zeus at Olympia no longer exist as they were melted down and used for other purposes.

Study questions

1 To what extent did the cult statue of Athena conform to other representations of the goddess?

2 Why would the Athenians decide to make a statue of Athena out of gold and ivory as opposed to marble?

The Temple of Zeus at Olympia

Location

The temple of Zeus was situated within the sanctuary at Olympia called the **Altis**. The building of Zeus' temple did not begin until around 472 BC. However, the Olympic

Altis the sacred area in the centre of Olympia that contained religious buildings

Study questions

1 How did the Parthenon show off Athens':
   a. wealth
   b. military strength
   c. piety?
2 'The Parthenon was more than just a temple, it was a monument to the greatness of Athens.' To what extent do you agree with this statement?

Games were believed to have been founded in 776 BC and the Altar of Zeus was known to have been there from at least that time. This highlights the importance of the altar over the temple building itself.

The Altar

The Altar of Zeus at Olympia was described by Pausanias:

> Some say that it was built by Heracles, others by the local heroes two generations later than Heracles. It has been made from the ash of the thighs of the victims sacrificed to Zeus . . . men only can ascend . . . to the highest part of the altar. Even when the festival is not being held, sacrifice is offered to Zeus by private individuals and daily by the Eleans . . . Every year the soothsayers . . . bring the ash from the town-hall, and making it into a paste with the water of the Alpheios they daub the altar therewith.
>
> Pausanias, *Description of Greece*, 5.13.8–11 (abridged)

As can be seen by Pausanias' account, the altar's origin was not known but what can be inferred is that the altar was one of the oldest structures in Olympia. The main sacrifice that Pausanias talks about was the sacrifice of 100 oxen that took place on the third day of the Olympics. This was called the **hecatomb**. The ash left by the sacrifice built up over time and by Pausanias' day, around 925 years after the Olympics was believed to have been founded, the altar was some 7 metres high. Importantly, the altar was present around 200 years before the temple of Zeus was built. This shows the relative importance of the altar and temple in Greek religion.

Plan

The temple of Zeus at Olympia was 64.1 metres in length and 27.7 metres wide. The temple had many similarities with standard Greek temples:

- It was orientated east to west.
- It stood on a three-stepped base.
- It was surrounded by a colonnade.
- It had a naos and opisthodomos.

Zeus and the temple

On the eastern pediment was the myth of Oinomaos and Pelops. In the centre stands Zeus. As god of justice he stands as judge in the centre of the scene. On either side stands the elder King Oinomaos and the younger Pelops. Either side of the men are the key female figures, the king's daughter Hippodamia and his wife Sterope. Next come the horses and, although slightly smaller than expected, the sculptor uses the natural body shape to follow the triangular shape of the pediment. He finishes the corners with two figures laying down, these are personifications of Olympia's two great rivers, the Kladeos and Alpheios.

The twelve labours of Heracles were sculpted onto the six eastern and six western metopes of Zeus' temple at Olympia (see also p. 31).

PRESCRIBED SOURCE

The Temple of Zeus at Olympia

Date: 472–456 BC

Architect: notably Libon

Dedicated to: Zeus

Material: local limestone

Style: Doric

Location: Olympia

Function: temple and treasury

Significance: the building and its decoration symbolised the importance of Zeus, Hercules, Pelops and the Greeks

FIGURE 1.31
Plan of Zeus' temple at Olympia.

EXAM TIP

You are expected to understand the context of Zeus' temple and altar at Olympia and their locations in the Altis. However, you do not need to know about the other buildings. See Figure 1.18 for a plan of Olympia.

EXPLORE FURTHER   Discuss

Look at Figure 1.32. Older reconstructions switch the statues of Pelops and Oinomaos around to different sides of Zeus. Why do you think this is?

Why do you think the sculptor chose to arrange the characters on the eastern pediment as he did?

The western pediment

The western pediment of the temple of Zeus at Olympia depicts the mythical battle between the Centaurs and Lapiths called the Centauromachy. The myth came to represent the victory of civilisation over barbarism and was a popular motif in temple architecture (see also p. 100).

Why would the architect of Zeus' temple at Olympia choose to include the Centauromachy in the sculpture of Zeus' temple at Olympia?

Study questions

1 How fitting was the decoration of Zeus' temple at Olympia for both the worship of Zeus and the glorification of Olympia?
2 'The Temple of Zeus at Olympia was far greater than the Parthenon.' To what extent do you agree with this statement?

Study questions

1 Why do you think that the Olympians would have chosen to place this story above the entrance to the temple?
2 Why do you think the architect decided to show the labours of Heracles on the metopes and the contest between Pelops and Oinomaos on the pediment and not vice-versa?

Study question

Compare the plan of the temple of Zeus in Figure 1.31 with the typical plan of a Greek temple in Figure 1.24.

a. What are the differences between the two?
b. Why do you think these differences exist?

FIGURE 1.32
Sculptures from the east pediment of the Temple of Zeus at Olympia as they exist today.

Study question

How do you know which part of Olympia was the Altis? Use Figure 1.18 to help you.

The cult statue of Zeus

Inside the temple stood the cult statue of Zeus, which was around 13 metres tall, as Pausanias wrote:

> The god sits on a throne, and he is made of gold and ivory. On his head lies a garland which is a copy of olive shoots. In his right hand he carries a Victory, which, like the statue, is of ivory and gold; she wears a ribbon and – on her head – a garland. In the left hand of the god is a sceptre, ornamented with every kind of metal, and the bird sitting on the sceptre is the eagle. The sandals also of the god are of gold, as is likewise his robe. On the robe are embroidered figures of animals and the flowers of the lily.

Pausanias, *Description of Greece*, 5.11.13

This statue was designed by Phidias, and created in his workshop which was situated to the west of the Altis (see also Figure 1.18). Phidias was also the sculptor who designed the statue of Athena that stood in the Parthenon. Given the huge distance between Athens and Olympia, it must be a great testament to Phidias' skill to have been asked to design both. The temple of Zeus was finished around 456 BC but the statue of Zeus was not added until 448 BC. In front of the statue was a pool of olive oil, this helped maintain the ivory on the statue and would have created a shimmering reflection of the light.

PRACTICE QUESTIONS: GREECE

Source A: *The Parthenon*

Source B: *The Temple of Zeus*

1. **a.** Describe what is shown on the Eastern Pediment of the Parthenon. [2]
   b. Why might the architect have chosen to place it there? [1]
2. Which temple fulfils its purpose better, the Parthenon or the Temple of Zeus? Use **Sources A** and **B** as a starting point **and** your own knowledge in your answer. [8]

ROME

The sanctuary

The **sanctuary** was a holy area in a city or town that contained a temple and an altar to a god. The sanctuary was usually separated from the rest of the city by a wall. Importantly, a sanctuary could have temples and altars to many gods, it did not have to be specific to one god or goddess. The sanctuary often also had a fresh water source at its entrance for people to wash their hands and feet. This was because it was important to the Romans that that their holy sites were not **polluted** as this could anger the gods.

The function of a Roman temple

A temple is a building dedicated to a god and was used to house the cult statue of that god. It may be more easily understood as a house of the god, and it gave the god a residence on earth for when they left Olympus. Unlike the Greeks, Roman priests were not appointed to a specific temple.

The altar

The most important part of the sanctuary for the populace was the altar. The altar could exist in its own right without a temple (see the Ara Pacis, p. 110). The altar was where sacrifices and offerings to the god took place. The sacrifice also was the most communal part of the gods' worship and, dependent on the type of sacrifice, could involve the whole city.

ACTIVITY

Construct replicas of the Temple of Zeus at Olympia and the Parthenon, including the sculptural detail.

FIGURE 1.33
An altar dedicated to Julia Victoria who died aged 10.

FIGURE 1.34
Plan of a typical Roman temple: 1 podium; 2 colonnade; 3 cella.

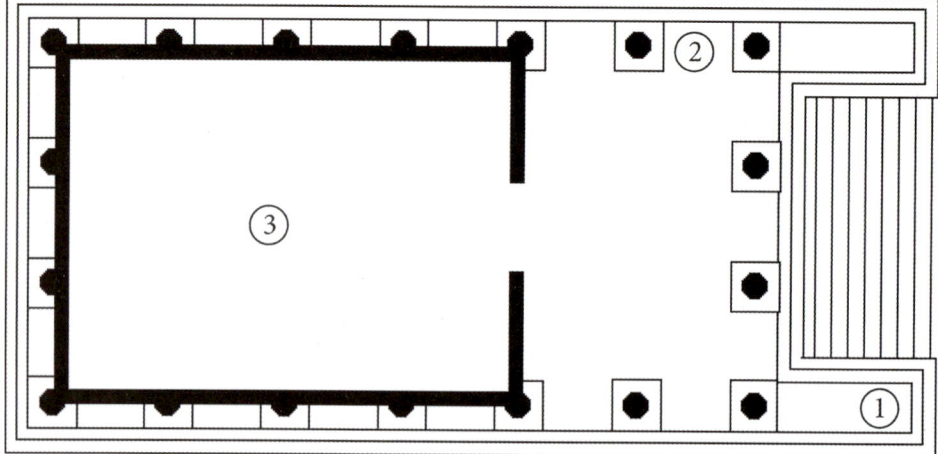

semi-engaged column a supporting column that is embedded in a wall, half protruding from it

pax deorum the peace of the gods

The temple building

Roman temple design was based on a mix of Etruscan and Greek styling. There were, however, anomalies that existed, most notable of these is the Pantheon in Rome (see also p. 63).

Figure 1.34 shows a plan of a typical Roman temple. The temple was usually orientated on an east to west axis. This was to allow the sun to shine on the temple's entrance in the morning. A Roman temple was placed on a podium (1), much like the Etruscan temples. This meant that you could only enter the temple from the front. The colonnade (2) stood on the podium and ran around the temple. In the Roman temple the side and rear columns were **semi-engaged**. The main room in a temple was the **cella** (3). This would contain the cult statue of the god.

Priests

In Rome the priesthood was an excellent example of the role of religion in society. The priest's role was to uphold the state religion by maintenance of the **pax deorum** (in Latin *pax* means 'peace' and *deorum* means 'of the gods'). This was done by uttering the correct prayer, completing the appropriate sacrifice and fulfilling their priestly roles at festivals. Unlike today, priests did not preach a way of life or moral code, it did not matter if a Roman killed or behaved poorly, provided the *pax deorum* was maintained. A good way of explaining the relationship between gods and men in the Roman world is shown in the Latin term *do ut des*, 'I give so that you give'. If the Romans offered sacrifice and offerings, then the gods would grant favour to them.

Unlike the Greeks, Roman priests were not assigned a specific temple or god. Additionally, they veiled their heads when engaging in their various religious duties (see Figure 1.35). Unlike priests today, a Roman priest worked part time. The rest of their time would have been spent engaging in business and politics. Becoming a priest could greatly increase political power and could help to progress a Roman's political career, thus many ambitious politicians would serve as priests at some point in their lives.

FIGURE 1.35
Augustus as Pontifex Maximus.

pontifex (pl. **pontifices**) a Roman priest in charge of protecting temples, regulating religious law and overseeing the religious calendar
Pontifex Maximus the head of the pontiffs, greatest pontiff

Rome had a series of priestly colleges. These groups of priests had different roles and responsibilities, but they all worked to ensure the *pax deorum*. The main colleges were:

- the pontifices
- the Augurs
- the Vestals.

The Pontifices

The **pontifices** were the most important college of priests in the Roman world. Although numbers varied through time the most common number of them totalled fifteen. The college of pontifices was headed by the **Pontifex Maximus**, a post which was life long and so gave the holder great power over the college. From Rome's founding, the Pontifex Maximus was always elected from the existing pontifices. However, from Augustus' election in 13 BC, the post was always held by the emperor. The term pontifex means bridge builder and may allude to the priest's role as mediator between man and god. The main roles of the pontifices were the protection of temples, regulation of burial and inheritance laws, and supervision of the religious calendar. Control of the calendar gave the priesthood immense power of when things could happen in Rome.

The Augurs

An augur's main job was 'taking the auspices', which meant reading the flight of birds, the behaviour of animals or direction of thunder to work out the will of the gods. The taking of auspices was commonplace in both state business and personal life. Most commonly they took place before a battle, marriage or business transaction. Writing in 20 BC, the Roman historian Livy recounted how Rome was founded. The story highlights the issues in reading such signs. Once grown, Romulus and Remus decided to found a city, but they argued as to where it should be built and so decided to take auspices to help them choose:

Since they were twins and could not be distinguished by age, it was decided that the one who protected those places should send an augury which would decide the name of the new city, and, when it had been built, who would govern it. Romulus took the Palatine as his place for observing the augury, and Remus, the Aventine.

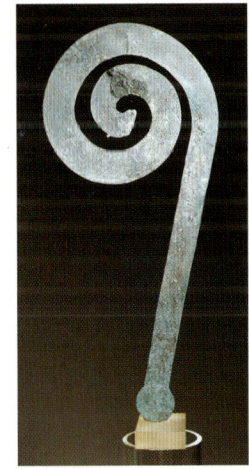

FIGURE 1.36
A **lituus**.

lituus staff used by a Roman augur

> Remus was the first to receive the augury: six vultures. Just as that omen had been reported, twice the number appeared to Romulus, and each king was saluted by their own followers: the first group prioritised time as a mark of honour, and the second, the number of birds. They entered a verbal conflict, which then turned to an angry struggle leading to bloodshed. In the ensuing clash, Remus was cut down.

Livy, *The Early History of Rome*, 1.7

Like other priesthoods and magistracies in Rome, the holders were accused of taking bribes or interpreting signs in favour of political allies for personal gain. While there is no proof of this, manipulation cannot be ruled out and, again, this explains why politics and religion in the Roman world were so closely tied.

The Vestal Virgins

> **Vestal** (pl. **Vestals**)
> female priests in charge of the cult of the goddess Vesta

The **Vestal** Virgins were a college of six priestesses who represented the only major female priesthood in Rome. As their name suggests, they were priestesses of the goddess Vesta, the goddess of the hearth (see also p. 15). The prestige of being a Vestal Virgin and the importance of their role was shown by their accommodation. The Vestals lived in the House of the Vestals, which was located in the Roman Forum, the hub of social and political activity in Rome (see Figure 1.37).

Selection

Selection to the college of the Vestals was a prestigious honour. When a position became available, the Pontifex Maximus would select a new priestess from the eligible girls. To

FIGURE 1.37
The Roman forum at the time of Augustus.

be eligible the girl needed to be between the ages of six and ten. She also needed to be fit and healthy with two living parents. The role was a big commitment, as a Vestal had to remain in the post for at least thirty years and take a vow of chastity. This would mean that the role would take up most of the girl's life. Like the pontifices, Vestals were taken from Rome's most prestigious families and the elite would hope that their daughter would have the opportunity to be a Vestal in her lifetime.

Duties, rewards and punishments

One of the Vestals most important roles was protecting the sacred flame for the safety of the state, which was housed in the Temple of Vesta. The flame was believed to have been brought from the ashes of Troy to Rome by the Roman hero Aeneas. It was believed that if the flame went out, Rome would fall. This temple also held important state documents, such as treaties and the wills of leading Romans. They also made the **mola salsa** that was sprinkled on the heads of the sacrificial animals in state sacrifices.

The Romans honoured the Vestal Virgins with several privileges. In addition to their house described above, they were also allowed front row seats at certain games. The Vestals were also freed from their father's authority, and able to make a will. These were all things that other women, Roman or otherwise, were not allowed to do.

The benefits given to the Vestals were matched by their punishments. If the flame of Vesta went out the Vestals were whipped. Additionally, if they broke their vow of chastity, they were buried alive while the male responsible was whipped to death.

mola salsa a mix of salt and flour made by the Vestal Virgins in Rome and sprinkled on the heads of sacrificial victims

FIGURE 1.38
The ruins of the temple of Vesta today.

FIGURE 1.39
Bronze model of an animal liver. This would be used by a haruspex to help him read the livers of sacrificial animals.

Both Julius Caesar and Mark Antony left their wills in the temple of the Vestals. After the breakdown in the relationship between Octavian and Mark Antony in 34 BC, Mark Antony left for Egypt where he met the Egyptian queen Cleopatra. Octavian retrieved Antony's will from the temple of the Vestals and read it to the senate. They were all shocked to read that upon his death Antony left the eastern provinces of the Roman Empire to Cleopatra and her children. This gave Octavian the fuel he needed to declare war on Antony.

Haruspex

While augurs had their origins in Greece, the haruspex was of Etruscan origin. A **haruspex** specialised in reading the entrails of sacrificial animals and was consulted at important sacrifices such as festivals and battles. To begin, the haruspex would watch how the animal fell to the ground once it was killed, he would then examine the smoke and flames when the sacrificial animal was burned on the altar. Finally, he would read the entrails of the animal. The most important of these was the liver, and the haruspex would use tools such as a model liver (see Figure 1.39) as a guide to reading it. The different parts of the liver meant different things, and the haruspex would check its consistency to see if it had any abnormalities, such as blood spots on its surface.

> **haruspex** (pl. **haruspices**) a Roman priest who read omens from entrails

Sacrifices

Roman sacrifices followed the same general procedure as Greek sacrifices, with blood sacrifices being the most common. The procedure of sacrifice was so important that if something went wrong the whole process would need to be started again.

The sacrifice can be divided into three parts:

- the preparation
- the kill
- the sharing of the sacrifice.

The preparation

In state sacrifices a pontifex would lead the ceremony, but in a smaller sacrifice it would be a private citizen. Once chosen, all the participants would ensure they were clean and

FIGURE 1.40
A relief showing a suovetaurilia.

well in order not to pollute the sacrifice. Additionally, they would dress in their best clothes. Next, the animal was prepared by gilding the horns if it had any or tying ribbons to its tail or horns. Attendants would then lead the animals to the altar (and it was a good omen if it went willingly). The presiding priest would veil his head with his toga. In order to obscure any noises that may scare the animal, flute players would join the procession.

The kill

Once at the altar the priest would sprinkle *mola salsa* on the animal's head, followed by wine, causing it to nod. Like the Greek sacrifice, it was important that the animal be seen to agree to the ritual. The priest would utter a prayer to the god, offering the animal into their care. At this point, a **popa** struck the animal on the head to stun it, and the **cultrarius** would slit the throat. It was important that the animal die with a single blow.

The sharing of the sacrifice

Once the animal was killed the feast began and the Romans ensured that none of the animal went to waste. The god received their share first as they were the most important. The priest would utter a prayer stating the god's name and the reason for the sacrifice. The entrails of the animal were read for omens by the haruspex and then cooked and offered to the gods. The remaining meat was then cut up, cooked and shared with the wider community. The communal aspect in Rome still had a hierarchy that was to be adhered to. In a state sacrifice the first to eat the sacrificial meat were the priests, followed by the senate, other elite citizens and so on. In a private sacrifice, only the participants of the sacrifice would share the meat. Despite the hierarchy, the sharing of the meat stressed the communal spirit and benefits of a sacrifice to those who participated. Meat was not a common part of the Roman diet and so was a further benefit to sacrifice for the participants.

The Temple of Portunus (Fortuna Virilis)

The temple has been given two names, as it was earlier wrongly attributed to Fortuna Virilis meaning *manly fortune*. It has more recently been correctly associated with Portunus, god of harbours. It was constructed during the Roman republic between 120 BC and 80 BC.

> **popa** an official at a Roman sacrifice who struck the sacrificial animal with a wooden rod
>
> **cultrarius** an official at a sacrifice who slit the throat of the sacrificial animal

> **S & C** The suovetaurilia was one of the most common sacrifices in Rome. It consisted of a pig, sheep and ox. The suovetaurilia was used when purifying something such as new land or buildings. Before the sacrifice took place, the animals would be led in procession around whatever needed to be purified. Then they were sacrificed by the usual method.

FIGURE 1.41
The temple of
Portunus as it stands
in Rome today.

PRESCRIBED SOURCE

The Temple of Portunus (Fortuna Virilis)

Date: 120–80 BC

Commissioned by: unknown

Architect: unknown

Dedicated to: Portunus (god of harbours)

Material: a locally found stone called tufa, and limestone covered with plaster to give the effect of marble

Style: ionic

Location: Rome, the Forum Boarium (cattle market)

Function: temple

Significance: best preserved temple in Rome after the Pantheon

Location

The temple of Portunus is located in the Forum Boarium, which was a cattle market between the Palatine and Aventine Hills. The temple stands next to the Tiber in an area that was a harbour during Roman times. It stands next to the circular temple of Hercules Victor and the site of the Great Altar of Hercules.

The altar

The altar for the temple no longer exists. However, like Greek temples, it stood at the foot of the temple steps. As in Greece, all worship would have taken place at the altar.

Plan

The temple of Portunus is one of the best existing examples of a Roman temple (see Fig 1.41). The Romans gathered inspiration from both the Etruscans and the Greeks. The Etruscan influence can be seen by the podium and steps that the temple stands on. The Greek influence can be seen in the inclusion of the porch and free standing columns that are at the front of the temple. A variation on the Greek style comes with the **semi-engaged columns** that are attached to the cella.

The Pantheon

The original Pantheon was commissioned by Augustus and built by his general Marcus Agrippa between 27 and 25 BC. However, this burnt down in AD 80. The Pantheon that stands today is the building rebuilt by the emperor Hadrian, completed around AD 125.

Pantheon means *all gods* (from the Greek *pan* 'all' and *theos* 'god') and so it is believed that the temple was dedicated to all the gods. However, even in the second century AD the name of the Pantheon was debated. A Roman Historian called Dio wrote:

> It has this name, perhaps because it received among the images which decorated it the statues of many gods, including Mars and Venus; but my own opinion of the name is that, because of its vaulted roof, it resembles the heavens.
>
> Cassius Dio, *Roman History*, 53.27.2

Location

The Pantheon is located in the ancient Roman Campus Martius, *Field of Mars*. This area was a large open space where the army met before campaigns, where elections took place and where Romans would engage in general exercise.

Plan

The Pantheon is good evidence that Roman temples did not always have to conform to a standard plan. From the front the temple follows the usual Roman plan, standing on a small plinth, the columns at the front are free standing and are followed by semi-engaged columns at the rear of the porch. The unique feature comes in the **rotunda** at the rear of the temple. This circular space is capped with a dome which has an **oculus** at the top. The Pantheon provided the first example of this type of building and was a feat of engineering in its time.

Decoration

Hadrian desired to link his own family with Augustus. When he rebuilt the Pantheon, he restored the original inscription that was on the frieze:

M·AGRIPPA·L·F·COS·TERTIVM·FECIT
M[arcus] Agrippa L[ucii] f[ilius] co[n]s[ul] tertium fecit
Marcus Agrippa, son of Lucius, built this when consul for the third time

The pediment shows signs that it once contained sculpture but that is now lost.

Cult statue

Much of the internal structure of the Pantheon has been updated and changed through time. From what we do know, the circular plan would allow for several statues of gods to be placed in the cella.

PRESCRIBED SOURCE

The Pantheon

Date: AD 125

Commissioned by: Hadrian

Architect: unknown

Dedicated to: debated (see also opposite)

Material: marble, brick and concrete

Style: Corinthian

Location: Rome

Function: debated (see also opposite)

Significance: one of the best preserved ancient Roman buildings, rotunda and oculus.

---

rotunda a round Roman building, especially one with a dome

oculus a circular opening at the top of a dome

ACTIVITY

Construct a replica of the Pantheon and temple of Portunus (Fortuna Virilis).

FIGURE 1.42
The Pantheon as it stands today.

FIGURE 1.43
Illustration of the Pantheon.

PRACTICE QUESTIONS: ROME

Source A: *A Roman sacrifice*

Source B: *The temple of Vesta in Rome*

Study **Source A**.

1. Who is the main official in **Source A** and how do you know? [2]

2. a. What happened **AFTER** the sacrificial animal reached the altar but **BEFORE** it was killed? [2]

  b. Why was this important to a sacrifice? [1]

3. Which do you think was a better way to honour a Roman god, building
a temple or conducting a sacrifice? [8]

Study **Source B**.

1. Specifically, where was the temple of Vesta in Rome located? [1]

2. a. Give **two** roles for the Vestal Virgins? [2]

  b. Why were they important to the Roman state? [1]

3. Who do you think were more important to Rome, the Pontifex
Maximus or Vestal Virgins? [8]

TOPIC REVIEW

You should be able to:

1. Describe the key features of a religious sanctuary, including:
   - the typical layout of a Greek and Roman temple and how they compare to the Parthenon and temple of Zeus at Olympia, the Pantheon and temple of Portunus
   - what happened during a Greek and Roman blood sacrifice
   - the names and roles of the various Greek and Roman religious officials.

2. Explain:
   - the role of a Greek and Roman priest in their respective societies
   - why blood sacrifice was important to the Greeks and Romans
   - the extent to which the Parthenon, temple of Zeus and Pantheon and temple of Portunus conformed to the typical layout of Greek and Roman temples
   - the role the Parthenon, temple of Zeus and Pantheon played in the worship of their respective gods.

PRACTICE QUESTIONS: COMPARING GREECE AND ROME

Greece and Rome

Source A: *An extract from Aeschylus' Seven Against Thebes*

And now here Eteocles makes his vow to the gods who guard our city's land, both those who dwell in the plain and those who watch over its meeting-place . . . I vow that, if things go well and the city is saved, the citizens shall redden the gods' altars with the blood of sheep and sacrifice bulls to the gods – this is my vow – and offer trophies, while I will crown their holy temples with the spoil of the enemy's spear-pierced garments.

Source B: *A piece of sculpture showing a Roman sacrifice*

1. Study **Source A** and **Source B**.
   a. Explain why the Greeks and Romans engaged in blood sacrifice. [3]
   b. Explain the role of the temple in honouring Greek and Roman gods. [3]
   c. Explain the importance of the role played by participants during a sacrifice. [3]
   d. Explain the importance of the animal in blood sacrifice. [3]
2. Who constructed more impressive temples, the Greeks or Romans? [15]

1.4 Myth and the City: Foundation Stories

TOPIC OVERVIEW

Ancient Greek and Roman belief about how Athens and Rome were founded by their associated heroes, including how and why the myths are depicted as they are; what these myths meant to the city; the role of the hero; the role of the gods.

Greece

- The naming of Athens: Poseidon and Athena
- The adventures of Theseus: as displayed on the Theseus Kylix

Rome

- The founding of the Roman Race: Aeneas' leadership of the Trojans, arrival and settlement in Italy, the founding of Alba Longa and the line of kings
- The founding of Rome: Romulus and Remus

Greece and Rome

- A comparison of Theseus and Romulus

The prescribed sources for this topic are:

- Livy, *The Early History of Rome*, 1.0–1.1, 1.3.7–1.4, 1.6.3–1.7.3
- Plutarch, *Parallel Lives: Comparison of Theseus and Romulus*
- Kylix showing the labours of Theseus

Don't forget that you will be given credit in the exam if you study extra sources and make relevant use of them in your answers.

In this topic we will learn about the myth surrounding the naming of Athens and the role Theseus played in the development of Athens. For Rome we will explore the role Aeneas and Romulus played in the founding of the city. While exploring both cities we will look at how and why the myths are depicted as they are and what they meant to Athenians and Romans.

MYTH AND BELIEF

Many cities in the Classical world sought to link their beginnings to the gods and heroes. Athens and Rome were no different. Stories of how cities were founded were passed down by oral tradition and were not written down until the cities were well established. In some instances, even when they were written down, opinions differed as to how the city was created. This means that one single version of a city's foundation did not exist. We saw this in the sculpture of Zeus' temple at Olympia and the involvement of Heracles and Zeus in the founding of the Olympic Games (see also p. 31). When we read the accounts of Athens' and Rome's founding we are again presented with the same issues. However, when reading the accounts of Livy and Plutarch, they appear aware of the problem when writing their own histories, and ancient writers in general saw no issue in presenting their opinion alongside that of others when writing their own accounts (see also pp. 76 and 81). With this in mind, did the Greeks and Romans actually believe these events happened? Again, we cannot be sure. Myths were recorded by men who had the time to engage in writing, such as the wealthy. We cannot be sure of the extent to which the peasant farmer, butcher or blacksmith would have engaged with these. A city's founding myth could give its population a sense of unity and patriotism. Irrespective of whether the whole population believed it, what we do know is that the stories were important enough that the men in power in Greece and Rome thought to record them in writing and represent them in their cities' architecture.

GREECE

The naming of Athens

The story of Athens' naming was not recorded in one definitive version. We have instead reconstructed it through examining the existing evidence. The story was sculpted into the western pediment of the Parthenon in the fifth century BC. Although it has not survived, its existence was recorded by the Greek geographer Pausanias in the second century AD. What is presented below is a modern interpretation of a number of ancient sources.

Attica the region around Athens in south-eastern Greece (see map, p. ix)

patronage the provision of help and support

When the legendary king Cecrops founded a city in **Attica** he needed a name for it. At this time the gods travelled the land seeking cities to lay their **patronage** on. As Cecrops gave worship to both Athena and Poseidon, both came to Cecrops' city to claim it for their own. Poseidon was the first to arrive and struck the centre of the Acropolis with his trident creating a hole in the ground. From this hole sea water sprang up. Athena was the next to arrive on the Acropolis and for her gift she planted an olive tree. In order to decide the winner of the contest Zeus and Cecrops judged the gifts. Poseidon gave water, but its salt content meant that it was largely unusable. On the other hand, Athena's gift of the olive was central to the Greeks' way of life, both as food and oil. Weighing up these points, Athena was judged the victor and she named the city after herself.

S & C

The Erechtheion

As part of Pericles' building programme on the Acropolis (see also p. 48), the Erechtheion was constructed in the 420s BC. The Erechtheion was a temple dedicated to Athena, Poseidon and a legendary king of Athens called Erechtheus. The temple contained a well that was believed to be the place where Poseidon struck the Acropolis with his trident. The temple also had a small walled garden that contained the olive tree believed to be planted by Athena. In addition to these two gods, the temple also held the graves of the legendary kings Cecrops and Erechtheus.

FIGURE 1.44
A drawing of the Erechtheion as it is believed to have looked in the fifth century BC. To the right stands the sacred olive tree.

kylix (pl. kylixes) a drinking cup

Theseus and Athens

Although not the founder of Athens, as its king Theseus united Attica under the political leadership of Athens and so was a great reformer. However, before he could become king he had to undergo a series of heroic adventures similar to those of Heracles. Some of these labours are recorded on a **kylix** now in the British Museum.

S&C

EXPLORE FURTHER   Plutarch's *Life of Theseus*

What follows is an account of the life of Theseus taken from the Greek biographer Plutarch (see p. 81). Plutarch's *Lives* are an excellent example of the fluidity of myth and an acceptance by ancient writers that, if he did exist, different people thought different things about Theseus.

Read Plutarch, *Life of Theseus*, 1–2

How useful is Plutarch as a source for the life of Theseus?

Birth

Aegeus, king of Athens, had been to Delphi, where he had been asking how to get an heir. On his way home, Aegeus went to King Pittheus of Troezen, a small city south west of Athens to ask if he could interpret the oracles riddling response. Pittheus realised that the next time Aegeus had sex he would conceive a son, so he got Aegeus drunk and induced him to sleep with his daughter Aethra. They slept together and Aethra conceived Theseus. That same night Aethra received a message from Athena in a dream that she should wade to the island of Sphairia that lay close to the Troezen shore. When she arrived there, she lay on the shore. Poseidon emerged from the sea and coupled with Aethra and so the child she carried contained both human and godly characteristics. After the child was born, Aegeus was worried that Theseus' cousins in Athens

FIGURE 1.45
Kylix showing the labours of Theseus.

PRESCRIBED SOURCE

Kylix showing the labours of Theseus

Date: 440–430 BC

Style: red-figure

Artist: the Codrus Painter

Current Location: British Museum, London

Image: central scene shows Theseus defeating the Minotaur; six further labours are shown around the outside

Significance: the kylix shows seven of Theseus' labours

Study questions

1 Why may Pittheus have wanted his daughter to conceive a child by Aegeus?
2 Compare the births of Theseus and Heracles. Which do you consider to be a birth more befitting a hero?

would be jealous of Theseus and kill him. To avoid this the king left Aethra in Troezen. Before he left, Aegeus placed his sandals and sword under a rock and told Aethra that if her son was worthy to be his heir he would lift the rock and bring the sandals and sword back to him.

When he came of age, Aethra led Theseus to the rock and told him of his true parentage. Not one to shy away from a challenge, Theseus put the rock to his shoulder and easily lifted it, removing both the sandals and sword. After he retrieved his father's items, Aethra told Theseus that if he returned to Athens with them, he would become king. There were two ways to Athens. The easiest was by boat, and both Aethra and Pittheus begged Theseus to take that route. The route via land was a full of peril, containing villains and monsters, as Pittheus told Theseus:

> Some of these creatures Heracles cut off and destroyed as he went about, but some escaped his notice as he passed by, crouching down and shrinking back, and were overlooked in their abjectness. And when Heracles met with calamity . . . in the regions of Hellas the old villainies burst forth and broke out anew, there being none to rebuke and none to restrain them.

Plutarch, *Life of Theseus*, 6.5

EXPLORE FURTHER   Periphetes

S&C

The first challenge for Theseus was Periphetes – the club bearer. This bandit would hide on the side of the road, jump out and beat travellers to death with his club. Theseus spotted him before he could pounce, grappled with him, then beat him with his own club. As a prize Theseus took the club and used it in his subsequent labours.

How does this story parallel Heracles' labours?

Instead of deterring Theseus, this encouraged him to take the land route, as he had long looked up to his cousin Heracles' labours, and longed to equal his achievements.

Study question
Whose reasons for undertaking his tasks were more heroic, Theseus' or Heracles'?

Sinis (1)

The second labour was Sinis – the pine bender. Sinis was a robber who would tie his victims to the ends of bent pine trees then release them tearing them to pieces. In one version of the myth Theseus tricked Sinis by asking for Sinis to help him bend a pine. Once both men had bent the pine back Theseus let go and flung Sinis to his death. In another version of the myth Theseus tied Sinis to two pines and he was torn in two. After he slew Sinis, Theseus courted his daughter Perigune and she bore him a son called Melanippus.

On the kylix Sinis is seated on a hill-top beside a tall pine-tree. Theseus has seized him by the right arm and with the other hand draws down the top of the pine-tree. Sinis has thrown one arm around the pine and presses his right foot against the rock. At the foot of the hill the outline of a tortoise has been drawn in error and left unfinished.

Crommyonian sow (2)

Unlike the previous two labours Theseus sought out the Crommyonian sow as, according to Plutarch:

> he might not be thought to perform all his exploits under compulsion, and at the same time because he thought that while the brave man ought to attack villainous men only in self-defence, he should seek occasion to risk his life in battle with the nobler beasts.

Plutarch, Life of Theseus, 9.1

Another version of the myth states that the sow actually referred to a female thief who was nicknamed 'Sow' on account of her beast-like behaviour. In both versions of the myth, Theseus killed the sow.

On the kylix the sow of Crommyon springs upward against Theseus, who advances with sword drawn back and left hand raised and wrapped in a mantle as a shield. Beside the sow an old woman stands, she has a long chiton and a mass of white hair. She is probably Phaea (the Grey One), the old woman who reared the sow.

Sciron (3)

Sciron was an old man who would sit on a path by the cliff's edge. He would ask passers-by to wash his feet. As they bent to wash them he would kick them into the sea. They would then be consumed by a giant turtle. Theseus caught the old man by the feet and threw him off the cliff.

On the kylix Theseus swings over his head the foot-stool to strike down Sciron, who has fallen backwards to the right on the hill in an attitude balancing that of Procrustes (5). He is bald over the forehead, and has shaggy hair and beard; at the foot of the hill is the tortoise, half seen, as though climbing up out of water.

Cercyon (4)

Next Theseus arrived at Eleusis, a city ruled by King Cercyon. As a show of strength, Cercyon would challenge passers-by to a wrestling match. The winner would become king of Eleusis. The geographer Pausanias noted about Cercyon:

> He is said to have treated strangers wickedly, especially in wrestling with them against their will. So even to my day this place is called the Wrestling Ground of Cercyon . . . Cercyon is said to have killed all those who tried a bout with him except Theseus, who out matched him mainly by his skill. For Theseus was the first to discover the art of wrestling, and through him afterwards was established the teaching of the art. Before him men used in wrestling only size and strength of body.

> Pausanias, *Description of Greece*, 1.39.3

Having defeated Cercyon, Theseus became king of Eleusis. Despite this, Theseus moved on to Athens.

On the kylix Theseus is pulling Cercyon's body towards him. His body position suggests that he is ready to throw Cercyon backwards across his thighs. The left arm of Cercyon hangs uselessly behind the back of Theseus. Beside the men, there is a club hanging up and a spear or staff leaning against the wall.

Procrustes (5)

Procrustes posed the last of Theseus' six labours on the way to Athens. This foe would invite visitors to stay a night on a 'magical' bed that would fit anyone. Once they accepted, he would lay them on the bed. If they were too small, he would use his mallet to stretch them out. If they were too tall, he would use his axe to chop off their feet and head. Theseus compelled Procrustes to lay in his bed to test it before he tried. When Procrustes lay on the bed, Theseus quickly chopped off his head and made him suffer the same fate as his many victims before him.

On the kylix Procrustes has fallen backwards on his bed, supporting himself with his right hand, and, with left hand and foot feebly raised, tries to ward off the blow which Theseus, swinging over his back the double axe, is dealing him.

Theseus in Athens

When Theseus arrived in Athens he found his father under the control of the witch Medea. In order not to arouse suspicion, Theseus did not reveal himself to his father until he had a plan of action. Unfortunately for Theseus, Medea knew who he was and convinced his father that the stranger posed a threat to Athens. Accordingly, she arranged for Theseus to prove his heroism by defeating the Bull of Marathon (6) that had terrorised Attica ever since Heracles brought it to king Eurystheus as part of his labours. Theseus accepted the challenge and easily mastered the bull and marched it through Athens before sacrificing it.

On the kylix the bull, charging fiercely, is being ridden by Theseus, who, with right leg supported against a rock and left knee pressed against the bull's shoulder, throws his weight back on a cord in his left hand, which is fastened to the animal's horns.

With her first attempt thwarted, Medea then arranged to have Theseus poisoned during the sacrifice. During the meal, Theseus pulled out his father's sword as if to carve the meat from the sacrifice. Aegeus immediately recognised the sword and in his excitement knocked over the poison. Aegeus legally recognised Theseus as his heir in front of the citizens of Athens so there could be no doubt of his right to the throne. The spilling of the poison exposed Medea's wickedness and she was forced to flee Athens.

Theseus and the Minotaur (7)

As a consequence of his son Androgeus' death, Minos, the king of Crete, demanded that seven girls and seven boys be sent each year from Athens to Crete as sacrifice to the Minotaur. Theseus' return coincided with this sacrifice. The youths for sacrifice were chosen by **lot** from the citizen families of Athens. Showing his courage again, Theseus volunteered for the sacrifice.

> **lot** the random drawing of a name from a pot

S & C

Apollodorus explains how the Minotaur was born:

> Poseidon did send him up a fine bull, and Minos obtained the kingdom, but he sent the bull to the herds and sacrificed another. But angry at him for not sacrificing the bull, Poseidon made the animal savage, and contrived that Pasiphae should conceive a passion for it. In her love for the bull she found an accomplice in Daedalus, an architect who had been banished from Athens for murder. He constructed a wooden cow on wheels . . . then he introduced Pasiphae into it; and the bull came and coupled with it, as if it were a real cow. And she gave birth to Asterius, who was called the Minotaur. He had the face of a bull, but the rest of him was human; and Minos . . . shut him up and guarded him in the Labyrinth.
>
> Pseudo-Apollodorus, *Library*, 3.1

When in Crete, Theseus met Ariadne, daughter of Minos. Having fallen in love with Theseus, Ariadne gave him a ball of wool so he would not get lost in the labyrinth and a sword so he could kill the Minotaur. On the kylix Theseus, with his sword in his right hand, moves to the left, looking back, and dragging with his left hand the Minotaur by the left horn out of a building. The Minotaur has apparently fallen forward, dying. Only his head, right arm and body to the waist are visible, the rest being concealed behind the building. Theseus was successful in his mission and left the labyrinth having killed the beast.

Ariadne ran off with Theseus when he boarded his ship to return to Athens. Theseus left Ariadne on the island of Naxos before returning to Athens.

There are several different versions of the Theseus myth. One says that Ariadne was pregnant with Theseus' child and while they rested on Naxos, Theseus went to secure the ship. Whilst on board he was swept away by storms and unable to return. At this point the women of Naxos looked after Ariadne until she gave birth to their son. She then lived out her life on Naxos.

Another version states that Theseus fell in love with another woman and abandoned Ariadne on Naxos, taking away his other bride instead.

EXPLORE FURTHER

Island of Naxos
Read Plutarch, *Life of Theseus*, 20.

What reasons does Plutarch give for Theseus leaving Ariadne in Naxos?

Study questions

1 Which of these stories regarding Ariadne do you find the more believable?

2 Which of these versions do you think the Athenians would rather believe? Give a reason for your answer.

A final version states that while on Naxos, Athena came to Theseus in a dream and told him that Dionysus had chosen Ariadne for his bride and that Theseus was to leave her on Naxos so she could be with the god.

Upon returning to Athens, Theseus was meant to remove the black sail of grief and replace it with a white sail that signified that he was safe and that his mission had been successful. Theseus forgot to show this sail and when Aegeus saw the black sail, believing Theseus to be dead, he threw himself from the city walls into the sea. When Theseus found out about this he was distraught and honoured his father with a state burial and sacrifices worthy of the king. Theseus was involved in a number of other adventures that became famous images of power for Athens.

Theseus as King of Athens

As king of Athens Theseus brought about a number of reforms to Attica. First, he realised that the region around Athens was made up of a lot of small warring towns. The region lacked unity and because of this it was weak. Theseus travelled to each of these towns and negotiated their allegiance to Athens. He won them over by promising that they would be not be ruled by a king but would take part in a democracy. This would give them the opportunity to vote for their leaders. Theseus would be commander in time of war and keeper of the laws, but in all else they would be equal. The towns agreed and so Athens the city was formed. To firmly place Athens at the centre of the alliance, Theseus destroyed all the town halls and council chambers in the smaller towns and built a new council chamber and town hall in Athens. To unite the religions of the area he initiated the Panathenaic Games. Within these games all Athenians would have an opportunity to contest and represent their tribe (see also p. 84).

Study questions

1 Compare the account of Theseus' labours to their representation on the British Museum's kylix. How appropriate is the scene chosen by the artist for each labour?

2 Compare the adventures of Theseus to those of Heracles.
   a. Which hero undertook the more dangerous tasks? Give reason for your answers.
   b. How similar were the ways in which each hero successfully completed his tasks?

3 Based on his tasks, who was the greater hero, Theseus or Heracles?

Death, burial and importance

After Theseus' death Plutarch states:

The Athenians were moved to honour Theseus as a demigod, especially by the fact that many of those who fought at Marathon against the Medes thought they saw an apparition of Theseus in arms rushing on in front of them against the Barbarians . . . And now he lies buried in the heart of the city, near the present gymnasium, and his tomb is a sanctuary and place of refuge for runaway slaves and all men of low estate who are afraid of men in power, since Theseus was a champion and helper of such during his life, and graciously received the supplications of the poor and needy.

Plutarch, *Life of Theseus*, 35.5–36.2

Therefore, although Theseus did not found Athens he was credited with uniting the city with the neighbouring towns. He introduced democracy, which made all citizens equal and marked Athens out from the other kingdoms that were ruled by a king. This trait gave Athens its identity in the ancient world and laid the marker that others followed, or tried to suppress. In Theseus, Athens thought it had a hero that could match the great Heracles. Indeed, many of his later adventures involved him fighting alongside Heracles.

EXPLORE FURTHER   Euripides' *Heracles*   **S&C**

The Athenian tragedian Euripides wrote *Heracles* in the late fifth century BC. The play attempts to explain the death of Heracles' family at his own hands. At the end of the play the hero is consoled by Theseus who helps convince Heracles not to kill himself.

Read Euripides, *Heracles*, 1167–1427.

What impression of Theseus do you get from these lines?

Study question

Who was more significant as a hero of a centre, Heracles at Olympia or Theseus at Athens? Give reasons for your answer.

ACTIVITY

You have been asked to speak in front of the Athenians at the funeral of Theseus. You must write a eulogy to honour the life of Theseus including his greatest achievements and what he did for Athens.

PRACTICE QUESTIONS: GREECE

Source A: *Greek kylix showing some of the labours of Theseus*

1. **a.** In the myth of the contest judged by Cecrops between Athena and Poseidon, what did Athena do to win? [2]
   b. What was the significance of this act to the Athenians? [1]

Study **Source A.**

2. Which of Theseus' labours is labelled A and how do you know? [2]

ROME

In this section we will be learning about the founding of Rome from the account of Livy. Therefore, it is important to understand a little about Livy and the strengths and weaknesses of his account before we start.

The life of Livy

Titus Livius (Livy) was born in Padua, northern Italy, in either 64 BC or 59 BC. Unlike many Romans of his social status he did not involve himself in a political career; instead he devoted his life to his literary works, most notably his *History of Rome*. The exact date he started writing the *History of Rome* is not known. However, due to references to historical events of the 20s BC, it is believed he started on the first five books around 24 BC.

Livy lived through great turbulence. He was born at the time of the Civil War between Julius Caesar and Pompey Magnus in 59 BC. He was 21 or 16 when Julius Caesar was assassinated in Rome. A year later, the adopted son of Caesar, Octavian, with the help of Mark Antony, defeated Caesar's murderers, Cassius and Brutus, at Philippi in Greece. After Antony met Cleopatra in Egypt, the relationship between him and Octavian soured, leading to the battle of Actium in 31 BC. After this battle Antony and Cleopatra committed suicide, leaving Octavian in sole charge of Rome. What followed was an age in which Octavian declared an end to civil war and ushered in a golden age of building, literature and politics. In 27 BC Octavian was given the name Augustus by the senate. Historians mark this as the beginning of the Empire, an age where the Emperor was at the head of the state.

Thus it can be seen that Livy lived through one of the most significant periods of Roman history. By his early thirties Livy had seen the fall of the Republic and the founding of the Imperial system under Augustus.

FIGURE 1.46
A modern statue of Livy (note Athena in the background). **PS**

Livy as a source for Roman history

We must be cautious when we use the term 'historian' when referring to ancient writers. Although Livy was a historian, he did not gather evidence in the same way a modern historian would. Likewise, he does not make regular reference to his sources of information. Livy would use the resources available to him. As Livy himself wrote, much of Rome was destroyed after it was sacked by the **Gauls** in 387/6 BC. Thus, it was believed many written records were lost. As Livy wrote:

> I do not know whether I would achieve anything worthy of the effort involved, if I were to write down the history of the Roman people from the foundation of the city. Nor would I dare to say it if I did know, since naturally I consider the theme to be not only old, but clichéd; as long as the constant succession of new writers believe either that the information they present is more accurate, or that their writing will surpass the primitive efforts of the ancient authors.
>
> Livy, *The Early History of Rome*, 1

> **Gaul** a Roman province to the west of the Alps encompassing much of modern-day France and northern Italy

This suggests a large margin of error was possible. In addition, many of Rome's legends were oral, thus leading to adaptation and manipulation over time. Again, Livy stated:

> Besides, my subject is one which involves huge exertion: it must look back over more than seven hundred years, and has advanced from small beginnings to the present day, where it considers itself burdened by its own greatness . . . It is not my intention either to confirm or deny the traditions which came before the city was founded, or whilst it was in the process of being built; they are more suited to decorating the stories of the poet than the uncorrupted records of the historian.
>
> Livy, *The Early History of Rome*, 1

Frustrating still is the fact that Livy saw no need to separate fact from fiction, noting that:

> This indulgence is granted to the ancients; by mixing human actions with divine ones, they might make the origins of cities more sacred. But, if it is appropriate for any nation to claim its beginnings are sacred and refer back to divine founders, then Rome is that nation.
>
> Livy, *The Early History of Rome*, 1

Aeneas' birth

Aeneas' birth is explained in detail in the *Homeric Hymn to Aphrodite* and rivalled that of the Greek heroes before him. Venus boasted to the gods that she had persuaded them to sleep with mortal women, causing all kinds of problems. As punishment for this boast, Jupiter placed in Venus' heart the desire for a mortal man. After travelling to Troy, Venus met Anchises who was described as rivalling the beauty of the gods. She fell in love with him and, disguised as a mortal woman, slept with him. In the morning she revealed to Anchises what she had done:

> Anchises, most glorious of mortals, have courage. Let not your heart be so afraid. There is no need to fear, you will not suffer harm from me nor from the other blessed ones, for you are loved by the gods. You shall have a dear son who will rule among the Trojans and children will be born to his children forever. Aeneas shall be his name because my anguish was so dreadful that I fell into the bed of a mortal man. Yet of all human beings those of your race are always the closest to the gods in their beauty and form.
>
> *Homeric Hymn to Aphrodite*, 192–201

> **ACTIVITY**
>
> Read Livy, *The Early History of Rome*, 1.
>
> Highlight specific sentences and sections that illustrate the weaknesses of using Livy as a source for the early history of Rome. Summarise your findings in a paragraph.

Therefore Aeneas was the son of a mortal man and goddess.

Aeneas and Troy

Having grown up in Troy Aeneas became a fierce warrior, and when the Greeks attacked Troy he fought in the war. Aeneas is mentioned throughout the *Iliad* as both a brave soldier and loved by the gods. He survived the ten-year onslaught.

The fall of Troy

After ten years of fighting the Greeks had been unable to defeat the Trojans. In a last attempt they turned to Odysseus, king of Ithaca. Odysseus devised a wooden horse that the Greeks filled with their own men. Once complete the horse was wheeled to the gates of Troy. The rest of the army got on their boats and sailed out of sight of Troy. Thinking it a peace offering from the Greeks, and in fear of the gods, the Trojans brought the horse into Troy. When night came the Greeks crept out of the horse and opened the city gates, letting in the rest of their army. The Greeks quickly killed the Trojan warriors and began to burn the city. In the process, they killed the Trojan king, Priam.

The wanderings of Aeneas

Having been unable to save Troy, Aeneas fled the city with his father Anchises, wife Creusa, and son Ascanius. In the confusion, he lost his wife. When she later appeared to him as a ghost, he realised that she had been killed by the Greeks. In addition to his family, Aeneas brought the **public Penates** with him. After Rome's founding, these were looked after by the Vestal Virgins (see also p. 58). After leaving Troy Aeneas travelled across the Aegean Sea to Macedon, from Macedon to Sicily, and finally from Sicily to the west coast of Italy (see map, Figure 1.10).

Throughout his journey Aeneas demonstrated his **pietas**. This term goes beyond our modern word 'piety'. Pietas was a Roman virtue and it encompassed respect for the family, gods and your city.

Having arrived in Italy Aeneas engaged in a huge war with a local tribe. After winning the war he made peace with King Latinus of Latium and founded a new city. He and his wife Lavinia had a son called Ascanius. Livy discusses this in another section of his history as it posed a problem for him. It was commonly known that Aeneas already had a son called Ascanius by his first wife Creusa. Therefore, we are unsure if this was a second son or a confusion of the ancient source material. Aeneas' first son by Creusa was also known by the name Iulus, so it may be possible that this second Ascanius was in fact a different person and indeed a second son of Aeneas.

The importance of Aeneas to Rome

As Livy states, Aeneas did not found Rome. So why was he important? Livy and Virgil wrote about Aeneas between 28 BC and 19 BC, the same time that Augustus was ruling

EXPLORE FURTHER **S&C**

The fall of Troy is not recorded in the epics of Homer. Only Virgil's epic, the *Aeneid*, describes how Troy fell.

Read Virgil's *Aeneid*, Book 2.

How heroic was Aeneas during the fall of Troy? Use evidence from the *Aeneid* to support your answer.

public Penates sacred objects dedicated to the city

pietas the most important heroic quality in the *Aeneid*, a Roman virtue that means 'sense of duty', and applies to a man's duty towards his family, gods and city

S & C

Virgil sought to explain the beginning of Rome in a version to rival the existing work of Homer. To do this he took a lot of inspiration from Homer's *Iliad* and *Odyssey*, and Aeneas' journey is comparable to the wanderings of Odysseus in the *Odyssey*. Like Homer's epics, Virgil's story is full of references to the gods and mythology of the ancient world.

Study questions

Read Livy, *The Early History of Rome*, 1.1.

1. Who was Antenor?
2. What city did Antenor found?
3. Livy tells two stories of how Aeneas and King Latinus came to peace.
   a. Describe each of those stories in detail.
   b. Which do you think is the more likely to have happened? Support your answer with information from the source.
4. How did the events of the alliance between Aeneas and Latinus show Aeneas' pietas?
5. What was the name of Aeneas' new settlement and why was it called that?

Study questions

Read Livy, *The Early History of Rome*, 1.3.7–1.4.

1. Why were King Tiberinus and King Aventinus important to Rome?
2. How did Amulius try to secure his reign against his brother Numitor?
3. How did making his niece a Vestal Virgin help Amulius secure his throne?
4. How did Rhea Silva fall pregnant?
5. Why might the Romans have favoured Mars as a father figure?
6. How did Amulius try to kill Romulus and Remus?
7. Having been saved from death, what happened next to the twins? What variation of the story does Livy offer?

Rome. Augustus was nephew and adopted son of Julius Caesar. The Caesars traced their family lineage back to Aeneas in order to legitimise their right to rule Rome. In Aeneas, Augustus could claim that he was related to the gods and that his family founded the Roman race.

Aeneas to Romulus

After Aeneas died, his son took control of Lavinium. Due to the gradual expansion of Lavinium, Ascanius founded a new city called Alba Longa next to it. This city spawned the line of kings that culminated in the birth of Romulus and Remus.

The founding of Rome

The grandfather of Romulus and Remus, King Numitor, was supplanted by his brother Amulius. When they came of age, Romulus and Remus took revenge on Amulius and killed him, returning the city to Numitor. Rather than continue to live in Alba Longa, the twins decided to found a new city because Alba Longa had, like Lavinium before it, become overcrowded.

Study questions

Read Livy, *The Early History of Rome*, 1.6.3–1.7.

1 What trait did Romulus and Remus share with their uncles? Why did this cause a problem for them?
2 How did the twins decide to resolve the issue?
3 Having decided how to resolve the issue where did each brother stand?
4 How successful was their solution?
5 Who won the right to name the new city and what did they call it?

PRACTICE QUESTIONS: ROME

Source A: *An extract from Livy about the meeting of Latinus and Aeneas*

From this point, there are two versions of the story. Some say that when Latinus was defeated in battle he made peace with Aeneas, and later, an alliance of marriage. Others claim that when battle lines had been drawn, Latinus advanced before the trumpet had sung the starting signal, and, surrounded by his generals, called the leader of the foreigners to a conference. Then he asked: who were they; where had they come from; what misfortune had made them leave their home; and what were they looking for when they came to Laurentum?

Livy, *The Early History of Rome*, 1.1

Source B: *An extract from Livy about Romulus and Remus*

Remus was the first to receive the augury: six vultures. Just as that omen had been reported, twice the number appeared to Romulus, and each king was saluted by their own followers: the first group prioritised time as a mark of honour, and the second, the number of birds. They entered a verbal conflict, which then turned to an angry struggle leading to bloodshed. In the ensuing clash, Remus was cut down . . . So Romulus gained sole power, and when the city was established, it took its founder's name.

Livy, *The Early History of Rome*, 1.7

Study **Source A**.

1. How did Aeneas respond to the following questions?
   a. Where did you (Aeneas and his men) come from?   [1]
   b. Why did you leave that place?   [1]
   c. For what purpose have you landed in Italy?   [1]

Study **Source B**.

2. **a.** What was the name given to a priest who could read bird signs and why did Romulus and Remus consult such men on this occasion? (lines 2–3)   [2]
   b. What problem does Source B highlight about using bird signs to make decision?   [1]

GREECE AND ROME

As we have seen, Theseus and Romulus were believed to be two of the great men in Greek and Roman history. Theseus, the great reformer, unified Athens and allowed it to expand into the great city it became. On the other hand, Romulus, after a turbulent upbringing, warred with his brother and founded the city of Rome. In the second century AD the Greek biographer Plutarch compared the lives of the two great men.

The life of Plutarch

Plutarch was born in Boeotia, Greece, sometime before AD 50 and he died sometime after AD 120. Despite the popularity of his literary work he spent most of his life in Greece, and from *c.* AD 90 he served as a priest of Apollo in Delphi. The period in which Plutarch lived was not as turbulent as that of Livy. He lived at a time when the rule of the emperor had been firmly established in Rome. Despite this there are several events that took place in the Roman world that bear note: during the reign of Nero in AD 64, Rome suffered a devastating fire that destroyed much of the city; in 79 Pompeii was destroyed by the eruption of Vesuvius, and in 80 the Emperor Titus finished the construction of the Colosseum in Rome.

Plutarch was a biographer and is best known for his *Lives*, a series of literary works that, as the title suggests, examined the lives of some of the most famous Greeks and Romans. In addition to his *Lives* he also wrote the *Parallel Lives*, in which he compared the life of a great Greek with that of a great Roman. It is the *Lives of Theseus and Romulus* that we will be examining.

Plutarch as a source for Greek and Roman History

Unlike Livy, Plutarch wrote biographies. With this in mind he was more concerned with character and the individual rather than compiling a narrative history of the time in which he lived. Plutarch was a prolific writer and read extensively. When writing his *Lives* he often used one main source and supplemented this with others as he went. Where evidence from the sources was lacking, he filled in the blanks with his own thoughts on the man he wrote about. As we saw above, the history of Rome's founding was largely based on myth and legend. Although many writers came before him, Livy's work became the 'go-to' source for those writing on early Roman history. There is no doubt that Plutarch used Livy when writing on the life of Romulus.

A comparison of Theseus and Romulus

Plutarch's comparison does not read like a modern essay. He does not outline what he will discuss and does not make clear who he thinks is the better of the two men. Instead, he compares the men in several different areas drawing on his various sources. His areas of comparison are:

PRESCRIBED SOURCE

Plutarch, *Parallel Lives: Comparison of Theseus and Romulus*

Date: AD 100–120

Author: Lucius Mestrius Plutarch (Plutarch)

Genre: biography

Significance: Plutarch directly compares the lives of Theseus and Romulus

Read it here: OCR sources booklet

- Section 1 – the greatness of their deeds
- Section 2 – their leadership
- Section 3 – the reasons for their misfortune
- Section 4 – their achievements
- Section 5 – their relationship to their family
- Section 6 – their relationship to women and the gods

At times it is clear that he favours one over the other, although his comparison lacks an overall conclusion and he leaves the reader to make up their own mind as to which of the men was the greater.

TOPIC REVIEW

You should be able to:

1. Describe:
   - the contest that took place between Athena and Poseidon for the naming of Athens
   - each of the scenes shown on the Theseus kylix in the British Museum
   - the events that led to Aeneas landing in Italy
   - the events that led to Romulus founding Rome.

2. Explain:
   - why the myth of Athena and Poseidon's contest was important to the Athenians
   - why Theseus was important to the Athenians
   - why Livy used Aeneas and Romulus' stories in his work
   - why Plutarch considered Theseus and Romulus good subjects for comparison in his work.

PRACTICE QUESTION: COMPARING GREECE AND ROME

Who was the greater man, Theseus or Romulus? Justify your answer. [15]

1.5 Festivals

TOPIC OVERVIEW

Greek and Roman festivals, including the origins of the festival; officials; sacrifice; the programme; the participants.

Greece

- The City Dionysia and the Great Panathenaia

Rome

- The Lupercalia and Saturnalia

There are no prescribed sources for this topic, but students are encouraged to draw on any other appropriate sources and evidence they have studied in the extended response exam questions. Here are some suggestions:

- Panathenaic amphorae and the Panathenaic frieze on the Parthenon
- Ovid, *Fasti*, 2.267–474: 15th Feburary, the Lupercalia
- a drawing from the Calender of Philocalus showing the Saturnalia (see p. 95)

In this topic you will study some of the key festivals that took place in Greece and Rome. For Greece you will examine the Great Panathenaia that was held to honour the city's patron goddess Athena. You will also study the City Dionysia held in honour of Dionysus, god of wine and revelry. For Rome you will study the Lupercalia held in honour of Lupercus and the Saturnalia held for Saturn.

When examining these festivals, you will need to draw comparisons between their origins, officials, the sacrifices that took place and the people who attended the festival.

FESTIVALS IN THE GREEK AND ROMAN WORLD

Although the Greeks and Romans divided their year into twelve months, they did not divide their week into seven days. In fact they did not even have weeks. To gain their rest days the Greeks and Romans scattered their months with numerous holiday days, in which they watched games and took part in religious festivals. Some festivals lasted just one day, while others could last a lot longer. Our seven-day week gives us roughly 104 days off per year. In Classical Athens around 140 days of the year were given over to religious celebrations, festivals and entertainment days. In Rome around 159 days were given over to these days.

GREECE

The Great Panathenaia

Panathenaia an annual Athenian festival celebrating Athena's birthday

Great Panathenaia an Athenian festival to Athena that took place every four years and contained more athletic and literary competitions than the annual Panathenaia

The **Panathenaia** was for all Athenians, and only Athenians and resident foreigners could take part. As Athena was the patron goddess of Athens, the celebration of her birthday marked the most important part of the year for the city. Theseus was believed to have founded the yearly Panathenaia in honour of Athena (see p. 74). From 566 BC every four years the Panathenaia was expanded to an eight-day festival called the **Great Panathenaia**, which contained more athletic and literary competitions.

The programme of events

Sources are not clear when it comes to the exact programme of the Great Panathenaia. However, the most commonly understood version is as follows:

Day	Event
1	Rhapsodic and musical contests
2	Boys' and youths' athletics
3	Men's athletics
4	Equestrian events
5	Tribal contests
6	All-night celebration, procession and sacrifice
7	Apobates and boat race
8	Prize-giving

Rhapsodic and musical contests

rhapsode (pl. **rhapsodes**) someone who recites epic poetry at a festival competition

The first events to take place were the rhapsodic and musical contests. The verses that were recited were taken from Homer's *Iliad* and *Odyssey*. As the work of Homer was part of the oral tradition, **rhapsodes** would have to have an excellent memory in order to correctly recite the sections chosen for the contest.

There were four main competitions in the musical contests, which revolved around two popular Greek instruments, the aulos (an oboe-like instrument) and kithara (a harp-like instrument from the same family as the lyre). The first of these were singers accompanied by the aulos, the second was soloists on the aulos, the third were singers accompanied by the kithara and the fourth was soloists on the kithara.

The sporting events

Three of the eight days of the Great Panathenaia were taken up by sporting events. The Great Panathenaia offered a wide variety of athletic events. While these events were almost exclusively for Athenians, there were a small number of events for non-Athenians to take part in. Women were not allowed to compete in the sporting events. Like the prizes for the musical and rhapsodic events, the sporting prizes were worth a great deal. Winners would receive a varied amount of **Panathenaic amphorae**. The amphorae would have a picture of Athena on one side and a picture of the event in which they were awarded on the other. This reinforced the importance and honour paid to Athena through the sporting competitions. The amphorae would be filled with olive oil, which was a valuable commodity in Greece as it was used for cooking and cleaning.

> **Panathenaic amphora** (pl. **Panathenaic amphorae**) storage jars containing olive oil given as prizes at the Great Panathenaia

The stadion

The stadion was a running event in which the competitors would run the length of the stadium.

Wrestling

According to myth Theseus was believed to have introduced wrestling as a sporting contest after he defeated King Cercyon of Eleusis. During the contest competitors would attempt to get their opponent down onto their back or shoulders, which was called a 'fall'. After three 'falls' the contest was over. To make it harder, the competitors would cover themselves in oil. Opponents were allowed to trip one another but there was no biting, kicking or punching allowed.

FIGURE 1.48
Panathenaic amphora showing wrestlers (left); on the other side is Athena (right).

EXPLORE FURTHER

In Homer's *Iliad* Achilles held funeral games for Patroclus. These included boxing, wrestling, a foot race, archery and javelin.

Read Homer, *Iliad*, 23.651–797, 850–883.

1. Which do you consider the more dangerous competition?
2. What role do the Greeks believe the gods play in athletic competition?

Support your answers with evidence from Homer's *Iliad*.

Boxing

Ancient boxing was very different from our modern version. Competitors would not wear any protective head gear. Instead of gloves the athletes would wrap leather strips around the knuckles, which was for the protection of their own hands, not the opponent's body. The object was to knock out your opponent, so many of the blows were not to the body but the head. This made boxing one of the most dangerous of the ancient competitions.

Pankration

The term pankration literally means 'all strength' and competitors certainly needed everything they had to compete in this event. The pankration was a mixture of boxing and wrestling with the addition of kicking moves. The competition only had two rules: no eye gouging and no biting.

Pentathlon

The ancient pentathlon consisted of the discus, javelin, long jump, stadion and wrestling. Three of these events did not take place as events in their own right, so they came first. If an athlete won all these three events then the last two events, the stadion and wrestling, did not take place.

Equestrian events

On the fourth day of the games the equestrian events took place. These included a four-horse chariot race. Another was a mounted javelin contest where riders would have to hit targets while riding their horses. The greatest of the equestrian events took place on the seventh day of the festival, which was the **apobates** (meaning *dismounter* in Greek). This race involved fully armoured charioteers dismounting their chariots while racing, running alongside them for a period of time, then mounting them again. Unlike all the other events, this meant that the prize for an equestrian event went to the owner of the horses, not the rider.

apobates in Greek means *dismounter* – a chariot race in which the rider would dismount and remount his chariot

Tribal contests

There were four events that made up the tribal contests. As their name suggests they were only open to the citizens of Athens, who competed in their ten tribes.

- The first of these events were a series of strength trials.
- The second was the boat race that took place in the nearby port town of Piraeus.
- The third was a war dance competition accompanied by the aulos (pipes).
- The fourth was a torch race to the altar of Athena on the Acropolis.

All-night celebration, procession and sacrifice

On the evening before the procession an all-night celebration took place on the Acropolis. The torch race involved a two-mile run from the Dipylon Gate to the altar on the

The ten tribes of Athens

In 508 BC an Athenian statesman called Cleisthenes reformed the constitution of Athens by changing its tribal system. Prior to his reforms Attica was divided into four tribes, which were united by familial ties. These ties of blood fragmented the Athenian political system as tribes sought only to progress the prestige of their family rather than Athens. To stop this, Cleisthenes divided Attica into ten tribes based on region rather than family. Each tribe was named after a hero of Athens and statues of the heroes were erected in the Athenian marketplace.

Acropolis. Each competitor would race with a lit torch, with the winner's torch being used to light the sacrificial flame used in the sacrifice to Athena the next day. No doubt this would have been an incredible honour for the winner and would have created great glory for the winning tribe. This would be followed by singing and dancing in honour of Athena, which involved maidens and young men.

The sixth day was the most important in relation to Athena as it was the day all Athens presented her with the **peplos**. The peplos was a Greek dress that was woven using saffron and purple cloth. Stitched in saffron thread were scenes from the great battle between the gods and the giants. In the mid-fifth century two peploi were made. The smaller of the two were presented to the wooden statue of Athena in the Erechtheion. The larger may have been presented to Athena Parthenos.

> **peplos** (pl. **peploi**) a Greek dress

The procession began at the Dipylon gate, travelled through the city on the Panathenaic way and ended at the foot of the Acropolis. The larger of the two peploi was used as a sail for a ceremonial boat that was pushed to the Acropolis before it was removed and taken up into the Acropolis. The procession ended at the altar to Athena Polias that was situated between the Parthenon and the Erechtheion.

The Panathenaic procession and the Parthenon

The Panathenaic procession was depicted on the Ionic frieze of the Parthenon (see Figure 1.49). The procession starts on the western (rear) part of the temple with cavalrymen mounting and riding their horses. The procession then follows two routes, the northern and the southern.

The sacrifice

Once the procession was complete the sacrifice began at the altar of Athena Polias. Only Athenians were allowed on the Acropolis and so a real sense of belonging would be felt by those at the sacrifice. No expense was spared at the Panathenaic sacrifice as up to one hundred oxen and other animals were sacrificed to Athena. Once the goddess had received her share of the animals, the Priestess of Athena and prominent Athenians would feast, then the rest of the community would receive the sacrificial meat.

> **Study questions**
>
> Gather some images from the Parthenon frieze.
>
> 1 Who took part in the procession?
> 2 Explain why the Ionic frieze was a good place to display the Panathenaic procession.
> 3 What is the most important image on the frieze? Justify your answer.

FIGURE 1.49
Scene from the eastern end of the Panathenaic frieze, showing the peplos bearers flanked by the goddess Athena and Hephaistos.

ACTIVITY

Phidias has been asked to build another temple to Athena in Athens. He has asked you to design six metopes to go over the temple entrance depicting the Great Panathenaia. You must choose the six most important parts of the festival and create metopes to celebrate the festival.

Study questions

1 How did the Great Panathenaia show off:
   a. the city of Athens
   b. the people in Athens
   c. the piety of the Athenians?
2 Imagine you are an ancient Athenian. What part of the Great Panathenaia would you have most enjoyed? Give reasons for your answer.
3 'The Great Panathenaia was more a celebration of Athens rather than Athena.' To what extent do you agree with this statement?

The City Dionysia

Origins of the festival

Eleutherae a town on the northern border of Attica

Although an exact date is not known, the City Dionysia, or Great Dionysia, was founded in the sixth century BC. The date coincided with the alliance between **Eleutherae** and Athens. As Pausanias wrote:

> The reason why the people of Eleutherae came over was not because they were reduced by war, but because they desired to share Athenian citizenship and hated the Thebans. In this plain is a temple of Dionysus, from which the old wooden image was carried off to Athens.
>
> Pausanias, *Description of Greece*, 1.38

When the statue originally came from Eleutherae the Athenians rejected it. Soon after this the city was hit with a plague that effected men's genitals. Linking the two events the Athenians accepted Dionysus into the city and from that point honoured him with drama and revelry and initiated the Great Dionysia. It was believed that as soon as they accepted Dionysus into the city the men were cured of their disease. As the god of revelry, wine and drama the Athenians honoured the god through their favoured form of entertainment, theatre. Due to the god being associated with rebirth, the festival took place in the spring over five days in mid-march. Although it started with a parade from the gates of Athens, the majority of the festival was based in the sanctuary of Dionysus.

The sanctuary of Dionysus

The sanctuary of Dionysus was built to the south side of the Acropolis. It contained the usual features of any other Greek sanctuary; the temple and altar were surrounded by a short wall. The sanctuary shows the communal importance of the altar as it sat in the centre of a large open area. The temple was relatively small and situated in the north-west corner of the sanctuary.

Officials

The eponymous archon

The organisation of the City Dionysia reflected the democratic nature of the city. One of the most important administrative jobs was undertaken by the **eponymous archon**, an elected official who had various administrative responsibilities over the year. The archon would select three tragic playwrights and five comic playwrights who would have to write plays, seventeen in total. After the playwrights were chosen the archon had to choose a **choregos** to finance the plays.

Participants

Even though competition between playwrights was fierce, the City Dionysia was far from elitist when it came to participation. First, the **dithyramb** competition saw 100 members from each tribe take part in a choral dance in honour of Dionysus. This meant 1,000 amateurs each year took part in the celebrations. The tragic and comic participants could be divided into two groups, professional actors and amateur chorus members. While the actors pursued theatre as a career, the amateur chorus members were drawn from the citizen body.

The night before the festival a torchlight procession took place. The procession recreated events that took place in the sixth century BC when Eleutherae allied with Athens with the wooden statue of Dionysus being brought into the city. As the statue travelled from a shrine just outside the city, to the city, it was accompanied by the military cadets.

The programme of events

Day	Event
1	Pompe, dithyrambic contests, komos
2	Opening ceremony, 5 comedies
3	3 tragedies, 1 satyr-play
4	3 tragedies, 1 satyr-play
5	3 tragedies, 1 satyr-play; Judging and prize giving

FIGURE 1.50
Plan of the sanctuary of Dionysus.

eponymous archon an Athenian magistrate elected for one year (eponymous meaning that the civil year was named after him)

choregos *chorus director* – the financial backer of a set of plays at the City Dionysia in Athens

dithyramb a choral dance in honour of the god Dionysus

Pompe, dithyrambic contests, komos

pompe a grand procession

On the morning of the first day, the **pompe**, or grand procession, took place. The procession accompanied the wooden statue of Dionysus in a boat on wheels from the city gates to the sanctuary of Dionysus. The procession resembled that of a carnival with drinking, dancing and general revelry taking place in honour of Dionysus. In addition to the more traditional sacrificial objects such as animals, fruits and breads people would also carry model phalluses in recognition of Dionysus' relationship to fertility and recreation.

After the pompe, the dithyramb competition took place in the theatre. Although little is known about the dithyramb, what is known is that it was a choral song and dance written in honour of Dionysus and that it predated tragedy and comedy.

komos meaning *revel* – a party that took place in the streets in honour of the god Dionysus

The **komos**, in which only men took part, was held in the evening of the first day. A central symbol to the celebration was the phallus, and participants would bring leather phalluses to present to the god. This celebrated Dionysus as a god of fertility. The komos involved singing, dancing and a lot of wine drinking.

Opening ceremony and the comedies

At the beginning of the second day was the opening ceremony. To start the proceedings the priest of Dionysus would sacrifice a piglet. Following this each of the ten generals of Athens poured a **libation** to the twelve Olympian gods.

libation a drink offering poured in honour of the gods

Theoric Fund a supply of money that was used to pay for the poor to attend the theatre in ancient Athens

The theatrical contests were not free. It cost two obols to attend them, which would have been a day's wage for an unskilled worker. The Athenians set up the **Theoric Fund** in the late fifth century BC to help the poor to attend the festival. Once the opening ceremony had taken place, the five comedies were shown. A single play could go on for around an hour and a half.

Comedy

Comedy developed later than tragedy and perhaps reflected the greater political freedom that was present in Athens in the fifth century BC. For this reason the themes of comedy were usually war, politics or social life. The characters in these plays would often have reversed roles, slaves would act superior to their masters, women controlled men, and politicians were openly mocked. With this in mind, comedy offered relief from the everyday world of Athens. It also allowed the playwright a chance to voice their feelings about contemporary issues in Athens. Although many playwrights wrote comedy, we only have eleven surviving plays from one comic playwright called Aristophanes (446 BC–386 BC).

The tragedies and prize giving

Unlike comedy, tragedies were performed in a trilogy plus a satyr-play. For this reason, a day each was devoted to three playwrights. This also suggests an emphasis on tragedy over comedy at the Dionysia.

Tragedy

Tragedy was inspired by well-known mythic and historical events of the past. As a genre, tragedy focused on human suffering and sought to ask questions about human nature. What makes a man great? What causes men to suffer? To what extent can man control his own fate? With this in mind the audience was meant to consider how what they were watching was reflected in their own lives, be it as an individual or as the city as a whole. Of the surviving plays we have plays by three great tragic playwrights: Aeschylus (525 BC–456 BC), Sophocles (497 BC–406 BC) and Euripides (480 BC–406 BC).

Satyr-plays

The Satyr-play formed part of four plays that were written by one playwright. It was intended as a comic respite after the three tragedies had been performed. The theme of the play was mythological and did not need to relate to the three tragedies.

The judging

On the fifth day after all the plays had been performed, each judge wrote the plays in order of preference and placed the list in a single urn. The eponymous archon then drew five of the ten lists. The playwright with the most votes was then declared victor and given a garland of ivy, a symbol of Dionysus.

Study questions

1 How did the events of the City Dionysia honour Dionysus?
2 'The City Dionysia showed off the greatness of Athens more than the Great Panathenaia did.' To what extent do you agree with this statement?

ACTIVITY

Produce a poster advertising the City Dionysia. The poster needs to inform Athenians what is going to happen during the festival and why they should attend.

PRACTICE QUESTIONS: GREECE

Source A: Section from a Greek frieze

Study **Source A:**

1. What event is shown in **Source A *and*** how do you know? [2]
2. Which do you think the Athenians would enjoy more, the Great Panathenaia or the City Dionysia? [8]

ROME

The Lupercalia

Origins of the festival

Although the origins of the Lupercalia were debated by ancient writers, the festival, as it had developed as Rome expanded, was originally derived from a festival of purification and fertility in honour of the god **Lupercus**. In Latin the word *lupus* means 'wolf' and so the festival also honoured Rome's founder Romulus. Indeed, when Romulus first founded Rome he was known as the King of the Shepherds. As Rome lost its identity as a nation of farmers, the importance of the shepherd decreased and the festival became more associated with the city's founder. The festival took place annually on 15th February.

> **Lupercus** a Roman god of fertility and purification

Officials

The priests were called the **Luperci** and were chosen especially for the day from the **noble** male population.

> **Luperci** a priest of Lupercus
>
> **noble** a member of the upper class in Rome

The programme

At the beginning of the festival the priests gathered in the **Lupercal**. This was a cave in the Palatine hill that was believed to be the place where Romulus and Remus were suckled by the she-wolf. Dionysius of Halicarnassus, who lived at the time of the emperor Augustus, described the cave:

> **Lupercal** the cave in the Palatine Hill of Rome where the Lupercalia took place

> This place the Romans call the Lupercal . . . Now, it is true, since the district about the sacred precinct has been united with the city, it has become difficult to make out by conjecture the ancient nature of the place. Nevertheless, at first, we are told, there was a large cave under the hill overarched by a dense wood; deep springs issued from beneath the rocks, and the glen adjoining the cliffs was shaded by thick and lofty trees. In this place they raised an altar to the god and performed their traditional sacrifice, which the Romans have continued to offer up to this day in the month of February, after the winter solstice, without altering anything in the rites then performed.
>
> Dionysius of Halicarnassus, *Roman Antiquities*, 1.32

DEBATE   **The Lupercalia**

The Romans themselves were not entirely sure of the origins of the festival. Two writers attempted to explain its origins. Plutarch links the festival with Archadian Lycaea, the feast of wolves (Plutarch, *Romulus*, 21.3). Ovid, on the other hand, links the festival with the Greek god Pan (Ovid, *Fasti*, 2.267–474: 15th February).

Read both writers' accounts. Which do you believe is a more likely story?

FIGURE 1.51
Scene from the Lupercal.

The cave contained an altar to Lupercus. The Luperci were divided into two teams and underwent a sacrifice in honour of the god. Once the sacrifice had taken place the two teams took part in a race around the foot of the Palatine Hill.

The sacrifice

On entering the cave the Luperci sacrificed dogs and goats to Lupercus. These animals were known for their virility and suited a sacrifice to a god of fertility. The animals were sacrificed by sprinkling *mola salsa* on their heads. Once the animals had bowed their heads in acceptance, their throats were slit. When the animals had been killed, a knife was dipped in the blood, which was dripped onto the foreheads of the participants. The blood was then immediately wiped off with wool soaked in milk. At this point the Luperci were expected to let out a laugh. Following the killing of the animals a haruspex would read their entrails for positive signs. If the entrails were positive, the participants would eat the sacrificial meat and drink large amounts of wine. Once the feast was consumed, the Luperci cut the skins from the animals into strips; some of these were used for covering parts of the body, while others were used during the race.

The reasons for the race and the participants' lack of clothing was explained by the Roman poet Ovid:

> Why, you ask, do the Luperci run, and since it's their custom, this running, why do they strip their bodies naked? The god himself loves to run swiftly on the heights, and he himself suddenly takes to flight. The god himself is naked, and orders his servants naked, since anyway clothes were not suited to that course.

> Ovid, *Fasti*, 2.283–288

S & C **Dionysius of Halicarnassus**

Dionysius was a Greek historian from Halicarnassus on the west coast of Asia Minor, modern Turkey. He lived from around 60 BC to around 7 BC. One of his major works was called *Roman Antiquities*, which focused on Rome from its mythical founding to the Punic Wars in the second century BC.

Study questions

1 How appropriately was Lupercus worshipped during the Lupercalia?
2 How inclusive was the Lupercalia festival?

The race

The race was the public part of the festival and involved the participants running around the foot of the Palatine Hill. Part of this route took them through the Roman forum, which was the centre of Roman business and politics. As the runners raced they whipped spectators with their leather strips to grant great fertility to those struck. As Plutarch wrote:

> Many women of rank also purposely get in their way, and like children at school present their hands to be struck, believing that the pregnant will thus be helped to an easy delivery, and the barren to pregnancy.
>
> Plutarch, *Caesar*, 61.2

The Saturnalia

Origins of the festival

The Saturnalia was held in honour of the Roman god Saturn. The festival celebrated a number of things:

- As Saturn was the Roman god of sowing and the seed, the festival celebrated the end of the winter sowing.
- The festival began at the Winter Solstice and celebrated the coming of new light, rebirth and the promise of a positive future.
- Saturn was believed to have ruled the earth during the Golden Age, a time when both men and gods lived together in prosperity as equals. The festival brought hope of a return to this Golden Age. The Saturnalia was considered unique amongst festivals because all levels of society took part, including men, women, children and slaves.

At its longest the festival lasted from the 17th to the 23rd of December. However, during the reign of Augustus (28 BC–AD 14), the festival was shortened to three days before being extended again to five days during the reign of Claudius (AD 41–54). The festival remained popular throughout the Roman period right through to the fourth century AD, when it became incorporated into the Christian celebration of Christmas.

In the fourth century a calendar was made depicting the important events of each month. The version of the calendar that survives today is from a seventeenth-century manuscript copy (Figure 1.52).

1. The top inscription reads, '*the Month December*'.
2. A mask. Although this suggests theatre, there is no existing evidence that any performances took place during the festival.
3. A table with dice and a dice tower, which was used to throw the dice.
4. The bottom inscription reads, '*I grant the subjects of the month of December to you*'.
5. Birds hanging from a hook.
6. A torch.
7. Unidentifed heart shapes.
8. The inscription written vertically on the right reads, '*Behold winter nourishes the seed thrown each year into the ploughed earth; all is wet with rain sent from Jupiter. Now let December call once more the golden festival for Saturn. Now you, slave, are allowed to play with your master*'.

FIGURE 1.52
Seventeenth-century copy of a fourth-century calendar page showing December.

Officials

In 497 BC the Temple of Saturn in the Roman forum was dedicated during the Saturnalia, and it was the priests of this temple that provided the religious officials. Religious officials were often elected for a single year (see also p. 56) and so the possibility of leading the sacrifice at the Saturnalia was a prospect for many leading Romans. The responsibility for the public feast fell to the Senate and state money was used to pay for it.

The programme

Despite the Saturnalia being the most popular festival in Rome, it has been poorly documented. For this reason we know what happened, just not when it happened. An exception to this was the sacrifice that took place on the first day. From the first day of the festival all business was suspended and the period declared a national holiday. This meant that the whole of the city was free to take part in the festivities.

The sacrifice

Unlike normal Roman sacrifices the priest took part in the sacrifice with his head uncovered in the Greek style. This no doubt alluded to the relationship between Saturn and Cronus, the Greek father of Zeus.

Study question
What can we infer about the Saturnalia from Figure 1.52?

The public feast

After the sacrifice the state paid for a public feast that took place throughout the streets of Rome. Given that all levels of society took part, this would have been an enormous expense to the Roman state and could have lasted for several days. The feast also included a statue of Saturn that would sit at the banquet table to signify the god's presence at the festival.

Private feasting

The private aspect of the Saturnalia provided another unique experience. The festival promoted equality, which meant that slaves and masters were equal for its duration. To support this, masters would remove their togas and all would wear party dress. Additionally, men would wear the small felt cap called a pileus as a symbol of freedom. An ancient writer called Macrobius explained the benefits to slaves:

> Meanwhile the head of the slave household, whose responsibility it was to offer sacrifice to the Penates [see. p. 78], to manage the provisions and to direct the activities of the domestic servants, came to tell his master that the household had feasted according to the annual ritual custom. For at this festival, in houses that keep to proper religious usage, they first of all honour the slaves with a dinner prepared as if for their master; and only afterwards is the table set again for the head of the household.
> So then, the chief slave came in to announce the time of dinner and to summon the masters to table.
>
> Macrobius, *Saturnalia*, 1.24.22–23

Another feature of the Saturnalia was gift giving. Much like our Christmas presents, Romans would give numerous and varied gifts to each other.

Study question S&C
To what extent do the Lupercalia and Saturnalia mirror the modern celebrations of Valentine's Day and Christmas?

S & C
Little is known about Macrobius. Although he lived in the fifth century AD and wrote in Latin, he was not born in Rome. He wrote two works that have survived, the *Saturnalia* and the *Commentary on the Dream of Scipio*. Though entitled the *Saturnalia*, the book contained a discussion of many other aspects of Roman myth and religion.

Study questions

1 How appropriately was Saturn worshipped during the Saturnalia?
2 Imagine you are a Roman slave. What would be your favourite part of the Saturnalia? Justify your answer.
3 'The Saturnalia was a more inclusive festival than the Lupercalia.' To what extent do you agree with this statement? Support your answer with evidence from both festivals.

ACTIVITY   The journal of Pausanias

As part of your travels you have spent a couple of months in Rome during which time the Lupercalia and Saturnalia have taken place. Write an account of the festivals from a first-hand perspective.

PRACTICE QUESTIONS: ROME

Source A: *A Roman sacrifice*

Study **Source A**.

1. How did the animal sacrifice that took place during the Lupercalia differ from the scene shown in **Source A**?   [2]
2. Do you think the Romans would have enjoyed the Lupercalia or Saturnalia more? Justify your answer.   [8]

TOPIC REVIEW

You should be able to:

1. Describe:
   - how the Great Panathenaia and City Dionysia were founded
   - what happened on each day of the Great Panathenaia and the City Dionysia
   - what happened at the Lupercalia and Saturnalia
   - the sacrifices that took place at each festival.

2. Explain:
   - why the Great Panathenaia and City Dionysia were important to the Athenians
   - how Athena and Dionysus where worshipped at their festivals
   - why the Lupercalia and Saturnalia were important to the Romans
   - how Lupercus and Saturn were worshipped at their festivals.

PRACTICE QUESTIONS: COMPARING GREECE AND ROME

Source A: *A plan of the Sanctuary of Dionysus in Athens*

Source B: *An account of Saturnalia and Lupercalia*

The Saturnalia

Meanwhile the head of the slave household, whose responsibility it was to offer sacrifice to the Penates, to manage the provisions and to direct the activities of the domestic servants, came to tell his master that the household had feasted according to the annual ritual custom. For at this festival, in houses that keep to proper religious usage, they first of all honour the slaves with a dinner prepared as if for their master; and only afterwards is the table set again for the head of the household. So then, the chief slave came in to announce the time of dinner and to summon the masters to table.

The Lupercalia

This place the Romans call the Lupercal . . . Now, it is true, since the district about the sacred precinct has been united with the city, it has become difficult to make out by conjecture the ancient nature of the place. Nevertheless, at first, we are told, there was a large cave under the hill overarched by a dense wood; deep springs issued from beneath the rocks, and the glen adjoining the cliffs was shaded by thick and lofty trees. In this place they raised an altar to the god and performed their traditional sacrifice, which the Romans have continued to offer up to this day in the month of February, after the winter solstice, without altering anything in the rites then performed.

Study **Source A** and **Source B**.

1. Explain the importance of the altar in ancient festivals. [6]
2. Explain why participants enjoyed ancient festivals. [6]
3. Explain why festivals were important for honouring the gods. [3]

1.6 Myth and Symbols of Power

TOPIC OVERVIEW

Links between myth and portrayal of power, including how and why myth might be presented in art to demonstrate power, and the significance of where it was sited/displayed.

Greece

- The Centauromachy: as depicted on the Parthenon
- The Amazonomachy: as depicted on the Bassae frieze

Rome

- The Prima Porta of Augustus
- The Ara Pacis of Augustus

The prescribed sources for this topic are:

- The Parthenon (metopes)
- Augustus of Prima Porta
- The Ara Pacis

Don't forget that you will be given credit in the exam if you study extra sources and make relevant use of them in your answers.

In this topic you will explore the links between myth and portrayal of power. To the Greeks and Romans world myths were more than just stories. Myths stood as symbols of power that were used to define a civilisation, city, family or even an individual. When combined with architecture and sculpture they could stand as statements of power for those exhibiting them. For the Greeks we will examine the Athenian use of the Centauromachy on the Parthenon. We will also examine the Amazonomachy as depicted on the temple of Apollo at Bassae. For the Romans we will examine the Roman emperor Augustus and how he used popular Roman mythology and sculpture to promote his bid for power in Rome. For these examples you will examine how and why myth might be recreated in art to demonstrate power, and the significance of where it was displayed.

EXPLORE FURTHER

S&C

The Roman poet Ovid included the battle between Centaurs and Lapiths in his poem *Metamorphoses*.

Read Ovid, *Metamorphoses*, 12.210–535.

How successfully does Ovid paint a vivid picture of the battle between the Centaurs and Lapiths?

GREECE

The Centauromachy

Lapiths and Centaurs

Lapiths a mythical race of men based in Thessaly, northern Greece

The **Lapiths** were a tribe of men that lived in Thessaly and were initially ruled by Ixion. Zeus invited Ixion to Olympus and when he was invited to the gods' table, Ixion took a liking to Hera. In order to trick Ixion, Zeus made an image of Hera out of the clouds. Fooled, Ixion coupled with the cloud and the next rains to fall gave birth to the Centaurs. Therefore, the Centaurs were the children of the Lapith king. Unlike the Lapiths, the Centaurs were savage beings that lived in caves, hunted wild food and fought with rocks. As wild creatures they were unskilled in the arts of men such as crafts, hospitality and religion.

KEY PLACE

Thessaly a region in central Greece (see map, Figure 1.10)

The battle between the Lapiths and Centaurs

Centauromachy mythical battle between the Centaurs and Lapiths

Centauromachy (from the Greek *centaur* plus *machy* meaning battle) means a battle between the mythical race of Centaurs and human Lapiths at the wedding of the Lapith king Pirithous, son of Ixion. As Plutarch explains:

> When Pirithous was about to marry Hippodamia, he asked Theseus to come to the wedding, and see the country, and become acquainted with the Lapiths. Now he had invited the Centaurs also to the wedding feast. And when these were flown with insolence and wine, and laid hands upon the women, the Lapiths took vengeance upon them. Some of them they slew upon the spot, the rest they afterwards overcame in war and expelled from the country, Theseus fighting with them at the banquet and in the war. Herodotus, however, says that this was not how it happened, but that the war was already in progress when Theseus came to the aid of the Lapiths.
>
> Plutarch, *Theseus*, 30.3

After a long battle Theseus and the Lapiths either killed or chased off the Centaurs from the wedding.

The story came to represent civilisation versus barbarism. As uncivilised creatures the Centaurs had no understanding of how to conduct themselves at a ceremony or how to correctly drink wine, drinking it unmixed with water. The Lapiths, seeking to make up for the exploits of Ixion, innocently invited their brothers to a wedding. They were then the victims of an unprovoked attack by the uncivilised Centaurs.

The Centauromachy and Greece

The Greeks were successful in defeating the Persians at Plataea in 479 BC (see also p. 48). From that point forward the Persians were seen as an image of barbarism and the Greeks took pride in depicting their victory over them. To do this they used the Centauromachy on their temples as a symbol of the Greek victory over barbarism.

The Centauromachy and Athens

No doubt the Centauromachy as a symbol of the Greek victory over the Persians held great significance to the Athenians. In 480 BC the Persians successfully sacked Athens and raised the city to the ground destroying an earlier temple to Athena on the Acropolis. When Pericles rebuilt the Parthenon in 449 BC, the inclusion of the Centauromachy on the metopes would have been a message to the world that Athens would never give up.

In addition to the general symbolism of civilisation versus barbarism, the involvement of Theseus in the myth would lead to an even greater importance for the Athenians.

The Centauromachy and the Parthenon

Of the ninety-two metopes that ran around the Parthenon, thirty-two depicted the Centauromachy. Although these are the best preserved, they are still heavily fragmented. The job of sculpting the metopes did not fall to one man. A team of sculptors would have been employed to complete the work. Due to this there is a great deal of variation in the quality and finish of the sculptures.

Analysing the success of a metope

The sculptor had several objectives to fulfil when sculpting the metopes. These were to:

- create a scene that could be easily recognisable
- create realism in his scene
- fill the space so as not to leave big blank areas.

We will use figure 1.53 for our analysis.

Create a scene that could be easily recognisable

The topic of the story makes this quite easy for the sculptor as the Centaur dominates the scene. Although lost, the Centaur may have been wielding a weapon. However, the sense of a battle can be easily seen through him standing triumphant over the Lapith. The metopes were positioned around ten metres up on the temple and so would have been viewed from beneath. This would have increased the drama as the Centaur rears above the Lapith, which appears to be rolling off the metope.

EXAM TIP

You will also need to comment on how successfully the sculptor has depicted the battle. For this you must form your own opinion based on the rules outlined here.

PRESCRIBED SOURCE

The Centauromachy Metopes

Date: 447–432 BC

Material: Marble

Location: On the external frieze of the Parthenon, now in the British Museum.

Significance: A highly detailed set of sculptures that represented the victory of civilisation over barbarism.

FIGURE 1.53
Metope from the southern side of the Parthenon.

> **Study question**
> Choose another metope from the Parthenon. How successfully has the sculptor depicted the Centauromachy in this metope?

> **Amazons** a mythical race of women from Asia Minor
>
> **Asia Minor** the western two thirds of modern Turkey

> **Amazonomachy** mythic battle between the Greeks and Amazons

Create realism in his scene

The sculptor has been very successful in depicting action in the scene. The left arm of the Centaur is carved in low relief, while the body is carved in high relief. This technique helped make the carvings visible from beneath. The semi-circular mark above the right shoulder suggests the arm held a pot. This creates depth to the scene. The same can be said of the front legs of the Centaur that are held above the fallen Lapith. When combined with the rear leg muscles and raised tail, the sculptor has successfully captured the Centaur as he rears to trample the Lapith. Regarding the Lapith, he has been captured in the moment of defeat. The body lies awkwardly twisted, this is due to him landing on his arms which are missing from sight. The right leg is raised with the left leg balancing on the leg of the Centaur. Although it is missing you can imagine a look of anguish on the face of the Lapith.

Fill the space so as not to leave big blank spaces

The rearing Centaur with open arms successfully fills the upper space of the metope forming a 'z' shape with the Lapith. Additionally, the sculptor has used the wild animal skin draped over the arm of the Centaur to fill the right-hand side of the metope. This also reflects the beastlike nature of the creature. The twisted body of the Lapith with bent knee is successful in filling the bottom part of the metope.

The Amazonomachy

The Amazons

The **Amazons** were a mythical race of women who came from **Asia Minor**. As a race they stayed clear of men, except when they needed to repopulate. When this time came, they coupled with men from a neighbouring tribe. If the women gave birth to a son, the baby was killed. However, if the baby was a girl, she was raised by her mother and became an Amazon. Many myths exist regarding the Amazons and ancient writers offered differing accounts of their battles. However, their commonality is that they always sided against the Greeks.

The battles between the Greeks and Amazons

Amazonomachy is used when discussing the mythical battles between Greeks and Amazons. There were two great battles between them. The first was between Heracles and the Amazon queen Hippolyte as his ninth labour. The second relates to the events after this labour, in which Heracles brought back an Amazonian bride for Theseus as a gift. Enraged that Heracles had done this, the Amazons declared war on Athens. This was called the Attic War. To defeat the Amazons, Theseus and Heracles led an army of Athenians against them. Like the Centauromachy, the Amazonomachy came to represent Greece's triumph over foreign people.

EXPLORE FURTHER

S&C

The Centauromachy was also depicted on the western pediment of the Temple of Zeus at Olympia (top) and the frieze at Bassae (bottom).

FIGURE 1.54
The Centauromachy from the Temple of Zeus at Olympia.

FIGURE 1.55
The Centauromachy on the Bassae frieze.

1 Why may the Greeks have decided to include the Centauromachy on the Temple of Zeus at Olympia?
2 What are the strengths and weaknesses of depicting the Centauromachy:
  a. on a metope?
  b. on a frieze?
  c. on a pediment?

The Amazonomachy Frieze

Date: *c.* 420 BC

Material: Marble

Location: On the internal frieze in the temple of Apollo at Bassae, now in the British Museum.

Significance: A unique example of a sculpted frieze inside the naos of a temple.

The Amazonomachy and Bassae

Bassae was a small town around 36 miles southeast of Olympia in the west of the Peloponnese (see map, Figure 1.10). As a small, geographically isolated town it may seem strange that its people built a temple. However, as Pausanias explained:

> Of the temples in the Peloponnesus, this might be placed first after the one at Tegea for the beauty of its stone and for its symmetry. Apollo received his name from the help he gave in time of plague, just as the Athenians gave him the name of Averter of Evil for turning the plague away from them.
>
> Pausanias, *Description of Greece*, 8.41.7

The temple was begun in 450 BC by Iktinos, the same architect who helped design the Parthenon; this may be why it received such admiration for its design and sculpture. It was dedicated to Apollo Epikourios, 'the helper'.

The Amazonomachy was twinned with the Centauromachy and depicted on a frieze that ran around the inside of the temple's naos. This is unique and allowed the viewer to take in the whole frieze standing in one place. This would make the narrative easier to follow. The choice of scene suited the space as battles provided a busy and interesting scene for viewers. The symbolism of Greek victory would also have been a suitable topic for the small town that wanted to celebrate its Greekness.

The scene runs around the east and south-east end of the frieze and shows the Heraclean Amazonomachy, which was Heracles' battle with the Amazons for the belt of Hippolyte. Heracles can be seen on one of the south blocks; he can be identified wearing his lion-skin cloak.

Analysing the success of the frieze

The objectives for the sculptor of a frieze were the same as that of a metope. These were to:

- create a scene that could be easily recognisable
- create realism in his scene
- fill the space so as not to leave big blank areas.

We will use Figure 1.58 for our analysis.

Create a scene that could be easily recognisable

The sculptor has successfully created a scene in which a man fights two women. The Amazons were frequently depicted with one bare breast; this can be seen on the Amazon on horseback.

Create realism in his scene

The drapery on the right-hand Amazon correctly depicts the movement of the woman towards the left. The shallow relief on both the horseback Amazon and Greek suggest a snapshot mid-flight in which the horseback Amazon tries to flee away from the Greek. The horse, although clearly in action, is rather small in comparison to the human figure.

Study question

Choose another scene from the frieze at the temple of Bassae. How successfully has the sculptor depicted the Amazonomachy in this scene?

ACTIVITY

Iktinos has been asked to build a temple that includes the Amazonomachy and Centauromachy as part of the design. He has asked you to design the Amazonomachy on the metopes and the Centauromachy for the continuous frieze.

FIGURE 1.56
On the left is the plan of the temple, on the right the internal view. The internal frieze can be seen above the columns.

Fill the space so as not to leave big blank areas

The sculptor has used action well to fill the space. The left- and right-hand characters mirror each other in pose. The bent knees suggest action, while fitting them neatly into the space. Although small, the rearing horse in the centre fills the entirety of the central area. The sculptor has cleverly depicted the horseback Amazon being pulled from her horse by the Greek. This allowed for her to fit neatly into the rectangular space.

FIGURE 1.57
Southern block of the Bassae frieze, showing Heracles in his lion-skin cloak.

FIGURE 1.58
Eastern block of the Bassae frieze.

PRACTICE QUESTIONS: GREECE

Source A: *A metope from the Parthenon*

Source B: *A metope from the Parthenon*

Source C: *Section from the Bassae frieze*

Source D: *Section from the Bassae frieze*

1. How successfully have the sculptors depicted the Centauromachy? Use **Sources A** and **B** as a starting point **and** your own knowledge in your answer. [8]
2. How successfully has the sculptor depicted the Amazonomachy? Use **Sources C** and **D** as a starting point **and** your own knowledge in your answer. [8]

ROME

Augustus

In 63 BC Augustus was born Gaius Octavius Thurinus, named after his father in the usual Roman custom. As a boy he enjoyed life in an aristocratic family. His life took a turn at the age of 19 when his great uncle Julius Caesar was assassinated by Brutus and Cassius. When Caesar's will was read out, Octavian was surprisingly named as his heir and adopted son. From this point, Octavian took the name Gaius Julius Caesar Octavianus.

As his opening vow he promised to avenge his father's death. Towards the end of his life Augustus recalled his early years:

> At the age of nineteen, on my own initiative and at my own expense, I raised an army with which I set the state free, which at the time was oppressed by the domination of a group . . . But the people made me consul in the same year, when both consuls died in battle . . . I drove the men who slaughtered my father into exile legally, punishing their crimes, and afterwards, when they waged war on the state, I conquered them in two battles.

Augustus, *Res Gestae Divi Augusti*, 1–3

When he speaks of a *group*, he is referring to Mark Antony, who, after Julius Caesar's death tried to control the state with Caesar's old army. Panicked, the senate asked Octavian to donate his troops to the senate's army. The battle was won by the senate and Octavian's troops, and as reward he demanded that he be made **consul**. The senate refused and Octavian marched on Rome with his army. With few other choices, the senate granted him the consulship under the guidance of Cicero, a senior Roman senator.

As consul, Octavian declared Brutus and Cassius enemies of the state. This created mixed feelings in the senate as many of its member were friends of Brutus and Cassius. In retaliation, the senate recalled Brutus and Cassius from the East, where they had gathered a huge army after fleeing Rome having assassinated Caesar.

Instead of being scared off, the young Octavian kept a cool head and formed an alliance with Mark Antony and Marcus Lepidus, a Roman general. Together they formed the Second Triumvirate. Combining their armies, they travelled to Greece where they

EXAM TIP

You will not be asked questions on Augustus' early life. However, it is important that you understand how he came to be emperor.

consul the most important public official in Rome after the emperor; two consuls were elected annually

EXPLORE FURTHER

S&C

Res Gestae Divi Augusti
(The Achievements of the Divine Augustus)
Towards the end of his life Augustus wrote his *Res Gestae Divi Augusti*. Once complete, it was placed at the entrance to his tomb in Rome. Although this copy is now lost, further copies were placed around the Roman empire. The version that survives today comes from Turkey.

Read the rest of the *Res Gestae Divi Augusti* to learn more about what Augustus thought were his greatest achievements.

Study questions

1 Why did Augustus feel the need to raise an army when he was 19?

2 How did Augustus become consul in 43 BC and what was his first decree?

3 How did Augustus come to beat Brutus and Cassius in 43 BC?

4 What was the turning point that allowed Augustus to declare war on Antony in 32 BC?

5 Why could Augustus claim that he 'exceeded all in authority, but none in power'?

defeated Brutus and Cassius in 43 BC at the battle of Philippi. Brutus and Cassius subsequently committed suicide.

With their enemies removed, the Triumvirate ruled Rome for ten years in relative peace. Greed and jealously led to a soured relationship. Lepidus was accused of inciting a revolt and was exiled in 36 BC leaving Antony and Octavian in control. Antony would not be as easy to remove as Lepidus. Antony was a war hero who fought alongside Caesar for the greatness of Rome; the people loved him. From 37 BC Antony had been based in Egypt inciting war against the Parthians. Despite huge losses his popularity in Rome did not decrease. Octavian's chance came when he obtained Antony's will from the Temple of the Vestals in 32 BC. The will revealed that he had married Cleopatra, and upon his death he left all of Rome's eastern provinces to her and his children by her. This enraged the Roman people and provided the evidence that Octavian needed to declare war. In 31 BC Octavian defeated Antony and Cleopatra at the Battle of Actium, and by 30 BC both had committed suicide.

At the age of 33, and after almost 60 years of civil war, Octavian was the last man standing. What followed was a period of careful self-promotion, aimed at placing himself at the head of the Roman state. Octavian learnt from his predecessors and avoided assuming any role or taking any title that would suggest he was a king or dictator. Instead, he invested in various forms of propaganda to promote his power and superiority. As he wrote towards the end of his life:

> After putting out the civil war . . . I handed over the state from my power to the senate and Roman people. And for this merit of mine, by a senatorial decree, I was called Augustus . . . After that time, I exceeded all in influence, but I had no greater power than the others who were colleagues with me in each magistracy.
>
> Augustus, *Res Gestae Divi Augusti*, 34

Importantly Octavian relinquished power and returned to the usual system of government. It was in 27 BC that the senate gave him the religious name Augustus, which means venerable, esteemed and respected. From this point on he used this name instead of Octavian.

The architecture of Augustan Rome

Augustus had several goals in his sculpture and architecture:

- **Recreate the Golden Age of architecture** Augustus saw fifth-century Greece as a high point in architectural and sculptural design. He was inspired by buildings like the Parthenon and he sought to recreate these styles in his own sculpture and architecture.
- **Pax Romana** The *Peace of Rome* was key to Augustan Rome. The Battle of Actium marked the end of civil war. Augustus sought to promote himself as a bringer of peace.
- **Pax Deorum** The *Peace of the Gods* was a key concept for Romans. If the gods were appeased Rome would flourish, if they were angered Rome would suffer.
- **Self and Family Promotion** Although Augustus gave the impression of Rome being a republic, he certainly wanted and needed to promote himself and his

family. To do this he emphasised his family's links to the gods, while promoting future heirs.

The Augustus of Prima Porta

As it exists now the Augustus of Prima Porta is a marble copy made around between 20 BC and AD 14 for Augustus' wife Livia. It was originally displayed in the town of Prima Porta, which sat on the main northern road into Rome.

Recreating the golden age of architecture

The Prima Porta was based on the Doryphorus (spear-bearer), sculpted by Polykleitos around 440 BC. The sculpture was praised as a depiction of the ideal man. Importantly, the Augustus of Prima Porta is not a direct copy, the sculptor has Romanised it to promote the Augustan ideal.

The Augustan statue differs in four ways:

- **The right arm** Augustus' right arm is raised in the pose a general or emperor would use when addressing his army.
- **The clothing** The breastplate worn by Augustus portrays him as a soldier. Unusually, the military breastplate has been combined with the senatorial toga, which Augustus holds around his waist. The breastplate contains several religious images. The gods depicted include Apollo, Augustus' patron god; Artemis, Apollo's sister; Tellus, mother earth, holding the cornucopia. Other deities are represented, although their exact identity is unknown.
- **The standards** The central figures represent the return of the Roman standards. The Roman standard was first lost by the Roman general Crassus in 53 BC. Another was lost by Mark Antony in the 40s BC. Finally, in 20 BC Tiberius negotiated peace with the Parthians and the standards were returned.
- **The statue of Cupid** At the feet of Augustus, Cupid sits on the back of a diving dolphin. Cupid was the son of Venus and the dolphin was one of her animals.

PRESCRIBED SOURCE

Augustus of Prima Porta

Date: 20 BC–AD 15 (debated, see left)

Commissioned by: the senate in honour of Augustus

Material: marble

Original Location: Livia's villa in Prima Porta, nine miles north of Rome

Current Location: Vatican Museum

Significance: excellent example of how Augustus wished to be seen by the Roman people

---

DEBATE **S&C**

The Augustus of Prima Porta shows Augustus bare footed. This was a pose reserved for heroes and gods, to the Romans a living man could not be a god. Upon Julius Caesar's death in 44 BC it was said that a shooting star was seen elevating to the heavens. Augustus took this as a sign that Caesar had become a god and started building a temple to the Divine Caesar in the Roman forum. We do not know Augustus' real motives for this. However, by making Caesar a god, Augustus became the son of a god. Indeed, from 42 BC Augustus added *divi filius*, son of a god, to his name.

If a living man could not be a god why does the Augustus of Prima Porta have bare feet?

DEBATE

Scholars disagree who the Roman is on the breastplate, some believe it is Tiberius as he returned the standard. Others believe it was Mars Ultor (the Avenger), god of war.

Which do you think is the more likely? Support your answer with you own knowledge of Augustus.

FIGURE 1.59
The Augustus of Prima Porta.

FIGURE 1.60
The Doryphoros of Polykleitos.

Study question

How successful was the Augustus of Prima Porta in promoting the power of Augustus?

S & C The Doryphoros shown in Figure 1.60 is a Roman copy made from marble. Polykleitos' original sculpture was made of bronze. As marble was a weaker material than bronze the Roman sculptor needed to add support struts to stop the marble from cracking and breaking off. These supports can be seen on the right arm and leg. A skilled sculptor would try and disguise these supports as part of the sculpture. In Figure 1.60 the leg support has been disguised as a tree stump.

The Ara Pacis

The Ara Pacis (Altar of Peace) was commissioned by the senate in 13 BC to honour the return of Augustus from **Hispania** and **Gaul**. As Augustus wrote towards the end of his life:

Hispania a Roman province covering the area of Spain

> After I returned to Rome from Spain and Gaul, having successfully accomplished matters in those provinces . . . the senate voted to consecrate the altar of Augustan Peace in the field of Mars for my return. Additionally it ordered the magistrates, priests and Vestal Virgins to offer annual sacrifices.

Augustus, *Res Gestae Divi Augusti*, 12

FIGURE 1.61
The Ara Pacis today from the outside, and showing the altar inside the enclosure wall.

 PS

FIGURE 1.62 **PS**
Side of the altar.

The altar

The altar itself was elaborately carved with scenes that related to the sacrifice that took place on it (see Figure 1.62). The scene shows the semi-nude slaves leading sacrificial beasts.

The enclosure wall

The altar was surrounded by an enclosure wall that was sculpted inside and out. The western and eastern walls contained a doorway into the enclosure. These walls contained scenes that linked the Augustan family to the founding of Rome and Rome's important gods. The northern and southern walls depicted the procession that took place to the Ara Pacis before the annual sacrifice. The northern and southern walls are stylistically similar to the frieze on the Parthenon that showed the Panathenaic procession (see also p. 87).

> **EXPLORE FURTHER** **S&C**
>
> To celebrate the completion of the Altar of Peace the Roman poet Ovid referred to it in his poems.
>
> Read Ovid, *Fasti*, 1.709–722.
>
> 1. In Ovid's eyes what did the Altar of Peace represent?
> 2. What can we learn about what happended at the altar from Ovid's hymn?

PRESCRIBED SOURCE

The Ara Pacis

Date: 9 BC

Commissioned by: the Senate to honour Augustus

Material: marble

Original Location: northeastern corner of the Campus Martius

Current Location: central Rome, on the bank of the Tiber

Significance: decorative friezes depict Augustus' ideal of Roman civil religion

The west frieze

FIGURE 1.63
The upper register of the west façade.

EXPLORE FURTHER

Use http://www.vroma.
org/images/
mcmanus_images/
index15.html

Which characters on the
Ara Pacis are believed to
be Augustus, Agrippa,
Livia, Tiberius, Lucius and
Gaius?

DEBATE

The left-hand image above is heavily fragmented and tenuously linked to the Lupercalia, the moment that the shepherd discovered Romulus and Remus being suckled by the she-wolf. The right-hand image has been interpreted in two ways. First, as Aeneas. If this is the case Aeneas stands offering sacrifice in front of his son Ascanius (Iulus). The Penates, which he brought from Troy, are housed on the hill behind him. Another interpretation is that the man represents Numa Pompilius, the second king of Rome. Numa was attributed with some important religious introductions. He built the Temple of Janus; when Rome was at peace the doors were closed, when at war they were left open. In his *Res Gestae* Augustus boasts that he closed the doors of the temple. Numa also created the office of the Pontifices.

1. Why may scholars have interpreted the left-hand frieze as the Lupercalia?
2. Which interpretation of the west frieze better suits the ideology of Augustus?

The east frieze

FIGURE 1.64
The upper register of the east façade.

DEBATE

The right-hand image (Figure 1.64 opposite) is heavily fragmented and tenuously linked to the goddess Roma (a personification of Rome) who sits on a throne of weapons. This has been decided based on coins depicting the goddess in that pose. The left-hand image is very well preserved. The veiled goddess in the centre has been variously identified as Tellus (Mother Earth), Venus and Pax (Peace). The goddess is surrounded by animals and is flanked by two semi-nude females.

1. Why may scholars have interpreted the left-hand frieze as Tellus, Venus or Pax? Which do you think is the most appropriate?
2. Why would Roma be a good goddess to depict in the right-hand scene?

Study questions

1 How successfully did the altar of peace fulfil Augustus' architectural aims?
2 'The Greeks were better than the Romans when expressing power through architecture.' To what extent do you agree with this statement? Use the architecture you have studied in your answer.

The north frieze

The north and south friezes are very well preserved and represent a religious procession to the Ara Pacis. The northern wall depicts senators and priests (Figure 1.65). One carries a jug and an incense box, which were both used in the sacrifice. Others carry laurel leaves, which were common in sacrifices. Several of the men have their heads veiled as was traditional during Roman sacrifices. The bottom of the frieze contained floral patterns.

The south frieze

The south frieze shows the imperial family on the far right (Figure 1.67), this includes Augustus' wife Livia, his lead general Agrippa and nephews Lucius and Gaius Caesar, and Tiberius, Livia's son. The family are preceded by priests, identified by their caps (Figure 1.66).

FIGURE 1.65
The north wall showing senators and priests.

FIGURE 1.66
The south frieze showing Augustus followed by priests wearing their characteristic caps.

FIGURE 1.67
The south frieze showing the imperial family.

PRACTICE QUESTIONS: ROME

Source A: *A scene from the Prima Porta*

1. Study **Source A**.
   a. What is shown in this scene? [2]
   b. Why did Augustus choose to use this scene on the Ara Pacis? [1]
2. Which was a better expression of Augustus' power, the Augustus at Prima Porta or the Ara Pacis? [8]

TOPIC REVIEW

You should be able to:

1. Describe:
   - the battle between the Centaurs and Lapiths
   - the battle between the Amazons and Greeks
   - the Prima Porta of Augustus, including its key features
   - the Ara Pacis, including its religious and mythological scenes.

2. Explain:
   - why the Centauromachy was used in the decoration of the Parthenon
   - why the Amazonomachy was used in the decoration of the temple of Apollo at Bassae
   - how the Prima Porta promoted the power and authority of Augustus
   - how the Ara Pacis promoted the power and authority of Augustus.

PRACTICE QUESTIONS: COMPARING GREECE AND ROME

Source A: *a metope from the Parthenon*

Source B: *an extract from Ovid's* Fasti *about the Ara Pacis (Altar of Peace)*

My song has led to the altar of Peace itself.
… Come, Peace, your graceful tresses wreathed
with laurel of Actium: stay gently in this world.
While we lack enemies, or cause for triumphs:
you'll be a greater glory to our leaders than war.
May the soldier be armed to defend against arms,
and the trumpet blare only for processions.
May the world far and near fear the sons of Aeneas,
and let any land that feared Rome too little, love her.
Priests, add incense to the peaceful flames,
let a shining sacrifice fall, brow wet with wine,
and ask the gods who favour pious prayer
that the house that brings peace, may so endure.

1. Explain which you think was a better expression of power: the Centauromachy or Ara Pacis? [3]
2. Which civilisation expressed their power better in their architecture, the Greeks or Romans? [15]

1.7 Death and Burial

In this topic you will learn about Greek and Roman practices and beliefs surrounding death and burial including the preparation, funeral procession and burial of the body. Remembrance of the dead was also an important part of family life and you will study some of the festivals of remembrance that the Greeks and Romans held.

GREECE

Preparation of the body

Death was an important issue to the Greeks. It was incredibly important that the dead were treated with respect and that everyone, no matter their social status or wealth, received a proper burial. Once the person had died, their eyes and mouth were closed. The body would be washed, perfumed and wrapped in a long white shroud. When this process was complete a coin would be placed on the deceased's mouth. This was payment for Charon, the boatman who ferried the dead from the land of the living to the underworld.

After the body was prepared, the **prothesis**, or laying out, took place. The prothesis lasted two days and gave the friends and family of the deceased a chance to come and pay their respects. As a death automatically polluted the house, a bowl of water was placed outside for people to wash themselves as they left. Once respects had been paid, the women of the family would start their **lament**. To do this they would cut their hair, dress in shabby black clothing and wail beside the deceased, beating their chests and flailing their arms.

> **prothesis** during the preparation of the body in the Greek world, the deceased would be laid out for two days to receive mourners
>
> **lament** a passionate expression of grief or sorrow
>
> **ekphora** the funeral procession in ancient Greece
>
> **Kerameikos** an area of Athens that included the main burial ground outside the city

Funerary procession

Before dawn on the third day, the **ekphora** took place. This was the funeral procession from the house of the deceased to the burial ground. Depending on the wealth of the family and distance they travelled, the deceased would either be carried on a wagon or carried by pallbearers. The procession included women, children and men from the family. As can be seen in Figure 1.68, the procession was also accompanied by an aulos player.

FIGURE 1.68
An ekphora scene from a Greek vase.

Burial of the body

It was vital that the final resting place of the deceased was outside the city to remove the chance of religious pollution (see also p. 44). Additionally, burial outside the city reduced the spread of any disease. In Athens the main burial ground was in **Kerameikos**, an area just outside the northwest walls of the city. Once the body reached the burial ground, it was either buried or cremated. In a cremation, a pyre would be built and the deceased laid on top. It would then be lit. After the body had burned, the ash would be collected in an urn and given to the family. This would then be placed in a shrine or grave. To assist the deceased in their journey to the underworld, the family would add burial gifts to the grave. This may be an item that was important to the deceased in life or food for their journey.

> **stele** (pl. **stelai**) stone slabs often with patterns or images carved on them most commonly used as tombstones

Depending on the wealth of the family, a **stele** may be set up for the deceased. This was important as it was vital that the deceased be remembered. If a family neglected the deceased's grave, they would dishonour their family memory. A stele may be equated to a modern gravestone and acted as a monument to the dead. The family of the deceased would employ a sculptor to carve a relief on the stele that reflected the deceased in life. This could be a display of the family's wealth and status as much as a commemoration of the deceased.

Once the deceased had been buried or cremated, a sacrifice would take place. This differed from a normal sacrifice, as the blood of the victim was released on the earth as an offering to Hades and Persephone.

Maintaining respect was very important to the Greeks. Once the deceased had been buried a period of mourning began that lasted for thirty days. There were three days in which the family were obliged to visit the deceased: the third, ninth and thirteenth. After this, the family visited the grave on an annual basis.

FIGURE 1.69
The funerary stele of Hegeso.

Festivals for the dead and the ancestors

Beyond private funerals Athens also celebrated other festivals to the dead, as it was vital that their memory be maintained. If grave stelai were left to become overgrown or damaged, the memory of that person would be damaged.

The first, called the **Anthesteria**, took place in late January and lasted three days. The festival celebrated the maturing of wine and was held in honour of Dionysus. The first day was believed to be a day the dead rose from the underworld and roamed the earth. During this day, the wine from the previous year was opened and libations were poured to Dionysus. On the second day, groups would gather for drinking contests and families would pour libations on the graves of their ancestors. The final day was dedicated to the dead. Families of the dead would make offerings to the god Hermes, as he was the only god, along with Dionysus, who could travel in both the world of the living and the world of the dead. Unlike normal offerings, the living were not allowed to eat any of the food. The ceremony marked the period that the dead had to leave Athens and return to the underworld.

Anthesteria a Greek festival to Dionysus and the dead held over three days in late January or early February

Genesia a Greek festival to the dead ancestors celebrated in late September

The second of these celebrations was the **Genesia**, which took place in late September. During this day, the Athenians would decorate the graves of the deceased with ribbons and offer food and blood sacrifice in honour of all their dead ancestors.

EXPLORE FURTHER   S&C

Figure 1.69 shows a Greek woman called Hegeso. In the scene, Hegeso is seated and accompanied by a slave girl. Hegeso admires a piece of her jewellery. We do not know how old Hegeso was when she died, but she has been captured in this image at a point of eternal beauty.

What can we learn about the deceased from Figure 1.69?

EXPLORE FURTHER S&C

Read Homer, *Odyssey*, XI.51–89.

What does the speech of Elpenor suggest about the importance of burial to the Greeks?
Read Homer, *Iliad*, 24.776–804.

How typical a burial did the Trojan prince Hector receive?

Study questions

1 How was the body prepared for the prothesis?
2 What role did women have in the preparation and burial of the deceased?
3 What happened once the deceased's body reached the burial ground?
4 How important was the grave stele to the burial process?
5 'Respecting the dead was more important for the individual family than the city.' To what extent do you agree with this statement?

PRACTICE QUESTIONS: GREECE

Source A: *A scene from a Greek funerary procession. Drawing from pottery.*

1. **Source A** depicts a funerary procession. Identify **two** types of participants in this procession. [2]
2. State **two** things that happened during the preparation of the body **before** the procession took place. [2]

ROME

It was incredibly important that the dead were treated with respect and that everyone, no matter their social status or wealth, received a proper burial. In the first century AD a Roman aristocrat called **Pliny** wrote to his friend regarding a ghost that was haunting a house:

> The next day he went to the magistrates, and advised them to order that spot to be dug up. There they found bones commingled and intertwined with chains; for the body had rotted away due to lying so long in the ground, leaving them bare, and corroded by the fetters. The bones were collected, and buried at the public expense; and after the ghost was thus duly laid the house was haunted no more.
>
> Pliny, *Letters*, 7

Like the Greeks it was important to the Romans that the final resting place of the deceased was outside the city to remove religious pollution and reduce risk of disease. In Roman towns, the wealthy were buried in tombs along roads that led into the city or town, which allowed passers-by to pay their respects.

S & C Pliny the Younger

Pliny the Younger was born around AD 61 and died around AD 113. He was a lawyer, magistrate and writer. Although he wrote no major surviving works, many of his letters survive and give us valuable information about the time in which he lived. One of these key events was the eruption of Vesuvius in AD 79, at which Pliny was an eye witness. His uncle, Pliny the Elder, died in the eruption while trying to save some of the population.

Wealth and status in Rome

As in many aspects of Roman life, status and wealth were important. The same was true in death. Wealthy families would invest heavily in the funerals of their dead. With this in mind, the vast majority of our evidence for funerals comes from the rich. However, the majority of the Roman population were working-class citizens, freedmen and slaves. These people did not always have the spare cash or social connections to spend on a funeral and so they sought other ways of ensuring that they were provided for in death.

The main option open to the less wealthy were **funeral clubs**. Those who could afford it would pay a monthly fee to join the club. The club met for meals and gatherings, giving members an opportunity of making social connections. Frequently, workers of the same trade would set up their own clubs, such as the baker's guild or blacksmith's guild. As the names suggest, these were open only to those craftsmen. Upon the death of one of its members, the club would pay for a funeral and provide mourners to ensure the deceased was not forgotten. In the case of larger clubs, members may be buried in a club tomb or burial ground.

> **funeral club** a social club set up to support the less wealthy members of Roman society

Preparation of the body

Much of Roman burial practice was similar to that of the Greeks. If possible, just before the moment of death a relative would capture the last breath of the person with a kiss. If at home those present would then call out the deceased's name. If the person died unaccompanied, this would be done ceremonially afterwards. The body was washed and perfumed then dressed in the deceased's finest clothes. A coin was then placed on the mouth of the deceased to pay the ferryman Charon.

If the family was wealthy, the body would then be placed in the **atrium** for eight days. This would give friends and relatives a chance to pay their respects. During this time the women of the house would lament the deceased while beating their chests.

> **atrium** the main room of the Roman domus where the family received friends and clients

Funerary procession

The funeral would take place eight days after death and involve a variety of people, including flute and horn players, the deceased's family, slaves and freedmen. Members of the family would wear wax **funerary masks** of the family ancestors. This was done to symbolise the acceptance of the deceased into the afterlife by their ancestors. If a family was wealthy but small, they would pay for professional mourners to join the procession, mourning and lamenting the dead. Wealthy families would also pay for actors to mimic the deceased as they were in life.

> **funerary mask** a mask made by placing wax on the deceased's face to take their image. When it was dry, it was taken off and stored in the family shrine

Burial of the body

Once outside the city the body would be either buried or cremated. The Romans followed the same custom as the Greeks with their cremations and burials. Again, the

FIGURE 1.70
A Roman funerary
procession.

Study question
Identify each of the
people represented in
Figure 1.70.

family's wealth determined the size of the tomb. A wealthy person could expect to be buried in the family tomb or an individual monument. The Romans built their tombs along the roads that ran into a town; this ensured the deceased would be remembered. It also meant that people avoided uniformity as they wanted their tomb to stand out. Figure 1.71 shows one of the main streets that led into Pompeii. The street is lined with tombs that resemble homes and temples. The super-rich would also place their dead in elaborately carved **sarcophagi**. These would contain reliefs of mythological battles and heroes.

Once the dead were buried they were not to be forgotten. To ensure the family member was correctly honoured, a marble bust would be made and placed in the house. The Romans believed that they turned into **Manes**. They needed to be fed and the deceased's family were expected to leave food and wine offerings at their tomb.

Manes meaning 'the
deified ancestors', these
were the spirits of the
dead in the Roman world

Festivals for the dead and the ancestors

The Parentalia

The Parentalia took place over nine days between the 13 and 21 February. During this time people were not permitted to marry, temples were closed and no official business was allowed to take place. Apart from a blood sacrifice by a Vestal Virgin on the first day, the Parentalia was a domestic festival, that is, one centred on the family rather than the State. Despite the apparent extravagance given to the deceased during their burial, the Roman poet Ovid states:

> Their shades (dead) ask little, pietas they prefer to costly
> offerings: no greedy deities haunt the Stygian depths. A tile
> wreathed round with garlands offered is enough, a scattering of
> meal, and a few grains of salt, and bread soaked in wine, and
> loose violets.
>
> Ovid, *Fasti*, 2.535–539

These offerings were taken to the tombs of the deceased during the first eight days of the festival. On the ninth day the family would meet and share a meal in the home. This gave them an opportunity to undo any wrongs that had taken place.

FIGURE 1.71
Tombs line a street into
Pompeii.

Study questions

1 How and why were funeral clubs important to certain Romans?
2 How was the body prepared for the funerary procession?
3 Who accompanied the deceased during their procession to the burial ground?
4 How could a wealthy Roman family show off their status through a funeral?
5 'Respecting the dead was more important for the individual family than the city.' To what extent do you agree with this statement?

EXPLORE FURTHER S&C

In the case of important political figures and leaders, the funeral procession was allowed to stop in the Roman forum, where a member of the family gave a speech in honour of the deceased. This honour was granted to Julius Caesar after he was assassinated. Mark Antony delivered the speech.

Read Appian, *Civil Wars*, 2.144–147.

What atmosphere did Antony create in his speech?

The Lemuria

The Lemuria was held over three days in May: the 9th, 11th and 13th. Like the Parentalia, people were not permitted to marry, temples were closed and no official business was allowed to take place. Unlike the Parentalia, which was aimed at honouring the family's deceased ancestors, the Lemuria was held to ward off evil spirits. Ovid described the ritual as follows:

> He who remembers ancient rites, and fears the gods, rises and makes the sign with thumb and closed fingers, lest an insubstantial shade meets him in the silence. After cleansing his hands in spring water, he turns and, first taking some black beans, throws them with averted face, saying, while throwing: 'With these beans I throw I redeem myself and my family.' He says this nine times without looking back: the shade is thought to gather the beans, and follow behind, unseen. Again he touches water, and sounds the bronze symbols and asks the spirit to leave his house. When nine times he's cried: 'Ancestral spirit, depart,' He looks back, and believes the sacred rite's fulfilled.

Ovid, *Fasti*, 5.431–444

EXPLORE FURTHER
The Rites of Muta S&C

Muta was a goddess of the Parentalia. She was said to have been made mute by Jupiter because she would not stop talking.

Read Ovid, *Fasti*, 2.571–582.

What strange rite do old women do as part of the Parentalia?

PRACTICE QUESTIONS: ROME

Source A: *Image from a Roman stone coffin (sarcophagus)*

1. **Source A** depicts a funerary procession. Identify **two** types of participants in this procession. [2]
2. **a.** Describe where the dead were carried to before they were buried or cremated. [2]
   b. What does this suggest about Roman attitudes to the dead? [1]

TOPIC REVIEW

You should be able to:

1. Describe:
   - what happened to a Greek from death to burial
   - what happened at the Genesia.
   - what happened to a Roman from death to burial
   - what happened at the Parentalia and Lemuria.

2. Explain:
   - why it was important that the dead were properly buried
   - how a funeral could show of the wealth and social standing of Greek and Roman families.
   - why it was important that the dead were buried outside the town or city
   - why festivals to the dead were important to the Greeks and Romans.

PRACTICE QUESTIONS: COMPARING GREECE AND ROME

Source A: *An Athenian grave stele dated c. 390 BC.*

Source B: *An extract from the biographer Suetonius describing how Rome planned the funeral of the emperor Augustus.*

From Bovillae, a party of Roman knights carried it to the vestibule of his own house in Rome. The senators vied with one another in proposing . . . honours for Augustus. Amongst the motions introduced were the following: that his funeral procession should pass through the Triumphal Gate preceded by the image of Victory from the Senate House, and that boys and girls of the nobility should sing his dirge; that on the day of his cremation iron rings should be worn instead of gold ones; that the name of the month 'Augustus' should be transferred to September, because Augustus had been born in September but had died in the month now called August . . . Although it was decided not to pay him excessive honours, he was given two funeral eulogies – by Tiberius . . . and by Tiberius' son Drusus. After which a party of senators shouldered the body and took it to a pyre on the Campus Martius, where it was burned. Leading knights then took his ashes and placed them in the family tomb.

1. Explain how funerals could vary dependent on wealth and importance. [6]
2. Explain why stelai and tombs were important to the burial process. [3]

1.8 Journeying to the Underworld

TOPIC OVERVIEW

Myths about journeys to the underworld, as told by Greek and Roman authors, including details of the myth and its plot; portrayal of characters; portrayal of the underworld; how the set texts depict and reflect ancient culture

Greece

- Persephone and Demeter as told in the *Homeric Hymn to Demeter*, 2.1–104, 2.301–474

Rome

- Orpheus and Eurydice as told in Ovid's *Metamorphoses*, 10.1–64

The prescribed sources for this topic are:

- *Homeric Hymn to Demeter*, 2.1–104, 2.301–474
- Ovid, *Metamorphoses*, 10.1–64

Don't forget that you will be given credit in the exam if you study extra sources and make relevant use of them in your answers.

The Greeks and Romans had various myths and beliefs regarding what happened to the dead once they left the world of the living. Neither civilisation believed in a heaven or hell. All the dead ended up in the same place, the underworld.

The underworld was the realm of Hades and the Olympian gods were not allowed to enter it. Hermes and Dionysus were exceptions to this rule. As the messenger of the gods, Hermes had reason to travel between the two. Due to the circumstances of Dionysus' birth, he too was a god that could, if needed, visit the underworld. Beyond these two gods, travelling to the underworld was something reserved for the dead and heroes. Indeed, both the Greek hero's Heracles and Odysseus, and the Trojan hero Aeneas, visited the underworld as part of their quests.

Myths surrounding the underworld were popular motifs on funerary monuments, as they gave the deceased hope that they too could successfully enter the underworld and gain favour from its King and Queen.

GREECE

What were the *Homeric Hymns*?

The *Homeric Hymn to Demeter* was one of thirty-three poems dedicated to the gods, including Heracles. The poems are called 'Homeric' as they share a similar style to the epics of Homer. However, if Homer actually composed them or not is unknown. With this in mind, for our purposes, we will refer to the poet as Homer. What seems certain is that, like the other works of Homer, the poems were part of an **oral tradition**, and they would have been sung to audiences across the Greek world. For this reason, scholars have dated the poems to the seventh and sixth centuries BC. In oral poetry stock phrases, or **epithets**, would be used to identify characters. In the *Hymn to Demeter*, the goddess is called 'Demeter with the lovely hair' and Persephone, the daughter with 'the slender ankles'.

Themes

There are two main themes in the *Hymn to Demeter*; the relationship between the gods, and the relationship between gods and men. The poem cleverly explores the nature of the gods. Although they existed separately from men, they experienced all the same emotions, such as love, hate, loss and fear. However, their actions could have disastrous consequences for men. When Demeter retires to her temple:

> She made the grimmest and most brutal year for men on the all-nourishing earth. No ground sent up seeds, for Lady Demeter kept them hidden. Many oxen dragged the bent ploughs over the fields in vain. Much white barley fell upon the ground to no purpose.

Homeric Hymn to Demeter, 2.305–309

Despite the power the gods held over men, men also had power over the gods. As Zeus realised:

> By means of painful famine, she would have destroyed the whole mortal race and deprived the glorious dwellers of Olympus the honour of gifts and sacrifices, if Zeus had not noticed and pondered upon this in his heart.

Homeric Hymn to Demeter, 2.310–313

Thus man, while he had to submit to the will of the gods, was needed by them to offer sacrifice.

The entrapment of Persephone: lines 1–18

The first section of the hymn deals with the abduction of Persephone by Hades.

PRESCRIBED SOURCE

Homeric Hymn to Demeter, 2.1–104, 2.301–474

Date: uncertain 7th–6th century BC (debated, see left)

Author: attributed to Homer

Genre: poetry

Protagonist(s): Demeter, Persephone and Hades

Significance: provides an insight into what the Greeks thought the relationship between gods and men was like

Read it here: OCR sources booklet **CW**

oral tradition the passing on of information by word of mouth rather than the written word

FIGURE 1.72
Sarcophagus showing the abduction of Persephone.

> I begin to sing of beautiful-haired Demeter, holy goddess – of her and her delicate-ankled daughter whom Hades snatched away, her having been given to him by far-seeing Zeus the loud-thunderer.
>
> *Homeric Hymn to Demeter*, 2.1–3

While out playing with the daughters of Oceanus, Persephone began to collect flowers in a field:

> Roses and crocuses and beautiful violets, irises also and hyacinths, and the narcissus; which Earth made to grow at the will of Zeus and to please Hades, as a snare for the bloom-like girl. A marvellous, radiant flower, it was a thing of wonder for both immortal gods and mortal men to see.
>
> *Homeric Hymn to Demeter*, 2.7–9

This scene highlights an important part of Greek society in that the head of the household, a male, was responsible for arranging the marriages of his children. Importantly, he did not need the permission of the mother, in this case Demeter. The purposes of such marriages would be to secure family links. In this instance, Zeus may have sought to improve the relationship between the underworld and Olympia.

The flower itself received a lot of attention from the poet.

> From its root grew a hundred blooms, and it smelled most sweetly, so that all wide heaven above and the whole earth and the salty sea laughed for joy.
>
> *Homeric Hymn to Demeter*, 2.10–13

While Persephone looked at the flower, Hades emerged from the Earth and took her to his kingdom in his chariot.

The abduction of Persephone: lines 19–39

Having distracted Persephone, Hades emerged from the earth, took hold of her and took her to the underworld in his chariot:

> He seized her against her will on his golden chariot and carried her away as she wailed. Then she cried out shrilly with her voice, calling upon her father, the Son of Cronos, the highest and the best.
>
> *Homeric Hymn to Demeter*, 2.20

No one except Helios and Hecate heard the cries of Persephone, who went protesting to the underworld. Before the earth sealed behind her she let out one last cry, which was heard by Demeter.

> So long as both the earth and the starry sky could be seen by the goddess, and the strong-flowing, fish-filled sea, and the rays of the sun, she still hoped to see her dear mother and the tribe of the immortal gods. So during this time her great heart was soothed by hope, distressed as she was.
>
> *Homeric Hymn to Demeter*, 2.33–39

KEY INDIVIDUALS

Demeter Goddess of the harvest, sister of Poseidon, Hades and Zeus, mother of Persephone. She is given the epithet *of the lovely hair*.

Persephone Daughter of Demeter. She is given the epithet *of the slender ankles*.

Hades Brother of Poseidon, Zeus and Demeter. In the *Hymn to Demeter* he is rarely called Hades, instead he has other epithets, which include *God Who Receives So Many*, *The Ruler of Many* and *Receiver of Many*.

Zeus Brother of Demeter, Poseidon and Hades. In the hymn he is also referred to as *Son of Cronos*. He has the epithets *loud thundering* and *far seeing*.

Daughters of Oceanus Daughters of the Titan Oceanus, god of fresh water.

Study question
How effectively does Homer describe the flower planted by Gaia?

Demeter searches for Persephone: lines 40–89

Despite her close relationship with Zeus, Demeter's lack of inclusion in the decision made by Zeus is made clear:

> A sharp pain seized her heart. She tore off the veil from her divine flowing hair with her own dear hands, hurled her dark cloak down from both her shoulders, and sped off searching like a bird of prey over land and sea.

> *Homeric Hymn to Demeter*, 2.33–39

Demeter sprang into action searching all over for her daughter. After nine days of searching, Hecate approached Demeter with news of Persephone's abduction. Unfortunately, she only heard Persephone's cries, but Helios may have seen what happened. Hearing this, the two goddesses visited Helios and asked him what happened. Helios told her that it was Zeus that had offered Persephone to Hades.

Demeter's lament: lines 90–104

Having heard Helios' words, Demeter became enraged and left Olympus. Her response shows how the emotions of gods and men were the same:

> A more terrible, more dreadful grief came upon Demeter's spirit. Therefore, in her anger at the son of Cronos of the dark clouds, she abandoned the assembly of the gods and high Olympus. She went among the cities and rich fields of men, for a long time disguising her form. Not one of the men who saw her, recognised her, nor did any of the deep-girded women.

> *Homeric Hymn to Demeter*, 2.90–95

Disguised as an old woman she took refuge under a tree and mourned for her lost daughter.

> **S & C**
> **Lines 105–300**
>
> After Demeter left the gods to live with men, she met a family who took her in. The family were unaware that she was a goddess and allowed her to look after their son. Instead of feeding the baby mortal food, she fed him the ambrosia of the gods to grant him immortality. As a final act, Demeter attempted to throw the child in a fire, to make him shed his human form and emerge as a god. Before this could be done, the mother of the child entered the room and, understandably panicked, snatched the baby from Demeter. Annoyed at the ignorance of humans, Demeter explained her plan. She demanded that the people of Eleusis build her a temple and altar so she could teach them how to worship her correctly. The townsfolk met and agreed to build the goddess a temple.

Demeter's rage and Zeus' intervention: lines 301–334

The completion of the temple by the Eleusinians shows how men needed to honour the gods, but Demeter's actions showed that the gods also needed humans:

KEY INDIVIDUALS

Helios God of the sun. He pulled the sun across the sky with his chariot.

Hecate Goddess of magic, witchcraft and the night.

Study questions

1 What is your impression of Persephone from her actions during lines 19–39?
2 Why may Helios and Hecate have been the only two to hear Persephone's cries?

Study questions

1 What impression do we get of Demeter from lines 40–89?
2 Why did Helios consider Hades a good match for Persephone?

Study question

What impression of Demeter do we get from lines 90–104?

EXAM TIP

You are not expected to know the plot between lines 105 and 300, although it is helpful to know why the people had to build Demeter a temple.

Study questions

1 How justified were the actions of Demeter?
2 To what extent was Zeus the cause of his own problem?

She (Demeter) made the grimmest and most brutal year for men on the all-nourishing earth. No ground sent up seeds, for Lady Demeter kept them hidden. Many oxen dragged the bent ploughs over the fields in vain. Much white barley fell upon the ground to no purpose. By means of painful famine, she would have destroyed the whole mortal race and deprived the glorious dwellers of Olympus the honour of gifts and sacrifices, if Zeus had not noticed and pondered upon this in his heart.

Homeric Hymn to Demeter, 2.305–313

Having realised the consequences it would have for the gods, Zeus decided to intervene and sent Iris to beg Demeter to return. Demeter refused and so Zeus sent all the gods to offer gifts to her. Demeter still refused and told Zeus that only the return of her daughter would bring her back.

KEY INDIVIDUAL

Hermes Son of Zeus. Also referred to as the Slayer of Argos.

Zeus' appeal to Hades: lines 335–385

Having realised that Demeter would not submit unless Persephone was returned, Zeus sent Hermes to the underworld to appeal to Hades:

Study questions

1 Why did Zeus choose Hermes to travel to the underworld?
2 How is the power and authority of Zeus shown in this section?
3 How appealing would it be to be the wife of Hades?

Dark-haired Hades, who rules those who have died, father Zeus ordered me to lead noble Persephone out of Erebus so that her mother can see her with her eyes and stop her terrible rage and anger against the gods. She is devising some great scheme to make the feeble tribe of earth-born men perish by hiding seeds below the ground, and thus bring an end to worship of the immortals.

Homeric Hymn to Demeter, 2.305–313

Interestingly Hermes' appeal focused on the damage done to the gods and only concerned humans when their destruction would harm the gods. Beyond this the gods do not seem bothered about humans.

Hades submitted to the request of Zeus and sent Persephone back to Demeter with Hermes. Hades' discussion with Persephone before she leaves again highlights that the arranged marriage is not always a mutually accepted thing:

Keep the spirit in your breast kindly; don't be too angry for all you could be. I will not be a shameful husband to you amongst the immortals, being the brother of Zeus the Father. Here you will rule all that lives and moves, receiving the greatest honours amongst the immortals. Those who do wrong and do not appease your power with sacrifices, reverently performing rites, and giving rich gifts, will have punishment for all their days.

Homeric Hymn to Demeter, 2.361–369

The final point Hades makes again highlights the relationship between men and gods. Men must ensure that they sacrifice to the underworld gods or, after death, they will live in eternal suffering.

Before she left, Hades gave her a pomegranate seed to eat. Persephone did not know that if she ate it she would be bound to stay in the underworld for a set period of time. Once she ate it, Hades gave her his chariot and Hermes led her back to Demeter.

Demeter and Persephone reunited: lines 386–474

After they left the underworld, Persephone and Demeter embraced each other. Demeter suspected some trickery by Hades and asked Persephone if she had eaten anything in the underworld:

> Child, you didn't eat any food while you were down below, did you? Speak out, don't hide anything, so that we both know. For if you have not, you shall come back from hated Hades and live alongside me and your dark-clouded father, the son of Cronos, honoured by all the immortals. But if you did eat, you will go back again to the depths of the earth, to live for a third part of the seasons each year. The other two parts however, you shall live alongside me and the other immortals. When earth blooms with the fragrant blossoms of spring of every kind, then from the murky dark again you will rise up, a great marvel to gods and mortal men.
>
> *Homeric Hymn to Demeter*, 2.394–402

PS

This was the Greek explanation for the seasons. During winter Persephone was with Hades, and Demeter was in mourning for her daughter and, therefore, sent no seed or harvest.

Persephone retold how she was captured and what had happened in the underworld. The next morning Zeus sent Rhea to retrieve Demeter. Before she came, however, she would have to agree that Persephone had to return to Hades for one third of the year. She agreed and returned the harvest to humans.

EXPLORE FURTHER

S&C

In Book 11 of Homer's *Odyssey* the hero Odysseus has to descend to the underworld to speak with the prophet Teiresias. While there he meets his mother and many deceased heroes of the past.

Read *Odyssey*, 11.

What impression of the underworld does Homer present in Book 11?

Study questions

1 What impression of Demeter do you get from this poem?
2 'Men were pawns that the gods manipulated for their own advantage.' To what extent do you agree with this statement?

PRACTICE QUESTIONS: GREECE

Source A: *Homeric Hymn to Demeter*, 2.361–369

Keep the spirit in your breast kindly; don't be too angry for all you could be. I will not be a shameful husband to you amongst the immortals, being the brother of Zeus the Father. Here you will rule all that lives and moves, receiving the greatest honours amongst the immortals. Those who do wrong and do not appease your power with sacrifices, reverently performing rites, and giving rich gifts, will have punishment for all their days.

1. Who is speaking in this scene and who were they speaking to?   [2]
2. Why was this myth important to the Greeks?   [1]

ROME

Orpheus

Like many Greek and Roman heroes, Orpheus had both godly and earthly origins. His father was believed to be either the Thracian king Oeagrus or the god Apollo, his mother was the **muse** Calliope. Apollo gave Orpheus a lyre and taught him how to use it. His mother Calliope taught him to sing.

Orpheus' song was said to enchant anyone who heard it, be that a god, human or animal. Orpheus' songs were even said to move inanimate objects such as stones and trees to tears. During his life he joined Jason on his quest for the Golden Fleece and saved the crew from the Sirens:

KEY INDIVIDUAL

Hymen God of weddings

> To the heroes, too, they sent forth from their lips a lily-like voice. And the crew were ready to dive out, had the Thracian Orpheus, son of Oeagrus, stringing in his hand his lyre, rung forth the hasty sound of a rippling melody so that their ears might be filled with the sound of his twanging; and the lyre overcame the maidens' voice.
>
> Apollodorus, *Argonautica*, 4.898–900

After his journey with Jason he returned home and fell in love with a young maiden called Eurydice. This is the story that the Roman poet Ovid used in his *Metamorphoses*.

Orpheus' wedding and Eurydice's death: lines 1–10

> Hymen, called by the voice of Orpheus, departed, and, dressed in his saffron robes, made his way through the vast skies to the Ciconian coast: but in vain. He was present at Orpheus's marriage, true, but he did not speak the usual words, display a joyful expression, or bring good luck. The torch, too, that he held, sputtered continually, with tear-provoking fumes, and no amount of shaking contrived to light it properly.
>
> Ovid, *Metamorphoses*, 10.4–7

FIGURE 1.73
Roman mosaic showing Orpheus surrounded by animals.

These ill-omens foreshadowed the death of Eurydice who, while walking along a riverbank shortly after their wedding, was bitten by a poisonous snake and killed by the venom.

Orpheus' journey to the underworld: lines 11–39:

Overcome with grief, Orpheus decided to descend to the underworld and retrieve Eurydice:

> When Thracian Orpheus, the poet of Rhodope, had mourned for her, greatly,
> in the upper world, he dared to go down to Styx, through the gate of **Taenarus**,
> also, to see if he might not move the dead. Through the weightless throng, and
> the ghosts that had received proper burial, he came to Persephone, and the lord of
> the shadows, he who rules the joyless kingdom.

> Ovid, *Metamorphoses*, 10.11–16

Orpheus began to play his lyre and made an appeal to them both. The appeal he made to Pluto and Proserpina highlighted the Roman beliefs about life after death:

> O gods of this world, placed below the earth, to which all, who are created
> mortal, descend . . . all things are destined to be yours, and though we delay a
> while, sooner or later we hasten home. Here we are all bound, this is our final
> abode, and you hold the longest reign over the human race.

> Ovid, *Metamorphoses*, 10.18, 32–35

Although Orpheus admitted that all men were fated to live with Pluto he argued that it was not fair that Eurydice had her years cut short. If they returned her to him he would not come back until it was his time to live in the underworld.

Pluto's answer and the tragedy of Eurydice: lines 40–64

Hearing the words of Orpheus, several men who had been subject to eternal damnation were temporarily stopped from their tasks:

> The bloodless spirits wept as he spoke, accompanying his words with the music.
> Tantalus did not reach for the ever-retreating water: Ixion's wheel was stilled: the
> vultures did not pluck at Tityus's liver: the Belides, the daughters of Danaüs, left
> their water jars: and you, Sisyphus, perched there, on your rock. Then they say, for
> the first time, the faces of the Furies were wet with tears, won over by his song . . .

> Ovid, *Metamorphoses*, 10.41–46

EXPLORE FURTHER

S&C

The underworld could be a place of great suffering and torment for those who had done wrong in their life. Some of the most famous characters were Tantalus, Ixion, Tityus, the Danaids and Sisyphus.

1. What did they do to deserve their punishment?
2. What was their punishment?

Study question
Why were torches important in a wedding ceremony?

Taenarus the traditional entrance to the underworld in the south of the Peloponnese

---

KEY INDIVIDUALS

Orpheus Thracian musician and poet

Eurydice Wife of Orpheus

Proserpina Queen of the underworld, daughter of Ceres and wife of Pluto

Pluto King of the underworld, husband of Proserpina. He was also called the *Lord of Shadows*

Study question
How does Ovid create sympathy for Orpheus in this section?

Study questions

1 What does Orpheus' journey suggest about his character?
2 What impression of the underworld does Ovid give us in this section?
3 How important is love to Orpheus' argument? Does it change your view of the underworld?

Both Pluto and Proserpina were so moved by his song that they brought Eurydice forward:

> The poet of Rhodope received her, and, at the same time, accepted this condition, that he must not turn his eyes behind him, until he emerged from the vale of Avernus, or the gift would be null and void.

Ovid, *Metamorphoses*, 10.50–51

As they came close to the Taenaran gateway, Orpheus was worried that Eurydice had fallen behind and was lost. He turned around and Eurydice was pulled back into the underworld:

> Dying a second time, now, there was no complaint to her husband (what, then, could she complain of, except that she had been loved?). She spoke a last 'farewell' that, now, scarcely reached his ears, and turned again towards that same place.

Ovid, *Metamorphoses*, 10.60–62

EXPLORE FURTHER   Aeneas in the Underworld

The Trojan hero Aeneas also had to enter the underworld as part of his quest. Read Virgil, *Aeneid*, 6.264–903.

What impression of the underworld does Virgil present in these lines?

PRACTICE QUESTIONS: ROME

Source A: *A Roman sarcophagus*

1. In the myth of Orpheus and Eurydice how does Orpheus persuade Pluto to release Eurydice and why does she not manage to return with him?   [2]
2. Why is this scene appropriate for a Roman sarcophagus?   [1]

TOPIC REVIEW

You should be able to:

1. Describe:
   - what happened in the *Homeric Hymn to Demeter* and Ovid's story of Orpheus and Eurydice
   - the characteristics of Demeter, Persephone, Hades and Zeus
   - the characteristics of Orpheus, Eurydice, Proserpina and Pluto
   - how the underworld is described by Homer and Ovid.

2. Explain:
   - why the myth of Persephone's abduction was important to the Greeks and Romans
   - why Orpheus' story was important to the Greeks and Romans.

PRACTICE QUESTION: COMPARING GREECE AND ROME

'The underworld was not something to look forward to.' To what extent do you agree with this statement? Use **both** the *Homeric Hymn to Demeter* **and** the myth of Orpheus in your answer.   [15]

Further Reading for Thematic Study: Myth and Religion

Beale, A. (2011) *Greek Athletics and the Olympics*. Cambridge: Cambridge University Press

Beard, M., North, J. and Price, S. (1998) *Religions of Rome Volume 1: A History*. Cambridge: Cambridge University Press

Beard, M., North, J. and Price, S. (1998) *Religions of Rome Volume 2: A Sourcebook*. Cambridge: Cambridge University Press

Boardman, J. (2005) *Greek Sculpture: The Classical Period*. London: Thames & Hudson

Bradley, P. (2000) *Ancient Rome: Using Evidence*. Cambridge: Cambridge University Press

Bradley, P. (2000) *Ancient Greece: Using Evidence*. Cambridge: Cambridge University Press

Burkert, W. (1987) *Greek Religion: Archaic and Classical*. Oxford: Blackwell

Cooley, M.G.L. (2008) *Lactor 17: The Age of Augustus*. London: London Association of Classical Teachers.

Croally, N. (2011) *Classical Literature: An Introduction*. Oxford: Routledge

Dugdale, E. (2008) *Greek Theatre in Context*. Cambridge: Cambridge University Press

Jones, P. and Sidwell, K. (1997) *The World of Rome: An Introduction to Roman Culture*. Cambridge: Cambridge University Press

Mikalson, J. (2005) *Ancient Greek Religion*. Oxford: Blackwell Publishing

Renshaw, J. (2015) *In Search of the Greeks*. London: Bloomsbury

Renshaw, J. (2012) *In Search of the Romans*. London: Bloomsbury

Shelton, J. (1998) *As the Romans Did*. Oxford: Oxford University Press

Spawforth, T. (2006) *The Complete Greek Temples*. London: Thames & Hudson

Walsh, P.G. (2000) *Livy: His Historical Aims and Methods*. Cambridge: Bristol Classical Press

Woodford, S. (1986) *An Introduction to Greek Art*. London: Duckworth

What to Expect in the Exam for Myth and Religion

This section aims to show you the types of questions you are likely to get in the written examination. It offers some advice on how to answer the questions and will help you avoid common errors.

THE EXAMINATION

This component of the GCSE examination is designed to test your knowledge, under-standing and evaluation of Myth and Religion in the Greek and Roman world. The examination is worth 90 marks and lasts 1 hour and 30 minutes. This represents 50% of the total marks for the GCSE.

There are **three** sections to the paper, one on Greece, one on Rome and the third on Greece and Rome. Each section is worth 30 marks. The question paper will consist of both short-answer and extended-response questions. You will be required to respond to literary and visual/material sources, some of which will be from the prescribed material, and some you will not have seen before. In the third section of the paper you will be required to compare two ancient sources, one Greek and one Roman, one of which will be literary, the other visual/material.

There are two Assessment Objectives in your GCSE in Classical Civilisation. Questions will be designed to test these areas. These Assessment Objectives are explained in the table below:

	Assessment Objective	Marks
AO1	Demonstrate knowledge and understanding of: • literature and visual/material culture from the classical world • how sources reflect their cultural contexts • possible interpretations of sources by different audiences and individuals.	58
AO2	Analyse, interpret and evaluate literature and visual/material culture from the classical world, using evidence and producing coherent and reasoned arguments.	32

For AO1 in this component, you will need to demonstrate the following:

- A good range of accurate and relevant knowledge of the prescribed myths and aspects of religion listed on the specification.
- An understanding of what the myths tell us about Greek and Roman beliefs in their gods, heroes and founding myths, and how they were utilised to promote the power of those using them.
- An understanding of how myth and religion affected the everyday lives of the Greeks and Romans, including temples, religious officials, sacrifices, festivals, death and beliefs in the afterlife.
- Different interpretations that can be made about these myths, and the different conclusions that can be drawn from these.

For AO2 in this component, you will need to demonstrate that you can analyse, interpret and evaluate the sources you have studied, giving opinions and backing them up with evidence, for example:

- Sound analysis of sources and factual evidence to reach and support reasoned opinions about the myths and aspects of religion in Greece and Rome.
- Appropriate evaluation of different sources and factual evidence to provide reasoned ideas.
- The ability to compare and contrast Greek and Roman ideas about myth and religion.

QUESTION TYPES

All questions, apart from extended-response questions (see p. 141), will be linked to an ancient source. These will be a mixture of literary and visual/material sources. Some will be prescribed sources that you will have studied beforehand and others will be 'unseen' sources, which you will see for the first time in the exam.

There are five types of questions that will feature in your exam. The question types are listed in the table below, which identifies where in the exam they will appear. They are arranged into two categories: knowledge and understanding, significance, and stimulus questions are all short-answer questions; detailed-response questions and extended-response questions, require a longer answer.

Section	Question type	Number of marks available
Section A: Greece	Knowledge and understanding questions	16
	Significance questions	6
	Detailed-response question	8
Section B: Rome	Knowledge and understanding questions	16
	Significance questions	6
	Detailed-response question	8

Section	Question type	Number of marks available
Section C: Greece & Rome	Stimulus questions	15
	Extended-response question	15

Knowledge and understanding questions

There will be 16-marks' worth of knowledge and understanding questions (all AO1). The 16 marks will be broken down into a series of short-answer questions, typically worth 1, 2 or 3 marks.

Some questions will require you to show your **knowledge** of a myth or aspect of religion. This may be done using a prescribed source or an unseen one. Other questions will require you to show **knowledge** and *also* demonstrate an **understanding** of these facts.

There will be a **source** to assist you. For example, you might be shown this image with the following questions:

Question: Who is depicted in this statue and how do you know?   [2]
Answer: Athena [1]. Because of her helmet/shield/snake cloak.   [1]

Correctly stating that this is Athena is a piece of knowledge, and you can then show further understanding of this object by explaining how you know this. This answer should be brief. There is in fact no need to write full sentences if it seems that only a single word or a phrase is needed, as is the case in the first part of the answer.

Significance questions

There will be two of these questions in both Section A and Section B. Significance questions are split into two parts. You will be asked to give two pieces of information (2 marks AO1) and state why one or both are important or significant, or what this knowledge tells us (1 mark AO2). Examples are given below.

Question: **a.** In the myth of the contest judged by Cecrops between Athena and Poseidon, what did Athena do to win? [2]

b. What was the significance of this act to the Athenians [1]

Answer: **a. Two** from:

She planted an olive tree [1] which gave them olives, oil and wood [1] which was more useful than the salt-sea Poseidon offered [1]

b. One from:

Explains why she was their patron goddess [1] explains why their city was named after her [1], olive trees were grown in Attica and were very important to the Athenians and so Athena's gift was important to them [1]

For part (a) we are looking for knowledge about the myth. For part (b) we are looking for why the myth was important.

Detailed-response questions

You will get one of these questions in both Section A and Section B, with one or more sources to prompt you. This stimulus is meant only as a starting point, and it will be clear from the question that you will need to bring in **extra information and examples**.

For knowledge and understanding there are **four** marks (AO1), and **four** marks are given for your analysis, interpretation and evaluation of facts and understanding (AO2). It is important to remember that for AO1 you will need to show knowledge and understanding of a source's context and the different ways people interpret the sources.

These questions are marked in a different way, however; you are not given one mark for each correct opinion and each piece of evidence, but the answer as a whole is marked using a Levels of Response Grid. A Levels of Response Grid explains to examiners what answers may look like to achieve a certain number of marks. An examiner will read the whole answer and check the grid to work out what level the answer belongs to. It is essential to remember that the quality of your answer is more important than the amount you have written. The Levels of Response Grid is included in the mark schemes for exam papers.

Remember that you can examine both sides of an argument. For example, if you are asked how heroic you believe Heracles to have been, there are likely to be arguments on both sides of the question. It may be that you believe Heracles to be an excellent hero but that he had some flaws, or that you believe him to have been a poor hero but that he had some redeeming features. If you do not examine both sides of an argument, you may have missed some key facts, and your answer may not show a full evaluation.

This question is not meant to be an essay. You are advised not to write an introduction that simply outlines how you will write your response as this will not add anything to your answer and will take up valuable time. You may find you have more to say than time allows, so you might have to be disciplined in moving on. Make your key points at the start, keep to the point, and if you do choose to have a conclusion, keep it brief, as you will ideally have answered the precise wording of the question throughout your answer. It is not necessary to have a conclusion to gain full marks.

An example of a question is given below.

Source A: *An extract from Livy about the meeting of Latinus and Aeneas*

From this point, there are two versions of the story. Some say that when Latinus was defeated in battle he made peace with Aeneas, and later, an alliance of marriage. Others claim that when battle lines had been drawn, Latinus advanced before the trumpet had sung the starting signal, and, surrounded by his generals, called the leader of the foreigners to a conference. Then he asked: who were they; where had they come from; what misfortune had made them leave their home; and what were they looking for when they came to Laurentum?

Source B: *An extract from Livy about Romulus and Remus*

Remus was the first to receive the augury: six vultures. Just as that omen had been reported, twice the number appeared to Romulus, and each king was saluted by their own followers: the first group prioritised time as a mark of honour, and the second, the number of birds. They entered a verbal conflict, which then turned to an angry struggle leading to bloodshed. In the ensuing clash, Remus was cut down. . . . So Romulus gained sole power, and when the city was established, it took its founder's name.

Question: Whom do you admire more as a founder of Rome, Aeneas or Romulus? Use sources A and B as starting points **and** your own knowledge in your answer.   [8]

To show your knowledge about Aeneas and Romulus you may include the following:

- Aeneas led the Trojans after their city was destroyed.
- Aeneas founded the line of Alban Kings.
- Romulus and his brother were almost killed by his uncle.
- Romulus killed his brother.
- Romulus founded the actual city of Rome.
- Rome is named after Romulus.

Remember you need to say whether this is an admirable characteristic or not, with possible ideas being:

- Aeneas is more admirable because he led the Trojans across the ocean to Italy after their home was destroyed, a very difficult task both physically and emotionally.
- Romulus founded the actual city, not just the line of kings, and therefore is more admirable as a founder of Rome.
- Romulus killed his brother, which makes him a lot less admirable than Aeneas who is very pious.

Half the marks are awarded for AO1 and for AO2, but this does not necessarily mean that you should give four facts and four explanations. Examiners will read your whole response and judge how good they feel it is overall.

Stimulus questions

These questions will only be asked in Section C, the **Greece and Rome** section of the examination. You will be given a series of questions that will ask you to identify something relevant from the stimuli given, and to analyse what you have recognised.

While your Literature and Culture exam also contains stimulus questions, the ones in Myth and Religion are slightly different as they have more marks for AO2 than AO1. To indicate this, they all use the command word 'explain', suggesting that you need to expand a little more on your analysis and explain your ideas more fully.

These questions will add up to a total of fifteen marks, with each question carrying **three** marks: **one** mark for AO1 and **two** marks for AO2. You will be given one literary **and** one visual source from the Greek **and** Roman world. Thus, if you are given a Greek literary source it will be accompanied by a Roman visual source, and vice-versa.

An example of a question is given below.

Source A: *Relief from a stone coffin (sarcophagus) with the abduction of Persephone/ Proserpina, use Fig 1.72*

Source B: *Homeric Hymn to Demeter,* **lines 267–277; 292–315; 399–406**

'I am Demeter, the honoured one, who for mortals and immortals alike has been made the greatest blessing and source of joy. But come, let all the people build me a great temple and an altar beneath it, below the steep walls of the city above Kallichoron, upon the rising hill. And I myself will inaugurate my mysteries, so that from now on you may perform them in all purity and be reconciled to my heart.' As the goddess said this, she changed her stature and form, throwing away old age . . . But as soon as dawn appeared they told powerful Keleos exactly what had happened, just as the goddess had commanded, Demeter with her lovely crown. So he called to assembly his innumerable people, and he ordered them to build for Demeter with the lovely hair a sumptuous temple and an altar upon the rising hill. They heard his voice and hurriedly obeyed him, building it as he commanded. And it grew as the goddess decreed.

Now when they were finished and done with their labour, each man went back to his house. But golden-haired Demeter sat there, far away from all the blessed gods, she stayed there, wasting with longing for her deep-breasted daughter. And she made the most terrible and cruel year for human beings on the deeply nourishing earth. The earth did not send up seed, for rich-crowned Demeter kept it hidden. Many times the oxen dragged the curved plough across the fields in vain, and many times the white barley fell upon the earth fruitlessly. So she would have destroyed utterly the mortal race of human beings, starving them to death, and depriving those who lived on Olympus of the glorious honour of gifts and sacrifices, if Zeus had not noticed it and reflected upon it in his heart.

After Hermes' intervention at the request of Zeus, Hades agreed to free Persephone but tricks her before she leaves. Demeter explains the result of the trick . . .

. . . But if you did eat anything you will have to go back again to the secret depths of the earth and live there for a third part of the seasons of the year, but for the other two parts you will be with me and the other immortals. But whenever in spring the earth blossoms with sweet flowers of every kind, then you will rise again from the realm of dusk and darkness and be a source of great wonder for mortals and for gods.

Question: Explain why Persephone/Proserpina and Demeter/Ceres were so important to both the Greeks and Romans.   [6]

Answer: **One** from:
Demeter/Ceres was a goddess of regeneration [1], fertility [1], the harvest [1].

Plus one from:
Persephone/Proserpina was goddess of death [1], queen of the underworld [1].

Four from:
Demeter/Ceres: agriculture/the harvest was vital for the survival of the Greeks and Romans [1], the favour of Demeter/Ceres can lead to a good harvest/fruitful life [1], childbirth was dangerous [1], having children was important; for the family line [1], to help out with the family's work [1].

Persephone/Proserpina: the deceased would want Persephone/Proserpina on their side when passing into the underworld [1], cannot save humans from death, but the favour of Persephone/Proserpina can enable a better afterlife [1], the favour of Persephone/Proserpina (in conjunction with Demeter/Ceres) can enable a more fruitful life [1].

As the question is out of six marks your answer needs to contain **two** marks for AO1 and **four** marks for AO2.

The question asks you about Persephone/Prosperina **and** Demeter/Ceres. Therefore your AO1 needs to address both goddesses, with **three** marks available per goddess. With this in mind, even if you were to list several correct points focusing only on Demeter/Ceres you could only get four of the available marks.

Extended-response questions

You will only need to do one extended-response question in this exam, and this is in Section C. This type of question is different from the other questions in two respects: there is no stimulus passage to introduce it, and you will be given a **choice** of questions to answer (there will be two on the paper, and you answer **one** of these). However, it is marked using a Levels of Response Grid in the same way as the detailed-response question.

Five marks are awarded for your knowledge and understanding (AO1), and **ten** marks are given for your analysis, interpretation and evaluation of facts and understanding (AO2). This means more marks are awarded for how good your argument is than for simply what you know. Therefore, you might want to spend a bit of time thinking about the structure of your answer. As for the detailed-response question, it is important to remember that for AO1 you will need to show knowledge and understanding of the literary and historical context of sources and the different ways people interpret them.

Extended-response questions will cover a wider area than detailed-response questions. You will be expected to bring together your knowledge and understanding of both Greek and Roman cultures, and will directly compare the societies with regard to a particular aspect of the course, and reach a judgement about them.

The following is an example of a possible extended-response question.

Question: Who had more enjoyable festivals, the Greeks or the Romans? Justify your response.   [15]

To answer this question you should mention the aspects of the festivals that would be exciting and those that may not. You might include some of these facts:

Greeks
City Dionysia

- Tragedy and comedy performances
- Plays could draw on current affairs
- Sacrifice to Dionysus
- Procession
- Celebration and drinking
- Chance for all citizens to take part (chorus, voting)
- Involved in voting for the winner
- Five days of festivities

Great Panathenaia

- Five-day festival
- Events for both Athenians and non-Athenians
- Procession
- Sacrifice and offerings to Athena

Romans

Lupercalia

- Links to the founder of Rome
- Only young boys were in the teams
- Sacrifice
- Drinking and feasting after the sacrifice
- Competition (race)
- Whipping of public (especially females) during race around the Palatine.

Saturnalia

- Sacrifice
- All business, schools and politics were suspended so all could take part.
- Free public banquet
- Masters and slaves treated as equals
- Presents exchanged

You then need to analyse why these aspects made either the Greek or Roman festivals more enjoyable. You should compare both cultures when you do this. You might draw conclusions such as:

- The Panathenaic sacrifice to Athena was most entertaining due to the variety of people involved and the scale of the event.
- You may make a distinction between the enjoyment of the ancient participants and what a modern person might enjoy; for example, the festivals involving animal sacrifice might offend modern sensibilities and so be less enjoyable.
- Some might make distinctions between social groups; for example, slaves might have particularly enjoyed the Saturnalia as they could be treated as equals for a time.

Remember that examiners will read your whole response and judge how good they feel it is overall.

Key points

The following applies to both detailed-response questions and extended-response questions:

- Your facts must be **relevant**. Do not merely state everything you know about a particular topic.
- It is a common mistake to over-narrate examples and to retell a whole story. You should instead **summarise** the main points of a story, or focus in detail on one or two parts of it. This is particularly important in your extended-response answer, where five marks are available for your knowledge, but ten marks are given for your evaluation, interpretation and analysis.
- Show that you **understand** things from an ancient point of view wherever possible. For example, people in ancient Greece and Rome had very different

views regarding prostitution from ours today. Show that you understand these differences in context through explanation of the facts.

- Evaluation is best done throughout the response. **Keep referring back** to the title in your essay to do this. If you give all your facts, and then give all your opinions, it is easy to miss something out, or to run out of time.
- Try to find a **balance** of ideas as the question will usually require you to argue both for and against an idea.
- Sometimes a piece of evidence can be taken two ways. If so, remember to give **both interpretations** in order to show a high level of understanding.
- You will not have a lot of time to do these questions and so it is always best to make your most important arguments first in case you find yourself running out of time.
- Ultimately make your conclusion **logical**, and supported by evidence from your whole answer, not just one part of it.

Look at these two extracts from an essay.

Question: Who had more enjoyable festivals, the Greeks or the Romans? Justify your response. [15]

Extract 1

The Greeks had more entertaining festivals. The Great Panathenaia was held in honour of Athena and the City Dionysia was held for Dionysus, two important gods for the Athenians. Both festivals had lots of events like a procession that involved the whole population, which made them more enjoyable. Likewise, the numerous sporting and musical contests that took place could make them more enjoyable to watch. On the other hand, the Roman festivals were not as enjoyable. The Lupercalia was linked to the founder of Rome, Romulus. The events were not as numerous as they did not have a procession and the race during the Lupercalia and did not directly involve most of the population of Rome. However, the feast that took place during the Saturnalia did involve everyone. Therefore, on balance the Greek festivals were more enjoyable.

Extract 2

The Greek festivals of the Great Panathenaia and City Dionysia were more enjoyable as they contained processions that involved all of Athens, from the poor to wealthy. The inclusion of the cavalry, religious officials, sacrificial animals and musicians in the Great Panathenaia would have created a real buzz and party-like atmosphere in the streets of Athens. Likewise, the nature of Dionysus' procession would also be really enjoyable as the adults would drink wine, sing and dance in honour of the god. On the other hand, the Roman festival of the Lupercalia would have been less enjoyable as it had no procession before the sacrifice, meaning only the officials directly involved took part. Furthermore, the numerous sporting events such as the tribal contests at the Great Panathenaia, and musical and theatre contests at the City Dionysia made the festival more enjoyable, as all of Athens would have the opportunity to take part in a dithyramb or play. The fact that they also took part in the tribe contests also added an aspect of competitiveness that would have made them enjoyable. Although the Lupercalia had a race around the Palatine, it only directly involved a few select men chosen from the upper classes, leaving the majority of the population to watch. However, it could be said that the communal feasting that took place as part of the Saturnalia made it enjoyable as people united. However, communal feasting after the sacrifice was also a part of the Great Panathenaia. With these points in mind the Greek festivals were more enjoyable than the Roman festivals.

Notice how the first extract spends more time on presenting the facts than giving opinions, and many of the facts are unspecific or unnecessary. The evaluation is not developed fully, and the statements regarding the gods are irrelevant to the question. The second extract is much more balanced. It argues both sides and flows smoothly from Greeks to Romans and vice versa, providing alternative interpretations of the festivals.

GENERAL EXAM SKILLS

When you are sitting the examination, read the instructions carefully so that you realise which questions are compulsory and which are optional (the only option you have is which of the two extended-response questions you choose to answer). Remember that the examination will have a range of difficulty of questions; some of it is designed to be challenging, and you should not be panicked if you cannot think of an answer immediately. The following pieces of advice may seem obvious, but you should not underestimate their importance:

- The examination lasts 90 minutes and is worth 90 marks. Do not assume this means you should spend a minute per mark: in reality a lot of short questions will take less than a mark a minute and you should spend longer than a mark a minute on the long questions.
- Each section is worth 30 marks. Do not spend too long on whichever you choose to do first, especially if you like the questions that have been set and feel you could say a lot.
- If you see a question that you do not know the answer to, move on quickly to another question and do not waste time thinking. Leave enough time to go back to it, as during the examination you might well remember the answer.
- Stick to the question: if you are asked for facts, do not give opinions and vice versa.
- Do not try to answer a slightly different question if you wish another had been set, or if you have practised a similar one before at school.
- For detailed-response and extended-response questions, present different interpretations.
- More marks are available in the paper for opinions than knowledge or understanding. It is vital that you do not over-narrate.

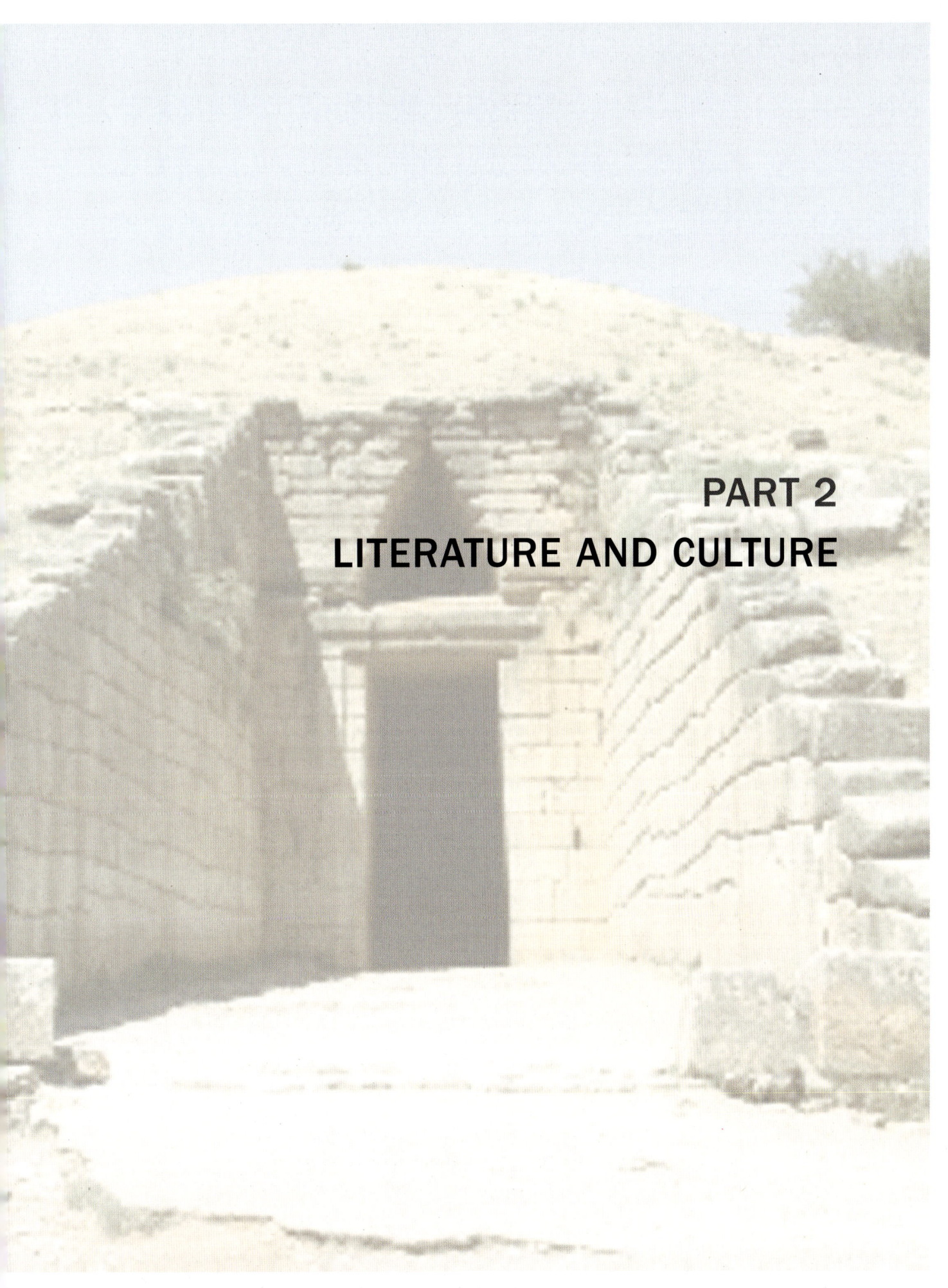

PART 2
LITERATURE AND CULTURE

Introduction to the Literature and Culture Options

Half of your GCSE in Classical Civilisation involves the study of an aspect of ancient culture combining a cultural depth study with reading and analysis of ancient literature in translation.

OCR offers the choice of one of three options:

The Homeric World	J199/21
Roman City Life	J199/22
War and Warfare	J199/23

The following pages of this textbook include all the content needed to study all three of these options, but you will only study one of them.

EXAM OVERVIEW

Your assessment for the Literature and Culture option will be:

50% of the GCSE	1 hr 30 mins	90 marks

50 marks will test AO1: demonstrate knowledge and understanding of:

- literature and visual/material culture from the classical world
- how sources reflect their cultural contexts, and
- possible interpretations of sources by different audiences and individuals.

40 marks will test AO2: analyse, interpret and evaluate literature and visual/material culture from the classical world, using evidence and producing coherent and reasoned arguments.

The Literature and Culture paper is divided into two sections:

Section A	Culture	45 marks
Section B	Literature	45 marks

Each section has five question types:

- knowledge-and-understanding questions
- significance questions
- stimulus questions
- 8-mark detailed-response question
- 15-mark extended-response essay

You can read more about these question types for each component in the three What to Expect in the Exam Chapters, pp. 233, 345 and 453.

L&C 1
The Homeric World

Introduction to the Homeric World

This component is based around life in ancient Greece just over three thousand years ago. The Culture half of the topic covers the ancient civilisation known as the Mycenaean Age. You will study some of the main Mycenaean sites and the items that made these places so remarkable. From tiny objects like rings, to huge city walls, you will study a variety of source material to find out what life was like at the time.

In the Literature half, you will read five books (the equivalent of modern chapters) from Homer's poem, the *Odyssey*. You will read some of the most important parts of the *Odyssey*, including the stories of the giant Polyphemus and the witch Circe, and Odysseus' encounter with his rivals, the suitors, in his palace. You will look at these characters, and other key figures, and the themes that feature throughout the poem, such as hospitality, civilisation and trickery. You will find out about how Homer composed the poem and the literary style he uses in it, which has influenced many writers throughout history.

EXAM OVERVIEW	J199/21

Your examination will require you to show knowledge and understanding of the material you have studied (AO1) and will require you to analyse and evaluate it (AO2), giving your opinions on areas such as characters in the literature or objects in the culture.

This component makes up 50% of your GCSE. In this component 50 marks will test your AO1 skills and 40 marks will test your AO2 skills.

There will be a distinct section of questions on the Mycenaean Age, and a distinct section on the literature. Neither section will ask questions requiring knowledge of the other: for example, you will not be asked how far the *Odyssey* confirms knowledge of what life in the Mycenaean Age was like.

In both sections you will be asked to answer a series of short factual questions, based around images or around passages from Homer. Some of these will also ask for your opinions. You will be required to write longer answers in each section, worth 8 marks and 15 marks, showing knowledge and giving opinions. There will be 45 marks' worth of questions on Mycenae, and 45 marks' worth on Homer. You will have a choice of longer questions worth 15 marks in each section, but all other questions will be compulsory.

Culture

2.1 Key Sites

Cities in the Mycenaean Age were small by modern standards, often having an area similar to a small village today. However, these cities had a lot of different areas packed into them, including palaces, defences and burial grounds. In this section you will read about some of the major cities of the Mycenaean Age.

THE CONCEPT AND DATING OF THE MYCENAEAN AGE

Mycenaean a civilisation that was powerful from around 1600 BC to 1150 BC, named after the city of Mycenae in southern Greece

The **Mycenaean** Age, named after the city of Mycenae in Greece, is a general term that describes the time when many separate independent cities in the Greek world were powerful. Mycenae was the most famous of these cities. They had a similar culture, buildings and administration, and had palaces at the heart of them. However, it is important to realise that they were totally independent from each other, and the term 'Mycenaean' is a modern one to link cities that had these similarities. There was no concept at the time of all the cities being in any way linked or united. These cities are found in many parts of the Mediterranean, and not only Greece; in fact, the country of Greece did not even exist at the time of the Mycenaeans, and whilst we cannot say how they felt for certain, it would seem very likely that they saw other cities as totally distinct from themselves.

The Mycenaean Age lasted from approximately 1600 BC to 1150 BC. This period is part of what is known as the Bronze Age, because it was in this time that tin and copper were first mixed together to make the alloy bronze, which is a much stronger material than the elements that were combined to make it.

As with many aspects of Mycenae, it is very hard to be more exact about these dates, as nothing can be precisely dated until much later in Greek history. Further complications are caused by the fact that the Mycenaean civilisation is very similar to the **Minoan civilisation**, which came just before it, and it is often hard to distinguish from which of these civilisations objects come.

In order to date the Mycenaean Age, historians look at pottery styles in Greece, comparing them to those in Egypt, where historical records were kept more accurately. Carbon objects, such as wooden objects and timbers, are also beginning to yield clues as scientists can date them using the radioactivity that is present in such materials.

The Mycenaean Age has been divided into three phases by historians:

- The early period (1600–1400 BC), in which burials were made in shaft graves (see pages 191–192).
- The palatial period (1400–1250 BC), when the great palaces are thought to have reached their peak.
- The later period (1250–1150 BC), when the palaces seem to have come under more attacks before suddenly being abandoned or destroyed.

> **Minoan civilisation** a civilisation based on Crete that influenced neighbouring areas. It lasted from around 3500 BC until around 1400 BC, overlapping in both time and area with the Mycenaean civilisation

S & C

Much debate has existed over the collapse of Mycenaean cities. In the final decades of the age, huge changes were happening throughout the Eastern Mediterranean. The kingdom of the Hittites to the east of Greece collapsed around 1200 BC, and written accounts from Egypt tell of 'Sea Peoples' attacking Egypt from the north. Moreover, the site of Troy was also destroyed around this time, although this is probably not the famous Trojan War, which is discussed on pages 161–163. There is evidence that some of the main Mycenaean cities strengthened their walls and defences around this time, presumably in fear of an attack. However, these measures did not prevent the destruction of the cities as there were huge fires in many of the sites, although we do not know what was the cause of these.

After the end of the Mycenaean Age, the Iron Age began. Iron, widely neglected by the Mycenaeans, was used for weapons and tools in this age. We have no written records at all from this period, and it used to be known as the 'Dark Age', as it was felt that we knew little about life at this time. Historians are now able to give more information about the period, and one idea is that the decline that was evident in the Mycenaean Age continued into the Iron Age, with large falls in the populations of some cities.

TIMELINE OF THE MYCENAEAN AGE

Date (BC)	Major events in the Mycenaean Age	Period
1675	First burials in Grave Circle B at Mycenae	Early
1600	First burials at Grave Circle A Destruction of Akrotiri	
1400	Start of major building at Mycenaean sites Treasury of Atreus built Development of the city of Tiryns End of Minoan Age	Palatial
1375	Shipwreck of Ulu Burun	
1350	Tombs of Clytemnesta and Aegisthus built Cyclopean Walls of Mycenae built	
1300	Western wall of Mycenae strengthened Eastern Gate and palace built at Mycenae	
1250	Further strengthening of walls and defences of Tiryns Building of Galleries at Tiryns Lion Gate built Destruction of Troy VIIa Decline of major Mycenaean sites	Later
1200	Destruction of Troy VI Damage to Mycenae from fire	
1075	Final destruction at Mycenae from fire	

THE LOCATION AND IMPORTANCE OF THE KEY SITES, INCLUDING MYCENAE, TIRYNS AND TROY

Mycenae is the most famous city of the Mycenaean Age, and in mythology it was the home of King Agamemnon, who led a Greek army against the city of Troy. The city is built on a hill, which is 40–50 m above the plains that it surrounds. It is a small area by modern standards, with a perimeter of around 900 m. Hills to the north and south and ravines surround the plains on three sides, and a spring less than 400 m away supplied water throughout the year.

An ancient city built on higher ground, and defended by walls, is known as a citadel. The term means 'little city', and these were indeed very small by modern standards, being more like small towns. For the sake of convenience, this chapter will use the term 'city' to describe the sites.

Evidence for the occupation of the site goes back a few thousand years beyond the Mycenaean Age. Archaeologists have traced the first Mycenaean burials to around 1650 BC, and believe the site reached peak prosperity from around 1400 BC to 1200 BC.

> **ACTIVITY**
>
> Imagine you are the person who decided where the city of Mycenae should be built. Explain why you have chosen the site as the location for your city.

FIGURE 2.1 PS
View of the archaeological site of Mycenae. You can clearly see the surrounding hills, and some of the huge walls that helped defend the city.

The Greeks believed that the hero Perseus, the man who killed the Medusa, first founded the city. He was given help in building the city by the mythical race of giants called the Cyclopes. The Greeks did not think that any human could have built such huge structures without help. According to legend, Agamemnon became king of Mycenae centuries later. Homer states that Agamemnon led an army gathered together from lots of Greek cities and islands against Troy, although the evidence for Agamemnon's existence and the war itself is debatable.

Mycenae is most famous for the tombs and the treasures that were found there. These tombs, together with the rest of the city, were excavated by a German archaeologist, Heinrich Schliemann, between 1876 and 1878.

Another important Mycenaean site is Tiryns, located around 10 miles from Mycenae. It had strong defensive walls, which were up to 8 m high and 13 m thick, and is famous for its palace, throne room and a series of arched galleries. Numerous frescoes have been found from Tiryns; one of these shows a youth somersaulting over a bull, which was an activity that was popular in the Minoan Age. The ancients believed that Tiryns was slightly older than Mycenae. It was supposedly founded by Proitos, whose brother was Acrisius. Acrisius' grandson was Perseus, the founder of Mycenae. It was also thought to be the birthplace of the hero Heracles (known as Hercules by the Romans).

Troy, the site of the famous war between the Greeks and the Trojans, is found in northwest Turkey. It is a city that was rebuilt several times in ancient history, with each new version built on top of the previous one. Much debate surrounds which version of the city existed at the time of the Trojan War (see pages 161–163). The city has revealed little evidence of the riches that Homer describes, but it is likely that it was an important site in Mycenaean times.

Study question
Why might the Greeks have wanted to believe that their mythological heroes founded their cities?

KEY PLACE

Mycenae the best preserved site of the Mycenaean Age, containing a significant quantity of gold, pottery, treasure and frescoes (wall paintings). It has huge defensive walls and the remains of a palace. The site also contains several different types of tombs and graves

KEY PLACE

Tiryns a strongly defended site, famous for its walls, palace, throne room and frescoes

megaron the central hall in the Mycenaean palace, used for banquets, worship and meetings

S & C There are a number of other important Mycenaean sites in and around Greece. One of these is Pylos, which is situated in the far southwest of Greece. It has excellent views to the sea to the west, as it is built on a small bank, a few metres higher than the surrounding area. To the west is a natural bay, and to the east are mountains. In Homer's *Iliad*, Pylos is the home city of Nestor, the aged advisor to the Greek army at Troy.

It is different from many Mycenaean sites as it does not show evidence of large perimeter walls, although it does contain a well-preserved palace. There is evidence that this palace was destroyed by a large fire in the thirteenth century BC. During a fire at the palace, hundreds of clay tablets were preserved that showed evidence of a written language known as Linear B (see pages 175–178). Other parts of the site include a **megaron** (see pages 166–167) with a central hearth and four columns. The site also contains a smaller megaron (possibly for the queen), a bathroom with a bathtub, storage rooms with jars sunken into the floor, and an armoury. You can find more information about it at http://www.ancientgreecejourney.co.uk/places/nestors.htm.

Another important site is Akrotiri. Akrotiri is on the island of Santorini, situated in the Aegean Sea. The site is famous for its wall paintings, which show a heavy influence from the earlier Minoan Age. These include paintings of ships, boxers, flowers, birds, priests and worshippers.

THE LAYOUT AND STRUCTURES OF THE SITES OF MYCENAE AND TIRYNS

FIGURE 2.2
Plan of Mycenae. **PS**

A Lion Gate	M Temple
B Granary	N Guest Chamber
C Ramp	P Court
D Grave Circle A	Q Staircase
E Ramp House	R Megaron
F Warrior Vase House	S Postern Gate
G South House	T Stair to Cistern
H House with the Idols	W Sally-port
J Tsountas House	Y House of Columns
K Palace Entrance	Z Tower
L Retaining Wall	

FIGURE 2.3
Aerial view of
Mycenae.

PRESCRIBED SOURCE

Site of Mycenae

Built: 17th–11th century
BC (approximately)

Location: northeast
Peloponnese, Greece

Materials: limestone and
conglomerate blocks

Significance: contains
important frescos,
tombs and treasure

Find out more here:
http://www.ancient.eu/
mycenae/

The palace of Mycenae is situated at the very top of the hill. The hill did not have a flat top, so the ground had to be artificially levelled. There were large terraces at the sides that would have been used for storage.

The **sally ports** were an important part of the defensive structure of the city. There were two of these; one at the north and one at the south of the city. These have been suggested to have been secret passages from which defenders could rush out and attack unsuspecting enemy soldiers. However, the south sally port is visible from a distance, which might question whether it was a defensive measure, or at least how effective it was, especially as the passage is only just over one metre wide.

The ports use a technique known as **corbelling**, which was a method of spanning a gap between two structures. At the top of both sides of the gap, increasingly larger blocks of stone would be placed one on top of the other until they joined at the top. Examples of this technique are the passage that leads to the underground cistern (see Figure 2.4 on page 156) and the roof of the Treasury of Atreus (see Figure 2.40 on page 193).

Next to the northern sally port is a passage that goes under the perimeter wall and leads to an underground cistern (a tank used to store water). The cistern itself is 18 m below ground level. It collected water through a series of clay pipes in the roof. This water came from the natural spring that lay close to the city. If attackers laid siege to the city and tried to cut off the water supply, the Mycenaeans could secretly get to a supply of water to enable them to hold out for a lengthy period.

The walls of Mycenae are an impressive feat of engineering and construction. In the first phase of wall building (from approximately 1350 BC), the walls only surrounded

sally port a gap in the outer wall through which defenders could rush out to surprise attackers

corbelling a technique used to span a gap between two walls by placing increasingly larger blocks of stone onto each other, thereby creating a vaulted roof (see also Figure 2.10 on p. 160)

FIGURE 2.4
Passage leading to the underground cistern at Mycenae. The walls and roof are an excellent example of the corbelling technique.

PS

---

relief (from the Latin verb 'relevo', 'to raise') a carving that projects from, and is a part of, the same background material; it has the effect of shading and being in 3D

Study question
Why do you think the rulers used a symbol of lions at the entrance to the city?

---

the top of the city of Mycenae, and little of this survives. The walled area was enlarged a century or so later, until the final perimeter wall was finished around 1200 BC, being around 900 m long.

The best preserved section of the wall at the north of the city ranges from 5.5 m to 7.5 m. thick. This thickness is the length of a large room in a house today. None of the walls survives to full height, but it is estimated that they reached around 12 m high. The section of wall surrounding the Lion Gate (Figure 2.5) is 8.25 m high.

To build these walls was a superhuman feat. Even the ancient Greeks could not work out how any human built them, as each block weighs around 2 tonnes. The ancient Greeks referred to them as the 'Cyclopean Walls', after the giant that Odysseus blinded, believing that only a huge giant could have moved such blocks.

The walls were made out of huge blocks of limestone piled on top of each other; the area around Mycenae is a good source of the stone. Mortar (to join the blocks) was not used, but smaller pieces of limestone filled the spaces between the blocks. Some blocks could have been moved from higher areas of the city by placing them on rollers. Other blocks would have been raised through the construction earth ramps. Larger blocks were used for the visible parts of the wall, while the inner core was made from earth and rubble. The wall generally followed the contours of the hill to make it easier to build.

The Lion Gate is probably the most famous feature of Mycenae and is one of the most impressive pieces of masonry in the Greek world. This was the main entrance to the city and was built in the thirteenth century BC, when Mycenae was at its most powerful. The approach to the gate was along an uphill path. The area surrounding the gate itself is not made of limestone, but of a different rock called conglomerate. This would provide an effective contrast with the limestone around the rest of the site as conglomerate is a shinier and smoother material than limestone.

The opening where the gate would have been is roughly a square whose sides are 3 m. The gate has large blocks at either side (the jambs) and above (the lintel). The lintel on its own weighs 20 tonnes. Above the edges of the lintel is a corbel arch. In the lintel and threshold, holes are visible for the doors and bar that would have locked the gates.

In the triangle created in the corbel arch is a slab of limestone, carved into the form of two lions in **relief**. The lions have their paws on altars, but their heads have not survived. These would probably not have been made of limestone, as it is very difficult to carve precise details in this medium. The columns above the altars are typically Minoan, being thicker at the top than the bottom. By showing the sides of the lions, but with their heads possibly facing forward, an air of solemnity and majesty was created. The Lion Gate would be an obvious area for attackers to focus on, but defenders on the walls would hurl missiles down to try to prevent enemies breaking through. The only other entrance to the city was through the northern gate, also known as the Postern Gate.

The tombs of Mycenae are probably the most famous in ancient Greece. This is due to the physical structures of the tombs themselves and the lavish treasures that they contained.

There are several different areas of tombs both in Mycenae itself and a short distance from the city walls. Full details of these tombs and their contents are given on pages 190–195.

The oldest tombs are those that are found in the area known as Grave Circle B (so called because it was discovered in 1952, while Grave Circle A had been discovered and named in 1876). Grave Circle B is an area around 200 m to the west of the city walls, and contains twenty-four graves, dated to the seventeenth and sixteenth centuries BC. It is enclosed within a stone wall, which had a diameter of 28 m. Just over half of the graves are thought to have been for members of the royal family, owing to the objects that were found within them. Part of the tomb of Clytemnestra was built over Grave Circle B around 300 years later.

Around thirty-five bodies of men, women and children have been found. The location of some of these are marked with upright stone **stelai**. An uncarved stele indicates the burial of a female, while carved ones indicate male burials.

Grave Circle A, situated in the southwest area of the city, is similar in many respects to Grave Circle B. It is also 28 m in diameter, and was originally surrounded by a low wall. It is thought to have been a royal burial site since the sixteenth century BC because the rich contents found within it were similar to those that had been dated to this time in Egypt. When the Lion Gate was built next to it, it was rebuilt with a new wall and the level of the ground was raised. At the time of the rebuilding, rulers were being buried in even grander tombs (see pages 192–193), and so it is thought the improvements to Grave Circle A were carried out to honour previous rulers. The original wall of smaller stones can be seen near the top of Figure 2.6, enclosed within the later double perimeter wall.

The area contained six shaft graves (see pages 191–192), in which a total of nine women, eight men and two children were buried at the bottom of shafts. These shafts are deeper and larger than those of Grave Circle B. The dead were buried with a vast quantity of precious objects, including gold objects weighing 14 kg, together with silver, amber, glass and ivory. Stelai, often elaborately carved, were set over the burials. Three of these depict chariot scenes. It is not surprising that Homer called Mycenae 'rich in gold' (*Iliad*, 11.25).

Outside the walls of Mycenae are even grander tombs; the 'so-called' tombs of Clytemnestra and Aegisthus and a tomb known as the Treasury of Atreus (treasury in this context means a place where treasure was stored). These were built around the fourteenth century BC. The

FIGURE 2.5
Lion Gate, Mycenae, 13th century BC.

> **stele** (plural **stelai**) stone slabs, often with patterns or images carved on them, most commonly used as tombstones

FIGURE 2.6
Grave Circle A, Mycenae.

tholos tomb a large domed tomb in the shape of an igloo, roughly circular in its floor space – also known as a beehive tomb

Study questions

1 What classes of people do you think would be buried in the graves of Grave Circle B?
2 Why do you think the shafts were deeper and larger than the earlier shafts of Grave Circle B?

construction of these is discussed fully on pages 192–193. Such tombs are known as **tholos tombs**, from a Greek word meaning 'domed'.

Despite their names, the tombs of Clytemnestra and Aegisthus never housed these legendary rulers. Clytemnestra was the wife of King Agamemnon in mythology and Aegisthus was her second husband after she had killed Agamemnon. The tombs were given their names in relatively recent times by local villagers. Atreus was the father of Agamemnon. It is possible (though unlikely) that this actually was the tomb of Atreus: it might date from the time when he was supposed to have lived, and there was a tomb with this name in ancient times as the Greek writer Pausanias tells us:

> In the ruins of Mycenae is a fountain called Persea; there are also underground resting places of Atreus and his children. Their treasure was kept in these chambers. There is the tomb of Atreus, and the tombs of those who came back with Agamemnon from Troy.
>
> Pausanias, *The Description of Greece*, 2.16.6

The tombs of Clytemnestra and Aegisthus are situated just to the west of the city, with the Treasury of Atreus a little further away. The tombs of Clytemnestra and Aegisthus each have a diameter of around 13 m, with the former also being an impressive 13 m high. The roof of the tomb of Clytemnestra collapsed in 1951 and the roof that can be seen there now is a reconstruction. No treasure remained in the tombs when they were excavated in the nineteenth century, as they had been robbed of their contents in ancient times.

Like Mycenae, Tiryns is built on a hill. This hill rises 18 m above the land that surrounds it. The city is 300 m long and is between 45 m and 100 m wide. The earliest buildings at Tiryns date from around 2500 BC, but the first Mycenaean phase of building occurred around 1400 BC, where the first city walls were built to the south of the site. Around a century later the Eastern Gate was added as the city expanded and the palace was constructed. This was further strengthened in the thirteenth century, and the wall on the western side was added with its curving defence, justifying the description in the *Iliad* of Tiryns being 'surrounded by walls' (*Iliad*, 2.559).

FIGURE 2.7

PS

Entrance to the Treasury of Atreus, Mycenae, 14th century BC. For a view of the interior of the tomb, see Figure 2.40 on page 193.

PRESCRIBED SOURCE

Site of Tiryns

Built: 15th–13th century BC (approximately)

Location: East Peloponnese, Greece

Significance: contains an important palace and throne room, frescoes and treasure

Find out more here: http://www.ancient.eu/tiryns/

FIGURE 2.8

Plan of Tiryns:
1 – Cyclopean Ramp,
2 – Gates, 3 – Galleries,
4 – Courtyard,
5 – Palace courtyard,
6 – Megaron and
Palace, 7 – West Gate.

The walls at Tiryns, like those at Mycenae, were thought to have been built by the Cyclopes, whom Proitos had brought in from Turkey to complete the task. They are around 7 m high now, but extended to as high as 10 m in Mycenaean times. The main approach to the walls was on the east side up a ramp, now known as the Cyclopean Ramp because of its size. Only a small part of this remains, giving little clue as to as its impressive nature in ancient times. From here it was a short walk to the main gate.

The gate was thought to be about 3 m high, although it is only half this height now, and is about 3 m wide, therefore being of a similar width to the Lion Gate at Mycenae. Pivot holes for the doors can still be seen, together with slots in the gate posts for a bar to lock the gates. Attackers could be trapped in the long, narrow passage between the two gates beyond the entrance. This would have been an ideal area into which defenders could hurl down objects on attackers.

Many of the walls around Tiryns are relatively straight, but the wall on the west of the city has a significant, and very deliberate, curve. There was also a stairway leading to a very narrow corridor.

The palace was built on the highest part of Tiryns, known as the Upper City. This was protected by its own defensive walls. A grand entranceway led to the megaron. The central hearth was surrounded by four wooden pillars, whose stone bases still survive. Towards the east of the megaron was a small platform on which the king's throne would have been. The floor was plastered and had images of octopi and dolphins on it. The walls were also covered with plaster, on which **frescoes** were painted, on damp plaster, of rich ladies and a hunting scene.

Around the megaron were a series of apartments and colonnades for the rulers, and even a bathroom whose floor was made of a polished limestone slab. Holes were drilled

Study question

The Cyclopean Ramp at Tiryns was long and uphill. Why do you think it was designed in this manner?

fresco a painting originally made on damp plaster in which the colours become fixed as the plaster dries

FIGURE 2.9
The entrance passage PS
and main gate of Tiryns,
13th century BC, looking
outwards from the city
towards the Cyclopean
Ramp.

FIGURE 2.10
Gallery, Tiryns, PS
13th century BC.

into the floor for drainage. There is also evidence of at least two stair-cases, revealing a second level to some of the parts of the megaron.

Some of the most famous features of the city of Tiryns are the galleries, which were built into the outer walls of the city. They used the technique of corbelling to create vaulted roofs. Some of these galleries were up to 30 m long. Leading off the galleries were a large number of rooms. At the end of the thirteenth century BC, the site was extended to the north by adding an extra loop to the wall, with the area containing workshops and houses.

Just over half a mile from Tiryns another tholos tomb has been found, built into the side of a hillside. It is about 6 m tall and 6 m wide, with an entrance 1.5 m high. Inside the tomb was discovered a large round stone, which might have been an altar. It has a superb corbelled roof and massive blocks of stone were used to hold up the roof of the entrance.

TROY

Of all the Mycenaean sites, the one that most people are familiar with is Troy. However, the knowledge that people have comes mostly from the *Iliad* of Homer, rather than the site itself. Indeed, some of the evidence from the site itself seems to contradict the impression of Troy in the *Iliad*.

EXPLORE FURTHER

There are some excellent websites on the history of Tiryns. Have a look at http://www.greek-thesaurus.gr/Mycenaean-Tiryns-Acropolis.html for a good description and http://ancient-greece.org/archaeology/tiryns.html for some excellent photographs.

For images of the tholos tomb, look at http://www.megalithic.co.uk/article.php?sid=15099.

The evidence for and against Troy VI and Troy VIIa being the site of Homer's Troy

While people were certainly living in the settlement that many believe was Troy during the Mycenaean Age, it is highly debatable this site formed the historical basis of the Trojan War. We no longer think that there was a Trojan War in the way that the myths of Homer describe. However, these stories may recall an actual historical siege of Troy. We know from archaeology that there were several wars fought at Troy in Mycenaean times, which might have been merged together, but the evidence for each of these does not match in their entirety what is in the myths of Homer. It may be there was no single war as described by Homer, but a series of conflicts over a much longer timespan, which Homer merged into one story.

The oldest settlement at Troy, called Troy I, dates back to 3000 BC, and the Mycenaean period at Troy occurs in the ruins of Troy VI and Troy VIIa (1900–950 BC).

There are several reasons why archaeologists think Troy VI could have been the site of Homer's Troy:

- It was destroyed around 1250 BC, with the Trojan War traditionally dated to 1200 BC.
- It seems to have been a rich city with numerous large houses.
- Its stone walls were over 7 m high, and the *Iliad* refers to the high walls of Troy.
- These walls seem to have had towers, with towers a feature of Troy in the *Iliad*.
- It extended over quite a large area with a suggested population of 10,000, which would indicate a thriving city as in the *Iliad*.

However, there is also some evidence that seems to contradict the mythological legend, including:

- Archaeologists also believe it was destroyed by an earthquake, not the fire that ancient literature suggests.

It was then succeeded by Troy VIIa, which seems to have been a settlement that existed for only around 30–40 years. There are several pieces of evidence that Troy VIIa could have been the site of the legendary war:

Study question

From the archaeological evidence, do you believe that Schliemann found the site of Troy?

ACTIVITY

Debate whether you would have preferred to have lived in Mycenae or Tiryns.

To extend this idea further, research what life was like in the city of Pylos and add this to the debate.

FIGURE 2.11
Sophia Schliemann wearing some of the treasures excavated from Troy.

- It too had large towers.
- It had single-storey houses, which were relatively crowded together and built in a short period. This would fit in with the idea of emergency housing for the Trojans when the Greeks were attacking the city.
- Storage jars were sunk deep into the ground. Were the people trying to store up food when under siege?
- It was destroyed by a large fire. The writings of the Roman poet, Virgil, describe the fires started by the Greeks when they destroyed Troy.
- Partial human remains of individuals have been found (possibly killed in warfare).
- Three bronze arrowheads have been found.

S & C

Troy was excavated in the late nineteenth century, by the archaeologist Heinrich Schliemann. He had long been fascinated by the legend of Troy. Of the many possible sites in Turkey that might have been Troy, he decided to excavate one near the village of Hisarlik. On excavating, he discovered a walled city, which had been rebuilt many times in history. Not only did he discover this, but he also found treasure, leading him to the conclusion that he had found Troy, and to calling what he had found 'Priam's treasure' (Priam was supposedly the king of Troy at the time of the Trojan War). He later wrote how his wife had smuggled it out of Troy in her clothing, rather than officially declaring what he had found. He even got his wife to model some of the jewellery for publicity. However, other evidence from the site where the treasure was found suggests that it came from over 1,000 years earlier.

Moreover, in digging through the layers of Troy, many later archaeologists believe that Schliemann caused considerable damage to the part that may have been Homer's Troy. This excavation was done quickly, and with very rough methods. Schliemann did not keep detailed records nor map his finds. Yet, in the nineteenth century, these methods were commonplace, and Carl Blegen, a later famous archaeologist at Troy, said that there was probably no other digger who was better than Schliemann in field work.

Troy was part of the kingdom of a people known as the Hittites. Some of their writings refer to a place to the west of their kingdom called Ahhiyawa. This perhaps sounds similar to Achaea, one of the words for Greece, in Homer. Moreover, the Hittite word for Troy, Wilusia, is similar to the Greek word for Troy, Ilion. From this it was generally accepted that where Schliemann had excavated was indeed Troy, although in recent years scholars have become more sceptical about these verbal connections.

As Troy developed as a city, each civilisation destroyed what had been there already, and built on top of the ruins. These layers reached a height of 32 m over the surrounding plains. As archaeologists have dug down, they have come across nine different periods of settlement at Troy, during which houses were built, occupied and finally destroyed (usually by a fire or earthquake).

EXPLORE FURTHER **CW**

For further ideas on the levels of Troy and the remains, an excellent source of information is http://www.dartmouth.edu/~prehistory/aegean/?page_id=630#L271.

Another important Mycenaean site is Pylos. Find out information about it at http://www.ancientgreecejourney.co.uk/places/nestors.htm.

All of this, while hardly conclusive, might seem to back up the view that this was the site of the actual war between the Greeks and Trojans. However:

- The houses were crammed together, which suggests the city was not rich, unlike the one described by Homer.
- The sunken jars might not indicate a siege, but simply a lack of space that people had in which to keep food.

All that can be said for sure it that there is no certain answer as to which of the two layers might have been Homer's Troy, although there has been more support from scholars in recent decades in favour of it being Troy VIIa.

FIGURE 2.12
Plan showing some of the buildings and defences of some of the layers of settlement at the city traditionally called Troy.

Main archeological layers of the site of Troy/Hisarlik

- Troy I
- Troy II
- Troy VI
- Troy VII

0   25   50 m

TOPIC REVIEW

You should be able to:

1. Describe:
   - the important stages in the history of the Mycenaean Age
   - the layouts of Mycenae and Tiryns
   - the key features of Mycenae and Tirnys
   - the findings in the different levels of Troy.

2. Explain:
   - why the cities of Mycenae and Tiryns were built in the locations that they were
   - why the cities of Mycenae and Tiryns developed as they did
   - what is particularly impressive about Mycenaean cities
   - the arguments for and against the archaeological levels of Troy VI and VIIa being the site of the Troy of the Trojan War.

PRACTICE QUESTIONS

Source A: *The entrance to Mycenae*

1. What is the name of this entrance to Mycenae? Why is it known by this name? [2]
2. Choose **two** features of the image in this source and say why they might be admired. [4]

2.2 Life in the Mycenaean Age

TOPIC OVERVIEW

- Palaces:
  - the typical palace complex and megaron (central hall)
  - their functions and use

- Everyday life; evidence for, and nature of:
  - hunting
  - armour and weapons
  - chariots
  - clothing
  - trade

- Linear B tablets:
  - how the tablets were preserved and what they record
  - the significance of the tablets

The prescribed sources for this topic are:

- Dagger blade showing hunting scene from Grave Circle A, Mycenae
- Mycenaean Warrior Vase, House of the Warrior, Mycenae
- the fresco of a Mycenaean lady holding a necklace from the House of the Chief Priest, Mycenae
- Linear B tablet showing the word 'tripod' in syllabic and ideogram forms, Pylos.

Don't forget that you will be given credit in the exam if you study extra sources and make relevant use of them in your answers.

In this section you will discover what life was like in cities for both rulers and their subjects by looking at the sites themselves and objects that have been found within them. These things tell us what priorities the Mycenaeans had in their daily lives, and show a very precise and advanced civilisation.

PALACES

Mycenaean cities were ruled by kings, and as such they contained palaces. These palaces, although small by modern standards, occupied a large percentage of the city. They

FIGURE 2.13

Plan of a typical megaron: A – entrance porch; B – front room; C – hearth.

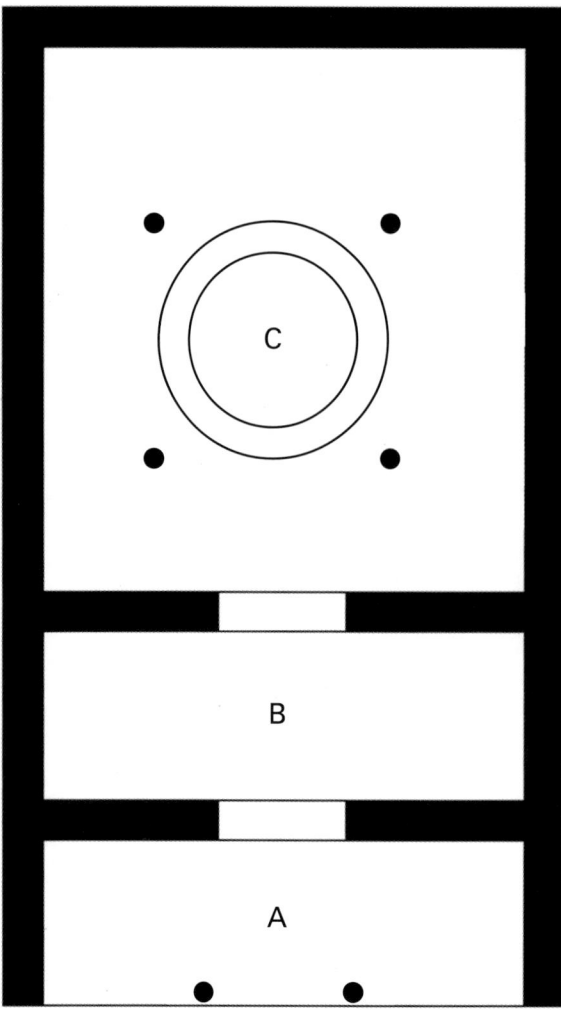

contained numerous pleasant areas, such as colonnades, but were more than just areas for the royal family to relax in. There is evidence that palaces contained rooms for official documents, shrines, potteries, oil press rooms, armouries and storerooms for food.

The most important part of the palace was the megaron. This was often in the highest part of the city, dominating the area. In many ways it had a similar design to later Greek temples as it was usually rectangular in shape, and had an entrance porch with two columns, with another room behind this (known as a vestibule). The megaron usually contained one or more courtyards.

The most important feature of the megaron was a hearth. The hearth was a stone area, usually circular in shape, on which a fire would be lit for religious purposes or cooking. Around this would have been four columns, which supported the roof. A hole in the roof would have allowed smoke to escape from the fire.

This room would also be where the king's throne would have been. The megaron would have been used for feasts, like the one described in the *Odyssey* during which the suitors are killed, and poetry would have been recited there.

FIGURE 2.14
Megaron from Pylos, showing central hearth and holes where two pillars would have been.

HUNTING

Animal hunting was an important activity in the Mycenaean Age. As most of Greece was unsuitable for farmland, and flat land was normally used for growing crops, hunting animals was essential if people were to eat meat. Many of the animals the Greeks liked to hunt lived on mountainous terrain.

Our evidence for hunting comes from frescoes, scenes on daggers and carvings on rings. The most famous piece of evidence comes from a dagger blade showing a lion hunt (lions lived in the wild in Greece in ancient times), widely known as the Lion Hunt Dagger. This was found in Grave Circle A in Mycenae.

The dagger in Figure 2.15 is too intricate and precious to have been used for combat, but is instead an ornamental object. It would have almost certainly belonged to a king as a status symbol. The hunting of a lion was the greatest challenge a hunter could face, and the image on the dagger highlights this as the hunter on the right has been felled by the

FIGURE 2.15
Detail of the Lion Hunt Dagger.

lion. One hunter has a bow and arrow, while the others have long spears. Two types of shield are shown; the ones in a figure of eight shape originate from the earlier Minoan age.

Other precious objects also provide vital evidence for the importance of hunting. Two cups from Vapheio, near Sparta, show the capture of bulls (see p. 186). A signet ring from Grave IV in Grave Circle A in Mycenae shows a miniature scene of a hunter and driver on a chariot, armed with a bow and chasing deer (see p. 170). A fresco from Tiryns shows the use of dogs in hunting.

ARMOUR AND WEAPONS

There is no doubt that battles played a huge part in the lives of the Mycenaeans, judging by the evidence from Homer and numerous objects found in Mycenaean cities. Different styles of armour and weapons have been found, leading to some uncertainty as to the exact nature of warfare, with helmets and shields changing significantly over the period.

It would seem that a major change was happening at the start of the Mycenaean period: the huge figure-of-eight shields and tower shields that the Mycenaeans used were being gradually replaced by smaller ones. The older style shields are shown on the Lion Hunt Dagger, and Homer describes a tower shield that was used by the Greek hero Ajax, made up of eight layers of leather and one of bronze (*Iliad*, 7.219–223). Painted shields, covering from the neck to the knees are also shown on the frescoes of Akrotiri, and the ones on the Lion Hunt Dagger covered all the way to the ankles, as did Ajax's shield in the *Iliad*. Agamemnon is also said, in the *Iliad*, to have had a shield that could cover a man (although it could be that Homer is inferring that Agamemnon was tall and that his shield would cover a lesser man than him).

FIGURE 2.16
Mycenaean boars' tusk helmet, Chamber tomb 515, Mycenae, now in the National Archaeological Museum, Athens.

S & C

As part of this component, you will read the story of the battle between Odysseus and the suitors, which gives some ideas of the weapons and armour that the Mycenaeans used. More traditional battles are shown throughout the *Iliad*. Read Book 16 of the *Iliad*, where the Greek hero Patroclus arms himself and goes out to fight the Trojans. Below is the passage where Patroclus arms himself. Read the rest of Book 16 and make a list of all the types of weapons and armour used.

At his words, Patroclus began to clad himself in gleaming bronze. First he clasped the shining greaves, with silver ankle-pieces, about his legs. Next he strapped Achilles' ornate breastplate round his chest, richly worked and decorated with stars. Over his shoulder he hung the bronze sword with its silver studs, and then the great thick shield. On his strong head he set the fine horse-hair crested helm, its plume nodding menacingly. Lastly he grasped two stout spears that suited his grip, though not peerless Achilles' own great, long and heavy spear that alone among the Achaeans he could wield, that spear of ash from Pelion's summit that Cheiron gave to the warrior's dear father Peleus, for the killing of men.

Homer, *Iliad*, 16.131–144

Helmets also changed significantly. The *Iliad* tells of a helmet that Odysseus once wore, made up of a leather cap, covered with felt, onto which boars' tusks were put. This seems to have been used in the early Mycenaean Age, and one of these helmets survives from Mycenae. The tusks are extremely strong and gave good protection, but each helmet would need the tusks of at least ten wild boars, and possibly many more. The hunting of these animals was extremely dangerous, as seen from the story of how Odysseus got badly injured when hunting a wild boar in the *Odyssey*, Book 19.

Several other boars' tusk helmets have been found at other sites, suggesting they were used fairly commonly in early Mycenaean times. One from Dendra, near Argos, even has bronze cheek pieces on it. However, most helmets in the *Iliad* are not like these. These are often described as gleaming, and having animal skin liners for comfort and some added protection. They often had throat straps and animal hair plumes on top, presumably simply to look impressive. Mycenaean wall paintings also regularly show plumed helmets.

One of the most famous pieces of pottery from Mycenae shows how far helmets and shields developed over the centuries. The Warrior Vase, from a house in Mycenae of the same name, depicts a series of soldiers in a battle-line.

On this vase, a group of almost identical warriors are shown marching. They carry long spears (for thrusting rather than throwing) and small round shields. They are dressed in tunics, called **chitons**, and wear breast-plates and greaves for protection. They also carry knapsacks on their spears, perhaps suggesting they have a long journey to make. The helmets have horns coming from them and seem to be relatively light. On the far left of the vase, a woman is shown, presumably saying farewell to the soldiers as they depart for battle. On the other side of the vase are more soldiers wearing spiky helmets (the helmets look like hedgehogs!) and carrying much shorter spears. Noting the similarities in the handles of the vase and the appearance of the soldiers to later depictions, some scholars suggest this vase is not Mycenaean, but is from the eighth century BC.

The Mycenaeans used a variety of weapons. Spears were commonly used, consisting of a wooden handle into which a bronze spearhead would be fitted. By the twelfth century

EXPLORE FURTHER

A detailed study of helmets in the *Iliad*, and drawings of how they may have looked, can be found at http://www.salimbeti.com/micenei/helmets4.htm.

chiton a large, loose-fitting, woollen tunic worn in ancient Greece

krater a large bowl used for mixing wine and water

PRESCRIBED SOURCE

Mycenaean Warrior Vase

Date: 13th century BC

Location: House of the Warrior, Mycenae

Material: clay

Original purpose: krater

Significance: weaponry and armour of Mycenaean soldiers

FIGURE 2.17
The Warrior Vase.

FIGURE 2.18
Sword found in a Mycenaean tomb.

BC spears had become shorter and could have been thrown. Evidence for spears also comes from Linear B tablets (see pages 175–178) from Crete which refer to forty-two bronze-tipped spears.

Many swords have been found in Mycenaean tombs, some with elaborate golden hilts (handles). Early swords also often featured a wooden pommel (a rounded end to the handle), covered in gold. They would have been much sharper than they now appear.

The more elaborate the sword, the less likely it was to have been used for actual combat. The sword would have been carried in a holder called a scabbard, and a wall painting from Akrotiri shows tassles on the end of the scabbards. Like spears, swords became shorter through the Mycenaean age, which would have been more useful in close quarter combat.

The earliest suit of armour in Europe comes from a Mycenaean site. A breastplate was found at Dendra, near the city of Argos, from the fifteenth century BC. It was made up of sheets of bronze for the chest and back, which were hinged together using strips of leather. Further plates of bronze protected the shoulders, neck and upper legs. Altogether fifteen separate plates of bronze make up the suit, which differs significantly from the armour shown on the Warrior Vase, which would probably have been made of leather. Found with this breastplate at Dendra were a boars' tusk helmet, a pair of greaves and a wrist guard. This armour would certainly have been heavy, but the protection it gave was far greater than other types of body armour.

Bows were certainly used in Mycenaean times, but were considered a cowardly weapon in the battlefield in the *Iliad*, as they could inflict death from afar with little risk to the archer. Odysseus kept his bow at home in the *Odyssey*, and none of the great warriors used one in the *Iliad*. The Lion Hunt Dagger shows the use of a bow, as does the image on the signet ring from Tiryns shown in Figure 2.19. Arrowheads have been found on several sites and bowmakers are recorded on the Linear B tablets from Pylos (see pages 175–178).

FIGURE 2.19
Signet ring showing a hunting scene, Tiryns, 15th century BC.

CHARIOTS

Figure 2.19 shows another key aspect of life in Mycenaean times; the use of chariots. Chariots are regularly shown in wall paintings, pottery and even stelai. They were used most often for chasing prey (as in the signet ring in Figure 2.19), or in war. In the *Iliad*, warriors are often driven to the centre of the fighting, before getting off the chariot to fight on foot. Generally, warriors did not fight other warriors from their chariots. After the fighting, the chariot driver would pick up the warrior to drive him elsewhere. Chariots also raced each other as part of funeral contests, as is told in the famous chariot race in *Iliad*, Book 23.

The earliest representation of a chariot is from one of the stelai of Grave Circle A at Mycenae (see Figure 2.38 on p. 191). It shows a man on a simple two-wheeled box chariot, chasing down another man, either during a race or in a battle. The wheels on this and other chariots regularly have four spokes.

A fresco from Tiryns shows that chariots were not just used for fighting or competition, but were a mode of transport. Figure 2.20 from Tiryns shows a very different type of chariot from the image on the signet ring in Figure 2.19. The chariot shown below is more spacious and covered in a red fabric or animal hide, and a fresco from Pylos shows a similar, if slightly lighter chariot covered in a yellow material. These chariots would presumably have travelled on roads, but little is known for sure about roads at this time.

FIGURE 2.20
Fresco showing a couple travelling by chariot, Tiryns, 13th century BC, now in the National Archaeological Museum, Athens.

EXPLORE FURTHER

To see the other chariots mentioned in this section, together with a full discussion of Mycenaean chariots, go to http://www.salimbeti.com/micenei/chariots.htm.

Study questions

1 What do you think it would have been like to have travelled in chariots in Mycenaean times?
2 Which class of society would need and use chariots?
3 Why do you think this was the case?

CLOTHING

As clothes are made from materials that decay over time, no actual clothing remains from Mycenaean times, and the descriptions of clothes in Homer's poetry do not give us much helpful information. However, we are able to gain an understanding of what Mycenaean people wore from art, and frescoes in particular (see above, p. 172 and p. 183).

The vast majority of garments in Mycenaean times were made from wool from sheep or goats, or linen, which is made from fibres of the flax plant. These were then dyed with natural products, with the colour being locked in through the addition of a substance such as vinegar or urine, which would preserve the dye when the garment was washed. Some garments were also made from silk, but these would have been rare.

The following table shows the possible origins of some of the dyes used by the Mycenaeans.

COLOUR	SOURCE
yellow	onion skins; saffron (a spice)
red	insect eggs; madder (a plant)
blue	indigo (a plant)
purple	shellfish ink

Some of the colours, such as blue and purple, were likely to have been expensive as they were harder to obtain.

The Linear B tablets from Pylos (see pages 175–178) are a valuable source of information on cloth making. They tell us of different workers who prepared, spun, dyed and wove the wool. Some of the workers were given rations from the palace, but whether this means they were slaves or not is unclear.

Women are regularly shown wearing wrap-around skirts. These skirts often had several thin layers, creating a tiered effect. They were often very colourful and would have required great skill to make. They would have been worn with an underskirt. Frescoes from Akrotiri show both longer and shorter versions of this type of skirt, while later versions from Mycenae and images on rings from shaft graves only show the longer garment. Perhaps this shows how fashion changed even in the ancient world?

Blouses were short-sleeved, but may not have covered the breasts: some frescoes show bare-breasted women, and in other ones the clothing seems designed to highlight the breasts. There is also evidence from frescoes that women wore robes, cloaks, shawls, ornate headbands and ankle bracelets. Archaeological discoveries also give us examples of different jewellery.

The most famous original fresco is known as 'the Mycenaean Lady'. It shows a thoughtful woman in a typically Mycenaean garment holding a necklace. This might have been a gift to her, leading some to believe that she is a goddess. She wears a short-sleeved top over a thin bodice, which has enabled the artist to show off her breasts. She has an intricate hairstyle and is wearing a fine necklace and bracelet. In her hand she holds another bracelet.

PRESCRIBED SOURCE

Fresco of a Mycenaean lady holding a necklace

Date: 13th century BC

Location: House of the Chief Priest, Mycenae

Significance: fresco colours and styles of female clothing and hairstyle, jewellery

FIGURE 2.21
A Mycenaean lady holding a necklace, 13th-century fresco from Mycenae.

EXPLORE FURTHER

Mycenaeans had elaborate hairstyles (at least on their frescoes). Young children seem to have had their heads shaved, except for a lock of hair at the top of their head and a pony-tail. As they reached puberty, they grew their hair more. Women had long hair, intricately tied with ribbons and beads, with strands of hair falling down to their shoulders. In some images headbands were worn on the fringe and the hair was generally short, but more often it seems the hair was allowed to grow long and was plaited. Men too had long hair which was elaborately arranged. The chariot fresco (Figure 2.20) shows a typical male and female hairstyle.

Men wore a braided, short-sleeved tunic, with a robe over it. There is also evidence that they wore a kilt-like garment, especially if they were soldiers, and a kind of loincloth for underwear. Leather boots were also worn, as shown on the Warrior Vase (see p. 169), but people may well have generally gone about barefoot (see Figure 2.22).

FIGURE 2.22
From left to right: male robe, tunic and kilt. Image from *Mycenae: Agamemnon's Capital*, Elizabeth French.

TRADE

The major Mycenaean cities developed strong trades links with many areas around the Mediterranean and beyond. This was essential for the growth and survival of their societies, as Greece does not have a rich supply of the mineral resources and metals that the Mycenaeans used. Much of the trade was done by sea as travel on land was slow due to mountain ranges and probably difficult due to bandits. The roads that existed would have been very basic and little could be carried on animals or chariots in comparison with boats.

We have evidence from a variety of sources of this trade, including the objects themselves in cities, written records on Linear B tablets, and even shipwrecks (see p. 174). As many of the Mycenaean sites are just a few miles from the sea, and there are many sheltered harbours, it was natural to import and export goods this way. However, such journeys were very hazardous, and a round trip would take many weeks. In ancient times it was only safe to sail for around half the year from early spring to the early autumn, and even then the weather in the Mediterranean could be very unpredictable. Journeys would not usually have been undertaken in one go, as ships were manned by rowers; as there are so many islands dotted around Greece, merchants would 'island hop' to get to mainland Greece from more distant places, and would probably both drop off and pick up cargo on the way. Most of the trade was with areas to the east, such as the islands in the Aegean Sea or Egypt, and the Middle East, but there was some trade with Italy and the surrounding islands. Some historians even believe the Mycenaeans imported amber and tin from Britain. Items were exchanged for other goods in a system known as bartering (in which, if a merchant wanted one type of item or service, he would offer something he already had), rather than sold for money, as there is no evidence that money existed at the time.

We can never be sure of exactly where products and raw materials came from, as the Mycenaeans did not keep such records. We have to look at where else was producing these materials and products at the same time and make a reasoned guess about trade. The following table suggests possible areas from which the Mycenaeans imported items.

PRODUCT	PLACE OF ORIGIN
Gold	Macedonia, Egypt, Thasos (Greek island)
Amber (for beads)	Denmark, northern Europe
Ivory	Africa, Syria
Lapis lazuli gemstones	Africa
Silver, lead	Attica (area around Athens)
Copper	Attica, Syria, Cyprus, Sardinia
Ostrich eggshells	Africa
Tin	Britain, Turkey, Afghanistan, Spain
Glass	Egypt

Some of these products are found in small quantities and are luxury items, but copper was perhaps the most crucial import as it is the main metal in the manufacture of bronze. Gold is probably the most famous import as some of the most famous objects in Mycenae were made from it.

It is much more debatable whether people were also imported as slaves. In the *Iliad*, people defeated in war were regularly turned into slaves, especially the women, and there are numerous mentions of workers in the Linear B tablets, though it is not known whether they had slave status or not. However, their native land is often mentioned, and many came from a long way away.

We should remember that trade was a two-way system; the Mycenaeans exported items throughout their known world. Pottery seems to have been their main export, with examples being found in Israel, Egypt, Sicily, Albania and Macedonia, amongst other places. Many pottery vessels would have contained olive oil, and some of these have been found in other parts of Greece. Large mixing bowls for wine, called kraters (such as the Warrior Vase on p. 169), were exported to Cyprus. One of the inhabitants of Mycenae seems to have traded wine and another one oil. Other items include a gold Mycenaean-style dagger found in Romania, and beads found in Egypt.

Around 1375 BC, a Mycenaean ship sunk off the coast of southwest Turkey, near Ulu Burun. We do not know where it was travelling to or from, but its cargo reveals a lot about trade at the time. The ship was carrying 10 tonnes of copper and 1 tonne of tin, which would have been used to make bronze, and is the correct proportion of each metal needed to make it. Around 150 jars of a type found commonly in the Middle East were also on the ship, with the majority filled with resin or olives, and one with glass beads. Other items included wooden logs, elephant tusks, hippopotamus teeth, tortoise shells, oil lamps and pottery, amber, drinking cups, weapons, food (including nuts, olives and spices), a trumpet, wooden tablets (possibly to be filled with wax for writing) and much else besides.

EXPLORE FURTHER

An excellent short video on the Ulu Burun shipwreck, showing numerous items from the wreck can be viewed at https://www.youtube.com/watch?v=7IZWOdY7fEk.

LINEAR B TABLETS

The Linear B tablets (there is an even older form of writing known as Linear A, which is yet to be deciphered) are a series of inscribed clay tablets from the Mycenaean Age. They are found at some of the major palace sites of the time, notably Pylos and Knossos on the island of Crete. Over 1,000 tablets have been discovered at Pylos, and even more at Knossos. Scholars have identified different sets of handwriting among the tablets, leading to the conclusion that up to 100 different individuals wrote the tablets at Knossos. Many of the tablets were kept in a special document room, assumed to be an archive room.

The tablets were simply pieces of damp clay on which written records were inscribed with a sharpened tool. These tablets were then left to harden in the sun to provide a semi-permanent record. As the clay was not fired in an oven to become pottery, it would eventually take on moisture from the air, then crack and crumble. In their natural state, it has been estimated that each tablet would last for several months at most.

So how have these tablets survived for over 3,000 years, if they were meant to only last for a few months? It is entirely down to luck: the sites where they have been found suffered major fires, and as a result the tablets were baked as if in a kiln and became hardened.

As other tablets only lasted for a few months, those that we have represent a moment in time, in much the same way as the site of Pompeii provides a snapshot of what life was like when Mount Vesuvius erupted in AD 79. Most have been dated to the end of the Mycenaean period.

It seems that the first stage in recording information was to inscribe the detail on a small piece of clay, designed to be held in the palm of the hand. Some of these are only about 3 cm in length. The information on these was then transferred to a larger thin horizontal tablet, known as a leaf tablet, and several of these could then be transferred to a larger document measuring up to 30 cm in length. Many of these were extremely fragile on discovery and some crumbled when touched.

There are two main types of symbol used in the Linear B tablets: syllables (parts of a word sounded as a single unit) and ideograms (pictures that represented what the item

Study question
Why do you think the Mycenaeans used clay to create the Linear B tablets?

FIGURE 2.23
A selection of Linear B syllables.

S & C For many years, the tablets could not be deciphered. An American, Alice Kober, made vital steps in working out combinations of symbols in words, and after many years of struggle, a Briton called Michael Ventris worked out what the symbols represented. He realised that many of the deciphered words were an early form of Greek whose alphabet developed a few hundred years later.

Investigate further into how Kober and Ventris managed to decipher the symbols.

looked like). Words could be shown using either of these. There were symbols for each of the vowels and a symbol for each consonant and vowel syllable.

In addition to the syllables above, there were also signs known as ideograms, where the picture represented a whole word. These could depict animals (e.g. rams or pigs) or objects (e.g. tripods or swords). Sometimes the syllable form and ideogram form of a word are inscribed next to each other, presumably to aid those reading the signs in Mycenaean times. The gender of the animal was shown by extra strokes on the ideogram, with two small extra horizontal lines indicating a male animal, and an extra vertical, or near vertical, line for a female. For example, look at the difference in the following symbols:

ewe   ram

(female) (male)

In addition, there were separate symbols for numbers, weights and measures.

FIGURE 2.24
Some Linear B ideograms.

FIGURE 2.25
A Linear B tablet together with a line drawing to show its inscription more clearly.

PS

The complete translation of the tablet reads:

2 tripod cauldrons of Cretan workmanship of the Aikeu type, tripod cauldron on one
foot with a single handle, 1 tripod of Cretan workmanship burnt from the legs up,
3 wine jars, larger sized goblet with 4 handles, 2 larger sized goblets with 3 handles,
1 smaller sized goblet with 4 handles, 1 smaller sized goblet with 3 handles, 1 smaller
sized goblet without handles.

PRESCRIBED SOURCE

Linear B tablet showing the word 'tripod' in syllabic and ideogram forms (number 641)

Date: 13th century BC

Material: clay

Original location: Archive room, Palace of Pylos

Current location: National Archaeological Museum, Athens

Significance: shows various syllables and ideograms, including the word for tripod

Ti-ri-po-de (syllable form)   Tripod (ideogram form)

This tablet is typical of those found. Most of the tablets list objects, and are probably best regarded as a way of keeping records of items that were in the palace, or transactions that were made.

The tablets are vitally important documents. We have no literature that was written in this period, and without the tablets we would know nothing of certain aspects of life, such as how cities were run or where some of the workers came from. The tablets also shed light on how the Greek language developed, and even some of its beliefs. For example, the tablets reveal the names of several of the main Olympian gods (Zeus, Poseidon, Hermes, Hera and Artemis appear on tablets), together with female versions of Zeus and Poseidon, called Diwia and Posidaia. These female identities of Zeus and Poseidon did not exist much beyond the Mycenaean age, showing that some, but not all, aspects of the Mycenaeans survived into later times.

Some of the words survived over the centuries and are found in ancient Greek with little change in spelling. For example, the word for gold in Greek is chrusos, which was written in Linear B as kuruso. Some English words derive originally from Linear B, such as the word pamako. This meant medicine, and has come to be used by us in English through ancient Greek: it is the origin of our word pharmacy. Tripod, as seen in Figure 2.25 is another example of such a word, being written as tiripode in Linear B. Until the decipherment of Linear B, it was generally thought that the arrival of later Greeks wiped out the language of the Mycenaeans.

The tablets tell us a lot about agriculture and food production in Mycenaean times. A tablet from Knossos tells us about wine production, mentioning 420 vines and the storage of 14,000 litres of wine. One tablet records the delivery of 518 litres of oil by Kolakas to Eumedes. Figs, wheat and barley are also mentioned. We read of an official who was in charge of honey production and of honey being used for religious offerings. Spices, such as saffron and coriander, are also mentioned.

Animals are mentioned in the tablets as well. Some plough oxen are even named, for example Dusky, Dapple or Whitefoot. Horses are listed as a part of military equipment, and goats and pigs appear in the tablets.

Some of the tablets record details about how the cities were run. There seems to have been a chieftain or king called a **wanax** at the top of each society. This corresponds to the word 'anax' in Homer, which means 'lord'. This word does not appear in later authors, suggesting that this position may only have existed in Mycenaean times. He had royal lands, special garments (often purple-coloured), and freedom from some taxes. Beneath him was an official called a **lawagetas**, whose estate at Pylos was a third of the size of the wanax. This title might be connected with the later Greek words for people and leader, which might suggest he was a military figure. Beneath both of these are a noble class known as the **hequetai**, who were perhaps followers of the ruler in war and a warrior class. These were landowners who may have owned slaves. Beneath these were the classes who did much of the work.

These workers fulfilled a variety of roles. There is mention of female religious workers and women who ground corn, spun, produced flax (from which the Mycenaeans made linen), and were waitresses and bath attendants. Often these are mentioned as coming from other parts of the ancient world, possibly suggesting that they were slaves. Other workers mentioned include headband makers for horses, musicians, sweepers, bakers, fire-kindlers, perfume makers and stonemasons.

Tablets telling of military organisation exist, and perhaps the details of the struggles of cities to survive. The tablets of Knossos tell us of forty-two bronze-pointed spears, while tablets from Pylos tell us that officials had to provide bronze for spears, arrows and ships, suggesting perhaps a greater focus on producing what would be needed in an attack. The tablets also tell us of chariot parts, such as wheels or frames, with those from Pylos mentioning 117 pairs of wheels. Tablets from Pylos mention 600 rowers and 800 coastal watchmen, which might suggest a major invasion was feared.

Offerings made to gods are mentioned in one tablet. Aside from gold items, some of which were offered at a shrine of Zeus, other offerings were made. There is much controversy about the translation, but many scholars believe that two men and eight women are mentioned as offerings for gods including Zeus, Hermes and Hera, indicating the custom of human sacrifice.

wanax the Mycenaean word for a chieftain or king

lawagetas the leader of the people in Mycenae, who was also probably the leader of the army

hequetai the nobles in Mycenae; they were probably also important troops in the army

TOPIC REVIEW

You should be able to:

1. Describe:
   - the appearance of a typical Mycenaean palace
   - how the Mycenaeans hunted animals
   - what Mycenaean chariots looked like and were used for
   - the weapons and armour of the Mycenaean age
   - what Mycenaean men and women wore
   - what items the Mycenaeans imported and the evidence for this
   - the syllables and ideograms of Linear B
   - what the Linear B tablets record and how they were preserved.

2. Explain:
   - the functions and use of a typical Mycenaean palace
   - the difficulties of travelling by chariot and hunting in the Mycenaean Age
   - the strengths and limitations of Mycenaean weapons and armour
   - how practical and comfortable the clothing was that the Mycenaeans wore
   - the difficulties and extensiveness of Mycenaean trade
   - the importance of Linear B tablets to our understanding of the Mycenaeans
   - the strengths and limitations of the evidence for daily life of the Mycenaeans

PRACTICE QUESTIONS

Source A: *Linear B tablet*

1. 'The Linear B tablets tell us little about the lives of ordinary Mycenaeans.' Using **Source A** as a starting point, how far do you agree with this assessment? [8]
2. What do the Linear B tablets say about religion? [2]
3. Why is this knowledge important to our understanding of how Greek religion developed? [1]

2.3 Decorative Arts

The quality of craftsmanship in Mycenaean objects has been greatly admired. The objects themselves, whether paintings, metalwork or items of jewellery, show very intricate and detailed manufacture. In this section you will find out how these items were made, what they were used for and why they are so admired.

FRESCOES

Some of the most famous pieces of artwork of the ancient world are Mycenaean paintings known as frescoes. These seem to have been influenced by earlier frescoes from Crete in the Minoan Age. Mycenaean frescoes are admired for their use of colour and attention to fine detail. They would originally have adorned palaces, but some are also found at houses, workshops and public buildings. While the grander buildings had frescoes of important individuals or detailed scenes, like the ship fresco from Akrotiri (see Figure 2.27), even small houses had walls where the plaster was painted, although in a much simpler fashion.

Initially a thick layer of lime plaster would have been put on a stone wall to be decorated. Then a finer layer of plaster would have been added. Before this dried, colours would be painted on using natural and manufactured products. String would have been used to set out lines during the composition, and faint lines from this string can be seen at times on the plaster.

A black colour could be gained from carbon, while the famous Mycenaean blue was manufactured from a copper compound. As it did not occur naturally, this blue colour would have been more expensive, and its use would have been designed to impress. Red was obtained from a mineral called haematite, white from lime, yellow from ochre, and green was obtained from mixing blue and yellow, or grinding a mineral called malachite. Some details in lighter colours were added later when the plaster dried, but these have faded over time. A white colour could have been achieved by cutting through to the backing plaster, or by adding more lime plaster.

There seem to have been common uses for these colours. Men are shown with a red skin colour and women with white. Red indicated a tanned skin, and white suggested a person spent more time indoors. Yellow was used for lions and blue for monkeys.

Many different subjects were painted on the frescoes. Those from Akrotiri have been especially admired. Akrotiri was a Minoan site destroyed by fire around the start of the Mycenaean period, so it is debatable how strong the link was between the two societies, but it is not unreasonable to think the Mycenaean frescoes, possibly indirectly, were influenced by those from Akrotiri.

Scenes from nature feature heavily at Akrotiri, such as a spring fresco, which features on three walls of a house. One part of this shows lilies or papyrus growing among colourful

FIGURE 2.26 Fresco of a fisherman with his catch, Akrotiri, 16th century BC, now in the National Archaeological Museum, Athens. Notice the shaved head painted blue, with the elaborate strands of hair, a sign of youth.

FIGURE 2.27 Fresco of a ship procession and a coastal town from Akrotiri, Santorini, 16th century BC, now in the National Archaeological Museum, Athens. The image, part of a longer scene on a river, is tremendously detailed, and notable for its use of colour.

Study question

Why do you think the Mycenaeans chose the subjects for frescoes that they did?

EXAM TIP

If you talk about a particular fresco, do not only talk in general terms about what you can see in it. You will need to explore areas such as the use of colour, the atmosphere of the composition, the realism and the shapes. There is no single correct interpretation, but you must be willing to give your opinions, positive or negative, on it.

ACTIVITY

Research a Mycenaean fresco and give a presentation to the rest of your class on it, stating the dating and location, what it depicts, and your reaction to it. If you are in a group, you could give a presentation on the frescoes from a particular room or house in a site.

rocks with swallows flying overhead. Another house has a fresco of blue monkeys climbing rocks to escape chasing dogs, and two boxers are seen to be fighting in another fresco. Women feature heavily in the frescoes, with some picking saffron in one example.

Perhaps the most famous fresco is the ship fresco shown in Figure 2.27. The full fresco contains eight large ships and three boats being rowed though a town. The ships are decorated with flowers, butterflies, swallows and lilies. Dolphins swim through the water. The town is shown in great detail, with even the clothes of the people individually highlighted. It has been suggested that the high-status clothes and abundance of flowers might show a festival in progress. Others note that helmets hang under the canopies of the ships, suggesting a scene of conflict.

Other common images in frescoes include animals such as octopi, cuttlefish, horses, bulls, lions, dogs, deer, boar and even creatures from myth, such as sphinxes and griffins. In some, men seem to be leaping over bulls, an activity which is shown famously in the earlier Minoan Age in the palace at Knossos.

There are also several examples of processions in frescoes. At Thebes, a fresco shows women carrying a vase, a pyxis and flowers. Images from war are seen too, with figure-of-eight shields depicted at several cities, including Mycenae. Repeated patterns are also found in some frescoes, such as swirls, spirals or wavy lines.

For all their beauty, the frescoes did have their limitations: the Mycenaeans did not use perspective in their pictures, and sometimes people or objects appeared disproportionately large or small; no attempt was made to give the pictures a three-dimensional feel; faces are shown with eyes looking forward, even if the head is facing to the side. However, all this should not take away from the incredible skill shown for the time in creating such frescoes.

The fresco in Figure 2.28 shows a use of contrasting colours to pick out the details of the woman. There is a significant level of detail, shown by the bracelets on the woman and the varied patterning of the brown fabrics. The blue bracelets are similar to one another, creating a consistency in the picture. Her facial features are very delicate and she gently grasps the saffron. She seems to have a slight smile, which helps create a sense of energy in the picture.

JEWELLERY

The burial sites of Mycenae and Tiryns have revealed a significant amount of jewellery, which may have been worn by men as well as women. Rings and beads have been found at the major graves. Rings are commonly made from gold, and beads were moulded from gold or carved from gemstones, amber, ivory or a form of glass.

Gold rings were often engraved with images on them. These are known as signet rings. Many of these show religious scenes, although the precise meaning of the images is often unclear.

One such ring from Tiryns shows a goddess seated on a folding chair holding a cup, with a hawk or eagle behind her, which may signify power. She is approached by strange lion-headed spirits carrying long-necked jugs perhaps with a drink offering in them. There are ears of wheat, and the sun and moon are also visible, possibly signifying a

FIGURE 2.28
Fresco showing a woman gathering saffron from Akrotiri, Santorini, 16th century BC, now in the National Archaeological Museum, Athens.

FIGURE 2.29
Fresco showing a goddess or priestess holding plants or flowers, Cult Centre, Mycenae, 13th century BC, now in the Archaeological Museum, Mycenae.

ritual connected with crops. Perhaps the most remarkable thing of all is to consider that all this detail could have been put onto a ring.

The details on Figure 2.30 would have been made using a technique known as **repoussé**. Using a hammer and nail, an elaborate pattern could have been worked on to metal to give a sense of depth. Usually the hammering would have been done from the inside of the object so that the scenes would face out. This can be seen from the ring showing a hunt on p. 170, the Vapheio cup on p.186 and the funeral mask on p. 195.

Many other undecorated rings, gold necklaces and diadems (a kind of royal head-dress) have been found at sites. The beads on necklaces were often worked into imaginative shapes, such as flowers or eagles, and moulds have been found at Mycenae to enable craftsmen to do this. Necklaces of gemstones and rock crystal have also been found. Some of these beads would have been imported, such as amber, ivory, glass and lapis lazuli.

> **repoussé** a technique where a design is hammered onto an object from the inside of it

> **Study question**
> What can you find to admire, or criticise, about Figure 2.29? Use the example of the analysis of the saffron gatherer fresco to give you ideas.

MODERN PARALLEL

Many people today wear signet rings. The images on them might show things about the wearer, and the same thing may well have been the case about the images shown on the Mycenaean rings, although fewer signet rings today have a religious significance.

FIGURE 2.30
Gold ring, Tiryns, 15th century BC, now in the National Archaeological Museum, Athens.

pyxis a box, often with a lid, to hold cosmetics or possibly jewellery

inlay a technique where one metal is put on top of another on an object

cloisonné the soldering of a wire onto metal and then putting glass or gemstones in the soldered pattern

granulation dropping molten metal onto an object to give a spotted effect

A particularly fine example of metalwork is a **pyxis** found in Mycenae. A pyxis is a small storage box. The inner part of this pyxis was a hexagonal wooden box, which is covered in twelve small plates of gold with filigree borders (made by twisting metal wire). The plates show lions chasing deer and antelope among palm trees. Spiral patterns and heads of cattle can be seen, whose bulging eyes stand out in the composition. Aside from the detail of the composition, which shows the use of the repoussé technique, the piece is also a very rare example of a wooden object surviving from the period. The item would have probably been used to contain cosmetics or jewellery.

Another technique used by the Mycenaeans was **inlay**, where one metal was heated and laid over another in an object. This is shown most famously on the Lion Hunt Dagger on p. 167. Swords, too, have been found on which the handle was covered and elaborately patterned with gold. The Mycenaeans also used a technique called **cloisonné** where a fine wire was soldered onto metal and inlaid with gemstones or glass. Tiny beads of gold could also be dropped onto an object to give a spotted effect, a technique known as **granulation**. An example of this is the rhyton on p. 187.

S & C
The ring in Figure 2.30 is thought to have had a religious meaning, although it is not clear what this may have been. The Mycenaeans worshipped many gods and almost certainly made offerings, sacrificed and poured drink offerings, known as libations, to them. Parts of the cities seem to have had a religious function with small shrines dedicated to worship, but there is no evidence of the huge temples of later Greek times.

Research further into the possible religious beliefs of the Mycenaeans and their shrines. Present your findings to your class.

FIGURE 2.31
Gold pyxis, Grave V, Grave Circle A, Mycenae, now in the National Archaeological Museum, Athens.

PS

DECORATIVE OBJECTS AND THEIR CREATION

Types of storage vessels and drinking vessels

The Mycenaeans were equally as talented in the manufacture of pottery as they were in the making of jewellery. This is not surprising as early in the period, before developing their own style, they imitated the Minoans, who were also excellent potters. The basic shape was made on a potter's wheel, with patterns then applied. An iron-rich slip (a mixture of water and clay used to give decoration to pottery) was then added. This became various shades from red to black depending on the temperature of the kiln.

The Mycenaeans made many different types of storage vessels. The largest were **pithoi**, which could be over 1.5 m high and weighed over 2 tonnes when filled. These would usually contain liquid or food, and could be partially buried in the ground to keep the contents as cool and fresh as possible. As they often contained oil, it is likely that they could become a fire hazard, and many ancient cities suffered greatly from huge blazes.

Another popular vessel were **amphorae**. These differed from pithoi in that they were much smaller, and had a much narrower neck. They often were more elaborately painted with geometric patterns or images from nature.

These amphorae show that the Mycenaeans liked to decorate their pots. A common style of decoration included marine and plant life, while others showed a simpler geometric pattern. In later Mycenaean jars, the neck and lower part of the amphora were painted in lines or a solid block, focusing the eye on the picture in the main part.

The most common form of storage vessel in Mycenaean times would seem to have been the stirrup jar. The jar gets its name from the handle, which resembles stirrups on a horse. Stirrup jars would have been used to store oil or wine. Figure 2.33 shows a stirrup jar decorated with a common form of precise geometric design that had a major influence on later Greek pottery.

In the early Mycenaean Age, double axes, spirals and leaves were commonly shown on vessels. As tastes changed, scenes might include chariot racing, bulls or human figures. The Warrior Vase on p. 169 is an example of such a scene. Other representations on later vessels include flowers, spiralled whorl shells, zigzags and vertical lines.

Other types of storage vessels included large **kraters** for mixing water and wine, squat three-handled jars made from alabaster, and miniature vases for perfumes. Even burial caskets and bath tubs were made from clay by the Mycenaeans.

Many other cups have been found. These often had long stems and two small handles. Such a cup is known as a **kylix**.

Vessels were also made from gold in Mycenaean times, including jugs and cups. Gold cups decorated with beautiful swirls were found in Grave Circle A at Mycenae, whilst two elaborately decorated cups were found at Vapheio, near Sparta.

One cup shows the capture of bulls with a man tying a rope around the bull's leg without any signs of a struggle. In the other cup (Figure 2.34) one bull is caught in a net while another two attack hunters, one of whom flees. It is possible that these cups were originally from Crete and were made in the Minoan times, as their quality surpasses other early Mycenaean cups. Unlike many cups, they are one handled, without stems, and are not curved.

PRESCRIBED SOURCE

Gold Pyxis

Date: 16th century BC

Original location: Shaft Grave V, Grave Circle A, Mycenae

Current location: National Archaeological Museum, Athens

Material: wood and gold

Image: lions chasing animals, heads of cattle (and spirals, not visible in Figure 2.31)

Techniques used: repoussé and filigree

Function: to hold cosmetics or jewellery

Significance: shows techniques in metalworking

---

pithos (pl. **pithoi**) a large clay storage jar

amphora (pl. **amphorae**) a clay storage jar, often containing wine or olive oil, with two carrying handles

kylix (pl. **kylixes**) a drinking cup

Study question
Why do you think amphorae differed in their style and decoration from pithoi?

FIGURE 2.32
Amphorae from Argos, 15th century BC, now in the
National Archaeological Museum, Athens.

FIGURE 2.33
Stirrup jar, Kalkani tomb, Mycenae, 12th century BC, now
in the Archaeological Museum of Mycenae. Note the
precise patterning on the jar using a clay slip.

FIGURE 2.34
Vapheio cup, Laconia, 15th
century BC, now in the
National Archaeological
Museum, Athens.

> **rhyton** (pl. **rhyta**) a vessel,
> either in the shape of a
> cone or animal head,
> probably for pouring liquid,
> and made from either
> pottery or metal

Another famous cup is a golden cup from Mycenae. In the *Iliad*, a Greek leader called Nestor had a famous gold cup, which was four handled and had a pair of golden doves around each handle (*Iliad,* 11.632–637). It was so heavy, it could barely be lifted when full. When Schliemann excavated the gold cup at Mycenae, he named it the 'cup of Nestor'. However, although Schliemann's name for it has stuck, it differs significantly in having a single falcon on each of its two handles, and being very easy to lift.

Other striking vessels include **rhyta**, which could have been made from pottery or metal. They are roughly cone-shaped, with many taking the form of animal heads. The liquid was designed to fall through a hole at the bottom or the mouth of the animal head.

The rhyton in Figure 2.35 is in the form of a lion's head, a fitting image for the rulers of Mycenae. It was made from sheets of gold, which were hammered into shape. Liquid would have been poured through the top of the head, with it flowing out through the muzzle. Another notable rhyton from Mycenae is a spectacular silver rhyton in the shape of a bull. This had gold horns, a multi-layered gold rosette on the top of its head, and gold plating on the nose. One hole was between the horns (presumably for filling) and another at the mouth (for pouring). When it was first discovered by the archaeologist Heinrich Schliemann, he thought the hole at the top was for putting flowers in. One pottery rhyton from near Athens was even in the shape of a shoe.

Gold rhyton

Date: 16th century BC

Original Location: Grave IV, Grave Circle A, Mycenae

Current location: National Archaeological Museum, Athens

Material: sheets of gold

Original purpose: container for pouring wine

Image: lion's head

Techniques used: hammering, granulation, repoussé

Significance: shows techniques in metalworking

FIGURE 2.35
Mycenaean gold rhyton in the shape of a lion's head.

Study question

Why do you think that most scholars believe that people did not drink out of a rhyton?

Animal figures, human figures and votive offerings

Many clay **figurines** of animals and humans have been found in private houses and tombs in Mycenaean cities. While some of the human figurines might have been toys, as they were found in children's tombs, it would seem that many had a religious significance, although what this was is unclear. It has been suggested that figurines were used in religious worship, or else were votive offerings to the gods in the hope of the fulfilment of a prayer. These figurines were usually small enough to be held in a hand.

> **figurine** a small statue of a person, god or animal

Three particular styles of human figurines are easily recognisable: the phi, psi and tau figurines. They get their names respectively from the Greek letters ϕ, ψ, and τ whose shapes the figurines resemble. It is thought that they may have represented female goddesses, with the phi and psi types usually showing females with prominent breasts. These goddesses were imported from Crete, probably in the Minoan Age.

Other pottery figurines are more recognisable as human and include a number with arms raised or holding implements. Female figurines often are painted wearing fine jewellery and with prominent breasts. Animal figures include numerous coiled snakes, which almost certainly had a religious significance, and miniature pottery cattle.

Ivory carving

We have already seen how the Mycenaeans used ivory tusks to make helmets (see p. 168), but they also used ivory from elephants, hippopotami and boars to make elaborate works of art. One of the most famous is a sculpture of a child (possibly a young god) with two bare-breasted women (possibly goddesses).

FIGURE 2.36
Left – Phi figurine, Mycenae, 13th century BC, now in the National Archaeological Museum, Athens; centre – Psi figurine, Mycenae, 13th century BC, now in the Ashmolean Museum, Oxford; right – Tau figurine, Mycenae, 13th century BC, now in the National Archaeological Museum, Athens.

FIGURE 2.37
Ivory sculpture showing two women and a child, 14th–15th century BC, Mycenae, now in the Archaeological Museum, Athens.

Other figures include a reclining lion and the head of a youth, both from the House of the Fresco in Mycenae.

Another very intricate piece of ivory carving is a comb from Attica. Above the teeth of the ivory comb are two bands containing sphinxes and a rosette. Ivory was also used to make a pyxis from Thebes, also depicting sphinxes, and a pair of chair legs from Thebes. Other items of furniture included ivory inlays of sphinxes, dolphins, columns, shells and shields.

TOPIC REVIEW

You should be able to:

1. Describe:
   - how frescoes were painted and what they showed
   - the types of jewellery that the Myceanaeans wore
   - the designs on Mycenaean rings and the techniques that were used in making them
   - the types of other metal objects such as storage boxes, cups and rhyta, and the designs on them
   - what the Mycenaeans used ivory for
   - the different types of pottery storage vessels that the Mycenaeans had
   - the appearance of pottery figurines and votive offerings.

2. Explain:
   - why Mycenaean frescoes are generally admired
   - what the designs on frescoes tell us about Mycenaean life
   - what the designs on jewellery and cups tell us about Mycenaean life
   - the different possible uses of rhyta and figurines.

PRACTICE QUESTIONS

Source A: *A gold pyxis from Mycenae*

1. How would an object such as the gold pyxis from Grave Circle A have been made? [2]
2. Give **one** reason why this particular object is unusual. [1]
3. 'We can gain a full understanding of the Mycenaeans from their metalwork?' How far do you agree with this assessment? [15]

2.4 Tombs, Graves and Burial

TOPIC OVERVIEW

- Burial customs
- Structure and use of cist graves
- Structure and use of shaft graves
- Structure and use of tholos and chamber tombs
- The use of funerary objects
- The contents of the graves of Grave Circle A and Grave Circle B at Mycenae

The prescribed source for this topic is:

- Gold death mask of Agamemnon from Shaft Grave V, Mycenae

Don't forget that you will be given credit in the exam if you study extra sources and make relevant use of them in your answers.

Honouring the dead was an important part of Mycenaean life. A significant area of Mycenae and the surrounding area is devoted to burial spaces, and the places where bodies were buried could be very grand constructions. In this section you will learn how the Mycenaeans buried their dead, and the types of graves and tombs that they used.

BURIAL CUSTOMS

Although the form of Mycenaean tombs changed, burial customs probably did not differ greatly over the period. We know that the body, if wealthy, would have been adorned with jewellery, as this has been found on the necks and wrists of skeletons. From this we can assume that bodies were clothed for burial too. A drink offering was almost certainly made to the gods as metal cups have been found badly damaged on the floor at the entrance to tholos tombs.

Bones of animals and sea-shells have also been found, suggesting a meal was eaten in honour of the dead. Gifts would have been offered, although these have often either decayed or were robbed in ancient times. A pair of horses was found slaughtered at both Marathon and Dendra, but there is no such evidence from Mycenae to suggest this was a common practice. However, the killing of animals does mirror a scene from the *Iliad*, Book 23, where two of Patroclus' dogs were slaughtered at his funeral.

Finally, the earth would have been filled in and a raised mound would then have covered the area so that it was visible from a distance. A stele would have been placed over the tomb, such as the one shown in Figure 2.38.

The mound would be dug again when another burial was made and bodies would be interred in the same area.

There is evidence that some bodies could have been put in a clay burial casket, as remains from Tanagra in central Greece show. The painted scenes on the caskets also tell us a lot about customs as we can see a funeral procession of women, many of whom are in elaborate dresses. Some women also wear an unusual feathered cap, and it is the women, rather than the men who have their hands raised to their heads, perhaps in a sign of grief. Women, not men, are shown near the bodies, all indicating they had the greater role in burial. On one casket, a body lies on a bed and the dead person is wrapped in a short tunic. On another casket a drink offering, known as a **libation**, seems to be poured in honour of the dead. However, these caskets are extremely rare, and it is hard to know whether what they represent was typical of Mycenaean funerals and burials.

FIGURE 2.38
Stone stele (grave marker) showing hunting from a chariot, Grave Circle A, Mycenae, now in the Archaeological Museum, Athens.

> **libation** a drink offering poured in honour of the gods

STRUCTURE AND USE OF CIST GRAVES

In the Mycenaean Age the most basic type of burial was one in a **cist grave**. These were used before the Mycenaean Age, but continued to be used at sites until the end of the period. In a cist grave, a shallow pit was dug in the earth, and the sides were covered in slabs of stone. A pile of stones was then placed at the bottom for the body to lie on. These pits were so small that the body had to be placed in a curved position.

Before the Mycenaean Age, these tombs were intended only for a single use. At the start of the Mycenaean Age they began to be grouped together with a mound of earth raised on top. The mound was opened up when a new body needed to be buried. These might be placed in pithoi, or in fresh pits, or in re-dug earth beside the original burial.

> **cist grave** a grave in the form of a stone-lined pit, dug into the earth, and covered up

> **Study question**
> Graves and tombs were re-used many times. Why do you think this was the case?

STRUCTURE AND USE OF SHAFT GRAVES

A second type of grave, known as a **shaft grave**, was also used at the start of the Mycenean Age. Grave Circle B contained fourteen shaft graves, together with ten cist graves.

> **shaft grave** a grave in which a deep shaft was dug and a space created at the bottom for a body, often re-used for later burials

FIGURE 2.39
Diagram of the excavation of
a shaft grave at Mycenae.
A = stelai; B = surface level;
C = roof support; D = brick.

EXPLORE FURTHER

Skeletons found in the shaft graves of Grave Circle B have been forensically analysed. The one from Grave Sigma was of a large man, aged about 55. He suffered from arthritis and possible problems with gall-stones, but only three of his teeth were diseased. The man in Grave Zeta was aged about 49 when he died, and his skull was notable for deep impressions, an indication that he suffered heavy blows to it. He had lived a violent life as his spine and one of his ribs show evidence of healing after fractures.

One of the five bodies in Grave Gamma was a man aged about 28. He was tall and had strong bones, but he had suffered an injury near the eye and had two fractures in the area. A hole had been drilled at the top of his skull in an operation, possibly to treat his injuries. However, the lack of any evidence of any healing on the bone suggests this failed.

A shaft grave is a natural development of a cist grave, but is larger and deeper. A narrow shaft was dug up to 2.5 m deep (the cist graves in Grave Circle B were only dug to up to 0.6 m deep). The largest grave (Grave Zeta) measures 3.4 × 3.9 m, the size of a typical bedroom today. At the bottom, a chamber with low rubble walls was created with a roof support. The pit of Grave Zeta has four post holes in the corners for beams to hold up the roof, which also rested on a rock ledge. Finally, the shaft that had been previously dug was filled in.

Bodies in shaft graves were usually laid on their backs. Multiple burials in the same chambers were common. When a second body was buried, the first was often pushed aside or moved to a corner to make room for the new one. A new stele might have been placed, but this was not a universal practice. Significant grave goods appear for the first time with the use of shaft graves.

STRUCTURE AND USE OF THOLOS AND CHAMBER TOMBS

tumulus a raised mound of earth under which bodies were buried

Study question
Why do you think tholos tombs were rarely created after the thirteenth century BC?

After the emergence of Grave Circle A, a new style of burial occurred in the fourteenth century BC, known as the tholos tomb. These derive from an earlier type of tomb, known as a **tumulus**, where a large mound was built over where a group of bodies had been buried. Tholos tombs were different from previous tombs as they were built from stone, rather than dug out the earth. As they are so monumental, they could only have been built for the most important members of a city.

The main part of the tomb consisted of a high-roofed dome (those at Mycenae were the tallest known domes in the world for over a thousand years), which would have been dug down from the top of a hill. A side chamber sometimes was dug to house the body. The stone at the bottom of the excavated area would then have been used to make the walls and roof of the structure, and the excavated earth would then have been placed over the top of the roof. These may have been constructed during the lifetime of the person intended to be

FIGURE 2.41
Drawing of the interior of the chamber tomb.

buried in it, as the construction of these tombs would have been a huge and time-consuming undertaking. Tholos tombs are rarely seen after the thirteenth century BC.

In front of the tholos was a long passageway with stone walls, known as a **dromos**. When a body had been buried, large stones would have been placed at the end of the dromos to block off the entrance. Earth would then have been put on the dromos to create an elevated slope.

At the end of the dromos was a richly decorated entrance, although no one could ever have entered it. Some of the entrance from the Treasury of Atreus has survived. There, two green limestone columns with a zigzag pattern framed the entranceway, and about the entrance there would have been a triangle of red stone where a triangular space now exists. This would have relieved the weight on the large block of stone above the doorway.

From the fourteenth century, less important Mycenaean nobles were buried in **chamber tombs** (a tomb dug from rock in which more than one body was buried in a chamber). They were similar to tholos tombs as they had a dromos, with a wall of stones to block the entrance. However, unlike tholos tombs, which were built from stone, chamber tombs were dug out of the earth, using the rock to form the roof of a square or rounded chamber. Several people could be buried in each, often in side chambers, and as such they were probably used as family tombs. These were used right up to the end of the Mycenaean period, but in the final years there is evidence of the resurgence of cist graves, possibly indicating a decline in prosperity in Mycenae.

> **dromos** a passageway leading to the tholos tomb

> **chamber tomb** a tomb, dug from rock, in which a body or bodies would be buried in a chamber

THE USE OF FUNERARY OBJECTS

Many of the shaft graves from Mycenaean cities are found to have contained valuable items, reflecting the importance of the people buried in them. Many ancient societies, such as the Egyptians, believed that the dead would use the items they were buried with in the afterlife. However, as we know virtually nothing of what the Mycenaeans believed happened after death, we cannot be sure that items would have been buried for the deceased to use. The items could have been buried simply to show off the status and wealth of the person during their lifetime.

Pottery items, whether vessels or figurines, are the most common objects found in tombs. These would almost certainly have contained oils, perfumes and other liquids. Military equipment, such as swords and daggers are also commonly found, presumably suggesting the deceased was a warrior. While inlaid weapons, such as the Lion Hunt Dagger, and ones with handles covered in gold are the most famous pieces of military equipment, the vast majority of items were simply made of bronze. Women were often buried with jewellery and sometimes with boxes for cosmetics, combs or bronze mirrors. If tombs were re-used, new items would have been placed in the tomb, with scraps of gold from previous burials found in the shafts.

THE CONTENTS OF THE GRAVES OF GRAVE CIRCLE A AND GRAVE CIRCLE B AT MYCENAE

The contents of Grave Circles A and B included some of the finest grave goods found anywhere in the world. While the goods of Grave Circle B are less spectacular on the whole than those from Grave Circle A, they still contain some remarkable pieces.

This vessel was found in a woman's grave, together with a quantity of jewellery. It is probably to keep cosmetics in. It may have come from Crete, where there are rock crystal quarries, and where there were similar objects in Minoan times. Other items found in graves include gold funeral masks, pottery, jewellery and swords.

The six graves in Grave Circle A contained a vast quantity of treasure. Some of the most famous items come from Grave V and include:

- two gold death masks (see below)
- gold cup with repoussé spirals
- gold necklace
- bronze dagger with the blade inlaid with gold spirals
- amber bead necklace
- wooden pyxis, covered with gold plates
- ostrich-egg rhyton with faience (a glazed ceramic) dolphins applied on to it
- swords with handles decorated with gold
- bronze sword decorated with griffins (a mythical creature)
- gold octopus brooch
- numerous other swords, pottery objects, items of jewellery.

FIGURE 2.42
Rock crystal vessel with a handle in the shape of a duck's head and neck, Grave Omicron, Grave Circle B, Mycenae.

The final picture in this section is perhaps the most iconic image from Mycenae, and comes from Shaft Grave V in Grave Circle A. When Schliemann saw the mask, he is alleged to have written 'I have gazed on the face of Agamemnon', believing he had unearthed the death mask of the legendary ruler of Mycenae at the time of the Trojan War, although many dispute if he ever said this. However, as was discussed on p. 162, many of the finds come from several centuries before his supposed existence.

A thick sheet of gold would have been heated to make it softer and easier to hammer into shape. This would probably have been done by placing the gold against a wooden background and hammering it to create a representation of the features of the deceased, using the

FIGURE 2.43

The famous death mask found at Mycenae and commonly attributed to Agamemnon.

PRESCRIBED SOURCE

Gold death mask of 'Agamemnon'

Date: 16th century BC

Original Location: Grave V, Grave Circle A, Mycenae

Current location: National Archaeological Museum, Athens

Material: sheets of gold

Original purpose: death mask

Image: face of the deceased

Techniques shown: hammering, repoussé

Significance: shows techniques in metalworking and burial customs

repoussé technique. A sharper tool would have been used for the facial details. Two holes near the ears indicate the mask was fixed over the face with twine when the deceased was buried. It illustrates the dignified and imposing features of a man, with its striking beard and moustache, and closed eyes. Due to the quality of the workmanship, it seems almost certain that it would have been used at the burial of one of the rulers of Mycenae. The mask is 17 cm high, 25 cm wide and weighs only 168 g, indicating the thinness of the gold and, therefore, the skill of the craftsman in being able to create such precise details on such a thin object.

Study question

Do you think Schliemann should be admired or criticised for the way he excavated Mycenae and Troy?

ACTIVITY

Research one of the shaft graves of either Grave Circle A or Grave Circle B, producing either a presentation or wall display. Individuals from a class could produce a booklet, with pages on each of the graves.

EXPLORE FURTHER

Some scholars doubt that this mask is a genuine Mycenaean object, pointing to stylistic differences between it and other masks from Mycenae. This mask has very distinctive facial features and a beard, unlike the other four masks uncovered from Mycenae. Contemporaries of Schliemann said that he planted objects at the site, so that he could later 'discover' them, and that he would make duplicates of objects to pass them off as genuine. He had earlier made an agreement to split his findings with officials in exchange for permission to excavate. He finished excavations three days after finding the mask, which might seem surprising if such a major find was genuinely made. He had left the site a few days earlier, but it was not known where he went. Could he have gone to obtain the mask from elsewhere, possibly Athens, where a relative of his wife was said to have been a goldsmith? The unnatural, upturned effect of the moustache would be very hard to create in Mycenaean times, so would not seem a logical way for a ruler to present himself.

While this may seem convincing, many scholars believe that despite these issues, it is a genuine Mycenaean artefact.

TOPIC REVIEW

You should be able to:

1. Describe:
   - how the Mycenaeans buried their dead
   - the forms of cist graves and shaft graves
   - the forms of tholos and chamber tombs
   - typical objects with which the dead were buried
   - the key objects found in Grave Circles A and B.

2. Explain:
   - why the Mycenaeans buried their dead in the manner that they did
   - the relationships between shaft and cist graves and between tholos and chamber tombs
   - how and why tholos and chamber tombs were constructed
   - what particular funerary objects tell us about the dead.

PRACTICE QUESTIONS

Source A: *Grave circle A at Mycenae*

1. Describe the appearance of a typical shaft tomb in Mycenaean times. [3]
2. 'Tombs and burials raise more questions about the Mycenaeans than they provide answers.' How far do you agree with this assessment? [15]

Literature

2.5 Literary Techniques and Composition

Homer is widely acknowledged as a master storyteller, and his influence on ancient and modern literature has been vast. His poem belongs to a class of literature called Epic Poetry, which you will discover more about in this section.

HOMER AS A STORYTELLER AND THE IDEA OF EPIC

KEY INDIVIDUAL

Odysseus King of Ithaca, who struggles to get home after the Trojan War. When he gets home, he then manages to defeat his enemies in the palace and reclaim his kingdom

The *Odyssey* is a poem in twenty-four sections, or books as they are generally known. It tells us of the adventures of the hero Odysseus sailing home after the Trojan War, and how he managed to reclaim his kingdom. This war, between the Greeks and Trojans, had lasted 10 years. Odysseus, despite wishing to stay at home with his wife Penelope and new-born son Telemachus, was bound by a promise he had made to go. He tried to back out of his promise by pretending he had gone mad when he was summoned to join the rest of the Greek forces. However, one of the other soldiers sent to fetch him placed his

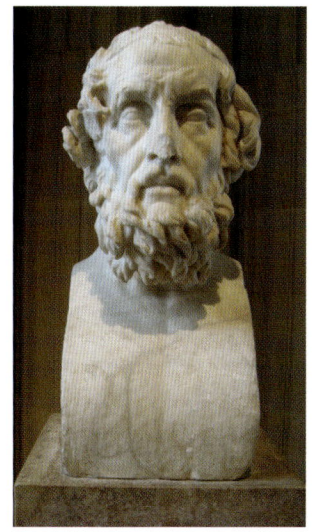

FIGURE 2.44
Marble head of Homer, Palazzo Caetani, Rome, 1st–2nd century AD, now in the Louvre Museum, Paris.

son in front of a plough. Odysseus snatched his son away as he was about to be trampled on, proving that he was sane after all.

During his time at Troy, Odysseus came up with the idea of the Wooden Horse by which the Greeks captured Troy. However, his voyage home from Troy and the reclamation of his kingdom was full of adventure and drama, and you will read some of the key episodes of these in the *Odyssey*. Together with Homer's other poem, the *Iliad*, the *Odyssey* considered to be amongst the greatest works of literature ever composed.

THE PLOT OF THE *ODYSSEY*

The plot of the *Odyssey* is a relatively simple one: a man, Odysseus, seeks to return home to the island of Ithaca (see map, Figure 1.10) after twenty years away. In his attempts to sail home, he gets lost and all his crew members die in horrific circumstances. When he eventually gets back, his problems are still not over; he has to reclaim his kingdom from his enemies, and convince his wife that he is the man she married, as he looks like a beggar, rather than her former husband.

You are not expected to know the whole of the *Odyssey*, but to make full sense of the books that you have to read, it is helpful to be aware of what happens in the rest of the story. However, you need to be aware of an added complication in the *Odyssey*; the chronological order of the events is not the same as the order that they occur in the story. This is because Homer uses a flashback technique, and the early books of the *Odyssey* describe events that occur near the end of Odysseus' 10-year journey home. This flashback is designed to make us to want to read on to find out about these adventures. Odysseus tells these adventures in Books 9–12.

Below is a brief summary of the key events of the *Odyssey* in the order they are written in the text.

S & C Another famous section of the *Odyssey* is Books 5–8, where Odysseus is on an island with the goddess Calypso, and is then entertained by the Phaeacians. These books are particularly worth reading to discover Odysseus' talents as a speaker.

Book 12 is also a famous book, which tells the adventures of Odysseus and his crew. It contains the famous story of Odysseus and the Sirens.

EXAM TIP

You will not get questions on sections other than the books of the prescribed reading, but reading other parts of the *Odyssey* will aid your understanding of characters and issues. You will be credited for your wider knowledge in the extended responses if you refer to other parts of the *Odyssey*, although you can still score full marks in questions without referring to these extra parts.

1) Odysseus' son, Telemachus, goes to Pylos and Sparta in search of news of his father, who has not returned home from Troy. It has been 10 years since the war has ended. He does not get any positive information (Books 1–4).

2) At a similar time, Odysseus leaves the island of the goddess Calypso, where he has been stuck for 7 years. He sails to the land of the Phaeacians, despite being hit by a storm sent by Poseidon (Books 5–8).

3) Odysseus tells the Phaeacians about what happened to him after leaving Troy. He tells of adventures with the Cyclops, Circe and various other encounters (Books 9–12).

4) Odysseus reaches home, disguised as a beggar. He bides his time, only revealing his identity to his son and a few slaves. He kills the suitors who wish to marry his wife, before being reunited with her (Books 13–24).

The chronological order of events is somewhat different.

1) After leaving Troy, Odysseus and his crew got lost at sea and had adventures in various places and with various creatures (Books 9–12).

2) After the crew die in a storm, Odysseus gets washed up on Calypso's island. He then sails to Phaeacia and is welcomed (Books 5–8).

3) While Odysseus leaves Calypso's island and is in Phaeacia, his son searches for news of him (Books 1–4).

4) Odysseus reaches home, disguised as a beggar. He eventually kills the suitors and is reunited with his wife (Books 13–24).

THE INDIVIDUAL BOOKS

Study questions

1 What qualities does Odysseus show in this passage?
2 Are these good qualities to have?

Book 9

At the start of your selection, Odysseus begins to tell of his adventures since leaving Troy to Alcinous, King of Phaeacia. The king had noticed that Odysseus was crying when a bard (a poet and storyteller) was singing about the Trojan War and questioned Odysseus. As a result Odysseus begins by telling Alcinous who he is, as Alcinous did not know the identity of his guest. Odysseus reveals his identity by saying:

> I am Odysseus, Laertes' son, known to all for my stratagems, and my fame has reached the heavens.

Homer, *Odyssey*, 9.19–20

Odysseus then goes on to tell of his adventures after Troy in Books 9 and 10, and he is famous for telling tales (and twisting the truth). This might make you wonder if all the stories that Odysseus narrates in these two books are completely or partially made up by Odysseus to create sympathy and gain help from the Phaeacians.

The first of these stories is his attack on the island of the Cicones. His men's insistence on staying an extra day to enjoy the successes of their initial victory result in a counter-attack by the Cicones on the next day and the loss of seventy-two of the crew. After a storm occurs, the crew lose their way and end up on the land of the Lotus-eaters, where a different danger awaits them – the loss of any memory of their home if they eat the lotus fruit. Three crew members do eat the fruit, but Odysseus uses all his strength and bravery to drag crew away, although a deadlier threat is in store.

We find out about the uncivilised land and inhabitants of the island as the suspense is built up by the long introduction to the encounter with the Cyclops, Polyphemus. The actual encounter is possibly the most famous part of the *Odyssey*.

On entering Polyphemus' cave, Odysseus and his men help themselves to his cheese. Polyphemus himself was out shepherding his flocks. His men want to steal the cheese and go, but Odysseus overrules them, staying in the hope of getting gifts from the cave owner. On his return, Polyphemus spots them and questions them about their identity and motives, before suddenly eating two of the men. After four more men are eaten, Odysseus devises a plan to get Polyphemus drunk, and blind him when he is asleep. He makes a huge stake while Polyphemus is out shepherding his flocks, and that evening, he gets Polyphemus drunk, tells him that his name is Nobody, and blinds him. Polyphemus shouts out that Nobody has blinded him, as a result of which the other Cyclopes do not come to help. That night, he and his men then cling on to the undersides of his flock until Polyphemus lets his animals out the next morning, not realising that men are clinging on to them. When they have escaped to their boats, Odysseus shouts out his name in triumph to Polyphemus, allowing Polyphemus to throw rocks at his fleet and curse him for the rest of his journey.

We are not given all the key information at once: we are not told Polyphemus is one-eyed until his eye is blinded, and whilst Odysseus knows why he is giving Polyphemus strong wine, and giving himself a false name, we do not know.

Book 10

The book starts off with more tales of fantasy with the story of the bag of winds. Aeolus, the keeper of the winds, traps all the winds in a bag, leaving out only the one that will blow Odysseus straight home. As the crew are within sight of Ithaca, Odysseus falls asleep for the first time in many days and his men open the bag, thinking that it is treasure; Odysseus had not told them of the contents, and he was guarding the bag very closely. They are driven back to Aeolus' island, but he refuses to help them a second time. At the next adventure at the land of the Laestrygonians, all of the men except for those on Odysseus' boat get trapped in the harbour and are slaughtered by the inhabitants.

The survivors then sail to Circe's island. Half of them, led by Eurylochus, travel to her home. When they arrive at her house they are seemingly given good hospitality by Circe, but she slips a drug into their food to turn them into pigs. Only Eurylochus, who had not eaten the food, retains his human form and travels back to Odysseus. Odysseus then sets off on a rescue mission and is given a magic flower by the god Hermes. This ensures that he remains unaffected when he meets Circe, who tries to turn him into a pig. She then becomes much more friendly, turning the pigs back into the crew and giving them all hospitality. After a year of relaxation, the crew persuade Odysseus that they must sail for home, and Circe helps with this too, preparing them for the next stage of the journey with gifts and advice.

Book 19

Odysseus is now in Ithaca and has been disguised as a beggar by Athena. Here he is verbally attacked by a maid. His wife, Penelope, comes to his aid, not knowing his real identity, and asks the beggar about his family. Odysseus, not wanting to risk the plans he has been making for revenge on the suitors (a group of men who assume Odysseus is dead and want to marry his wife; see also p. 224), makes up a false tale about his background. He convincingly adds in a few true details from an alleged meeting with Odysseus, which causes Penelope to weep.

Penelope asks Eurycleia, Odysseus' former nurse from his youth, to wash him. She spots a scar that causes her to realise the beggar is really Odysseus. At this crucial moment, Homer stops the story for over two pages while he tells us of how Odysseus got the injury in his youth when hunting a boar.

Odysseus then warns Eurycleia not to reveal his true identity:

> Keep it from all the rest of the house. Otherwise I say, and it shall be so, that if a god delivers the noble suitors into my hands, I will not spare you, though you nursed me, when I kill the other serving women in the palace.

> Homer, *Odyssey*, 19.486–489

Penelope then tells the stranger of a dream she had. Odysseus interprets this as a sign that her husband will soon return. Finally, she announces the contest that will lead to her marrying one of the suitors, as she can hold out no longer against their pressure.

Book 21

Penelope announces the contest to string Odysseus' bow and fire an arrow through twelve axes. Only Odysseus had been able to string the bow, and so if any suitor can do it, he will be a worthy husband for her. Penelope and Odysseus' son, Telemachus, has the first go, but he cannot quite manage to string it. Odysseus, needing help to put his plan into action, reveals his plan to some of his loyal slaves and to Telemachus. One of the leading suitors, Eurymachus, fails to string the bow, and the other suitors decide to take a break. It is at this moment that Odysseus asks to have a go at it. Despite the outrage of the suitors, Telemachus insists that the beggar is given a go. While this is going on, Eurycleia locks the doors in the palace so that the suitors cannot escape.

At this most tense moment of the whole *Odyssey*, Homer writes:

> So they chattered, but once wily Odysseus had flexed the great bow and checked it all over, he strung it easily, as a man skilled in song and the lyre stretches a new string onto its leather tuning strap, fixing the twisted sheep-gut at either end. Then

Study questions

1 Why do you think Homer has Odysseus disguised as a beggar during his time in Ithaca?
2 Why does Homer spend so long giving us the details of how Odysseus got his injury?
3 Do you consider Odysseus' reaction to his identity being discovered appropriate? Explain your views.

Study questions

1 Why do you think Homer uses the simile about the man skilled in song at this point?
2 How are the ideas in the simile developed in the sentence?

grasping the bow in his right hand, he plucked the string that sang sweetly to his touch with the sound of a swallow's note.

Homer, Odyssey, 21.404–411

Book 22

Odysseus shoots the leading suitor, Antinous, who dies in a gruesome manner. Even now, the suitors do not realise who the beggar is, assuming Antinous' death to have been accidental. Odysseus finally reveals his identity at this point. Despite Eurymachus' attempts to avoid his punishment by blaming the behaviour of the suitors on Antinous, he too is slaughtered. A massacre follows when the suitors are unable to escape from the hall, with Athena encouraging Odysseus in the battle. Telemachus and the loyal servants play an active part in the killing of the suitors. When all the suitors are killed, the disloyal maids are hung and the evil slave, Melanthius, also dies in a horrific manner. The loyal slaves are all spared.

HOW THE *ODYSSEY* MIGHT HAVE BEEN COMPOSED AND PERFORMED

So how did the *Odyssey* reach us, if there was such a long gap between the war and its composition? The answer lies in the way that it was composed. At the time of the events of the *Odyssey*, the ancient Greeks did not have a written alphabet, and so it would have been impossible for the story to have been written down at the time that the events might have happened. The *Odyssey* does mention professional singers, known as **bards**, who recited myths. Such singers would have recited tales while playing a stringed musical instrument known as a lyre. This would probably have happened after banquets, and the *Odyssey* itself describes such a situation in Book 8. One part, perhaps equivalent to a book of the *Odyssey*, might well have been recited after a meal. Thus, the *Odyssey* is known as an **oral poem**.

It would seem that this is what happened with the *Odyssey*; someone recited these stories originally, possibly on lots of different occasions, which were passed on through generations of singers and continually adapted. Several centuries later, when the Greeks had developed their written alphabet, the stories were written down.

> **bard** a public storyteller who recited vast amounts of poetry to the accompaniment of the lyre, often during banquets
>
> **oral poem** a poem that is composed and told without the aid of writing

Narrative and structural features of epic poetry

When people today think of an epic story, perhaps the saga of Beowulf or the Bible come to mind, or in a more modern context, the stories of Harry Potter or the Lord of the Rings. All have elements of epic in them. An epic might be regarded as having some or all of the following elements:

- it is long
- it contains a central figure or hero
- it tells of a quest or mission for the central figure

- it features amazing deeds
- it starts in the middle of the story (known by the Latin phrase 'in medias res')
- it has monsters, magic and gods ·
- it is set in lots of different places
- it has certain literary features (e.g. epithets and similes) within it.

The *Odyssey* has all these elements.

Descriptive techniques

The *Odyssey* contains over 12,000 lines of poetry and the *Iliad* contains around 3,000 more. We might ask how a bard was able to remember such an extraordinary amount. Part of the answer is that the poems have a number of repetitive elements; in fact, about a third of the lines of the poem are repeated wholly or in part. Moreover, it seems that each poet would develop his own version each time he presented it – he could use the repetitive elements as a starting point, and then insert his own lines around them, or use lines with which he was already familiar. The repetitive elements therefore acted as building blocks for each poet to work from, and allowed him to improvise each time he gave a performance.

Characters are regularly given descriptive phrases, called **epithets**, to highlight key aspects of their character. For example, Odysseus is often called 'noble Odysseus', 'resourceful Odysseus' or 'Odysseus of the nimble wits'.

Sometimes the epithet fits the situation perfectly. For example, when Eurycleia first notices a likeness between Odysseus and the beggar, and reveals this to him, Odysseus replies:

> "Old woman," said the quick-witted Odysseus, "that is what everyone says who has set eyes upon us both."

> Homer, *Odyssey*, 19.383–384

> **epithet** an adjectival word or phrase regularly added to a name to denote a personal or physical quality

> **Study question**
> Why is the epithet 'quick-witted' appropriate here?

Different epithets could be fitted it in to different parts of a line simply to fit to the rhythm of epic poetry. Longer phrases, often amounting to a line or more, could also be repeated. These are known as **formulae**.

The most famous example is Homer's description of Dawn, which is always fresh and rosy-fingered. This phrase occurs repeatedly to mark the start of a new day.

One very important feature of epic poetry is the **simile**. This helps the reader to visualise a situation. To analyse a simile properly, you need to consider the individual points of comparison between the simile and the story.

Some similes are simple, such as Penelope coming down from her apartment looking like Artemis or Aphrodite in Book 19, but others are more developed like this one about the hanging of the maids:

> **formula** (pl. **formulae**) a section of an epic poem, longer than an epithet, that is regularly used to describe a person, place or object
>
> **simile** a figure of speech whereby one thing is compared to another thing of a different kind in order to make a description more vivid

> The row of women held up their heads, and the rope was looped round their necks so they might die pitiably, like long-winged thrushes or doves, that are caught in a snare as they try to roost in their thicket, and are welcomed to a grimmer nest. For a little while their feet twitched: but not for long.

> Homer, *Odyssey*, 22.468–472

S & C

Even with these simple little ways to fill in some parts of the story, many people still doubted whether it was humanly possible to memorise all the story, let alone make it fit a particular rhythm. But in the 1930s, studies were made on poets at that time in Bosnia, in eastern Europe, where poems were recited from memory. One illiterate poet was able to recite a 12,000-line poem from memory, proving that what had been done in Greek times in the *Odyssey* was possible with practice.

Find a poem that is at least 10 lines long and learn it. After doing so, consider how long it was compared to the *Odyssey*. What problems did you have, and what helped you to memorise the poem successfully? Think also about learning lyrics to songs. Why are the lyrics of some songs easier to remember than others?

MODERN PARALLEL

Many forms of music use similar techniques in composition. Jazz musicians and rap artists often make up melodies or lyrics on the spot that they insert into their performances. These sections are made up from smaller units in much the same way as Homer used epithets and formulae to create a section.

The women, like birds, are caught in a situation they cannot escape from. They had probably been thinking of going to sleep with the suitors (108 local noblemen who wish to marry Penelope, believing Odysseus is dead), just as the birds had been about to roost, before being caught unexpectedly. They twitch in the final moments in the same way as birds in a trap flutter for a while.

Not every element of the simile has to match up: the women are not literally caught in a trap. Perhaps too we feel sympathy for the birds, unlike the women, though trapping birds was a way of life in the ancient world. These differences do not stop the simile being effective, but if there are too many differences, or it is too hard to imagine, you may find it less effective.

There are also longer sections of recurring situations, known as **topoi**, such as welcoming a guest or making a prayer. Many people feel that the repetitive elements add to the charm of the poem and create a sense of familiarity.

We have already seen how Homer uses similes, epithets, formulae and topoi in his narrative, but there are several other ways that he makes his story exciting.

Gory detail features in several books as Odysseus has to show himself to be a great warrior at various points. This is the same kind of appeal that horror and action films have, and the appeal was probably no different in Homer's time. A good example is the death of Antinous:

EXAM TIP

If you comment on a simile, do not simply write that 'it helps us to visualise the scene better'. That is the function of similes in general and does not show understanding of a particular simile. If you comment on the exact parallels, as in the quotations on p. 204 and p. 206, you will score more AO2 marks for your evaluation.

> The point passed clean through the tender throat, and Antinous sank to one side, the cup falling at that moment from his hand, while a thick jet of blood gushed from his nostrils. His foot kicked the table away, dashing the food to the floor, and the bread and meat were fouled.
>
> Homer, *Odyssey*, 22.16–21

PS

topos (pl. **topoi**) a poetic scene that occurs regularly, which is made up of a series of standard elements

In a few lines we can see each separate moment of his death. The twitching of his foot and the kicking of the table are well-chosen details, and the ordinariness of the food on the ground provides a contrast to the blood gushing out.

Dramatic irony is used at various points, especially towards the end of the story. The disguise of Odysseus provides numerous examples, as characters talk to the beggar about Odysseus, without realising his true identity. Examples include the occasion on which

dramatic irony when a character does not know the full significance of what is happening or being said, but the readers do

Eumaeus and Philoetius pray that Odysseus returns in a speech to him in Book 21, or when Antinous says that the bow will seal the suitors' fate in Book 22.

Detailed description is also a feature of this scene. It helps the reader to picture the scene completely and get more involved in the story. Look also at the description of the flocks of Polyphemus, the Cyclops. The precise detail that we are given of the separation of the animals and the making of the cheese helps us to see him as something more than just a monster.

Ordinary scenes and objects are raised to a higher status by the way they are described, such as the history of the bow that will seal the fate of the suitors. Homer often uses such descriptions to tell us how important an object is going to be. Sometimes it is not immediately clear why an object is described at length; for example, as Odysseus sets off towards the cave of Polyphemus, Homer tells us about the wine he takes. We are told of where he got it and there is an emphasis on how it is normally diluted heavily with water. When we read these details, we do not realise how the wine will be crucial later in the story, but when we get to the plan to blind Polyphemus, everything fits into place.

At times, detailed description of action creates a sudden dramatic effect:

PS

"Devoid of pity, he was silent in response, but leaping up laid hands on my crew. Two he seized and dashed to the ground like whelps, and their brains ran out and stained the earth. He tore them limb from limb for his supper, eating the flesh and entrails, bone and marrow, like a mountain lion, leaving nothing. Helplessly we watched these cruel acts, raising our hands to heaven and weeping. When the Cyclops had filled his huge stomach with human flesh, and had drunk pure milk, he lay down in the cave, stretched out among his flocks."

Homer, *Odyssey*, 9.287–298

The sudden action of 'leaping up' comes as a shock after the silence at the start of the passage. It shows Polyphemus' aggression and speed at this point. The simile of the whelps shows the helplessness of the men against the monster, who himself is compared to a lion, highlighting his animalistic behaviour. This is shown as he eats every bit of the men, even the parts such as bones that would seem inedible. The men pray to Zeus as they can do nothing; for battle-hardened soldiers to act in this

---

EXAM TIP

If you are asked what makes a passage exciting or dramatic, try to avoid simply saying there is a detailed description in it. Such comments are too generalised and could apply to most sections of the text. They do not show that you have fully appreciated what Homer is doing. Try instead to focus on what makes something detailed, such as the use of colours in a passage, the appeal to a particular sense, or what the details suggest about characters or objects. If you do this, you will gain more AO2 marks. An example of a dramatic passage, together with analysis of why it is dramatic, is given above.

way shows this is no ordinary enemy. After all this action the passage ends calmly, which provides a strong contrast to the violence of the deaths.

If this were an answer, it would score full marks for AO1 as it demonstrates a detailed knowledge and understanding of the text and full marks for AO2 as each time there is a reference, analysis is given of how it adds to the drama.

The pace of the story is crucial in keeping up the interest of the readers, and Homer changes this regularly. There are times when the pace slows right down with lengthy descriptions of settings, such as Odysseus' arrival on the islands of Polyphemus and Circe. We suspect by the slow build-up that something big is going to happen, so the situation is tense. Clues are given that all is not well, such as the strange animals outside Circe's home, or the introduction to Polyphemus and his home:

> There a giant spent the night, one that grazed his herds far off, alone, and keeping clear of others, lived in lawless solitude. He was born a monster and a wonder, not like any ordinary human.
>
> Homer, *Odyssey*, 9.187–190

'Lawless' and 'formidable' tell us how threatening Polyphemus will be, but Homer makes us wait to read what Polyphemus does to justify this description. It might seem frustrating to have to wait a few pages to find out, but it allows the reader an emotional breather before the action really gets going.

Everything leads to the climax of the story, which is slowly built up. Odysseus arrives back in Ithaca in Book 13 and we have to wait until Book 19 for Penelope to announce the contest of the bow and we are further made to wait until the end of Book 21 for it to be strung.

Pathos is to be found at various points in the story. When Odysseus' men are killed in the harbour of the Laestrygonians, Odysseus tells us that the groans of his dying men were appalling. We feel sorry for the victims and those who have to witness these events. Just a short while later his men break down in tears remembering what has happened, but get no comfort from Odysseus, although we might well sympathise with them.

But it is not just Odysseus and his crew that readers often feel sorry for. Pathos is a very personal feeling, and many people feel sympathy for the sufferings of Polyphemus (who ends up blind and having lost his flock) and some of the slaves of Odysseus, even though these are generally unlikeable characters. It is a rare skill for an author to make us sympathise with villains in a story.

Use of myth (or stories) is something that features heavily in the stories. Books 9 and 10 are a series of myths, told by Odysseus himself, but other parts feature backstories. When Eurycleia notices the scar on Odysseus' leg, Homer describes how he got this injury. In the same way, when Penelope fetches the bow, we are told how Odysseus got the bow in a myth. We are meant to focus on the history of the bow, just as the bow causes Penelope to reflect on the past. Antinous' tale of the centaur Eurytion is entertaining in itself, but as with many stories in Homer, it is used to give a moral lesson (on this occasion about the dangers of drink). As a storyteller himself, it is perhaps not surprising that Homer gets his characters to tell stories themselves.

MODERN PARALLEL

In the past hundred years, doctors have recognised the mental suffering that soldiers feel in and after war situations. This has been known as shell-shock since the First World War. Are Odysseus' men suffering from this same effect?

pathos literally 'suffering' in Greek, an appeal to the reader's emotions by inviting them to feel pity and sadness

ACTIVITY

Think of a book, film or TV programme where you have some sympathy for an evil character or group of evil characters. What made you feel sympathy for the character(s)?

ACTIVITY

Choose a passage of about half a page that you think is particularly memorable. Give at least three ways that Homer makes it memorable, using the ideas from the previous pages. Then do the same to say which book is your favourite.

Direct speech makes up a lot of the *Odyssey*. In fact, all of Books 9 and 10 are direct speech as Odysseus retells his tale to King Alcinous, and within this speech are speeches of other characters. It is easy to overlook the power of direct speech as we are so used to it, but it allows us to see the real thoughts of characters. Telemachus, in deciding the fate of the disloyal maids says:

"These women who poured scorn on my mother's head and mine, while they slept with the suitors, shall not die cleanly."

Homer, *Odyssey*, 22.462–464

TOPIC REVIEW

You should be able to:

1. Describe:
   - an outline of the events of Books 9, 10, 21, 22 and 23 of the *Odyssey*
   - how the order of the events in the book differs from the chronological order in which they occurred
   - the methods by which the *Odyssey* was composed
   - common features of oral poetry such as epithets, similes and formulae
   - other storytelling techniques used by Homer.

2. Explain:
   - what is meant by oral poetry and epic poetry
   - how the order of events in the poem affects our appreciation of the story
   - how common features of oral poetry add to our understanding and enjoyment of the text
   - how Homer's storytelling techniques add to our understanding and enjoyment of the text
   - what makes a particular passage interesting, dramatic or exciting.

PRACTICE QUESTIONS

Source A: Homer, *Odyssey*, 9.382–388

"They held the sharpened olivewood stake, and thrust it into his eye, while I threw my weight on the end, and twisted it round and round, as a man bores the timbers of a ship with a drill that others twirl lower down with a strap held at both ends, and so keep the drill continuously moving. We took the red-hot stake and twisted it round and round like that in his eye, and the blood poured out despite the heat."

1. How does this simile help us to understand the situation better at this point of the *Odyssey*? Make **two** points with references to the text. [4]

2. a. Give **two** details about the quality of the wine that Polyphemus is given. [2]

   b. Why is the quality of the wine important? [1]

2.6 Themes

There are several key themes that occur throughout the *Odyssey*. Many of these concern values that we are very familiar with today, such as revenge and justice. Others, like having to live away from home (as is the case for refugees) are things that are often in the news.

XENIA (GUEST-FRIENDSHIP)

Odysseus is in a very difficult situation in Books 9 and 10: he is hit by a storm, and soon his boats get lost. Hotels did not exist at this time, and he is forced to depend on the hospitality that strangers might offer for food and accommodation if he is to survive.

> **xenia** in Homer, hospitality given unconditionally to a traveller, involving the giving of any help needed; known as 'guest-friendship'

The Greeks had a solution to this problem that would encourage hosts to help visitors. They believed in a custom called **xenia**, where travellers would be given a bed, food and other help for as long as they needed it.

MODERN PARALLEL

It is very rare today that a complete stranger would turn up at a house and be given any form of hospitality, but there are ways in which people today show generosity to those in need. Food banks help many people survive who are in difficult situations. Odysseus too is given food when he desperately needs it on many occasions in the *Odyssey*.

When the traveller wanted to leave, he could be given help for the next stage of his journey, and possibly a leaving present. If the stranger were able, he would give something in return to the host. This was such an important idea in the ancient world that the Greeks decided that Zeus was the god who was in charge of this arrangement. As Odysseus said, when he met Polyphemus:

"Good sir, do not refuse us: respect the gods. We are suppliants and Zeus protects visitors and suppliants, Zeus the god of guests, who follows the steps of sacred travellers."

Homer, *Odyssey*, 9.269–271

Study questions

1 How does Odysseus try to persuade Polyphemus to give him hospitality?
2 Why do you think the Greeks might have made Zeus the god of hospitality?

Such reasoned arguments have no influence over a monster like Polyphemus, who does not follow the normal behaviour of the Greeks. We are not expecting him to follow the custom of xenia, because as soon as he spotted the men, he asked who they were. A key component of the custom of xenia was that you did not ask your questions to your guests before deciding whether to give them help.

Thankfully for Odysseus, other characters are far more helpful. The first example Odysseus experiences of good xenia is given in Book 10 by Aeolus, who fed Odysseus and his crew for a whole month and then gave a gift of a bag of winds to get them home. However, when Odysseus came back a second time, Aeolus refused to help again.

After his travels, Odysseus turned up at his own palace, disguised as a beggar by Athena. The custom of xenia demanded that he should be given help. Indeed, there was already a beggar in the palace whom Odysseus is made to fight as the suitors are only willing to assist one of them. The help that is offered should be unconditional, and not dependent on proving your strength or providing entertainment. The suitors even feel that the food they give, together with the opportunity merely to hear their conversation, should be enough for the beggar.

Study questions

1 Why does Aeolus refuse to help Odysseus when he comes back for a second time? Is he right to do so?
2 Why do you think Odysseus does not get home at this point in his journey?

As we would expect, Penelope is a perfect hostess. After she hears the beggar tell his false tale in Book 19, she offers him a bed, a bath and a seat with Telemachus at breakfast. In Book 21 she says that if he can string the bow, she will give him generous gifts and help him get to his next destination. She realises the importance of helping others when she says:

"But the fame of a good man, with a kind heart, his guests spread far and wide among men, and people sing his praise."

Homer, *Odyssey*, 19.332–334

ACTIVITY

Copy out and complete the table to show which characters offer xenia and which characters do not.

	Food offered	Bath given	Questions asked	Gifts offered
Aeolus	Fed for a month, presumably on the delicacies and roast meat that Aeolus and his family ate	We are not told	Odysseus is questioned on everything about Troy and his journey	A bag of winds when Odysseus leaves the first time, but nothing the second time.
Polyphemus				
Circe				
Penelope				

In some cases, characters offer xenia in a distorted way. In Book 10, the Lotus-eaters had no intention of harming Odysseus, and gave lotus as a gift to the crew. However, the lotus caused the crew members to forget about their home and wish to remain on the island. Circe too offers those who visit her something to eat, but this turns out to change Odysseus' men into pigs. However, when Odysseus proves to be immune to her magic, she turns out to be much more hospitable, entertaining the men for a year. Polyphemus' 'gift' of eating Odysseus last in Book 9 is hardly a gift at all, and shows a total disregard for the concept of xenia.

DECEIT AND TRICKERY

Odysseus was admired in the ancient world for his trickery and lies, and the *Odyssey* is full of examples of him not telling the truth. Indeed, it is impossible to separate truth from reality in the tales of Books 9 and 10 as we only have Odysseus' account of what happened, and he was famous for telling lies. His lies were often told with a view to gaining sympathy or help, and as such might be seen as necessary.

Some of the clearest examples of deceit and trickery come during Odysseus' time in Ithaca. He is turned into a beggar on his arrival by Athena, and he keeps up this pretence until he strings the bow. He even lies to his own wife about where he is from, even claiming to have met Odysseus. His tale makes Penelope weep, which in turn affects Odysseus:

But though Odysseus pitied his wife's distress, he gazed steadily from beneath eyelids that might have been made of horn or iron, and deceitfully repressed his tears.

Homer, *Odyssey*, 19.209–212

ACTIVITY

Have a discussion with a partner as to whether or not Odysseus is right to not reveal his identity to Penelope at this point, taking different sides of the argument. Write down the arguments that each person gives.

Perhaps the most famous examples of Odysseus' trickery come during his encounter with Polyphemus in Book 9. He lies about what has happened to his ship to prevent Polyphemus destroying it and finding the rest of his crew. Moreover, he is proud of having spotted Polyphemus' attempt to trick him with his questions. He goes on to state his name is Nobody, which results in the other Cyclopes not going to help Polyphemus later in the story. They logically think that if Nobody has blinded him, then he must not need any help.

But it is not just Odysseus that uses deception. Penelope proves a match for him in her tricking of the suitors. We are told in Book 19 that she put off marriage to one of them for years by saying she would only get married when she had finished a funeral shroud for Odysseus' father. Each night she would unpick the work that she had done during the day. This went on for several years until she was caught by her disloyal maids. Even though the trick did not work out, it bought her just enough time to delay her marriage until Odysseus arrived back home.

CIVILISATION AND BARBARISM

One important feature of civilisation that has been mentioned before is the giving of xenia (see pages 209–211). In the same way, those who do not give xenia can be regarded as barbaric. But there is more to characters being civilised than simply whether they give hospitality or not.

The Greeks would have been as horrified as we are today with the idea of eating people. Polyphemus and the Laestrygonians both eat crew members, and Polyphemus does so with the raw savagery of a lion, having bashed his victims' heads on the ground first. The Laestrygonians are no better as they carry off their helpless victims like fish on a spear.

The Laestrygonians' behaviour might come as more of a shock as we are not led to believe they are barbaric when the crew first meet them in Book 10:

Once ashore, they found a well-worn track down which wagons carried wood to the city from the mountain heights. Near the citadel they came across a girl drawing water, the sturdy daughter of Laestrygonian Antiphates.

Homer, *Odyssey*, 10.103–106

Aside from living in a community, with a reasonable transport system and a ruler who has a palace, they also have an assembly-place. These are all hallmarks of a civilised place, but are overshadowed by the behaviour of the population. Similarly, the skills that Polyphemus shows as a farmer, another sign of civilisation, do not compensate for his brutality.

The Cyclopes in Book 9, as a race, show a lack of civilisation. They have no assembly meetings to help the inhabitants rule in harmony, no laws or communities. To the Greeks,

FIGURE 2.45
Odysseus' men meet the daughter of Antiphates, the Laestrygonian, 1st century BC, fresco, now in the Vatican Museum, Rome. Note the fine jug she holds and her elegant clothing, signs of her civilisation. She appears very tall, even accounting for the slope.

who prided themselves on community life, this must have appeared shocking and primitive. What makes the Cyclopes' lack of civilisation worse is that they had everything they needed for a perfect life. There was a neighbouring island with a seemingly limitless supply of goats. Their island could support agriculture, if only the Cyclopes could be bothered to farm it. The natural, almost magical harbour, could have been perfect for trading opportunities, but the Cyclopes had no contact with any other community and did not bother to make ships. In some respects, they might be simply regarded as independent farmers, but that is not how the Greeks would see it. The people of Homer's time and Odysseus' age had strong trade links and were seafaring people, and would expect any civilised character to be the same.

Ithaca is a far more civilised place; it has a fine palace and command structure, although that seems to have collapsed in the absence of Odysseus; having slaves with clearly defined duties (such as the slaves who look after the swine, cattle and goats) and feasts are things that the Greeks would have expected in their ruling classes; the presence of the bard, Phemius, shows the people value music and song; Penelope also conforms

S & C The Phaeacians are another society in the *Odyssey* which is very civilised. They have a monarchy and decisions are made in a council. Their queen, Arete, can settle disputes, and a princess, Nausicaa, follows all the expected patterns of a good Greek woman, as she is modest, concerned about her reputation and does the traditional female task of washing clothes. They respect the gods, are fine sailors and sportsmen, and are ultimately very hospitable to Odysseus. Find out more about Nausicaa and the Phaeacians by reading Books 6–8 of the *Odyssey*.

to expected Greek standards of behaviour in weaving, which was seen as something a good Greek wife should do.

REVENGE AND JUSTICE

From the moment that Odysseus reveals his name to Polyphemus in Book 9, his crew are doomed to die at sea, and Odysseus is doomed to return to a palace in turmoil. Polyphemus curses Odysseus by raising his hands and praying to the god Poseidon at the end of the book, and as Poseidon is his father, the curse comes true. At the time of the curse, the suitors had not invaded Odysseus' palace, and so we are meant to think that Odysseus brings all his troubles on himself. That is not to say that the crew should not take responsibility for their actions. They have brought about their own downfall by eating sacred cattle in Book 12.

Attitudes to revenge have changed very much over the centuries. Many religions now advise forgiveness and not harming your enemies, but the Greeks would generally not have shared these ideas. The gods regularly punished humans for their wrong-doing, and there was even a goddess of revenge, **Nemesis**, whose name meant revenge in Greek.

> **nemesis** the concept of revenge

Odysseus' and Telemachus' punishments of the maids and suitors would probably not have been questioned by the ancient Greeks. Even begging for forgiveness, as happened with the priest Leodes in Book 22, does not save his life. The severity of the punishments reflect the severity of the wrong-doings.

Eurcyleia felt like crying out in triumph at the death of the Suitors, but Odysseus stops her, saying it is wicked to gloat. To him, the suitors deserved to die, but it is no cause for celebration. He feels that he is acting with justice and divine right, not with feelings of revenge.

However, in the case of Melanthius, the goat-herd, it might be argued that the punishment goes beyond what could be classed as mere revenge. He is subjected to a horrific death in having his nose and ears cut off, and his genitals are ripped away to be fed to the dogs. No doubt such a key slave should be loyal to the ruling family, but the anger of Telemachus and the loyal slaves is clear when Homer says:

> . . . lopped off his hands and feet in their deep anger.

> Homer, *Odyssey*, 22.477

Likewise, it is not enough that the disloyal maids merely die, as Telemachus declares before hanging them that he is unwilling to give them a decent death. The epithet given to Telemachus before he hangs them is 'wise'. This suggests that he has carefully considered the best course of action under the circumstances.

> ### Study questions
>
> 1 Why do Odysseus and Telemachus kill all the suitors and disloyal slaves?
> 2 Are they right in giving these punishments?
> 3 Do you think an ancient Greek would have shared your views?
> 4 Do Odysseus and Telemachus behave like tyrants in deciding punishments?

NOSTOS

Nostos is the name given to the desire to return home, and is the root of our word nostalgia, which literally means 'the pain felt from missing home'. It is essential for Odysseus to have this goal permanently in his mind to keep him focused on the journey he is undertaking, but things are never simple for him.

nostos the desire to return to your homeland

In Book 10, the Lotus-eaters may seem harmless, but the danger they present is as great as any monster or witch that Odysseus could face. The easy life that their island offers could be tempting, but at this point his desire to return home is strong and so he overcomes the threat relatively easily. His nostos remains fairly powerful when he is hit by a storm after his men open the bag of winds, as he decides to endure the storm rather than fight, although he did have a moment's hesitation in wondering whether to jump overboard and drown himself.

Later on in the book his determination can be questioned when his men have to ask him to leave Circe's island after spending a year there. When he is told near the end of Book 10 that he has to venture to the underworld, he again feels like giving up. Later in his journey, Odysseus is trapped on the nymph Calypso's island for seven years, and seems to have given up hope of his home before the gods arrange his release. This story is told in Book 5.

FATE

We might always feel that Odysseus is bound to get home and reclaim his kingdom, but this is not what is meant by fate. Many Greeks believed that key events in your life were pre-arranged by the actions of the gods, and this does seem to happen to a degree in the *Odyssey*. The key evidence for this occurs in the curse that Polyphemus delivers as Odysseus sails away from his island:

> "If he is destined to see his friends and his fine house in his own country, may he come there late and in sore distress, in another's ship, losing all comrades, and let him find great trouble in his house."
>
> Homer, *Odyssey*, 9.532–535

This all ends up coming true:

- It takes him ten years to get home.
- He suffers hugely on his journey, losing everything.
- All his men die (as told in Books 9–12).
- He gets to Ithaca in a boat provided by the Phaeacians.
- The suitors are competing to marry his wife and are plotting to kill his son.

However, it is important to distinguish between what is fate, and what are the actions of the gods. The gods do ensure that fate happens (such as when Zeus kills the remnants of the crew in Book 12 for eating sacred cattle), but just because they act at other times, this is not usually connected with fate.

Similarly, characters have to take responsibility for their actions. Could Elpenor blame his death in Book 10 on the curse of Polyphemus, or was it due to his own foolishness and drunkenness. Others die as a result of mistakes they or Odysseus make. At other times we are told what will happen to characters: we are told in Book 21 that Antinous will be the first suitor to die before the contest even started. However, this is not the same thing as him being fated to die.

TOPIC REVIEW

You should be able to:

1. Describe:
   - occasions when Odysseus is given or refused xenia
   - situations where Odysseus and other characters use trickery or deceit
   - barbaric or civilised features in the locations and characters of the Odyssey
   - the ways in which Odysseus seeks justice and gains revenge over the suitors and his attitude to his slaves
   - instances where Odysseus shows a strong desire, or a lack of desire, to return home
   - parts of the story where fated events occur.

2. Explain:
   - what is meant by the concept of xenia
   - why trickery and deceit were acceptable and what they reveal about characters
   - why having certain features made locations and characters civilised or barbaric
   - why Odysseus is keen to gain revenge, and how his actions would have been regarded
   - the importance of the homeland and fame to a hero
   - whether fate is the sole factor in determining what happens to characters.

PRACTICE QUESTIONS

Source A: Homer, *Odyssey*, 22.461–473

Then wise Telemachus spoke: 'These women who poured scorn on my mother's head and mine, while they slept with the suitors, shall not die cleanly.'

So saying, he took a cable from a dark-prowed ship, tied it to a tall pillar, high-up, and noosed it over the round house, so that their feet would not reach the ground. The row of women held up their heads, and the rope was looped round their necks so they might die pitiably, like long-winged thrushes or doves, that are caught in a snare as they try to roost in their thicket, and are welcomed to a grimmer nest. For a little while their feet twitched: but not for long.

1. Do you feel any sympathy for the fates of Odysseus' disloyal slaves? Use the passage as a starting point and explain your answer. [8]
2. How civilised are the places that Odysseus visits on his way home to Ithaca? Explain your answer. [15]

2.7 The Character of Odysseus

TOPIC OVERVIEW

- The qualities of Odysseus as a leader, husband and father
- The presentation of him as a warrior and hero
- His intelligence and oratorical skills
- His relationship with Athena

The prescribed source for this topic is:

- Homer's *Odyssey*, Books 9, 10, 19, 21, 22

Don't forget that you will be given credit in the exam if you study extra sources and make relevant use of them in your answers.

Odysseus is a very complex character. At times he seems considerate of others, heroic and intelligent, but at other points he seems selfish, weak and foolish. He makes mistakes in the story, but whether you lose sympathy for him is a very personal matter. It is the contradictions in his character that are at the heart of your study of him, and made him such a fascinating character for the Greeks.

To many modern readers, Odysseus is a womaniser. He seems to love his wife truly and be desperate to be with her, but he also has sex with Circe in Book 10 (and with another goddess Calypso earlier in the *Odyssey*). Is he simply thinking that he can get away with his unfaithfulness? Is he too weak to resist temptation when it is offered? As often, it is not as obvious as it may seem.

In the first case Hermes advises him of how he must deal with Circe:

"When Circe strikes you with her length of wand, draw your sharp sword and rush at her, as if you intend to kill her. She will be seized with fear. Then she'll invite you to her bed, and don't refuse the goddess' favours, if you want her to free your men, and care for you too."

PS

Homer, *Odyssey*, 10.293–298

So it seems Odysseus has no choice in the matter and is forced to sleep with Circe. To refuse her, and go against Hermes' orders, would have been extremely foolish. Homer

FIGURE 2.46
Marble head of Odysseus, 1st century AD, National Archaeological Museum, Sperlonga, Italy.

kleos the glorious reputation a Homeric warrior hopes to win

FIGURE 2.47
Odysseus threatens Circe, with Circe's 'animals' looking on, 4th century BC, sarcophagus, Claudio Faina Museum, Orvieto, Italy.

S & C To understand fully Odysseus' relationships with women, read Book 5 to see him with Calypso. Odysseus is described as a 'cold lover' and it seems he gets little pleasure from sleeping with her.

does not tell us if he sleeps with her after this occasion, but he does stay for a year and so it does seem highly probable. He certainly slept with Calypso many times during his seven-year stay.

Moreover, to sleep with a goddess would make him more heroic to the ancient Greeks, as goddesses would not usually sleep with mere mortals. This would increase his fame, or **kleos** as the Greeks called it. Heroes aspired to everlasting fame, and as books did not exist at the time, the only way to achieve this was to ensure that people would talk about you after your death. Odysseus achieved this kind of immortality through his actions, and sleeping with goddesses was one of the things that created his fame.

In Homeric times, it was a key role for a father to provide instruction and inspiration for his son, and Odysseus does all he can to be a good role model. He gives clear instructions to Telemachus about removing the weapons from the hall, even telling him plausible words to say to the suitors to stop their suspicions. The pair of them work together as a team to remove the items, before Telemachus goes to bed on the instruction of his father.

The clearest signs of Odysseus giving his son guidance are in the battle in Book 22. They decide together on Telemachus getting more weapons, and on the strategy for fighting the suitors. When the carnage is complete, Telemachus goes off to fetch Eurycleia when Odysseus tells him to.

Throughout the books that you read in the *Odyssey*, Odysseus always has people to lead: he leads his crew in his journey home in Books 9 and 10; he leads his son and slaves in the preparations for the battle in the hall in Books 19 and 21; and finally he leads them in the battle itself in Book 22. We might expect a great king like Odysseus to show perfect leadership, but this is not always the case, especially during his adventures in Books 9 and 10. Also remember that Odysseus is telling us this part of the story, so he might put a particular spin on the tales to make himself look better.

Odysseus has a very mixed relationship with his crew. At many points in the story the crew do exactly as he says, showing obedience and trust in him as a leader. When he tells them to leave the land of the Lotus-eaters in Book 9, his men immediately obey, and he gets no opposition from his plan to sail over to the island of the Cyclopes later in the book.

The blinding of Polyphemus shows Odysseus and his men working as a team. It is Odysseus that comes up with the plan, but he gives his men specific tasks like smoothing the wood and driving it into Polyphemus' eye. Similarly, the men on his ship obey him when he tells them to sail away from the Laestrygonians in Book 10.

As any good leader should, Odysseus tries to provide for his men. He achieves seemingly superhuman feats, such as killing a huge stag in Book 10 and managing to drag it back single-handedly to his crew on Circe's island. He realises the importance of feeding his men too, when the men eat the flocks of Polyphemus shortly after escaping under them.

In general, Odysseus comes across as a fair leader, even if his crew might disagree with this idea at certain points in the story. The first glimpse of Odysseus with his crew in your reading is in Book 9, on the island of the Cicones, where Odysseus says:

> "I sacked the city and slew the men, and the women and riches we split
> between us, so that as far as I could determine no man lacked an equal share."
>
> Homer, *Odyssey*, 9.40–42

He also divides up evenly the flocks that they steal from Polyphemus later on in the book. Clearly, he could not eat all the animals himself and his men do need feeding, so we would hardly expect him to do anything else. Even these acts do not stop his men being suspicious about him keeping treasure for himself when they leave Aeolus' island in the next book, but there is little evidence in the text to support their view in other stories that Odysseus is greedy.

Odysseus is often quite sensible in what he does when he gets to a new island. If it is clear that he needs to fight, as is the case in the city of the Cicones in Book 9, then all his men get involved and a battle occurs. If there is no immediate sign of danger, he sends a group to investigate. At the lands of the Lotus-eaters and Laestrygonians, in Books 9 and 10, he sends two men and a messenger or herald to do this and report back (see Figure 2.45 on p. 213). On the island of Polyphemus, where he has only taken his boat across, he selects his twelve best men, whilst on Circe's island, lots are drawn to see whether his group or Eurylochus' should investigate.

THE PRESENTATION OF ODYSSEUS AS A WARRIOR AND HERO

Odysseus shows himself to be a traditional Greek hero on a number of occasions. The Greeks would regard a hero as someone who defeats his enemy in a battle, so it is significant he achieves this the first time we see him with his whole crew at the land of the Cicones.

On this occasion there is no investigative group sent, nor any attempt to gain xenia. It is the idea of 'might is right', where the victory justifies the means that is used to achieve it.

Moreover, when Polyphemus spots Odysseus in his cave, he immediately asks him:

> "Where do you sail from over the sea-roads? Are you on business, or do
> you roam at random, like pirates who chance their lives to bring evil to
> others?"
>
> Homer, *Odyssey*, 9.252–255

FIGURE 2.48
Odysseus and his men work together to blind Polyphemus, 6th century BC, black-figure water-jar, now in National Etruscan Museum of the Villa Giulia, Rome.

Study questions

1 How would you describe Odysseus' feelings for Circe? Should we ignore, excuse or criticise his affairs?

2 What is the significance of Odysseus being allotted the great ram by his crew?

3 Do you think Odysseus was right to send just three of his crew to the Lotus-eaters and Laestrygonians?

4 Look again at the quotation on p. 219. How do you feel about Odysseus' attitude to his victory and achievement?

ACTIVITY

The trial of Odysseus

Imagine Odysseus has been put on trial for being a bad leader and guilty for the deaths of his men. Act out a trial, with people taking the role of the characters of Books 9 and 10, and Odysseus himself. You will also need a prosecution, defence and judge. Will you find Odysseus guilty or not? You could also read Book 12 and find out a bit more about his leadership of the crew.

MODERN PARALLEL

Women and children are still today innocent victims in human conflict situations. In 2014 an extremist group in Nigeria, Boko Haram, kidnapped 276 girls from a school in Chibok. Their leader at the time declared that he intended to sell the girls into slavery, and he later declared that they had been 'married'. Odysseus' behaviour towards the women of the Cicones might be regarded by some as similar, as he takes prisoners from their homeland to use as he sees fit.

ACTIVITY

With a partner, improvise a scene between Odysseus and Penelope. One of you should take the role of Odysseus and explain your relationship with Circe, and the other should take the role of Penelope, saying what you think about Odysseus' behaviour.

In Homer's other work, the *Iliad*, Greek warriors regularly plunder towns near Troy, killing men and taking the women as slaves, and this was seen as normal behaviour at the time. Indeed, Odysseus seems rather proud of doing such a thing to the Cicones in Book 9. Today, piracy has been eliminated from most parts of the world as we see it as unacceptable, but as recently as 2013, pirates captured other ships off the coast of Somalia in Africa, taking the people on board as hostages.

The ancient Greeks would almost certainly have felt admiration for Odysseus for his defeat of the suitors, as they had behaved in an arrogant, greedy and threatening manner in the palace. If Odysseus had not fought them, there is every chance that he would have been killed by them. The opening lines of Book 22, where Odysseus throws off his rags and leaps on to the threshold, reveal a brave and determined hero, and in the battle that follows, he and his men defeat a force of 108 men by a combination of skill and strength.

ODYSSEUS' INTELLIGENCE AND ORATORICAL SKILLS

In the ancient world, Odysseus was most famous for his speaking skills and his clever plans, and your selection of books shows these. There are several occasions where Odysseus gets himself out of trouble with a clever speech. The most famous of these is with Polyphemus in Book 9. When confronted with Polyphemus, Odysseus is the only one who has the courage to answer his questions when the men are spotted, and his answers are designed to make Polyphemus both respect and fear them. In mentioning being part of the victorious Greek forces, Polyphemus should be in awe of them. Odysseus then goes on to tactfully remind Polyphemus of his obligations by reminding them of the rules of hospitality (see the quotation on p. 210).

Later, when Polyphemus tries to get Odysseus to tell him about the rest of his fleet, Odysseus realises a trap that is being laid for him, and convincingly lies about what has happened to his boat. When he gets back to Ithaca, Odysseus is also very careful about what he says. When he speaks to his wife in Book 19, he compliments her fame, and goes on to very tactfully request that she does not ask him about his troubles. He is asked a little later in the book to recount how he (as the beggar) spent time with Odysseus, and then he gives a very detailed story, managing to give Penelope hope by mixing in true facts about Odysseus' appearance and clothing with the lies.

His intelligence is further shown in the events leading up to the battle when he asks his loyal slaves in Book 21 how they would feel about fighting for Odysseus. He is not prepared to reveal his identity until he has very firm support from them. He then goes on to casually request a go at stringing the bow, which would normally be seen as outrageous. Unsurprisingly, the suitors do take offence, but Odysseus convinces Penelope that he is only doing it to test out his strength and has no desire to marry her.

There is no doubt that Odysseus can be a very proud and confident individual. It is a fine line between confidence and arrogance, and you have to decide for yourself which side of the line Odysseus is on at times, such as when he tells Alcinous about himself at the start of Book 9 (see the quotation on p. 200).

Sometimes you might question Odysseus' intelligence. When Polyphemus drank three bowls full of Odysseus' wine, Odysseus refers to him as a fool and he calls him an idiot for not realising they were escaping under the flocks. He also laughs to himself at how the plan of his false name has worked, and goes on to reveal his name during his escape. This is foolish as it allows Polyphemus to be able to identify who has blinded him to Poseidon.

What Odysseus does not say can help us to form opinions of him. When his men are upset by Odysseus' plain assessment of the situation after feasting on arrival on Circe's island in Book 9, Odysseus' reaction is emotionless:

> They groaned aloud, and wept great tears. But all their lamentation did no good.
>
> Homer, *Odyssey*, 10.201–202

The men react similarly later in the book to the news of their journey to the underworld, with the same lack of comfort given by Odysseus. He had burst into tears when he heard the news and felt suicidal briefly, before pulling himself together. He is tough with his men, and here again it is up to you to decide if you think his approach is right.

ODYSSEUS' RELATIONSHIP WITH ATHENA

Athena is the main source of divine help for Odysseus. This is perhaps not surprising as she is the goddess of wisdom, and Odysseus is a hero who is famed for this quality.

If Athena had not changed Odysseus' appearance into that of a beggar, he would surely have been killed in Ithaca by the suitors before he had a chance to kill them. She helps Odysseus in the battle in the hall, by making the suitors' spears miss and by scaring them when she raises her aegis (a goatskin cloak which was her symbol). During the battle, Homer writes:

Study question

If you were in Odysseus' situation when he is questioned by Polyphemus, what would you have done?

Study questions

1 How do you feel about Odysseus' gloating about his success over Polyphemus?
2 Odysseus stops Eurycleia from gloating over the death of the suitors. Is he right to do so, especially when he gloated over the blinding of Polyphemus?

Study question

Does Odysseus come across as too uncaring towards the sufferings of his men?

Study questions

Odysseus does not mention any help that Athena gave him in Books 9 and 10, although he is in many life and death situations.

1 Why do you think this is the case?
2 If Athena deliberately chose not to help Odysseus, why do you think this was so?

Yet despite her words she still withheld from him the power to determine the course of the fight, and continued to test the strength and courage of Odysseus and his noble son.

Homer, *Odyssey*, 22.236–258

This enables us to feel that Odysseus has really earned his victory, rather than being gifted it by the gods.

TOPIC REVIEW

You should be able to:

1. Describe:
   - situations where Odysseus shows good leadership and fighting skills
   - situations where Odysseus shows weaknesses as a leader or hero
   - what Odysseus says to Penelope in Book 19, and what he does with Telemachus during, and after, the battle in the hall
   - parts of the story where Odysseus shows intelligence or an ability to speak effectively
   - instances where Athena appears in the story.

2. Explain:
   - why you might conclude that Odysseus shows good leadership and fighting skills in particular stories
   - why you might conclude Odysseus is a poor leader on occasions
   - how his relationships with Penelope and Telemachus should be regarded
   - what makes Odysseus an effective speaker and a man of intelligence
   - why Athena appears in some of the stories.

PRACTICE QUESTIONS

Source A: Homer, *Odyssey*, 19.172–189

'Out in the wine-dark sea lies a land called Crete, a rich and lovely island. It is filled with countless people, in ninety cities. They are not of one language, but speak several tongues. There are Achaeans there, and brave native Cretans, Cydonians, three races of Dorians, and noble Pelasgians too. One of the ninety cities is mighty Cnossus, where Minos ruled, and every nine years spoke with mighty Zeus. He was brave Deucalion's father, and so my grandfather. Deucalion had two sons, Lord Idomeneus and me. Idomeneus, my older brother, and a better man than I, sailed with the sons of Atreus in the curved ships to Ilium, so I the younger, Aethon is my name, was left behind, there to meet and entertain Odysseus. The wind had driven him to Crete as he headed for Troy, and blew him off course by Cape Malea. He anchored at Amnisus, a tricky harbour, near the cave of Eileithyia, and barely escaped shipwreck.'

1. How does Odysseus show himself to be a good storyteller in this passage? Make two points, giving evidence from the passage. [4]

2. Why does Odysseus feel he needs to tell this tale to Penelope at this point in the *Odyssey*? [3]

2.8 The Portrayal of Key Characters

TOPIC OVERVIEW

The portrayal of key characters

- The role of the gods
- The portrayal of the suitors
- The portrayal of the crew of Odysseus
- The portrayal of Polyphemus as a monster and keeper of livestock
- The portrayal of Circe as a witch and host
- The portrayal of Penelope as a host, wife and queen
- The portrayal of Telemachus as a son and hero
- The loyalty of Odysseus' slaves

The prescribed source for this topic is:

- Homer's *Odyssey*, Books 9, 10, 19, 21, 22

Don't forget that you will be given credit in the exam if you study extra sources and make relevant use of them in your answers.

There are numerous other key characters in the *Odyssey*, apart from Odysseus himself. Many of them make life very difficult for him, but there are a similar number that try to help him in his missions. In this section, you will find out more about some of these characters.

THE ROLE OF THE GODS

The gods and goddesses of the *Odyssey* are an intriguing set of characters. Zeus is the god who has the ultimate control over the action, and is held responsible (at least by Odysseus) for some of the problems on the journey. He claimed that the Cicones fought back in Book 9 as Zeus wanted the men to suffer, and just a few lines later he also blames him for the storm which drove the crew off course. This might reflect the typical view of the Greeks in trying to ascribe to the gods events for which they could not find a

KEY INDIVIDUAL

Zeus king of the gods. He has a key role as the god most associated with justice and xenia, and has the final say in the fate of Odysseus and his crew

S & C Some scholars have said that Homer's gods behave like humans.

What do you think is meant by this statement? To what extent do you agree with it?

KEY INDIVIDUALS

the suitors a group of 108 men who wish to marry Odysseus' wife Penelope. They set up permanent residency in Odysseus' palace, abusing the royal family's hospitality and its slaves

rational cause. Zeus is definitely responsible for the storm that killed the crew of Odysseus' boat as a punishment for eating the cattle of the Sun-god, an event referred to in Book 19.

However, he can be equally helpful to Odysseus; as the god most associated with justice, he gives a thunderclap of approval to encourage Odysseus when he strings the bow at the end of Book 21.

Other gods are involved at several points in the story. The goddess Circe has a pivotal role in the story and will be discussed separately, and Athena also features prominently (see pages. 221–222). Hermes too has a minor, but crucial, role in helping Odysseus avoid Circe's magic in Book 10 by giving him the antidote to her drugs.

THE SUITORS

It is difficult to say much that is positive about the suitors: for years they have been pressurising a woman, who is still convinced that her husband is alive, to marry one of them; they seem to have set up camp in the palace; they give orders to the royal family and have sexual intercourse with some of Odysseus' female slaves; they consume food and drink that is not theirs; they plan to murder Telemachus earlier in the story and Telemachus says in Book 2 that they would kill Odysseus if he came back; and they treat the beggar appallingly.

Their ringleader is Antinous. He makes several of the key suggestions in the contest of the bow, such as who should try first, and later proposes a postponement in the contest, both of which the other suitors agree to. He even suggests they can sacrifice some of Odysseus' own flocks to Apollo. He attacks Eumaeus and Philoetius for crying when handing over the bow in Book 21, calling them 'snivelling peasants'. When Odysseus asks for a go, he is threatened with violence by Antinous. Antinous even throws his weight about with the other suitors, abusing Leodes in Book 21 for his weakness and saying the other suitors are better than him at stringing bows.

EXAM TIP

If you are asked why the gods are interesting characters, do not simply state how they help and hinder Odysseus. This will not score highly on AO1 as you will not be showing a full understanding of their roles. Their help towards Odysseus is only one aspect of the issue. Think also about:

- how they are like humans
- their superhuman powers and use of magic
- how they choose to interact with each other and Odysseus. Do they appear in their usual form or disguise? Do they choose to help Odysses or not? If not, what does this show about them?

Eurymachus is the second most important suitor. He seems particularly concerned about his reputation, which is rather ironic as he seems to do everything he can to destroy it by his actions:

> "It's not that I'm bothered about the marriage, though it grieves me. There are plenty of other women in Achaea, in Ithaca's isle, and in other places. No, it's more that our strength falls so short of godlike Odysseus' that we can't even string his bow. It's a disgrace that posterity will hear of."

> Homer, *Odyssey*, 21.251–255

His speech suggests he is more interested in the status of being king, than any genuine feelings for Penelope, or else perhaps he is just trying to appear less bothered at his weakness. He also will do whatever it takes to get out of a tight spot, blaming all the suitors' actions near the start of Book 22 on the dead Antinous. He later attempts to make amends by raising money from taxing the people for all they have eaten and drunk in the palace. This would enable him to keep his wealth and further show his power over people.

One other suitor deserves a special mention: Leodes the priest seems a little out of place with the rest of the suitors. He is certainly no archer, and is the only one to beg Odysseus for mercy in Book 22, claiming to have tried to stop the suitors from their villainy. We see no evidence of this in the story, and so could feel that Odysseus' killing of him is as justified as any of the other suitors. In fact, as a religious figure, some might feel that he should have been more able than anyone to see the wrongs in his actions.

Study question
Who is the worst of the suitors? Explain your answer.

ODYSSEUS' CREW

Odysseus' crew, rather like the suitors, are a group with a leading individual, while the rest of the men are largely anonymous. This is perhaps not too surprising as there were around six hundred men at the start, fifty on each of twelve boats. Six from each boat get killed on the island of the Cicones, with a further six men in total falling victim to Polyphemus. Later the men from all the boats except his own die in the harbour of the Laestrygonians. Elpenor is the final crew member to die in the prescribed books, leaving Odysseus with forty-three crew members at the end of Book 10.

Eurylochus is the second in command on Odysseus' boat, and he leads the party to Circe's house in Book 10. He shows more suspicion than the rest by not entering, but you might question his leadership in allowing his fellow soldiers to go in while he waits outside. Later he is in tears when reporting the story and asks not to be taken back. Indeed, he suggests they leave the men, half of the crew at the time, with Circe on the island. This can be contrasted with Odysseus who personally drags three men back from the Lotus-eaters in the previous book.

When Odysseus wants to take the rest of the crew to Circe's house, Eurylochus says:

> "Remember how Cyclops too behaved, when our friends entered his cave with reckless Odysseus, this man through whose foolishness they died."

> Homer, *Odyssey*, 10.435–437

FIGURE 2.49
Odysseus (standing) and his men, 3rd century AD, mosaic, now in Bardo Museum, Tunis.

Whether Odysseus' reaction to this is appropriate, and whether there is some truth in the comment, it might be felt that this act of mutiny is not appropriate at a time when Odysseus is seeking to do the right thing in rescuing his men.

The crew as a whole do not always share the same viewpoint as their leader. Their decisions to stay an extra day on the island of the Cicones and to open the bag of winds both result in disaster as seventy-two men are killed in the first instance, and they are blown away from Ithaca in the second. However, they can act more sensibly than their leader, especially when they suggest not waiting for Polyphemus and trying to stop Odysseus from revealing his name. On other occasions, they follow his instructions carefully, and they are called 'loyal' by Odysseus in his adventures with Polyphemus and the Lotus-eaters.

POLYPHEMUS AS A MONSTER AND KEEPER OF LIVESTOCK

The man-eating giant is a standard element of folk tales – think of the giant in the story of Jack and the Beanstalk. But Homer's creation of the Cyclops Polyphemus is more balanced than we might have expected.

Before even meeting him in Book 9, his cave shows an impressive level of organisation and he seems a good farmer. He knows how to make cheese, and does not just kill his animals for meat. All his animals are kept according to age in separate pens, and his vessels and bowls are full of whey (a liquid created in making cheese). He shows genuine tenderness with his flock, milking them efficiently and putting each animal with its mother, all the time leaving the males outside. The affection is shown even more clearly when he talks to the large ram under which Odysseus is clinging, saying:

"My fine ram, why leave the cave like this last of the flock?"

Homer, *Odyssey*, 9.447–448

However, this speech also shows Polyphemus' brutal side, when just seconds later he says he wishes to splatter Odysseus' brains. It is this contradiction in his character that makes him so fascinating.

Perhaps the most brutal part of the story is where Polyphemus kills the first two crew members. See p. 206 for a full analysis of this scene.

His uncivilised nature is shown in numerous other ways in the story:

- He lives alone in a cave, and has no contact with his neighbours, the other Cyclopes.
- He drinks milk rather than wine as a normal drink.
- He thinks his race is better than that of the gods (even though Zeus is an uncle).
- He has no respect for xenia, and makes a mockery of it by his 'gift' of eating Odysseus last.
- He traps the men in the cave.

- Dung is in heaps in his cave.
- He gets drunk too easily and falls for Odysseus' trap.

As Odysseus says, perhaps with a touch of desperation:

> "why would anyone on earth ever visit you again, when you behave so badly?"

> Homer, *Odyssey*, 9.351–352

Homer has created a memorable character, in making the most monstrous individual in the book a figure whom we can also admire and be sympathetic towards.

CIRCE AS A WITCH AND HOST

Circe is a rather odd character. Despite being a goddess, she is a stereotypical ideal Greek mortal woman who weaves and sings. As such, we would expect her to be a rather powerless and gentle figure, but this is hardly the case. She is most famous for her witch-craft in turning Odysseus' men into pigs in Book 10, and has done the same to others, making them the wolves and lions who prowl about her house. Homer gives us no clue as to why she does this, and it is hard to find a reason for her doing so.

> **Study question**
> 'Circe acts like an ordinary mortal woman.' In what ways is this statement true, and in what ways is it false?

Although this is only a small part of the section in which she appears, it is the one thing that everyone remembers about her. She does go on to be the perfect hostess, giving food, a bath, clothes, lodgings, advice and gifts to Odysseus and his crew. Her hospitality is such that Odysseus stays for a year, and would probably have stayed longer had it not been for his crew's request to leave. She represents to Odysseus danger, temptation and relief from his troubles, but ultimately her contribution to Odysseus' mission is huge as she tells him to go to the underworld for advice about his journey.

PENELOPE AS A HOST, WIFE AND QUEEN

In an age where women were supposed to know their place and be supportive to their husbands, Penelope is the standard that all women in Greece (and those in mythology) were expected to match. Under immense pressure, she has held out against the suitors' imposition of marriage for three years, with all logic suggesting Odysseus has died, and custom suggesting she should remarry. As a good hostess, she is always polite and gener-ous to the suitors. You might feel she should have expelled them from her home earlier. However, a Greek woman would not have the authority to force a group of men out, and her son Telemachus is also too young at the time to make a stand.

> **KEY INDIVIDUAL**
> **Penelope** the wife of Odysseus, famed for her patience in waiting for her husband to return home from Troy

That is not to say that she does not speak her mind. When Antinous abuses Odysseus, she declares:

> "It is neither right nor just, Antinous, to deny his due to a man who came to Telemachus' house as a guest."

> Homer, *Odyssey*, 21.312–313

She speaks politely, but with firmness, putting Antinous in his place, and does similarly when Eurymachus tries to save his own reputation shortly after (see the passage on p. 225).

S & C Many scholars believe Penelope actually realises the beggar is Odysseus. They note that in Book 18 Penelope suggests for the first time that the suitors should bring her gifts. Is it a coincidence that she does this just as the beggar arrives on the scene? She suggests she might be ready to marry one of them. Odysseus is delighted by his wife's attempts to win gifts while 'her heart was set on something quite different' (18.280). Does the phrase 'quite different' really refer to her reunion with the beggar, whom she suspects is Odysseus. This is far from certain, but it is a real possibility. (Read page 246 of the *Odyssey* to see this part of the story in full.)

These scholars also tend to feel that she issues the challenge at this point, knowing only one man could do it. It is a chance for her to test Odysseus, and gives him the opportunity both to reclaim his kingdom in a blaze of glory, and get rid of the suitors. Even if she does not suspect it is Odysseus, she may set the challenge knowing none could possibly do it. This would buy her even more time, further showing her intelligence. Even when the suitors are dead, she tests the beggar's identity further in Book 23 by getting him to reveal a secret that only Odysseus would know about – how one of the posts of their bed was made from a living tree.

Study question

How does Homer suggest that Telemachus is acting reasonably in sending Penelope to her room? What does this suggest about his position in the household?

suppliant a person who begs for something from someone in a position of authority

Penelope tells him that the suitors have already damaged their reputation, and Eurymachus does not answer her back. In the end, Telemachus orders her to her room, and as he is now the leading man in the house, she obeys dutifully.

She is also generous and compassionate. When the beggar tells her his story in Book 19, she is overcome with grief, and her tears are compared to a river in full flood. She also bursts into tears when she fetches the bow in Book 21. This seems to add to her beauty, and her loyalty to Odysseus is touching. She protects Odysseus from the abuse he gets from the slave-girl Melantho in Book 19, and promises him gifts for the tale that he tells and further gifts if he can string the bow. We sympathise with her when she feels she is neglecting her guests, **suppliants** and messengers, which she declares to Odysseus after he has been abused by Melantho.

She knows what she must do, but is too grief-stricken and harassed by the suitors to fulfil her role as queen as effectively as she might wish.

She proves to be a perfect match for Odysseus. She shares his intelligence, and has managed to delay her marriage to any of the suitors for many years by her cunning ploy of unpicking a funeral shroud every night after having worked on it during the day. (It had been agreed that she would decide whom to marry when it had been completed.) Her weaving conforms to the expected behaviour of a Greek woman and she also covers her face when confronting the suitors after crying, highlighting her modesty. She sets the suitors a difficult task to complete, but one that would make them an equal of Odysseus if managed.

TELEMACHUS AS A SON AND HERO

At the time of Odysseus' return, Telemachus is at a key point in his life. He was born shortly before Odysseus left for Troy, and so is now about twenty years old, and as such is beginning to take his first tentative steps as heir to Odysseus' kingdom and reputation.

His newly found assertiveness in Book 21 largely springs from the fact that he knows who the beggar is, and that the plans to kill the suitors have been made. He puts on a show of surprise to Penelope's news of the contest, and invites the suitors to try, confident in the knowledge that none will succeed. He has the first go, after setting up the axes for the contests. Even his arch enemies, the suitors, feel a grudging admiration for how he went about his business.

When he attempted to string the bow, he nearly did it, and might well have done so if Odysseus had not stopped him in his fourth attempt. It would be an anti-climax if anyone other than Odysseus did string it, and it might have ruined the plan, but it does show him as a son in his father's image, and ready to become a great hero himself.

As the contest progresses, he continues to exert his authority:

> It was wise Telemachus who spoke to her then: "Mother, none of the Achaeans – those who rule in rocky Ithaca or in the islands seaward of the horse pastures of Elis – have more right than I to give or refuse the bow to whoever I wish."
>
> Homer, *Odyssey*, 21.343–345

All that remains for Telemachus to be a true hero is to prove himself in battle, and this he does in killing Amphinomus in Book 22. However, he shows that he still has a little bit to learn in leaping back when he hits his victim, leaving the spear in the body, although he might also be seen as sensibly cautious. He also shows his inexperience in leaving the store-room door open later in the book, but he remedies it in sending slaves to stop Melanthius getting more weapons for the suitors.

He proves himself equal to Odysseus, fighting alongside his father, and also proves himself to be his equal in dealing with those who deserve punishment, and in brutally killing the disloyal maids.

THE SLAVES' LOYALTY AND DISLOYALTY

Odysseus' slaves fall into two categories: those who are loyal and those who are not. There is no middle ground.

The loyal slaves that play a significant role in the story are the more experienced ones, and no one seems older or more experienced than Eurycleia, who has brought Odysseus up from his early years. She is the most trusted non-royal female in the palace, and Odysseus asks for her views about which female slaves have been loyal, even though in Book 19 he claimed he did not need her views to pick out the guilty ones. She is equally respected by Penelope who chooses her to wash Odysseus' feet. She is able to keep the secret of Odysseus' identity and is totally obedient to Odysseus; she locks suitors in the hall and later purifies the palace after the battle, both after requests made by him.

Odysseus' swineherd, Eumaeus, and his cowherd, Philoetius, are also very loyal. Eumaeus is the first man in Ithaca to welcome Odysseus in Book 14, and both of them are used by Odysseus and Telemachus to see to practicalities, such as passing the bow to Odysseus in

KEY INDIVIDUAL

Telemachus the son of Odysseus, who is just about ready to step into his father's position. He is strong, if inexperienced, but able to exert some authority over the suitors and household

KEY INDIVIDUALS

Eurycleia Odysseus' nurse, who recognises the beggar from a scar on his leg he gained whilst hunting

Eumaeus Odysseus' swineherd (man in charge of his pigs), who helps Odysseus in the battle both to get the bow and kill the suitors

Study question
Why else do you think that Homer chose to have Phemius spared?

Book 21 and fetching more weapons in Book 22. When the need arises, they both fight in the battle and kill suitors, and together with Telemachus, they later kill Melanthius.

Another slave worth considering is Phemius. He is spared in the aftermath of the battle as he had been an unwilling performer at the banquets of the suitors.

His survival shows that Odysseus and Telemachus are fair in distinguishing between who deserves punishment and who does not.

Homer's disloyal slaves are presented as thoroughly evil; the slave girl Melantho verbally attacks the beggar at the start of Book 19 and is presumably among the twelve maids who are hung for answering Penelope back, and the goat-herd Melanthius provides weapons for the suitors. It is worth noting that both their names come from the Greek word 'melas' that means 'black', and this colour was associated with evil in ancient Greece.

ACTIVITY

Form a group and get each individual to take a different character in the story. Make a 'Top Trumps' card for your character. Find, or draw, a picture of them and give them a score out of 100 for qualities such as strength, beauty, appearance, importance to the story and goodness. If Homer does not tell us all these details about your character, use your imagination.

Then justify the scores you gave to the rest of the group and play the game!

TOPIC REVIEW

You should be able to:

1. Describe:
   - the actions of Zeus and the other immortals in the story
   - what the suitors do in the story
   - the actions of the crew of Odysseus in Books 9 and 10
   - what Polyphemus does and says to Odysseus and his crew, and the consequences of this
   - what Circe does and says to Odysseus and his crew
   - what Penelope says to the beggar, the suitors and Telemachus, and the contest that she proposes
   - what Telemachus does leading up to, during and after the contest
   - what Odysseus' slaves do and say to the beggar before, during and after the contest.

2. Explain:
   - why the gods act as they do in the story, and how this affects our views of characters and events
   - why the suitors' behaviour is regarded as appalling
   - the relationship, and the reasons for it, between the crew and Odysseus
   - the positive and negative qualities that Polyphemus shows
   - the positive and negative qualities that Circe shows
   - the qualities of Penelope as a mother, wife and queen
   - the development of Telemachus as a prince and hero
   - how the actions of the slaves should be regarded.

PRACTICE QUESTIONS

Source A: Homer, *Odyssey*, 10.438–448

'Those were his words, and I felt like drawing the long sword strapped to my sturdy thigh and striking his head to the ground, though he was a kinsman of mine by marriage, but my friends each checked me with soothing words: "Scion of Zeus, let's leave him behind, if you will, to stay and guard the ship, while you lead us to Circe's sacred house."

So we left the ship and shore, but Eurylochus did not stay behind by the hollow hull, he came with us, fearing my stern rebuke.'

1. What had Eurylochus just said? [2]

2. Give **one** reason why this had upset Odysseus. [1]

3. How typical is the relationship in this passage between Odysseus and his crew compared to their relationship at other points in the poem? [8]

Further Reading for Literature and Culture 1: The Homeric World

Mycenae

French, E. (2002) *Mycenae*. London: Tempus Publishing

McCabe, R. and Cacouri, A. (2016) *Mycenae*. New York: Abbeville Press

Mylonas, G. (2006) *Mycenae*. Athens: Ektodike Athenon

Wardle, K.A. and Wardle, D. (2013) *The Mycenaean World*. Bristol: Bristol Classical Press

Homer's *Odyssey*

Graziosi, B. (2016) *Homer*. Oxford: Oxford University Press

Griffin, J. (2010) *Homer: The* Odyssey. Cambridge: Cambridge University Press

Jenkyns, R. (2012) *Classical Epic*. Bristol: Bristol Classical Press

Thorpe, M. (2013) *Homer*. London: Bloomsbury

York Notes (2001) *The Odyssey*. London: Longman

What to Expect in the Exam for The Homeric World

This chapter aims to show you the types of questions you are likely to get in the written examination. It offers some advice on how to answer the questions and will help you avoid common errors.

THE EXAMINATION

This component of the GCSE examination is designed to test your knowledge, understanding and evaluation and analysis of the Homeric world. The examination is worth 90 marks and lasts 1 hour and 30 minutes. This represents 50% of the total marks for the GCSE.

There are two sections to the paper, one focusing on the Mycenaean Age (the 'Culture' topics and sources), the other focusing on Homer (the 'Literature'). Each section is worth 45 marks, and is therefore worth 25% of your GCSE. The question paper will consist of both short-answer and extended-response questions.

For the 'Culture' section, you will be required to respond to visual and material sources. Some of these will be the prescribed sources you have studied in class, and some of these you will not have seen before. Sources for the 'Literature' section will only be from the five prescribed books of Homer that you have studied.

There are two Assessment Objectives in your GCSE in Classical Civilisation. Questions will be designed to test these areas. The Assessment Objectives are explained in the table below:

	Assessment Objective	Marks
AO1	Demonstrate knowledge and understanding of: • literature and visual/material culture from the classical world • how sources reflect their cultural contexts • possible interpretations of sources by different audiences and individuals.	50
AO2	Analyse, interpret and evaluate literature and visual/material culture from the classical world, using evidence and producing coherent and reasoned arguments.	40

For AO1 in this component, you will need to demonstrate the following:

Culture

- A good range of accurate and relevant knowledge of the Mycenaean Age.
- How the sites and objects tell us about life at the time.
- An understanding of the way the Mycenaeans lived, why their cities were built and developed in the way they did, and the creative skills that the Mycenaeans had.
- Different interpretations that can be made about the objects from the Mycenaean world, and the different conclusions that can be drawn from these.

Literature

- A good range of accurate and relevant knowledge of the plot of the *Odyssey*.
- Knowledge and understanding of customs and values in the story.
- An understanding of the literary style of Homer, the themes of the *Odyssey*, and the way characters behaved.
- Different interpretations that can be made about the *Odyssey*, and the different conclusions that can be drawn from these.

For AO2 in this component, you will need to demonstrate the following:

Culture

- A range of reasoned opinions about life in the Mycenaean Age.
- Appropriate evaluation of different sources to provide reasoned ideas.

Literature

- A range of reasoned opinions about the characters, themes and manner of composition of the *Odyssey*.
- Appropriate analysis of the characters, themes and manner of composition of the *Odyssey*.

QUESTION TYPES

There are five types of questions that will feature in your exam. Each type will appear in both the Culture and Literature sections, and together will be worth 45 marks in each section. With the exception of the extended-response questions (see pp. 239–242), each will be linked to a picture of a site or an object from the Mycenaean Age or a passage from Homer.

The question types are listed in the table below. They really fall into two categories: the first three types (knowledge and understanding, significance, and stimulus questions) are all short-answer questions. The final two types (detailed-response questions and extended-response questions) require a longer answer.

The final two types will usually be the final questions of each section. The short-answer questions can come in any order. For example, there could be a two-mark knowledge and understanding question, followed by a four-mark stimulus question, followed by a three-mark significance question.

The questions will not necessarily be in the same order as here, but the extended-response questions will always be at the end of each section.

Question type	Number of marks in each section for each question type
Knowledge and understanding questions	9
Significance questions	3
Stimulus questions	10
Detailed-response questions	8
Extended-response questions	15

Knowledge and understanding questions

There will be 9-marks' worth of knowledge and understanding questions (all AO1). The 9 marks will be broken down into a series of short-answer questions, typically worth 1, 2 or 3 marks.

Some questions will require you to show your **knowledge** of Homer or a Mycenaean object or site. Other questions will require you to show **knowledge** and *also* demonstrate an **understanding** of these facts.

There will be a **source** (a passage or an image) to assist you. For Literature, this will be a passage from Homer. For Culture, it could be a prescribed source you have studied, or it could be one that you have not seen before. For example, you might be shown the figurine on the right with the following questions:

Question:	**(a)** Name this style of figurine	[1]
	(b) Explain why it is known by this name?	[1]
Answer:	**(a)** A phi figurine.	[1]
	(b) It has the same shape as the Greek letter phi.	[1]

Knowing that this is a phi figurine is a piece of knowledge, and the fact that it gets this name from a Greek letter shows your understanding as to how it got this name. This answer should be brief. There is, in fact, no need to write full sentences for this type of answer if it seems that only a single word or a phrase is needed, as in the first part of the answer.

The following represents a typical Homer knowledge and understanding question, together with its answer:

Source A: Homer, *Odyssey*, 9.272–280

> "Stranger, you are a foreigner or a fool, telling me to fear and revere the gods, since
> the Cyclopes care nothing for aegis-bearing Zeus: we are greater than they. I would

spare neither you nor your friends, to evade Zeus' anger, but only as my own heart prompted.

But tell me, now, where you moored your fine ship, when you landed. Was it somewhere nearby, or further off? I'd like to know."

Question:	**(a)** What did Odysseus tell Polyphemus had happened to his ship?	[2]
	(b) Why do you think he told him this?	[1]
Answer:	**(a)** It had been destroyed [1] by Poseidon.	[1]
	(b) to stop Polyphemus going after his crew [1] or to stop Polyphemus destroying it and trapping the men on the island.	[1]

The first part is asking for two pieces of factual knowledge concerning the speech and the other mark is for your understanding of why he said this. In this case, there is more than one acceptable correct answer, and you will not be penalised for making more points than the number of marks available. However, if you are asked to give only a certain number of facts, or make a certain number of points, you should stick to the instructions.

In this type of question, each correct fact or opinion is worth one mark. You will not be asked to evaluate ideas (e.g. whether you think the story that Odysseus told was a clever idea, or whether you think the figurine is well made), so do not waste time in doing so.

Significance questions

There will be one of these questions in each section. It will be split into two parts. You will be asked to give two pieces of information (2 marks AO1) and state why one or both are important or significant, or what this knowledge tells us (1 mark AO2). Examples are given below.

Source A: Homer, *Odyssey*, 21.68–75

"Noble Suitors, listen to me. You have battened on this house, with its master long gone, eating and drinking endlessly, and you could find no better excuse to offer than the desire to win me as a wife. Well come now, my Suitors, your prize stands here before you, clear to see. Godlike Odysseus' mighty bow is the test."

(a) What does Homer tell us about the history of Odysseus' bow? [2]

(b) What does this tell us about Odysseus? [1]

There are various possible answers for the first part, including that Odysseus was given it by a friend, and he kept it at home in memory of his friend. For the second part, this might lead to the idea that Odysseus regarded the friendship as important or that he was sentimental about it, either of which would gain the mark available.

In the culture section the question might look something like this:

Ta 641

(a) Identify two things that we can learn about Mycenaean written language from the Linear B tablets. [2]

(b) Give one way that Linear B showed a link between the written language and later Greek. [1]

Two marks would be gained for saying that Linear B used ideograms and syllable combinations. The third could be gained for showing that some words came directly into later Greek from Linear B, or that both scripts write the same language.

Stimulus questions

These questions will require candidates to identify something relevant from a stimulus passage or image, and to analyse what you have recognised. Each **relevant** quotation or feature of the image that is picked out will be worth a mark, as will each piece of analysis. Therefore, these questions are each worth equal amounts of AO1 and AO2.

In the culture section, you might be given a picture of a rhyton and asked:

Question: Select **two** features of the design of this vessel, and suggest what each tells us about the Mycenaeans. [4]

Answer: To gain the first two marks (AO1), you might identify any two of the following features: it uses both gold and silver; it is not the most practical container for drinking from; it is made in the shape of a bull; it looks very Minoan in form.

To gain the next two marks (AO2), you might make the following suggestions:

- as gold and silver are not found on Mycenae they must have traded items
- they must have used this for something else, perhaps simply to show off wealth or for a libation
- the bull must have been important in Mycenae
- there were probably links between Mycenae and Crete.

Part (a) requires two pieces of knowledge and part (b) asks you to give your opinions of the evidence. You should be careful not to simply show an understanding of how it was used in the second part, but must give your own ideas based on the evidence.

In the Homer section, you will be given a passage and might be asked for your opinions on a character or for how the passage is made exciting. For example, you might be given this passage and asked how Homer makes it dramatic, for 4 marks.

Source A: Homer, *Odyssey*, 9.287–295

"Devoid of pity, he was silent in response, but leaping up laid hands on my crew. Two he seized and dashed to the ground like whelps, and their brains ran out and stained the earth. He tore them limb from limb for his supper, eating the flesh and entrails, bone and marrow, like a mountain lion, leaving nothing. Helplessly we watched these cruel acts, raising our hands to heaven and weeping."

You would be expected to make two points of analysis, giving your opinions. You might say that the victims are helpless and that Polyphemus is totally brutal. Two points of evidence to back this up would be the simile comparing them to whelps and the fact that he ate every last bit of the men.

Look at the number of marks available. If there are two pieces of evidence and two pieces of analysis required, do not give more than this amount. You will be using up time that would be better spent in detailed-response and extended-response questions.

Detailed-response questions

You will get one of these questions in each section with one or more stimulus passages or images to prompt you. This stimulus is meant only as a starting point, and it will be clear from the question that you will need to bring in **extra information and examples**.

Four marks are awarded for your knowledge and understanding (AO1), and four marks given for your analysis, interpretation and evaluation of your facts and understanding (AO2). These questions are marked in a different way, however; you are not given one mark for each correct opinion and each piece of evidence, but the answer as a whole is marked using a Levels of Response Grid. A Levels of Response Grid explains to examiners what answers may look like to achieve a certain number of marks. An examiner will read the whole answer and then check the grid to work out what level the answer belongs to. It is important to remember that the quality of your answer is more important than the amount you have written. The Levels of Response Grid is included in the mark schemes for exam papers.

It is also important to remember that for AO1 you will need to show knowledge and understanding of a source's context and the different ways people interpret the sources. Remember that you can examine both sides of an argument. For example, if you are asked whether you admire a character's behaviour in a particular section of the *Odyssey*, there are likely to be arguments on both sides of the question. If you do not give a balanced argument, you will probably have missed some key facts, and your answer will not show a full evaluation.

This question is not meant to be an essay. You are advised not to write an introduction that simply outlines how you will write your response as this will not add anything to your answer and will take up valuable time. You may find you have more to say than time allows, so you might have to be rigorous in moving on. Make your key points at the start, keep to the point, and if you do choose to have a conclusion, keep it brief, as you will ideally have answered the precise wording of the question throughout your answer. It is not necessary to have a conclusion to gain full marks.

For example, on the paper you might be given a source of a fresco, and then you might be asked the following question:

> What do you think is most impressive about Mycenaean frescoes? Use the source
> as a starting point and your own knowledge in your answer.　　　　　　　　　[8]

In order to show you know about frescoes, you might include some of these facts:

- frescoes were painted on a fine lime plaster
- sometimes on a thicker coarse backing
- mostly done when wet

- a range of colours from natural minerals
- a blue colour was manufactured
- men have red skin colour, women white, lions yellow
- representation of animals, flames, spirals etc.

You then need to weigh up how impressive frescoes were:

- some colours (e.g. blue) were rare and expensive; the use of them was unusual and could be used to show off wealth
- regularity of use of colour creates a very impressive effect
- sense of depth created by overlapping figures
- fine detail in clothing and hairstyle is impressive
- use of friezes is very effective
- use of symmetry/repetition makes the frescoes seem very precise
- division of walls into distinct bands is an impressive feature
- frescoes on floors create a different, interesting effect
- perspective was not always shown effectively
- faces always shown with eyes looking forward, even if the head was facing to the side.

Half the marks are awarded for AO1 and for AO2, but this does not necessarily mean that you should give four facts and four explanations. Examiners will read your whole response and judge how good they feel it is overall.

In Section B, on Homer, a question might ask you about the importance of a theme, or the portrayal of one particular character or episode.

Extended-response questions

This type of question is different from all the other questions in two respects: there is no stimulus passage to introduce it, and you will be given a **choice** of questions to answer (there are two extended-response questions in each section, and you must do **only one**). However, it is marked using a Levels of Response Grid in the same way as the detailed-response question.

Five marks are awarded for your knowledge and understanding (AO1), and ten marks given for your analysis, interpretation and evaluation of your facts and understanding (AO2). This means more marks are awarded for how good your argument is than for simply what you know. Therefore, you might want to spend a bit of time thinking about the structure of your answer. As for the detailed-response question, it is important to remember that for AO1 you will need to show knowledge and understanding of the literary and historical context of sources and the different ways people interpret them.

Extended-response questions will cover a wider area than detailed-response questions and will draw upon material from across topics of either the Literature or the Culture sections. These questions however, will never cover both Literature and Culture. For example, whereas you might be asked a question, as shown on p. 238 about frescoes in a detailed-response question, an extended-response question might ask about Mycenaean craftsmanship, allowing you to talk about metalwork and pottery too.

The following is an example of a possible extended-response question.

How similar are the characters of Telemachus and Odysseus in the Odyssey? [15]

To answer this question you should look for evidence where Telemachus and Odysseus can be compared (remember too that you can get credit for introducing material from outside the prescribed sources, so if you have read other books you could draw on these too). You might include some of these facts:

- both of them plan the murder together
- Telemachus seems to lead the suitors on in their demise in promoting the challenge. Odysseus does not stop the challenge either
- Telemachus might have strung the bow the fourth time. Odysseus strung it first time
- Telemachus orders Penelope to her room as Odysseus had ordered him to go previously
- both fight side by side and kill the suitors
- Odysseus kills Leodes, and Telemachus kills Melanthius and the maids
- epithets ('thoughtful Telemachus', 'Odysseus, master of stratagems') suggest both are cunning.

You then need to analyse how similar Telemachus and Odysseus are. You might draw conclusions such as these:

They are similar because:

- both make cunning plans to defeat the suitors.
- Telemachus is almost as strong as his father as he nearly strings the bow.
- both act as master in ordering members of the family to their room.
- both are merciless and merciful as appropriate to the slaves.

They are different because:

- Odysseus does not make mistakes in the fight, but Telemachus does leave the store-room door open.
- Odysseus strings the bow with ease, but Telemachus fails in three attempts.
- Telemachus leaves a spear in the enemy, through uncertainty, but Odysseus is more experienced and does not.
- Odysseus seems arrogant and greedy during his adventures with his crew, but Telemachus does not show such traits.

Key points

The following applies to both detailed-response questions and extended-response questions:

- Your facts must be **relevant**. Do not merely state everything you know about a particular topic.
- It is a common mistake in the literature to over-narrate the plot and to retell a whole story. You should instead **summarise** the main points, or focus in detail on

one or two parts of it. This is particularly important in your extended-response answer, where five marks are available for your knowledge, but ten marks are given for your evaluation, interpretation and analysis.

- Show that you **understand** things from an ancient point of view wherever possible. For example, characters in the *Odyssey* may have had different attitudes to revenge to modern attitudes, or certain colours that seem to us very ordinary (such as blue) were seen as very luxurious by the Mycenaeans.
- Evaluation is best done throughout the response. **Keep referring back** to the title in your essay to do this. If you give all your facts, and then give all your opinions, it is easy to miss something out, or to run out of time.
- Try to find a **balance** of ideas as the question will usually require you to argue both for and against an idea.
- Sometimes a piece of evidence can be taken two ways. If so, remember to give **both interpretations** in order to show a high level of understanding.
- You will not have a lot of time to do these questions and so it is always best to present your most important arguments first in case you find yourself running out of time.
- Ultimately make your conclusion **logical**, and supported by evidence from your whole answer, not just one part of it.

Look at these two extracts from an essay:

Question: How important is the theme of justice in the *Odyssey*?   [15]

Extract 1

Justice is very important in the *Odyssey*. Characters are often punished or rewarded for their actions. Those who help Odysseus are rewarded, while those who hinder his mission often suffer death. An example of someone who is harmed for acting badly is Polyphemus. Odysseus had turned up at his cave and helped himself to cheese. When Polyphemus turned up, he ate two of Odysseus' men who are compared to puppies. Odysseus then made a plan to call himself Nobody, and got Polyphemus drunk. When Polyphemus was drunk, Odysseus blinded him and escaped with sheep. Polyphemus clearly deserved his punishment as he had acted in a barbaric fashion. However, I think that other themes, such as hospitality, are far more important in the *Odyssey*.

Extract 2

Justice is first seen in the story of Polyphemus. Clearly Polyphemus pays the penalty for eating six of Odysseus' men by being blinded and losing his flock. However, Odysseus also suffers for his mistakes in being cursed by Polyphemus. His arrogance in calling out his name in triumph could be said to lead to the deaths of his men, and him arriving home alone. It might seem unjust that because of his mistake here, a chain of events occurs, causing grief to innocent victims. His wife, son and slaves are harassed by the suitors for years. Some might even suggest that all the men have to die (such as Elpenor in Circe's palace) to fulfil the curse and that there is no justice in this, although Homer does make it clear that they made significant mistakes (no one forced Elpenor to get drunk and climb on a roof).

Notice how the first extract spends more time on presenting the facts than giving opinions, and many of the facts are unnecessary. The evaluation is not developed fully, and the final statement is irrelevant to the question. The second extract is much more concise, and is much more balanced. It argues both sides and flows smoothly from one story to another, providing alternative interpretations of episodes.

GENERAL EXAM SKILLS

When you are sitting the examination, read the instructions carefully so that you realise which questions are compulsory and which are optional (the only option you have is which of the two extended-response questions you choose to answer). Remember that the examination will have a range of difficulty of questions; some of it is designed to be challenging, and you should not be panicked if you cannot think of an answer immediately. The following pieces of advice may seem obvious, but you should not underestimate their importance:

- The examination lasts 90 minutes and is worth 90 marks. Do not assume this means you should spend a minute per mark: in reality a lot of short questions will take less than a mark a minute and you should spend longer than a mark a minute on the long questions.
- Both the Culture and Literature sections are worth 45 marks. Do not spend too long on whichever you choose to do first; this is especially tempting if you like the questions that have been set and feel you could say a lot.
- If you see a question that you do not know the answer to, move on quickly to another question. Leave enough time to go back to it; during the examination you might well remember the answer and will not have wasted too much time thinking.
- Stick to the question: if you are asked for facts, do not give opinions and vice versa.
- Do not try to answer a slightly different question if you wish another had been set, or have practised before at school.
- For longer extended-response questions, try to find a balanced argument.
- More marks are available in the paper for opinions than knowledge or understanding. It is vital that you do not over-narrate, especially in your Homer answers.

L&C 2
Roman City Life

Introduction to Roman City Life

Imperial Period the period of Roman history from 30 BC, when Rome was ruled by emperors

In this component, learners will explore everyday life in Roman cities, with a particular focus on the **Imperial Period** and on popular sites and artefacts from Pompeii, Herculaneum, Ostia and Rome, as well as on four Roman authors who lived during this era.

The Culture section of this component allows you to study a variety of aspects of Roman society. It is sub-divided into the following key topics: Roman Housing, The Roman Home and Family, Society, and Leisure and Entertainment. An examination of topics such as Roman housing, education and citizenship gives us a window into how people in the Roman world lived their lives on a daily basis, and how their society was ordered on a strictly hierarchical foundation, from wealthy aristocrats to lowly slaves. Moreover, the study of Roman entertainment shows both the creativity and the cruelty of the Roman world.

In the Literature section of this component you will read from four authors who offer an insight into life in the Roman world. Two of these, Horace and Juvenal, are poets who wrote satires about the society they lived in. Their satires are quite different in tone from each other, with the light-hearted Horace offering a great contrast to the angry Juvenal. Petronius also satirised the society he lived in, and in particular he focused on the stereotype of the wealthy but vulgar freedman. Finally, Pliny was a successful Roman public official, whose letters to his friends give us a fascinating insight into his life and values.

EXAM OVERVIEW	J199/22

Your examination will require you to show knowledge and understanding of the material you have studied (AO1) and will require you to analyse and evaluate it (AO2), giving your opinions on areas such as characters in the literature or objects in the culture.

This component makes up 50% of your GCSE. In this component 50 marks will test your AO1 skills and 40 marks will test your AO2 skills.

There will be a distinct section of questions on the Culture section of this component, and a distinct section on the Literature material. Neither section will ask questions requiring knowledge of the other: for example, you will not be asked how far Pliny's *Letters* confirms knowledge of what you have learnt in the Culture section of Roman city life.

In both sections you will be asked to answer a series of short factual questions, based around quotations or images concerning the Culture material, or around passages from the prescribed authors. Some of these will also ask for your opinions. You will be required to write longer answers in each section, worth 8 marks and 15 marks, showing knowledge and giving opinions. There will be 45 marks' worth of questions on the Culture section, and 45 marks' worth on the Literature section. You will have a choice of longer questions worth 15 marks in each section, but all other questions will be compulsory.

Culture

3.1 Roman Housing

TOPIC OVERVIEW

- The layout and decoration of a typical Pompeian, atrium-style *domus*
- The design of apartments/blocks of flats (*insula/insulae*)
- Evidence for living conditions of the rich and the poor
- Comparison of the different living conditions in each setting

The prescribed sources for this topic are:

- The Insula of Diana at Ostia
- The House of the Wooden Partition at Herculaneum
- The House of Menander at Pompeii
- The House of Octavius Quartio at Pompeii

Don't forget that you will be given credit in the exam if you study extra sources and make relevant use of them in your answers.

This topic examines two main types of housing in the Roman world – the smart town house and the block of flats. It will cover the typical design features of each, and challenge you to think about the living experience of the inhabitants.

EXAM TIP

Remember that you may be required to answer about the how rich and poor experienced their living conditions, as well as being able to compare the two groups – and indeed to make comparisons between the living conditions of all the types of apartments and houses that you study. While you are studying this topic, therefore, keep asking yourself the question: what would it have been like to live here?

THE INSULA

When people think of Roman houses, they are most likely to think of a large, well-designed house with an internal garden, decorated with beautiful art, and containing plenty of living space and rooms for entertaining guests. However, this type of house, known as a **domus**, was only for the very wealthy, and the number of Romans who lived in such luxurious homes was very small. In fact, in a city such as Rome, the vast majority lived in apartment blocks; the literary sources suggest that these were often cramped and dangerous, although the evidence from nearby Ostia suggests that this was an exaggeration, and that they varied in size and quality. An apartment block was known as an **insula** (the word 'insula' literally meant 'island' in Latin, and presumably the link was that an apartment block was originally a large self-contained building all of its own). One fourth-century AD source records that the city of Rome had fewer than 2,000 domus-type houses but more than 40,000 insulae. To understand the living conditions of the average Roman, therefore, we need to examine what it was like to live in an insula.

Hardly any insulae have survived in Rome itself, and the best evidence can be found in Rome's port town of Ostia, located about twenty miles away. An insula commonly consisted of three to five storeys, although we even hear of insulae six or seven storeys high. Access to the upper floors came from external staircases leading off the street, some of which had impressive doorways, and sometimes from internal staircases as well. From the late first century AD, insulae were usually constructed of brick-faced concrete; roofs were made of wooden beams covered with flat terracotta tiles; at Ostia, examples of large glazed windows have also been found on the upper floors. Ground-floor rooms that faced onto the street tended to be shops, which often had an upper mezzanine level used for storage or even as living space (a **mezzanine** is an intermediate floor of a building, which is open to the floor below).

At Ostia, a few blocks were clearly designed for wealthy occupants: there are some examples of large apartments, which might have two large reception rooms together with a few other smaller rooms, including a kitchen and toilet facilities. However, this was not the standard type, and the city has many more examples of apartments with two to four rooms, both on the ground floor and on upper floors. There is also one interesting example in the Insula of Diana (see below) of small individual rooms in a communal living area.

A number of Roman writers mention how unsafe insulae could be, including Juvenal in a well-known passage discussed on p. 309. Such writers tend to focus on two concerns: that the buildings were poorly constructed and therefore prone to collapse, and that they were likely to catch fire. The wealthy statesman Cicero, who had his own property portfolio in Rome, made the following joke in a letter to a friend:

> Two of my buildings have fallen down, and the rest have large cracks. Not only the tenants, but even the mice have moved out!
>
> Cicero, To Atticus 14.9

> **domus** a large Roman private house in a city or town

> **insula** (pl. **insulae**) the Roman name for a block of flats

> **mezzanine** an intermediate floor of a building, open to the floor below

FIGURE 3.1
The remains of an insula near the Palatine Hill in Rome.

Fire was also a very real hazard. Aulus Gellius, a writer who lived in Rome in the second century AD, here reflects a wealthy man's concern about the dangers of buying property in Rome:

> We were accompanying him home when, while climbing the Cispian Hill, we saw a tall multi-storey block of flats overrun with flames, and all the neighbouring buildings burning in a great fireball. Then one of Julianus' companions said: "The income from urban property is great, but the dangers are far greater. But if some solution could be found to stop houses in Rome from catching fire all the time, by the gods I would sell my country property and buy in the city."
>
> Aulus Gellius, *Attic Nights*, 15.1

The Insula of Diana at Ostia

One of the best preserved (and most reconstructed) insulae at Ostia is the Insula of Diana, which takes its name from a relief depicting the goddess Diana on a wall of the inner courtyard. The dimensions of the insula are about 39 × 23 metres; the south and west walls faced out onto the street, while the other two backed onto other buildings, so that they contained no doors or windows. A central, roofless courtyard allowed light into the building, and it contained a cistern which provided water for the inhabitants since individual apartments did not have their own water-supply.

The ground floor contained a number of shops, which opened out onto the street on the south and west sides; they each had mezzanines and some also had a small back room. On the other two sides of the floor were apartments, some of which had elaborate decoration – the remains on one wall still show painted yellow panels divided by borders of red and green. The floor also had its own shared toilet facilities, which were probably available to all the tenants.

FIGURE 3.2
A cut away reconstruction of the Insula of Diana at Ostia.

There were three staircases, two external and one internal, which led to the upper floors – the building probably had four storeys in all. On the first floor, only the lowest few centimetres of the walls have survived, but from these we can form a good idea of the layout. On its south and west sides were some fairly large four-roomed apartments, while on the other sides was a communal living area. This consisted of a long corridor off which were small, poorly lit rooms; at one end of the corridor was a larger room that was probably a shared living space. It is also likely that there were communal toilet facilities on this floor too, immediately above the ones below.

It is interesting to speculate as to who might have lived in these apartments. Insulae were mainly rental properties owned by the wealthy (who could make a good profit on the rental income). The four-room apartments may have been rented by people who might be thought of as moderately wealthy, and who may have taken out leases of six months or a year. By contrast, the small rooms in the communal area were perhaps rented by the day or week, most likely to people who were passing through the busy harbour city, or working there for a short period of time.

THE DOMUS

Although the number of large domus-style houses in any Roman city was relatively small, they played a disproportionate role in daily life, since wealthy men used their living space to work, greet friends and clients, and conduct politics – as a general rule, there were no such things as offices where people went to work. Our best evidence for the domus comes from the preserved ruins of Pompeii and Herculaneum, where many such houses have survived. The rooms in these houses have traditionally been given names by archaeologists in the same way that we name rooms in our houses (e.g. kitchen, living room, study, bedroom), but we should be careful not to assume too much about what each room was actually used for: the evidence suggests that many rooms could be used in a variety of ways (in fact, this is not so different from today: a modern living room might be used to work, relax, or eat, etc.).

Figure 3.3 outlines the layout of a typical house with its key features. The design is focused around two important areas – the **atrium** (reception hall) and, beyond this, the **peristyle** (colonnaded garden). The atrium was the most public area of the house, and it was here that the owner would meet his visitors and guests, including his clients. The owner of the house might use this room to display signs of his wealth – one Pompeian house had large chests of money in the atrium. In the centre of an atrium was usually an **impluvium** – a rectangular pool into which rain water fell from a specially designed opening in the roof (the **compluvium**). This was a source of water supply for the house since the impluvium was linked to a reservoir below. The atrium might also contain a shrine to the household gods, while according to ancient sources ceremonial wax masks of the family's ancestors could be kept in the open recesses on each side of the atrium. The whole space could therefore be designed to hold the presence of the living, the ancestors and the gods.

The peristyle was a colonnaded garden which aimed to provide a feel of the country. If the atrium was for business, then the peristyle was for relaxation and pleasure. The

Study question
How similar was a Roman insula to the types of apartment blocks we see today?

ACTIVITY
Based on what you have studied of the Insula of Diana, create a drawing of what you think it might have looked like from the outside, and of what you think certain rooms or spaces might have looked like inside.

atrium the main room of the Roman domus, where the family received friends and clients

peristyle a colonnaded garden within a Roman domus

impluvium the pool in the centre of the atrium of a Roman domus that gathered rainwater

compluvium an opening in the roof of the atrium to allow rainwater to fall into the impluvium

FIGURE 3.3
Plan of a typical domus.

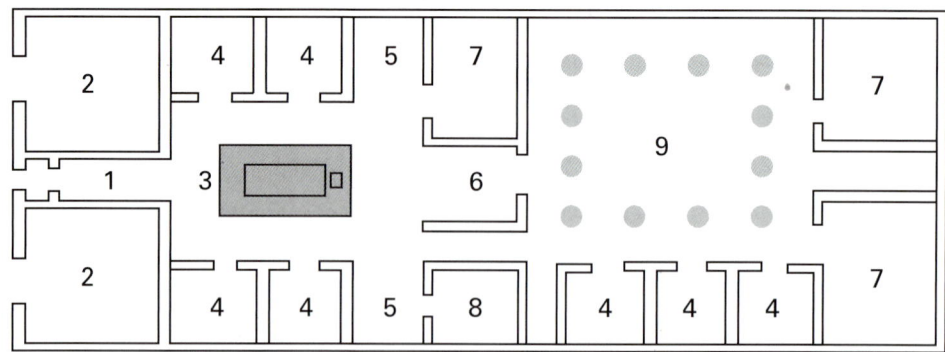

1	entry passage	This led into the atrium, and its walls could be painted ornately; some houses have signs or mosaics in the floor saying 'cave canem' – 'beware of the dog!'
2	shop	External rooms of a house, particularly at the front, were often turned into shops or workshops, either to be rented out to local tradesmen or to be managed by the family itself.
3	atrium	The atrium was the most public and formal part of the house, designed to welcome and impress visitors.
4	bedroom/ private room	These small private rooms could be used for private meetings or for sleeping. Such a room was just big enough for a bed and chair.
5	recess	A small room with one side open.
6	tablinum	This was often located between the atrium and the peristyle. It may have been used as the master's study or the main bedroom.
7	triclinium	The dining room was a key room in a domus: a typical Roman dinner party is described on pp. 262–263.
8	kitchen	This was often quite small and cramped, with a cooking hearth.
9	peristyle	The colonnaded garden was often ornately decorated with a rich variety of flowers, shrubs and trees, as well as fountains and statues.

> **triclinium** a dining room in a Roman domus
>
> **tablinum** a reception room in a Roman domus, often used as the master's study

peristyle may contain an ornate fountain, as well as a variety of flowers, plants and shrubs. The art work on the nearby walls could reflect the theme, with scenes from the countryside carefully painted. Very often rooms used for private hospitality, such as a dining room, known as a **triclinium**, opened onto the peristyle. The other rooms of the house were built around these two spaces. One important room was the **tablinum**, often located between the atrium and peristyle; some ancient sources claim that this was the master's study, where he could conduct private business (although other sources claim quite differently that it was where the matrimonial bed was placed). At the front of the house, rooms giving out onto the street could be converted into shops, which could provide the family with an extra source of income.

A house had a number of small private rooms, which may have been used as bedrooms – but the bedroom was not the important private space that it is in our homes today, it was simply just a place where one slept. Moreover, the activities of a house probably spilled over into a number of places. For example, a kitchen was often too small to cope with the preparations for a dinner party, so slaves might have used the peristyle to prepare food (and probably also to do the washing up afterwards). Similarly, it is unlikely that slaves had their own sleeping space, and so they probably lay down in out of the way corners.

There are some aspects of life in a domus that is especially hard for us to know about with any certainty. For example, there are only relatively few preserved examples of rooms on an upper floor (the House of the Wooden Partition, described below, is one house where there is evidence). These rooms were typically not grand, and were probably used for sleeping or storage; they may even have been rented out as living accommodation. We can also only guess at how many people lived in a domus, but it would usually have consisted of a family with some close relatives, as well as the attached slaves and perhaps freedmen. The total may, therefore, have been twenty or more.

One feature of a domus that we do know a good deal about is the art and furnishings, thanks to the preservation of houses in Pompeii and Herculaneum. Wall paintings here often come in vivid colours, most commonly red, orange and blue-green, but also yellows, purples and black. Onto these were painted scenes, frequently taken from Greek mythology (a source of great fascination for the Romans, who borrowed much of their own mythology from the Greeks) or country landscapes; still-life scenes such as flowers, fruit and animals. In many houses, painters represented architectural features such as buildings and pillars, giving the images greater perspective and suggesting that the room was more spacious than it really was.

In terms of furnishings, evidence from Pompeii and Herculaneum indicates that houses had many of the items, generally made of wood, which we might use in our homes today: tables, chairs, beds, screens, shelves, chests and cupboards. In one house in Pompeii, the contents of a large cupboard were found in the atrium, including bronze jugs and plates, a bronze basin and cake mould, two bronze signet rings and other pieces of jewellery, nine dice and bits of gaming equipment, as well as some coins made of gold, silver or bronze.

DEBATE

A Roman writer called Vitruvius, who lived in the first century BC, wrote a book called *On Architecture* in which he described the characteristics of what he defined as a typical domus. His work has been very influential in the modern era, and for years many books have based their description of a Roman domus on the names, and likely purposes of rooms, on what Vitruvius wrote. However, more recently archaeologists have argued against this approach, stressing that we should not assume that the work of one Roman author speaks for all Roman houses at all times. That is why it is important to remember that rooms in Roman houses often had a variety of functions.

You can read Vitruvius' description of a typical domus in Chapter 6 of his work, an English translation of which can be found on the Companion Website.

PRESCRIBED SOURCE

House of the Wooden Partition

Location: Herculaneum

Significance: a particularly well-preserved Roman domus with a conventional plan

Name: the house takes its name from the preserved wooden partition that separates the tablinum from the atrium.

The House of the Wooden Partition

This house is a classic example of the atrium-tablinum-peristyle domus. It is also better preserved than many other houses in Pompeii and Herculaneum, and it is a good example of a house where the upper storey has survived. Moreover, carbonised remains – caused by wood being turned into carbon by the intense heat of the eruption of Mount Vesuvius – give us an insight into household design and furnishings.

The house's façade is remarkably well-preserved; indeed, what can be seen today – a two-storey front with roof beams still in place at the top – is probably very similar to what was visible in the first century AD. Outside the front door are the benches for clients; high in the walls above them, small windows look out onto the street from the upper floor, while carbonised wooden beams supporting the roof are still in place. Moving into the house through the entrance way, one walks into an impressive atrium, decorated with red, black and yellow panels. In pride of place was a marble display table in front of the impluvium, while the impluvium itself, with a fountain at its centre, was also lined with marble.

The item of most interest is at the back of the atrium: the 'wooden partition' from which the house takes its name. It is assumed that this was used as a screen to separate the tablinum from the atrium, giving the owner some privacy when required. The partition was originally made of three beautifully panelled sliding double doors, although the middle panel was hacked through by early excavators. Thankfully, the other two panels have survived in carbonised form, together with their hinges and bronze lamp supports, each in the form of a ship's figurehead. Another carbonised relic can be seen in a small room on the west side of the atrium – a bed or couch, which stood on legs shaped by a lathe.

Beyond the tablinum, the peristyle was colonnaded on three sides. There were small family rooms around it, and the house's main dining room lay the other side of it. One of the rooms off the peristyle linked through to one of the various shops bordering the house; these would still have been owned by the owner of the house. At the back of the house was a flight of stairs, which led to a set of rooms above. Steps too can be found in the shop on the front side of the house, and these led up to a small apartment, perhaps the living space of the person who ran the shop – it is unclear if this was attached to the house or not.

FIGURE 3.4
A plan of the House of the Wooden Partition.

Key

A. Main entrance	C. Ala	E. Triclinium	G. Peristylium	J. Tabernae
B. Cubiculum	D. Atrium	F. Tablinium	H. Triclinium	

FIGURE 3.5
The front of the House of the Wooden
Partition from the street.

FIGURE 3.6
The wooden partition in place at the back of the atrium.

The House of Menander

This house is one of the largest and most impressive in Pompeii. It is named after a portrait on one of the walls of the peristyle of the Greek comic playwright Menander, who greatly influenced the Roman comic playwrights Plautus and Terence (see p. 286). Scholars are not clear who owned the house at the time of Pompeii's destruction.

The nucleus of the domus had the classic atrium-tablinum-peristyle design, and it seems to have grown out from this core, acquiring neighbouring buildings and incorporating them into an even larger house. From the entrance, one could see right the way through to the back wall of the peristyle. The impressive atrium contained an elaborate household shrine, next to which was a staircase to an upper floor. The recess off the atrium had complementary paintings on its three walls, each one depicting a scene from the Trojan War, including the arrival of the wooden horse at Troy in one of them. The south end of the atrium led into the tablinum, which itself led through to a large peristyle.

The focus of the house was the peristyle and the impressive reception rooms around it. In the north-west corner was a room coloured predominantly in green, with a floor mosaic depicting scenes from the river Nile. In the south-west corner was a suite of baths – only the very wealthiest houses could afford to have their own private set of baths like this. On the south end of the peristyle was a second household shrine, as well as three frescos – one the famous image of Menander, another depicting theatrical masks, and a third another portrait, perhaps of the Greek tragic playwright Euripides. On the east side of the peristyle was a vast dining room, one of the largest reception rooms discovered in Pompeii.

FIGURE 3.7
A plan of the House
of Menander.

House of Menander

Location: Pompeii

Significance: one of the largest and most impressive houses in Pompeii

Name: the house takes its name from a wall painting of the Greek comic playwright Menander

Key
1. Main entrance
2. Staircase to top floor
3. Recess
4. Atrium
5. Tablinum
6. 'Green' reception room
7. Peristyle
8. Second atrium
9. Dining room
10. Service quarters and stable
11. Niche with Menander fresco
12. Small atrium of baths
13. Kitchen quarters

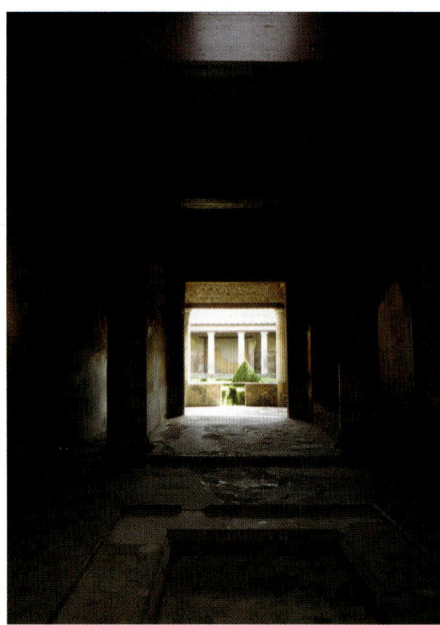

FIGURE 3.8
The atrium in the House of Menander, with a view through to the tablinum and peristyle.

FIGURE 3.9
The peristyle of the House of Menander.

The house was so large that it even had two service areas. To the east side was a long corridor with a number of small rooms; at one end was a large stable, where a wagon and many amphorae were found, suggesting that the owner may have had a large farming estate as well (agricultural implements were also found in the house). At the other end of the corridor was another small atrium, which may have been the headquarters for the house's steward, or head slave. The other service area, on the west side of the house, consisted of a kitchen, latrine and service rooms, with access to cellars below. It was here that the house's silver service was found by excavators – a large collection of decorated silver vessels, wrapped in cloth and neatly stacked, including plates, trays, spoons, ladles, bowls and cups.

The House of Octavius Quartio

The design of the house of Octavius Quartio shows how, over time, the design focus of a domus could move away from the atrium to the peristyle. The greatest feature of this house was its large and wonderful garden, enhanced by impressive water features, shrines and fountains.

The house is found on one of Pompeii's main streets. Outside the front was stone seating, which may have been used by clients, while the two front rooms opened out onto the street as shops; it is in one of these that a signet ring with the name 'Octavius Quartio' was found, giving the house its modern name. The entrance passage led into a rectangular atrium; its impluvium had a fountain jet and was surrounded by flower boxes, hinting at the beautiful garden that lay beyond. The rooms around the atrium were standard; the south side led directly into a small peristyle, colonnaded on three sides.

The fourth side of the peristyle opened onto a pergola that overlooked the garden. Under the pergola ran a narrow canal, lined with garden statues and probably home to fish; mid-way along was a bridge. Painted on the walls at the west end of the pergola were two scenes from the myth of Diana and Actaeon – Actaeon discovering Diana bathing, and then about to be ripped to death by his own hunting dogs. A large reception room, probably used for dining, opened onto the north side of the pergola; its walls were

FIGURE 3.10 PS
A plan of the House of Octavius Quartio: 1 atrium, 2 triclinium, 3 peristyle, 4 outside dining area, 5 pergola, 6 garden pergola.

PRESCRIBED SOURCE

House of Octavius Quartio

Built: substantially renovated in the AD 60s–70s

Location: Pompeii

Significance: the focus of this domus is its magnificent garden and water features.

Name: the house is named after Octavius Quartio, whose signet ring was found there.

S & C Find out about the largest domus in Pompeii, the House of the Faun. How does this compare to the houses you have studied?

decorated with scenes from the life of Hercules, as well as from the Trojan War. On the outer north wall of the pergola were painted hunting scenes, and to its east was an outside dining area, with space for two couches rather than the conventional three. Next to the couches on the east wall was a small household shrine flanked by two more paintings – to the left the myth of Narcissus, to the right the story of Pyramus and Thisbe.

The south side of this pergola led off into the garden, which was on a lower level. It was divided by a second, longer pergola and canal. Where the two pergolas met was a fountain shrine dedicated to Diana and Actaeon. The lower canal ran all the way along the garden, about 50 metres in all, and it too was decorated with statues, paintings and crossing bridges. Midway along this lower canal was another fountain, and beyond that a small temple. The garden on either side was planted with ordered rows of acanthus and fruit trees and in the wall at the back was another entrance to the property.

Study questions

1 How does the layout of a domus compare to that of houses today? How important is it to have personal space within a house?
2 How does the decoration in a typical domus compare to a house today?
3 Which of the houses described in this topic would you have liked to live in and why?
4 How important do you think it was for a house to have outside space for entertaining guests?

FIGURE 3.11
A view down to the garden pergola in the House of Octavius Quartio.

FIGURE 3.12
The outside dining area in the House of Octavius Quartio.

TOPIC REVIEW

You should be able to:

1. Describe:
   - the layout and key features of the Insula of Diana
   - the layout and key features of the House of the Wooden Partition
   - the layout and key features of the House of Menander
   - the layout and key features of the House of Octavius Quartio.

2. Explain:
   - the living conditions for the poor in a Roman city
   - the uses of key rooms in a Roman domus
   - what the art and furnishing in a domus can tell us about the lives of its inhabitants
   - how different you think the lives of the rich and the poor were in a Roman city.

PRACTICE QUESTIONS

Source A: *The house of Menander, Pompeii*

Study **Source A**.

1. Which part of the house is shown in this picture?   [1]

2. Identify **three** rooms adjoining this part of the house, and explain how each was important for the inhabitants.   [6]

3.2 The Roman Home and Family

This topic examines a variety of subjects related to the household, starting with the role of the male head of the house. It then moves on to focus on the education system such a man would want to put his son through, and then finally explores how he would seek to entertain and impress guests at a dinner party.

THE PATERFAMILIAS

> **paterfamilias** the male head of a Roman family

The **paterfamilias** was the oldest living male in a Roman family, and the head of a Roman household. The term meant 'the father of the family', although the Latin word 'familia' meant more than our concept of 'family', because it also included the slaves and property of the house. The paterfamilias had legal power over his entire household;

in early Roman times, this included the power of life and death, although by the time of the empire, this was only really the case for a new-born child. Indeed, one duty of a paterfamilias was to inspect a new-born baby; if it was unwanted or illegitimate, then the paterfamilias could order for it to be abandoned and exposed (left out to die).

The paterfamilias was responsible for the welfare of his family. He had a duty to raise his children to be good citizens of Rome; he would therefore want to oversee the education of his children, especially his sons, and would normally appoint an educated slave to act as a tutor. When his daughter reached puberty, he was responsible too for arranging a suitable marriage – very often this happened without the girl having any say at all. He would expect his wife to be loyal and hard-working in the home, and would manage the purchase of any slaves for the household. The paterfamilias was also the religious head of the family, and would lead worship at the family's household shrine, where the spirits of the family's ancestors, the **Lares**, were believed to reside. Other religious duties might involve him overseeing suitable offerings to the gods at important moments such as birth, marriage and funerals.

Patrons and clients

If he was wealthy enough, then the paterfamilias might also act as a **patron** to **clients**. Roman society was based around this patron/client relationship. Poorer Romans in need of money would attach themselves as clients to a wealthy man, the patron. Clients were expected to appear at their patron's house at dawn every morning; later, they might be required to accompany him to the forum or to the baths. In the city, they acted as their master's supporters and were expected to vote for him if he ran for political office. In return, clients would hope for a small hand-out of money or a gift each day, or perhaps a business opportunity; if they were particularly lucky, they might even be invited to dine with their patron in the evening.

In Roman society, almost everyone seems to have been a patron or a client – indeed, many people were both at the same time, receiving help from those wealthier than them, and providing help to those less wealthy. The system was the oil in the wheels of Roman society.

An inscription of a client supporting a patron

One example of a client publicly supporting his patron can be seen in an election notice carefully painted on the wall of a street in Pompeii, where a man, Thalamus, identifies himself as the client of Publius Paquius Proculus and thereby encourages others to vote for his patron as duumvir, the highest political office in the town:

> Thalamus, his client, elects Publius Paquius Proculus duumvir with judicial power.
>
> CIL IV 933

THE EDUCATION OF BOYS

In early Roman times there were no schools as we would understand them. Children simply learnt from their parents – fathers would teach their sons their own trades, as well as some

Lares the Roman family's household gods, representing the spirits of the family ancestors

patron a Roman who gives financial or other such support to a client in return for work and favours

client a Roman who would attach himself to a wealthier patron in order to boost his income and business opportunities

Study questions

1 Is it common for people to have religious shrines or objects at home today?
2 Is there anything similar to the patron/client system in our society today?

PRESCRIBED SOURCE

Cooley and Cooley, *Pompeii: A Sourcebook*: H45 (CIL IV 8562)

Location: Pompeii, Large Palaestra

Description: an inscription by a teacher referring to being paid

Significance: evidence for the presence of a school at the side of an exercise ground

basic literacy and numeracy, while mothers would teach their daughters how to manage the household. Children were also taught the values of being a good citizen. However, as Rome grew more powerful, it started to be influenced by Greek civilisation, which had a long educational tradition in disciplines such as literature, history, mathematics and philosophy. As a result, the Romans came to model their education system on that of the Greeks.

Schools therefore began to emerge, although not as we would recognise them today – there were no buildings with classrooms, assembly halls and playgrounds. School fees were cheap so a teacher had to find a simple room to hire – perhaps the back room of a shop, with customers coming and going, or a room in a house or apartment building. We even hear of teachers meeting their students in public places, where they would have had to compete with the noise in the streets.

An inscription by a teacher

The following graffito was found scratched on a column on one side of the large palaestra (exercise ground) in Pompeii:

> Whoever has paid me the fee for teaching, let him have what he seeks from the gods.

CIL IV 8562

Besides suggesting that the teacher met his students in a colonnaded part of the palaestra, it is also interesting because the teacher is thanking the pupils who have paid him (or whose parents have) – this of course implies that there were some pupils whose fees were overdue.

In the following passage, the satirist Martial complains about being woken up by a teacher holding an early morning class in the street just outside his block of apartments:

> What do you have against us, spiteful schoolteacher? We know you are hated by all the boys and girls you teach. Before the crested cockerel has even crowed, you shatter the silence with your harsh voice and the lashes of your whip . . . Would you be willing, you old windbag, to accept the same pay for being silent as you now receive for shouting out lessons?

Martial, *Epigrams*, 9.68

FIGURE 3.13
Drawing of a fresco from the Estate of Julia Felix depicting a boy being caned.

It is interesting to note that in this passage school begins before dawn – presumably this allowed the teacher to make the most use of the quietest time of day, before the streets filled up with people conducting their business. The words quoted here also refer to corporal punishment, and this seems to have been common – Horace (see pp. 295ff.) even refers to his old teacher as 'Orbilius the flogger'. Despite this, Orbilius actually had a high reputation as a teacher, but teachers generally must have varied greatly in quality: they did not need any special qualifications, and so in theory anyone could set himself up in the role. They were often poorly paid and drawn from the lower rungs of society – perhaps freedmen or foreigners. It is also very hard for us to know how much progress pupils made in their classes – there were no exams, and therefore no results for us to inspect, and we have no evidence for any other forms of assessment.

The Roman school system in Rome consisted of three stages. The first, between the ages of seven and about eleven, was a type of primary school with a teacher known as the **litterator**; after this, pupils progressed onto a secondary education with the **grammaticus**, followed by tertiary education at the age of sixteen with a rhetoric teacher, the **rhetor**, who taught them the art of public speaking. It is hard to know exactly what proportion of children went to school, and it is likely that it was mainly the preserve of the wealthy; interestingly, it is clear that some girls did attend lessons with the litterator as well as boys. By the age of fourteen, girls were preparing to get married and boys from poorer families had started working. Evidence suggests that the literacy levels amongst the population were very low, although there may have been a higher level of 'functional literacy', whereby people had a limited ability to read and write where they needed to.

The litterator

The first stage of a Roman education was at the school of the litterator. Boys and girls would attend his lessons from the age of seven and learnt reading, writing and some basic arithmetic. The education was very repetitive at this stage – pupils had to practise writing letters endlessly and, once they had mastered the alphabet, they were forced to copy out useful phrases such as 'Seek advice from a wise man'. We even have a diary extract from a Roman schoolboy that tells us about learning at this age:

> My slave who carries my books handed me my waxed tablets, my writing box, and my writing instruments. Sitting in my place, I smoothed over the tablets. I printed the assigned sentence. When I had finished it, I showed it to the teacher. He corrected it, wrote over my errors, and told me to read it aloud. So instructed, I recited it to another student.

CGL III, pp. 645–647

The boy's words tell us a lot about the equipment used by Roman pupils. They first used wax tablets – thin sheets of wood covered with wax, on which pupils could write with a **stilus**, an implement with a sharp end for marking the wax and a flat end to rub the wax out and smooth

litterator a teacher for primary-aged children in the Roman world

grammaticus a teacher for secondary-aged children in the Roman world

rhetor a teacher for tertiary-aged boys in the Roman world

EXPLORE FURTHER

Figure 3.13 is a drawing of a wall-painting from a large residence in Pompeii, the Estate of Julia Felix. The whole scene is set under a colonnade in the forum and depicts a pupil being beaten while others get on with their work. What does this painting suggest about Roman education?

stilus a pen-like implement used to write on wax tablets

FIGURE 3.14
A relief of a boy arriving late to school.

it over again. When pupils were competent writers, they would be allowed to move on to write with a pen and ink on a papyrus, thick reed paper invented in ancient Egypt.

Another feature of this passage is that the pupil has a slave to accompany him to school – if a family was wealthy enough, it would appoint an educated slave to supervise a boy's studies and act as his private tutor.

The grammaticus

FIGURE 3.15
Roman writing implements.

If parents could afford it, then their sons moved onto the grammaticus at the age of about twelve. The basis of the studies was Greek and Roman literature. The first century BC saw the emergence of some of Rome's greatest writers, such as Cicero, Virgil, Horace and Ovid. In the grammaticus' class, writers such as these were studied; in particular, Virgil's *Aeneid*, which told of the escape from Troy to Italy by Aeneas (whom the Romans believed to be their ancestor), was a standard text, much as the works of Shakespeare have been in the English-speaking world. Pupils were taught to learn and recite passages by heart, and to comment on matters such as grammar, figures of speech and the poet's use of mythology. The development of a strong working memory was emphasised at this stage of the curriculum.

In addition, a pupil would start to learn Greek at this time. This was considered the language of educated people, partly because there had been so many great thinkers and writers in the ancient Greek world – poets such as Homer, philosophers such as Plato, historians such as Herodotus, and orators such as Demosthenes. Moreover, it was also important to learn Greek because the eastern half of the Roman empire was predominantly Greek-speaking; Greek was the language of government and law there, and a Roman provincial official would have needed to know Greek fluently.

Other subjects were also studied at this stage too: one source speaks of a curriculum including music, astronomy, philosophy and natural science. However, these subjects were all secondary to the study of literature – for example, astronomy was studied so that a pupil could be better informed when a poet referred to the stars.

Study questions

1 Are there any similarities between Roman schools and schools today?

2 Why do you think teachers were so undervalued when they played such an important role in society?

3 Do you think that there should be courses in rhetoric today? What would be the advantages and disadvantages of such courses?

The rhetor

At the age of sixteen, the privileged few would move on to lessons with the rhetor. He taught them the art of public speaking, a crucial skill in a world without the various means of communication which we have today, such as newspapers, email, the internet, radio and television; a successful public figure in Rome had to be able to speak well in front of a large crowd of people. Pupils therefore learnt to compose and deliver speeches; one type of exercise required them to debate an event from history or literature, such as 'Should Hannibal have invaded Italy?' or 'Should Dido have committed suicide?' (Hannibal was the great Carthaginian general who almost defeated the Romans in the late third century BC, while Dido was a famous character from Virgil's *Aeneid* who had a doomed love affair with Aeneas.) Another type required them to analyse a specific legal case and argue either for the prosecution or for the defence. Pupils were taught to deliver their speeches with facial expression and hand gestures; their training was therefore similar to a barrister's training today, and it is no surprise that many of Rome's leading politicians were also accomplished lawyers.

In the following passage, the statesman Cicero outlines some of the qualities he feels a pupil should acquire through this training:

> The student must develop his style by careful attention not only to word choice but also to sentence construction. He must be thoroughly acquainted with all the emotions which nature has given to the human race because he must use all his power and ability at speaking to calm or, alternatively, to stir up those that listen to him . . . Delivery of speech must be reinforced by bodily movement, gesture, facial expression, and by modulation and variation of the voice.
>
> Cicero, *About the Orator*, 1.17–18

> **cena** the Roman word for a dinner

THE DINNER PARTY

A Roman dinner party, known in Latin as a **cena**, was an important social occasion for the affluent. Roman society did not have restaurants as we know them, but merely fast-food bars, which served food of moderate quality. Therefore, a respectable Roman would have eaten at home, and hosting a good dinner party became an important way for a paterfamilias to promote and confirm his social status. He would want to entertain friends and make new business and social contacts, while as a patron he would have been expected to invite his clients and freedmen to dinner from time to time.

FIGURE 3.16
A fresco of a Roman dinner party from Pompeii. The slaves are depicted as smaller in stature than the guests.

A dinner party was full of ritual and formality. It might typically begin in the late afternoon, after the host and guests had spent time at the baths. When the guests arrived at the host's house, wearing formal evening clothes, they might first admire its art and paintings before being shown by a slave into the triclinium. The word triclinium literally meant 'three-couch room', since it contained three long couches laid out in a U-shape. Guests would recline on these couches as they ate, normally with three guests to a couch. Couches were covered in mattresses for comfort and each place was divided by cushions. Guests lay in the reclining position, leaning on their left elbows. They took their food from the central table, which was kept supplied by the slaves, who would also walk round pouring wine and offering basins of water for diners to wash their hands in.

The seating plan was a matter of great precision and a sign of the social status of the guests. The plan in Figure 3.17 shows the layout of the three couches, which were called 'high', 'medium' and 'low'; each of the three seats on a couch was also divided into 'high', 'middle' and 'low', working from the right as you look at the couch. The place of honour was Y, at the low end of the medium couch. This was no doubt because the middle couch faced out towards the entrance to the triclinium and, leaning on one's left elbow,

FIGURE 3.17
A triclinium seating plan.

S & C Find out about the Roman cookbook that has survived under the name of 'Apicius'. Are there any recipes there that you would like to try at home?

mulsum a type of Roman wine sweetened by honey

FIGURE 3.18
A fresco from Pompeii of a plate of eggs, dead thrushes and bronze pitchers.

PRESCRIBED SOURCE

Cooley and Cooley, Pompeii: A Sourcebook: D80 (CIL IV 7698a–c)

Location: Pompeii, House of Sallust

Description: three inscriptions on the wall of a summer dining-room

Significance: instructions for guests about how to behave at a dinner party

this usually offered the best view of a garden or works of art opposite. Next to the guest of honour normally sat the host at position X, the high position on the low couch, which allowed him to speak with his most important guest. Also on the low couch would likely be the host's clients or freedmen. Other guests would recline on the medium and high couches, with the guest of honour perhaps having his clients or freedmen next to him.

A dinner party typically had three courses. The first might be made up of light appetisers, such as eggs, olives or salads; these were followed by **mulsum**, a type of wine sweetened by honey. The second, the main course, was typically a selection of meats or fish accompanied by vegetables and a variety of sauces. The final course was dessert, which might consist of fruit, nuts or simple sweet-cakes. The host would want to show off throughout by serving a variety of foods and recipes, as well as good quality wine, both red and white.

A number of sources suggest that some hosts served different quality food and wine at the same meal: what you received depended on your social status. You will read one example of this in your prescribed literature (see p. 322), while another famous example comes from the satirist Juvenal, who writes in a poem (Satire 5) of dining with his patron. The dinner party had three categories of guest: the host Virro and his friends; Virro's clients; and the freedmen. Like Pliny, some wealthy Romans clearly disapproved of this practice.

A good host would also put on entertainment during or after the meal. One possibility was an extended session of drinking wine. This was not simply a short-cut to getting drunk, since the Romans always watered down their wine, perhaps by adding as much as four-fifths of water to one-fifth of wine. Other entertainment might include dancers, acrobats and clowns, while we also hear of guests playing games similar to dice and backgammon. Some hosts might organise more intellectual activities, such as a discussion about literature or philosophy. Whatever the case, a host would have hoped that his guests would mix well and behave appropriately.

An inscription by a dinner party host

The following inscriptions found on the wall of the summer dining room of one Pompeian house make clear the standards one host expected from his dinner guests:

> Let water wash your feet clean and a slave wipe them dry;
> Let a cloth cover the couch, take care of our linens.

> Remove lustful expressions and flirtatious tender eyes
> From another man's wife; may there be modesty in your expression.

> [. . .] postpone your tiresome quarrels
> If you can, or leave, and take them home with you.

CIL IV 7698a–c

The first inscription refers to the preparations at the start of the dinner party: guests should have their feet washed by slaves and take care not to dirty the furniture. The second inscription warns male diners not to flirt with another man's wife, while the third one tells diners to go home if they are likely to start an argument.

Study questions

1 How common is it for food to be used to denote social status today?
2 What benefits do you think a host would gain from holding a good dinner party?
3 What would you have enjoyed about dining in the Roman style? What would you have found strange?

ACTIVITY

Imagine that you are going to host a Roman dinner party. Design a menu sheet for the occasion (although it should be noted that there is no evidence that the Romans did this, just as it is unusual for us to do this for a private dinner party today).

TOPIC REVIEW

You should be able to:

1. Describe:
   - the powers and responsibilities of a Roman paterfamilias
   - the patron and client system
   - the three stages of the Roman education system
   - the structure and features of a typical Roman dinner party.

2. Explain:
   - how a Roman household was structured
   - why the patron/client system was important for Roman society
   - the strengths and weaknesses of the Roman education system
   - why a Roman dinner party was important for the reputation and social status of the host.

PRACTICE QUESTIONS

Source A: *CGL III*, pp. 645–647

My slave who carries my books handed me my waxed tablets, my writing box, and my writing instruments. Sitting in my place, I smoothed over the tablets. I printed the assigned sentence. When I had finished it, I showed it to the teacher. He corrected it, wrote over my errors, and told me to read it aloud. So instructed, I recited it to another student.

1. What was a waxed tablet and how was it used by school children? [2]
2. Evaluate whether a modern student would have enjoyed studying in a Roman school? Use the source as a starting point **and** use your own knowledge in your answer. [8]

3.3 Roman Society

This topic looks at the different social groups in Roman society, from those at the top rungs, the senators and equites, to those at the other end – the slaves. In between were the ordinary citizens and, below them, freed slaves who are referred to as freedmen.

CITIZENS

Roman society was strongly divided by class and status. All citizens had a wide range of privileges, including protection under Roman law. Full citizenship was only open to men. Women were given a limited form of citizenship and were regarded as minors in Roman law, holding the same status as children; they could not vote and had no say in the Roman political system.

Citizens were entitled to some benefits, including free entry to the public games and free or heavily subsidised use of the public baths; moreover, poorer citizens in the city of Rome were provided with free corn out of public funds. The majority of citizens belonged to the classes beneath the senators and equites described below; many were relatively poor and ill-educated, and engaged in any number of trades and roles to make ends meet. We can learn a great deal about such types of work from surviving paintings and inscriptions, especially in the well-preserved cities of Pompeii and Herculaneum. Moreover, there is also some literary evidence: in the following passage by the comic playwright Plautus, one wealthy character complains about the number of tradesmen he has to pay:

> On your doorstep stand the clothes cleaner, the clothes dyer, the goldsmith, the wool weaver, the man who sells lace and the man who sells underwear, makers of veils, sellers of purple dye, sellers of yellow dye, makers of muffs and shoemakers who add balsam scent to their shoes, linen retailers, bootmakers, squatting cobblers, slipper makers, sandal makers, and fabric strainers. They all demand payment . . . and just when you think you've paid them all, they leave, but others appear, three hundred more, demanding payment – purse makers, weavers, fringe makers, manufacturers of jewellery cases – all cluttering up your atrium!
>
> Plautus, *The Pot of Gold*, 507ff.

In addition to these trades, many men chose to serve in the Roman army.

Above the lower classes, there were two elite classes of Roman society: the senators and the equites.

SENATORS

The highest group in the Roman class structure were the **senators**, who sat in the Senate. For centuries, this was a powerful body within the Roman political structure, although by the time of the emperors its power had been reduced; nonetheless, it continued to influence decisions and had the power to confer the title of emperor. By the first century AD the number of senators was fixed at 600; to qualify, a man had to be born into the senatorial class (meaning that his father had been a senator) or he had to have been elevated to the senatorial class by the emperor. In either case, a senator had to own property worth more than one million sesterces – a vast amount of money in the Roman world. The sons of senators were automatically eligible to be elected to the senate at the age of seventeen, but over time some families fell out of the senatorial class, perhaps through a loss of wealth, perhaps through lack of a male heir, or perhaps through falling out of favour with the emperor. Therefore, in each generation new senatorial families were elevated by the emperor.

Senators had a number of rights and responsibilities. They were not allowed to engage directly in trade and commerce (although evidence suggests that this rule was sometimes ignored), nor were they paid for being senators, and so their wealth came largely from their property. As a result, men of senatorial rank were free to give their time to politics and public service; they were the only citizens who could stand each year for election as **magistrates** – politicians who held the main legal and political offices. The two most important such offices were those of **consul** and **praetor**.

senators members of the highest social class in Rome; a senator had to own property worth at least one million sesterces

magistrate an elected politician in Rome

consul the most important public official in Rome after the emperor; two consuls were elected annually

praetor the second highest category of public official in Rome, responsible for the law courts and imperial administration

equites members of the second social class in Rome; an equestrian had to own property worth at least 400,000 sesterces

Two consuls were elected each year, and they were the most important officials in Rome after the emperor. In the time of the emperor Augustus, twelve praetors were elected each year, and they were responsible for the legal system and imperial administration. In addition to these positions, the emperor could appoint a senator to a number of other roles, including commanding a legion of the army, governing a province, supervising public services in Rome or holding an important public priesthood. Senators had a number of privileges, including reserved seating at public games and the right to wear a broad purple stripe on the border of their toga to mark their rank.

EQUITES

The second elite group in Roman society was made up of **equites**, or the 'equestrian order'. The word 'equites' literally means 'knights', and in the early days of Rome's history the term applied to those men wealthy enough to own a horse. However, by the first century AD, membership of the equites was open to men who had property worth 400,000 sesterces. The equites were often successful businessmen, since they could engage in trade and commerce where the senators could not. They were also used by the emperor to fill many roles in the civil service in Rome or the provinces, such as managing financial affairs. Equestrians could even be appointed governors of small provinces – one famous equestrian is Pontius Pilate, who was governor of the province of Judaea at the time of the trial and execution of Jesus Christ.

Equites were allowed to signify their rank by wearing a toga with a narrow purple stripe, as well as a gold finger ring. They could also be promoted to the senatorial class if they had enough property wealth and if a vacancy came up.

FIGURE 3.19
A Roman senator wearing a toga.

SLAVES

Slavery was an accepted part of life in the Roman world, as it has been in most societies until recent times. The labour of slaves was central to supporting the Roman economy and it could not have survived without it. There were various ways in which people fell into slavery:

- **Born a slave** This was perhaps the most common route into slavery: any child born to a slave mother automatically held slave status, even if the father was a citizen, as often happened.
- **Captives of war** As the Romans conquered new lands, their victories produced a significant supply of slaves and a great market for slave dealers. However, this supply dried up significantly in the second century AD, by which time the Romans had nearly reached the extent of their conquests.
- **Exposure** Babies abandoned by their parents at birth might be saved and brought up as slaves.
- **Kidnapping** Some were captured by kidnappers or pirates and sold into slavery; some remote parts of the Roman world were particularly dangerous for travellers.

- **Criminals** Some convicted criminals could be condemned to slavery, and sent to train as gladiators or to work in the mines.

Newly captured slaves were taken to a slave market. There were many of these in the Roman empire, but one or two were particularly large: on the Greek island of Delos, 10,000 slaves could apparently be sold on just one day. At the market, the enslaved people were put on platforms with placards hanging around their necks; these advertised their qualities and characteristics such as age, place of origin, level of education, and state of health.

Once bought, the life a slave lived was somewhat dependent on their skills and talents. There were broadly three groups of slaves in the Roman world:

- **Domestic slaves** It was probably preferable to live in a private household: an educated Greek slave might be highly valued as a tutor for children, while women were bought to help with domestic tasks such as childcare, cooking, weaving and shopping; male domestic slaves would be required to work for the paterfamilias, perhaps doing his accounts, accompanying him to the baths, or running errands.
- **Industrial slaves** Stronger male slaves might be marked down for more challenging or dangerous tasks: working in mines, factories, on large farming estates or as rowers on galleys. In each case, the conditions were grim and life expectancy was relatively short.
- **Public slaves** These were owned by the state rather than a private individual. They could perform a number of roles in a town or city, such as seeing to the upkeep of temples, baths and other public buildings. They might also work on public construction or maintenance projects on public facilities such as roads and aqueducts. Educated slaves could work as scribes in the Roman civil service.

Slaves were legally classified as property and a master had total rights over a slave, including the power of life and death. To stop them running away, some masters branded their slaves. Moreover, some metal identification collars dating to the late Roman period have survived; these would have been fixed around the necks of slaves, and one such collar has the following inscription:

> I have run away. Capture me. When you have returned me to my master, Zoninus, you will receive a reward.

CIL XV 7194

A slave had no legal or political rights, nor could they marry or own property, and so the quality of their treatment depended heavily on the master's character. Some masters were incredibly cruel, subjecting their slaves to frequent physical and sexual abuse. One example of a cruel master was Larcius Macedo, who you will read about in your prescribed literature (see p. 323). Some of the slaves in his large household conspired to kill him, and after his death the usual punishment was applied – every slave in the house was put to death, whether they were innocent or guilty of the crime.

Nonetheless, we also hear of warm and trusting slave/master relationships. One famous example was Cicero's loyal secretary Tiro, who

FIGURE 3.20
Relief showing slaves working at a wine-press.

S & C Slavery might not be legal today, but it still exists worldwide in many forms. Look up the following website: http://www.antislavery.org/english/, and list the ways in which people are enslaved today. How are governments and organisations trying to combat this?

PRESCRIBED SOURCE

Cooley and Cooley, *Pompeii: A Sourcebook*: F15 (CIL IV 910)

Location: Pompeii, Via della Fortuna

Description: a declaration of support by a freedman for an election candidate

Significance: may well show a freedman supporting his former master in his campaign

Augustales Roman public officials connected to preserving the honour of the emperor. They were largely drawn from the ranks of freedmen

was a close adviser of the great statesman, while Pliny, who relates the story of Larcius Macedo's murder with disapproval and horror, admits elsewhere that he could feel great grief at the death of his slaves.

FREEDMEN

Roman society was unusual in that it offered the hope of freedom to slaves. Slaves were able to earn some money, which they could put away to buy their freedom after a long period of service – this was designed to motivate slaves to work hard. In addition, a master might actually choose to free a slave if he had served him well or if he had performed a particularly outstanding act. We even hear of masters who freed slave-girls in order to marry them, especially if they had borne them a child. Some masters had more selfish reasons for freeing slaves: it was often cheaper to free elderly slaves who were too weak to work than to look after them in old age; there was little hope for such ex-slaves being able to support themselves.

Once free, ex-slaves had the status of 'freedmen'; they were allowed to wear a special felt cap to symbolise their liberty. Freedmen were classified as Roman citizens, although they were not allowed to run for public office or to become members of the senatorial or equestrian classes even if they made enough money to do so. However, the children of freedmen had the full rights of citizenship – as we have seen above, Larcius Macedo was the son of a freedman who became a senator. A freedman was still tied to his former master as a client, and required to work for him for a number of days each year, and many would have continued to work for their former master full time as a client.

An inscription by a freedman for an election candidate

In this inscription, Ceratus identifies himself as a freedman and declares his support for Publius Vedius Nummianus as aedile, the second highest political office in Pompeii. Given that he identifies himself as a freedman, it is likely that Nummianus is the former master he still works for:

> Ceratus, freedman, asks for Publius Vedius Numm[ianus] as aedile.
>
> CIL IV 910

However, besides working for their former master, freedmen could also go on to a variety of fields of trade and business, and a few became highly successful. They could also play an important civic role in their city by serving as one of the **Augustales**. Evidence from Herculaneum suggests that these were public officials with a status in the town second only to the magistrates. They could even display the symbols of a magistrate (including a bordered toga), and in return for their status they were expected to repair buildings, erect statues and pay for games. They also performed religious duties, and so have sometimes been thought of as priests. A key point about the Augustales was that they were largely drawn from the ranks of freedmen. The term 'Augustalis' came from the emperor Augustus; the Augustales seem to have been connected with preserving the dignity and honour of the emperor of the day. Becoming an Augustalis therefore gave a freedman the opportunity to hold high public office and show their loyalty to the empire which had freed him.

By the late first century AD, it is likely that the vast majority of the citizen population of Rome had some ancestors who had been slaves or freedmen. It was one impressive feature of Roman society that it was able to give hope and opportunity to people who were legally no different from items of property.

FIGURE 3.21
A marble relief of two freedmen, Publius Licinius Philonicus and Publius Licinius Demetrius. On the left are the rods and axes used in the ceremony of freeing a slave. The tools of a smith and a carpenter can also be seen.

The tomb of Naevoleia Tyche

One real-life example of a freedman and freedwoman who became very wealthy can be found in Pompeii. In the AD 60s, the freedman Gaius Munatius Faustus built a tomb outside the city for himself and his wife, the freedwoman Naevoleia Tyche. However, after Munatius' death, when Naevoleia seems to have inherited his wealth and property, she soon had another, far grander tomb built outside the other side of the city (burial grounds were always located outside the walls of a city for reasons of public health and religious duty).

Building an elaborate tomb was one way to show off wealth in the Roman world, since it was beyond the means of most Romans. Naevoleia was clearly more determined than her husband to show off both their combined wealth and the influence that Munatius had wielded in the city. The new tomb, made of marble, took the shape of a raised altar and was located within an enclosure. On one side of the tomb was sculpted an image of a ship, on the opposite side a ceremonial seat and footstool. On the front of the tomb was carved a detailed scene showing some sort of public ceremony, with an inscription and an image of Naevoleia above it. The inscription translates as follows:

> Naevoleia Tyche, freedwoman of Lucius, for herself and for Gaius Munatius Faustus, *Augustalis* and Country District Dweller, to whom the town councillors with the consent of the people decreed an honorific chair for his merits. Naevoleia Tyche had this monument in her lifetime for her own freedmen and freedwomen and for those of Gaius Munatius Faustus.
>
> CIL X 1030

We can establish a number of details about the life of Munatius from this tomb. The image of the ship suggests that he made his money through shipping; he clearly became an influential figure in the city, and the public ceremony may even depict a distribution of money or grain that he made to the people of Pompeii. Moreover, he served as an Augustalis, and was awarded a ceremonial seat most probably at public games or performances, for his services to the city.

FIGURE 3.22
A set of drawings showing the sides of the tomb of Naevoleia Tyche and its most important imagery.

FIGURE 3.23
The tomb of Naevoleia Tyche today.

PRESCRIBED SOURCE

The tomb of Naevoleia Tyche, including inscription

Built: AD 60s

Location: Pompeii (outside the Herculaneum Gate)

Name: named after the wealthy freedwoman who had this built for herself and her husband

Significance: a large tomb illustrating how successful freedmen and freedwomen could become in Roman society

Inscription: this identifies the tomb as belonging to Naevoleia and her husband Gaius Munatius Faustus and lists some of his achievements.

It is also important to reflect on the image that Naevoleia projects of herself on the tomb, since it draws attention to her own wealth and status in the city. The inscription itself emphasises that she is the one who has had the tomb built, while an image of her is depicted above the main scene. We learn too that, like her husband, she has other freedmen and freedwomen as her clients; even a freedwoman could play a significant role in Pompeian society.

TOPIC REVIEW

You should be able to:

1. Describe:
   - the nature of citizenship
   - the responsibilties and privileges of the senators and equites
   - the key features of Roman slavery
   - the rights of freedmen.

2. Explain:
   - the importance of citizenship to a Roman
   - the ways in which the senators and equites helped the running of Roman society
   - what life may have been like for different types of slave in the Roman world
   - the extent to which freedmen could be independent and successful.

PRACTICE QUESTIONS

Source A: *CIL IV*, 910

Ceratus, freedman, asks for Publius Vedius Numm[ianus] as aedile.

Study **Source A**.

1. What is the relationship between the two men named in this inscription, and how do you know?   [2]

2. 'Freedmen could play an important role in Roman society.' To what extent to you agree with this statement? Use the source as a starting point **and** use your own knowledge in your answer.   [8]

3.4 Leisure and Entertainment

TOPIC OVERVIEW

- The amphitheatre, including:
  - design of amphitheatre buildings, including the *Colosseum*
  - types of shows
  - sponsorship of games by the Emperor or politicians
  - gladiators; their status, training and types
  - audience involvement
- The chariot races, including:
  - design of the *Circus Maximus*
  - teams, colours, charioteers, horses and their status
  - public attitudes and audience involvement
  - the social significance of such events
- The theatre, including:
  - the design of theatre buildings and use of sets, costumes, masks
  - Roman comedy and its stock characters; mime and pantomime
  - actors and actresses; their reputation and social standing
- The baths, including:
  - the reasons people used bath complexes
  - design of bath buildings, and the different types of bath
  - activities at the baths, including the use of the *palaestra*

The prescribed sources for this topic are:

- the Colosseum
- the Circus Maximus
- the Large Theatre at Pompeii
- the Central Baths at Herculaneum
- inscription D51 (CIL X 833, 834) ⎫
- inscription D16 (CIL IV 1189) ⎬ from Cooley and Cooley, *Pompeii: A Sourcebook*

Don't forget that you will be given credit in the exam if you study extra sources and make relevant use of them in your answers.

This large topic examines four different types of leisure and entertainment. Three of them – amphitheatre shows, theatre shows and the chariot races – have a number of similarities, not least in the way that politicians funded them in order to win favour from the people. The fourth, baths, focuses on a central aspect of Roman daily life.

THE AMPHITHEATRE

Design

We first hear of gladiatorial fighting in the third century BC. It grew in popularity and by the late first century BC it was an established and popular part of Roman life. Gladiatorial fights were held in an amphitheatre, a word derived from the fact the stadium was a doubled-up version of a semi-circular theatre (*amphi* meant 'both', so that 'amphitheatre' really meant 'a theatre on both sides'). Today the terms 'theatre' and 'amphitheatre' are often confused – it is simplest to remember that a theatre had a 180-degree viewing area, while in an amphitheatre it was 360 degrees. Amphitheatres were not completely round but rather oval in shape. Most Roman cities of any size had an amphitheatre, and the remains of many more than 200 have been found throughout the Roman world.

The Colosseum

The most famous Roman amphitheatre was of course the Colosseum, situated in the heart of Rome. In fact, Romans never called it by this name (which was first used centuries after the Roman Empire fell). To them, it was the 'Flavian Amphitheatre', from the name Flavius, which was the family name of the emperor Vespasian, who reigned from AD 69 to 79. It was Vespasian who commissioned this enormous building project in the AD 70s, since he wanted to provide a wonderful stadium for the people in order to ensure his popularity. It took about ten years to build, and at its completion his builders had produced easily the largest amphitheatre in the Roman Empire. The capacity is estimated to have been around 50,000 (for comparison, the amphitheatre at Pompeii could hold an estimated 20,000). Its outer dimensions were 188 metres by 156 metres, while the outer wall rose to about 48 metres in height.

    The basic design of the Colosseum was based on a series of concentric circles, leading in from a huge outer wall to the arena inside. The outer wall consisted of four storeys: the first three had open archways looking out, while the fourth had small windows. The outer wall was built largely of hard travertine rock, a limestone quarried near Rome. Between the outer wall and the arena at ground level there were four circular corridors, as you can see from Figure 3.24. These had facilities such as water fountains and toilets, while they also led to staircases and the seating above. The whole design was cleverly constructed using archways, since arches provided a very stable support for the weight above. These arches were constructed of bricks and concrete – the Romans had invented concrete, which enabled the construction of a strong arch since the concrete allowed the bricks to stay in place at an angle.

FIGURE 3.24
A cut away reconstruction of the Colosseum.

---

vomitoria the staircases of the amphitheatre, via which people could pour out of the stadium in great numbers

---

The many staircases and walkways allowed spectators to get in and out of the building quickly and efficiently. Collectively, the staircases were known as **vomitoria**, which is linked to our word 'vomit', since the people could pour out of the seating area in great numbers. The amphitheatre had eighty entrances, with four especially ornate ones on the main axes – the two on the long axis are generally thought to be the performers' entrance and exit, while the two on the short axis were probably the entrances that VIPs used. There is evidence that these two were monumental entrances, beautifully designed with stucco – a type of plaster that it is easy to paint over. In fact, it is likely that stucco was used in many areas of the building, which allowed it to be decorated with beautiful paintwork.

This was not the only impressive design feature – if it became too hot, a huge awning could be pulled over the top of the seating area to protect two thirds of the crowd from the sun. In the seating area, up to the third storey was made of marble, which must have given the stadium a very impressive look. The seats at the level of the fourth storey were of wood, to reduce the downward weight and the pressure on the outer wall. All the seating was steeply tiered so that everyone could get a good view while sitting down. Nonetheless, spectators were seated rigidly according to social class: the more status you held, the nearer to the action you would be. Therefore, on the level podium nearest to the arena was the imperial box for the emperor, special seats for the Vestal Virgins, and seating for the senators. Above that there were three main tiers of seating: the equites sat in the first tier, behind them were the ordinary citizens, and at the top level sat those from society's marginalised groups – women, slaves and the poor.

The arena itself was surrounded by a wall of 4 metres in height. Above it was a metal fence, while during the shows archers stood guard to shoot any animal that threatened the spectators. In the arena itself, the ground was covered in sand, which could soak up the blood of victims (in fact, *harena* in Latin meant 'sand', which is where our word 'arena' comes from). Beneath the arena floor was an underground network of tunnels, cages and lifts, where animals were held before being sent into action through trapdoors. This underground area was also linked by a tunnel to a point outside the stadium, so that the spectators would not know what to expect before the animals appeared.

Sponsorship of the games

The gladiatorial games in Rome were closely associated with the power of the emperor. Even before the time of the emperors, senior politicians had campaigned for votes by promising to fund impressive games – it was a fine way to win public popularity. In the time of the emperors, this became a way for the emperor to promote himself and to show off his power. Senior politicians also continued to sponsor gladiatorial shows, although successive emperors passed laws ensuring that they alone could give far more spectacular shows than anyone else. We hear of some remarkable shows – the most extravagant, which was certainly not typical, came early in the second century AD when the emperor Trajan celebrated the military victories he had won by holding games over a 123-day period, during which 10,000 gladiators and 11,000 animals were apparently used.

The link between public shows and political sponsorship also remained strong in the provincial cities of the Roman Empire. Each city had its own council with elected representatives, and the evidence shows that they too paid for impressive shows in order to win public favour from the local population.

FIGURE 3.25
The network of tunnels under the amphitheatre at Puteoli.

An inscription advertising the games in Pompeii

This inscription, which was painted in red on the outside wall of a very large building on one side of the forum, shows a Pompeian politician advertising the games he is soon to put on for the people:

> The gladiatorial troupe of Aulus Suettius Certus, aedile, will fight at Pompeii on 31 May. There will be a hunt and awnings.

CIL IV 1189

The inscription was discovered painted on a wall close to the forum, which faced onto one of Pompeii's largest streets. Clearly Aulus Suettius Certus, who as one of two aediles jointly held the second most powerful position in the city, wanted to advertise his games in a very prominent place. It is also interesting to note that he promised both gladiators and wild beasts (the 'hunt'), as well as an awning to protect spectators from the heat of summer.

Types of shows

There are a variety of references to the gladiatorial games by Roman writers, and so it is possible to piece together the events of a day at the amphitheatre. The action started early in the morning and lasted until evening, so it was vital for the sponsor to make sure that he provided plenty of variety. It seems that the morning events were often dedicated to shows involving animals, while the gladiatorial contests came later in the day. At some point, too, there were often public executions of convicts – one writer refers to these happening at midday on one occasion, although we cannot be sure that this was always the practice. Indeed, we should be careful not to think that a day at the amphitheatre always followed exactly the same pattern.

Wild animals

Wild animals were a key feature of the games. It was a source of pride for an emperor in particular to bring the most exotic and dangerous beasts from all over the Roman Empire and beyond to the Colosseum – sources refer to animals such as giraffes, crocodiles and hippopotami. Most spectators would never have seen such animals and must have been amazed at the sight of them. Some were trained to perform tricks, just as circus animals do today. Sources speak of teams of panthers drawing chariots, of a tigress tearing a lion to pieces and then going to lick its trainer's hand, and of elephants bowing in front of the imperial box.

FIGURE 3.26
A Bestiarius fights a tiger.

Another form of entertainment was to set two different types of animal against one another, such as a bear and a buffalo, or an elephant and a rhinoceros. Very often, however, a human fighter would line up against such animals. He was known as a Bestiarius ('beast fighter') and his weapons gave him a significant advantage over the animals, despite their ferocity, so that he was expected to dispatch them in a variety of ways. Such slaughter was more than just mere entertainment. By introducing all these animals into the arena, an emperor was able to make two political points – first of all, that the empire had power over nature, just as it did over human beings, and secondly that such a great range of animals demonstrated just how far and wide the Romans had conquered.

Executions

During the middle of the day events often took an even more gruesome twist, when convicted criminals were brought out to be executed. Although these executions were presented as entertainment, they also served as a warning to the people to obey the emperor and of the dangers of criminality. The convicts were usually killed by being exposed to the wild animals, either tied to stakes or being made to fight them, but we also hear of criminals being made to fight each other to the death.

Gladiatorial combat

When it was time for the gladiator fights, the proceedings typically began with a procession around the arena, which was accompanied by the music of an orchestra – one mosaic shows musicians playing a water organ, trumpets and horns. When the procession was over, weapons were examined, and the fighters moved off to prepare for their bouts, which were mainly between individual fighters, although it seems that group fights also took place at times. Most bouts were overseen by a referee who also had an assistant on hand; they carried long staffs to separate the fighters if necessary.

A fight between two gladiators might last for as long as fifteen or twenty minutes, but when one man could go on no longer, he signalled defeat by raising a finger. His opponent now stood over him and looked for a signal from the emperor – to kill or to spare. The emperor would listen to the noise of the crowd and make his decision. He indicated this by giving a sign with his thumb – it is not clear if a 'thumbs up' meant 'let him die' or 'let him live'; another theory suggests that if he chose death he put his thumb out

ACTIVITY

Imagine that you are a Roman politician about to pay for a day at the amphitheatre. Design an advertisement notice to make the people aware of what you are going to offer.

MODERN PARALLEL

Are there any modern examples of politicians or public figures funding public entertainment in order to win popularity or support from a large number of people?

sideways to indicate a cutting sword. However, the key point is that at this moment the emperor was seen to engage with his people and to have the power of life and death.

In reality, defeated gladiators were probably not killed that often – evidence suggests that it may only have been one in five. It was very expensive to train gladiators, and a trainer would not have wanted to lose a good one. However, if a defeated gladiator was to be killed, he was trained not to flinch, nor to ask for mercy. Once he was slain, an attendant came out and hit his head with a mallet, while another dressed as Mercury, the god who escorted souls to the underworld, prodded the corpse with a hot rod. It was then removed from the arena, and the throat was cut to make sure that the man was dead. Back in the arena, other attendants raked over the bloody sand.

The gladiators

Gladiators came from a variety of backgrounds. Some would be strong slaves, others prisoners of war, and some convicted criminals; there were even free men who signed up to try to escape poverty. All gladiators had to train in a gladiator school, which was run by a trainer. He would hire out his fighters to a magistrate wishing to fund a gladiatorial show as its sponsor. Training was intensely tough; the men would spend hours practising fighting drills with blunted wooden swords, while they would also be taught how to face death bravely. Much expense was spent on the gladiators: they had access to high quality medical care and were given a high-energy diet of food such as barley, beans, oatmeal and fruit. A trainer had the power of life and death over his trainees, who held a very low social status and did not have the protection of the Roman legal system – a gladiator was regarded as being **infamis**.

The name 'gladiator' comes from the Latin *gladius*, meaning a sword. However, gladiators did not all use the same equipment: there were various types who were distinguished by their armour, their weapons, and their fighting style. The crowds loved to see different fighters pitted against one another, each one using his distinct skills and weapons. Most types of gladiators can be divided into one of two categories: heavily armed and therefore hard to wound, or lightly armed and quick on their feet.

Scholars have examined the evidence carefully for the different types of gladiator – their names and the equipment they used. While we cannot have certainty on these matters, in the box overleaf you can see details of what are believed to be some of the most common types of gladiator. Some were heavily armed, others lightly armed, and it seems that it was common for the different types to be pitted against one another in order to watch a clash of styles and weapons. So, for example, a retiarius might be matched against a secutor.

In addition to the normal types of gladiatorial fighting, some sponsors liked to put on shows that were more unusual and strange, and which brought novel interest for the audience. One example comes in the evidence that there were some female gladiators, while another is found in a number of

FIGURE 3.27
An imagined fight between a secutor and a retiarius.

EXPLORE FURTHER

There is a famous story of a riot in the amphitheatre of Pompeii in AD 59, when rival factions of supporters from Pompeii and a nearby town, Nuceria, broke into a fight with each other. Read the historian Tacitus' account of the riot in *Annals*, 14.17, and examine the details of the wall painting in the House of Actius Anicetus, which seems to depict the event.

infamis literally 'shameful' or 'disgraceful', the very low legal status given to a number of groups in the Roman world, including gladiators, charioteers, actors and prostitutes

FIGURE 3.28
A gladiator's helmet.

KEY TERMS   Gladiators

Murmillo A gladiator who was heavily armed rather like a Roman legionary soldier. He had a fish-crested helmet without a visor ('murmillo' means 'fish head'), short greaves, the curved rectangular shield of a Roman legionary, and also the legionary's short sword.

Secutor A heavily armed fighter who had a distinctive helmet with a visor containing two small eye-holes, so that his face would be protected from a trident thrust. He also had a greave on his left leg, an arm guard, a legionary-style shield and a short sword. The secutor usually fought against the retiarius.

Hoplomachus A heavily armed fighter who looked like a Greek hoplite, with a large crested helmet with visor, a thigh-length greave on his left leg, a spear and a round shield. He was often pitted against a murmillo in a re-enactment of Rome's wars against the Greeks.

Retiarius The name means 'net-fighter'. He was lightly armed with a large net, a trident, an arm guard, a shoulder guard and a dagger. The retiarius was the most lightly armed gladiator and the only one whose head and face were uncovered.

Thracian A lightly armed fighter who wore a crested, broad-brimmed helmet with a visor, armoured greaves on both legs, a protector on his sword arm and shoulder, a small shield, and a curved short sword designed to slash the opponent's flesh.

Bestiarius A special type of fighter trained to fight wild animals. Technically he was not really a gladiator since he did not carry a sword. He did not usually wear armour, but carried weapons such as whips, spears, or even bows and lances.

references to dwarfs fighting in the arena. In both cases, we can see members of marginalised groups being offered up to the audience as spectator sport.

CHARIOT RACING

Chariot racing was a central part of Roman society, and the Romans themselves liked to believe that it had been introduced to the city by its founder, Romulus, in the eighth century BC. Although today the gladiatorial games are most commonly associated with sporting entertainment in the Roman world, it was really chariot racing which played the same central role in Roman society as sports such as football do in ours today; then, as now, obsessive fans wore their team's colours and became very emotionally involved in the action and the drama of events.

The Circus Maximus

A stadium for chariot racing was known as a **circus**, from where we get the word 'circuit'. There was more than one circus in Rome, but by far the biggest was the Circus Maximus ('The Greatest Circus'), which was located in a small valley in the centre of the city – today

FIGURE 3.29
A reconstruction of
the Circus Maximus

PRESCRIBED SOURCE

The Circus Maximus

Built: first built in the 6th
century BC, rebuilt
a number of times,
particularly by the
emperor Trajan in the
early 2nd century AD

Location: Rome

Capacity: *c.* 250,000 in
the 1st century AD

Significance: the largest
stadium in the Roman
Empire

---

spina the thin dividing
bank down the middle of a
Roman stadium's racing
track

metae the set of three
turning posts located at
each end of the spina

carceres the starting
cages for the chariots –
there were twelve in all

---

the area is a public park, and the outline shape of the track is still visible. In fact, the Circus Maximus was an extraordinarily large stadium, the largest edifice in the Roman Empire; it also remains the largest sporting arena in recorded history. In the first century AD, its capacity was about 250,000, more than twice the size of the largest stadia in the world today.

The track was about 600 m long and 150 m wide, and down the middle was a narrow dividing bank called the **spina** ('backbone'). The curved turning point at either end of the spina was decorated with three posts, known as **metae**, which were made of gilded bronze. Along the spina were various monuments, including a large red granite obelisk from Egypt, which depicted Rameses II and dated to the thirteenth century BC. The emperor Augustus had this placed there to mark his conquest of Egypt. There were also symbols of the gods, since the chariot races were often put on as part of religious festival holidays; in particular, racing fans would have wanted to honour Neptune, the Roman god of horses. Also on the spina were seven large wooden eggs, which were lowered to indicate how many of the seven laps of a race had been completed; one emperor added seven bronze dolphins to do the same job.

Another important feature of the stadium was the starting cages, known as **carceres** ('cells') which worked in a similar way to the starting gates used in horse racing today. They were constructed to allow a staggered start for chariots, since some cages had a better starting position than others. There were twelve cages, each one with a spring-loaded starting gate; when the signal was given to start the race, all were released at the same time and the chariots flew out.

The substructures of the Circus Maximus were made of brick-faced concrete. Above them, seating wrapped round three sides of the stadium and contained three tiers – the lowest built in marble and the other two in stone. The lowest was reserved for VIPs: state priests, senators and wealthy equites. The next tier was available for anyone – unlike at the amphitheatre, there seems to have been little segregation at the circus, which meant that men, women and children from different sections of society could sit together; the top tier may have been standing room only. On one side of the stadium was the imperial box, built of marble, where the emperor watched the races. This also gave him an important opportunity to be seen by his people in the heart of the city.

EXPLORE FURTHER

The fact that men and women could sit together at the Circus Maximus gave some people the chance to try to strike up a romance. The Roman love poet Ovid twice writes about flirting with a woman at the races: read *Amores*, 3.2 and *Ars Amatoria*, 1.135–162. What can we learn about the chariot races from these poems?

The races

As at the gladiatorial games, a day at the Circus Maximus was paid for either by the emperor, or by a senior politician, who would look on this sponsorship as a chance to win popularity. As the sponsor of the games, he led the entry parade that began the day's events. Behind him came the charioteers and horses, as well as musicians and soldiers, who carried images of the gods and goddesses believed to be present at the races. These images were carried to a shrine in the imperial box.

The races would then start: each one consisted of seven laps of the track in an anti-clockwise direction and lasted for about ten to fifteen minutes; there were typically twenty-four races in a day. Chariots were normally drawn by teams of four horses (although we hear of races involving larger teams of horses – the emperor Nero apparently even took part in a ten-horse chariot race in the Olympic Games of AD 67). Before the race, the charioteers were allotted their position in the starting cages. They then lined up and waited for the sponsor to give the starting signal – he did this by dropping a white cloth, at which point the gates sprung open.

Once the race had begun, tactics were all important. A charioteer would wear a tunic, colour-coded to his team, and a leather helmet, and he would also carry a whip. Rather than holding the reins as we would expect, he wrapped them around his body and steered by transferring his weight from one side to another; therefore, if he crashed he was in danger of being dragged along by the reins and so he carried a knife with him to cut himself free. The most difficult section of the circuit was turning around the metae: a charioteer would have to find a balance between not going out too wide, thereby wasting

FIGURE 3.30
A chariot race in action.

valuable seconds, and not drawing too close to the spina, so risking a crash. Most accidents happened round the metae, and they could result in appalling injuries to both charioteers and horses.

When the race was over, the sponsor of the games presented the winning charioteer with a palm branch, while the payments to him and his team were made at the end of the day.

Charioteers and horses

A huge amount of time and money was invested in preparing the horses and charioteers to be race-ready. There were only four teams that competed in Rome – the Reds, the Whites, the Blues and the Greens – and since as many as twelve chariots could take part in a race, each team might field up to three chariots. We could therefore compare this system to Formula One racing today, where teams often put out two cars, which might try to work together. Each team was overseen by an owner, who could be compared to a modern football club chairman. He supervised his team's set of stables and employed many staff, including stable-boys, trainers and vets. However, his most valuable employees were the charioteers. As today, owners often paid huge prices to sign up the very best.

Charioteers were usually of low-born origin – either freedmen, or slaves who might be able to pay for their freedom after a few victories; like gladiators, they held the status of being infamis. However, as with exceptional modern sportsmen, an outstanding charioteer was able to win great wealth and fame. Perhaps the most celebrated charioteer in Roman history was Diocles, a Spaniard who competed for twenty-four years and apparently won 1,462 of his 4,257 races, becoming the Roman equivalent of a multi-millionaire in the process. However, Diocles was very much the exception rather than the rule: charioteers could be killed or seriously injured and few won great riches from the sport.

Supporters followed horses just as much as racers, and kept statistics about them, such as their breed and pedigree. Racehorses were purpose-bred on stud farms, which could be found in many parts of the empire, with a particularly high concentration in North Africa and Spain. Many inscriptions have survived on pottery and mosaics that bear witness to the popularity of some horses; for example, one describes a horse called Victor, which won 429 times.

FIGURE 3.31
A charioteer from the Red team holds the palm of victory mosaic.

The spectators

Supporters of chariot racing were just as passionate as many sports fans are today. It was common for fans to wear the colours of their favourite team, while there was also heavy betting on the results. For one obsessed fan, the races were even a matter of life and death: a Roman writer records that at the funeral of a

S & C Find out more about curse tablets in Roman Britain by visiting http://curses.csad.ox.ac.uk/. What sort of things do people put curses on? Are there any modern comparisons to this practice?

curse tablet a tablet on which someone wrote a prayer to the gods asking them to put a curse on an enemy

Study questions

1 What similarities can you find between chariot racing and modern horse racing?
2 Why do you think that fans become so passionate about the sports they follow?
3 How does the Circus Maximus compare to a modern sports stadium?

PRESCRIBED SOURCE

Large Theatre

Built: 2nd century BC, renovated at the end of the 1st century BC

Location: Pompeii

Capacity: c. 4,000

Significance: a very good example of a Roman theatre

Red charioteer, a supporter was so devastated that he threw himself onto the funeral pyre. This was an extreme case, but there is no doubt that many fans were overflowing with passion; you will read in your prescribed literature a letter by Pliny describing the behaviour of the spectators at the races (see p. 324). Other evidence for the obsessive nature of fans' behaviour comes in the form of **curse tablets** – some supporters even put curses on horses and riders they wanted to lose. This one was found in North Africa:

> I call upon you, o demon, whoever you are, and ask that from this hour, from this day, from this moment, you torture and kill the horses of the Green and the White factions, and that you kill and crush completely the drivers Clarus, Felix, Primulus and Romanus, and that you leave not a breath in their bodies.

> ILS 8753

THE THEATRE

Roman drama was strongly influenced by the drama of ancient Greece, partly because many Greeks had settled in cities of southern Italy, and there was close cultural contact between the two peoples. The Greeks had invented the genre of drama, and their plays were the source of much inspiration for the Romans. In particular, like the Greeks, the Romans often put on plays during religious festivals. They were usually paid for partly out of public funds, and partly by senior politicians responsible for running the festivals – therefore, the funding of plays offered politicians and public figures the opportunity to gain popularity, just as it did with the chariot races and gladiatorial games. Moreover, it was not just the plays themselves that wealthy men funded – there are a number of examples of benefactors paying for the building or upgrading of theatre buildings and facilities.

Theatre buildings

The first major stone theatre in Rome was not built until the middle of the first century BC, although permanent theatres had appeared much earlier in the cities of southern Italy that had closer contact with the Greeks – Pompeii was one of these. Today, we can learn about the design of Roman theatres both by looking at the remains of those that have survived, and from what Roman writers have said about them.

The large theatre at Pompeii

Pompeii had its own 'theatre district', with two theatres next to each other at the southern end of the city. The larger of the two had an estimated capacity of 4,000 and was first built in the second century BC. It was extensively modified at the end of the first century BC, when two members of a very prominent Pompeiian family, the Holconii, commissioned major improvements.

FIGURE 3.32
The large theatre at Pompeii.

FIGURE 3.33
A reconstruction of the large theatre.

Two inscriptions by the benefactors of the theatre

Two versions of the following inscription were found prominently in the area of the stage:

> Marcus Holconius Rufus and Marcus Holconius Celer (built) at their own expense the crypt, boxes, and theatre seating.

CIL X 833, 834

The two Holconii mentioned here were probably brothers, although it is possible that they were father and son. They clearly wanted to leave no Pompeiian in any doubt as to who had paid for the upgrade to their theatre – each inscription was more than six metres long! The inscription refers to three areas that were improved, and these can all be identified in the remains of the theatre today. The main seating area is made of marble, there is a narrow upper section of seating, supported by vaulted passageways, while two marble 'boxes' have been identified above the spectators' entrances at either end of the orchestra (see below) – these may have been reserved for the most privileged spectators or the sponsors of the shows.

Apart from the upper section of seating, the rest of the seating area of the theatre was built into a hillside, following the Greek fashion, although many other Roman theatres were free-standing. The seating area was semi-circular, and there were a number of aisles, which enabled people to reach their seats easily. As at the shows at amphitheatres, there was a clear hierarchy as to who sat where: VIPs sat in the lower rows made of marble; behind them sat other free citizens, and at the back sat freedmen, slaves and women. The theatre had an awning to shade spectators from the sun when necessary.

The spectators looked down onto the performing area, which had three distinct elements: an elaborately decorated back wall, a stage, and a semi-circular area in front of the stage. The back wall was known as the **scaenae frons** (literally meaning: 'front scenery') and usually consisted of two storeys and many columns (the scaenae frons of

scaenae frons the back wall of a stage set in a Roman theatre, usually two or three storeys tall and with elaborate decoration some Roman theatres even had three storeys); it would have been painted and adorned with beautiful statues. It matched the height of the seating area and attached to it on both sides. It also had three doors, each of which led onto the stage by a small set of steps.

The stage itself was made of wood and set on pillars; the area below it would be used to manoeuvre stage machinery and props. The front wall of the stage was normally a little over a metre high and made of elaborate stone. In front of the stage was a semi-circular area, known as the **orchestra**; it seems that this was rarely used for acting in Roman times – it was really a hangover from the era of the Greek theatre, when actors had performed there. In Pompeii, it might have been used for acting if there were revivals of Greek plays, but it seems that most of the time it served as another seating area reserved for VIPs. A further feature of Roman theatres such as this was that there was a curtain that came down at the start of the play, rather than up as we would expect today.

orchestra in a Roman theatre, the semi-circular area in front of a stage normally reserved for VIP seating

Types of plays

There is no conclusive evidence about what types of plays were performed in the Large Theatre of Pompeii. However, drama was clearly popular in the city, since many mosaics, paintings and graffiti relating to the theatre have been found. It is likely that the performances reflected the pattern elsewhere in the Roman world, and this involved great variety.

As the Romans had been influenced so much by Greek theatre, it is no surprise that tragedy and comedy were featured on the Roman stage. However, little has survived of Roman tragedy, and it seems that by the first century BC it had declined in popularity. We have very few surviving texts, and so it is hard to know much about it with any confidence. However, the same is not true of Roman comedy, about which we know a great deal.

Comedy

The two greatest writers of Roman comedy were Plautus and Terence, who both wrote in the first half of the second century BC. Both based their plays on earlier Greek models, and in particular on the plays of Menander – the Greek playwright whose portrait was painted prominently in the Pompeian house that today is named after him (see p. 253). In some ways, the comedies of Plautus and Terence were forerunners to modern sit-coms – their plots were often based around everyday social situations and behaviour. Although the plays have a variety of plots, they have many similar features: love affairs, confusions of identity, conflicts between fathers and sons, or clever slaves who outwit their masters. They contained typical **stock characters**, such as the flatterer, the lecherous old man or the boastful soldier. Music was often composed to accompany the plays.

stock character a character in a work of literature or drama who is easily recognisable as a particular type of person from certain behaviour traits

The comedies of Plautus and Terence were performed in a very similar style to Greek plays. This meant that there were no female actors; rather female parts were played by male actors (as they were even in Shakespeare's day). Actors wore Greek-style costume, often a tunic and cloak for male characters, and a dress and cloak for female characters. A costume and accompanying props could give information about a character type to the audience: for example, an old man might wear white and carry a stick; a cook might hold a knife, spoon or some sort of dish; while a slave-dealer would usually carry a money-bag.

To complete the Greek style of costume, actors wore masks, and these too were designed to indicate a specific type of character – one ancient writer even lists forty-four different types of comic mask. They were all designed to cover the front of the head, while hair was also attached to denote character: for old men, it was white or grey, younger characters were typically given dark hair, while for slave characters the colour was red. Another convenient feature of the masks was that they allowed actors to play more than one part.

Very few comedies were written after the second century BC, but the plays of writers such as Plautus and Terence remained popular for centuries, and scenes from them could be performed or recited at private dinner parties or gatherings as well as in the theatre. One example of this comes in your prescribed literature (see pp. 323–324), when Pliny the Younger writes about the qualities of a favourite freedman, Zosimus, whom he describes as an excellent 'reciter of comedies'.

FIGURE 3.34
A fresco from Pompeii showing actors in a comedy.

Mime and pantomime

By the first century AD, the popularity of both comedy and tragedy had been overtaken by two other forms of dramatic performance: mime and pantomime. Both names can be confusing to a modern reader. Unlike modern mime performances, Roman mime involved actors speaking. Moreover, the Roman pantomime has no similarity or link to modern pantomimes, which are staged during the Christmas period. Both mimes and pantomimes could be presented in the theatre, in other public places, or at a private performance.

Mime originated in Greece and initially was simply a variety show including acrobatics, song and dance, jokes and conjuring based around a simple plot. The subject matter was often obscene, with the emphasis on sex, parody of town and city life, and general silliness; some mimes were political, others presented scenes from everyday life. We hear of plots involving kidnappings, cuckolds and lovers hidden in convenient chests.

FIGURE 3.35
A Roman mosaic showing theatrical masks.

The mime could be presented in a number of settings: on its own, as an interlude to another play, or as part of another public or private form of entertainment.

If mime was similar to comedy, then pantomime seems to have replaced tragedy. A pantomime performance was essentially a form of ballet, but one in which all of the parts were played by a single actor. The actor did not speak or sing, but could be accompanied by musicians or a singer. A pantomime show often performed a scene from a Greek tragedy; the pantomime actor had to show great versatility to play all the roles – male and female, young and old – in a series of solo scenes which might require him to change into and out of a variety of costumes and masks. All the evidence suggests that pantomime was wildly popular in Rome, and that famous pantomime actors attracted a huge fan base.

Actors and audience

Like gladiators, actors held a very low social status and were legally defined as infamis. However, despite their low social status, a few highly successful actors could gain both fame and great wealth; at Pompeii, there are a number of graffiti that refer lovingly to an actor called Paris, including one that refers to him as 'Paris, pearl of the stage'.

Actors were typically organised into a troupe under the charge of a troupe leader. They were usually either drawn from the ranks of slaves or from the lower classes, although of course they had to be skilled enough to act and sing in a variety of different roles. Competition between the troupes seems to have been fierce – prizes were awarded to troupes or individual actors, and sources tell of how they stationed their supporters throughout the theatre with instructions to applaud at the right moment.

Sources suggest that audiences could either be wildly supportive or brutally critical. On the one hand, we hear of spectators learning the songs of the theatre and then singing them by heart; on the other hand, there are stories of actors making mistakes and being hissed or booed off stage. One source speaks of the bad behaviour typical in a theatre audience, with ushers walking in front of spectators, people arriving late, slaves sitting in seats reserved for free men, and mothers bringing crying babies who disturb the performance.

THE BATHS

The baths were a fundamental part of life in any Roman town. In Rome itself, one fourth-century AD source claims that there were nearly a thousand bath complexes. Some of these were absolutely huge; for example, the emperor Caracalla had baths constructed that could hold 1,600 bathers at any one time. However, most bath houses in the city were quite small. Going to the baths was just as popular in other parts of the empire – the well-preserved remains of a huge Roman bath complex can, of course, still be seen in the English city of Bath today.

Going to the baths was a daily routine for free Romans of all classes. Most people did not have bathing facilities at home and so the public baths were vital to keeping the population healthy and warding off disease. For this reason, many baths were subsidised by the state, and were very cheap to visit. It seems that men would work in the morning and head for the baths in the afternoon, and it was common for people to stay there until it was time to go home for dinner.

However, the baths were far more than a place where people went simply to keep clean. In fact, they were more like a cross between a modern gym and spa. Many bath houses also had an exercise ground where people could work out or play games, just as people might go to the gym on a daily basis today. Moreover, the baths were a focal point for Roman social life, and a place where people went to see and be seen. Wealthy men would arrive at the baths accompanied by a following of freedmen and slaves in a show of power and status, and it is likely that business meetings were held there. The baths were sometimes also used by the less affluent as a place to latch onto their social superiors, hoping to get an invitation to dinner that day.

Beyond this, the baths were simply just a place to meet up with friends and relax. Bath complexes would normally have shops attached to them where people could buy snacks: scrawled onto the wall of a bar near one set of ancient baths is a list of items for sale, including nuts, drinks, hog's fat, bread, cutlets and sausage.

As there were so many bath houses in the Roman world, no two of them were designed in exactly the same way. However, there were some key rooms and spaces that were common to all. Many baths had separate facilities for men and women, including the Central Baths of Herculaneum, which are featured overleaf. Men's facilities were usually more extensive than those of women. However, if there were no such separate facilities, men and women would typically bathe at different times of the day, with women bathing in the morning and men in the afternoon.

Arriving at the baths, a visitor would first have to pay the entrance fee. This was normally very cheap, perhaps just a quadrans, the smallest coin in the Roman currency system. He would then head to the changing room, or **apodyterium**, where he would leave his clothes in one of the niches along the walls, keeping on some light clothing for the exercise ground. He would then head to the exercise ground to work up a sweat. This area was known as the **palaestra**. Sources speak of various games being played there: one such game was called harpastum ('snatch-ball'), which seems to have been a bit like 'piggy in the middle', in which one player had to seize a ball stuffed with sand from others holding on to it and throwing it around. Some writers speak of men fencing against a post, others of men wrestling with one another, while there even seems to have been a form of tennis played with the hand.

After exercising, the bather would head back to the changing-room and remove the rest of his clothes in preparation for the bathing process. The number of bathing rooms would depend on the size and status of the bath house, but all baths had three fundamental rooms: the **tepidarium** ('warm room'), the **caldarium** ('hot room') and the **frigidarium** ('cold room'). More extensive bath houses may have had other facilities, a 'sweat-room', which was similar to a modern sauna, or a swimming pool – however, this would not have been used for exercise, since there was no culture of swimming laps in the Roman world; bathers would simply have got in to relax and freshen up.

We cannot be sure about the order in which a bather typically visited these rooms, or even if there was ever a set order. However, a bather would usually head to the tepidarium

EXPLORE FURTHER

The Roman writer and philosopher Seneca lived above a bath house and, in a famous letter, complains about the noise, which constantly disturbed him. Read his letter (Seneca the Younger, *Letters*, 56.1–2), and make a list of all the different activities he mentions taking place in the bath house.

apodyterium changing room in a baths complex

palaestra exercise ground

tepidarium the warm room in a baths complex
caldarium the hot room in a baths complex
frigidarium the cold room in a baths complex

FIGURE 3.36
The remains of a Roman hypocaust.

strigil a curved scraper used to remove oil and dirt from the body

hypocaust underfloor heating system

or caldarium first, where he would build up a sweat. At this stage of the bathing process, he would have oil rubbed all over his body (wealthy Romans would bring a slave to do this). Soap was unknown to the Romans, and so olive oil was used to wash the body. The hot atmosphere of the room opened up the pores of his skin, allowing the oil to penetrate thoroughly; the bather might move between any of the warm or hot rooms at this stage. After some time, he ordered his slave to scrape the oil (and dirt) from his body with a curved implement called a **strigil**. He would then head to the cold plunge-pool of the frigidarium, where the cold water closed the pores of his skin, so completing the cleansing process.

The warm rooms of a bath house were heated by a very clever design process that blasted hot air into gaps under the floor and behind the walls. This system of artificial heating was known as a **hypocaust**; the floor was raised above the ground by pillars and spaces were left inside the walls so that hot air and smoke from a nearby furnace (tended by slaves) could pass through these enclosed areas. The caldarium would be located nearest to the furnace, since it required the most heat.

The Central Baths of Herculaneum

We can get a good idea of how a set of baths were laid out from the Central Baths in Herculaneum. They were built in the late first century BC, and located near the middle

FIGURE 3.37
The palaestra of the Central Baths at Herculaneum.

of the town; they have also been known as the Forum Baths, since they are believed to have been located close to the city's forum, which is as yet undiscovered to the north. The baths occupied the southern end of a whole block and opened onto three different streets – this allowed for a number of different entrances. The men's section of the baths is bigger and more extensive than the women's section, but both derive their heat from the furnace room.

The men's apodyterium led off from the palaestra. The apodyterium has a marble bench running along three sides, and above it niches for storing clothes. At one end are two basins – a low one for washing feet, and a grander one made of marble for washing hands. An entrance leads from the apodyterium into the tepidarium. This had marble benches and shelves on all four sides, and the floor has been elevated to allow for the hypocaust – today part of the floor has collapsed and so the hypocaust is visible; the floor contains a black mosaic depicting a Triton (a sea monster) whose legs turn into curling sea serpents, while four dolphins surround him.

A further entrance leads into the men's caldarium. Much of the curved roof here has collapsed, and so it is possible to see hot-air pipes built into the walls. At one end is a large round marble basin, which contained cold water for bathers to splash their faces or bodies if they became too hot and sweaty. At the other end is a hot water bath, which bathers could lie in or sit beside. After completing his bath, a bather would walk back through the apodyterium to the frigidarium, where there was a plunge-pool. On the curved roof are painted various fish and sea-creatures, such as fish, lobsters and even an octopus.

The women's section of the baths has a similar structure, and the apodyterium has a black mosaic of a triton surrounded by dolphins very similar to that in the men's tepidarium.

PRESCRIBED SOURCE

The Central Baths of Herculaneum

Built: late 1st century BC

Location: Herculaneum

Key features: a separate suite of baths for men and women

Significance: a very good example of a bath house with separate bathing areas for men and women, as well as a palaestra

FIGURE 3.38
The Central Baths at Herculaneum:
A – Men's entrance;
B – Men's frigidarium;
C – Men's apodyterium;
D – Men's tepidarium;
E – Men's caldarium;
F – Women's caldarium;
G – Women's tepidarium;
H – Women's apodyterium;
J – Furnace;
K – Women's entrance.

Palaestra

FIGURE 3.39
The men's apodyterium in the Central Baths at Herculaneum with the two marble basins clearly visible.

PS

> **Study questions**
>
> 1 How do the baths compare to a modern spa or sports club?
> 2 For what reasons were the baths such an important aspect of Roman city life?
> 3 What would you have enjoyed, and what would you have disliked about a visit to the baths?

However, one notable point about the women's section is the lack of a frigidarium. Presumably women cooled down by leaving the baths and heading into the open air.

TOPIC REVIEW

You should be able to:

1. Describe:
   - the experience of watching the games at the amphitheatre
   - what it was like to spend a day at the chariot races
   - the experience of watching a play at the Roman theatre
   - a typical visit to the Roman baths.

2. Explain:
   - why the games were important for Roman politicians
   - how society viewed and treated gladiators, charioteers and actors
   - why Romans found these games so entertaining
   - why the baths played such an important role in Roman society.

PRACTICE QUESTIONS

1. **a.** Give **two** details about the content of the inscriptions of the Holconii in the large theatre at Pompeii. [2]
   b. Why was it important for people to see these inscriptions? [1]
2. 'Most Romans would have enjoyed visiting the Circus Maximus more than the Colosseum.'
   Do you agree with this statement? Give reasons for your answer. [15]

Literature

3.5 Satire and Fiction

TOPIC OVERVIEW

- The origins and purposes of satire
- The style and characteristic approach of each of the authors
  - Horace as the smiling satirist
  - Juvenal as the angry satirist
  - the nature and purpose of Petronius' *Satyricon*

- Narrative and descriptive techniques
- Use of humour and exaggeration
- Choice of themes and examples

The prescribed sources for this topic are:

- Horace, *Satires*, 2.2, 2.6, 2.8
- Juvenal, *Satire*, 3.190–322
- Petronius, *Satyricon: Dinner with Trimalchio*, 29–33; 37–38; 49–50

Don't forget that you will be given credit in the exam if you study extra sources and make relevant use of them in your answers.

This topic focuses on the literary genre of satire. It will first explore what satire is and how it developed in the Roman world, and then move on to examining three of your prescribed authors, Horace, Juvenal and Petronius, reflecting on how they produced entertaining and interesting works of literature.

THE ORIGINS AND PURPOSES OF SATIRE

> **satire** a form of writing that aims to show up hypocrisy, pretence or other character flaws through the use of humour

What is **satire**? Today, satire often attempts to mock public figures such as politicians and celebrities; usually, this attempt to make fun also has the intention of showing up hypocrisy, pretence or other character flaws in the people being satirised. Therefore, it is not just individuals who can be satirised – satire can focus more generally on social attitudes and everyday behaviour too.

Roman satire was not very different from this – in fact it was the Romans who invented satire as a **genre**. The first satirist we hear of is Lucilius, who lived in the second century BC; he was later recognised by the Romans as the founder of verse satire (satire written as poetry). Lucilius was an angry and outspoken social critic, whose biting verse aimed to show up corruption among the politicians and public figures of his day. One interesting point about him was that he was the first poet we know of from the Roman upper classes – he was a member of the equites. This suggests that it was at this time that writing poetry was first taken seriously by the Roman educated elite, who were Lucilius' target audience and friends.

Lucilius composed in a specific poetic metre, the hexameter. The hexameter might be thought a surprising choice for satire, since it was traditionally the metre of the great epic poems of Homer and others. These poems had a very different tone: where satire was down to earth and focused on everyday life and behaviour, epic poetry recounted great tales of heroism from the mythological past. In some ways, the two genres could not have been more different.

As satire developed after Lucilius, it came to be written in prose as well as in verse – in your prescribed literature, two satirists write in poetry, Horace and Juvenal, and one, Petronius, writes mainly in prose but also in poetry at times. The poetic satirists followed Lucilius by composing in the hexameter. They too were aware of the difference between the two hexameter genres of satire and epic. Horace reflects on this in Satire 2.6 when he describes the genre of satire with the Latin adjective 'pedester', which literally meant 'going on foot'. In other words, while other types of poetry, such as epic, had lofty aspirations of describing noble tales of legendary heroes, satire remained firmly grounded in the day-to-day and the real world.

One key feature of Roman satire was its variety. Indeed, the word 'satire' is probably derived from a Latin phrase, 'lanx satura', which literally means a 'full plate' and referred to a large plate brimming with a wide variety of first fruits offered to the gods (the 'first fruits' were the first agricultural produce of a harvest given to the gods as a thanks offering). The name 'satire' therefore seems to recognise that the genre could focus on any number of different topics and themes, and also that satirists could use a variety of techniques in their poems. Juvenal describes his satires as presenting a whole mixture of vices and immoral behaviours seen in the Rome of his day.

As a result, satire can seem quite gossipy – it is interested in what people are doing, and what they are talking about, in public places such as the forum, the theatre and the sporting arenas, as well as in private places such as dining-rooms and bedrooms.

HORACE

Horace had a remarkable life; he was born the son of a freedman in the small town of Venusia in southern Italy, and yet he grew up to become one of the leading poets in the Roman world. He lived during very troubled times; the Roman world was convulsed by

---

genre a category of literature – examples of literary genres might include epic, tragedy, comedy, history and satire

Study questions

1 Who are the best satirists in our society today, in your opinion?
2 What sort of things do they satirise, and what makes them effective?
3 Do they play a helpful role in society?

EXPLORE FURTHER

Find out more about Lucilius. How much do we know about his life and his writings? What do later writers say about him?

S & C The scholar Niall Rudd has identified three key features of Roman satire: attack, entertainment, and preaching. Does this seem to be a good basis of defining satire to you? To what extent does each of these features appear in your prescribed literature?

PRESCRIBED SOURCE

Horace, *Satires*, 2.2, 2.6, 2.8

Date: late 30s BC

Author: Horace (65–8 BC)

Genre: verse satire

Significance: three poems reflecting on life in the town and country, as follows:

- 2.2: A reflection on the virtue of the simple country life, as promoted by the peasant Ofellus.
- 2.6: Horace contrasts his enjoyment of the country life with the stresses of living in the city.
- 2.8: An account of a dinner party in Rome told to Horace by his friend Fundanius.

Read it here: OCR source booklet

KEY INDIVIDUALS

Octavian/Augustus: (63 BC–AD 14) a leading Roman aristocrat who was Julius Caesar's adopted heir. In 30 BC he became the sole ruler of the entire Roman world, and is regarded as the first Roman emperor

Maecenas: (*c.* 64–8 BC) a close adviser to Octavian who was appointed his patron of the arts. He welcomed Horace into his circle of poets, and became his mentor and close friend

civil wars for the first decades of his life. In 44 BC, Julius Caesar, the leader of the Roman world, was assassinated, but his assassins were soon hunted down and defeated. Two of Caesar's closest followers, his deputy Mark Antony and adopted heir **Octavian**, tried to share power between themselves and one other, Lepidus. The arrangement soon broke down, and this led to further civil wars during the 30s. Octavian became powerful in Italy and the western Mediterranean and by 30 BC he had become the sole ruler of the Roman world. Soon afterwards, he took the name of Augustus, and he is thought of as the first Roman emperor from this point on.

Although Horace had fought on the side of Caesar's assassins, he benefited from a general amnesty after their defeat at Philippi in 42 BC. He returned to Rome and in 38 he was introduced to **Maecenas**, a close adviser to Octavian who was responsible for promoting his regime. To do this, he aimed to nurture poets who would write poetry sympathetic to Octavian and the regime. Horace had already started writing poetry, and was welcomed into Maecenas' circle of poets. This was a big break for him. It was in the years after this that he composed his satires. Maecenas features in some of them, and is the guest of honour at the dinner party described in Satire 2.8.

In the mid-30s BC, Maecenas presented Horace with a wonderful gift: a villa and farm in the Sabine Hills, about 25 miles outside Rome. Soon after this, Horace wrote his second book of satires, and it seems that he loved to escape from the city to write, relax and reflect at this country estate. One of the key themes of the book is the contrast between life in the city and life in the country. In two of our poems, 2.2 and 2.6, he reflects on what makes a good life – and seems to conclude that the simple and humble life of the countryside is far richer and more fulfilling than life in the city.

Horace sets himself up as a particular type of satirist; in particular, he distances himself from the aggressive and angry tone of Lucilius. There is an obvious reason for this: while

Lucilius had been very critical of the leading politicians of his day, Horace did not have the scope to do this given that a senior political figure, Maecenas, was his patron. Therefore, he does not attack public figures, but focuses instead on the behaviour and customs of those whom he comes across in his daily life. Even here, he shows little anger or bitterness: his satires are light-hearted, and he makes fun of himself as well as others. In fact, he even claims, in a charming analogy, to use laughter in order to get his point across:

> What stops someone from telling the truth while smiling, as teachers sometimes give children cookies to tempt them to learn the alphabet?
>
> Horace, *Satires*, 1.1.24–25

His laughter, therefore, recognises that people are all flawed and gently encourages them to do better. As a result, he is sometimes referred to as a 'smiling satirist'. A related message of his satires is that we should remember not to take ourselves too seriously.

A further key feature of Horace's satires is their conversational tone; in fact, he often referred to them as 'sermones', a Latin word that can simply mean 'conversations'. In some of them, the poet appears to be speaking directly to the reader in a chatty tone; others report conversations that have taken place, or are taking place, between characters in the poem. As readers, we might therefore feel that we are listening in on a conversation or discussion.

Who was Horace writing for? It is clear that he was writing to be published, and his satires would have been read on papyrus scrolls. However, it is important to remember that only a small minority of Romans had a high level of literacy, and so we might say that he was writing for the educated elite. Of course, his most immediate target audience was the circle of Maecenas, which was close to the emperor Augustus. It is quite likely that when Horace first wrote his satires he gave some recitals of them himself. Horace says in Satire 1.10 that he is happy to have a small circle of readers, and does not want his satires to become so popular that they are studied in schools. If we take him seriously in this, then it is ironic that his satires are being studied in schools more than two thousand years after his death!

FIGURE 3.40
A modern statue of Horace in Venosa (ancient Venusia).

Satire 2.2

In this poem Horace gives a lecture on the benefits of the simple country life, and this introduces a common theme in his poetry – the contrast between life in the town and life in the country. He credits the ideas he puts forward to Ofellus, a peasant farmer whom he knew from childhood in Venusia. The audience is imagined and the lecture takes place in the morning – Horace specifically rejects discussion of this topic over the dinner table.

A key idea is that it is wrong to seek pleasure through over-indulging in luxurious foods; rather, true pleasure comes from simpler satisfactions. Horace criticises gluttony (eating or drinking far too much), and in particular people who follow the latest fashions in eating expensive food. However, he also emphasises that eating simply does not involve having to be stingy and ungenerous. He gives a sketch of a famously mean character, Avidienus, who represents a character type – the miser. Horace rejects this way of living too – his ideal character lives in balance between being a miser and being a glutton.

EXPLORE FURTHER

Horace's country villa has been identified and excavated. You can find out much more about it on this dedicated website: http://www.frischerconsulting.com/bf3e/horaces-villa/contents.html.

FIGURE 3.41
This ruined villa may be the remains of Horace's Sabine farm.

Epicureanism a philosophy of life that encouraged people to live for simple pleasures and to reduce anxieties as much as possible

Horace goes on to list the benefits of the simple diet: it promotes good health, good sleep and a feeling of wellbeing, and allows for better health in old age. He next suggests that wealth could be spent more profitably on good causes: by giving money to friends in need, or for the upkeep of temples or other public buildings. The poem finishes with Horace quoting Ofellus himself, as he outlines his philosophy of simplicity and self-sufficiency, which still allows for generosity on a special occasion. Even after he loses his farm, Ofellus is still able to live happily.

The ideas of the poem

There are some key themes that emerge in this poem. Central is the question of what is the good life – and Ofellus' recipe is put forward. Despite the fact that he is a simple farmer who is not highly educated, Ofellus represents ideas that can be found in the philosophical school of thought often advocated by Horace, **Epicureanism**. Epicureans believed that the purpose of life was to live for simple pleasures, and to avoid worries as much as possible. An important way to do this, so the thinking went, was to keep life in balance and not to adopt extremes of behaviour; in this poem, such extremes are represented by the glutton introduced at line 21, and the miser Avidienus introduced at line 55. Horace draws out the contrast between the two ways of living, which he believes are equally valueless:

> Ofellus judges that a mean life is different
> From a plain one: so it's foolish for you to avoid
> One fault and steer towards another.

Horace, *Satires*, 2.2.53–55

Ofellus himself represents the mid-point between the two – in his speech he talks of eating a simple diet, but of being generous in his hospitality to friends or neighbours who pay him a visit. The fact that he keeps his life in balance and that he has learnt to live on little means that he is self-sufficient and so can cope with the loss of his farm.

Speakers and audiences

One of the most impressive techniques used by Horace in this poem is the range of voices speaking to a range of audiences – this is a very conversational satire. You might think about the following:

- **Horace and his friends** The poem starts with Horace directly addressing his friends. We are not told who these friends are, but we can imagine that they are meeting somewhere in Rome. Horace reveals that the conversation takes place in the morning – the best time to think about such matters. In line 7, a new voice is

PS

introduced, presumably one of Horace's friends (or more than one), asking what the point of listening to this is – or at least showing his confusion by the look on his face.

- **Horace and the glutton** Horace goes on to outline Ofellus' ideas – notice that he has distanced himself from them so that they do not necessarily represent his own thoughts. In line 21 he reflects on the behaviour of a typical glutton, and in line 23 he moves from talking to his friends to speaking directly to the glutton, as though he was there among them. He questions this imaginary figure, and even calls him a fool in line 33! In lines 39–40, another glutton's own words are even reported, after which Horace seems to return to speaking to his friends again.

- **A rich man and Horace** At line 99, Horace again introduces a new speaker who is clearly another imagined figure and not among his friends. This speaker is a very wealthy man who believes that there is little danger of him falling into poverty. Horace advises him to spend his money for the benefit of others. Then, at line 107, he returns to speaking to his friends again.

- **Ofellus' speech** The poem finishes with Ofellus being given his own speech (lines 116–136), presumably delivered to Horace or anyone else who asks his views. However, in line 128 we learn that he has other company, as he turns to his sons to ask them a question.

How does this variety of speakers and audiences enrich the poem? Two points could be made. First of all, it allows Horace to represent different perspectives. As readers, we are invited to judge the characters through listening to their own words. Secondly, it fosters an atmosphere of debate and discussion in the poem. If you ask the question: 'What is a good way to live your life?' you are likely to have a range of opinions and therefore

---

KEY INDIVIDUAL Ofellus

Ofellus is presented as a figure of simple common sense in this poem – a countryman who, although not highly educated, has learnt through experience how to live well. We do not know if he was a real person, but it is interesting that his name is very similar to the Latin word 'ofella', meaning a 'small mouthful', which is appropriate to his character.

The poem concludes with Ofellus' speech (lines 116–136). He outlines how his principles have served him well in life and enabled him to survive a reversal of fortune, the confiscation of his farm (lines 128–134). Here Horace is referring to events of his own day – during the civil wars, Octavian rewarded veterans who had served in his army by allotting to them farms in various districts of Italy. He had earlier confiscated these farms and thrown the owners off their land. This must have been an issue close to Horace's heart, since his own family farm had also been confiscated in the aftermath of the battle of Philippi.

> **Study questions**
>
> 1 How does Horace satirise gluttony in lines 21–52? Think about the variety of words and ideas that he uses here to bring his point home.
> 2 How does Horace make his characterisation of the miser Avidienus effective in lines 55–62?
> 3 How does Ofellus come across in lines 116–136? Do you find him admirable?
> 4 How many different types of food and drink are mentioned in this poem? How often does food represent or symbolise a human quality or characteristic?
> 5 Find out about Epicureanism. Does it seem to you to offer a recipe for a life well lived?

agreements and disagreements. Horace's conversational tone allows us to feel that we are part of a debate, rather than simply listening to his own views.

Satire 2.6

This satire was written in 31 BC, a few years after Maecenas had presented Horace with the Sabine Farm. In the poem, he contrasts life in the city with life on the farm; he clearly prefers the latter, since it allows him to live as he wants, comfortably, simply and peacefully, and with the time and space to write poetry.

The poem opens with a prayer of thanks to Mercury, in his role as the bringer of wealth, and Horace explains how grateful he is with his lot in life. He goes on to outline all the unwanted distractions in the city that prevent him from getting down to writing poetry. In particular, because Horace is associated with Maecenas, many people in the city want to speak with him and ask favours. His close friendship with such an important man also arouses envy in others.

Horace then moves on to contrast this with his life in the country. Here, he can live simply, eating and sleeping well. In particular, he contrasts city dinner parties with those in the country, which are relaxed, intimate and full of rich conversation. He concludes by relating a fable that his country neighbour Cervius sometimes tells: the town mouse and the country mouse. While the town mouse has a more luxurious lifestyle, this comes at a cost of losing his freedom and peace of mind. The country mouse, on the other hand, enjoys the simple, self-sufficient life so valued by Horace.

Themes

This satire brings into sharp view two contrasts that often feature in Horace's poetry: city/country and public/private. Horace is the narrator of the first two thirds of the poem, after which he hands over to Cervius. The sentiments he puts forward in the first fifteen lines reflect the views put forward in 2.2 – to be happy with what you have, and not to be envious of others. At line 16, we learn that he is on his Sabine farm, from where he can reflect on the differences between life there and life in the city.

Horace continues by giving a flavour of what his life is like back in Rome, particularly given that he is closely associated with Maecenas. Although Horace does not state this, we can tell from the poem that the events must happen between late 31 and early 30 BC, when Octavian had left Maecenas in charge of affairs in Rome while he was away in the east. As Horace makes his way up to Maecenas' magnificent house on the Esquiline Hill (see map, p. viii) in the heart of the city, he is plagued by the clients and hangers-on who want access to Maecenas. Horace uses a number of different voices in direct speech to communicate the range of these people and their demands. A contrast then comes in lines 40–46, when we are given a private view into Maecenas and Horace's conversations about more trivial things, such as the weather or gladiatorial fights. Yet even these conversations cause problems for Horace, since others are envious of his closeness to such a powerful man.

FIGURE 3.42
A view of the Sabine Hills and the surrounding countryside today.

In line 60, Horace cleverly returns the focus to the countryside again – imagining himself in the city and longing for the country. (But remember that he is actually narrating the poem from the country and thinking about the city!) The theme of simplicity soon emerges as he talks about country dinner parties which do not have the formalities or anxious and envious chatter of those in the city. Once again, the theme of how to live a good life emerges, in relation to food – he and his friends have a philosophical discussion about the meaningful things in life. This is the point at which he introduces the fable told by Cervius, one of his country friends who can be compared to Ofellus in 2.2 – a countryman of simple common sense. We can almost imagine that we are present at one of these country dinner parties where Cervius is telling his tale.

A parody of epic

During Cervius' fable, Horace uses another literary device, **parody**, to make fun of the town mouse. A parody is an exaggerated and comic imitation of the style of a particular writer or genre. Consider the following lines:

parody an exaggerated and comic imitation of the style of a particular writer or genre

> ... His words stirred the country mouse,
> Who scrambled lightly from his house: then the two
> Took their way together as proposed, eager to scurry
> Beneath the city walls in darkness. And now night
> Occupied the zenith, as the pair of them made tracks
> Through a wealthy house, where covers dyed scarlet
> Glowed on ivory couches, and baskets piled nearby
> Held the remains of all the courses of a magnificent
> Feast, that had been celebrated the previous evening.

Horace, *Satires*, 2.6.95–103

The line 'And now night occupied the zenith' would have been immediately recognisable to Roman listeners and readers, since it is typical of an epic poem such as

EXPLORE FURTHER

The story of the town mouse and the country mouse first appears in Aesop's fables, and his version was clearly well known to Horace and his audience. Aesop was a Greek storyteller who is believed to have lived in the seventh or sixth century BC. Are there any other fables or stories you know which have a similar moral message to this one? Why might stories and fables be an effective way to put forward a moral message? Why might using animals to tell a story be a good way of doing this?

EXAM TIP

Literary analysis

Horace makes the following observation about how safe he feels in the country now that he is away from the dangers of Rome:

> I'm not cursed here with ambition, leaden sirocco,
> Or oppressive autumn, deathly Libitina's gain.

Horace, *Satires*, 2.6.18–19

Libitina was the old Roman goddess of burial: Horace is happy to be away from Rome during the autumn when a particular wind blows from the south, the sirocco, bringing cool wet weather to Europe. Even today, people associate it with illness because of the conditions it brings.

These two lines are skilfully written. If you are asked to comment on a passage including lines such as these, think about the following points:

- The lines contain three powerful adjectives, each describing a different noun. Writing a sentence with so many adjectives ensures that it is full of imagery.
- You must explain why a word is powerful, rather than simply saying 'it is powerful'. Therefore, you could say that by describing the south wind as 'leaden', Horace stresses the heaviness of the weather conditions which it brings, as well as the grey skies. Why do you think the adjectives 'oppressive' and 'deathly' might be powerful?
- The sentence concludes with Libitina personifying death. A **personification** is a figure of speech by which something non-human is given human characteristics. We might say that this personification is powerful because it is frightening for a reader to think of what a person representing death might look like (the modern concept of 'the grim reaper', and the imagery which commonly goes with that, is similar). Horace is also clever in leaving his description of Libitina to the end, as this allows him to suggest that ambition, the sirocco and the autumn all lead to death.

personification a figure of speech by which something non-human is given human characteristics

Study questions

1 What are the key differences between Satire 2.2 and Satire 2.6?
2 Using the example on pp. 298–299, make a list of all the different voices and audiences present in this poem. How does this make the poem interesting and effective?
3 How does Horace bring out the contrast between his life in the city and his life in the country? You could draw up a table listing the advantages and disadvantages of each.
4 What is the main moral message of Cervius' fable? How does the story communicate this message well?
5 Do you think that town and country life today are as different as Horace suggests they were in Roman times?

Virgil's *Aeneid*. Remember that Horace is able to do this successfully since epic and satire share the same poetic metre. The epic tone continues with the description of the luxurious house and the grand banquet in the following lines – it feels as if we are in the palace of a great king or queen.

The point of the humour here is of course that Horace is describing two mice, who are about as far from being epic heroes as it is possible to be! Indeed, their lack of heroism is emphasised in the preceding lines, when they have to creep up to the city walls under cover of darkness so as not to be detected. Moreover, in the house that they arrive at, they are not honoured guests but unwanted intruders who dine on the leftovers. The joke here is surely on the town mouse. He has come across as superior and self-important, and would no doubt like to think of himself as an epic hero, as Horace's parody of epic poetry suggests. Yet Horace's parody also shows up how ridiculous the town mouse's pretensions are.

Satires 2.2 and 2.6

Finally, it is worth comparing 2.2 with 2.6. There are a number of similarities and overlaps, including:

- Both place a value on a self-sufficient life in the country.
- Both poke fun at life in the town.
- In both, the food eaten reflects the lifestyle of the diners.
- In 2.2 a farm has been lost; in 2.6 Horace celebrates receiving a farm.
- Both end with the quoted words of a simple but wise countryman.

Satire 2.8

This satire describes a dinner party given by **Nasidienus Rufus**, a very wealthy man but one who is desperate to be seen to be a good host and to show off his sophisticated knowledge of food to his guests. Sadly for him, however, the dinner party goes disastrously wrong, much to the amusement of the other guests. We have no way of knowing if the story is made up or if it really happened, although Maecenas and other real-life characters are mentioned.

The poem starts with a conversation between Horace and his friend Fundanius, who is a comic playwright; Horace asks him how Nasidienus Rufus' dinner party went. The rest of the satire is Fundanius' account of the evening's events. He starts by giving an account of the food, wine and service, and then lists the guests' names and the seating plan. He focuses on the behaviour of Nasidienus and his clients Nomentanus and Porcius, as well as on that of the two clients of Maecenas, Vibidius and Balatro. Nomentanus has been appointed by his patron to explain the food in detail to the guests. However, Vibidius and Balatro soon become fed up with talk about the food and, to Nasidienus' great horror, rudely decide to drink as much of his fine wine as they can as quickly as possible. The other diners follow suit, apart from Nasidienus and his clients on the lower couch.

Nasidienus tries to retrieve the situation by giving further detailed description of the lavish foods that are served. However, before the guests have time to taste the fare, disaster strikes: a tapestry that is suspended above their heads falls down onto the food, covering it with dust in the process. Nasidienus reacts as if it is a great tragedy. Nomentanus shows great sympathy, but Balatro plays up to Nasidienus' self-importance by commiserating ironically with him. They try to continue the dinner party, but it has descended into farce. Vibidius complains that the supply of wine has stopped, while Balatro continues to make fun of the whole situation: both are perhaps drunk. Nasidienus returns, with a new series of dishes, but the guests cannot bear to go through more of the same commentary on the food again and so do a runner.

> **KEY INDIVIDUAL**   Nasidienus Rufus
>
> Nasidienus Rufus is obsessed by food. Today, we might call him a 'foodie' – someone who loves food and who loves to talk about food. In his case, however, it goes too far. He wants to make sure that his dinner guests understand just how special their food is, and just how carefully it has been prepared. In part, this is no doubt so that he can also show off just how much he knows about food; this theme reaches its peak in lines 43–53, where Nasidienus is quoted describing the food on the table in great detail. Sadly for him, his attitude only succeeds in boring and irritating his guests, and it is why they find the collapse of the tapestry onto the food so funny.

The names

Horace shows a sense of humour in the names that he gives some of the characters in this satire. We know that some of those present were real people – Maecenas and Fundanius, as well as Viscus and Varius, who are literary friends of Maecenas. However, the other five characters are apparently fictional, and four of them seem to have names that reflect their personalities: Balatro means 'buffoon' in Latin, and he plays the joker; Porcius means 'pig' or 'hog' and he scoffs down his food; the name 'Nomentanus' is linked to the Latin word for 'name', and it seems no coincidence that his job is to name and explain the food; finally, Nasidienus' name is linked to the Latin word for 'nose' – which seems fitting for a host who seems almost to be sniffing the food and wine to confirm their quality.

Themes

After describing dinner parties in the country in 2.2 and 2.6, in this poem Horace turns to satirising a city dinner party. Once again, this satire is rich in dialogue, with a number of different speakers, and it is set up by a conversation between Horace and Fundanius. Fundanius describes a dinner party that goes comically wrong – indeed, it is fitting that the tale is told by a comic playwright. It is also interesting that Horace was not at the dinner party himself – perhaps this is a way for him to distance himself from the events and the behaviour of both host and guests, just as he distances himself in 2.2 and 2.6 by presenting the speeches of Ofellus and Cervius.

The events of the dinner revolve around the behaviour of the host Nasidienus Rufus. Although Maecenas is the guest of honour, he never speaks and is hardly mentioned – all the focus is on Nasidienus and Nomentanus on one side, and Vibidius and Balatro on the other. Nasidienus is clearly very keen to impress such an important guest, and yet his keenness is self-defeating. He is a gourmet who is obsessed by the food and drink he serves, and his desire to explain it in great detail ruins the occasion.

Nasidienus next comes across as a show-off by telling Maecenas that if he is not satisfied with the extremely expensive wines he serves, he has other varieties that he can offer him. This brings an ironic reply from Horace, who claims that it must be tough being so wealthy. Indeed, the wines emphasise the lavishness of the feast. Caecuban was well known as the best Roman wine; it was a white that came from a single vineyard near the coast south-east of Rome. Chian was a red that came from much further afield – the Greek island of Chios in the Aegean Sea – and had long been recognised as one of the finest wines in the Greek world. Thus, when Nasidienus suggests that Maecenas would not enjoy these wines, he is really focusing attention on how good they are. Moreover, he proposed substitutes – Falernian or Alban were the best two Roman wines after Caecuban.

The second half of the satire is defined by the disaster that happens at lines 54–56. It is important to focus on the reactions of the main characters – Nasidienus weeping, Nomentanus trying to console him sympathetically, and Varius and Balatro struggling to contain their giggles. In lines 65–74 Balatro pretends to sympathise with the host, but in fact he is using great **irony** – he thinks the whole thing is highly amusing. However, Nasidienus does not spot Balatro's tone, and thanks him warmly for his kind words – showing just how naïve he is.

After this, we get a quick reminder of the start of the satire, as Horace reappears in the narrative to react to what he is hearing – he is finding the story hilarious. Fundanius then finishes the tale, as Nasidienus once again brings in fine food but spoils it by going into a detailed analysis. The satire ends abruptly as the guests run off – we are left to guess how the fragile Nasidienus might have responded to this.

> **irony** a way of expressing what you mean by using language that normally suggests the opposite

> **simile** a figure of speech whereby one thing is compared to another thing of a different kind in order to make a description more vivid

---

LITERARY ANALYSIS   Similes

Horace and Fundanius mock Nasidienus' behaviour almost from the start of the satire. One example can be found in Fundanius' description of the entry into the dining room of the two slaves bringing the wine, Hydaspes and Alcon:

> . . . then in came
> Dusky Hydaspes with the Caecuban wine, just like
> An Attic maiden carrying Ceres' sacred emblems,
> And Alcon with a Chian needing no added brine.
>
> Horace, *Satires*, 2.8.14–15

Horace uses a **simile** here to emphasise the pomposity or self-importance of the moment. The slaves' entrance is compared to a solemn religious procession in ancient Athens in which young women carried baskets of offerings to the goddess Ceres. Nasidienus is taking himself – and his dinner party – far too seriously. He will continue to do so when it all goes disastrously wrong – he reacts by weeping as if he had lost his own child.

ACTIVITY

Stage your own short play re-enacting the dinner party hosted by Nasidienus Rufus – you could even write your own script. How many different parts would you need to create? What props would you need? How would you develop each character as he is presented in Horace's poem?

Study questions

1 How much sympathy do you have for Nasidienus in this poem?
2 Do you think that Vibidius and Balatro's behaviour is acceptable in the circumstances?
3 Using the example on pp. 298–299, make a list of all the different voices and audiences present in this poem. How does this make the poem more interesting and effective?
4 What type of behaviour do you think that Horace is satirising in this poem? How successfully does he do this?
5 How does this dinner party compare to the dinner parties described in 2.6? Are there similarities in character between Nasidienus and the town mouse?

JUVENAL

We know very little about the life of Juvenal, although it seems likely that he was a lawyer who lived in Rome between *c.* AD 55 and *c.* AD 130, and who was an excellent public speaker. His sixteen satires are most likely to have been composed between the years AD 110 and AD 130. Early in the first satire he explains what drives him to write his poems:

> It's not hard to write satire. For who is so long-suffering of this unjust city that, leaden-heartedly, he can hold himself back . . .?

> Juvenal, *Satires*, 1.30–31

Juvenal's anger with life at Rome is a key theme of many of his poems. In fact, anger and indignation were key features of his writing, and so he rejected the gentler satire of Horace. Juvenal himself recognised this. A few lines after the quotation above, he coins a neat Latin phrase: 'facit indignatio versum', which translates as 'my indignation inspires my poetry'. If Horace was a smiling satirist, then Juvenal was an angry one who looked back to the example of the aggressive Lucilius.

Juvenal seems to have a love/hate relationship with his home city of Rome. While his poetry often savagely criticises life there, it is notable that he never chooses to move away and live elsewhere. Perhaps it was a case of 'I can't live with you, and I can't live without you'. His satires focus especially on the immoral, selfish and hypocritical behaviour of the Roman elite: he seems to believe that traditional Roman values had

---

PRESCRIBED SOURCE

Juvenal, Satire, 3.190–322

Date: sometime between AD 110 and 130.

Author: Juvenal (*c.* AD 55–130)

Genre: verse satire

Significance: a poem that relates bitter criticism of the quality of life at Rome.

Read it here: OCR source booklet

S & C

Juvenal has given us two particularly famous Latin phrases that are still quoted in English:

mens sana in corpore sano a healthy mind in a healthy body
quis custodiet ipsos custodes? Who will guard the guards?

Find out how these two phrases are used in English today. Do you agree with the sentiments that they communicate?

FIGURE 3.44
The remains of a Roman street alongside Trajan's Market in the heart of Rome.

disappeared from view. The assassinated emperor Domitian (who ruled Rome from AD 81 to 96) is a particular target. Yet even Juvenal's angry satire has its limits: he explains that he will not name any living individuals for fear of getting himself into trouble.

Since so many details of Juvenal's life are obscure, it is not clear who he was writing for. However, he was writing during a period when Greek as well as Roman orators, thinkers and philosophers were giving popular talks in Rome, and so he may have been in competition with them. As with Horace, he would have been writing for the educated elite, which would have been larger in Juvenal's day, although behaviour was still closely monitored by the emperor's circle. It seems that he was trying to provoke his readers into social change and improvement, and it is interesting that he is so ready to criticise the sort of wealthy men who may have made up much of his audience.

Juvenal's Third Satire

Juvenal's third satire focuses on how difficult life is in Rome. At the beginning of the poem, he addresses the reader directly and explains that his old friend Umbricius has chosen to leave Rome to live in Cumae, a small town near the Bay of Naples. While Juvenal is sad to see him leave, he does not blame his friend for his decision to abandon the capital. After this short opening, Juvenal quotes Umbricius directly – in a long monologue, he outlines the grievances with life in Rome which have driven him away. Therefore, only the first twenty lines of the 322-line poem are in the voice of the narrator – the rest belong to Umbricius. We should immediately be aware, therefore, that the views put forward in the poem are not presented as those of Juvenal, while it is hard to know just how much we can trust Umbricius as a reliable source of information about Roman life – his name even means 'shady'. It may even be that we are meant to laugh at Umbricius and his complaints and prejudices as much as at anything else.

Between lines 20 and 190, Umbricius complains about the difficulties of making a living in Rome. First, he laments the fact that there is no longer a place for an honest man in the city. He goes on to bemoan what he sees as his city overrun with foreigners – claiming that Greeks and Syrians are now everywhere, and presenting them as liars and cheats who have brought their cultural habits with them and taken jobs and opportunities for patronage from local Romans. Finally, Juvenal's departing friend claims that Rome is an awful place to be poor: the law protects the rich and abandons the poor, who are also evicted from their seats in the theatre and struggle to find women willing to marry.

The prescribed lines: 190–322

In these lines, Umbricius turns to listing the discomforts and dangers associated with life in Rome. They can be broken down into four distinct sections as follows:

- 190–231: falling buildings and fire
- 232–267: crowds and traffic
- 268–314: the dangers of the night
- 315–322: Umbricius' farewell.

Lines 190–231

In his attack on the dangers of falling buildings and fire, Umbricius first contrasts the relative safety of buildings in the country with those in the city. The four towns he mentions in lines 190–192 are all in the countryside beyond Rome, and Umbricius brings out a contrast between city and country here – the houses in the city are far more prone to collapse.

Umbricius then moves on to one of his main themes – that there is one rule for the rich, and one rule for the poor. He gives an example of the poor man Cordus, who has a bed so small that the dwarf Procula could not fit into it (an exaggeration to make his point), and who has very little to lose, but loses it nonetheless. At this point he is destitute, but has no support system – this seems to be a criticism of the patron/client system, which was supposed to help poor men support themselves.

LITERARY ANALYSIS

As Horace does in 2.6, Juvenal sometimes parodies epic poetry to further his satire. Consider the following lines:

> The place to live is far from all these fires, and all these
> Panics in the night. Ucalegon is already summoning a hose,
> Moving his things, and your third floor's already smoking.
>
> Juvenal, Satire 3.197–199

These lines only take on their full significance when we understand who Ucalegon is. A Roman reader would likely have spotted the reference to a minor character in Virgil's *Aeneid*, the greatest epic poem of Latin literature. In the *Aeneid* (2.311–312), Ucalegon is a noble Trojan whose house is torched by the Greeks on the night of Troy's sacking. Umbricius chooses to use the name to represent a typical lower class Roman whose apartment block is burning down.

What is the point of this comparison? The Romans liked to believe that they were descended from the Trojans, and so in some sense Virgil's Ucalegon is an ancestor of Juvenal's Ucalegon. Both lose their homes to fire, but that is where the similarity ends. The difference between them is just as important: while Virgil's Ucalegon is a noble Trojan with an impressive house, Juvenal's is a poor Roman living in a cramped apartment block. Therefore, the suggestion is that many of the descendants of the great heroes of Troy have ended up poor and helpless.

Moreover, Juvenal's Ucalegon is seen to be well-prepared to fight the fire and move his possessions, presumably from the ground floor. By contrast, the imagined person being addressed by Umbricius is on the third floor, where his apartment is already going up in flames. There is a suggestion that Juvenal's Ucalegon has learnt the lesson of his namesake in Virgil's poem, and this time is ready to protect his possessions.

S & C

Pliny the Younger, who is introduced on p. 319, also mentions disapprovingly the practice of Romans giving gifts to those who do not need them, while ignoring the poor. Read his letter 9.30 to find out more.

By contrast, if the house of the rich man Asturicus burns down, then important people rush to support him with gifts of new building materials. Umbricius once again uses exaggeration to emphasise how others respond to the news of Asturicus' house: women go dishevelled (a sign of mourning), nobles wear funeral clothes, and the praetor closes his court. Of course, none of these things literally happened – the courts were only closed in a time of national crisis. Umbricius ends this section of his speech by returning to his praise of life in the country, commenting that property is much cheaper there and you can buy a house that comes with a garden and proper quality of life.

Lines 232–267

These lines focus on the crowds, noise and traffic in the streets. Although Juvenal does not state this, we know from other sources that at that time the only vehicles allowed in Rome's streets during a normal day were those carrying materials for public building works, so that at night the streets were full of other traffic. In the poem, Umbricius claims that this prevents people from sleeping properly, and he even uses the comic example of a past emperor, Claudius (whom he refers to as Drusus) who was apparently famous for his drowsiness. Even Claudius would struggle to sleep, he claims! He follows this with a ridiculous parallel: seals – animals the Romans thought were just as drowsy – would also struggle.

At line 239 he gives us a detailed description of a scene in the streets, with a wealthy man being carried in a **litter** at his leisure, completely unaffected by the crowds around him. A litter was a portable taxi carried by slaves that only the wealthy could afford. Here the litter is compared to a **Liburnian galley**, a Roman warship that was more than 33 metres long and 5 metres wide. In these lines is another strong contrast between the experiences of rich and poor – if you are wealthy enough to afford a litter, you can have a relaxing journey through the streets; for the rest, it is an uncomfortable crush. Perhaps out of envy, Umbricius fantasises about a cart load of marble collapsing and crushing a patron and his followers. Back at the patron's house, slaves continue preparations for a dinner party unawares, while the master lies dead in the mud, unprepared for his journey to the underworld. This is a reminder of a truth which other Roman sources often mention – that there is no escape from death, whether you are rich or poor. Perhaps this thought gives some comfort to Umbricius.

Lines 268–314

Umbricius now starts to focus on other dangers of the city. One of these comes from up above: falling tiles and, amusingly, chamber-pots (bowls used as a toilets) emptied out of windows – perhaps this can be seen to symbolise Umbricius' own ranting and pouring out his views on the problems of life in Rome. He then moves on to discuss the threat posed by a burly drunkard in the streets, joking that he cannot sleep unless he has a fight first. He makes a ridiculous comparison with the great Greek warrior Achilles.

Umbricius goes on to explain why he himself is particularly in danger. The drunkard will avoid picking a fight with a wealthy man (identified by his expensive scarlet cloak) who has an escort of men carrying torches, but as Umbricius is poor – and his only escort

litter a portable taxi carried by slaves in the Roman world

Liburnian galley a Roman warship

FIGURE 3.45
A drawing showing a Roman litter.

is the moonlight or perhaps a candle he carefully preserves – he is easy prey. Umbricius' poverty is emphasised by the questions the drunkard asks him, suggesting that he has been to a dinner where he has drunk sour wine and eaten beans. Both were signs of a very cheap meal. The episode finishes with another reflection by Umbricius on the lot of the poor man – his only freedom is to plead to be allowed to go home with a few teeth left.

Umbricius' next danger in the streets of Rome at night is the one posed by thieves. He refers to the Pontine Marsh near Rome and the Gallinarian pine-forest near Cumae, both

LITERARY ANALYSIS

Juvenal again parodies epic poetry in lines 279–280. This time the reference is to the *Iliad*, the great poem of the Greek Homer recounting an episode near the end of the Trojan War. At the start of the twenty-fourth and final book of this poem (lines 3–11), Achilles is described mourning his beloved friend Patroclus, who has been killed in battle. Achilles himself feels responsible for his death, since he allowed him to go out to fight dressed in his (Achilles') armour. Achilles is therefore overwhelmed with grief and Homer describes him being unable to sleep, tossing and turning in the night while others slumber. Umbricius compares the situation of the drunkard in the street to that of Achilles – except that in the drunkard's case his mourning and lack of sleep is caused by having no one to fight with. It is a ridiculous comparison!

ACTIVITY

Imagine that you are Umbricius. Write a letter to the magistrate at Rome responsible for the upkeep of roads and streets outlining your complaints and making suggestions for how things could improve.

of which were well known to harbour many robbers and criminals because they were sparsely populated and it was easy to hide there. From time to time Roman troops were sent to clear both areas of criminals, but Umbricius claims that it only has the effect of sending them all to Rome, which is metaphorically described as being 'like a game preserve' for them. In another great exaggeration, Umbricius complains that Rome will soon run out of iron for farm implements as it is all being used to make chains for criminals. Once again, he suggests that Rome was much better in times gone by.

Lines 315–322

He concludes by driving his cattle out of the city, and suggests that when Juvenal himself escapes Rome to his own house in the country at Aquinum, he will come to visit and listen to his satires. This final point illustrates his divorce from life in Rome – he is only prepared to see Juvenal again when he is outside the city.

Study questions

1 Suggest three ways in which Juvenal's style of satire is different from that of Horace.
2 To what extent do you think that Umbricius might himself be being satirised in this poem, as a 'type' who loves to complain about his city?
3 Identify three ways in which Juvenal uses exaggeration in this poem. Do you think that this helps him to get the force of his message across?
4 Juvenal has structured lines 232–314 very cleverly to cover the period of an entire day: 232–238 refer to the nightime, 239–248 to the morning, 249–261 to the main part of the day, 261–267 to the late afternoon, 268–301 to the evening, and 302–314 to the nightime again. How do you think that this structure adds drama and atmosphere to the poem?
5 How accurate a reflection of Roman life do you think these lines give? What elements of the narrative seem to you to be likely?

ACTIVITY

Write two satires of your own, one of which imitates the 'smiling satire' of Horace, and the other the 'angry satire' of Juvenal. If possible, choose a topic or set of characters who you would like to satirise, and base both satires on it.

PETRONIUS

The author of the *Satyricon*, Petronius, was probably an influential aide to the emperor Nero (who reigned from AD 54 to 68), although there is not enough evidence to prove this conclusively. Nonetheless, there are a number of features of the world of this novel that are consistent with this exact period in Roman history. This Petronius is described in some detail by the historian Tacitus. He served as a consul in AD 62, while at the court of the emperor he was Nero's 'judge of taste', a role suggesting that he enjoyed luxurious living. We might even say that he acted as Nero's fashion advisor, in a similar way to how Maecenas had been Augustus' 'Minister of Culture'.

Petronius' novel attempts to show up and satirise social attitudes and pretensions rather than to attack specific individuals. One key difference between his work and the satires of Horace and Juvenal is that it was written largely in prose (although there are sections where poetry is quoted extensively). Moreover, it is a continuous novel with a plot, and so this gives it a very different feel from the poetic satirists. However, it is also clear that Petronius was influenced by the satirists, prose and poetic, who had come before him. When he wrote the account of Trimalchio's dinner party he must have kept in mind, for instance, Horace's account of the disastrous dinner party that he relates in 2.8.

Much of the Satyricon has been lost. It may have been twenty books long (in this sense, a 'book' is what we would think of as a chapter), but sections survive only from books 14, 15 and 16. For this reason, it is hard to reconstruct the outline of the plot, but it clearly centres on the adventures and misadventures of the main character Encolpius, who narrates the story, and his companions, his lover Giton, and Ascyltos, a rival for Giton's affections.

As with Juvenal, it is hard to know exactly who Petronius was writing for, but the novel's language is even more reflective of everyday speech than the language of Horace, and so he was probably aiming at a wider audience than just a small elite. None the less,

EXPLORE FURTHER

You can read Tacitus' account of Nero's aide Petronius in Tacitus' *Annals*, 16.17–20.

DEBATE

Scholars do not agree about what genre of literature the *Satyricon* belongs to. While it clearly has strong elements of satire, it also seems to be modelled on a variety of other genres, including Greek romance, epic poetry, comic drama and love poetry. What literary influences can you find in the sections you read?

S & C Modern works of satire

Find out about two works of satire in the modern era: *Gulliver's Travels* by Jonathan Swift and *Animal Farm* by George Orwell. Which groups of people and attitudes were being satirised by each author? How comparable is this to the focus of Petronius' satire?

PRESCRIBED SOURCE

Petronius, *Satyricon: Dinner with Trimalchio*, 29–33; 37–38; 49–50

Date: AD 60s

Author: Petronius (*c.* AD 66)

Genre: prose satire

Significance: a satire of a nouveau-riche freedman who holds an extravagant dinner party

Read it here: OCR source booklet

FIGURE 3.46
A view across the Bay of
Naples towards Mount
Vesuvius.

it is likely that his work was read by Nero and his circle, and may well have raised knowing smiles at a time when wealthy freedmen were prominent in Roman society.

Dinner with Trimalchio

Book 15 of the *Satyricon* has survived almost completely, and it tells of the dinner party at the house of Trimalchio, a wealthy but extremely vulgar freedman. Encolpius and his companions are citizens of relatively low social status, but have been invited as hangers-on to Agamemnon, a rhetoric teacher they have come to know. Agamemnon is invited as an honoured guest, since he is so intelligent and well-educated. The narrative satirises Trimalchio for his pretensions to high status, but also his inability to get things right. Also satirised, however, is the snobbery of Encolpius as he reacts to what he sees. A reader therefore needs to be alert to the fact that the narrator of the story is flawed too, and his own faults are also on display.

The dinner party takes place in a town somewhere around the Bay of Naples, a fashionable area for wealthy Romans to keep holiday homes. Just before the first prescribed passage (29–33), Encolpius has met Trimalchio for the first time when he finds him relaxing at the baths in the afternoon in preparation for the dinner. Immediately, it is clear that Trimalchio's behaviour is tasteless in the extreme – as he plays a ball game in the palaestra, a slave stands next to him with a silver chamber pot. Encolpius relates a particular incident:

> Trimalchio clicked his fingers. At the signal the eunuch held out the chamber pot for him while he carried on playing. He emptied his bladder, asked for water to wash his hands, splashed his fingers a little and wiped them on a slave's head.

> Petronius, *Satyricon*, 27

This episode epitomises the character of Trimalchio throughout the novel – his behaviour is often shocking and disgusting.

Sections 29–33

Section 29 begins with Encolpius arriving at Trimalchio's house and examining the paintings on the wall of the entry-passage: a warning to 'beware the dog', scenes from Trimalchio's career, and scenes from the *Iliad* and the *Odyssey*. The placement of these paintings next to each other is an obvious attempt by Trimalchio to place himself in the same company as the great heroes in the age of the Trojan War.

The guests are then led to the dining room. As they enter the dining room, a slave superstitiously reminds them to cross the doorway with their right feet first. (A similar modern superstition might be refusing to walk under a ladder for fear of bad luck.) Another slave then falls at their feet, begging them to rescue him from the whipping he is about to endure. The irony here is that the whipping has been ordered by a more senior slave: Trimalchio's steward is angry that his valuable clothing, given to him by a client, has been stolen in the public baths. The steward here is overstepping the mark just as

LITERARY ANALYSIS

Trimalchio himself (with hair) was holding Mercury's staff and was entering Rome, led by Minerva . . . Now indeed, where the colonnade was running out, Mercury was carrying him off, lifted by the chin, to a lofty tribunal. Fortune was there with her abundant cornucopia, and the three Fates, spinning their golden threads.

Petronius, *Satyricon*, 29

What can we learn about Trimalchio's character from these lines?

The art described here reflects Trimalchio's enormous sense of self-importance. The goddess Minerva represents wisdom and also military victory, while Mercury is there as the god of trade and profit (although it is ironic that he is also the god of thieves). Trimalchio believes that both are guiding his life. His sense of being divinely blessed does not end there: there are also images of Fortune and the three Fates. In Greek mythology, the three Fates were responsible for choosing the length of a person's life, and they usually appear in literature to warn people that death can come at any time. Here, though, Trimalchio presents them as allies who will allow him to live a long life. This is very arrogant of him, and suggests that he believes that he is immune to ill-fortune.

There is a further sense in which Trimalchio overvalues his achievements here. The reference to the magistrate's platform ('lofty tribunal') means that he has become an Augustalis (see p. 270). While this was the only major civic post a freedman could gain, it was not comparable to one of the major political offices, and so it was not worthy of the great ceremony that is depicted.

much as his master has done – slaves could neither own property nor could they have clients! Nonetheless, the steward decides to let the guilty slave off his punishment.

Once the guests have taken their seats in the dining room, a magnificent first course is presented, which Encolpius describes in detail. The guests are already eating when Trimalchio grandly arrives to the accompaniment of music. He takes his place in the seat reserved for the guest of honour – contrary to the usual custom – and rudely announces that he needs to finish the game he is playing, which has already caused him to be late. At this point, more food is brought in, and the guests witness their first culinary trick.

Sections 37–38

Fortunata, the wife of Trimalchio, is the focus of these sections. Encolpius has turned to another diner to ask about her. He learns that she is now fabulously wealthy, having once been a lowly slave girl and prostitute. Like Trimalchio, she is presented as someone who has come into extraordinary wealth and an extravagant lifestyle – her name, meaning 'Lucky', reflects this.

We then hear more about the extraordinary wealth of Trimalchio. All of his food is home-grown, and he goes to great lengths to import the best raw materials: bees from the region of Attica around Athens (long known for its honey) and mushroom spores all the

LITERARY ANALYSIS Symbolism

Petronius uses symbolism to emphasise Trimalchio's pretensions. As the guests walk into the dining room, they see above the door rods and axes with a miniature ship's beak protruding from the bottom. Rods and axes were symbols of senior magistrates, to illustrate their power to flog or execute. As an Augustalis, Trimalchio was allowed to display them as well, and he makes sure that they are prominently placed. Meanwhile, the ship's beak reflects the beaks that were attached to the main speaker's platform in the Roman forum, from where the city's leading politicians spoke. Again, he wishes to suggest that he is a leading man in the community.

Trimalchio's attire also reflects this desire to show off his status. As an Augustalis, he was allowed to wear a purple-bordered toga and a gold ring. In his case, he draws attention to this privilege by being unconventional: the purple stripe is on his napkin and the ring is gold and bronze.

way from India. The other freedmen at the dinner, while not as wealthy, are still very rich in their own right. As often in Petronius' account, great exaggeration is used to describe the characters, as in this sentence to describe the wealth of one of the freedmen guests:

More wine was poured under the table than another man has in his wine cellar.

Petronius, *Satyricon*, 38

This cannot literally be true, but the narrator (at this point one of the other guests) uses the exaggeration to emphasise just how wealthy this freedman had once been.

Sections 49–50

In section 49, Trimalchio plays another trick on his guests. The pretence that he arranges with his cook – that the cook will pretend not to have gutted the pig – allows Trimalchio to show anger with the cook and threaten to beat him. In turn, the guests beg the master to spare the cook. This episode is all about Trimalchio holding power – he is showing the guests that he has power over his household. More than that, however, the trick allows Trimalchio to have power over the guests, whereby they ask for his mercy almost as if a crowd at the amphitheatre might ask the emperor to spare

FIGURE 3.47
A fresco from Herculaneum showing a dining scene.

a fallen gladiator. When they see that they have been fooled, he has power over them again.

In section 50 Trimalchio is shown twice by Encolpius to be uncultured and lacking in class. The first example comes with his play on the term 'Corinthian bronze'. Bronze

EXAM TIP

Similes

Fortunata is described as having a nasty mouth on her and uses bad language, like a 'magpie on his couch'. How is this an effective image?

- A magpie is a bird that squawks loudly – one imagines Fortunata talking loudly and annoyingly.
- A magpie is a bird that collects loose bits of jewellery and takes them to its nest – the suggestion is that Fortunata also loves jewellery, some of which might not match well.
- A magpie is not usually found on a smart couch. This suggests that she does not deserve her current status of having great wealth.

tableware from the Greek city of Corinth was regarded as the finest that one could buy, and Trimalchio has some of it at his dinner party. Yet Trimalchio makes a very feeble joke about being the only person who has 'real' Corinthian bronze, since he bought it from someone called Corinthus. It would be one of those moments where the punchline to a joke falls flat, but the guests no doubt had to play along with it.

The second way in which Trimalchio embarrasses himself is in his knowledge of Greek and Roman history and literature. He talks about Troy being captured and looted by Hannibal. Yet the Trojan War – which involved Greeks and Trojans – happened so far back in history that it could not be dated (modern estimates are about 1200 BC), while Hannibal was a Carthaginian who fought against the Romans in the late third century BC. Trimalchio tries to show himself to be an educated man but in doing so proves to be the opposite.

Study question

The nineteenth-century US President Abraham Lincoln once said: 'Better to remain silent and be thought a fool than to speak out and remove all doubt.' Do you think that this sentiment applies to Trimalchio in this passage?

Study questions

1. What can we learn about the design of a Roman house from Petronius' satire?
2. Do you think that the readers of this satire were meant to find the story and its characters recognisable or believable? To what extent are they exaggerated?
3. Which parts of Petronius' satire do you find particularly funny? Do you think that a Roman reader would have found the same things funny as we do today?
4. To what extent do people today use food and dining to show off their wealth or status?
5. What impression do you form of the narrator Encolpius in this satire?

ACTIVITY

What do you think the main characters at Trimalchio's dinner party might have looked like? Choose three characters and draw or paint your own portrait of them. You could even exaggerate their features for comic effect and create a caricature.

TOPIC REVIEW

You should be able to:

1. Describe:
   - an outline of the storylines of Horace's *Satires*, 2.2, 2.6 and 2.8, and their key characters
   - an outline of the storyline of Juvenal's *Satire*, 3 (particularly lines 190–322), and its key characters
   - an outline of the storyline of Petronius' *Satyricon*, 29–33, 37–38, 49–50, and its key characters
   - the cultural context in which each author was writing.

2. Explain:
   - the key themes of each of Horace's satires, and the ways in which he creates humour
   - the key themes of Juvenal's third satire, and the ways in which he creates humour
   - the key themes of Petronius' account, and the ways in which he creates humour
   - the ways in which the style of each author is different.

PRACTICE QUESTIONS

Source A: Horace, *Satires*, 2.2, lines 112–128

You'll credit it more if I say that when I was a lad
Ofellus, as I know well, spent no more widely, then,
When his wealth was intact, as now it's reduced.
You can see him there with his sons and herd, a solid
Tenant on his lost farm. 'I was never one,' he says,
'To eat rashly on working days, no more than greens,
A shank of smoked ham, and if friends came to visit
I'd not seen for ages, or if I welcomed a neighbour
On a wet day when I couldn't work, we dined well,
Not on fish from town, but a kid or a pullet: then
Raisins and nuts and split figs graced our dessert.
After it, drinking matches with a forfeit for losing,
And with a prayer to Ceres: 'May she raise the stalks high',
She smoothed care from our furrowed brows with wine.
Let Fortune's winds blow, let her stir a fresh tumult:
How can she lessen this? How much worse off have I
Or you been, my lads, since this new landlord arrived?

1. Why has Ofellus lost his farm? [1]
2. How does Horace create a sense of Ofellus' character in this passage?
   Make **three** points. [6]

3.6 Pliny and his Letters

This topic focuses on Pliny the Younger. It will first outline who he was and what he achieved in his career, including his writings. It will then reflect on each of your six prescribed letters in turn, focusing on how his character comes across in them, and what they tell us about Roman life in his day.

THE LIFE OF PLINY

Gaius Plinius Caecilius Secundus was born into a wealthy family in Comum in the north of Italy in AD 61. Today, he is commonly known as Pliny the Younger to distinguish him from his uncle, Pliny the Elder. He was actually brought up by his uncle, and this automatically gave him access to the Roman elite, since Pliny the Elder was an admiral in the Roman navy. One of Pliny the Younger's most famous letters relates the death of his uncle during the eruption of Mount Vesuvius in AD 79, an event to which both men were eye-witnesses.

Pliny the Younger had an excellent education, and as a young man embarked on a career as a lawyer. He soon also rose through the ranks of Roman politics, and was appointed to the senate in the late 80s. Thereafter he held a series of high positions at Rome: most notably, he served as praetor in 93 and consul in 100. In about 111, he was appointed by the emperor Trajan to govern the province of Bithynia-Pontus, a

EXPLORE FURTHER

You can read about the eruption of Mount Vesuvius in AD 79 – including the death of Pliny the Elder and the escape of Pliny the Younger – in Letters 6.16 and 6.20.

FIGURE 3.48
A nineteenth-century painting of the eruption of Mount Vesuvius.

S Pliny has given his
& name to a certain type
C of volcanic eruption
called a 'Plinian
eruption'. Find out
about Plinian eruptions
and how they came to
be named after Pliny.

FIGURE 3.49
A medieval statue of Pliny on the side of the cathedral at Como (the modern name for Comum).

region roughly corresponding to a large section of northern Turkey today. He apparently died in office there in about 112.

We know a great deal about the life of Pliny through his surviving letters. Since he held so many important posts, they give us a very helpful picture as to what it was like for a senior Roman official to serve under an emperor; we also gain a valuable insight into elements of Roman society such as the patron/client system. However, the letters also give us a helpful lens onto his life away from the public eye; in particular, he writes in 1.9 with great fondness for life on his country estate. He writes in great detail about it in another letter, 2.17; it was a very large estate in Laurentum, about seventeen miles south-west of Rome, and clearly acted as something of a sanctuary for its owner.

PLINY AS A WRITER

Pliny was active as a writer throughout his life. He was a keen poet, although we have only quotations from his verses. He also wrote speeches, one of which has survived. However, Pliny has become best known for his letters, many of which have survived. He published nine books of letters at intervals between about 99 and 109, and they were addressed to a number of friends and acquaintances about many areas of his life, both private and public. A tenth book was published after his death and contains letters to the emperor Trajan while he was governor in Bithynia-Pontus. His letters tend to focus on a single subject or theme, and are relatively short.

Although the letters are centred on Pliny's day-to-day life, it is very important to understand that they are more than simple records of correspondence. In fact, Pliny wrote them to be published as short works of literature; some scholars even credit him with creating a new literary genre, the literary letter. Rather than writing history, it seems that Pliny wished to give a picture of his times through his letters – this obviously allowed him to write about and record the private lives of himself and others in a way which is rarely done by conventional historians. A further key feature of the letters is that they typically have a strong moral tone: Pliny wished to display through his letters how he felt people should behave, and where he felt that society had gone wrong. In this, there is an interesting overlap with Roman satirists, who also aim to point out society's flaws.

When we study Pliny's letters, therefore, we need to think not just about the content of what he is saying, but also how he has structured the letter; how the language he uses brings out his points; and what moral view or idea he is putting forward.

PRESCRIBED SOURCE

Pliny, *Letters*, 1.9, 2.6, 3.14, 4.19, 5.19, 9.6

CW

Date: *c.* AD 99–109

Author: Pliny the Younger (AD 61–*c.* 112)

Genre: literary letters

Read it here: OCR source booklet

Significance: letters that reflect on a variety of themes about life at Rome and in the country, as follows:

- 1.9   On the pleasures of spending time on his country estate
- 2.6   On an unkind dinner party host
- 3.14   On the murder of Larcius Macedo by his slaves
- 4.19   On the excellence of his new young wife
- 5.19   On his concern for the health of his freedman Zosimus
- 9.6   On his dislike of the chariot races

COMMENTARY

In the short commentaries that follow, each letter is summarised along with suggestions for what it might tell us about the following topics:

- the commentary Pliny offers on Roman life
- Pliny's use of language
- the purpose of the letter
- how Pliny reflects his position in Roman society
- the image Pliny projects.

However, it is important to realise that these commentaries are not exhaustive – by no means do they cover everything you could learn about the topics above. Rather, they are meant to give you examples and guide you in your own reading, so that you can develop other arguments and interpretations yourself.

Letter 1.9

Pliny writes this letter to his friend Minicius Fundanus, who was consul in 107. In the letter, Pliny reflects on the contrast between his life in Rome and the life he enjoys on his country estate at Laurentum. In Rome, he finds himself always busy with duties that seem important at the time, but soon seem insignificant. However, on his estate, he has time to relax, he becomes more even-tempered and he can focus on his writing, drawing inspiration from the natural beauty that surrounds him. He therefore encourages Fundanus to leave the city behind too, and summarises his thoughts with a pithy comment by his friend Attilius – it's better to relax than to be busy doing nothing.

Study questions

1 Compare this letter with Horace's Satire 2.6. What do each find tiresome in the city? What do each value most in the country?
2 What do we learn about Pliny's emotional state from this letter?

This letter presents the city/country contrast in a similar way to Horace in Satire 2.6. Like Horace, Pliny finds time on his country estate to clear his head, and this allows him to read, write and exercise. Pliny shows himself to be very self-aware, as he reflects on his changed emotional state – he does not speak harshly to anyone at his farm, which of course suggests that he does when he is in the city. Indeed, the only person he is harsh on is himself when he does not meet the very high standards he sets himself in his writing.

Pliny uses language carefully to get his point across. Reflecting on his life at Laurentum, he says:

> What a good and honest life! What delightful and virtuous leisure time and more wonderful than almost all business.

> Pliny, Letter 1.9

exclamation a figure of speech in which a writer seems to exclaim words aloud

This figure of speech is called an **exclamation** – it is as if we as readers can hear him exclaiming these words out loud, and it serves to draw greater attention to the point he is trying to make.

In the final paragraph, Pliny addresses Minicius Fundanus directly again, and the purpose of the letter becomes clear: he is advising his friend to leave the city so that he can rest or study, just as Pliny is doing. We do not know what pressures Fundanus is under, but in another letter Pliny refers to him as a learned man and a philosopher, so he is clearly keen for him to allow more time for this aspect of his character. Pliny finishes the letter by quoting a neat **aphorism** by an old friend, Atilius, who was well known for such sayings. The letter therefore ends in a suitably philosophical tone.

aphorism a short saying that communicates a common truth

Letter 2.6

This letter is written to Avitius, a younger friend of Pliny. We learn that he had recently attended a dinner party where the host's behaviour left him deeply unimpressed. The guests were divided into three categories: the privileged few, the clients and dependants of the host, and the freedmen. The first group were served excellent food, the rest ordinary fare in small portions; moreover, the wine was arranged and served in three categories by quality. Pliny voices his strong disapproval of the practice of offering different qualities of food at the same dinner party, partly through a conversation he reports with another guest. His own practice is to serve everyone the same, but not to go to great expense. The letter finishes with Pliny speaking as a mentor to Avitius, urging him to follow his own example.

It is clear what the purpose of this letter is – Pliny wishes to offer advice to a younger man about how a Roman of high status should treat those lower than him on the social ladder. We have seen on p. 264 that other writers talk about this practice of serving different foods to guests of varying status at a dinner party; Pliny takes a strong moral line on this, which he wishes Avitius to follow. Pliny therefore sets himself up as a wise mentor who has a clear set of principles.

One important way in which Pliny varies his language is by introducing a reported conversation with another guest half-way through the letter. This serves to magnify the sense of disapproval, since the discussion takes place quietly at the dinner party – there is the sense that the reader is invited to listen in on a confidential chat.

Letter 3.14

The addressee of the letter is Acilius, who is clearly away from Rome and unaware of the city's social problems. Pliny recounts the murder of Larcius Macedo, the son of a freedman who had become a senator. While Pliny admits that Macedo was a cruel master, he is horrified by the killing and approves of the punishment meted out to the slaves. He never says explicitly what this punishment was, but there was a precedent in such situations for every slave in a household – innocent or guilty – to be executed. Towards the end of the letter, Pliny turns to an earlier mishap which had befallen Macedo, when he was slapped by an equestrian at the baths.

It is interesting that Pliny, who is normally so humane, approves of the punishment and suggests that slaves can never be trusted. This attitude is in great contrast to how he speaks about his own household in Letter 5.19. Pliny's language reflects the violence of the murder, with a detailed description of the various parts of his body which were assaulted, followed by his being thrown on a hot pavement to see if he was still alive. During this description, Pliny uses an aside – 'shocking to say' – to illustrate just how repulsed he is by the event.

In the last section of the letter Pliny claims to be filling space left on his paper, but he does give a reason for linking the two stories related to Macedo's ill-fortune. Pliny describes the incident at the public baths as 'portentous' – in other words he believed that it was an omen of what lay in store for him at the hands of his slaves after he had taken a bath at home. Clearly, even this educated Roman believed in signs and omens that foretold the future.

Letter 4.19

This letter gives us an insight into the relationship between Pliny and his new young wife. The person addressed is Calpurnia Hispulla, her aunt (while Pliny does not name his wife in this letter, we know that she was also called Calpurnia). In the letter Pliny reports enthusiastically on her qualities as a new wife, and how they are both thankful for each other. A key point, which Pliny alludes to, is that Calpurnia is Pliny's third wife, and there is a huge age gap between them. She is likely to have been 15 or 16 at the time of their marriage, while Pliny is about 30 years older.

This letter gives a view into the expectations for an upper-class Roman wife. Pliny is pleased that Calpurnia is efficient in running the household, but also that she is a musical and literate young woman. As a consequence, Pliny almost presents her as a star-struck fan, one who memorises his books and listens out of sight when he is giving recitations. It could be argued that he is coming across as rather vain and self-important here.

The final section of the letter reveals its purpose. He wishes to thank Calpurnia Hispulla doubly – once for the role she played in his own upbringing, setting him high standards of behaviour, so that her niece admires him so much; and secondly for bringing them together – in Pliny's eyes, Hispulla is a matchmaker par excellence.

Letter 5.19

Pliny writes to his friend Valerius Paulinus, who was consul in 107, about his concern for the health of his freedman, Zosimus. This letter gives us an insight into the humane way in

Study questions

1 How does Pliny make clear his disapproval of the host's behaviour?
2 Why do you think that it was important to Pliny to act as a good mentor to Avitius?
3 In these first two letters, Pliny has the role of an adviser. What words and phrases from the two letters highlight this fact?

Study questions

1 Pliny admits that Macedo is a cruel master, yet fully approves of the punishment of all his slaves. Does this surprise you? Why do you think that wealthy Romans might have had such attitudes?
2 How does Pliny make his narrative vivid and graphic?

Study questions

1 Does this seem like a loving relationship? How can you tell?
2 What do we learn about Pliny's own upbringing from this letter?

ACTIVITY

Imagine you are Pliny's wife Calpurnia. Write a letter in the style of Pliny to your aunt, Calpurnia Hispulla, outlining what your life is like and how you feel about your marriage.

Study questions

1. Why do you think that Pliny is so keen for Zosimus to be restored to health?
2. Do you think that Pliny's comparison of himself with Odysseus is impressive? What do you think he was trying to say about the way he treats his household?

which Pliny treated members of his household, and so provides a contrast to his comments about slaves in 3.14. We hear about Zosimus' talents, and Pliny's fondness for him. We learn that he has already sent him to Egypt to help him recover from illness once before, and this time he asks Paulinus to host the freedman at his estate at Forum Iulii (modern Fréjus in Provence, France), so that he can relax and recover in the healthy country air.

We learn a great deal about Pliny's literary and cultural world from this letter. Near the start he quotes Homer to illustrate his own approach to the treatment of his household. Two points could be made about the quotation:

- Pliny is seeking to present himself as a cultured man. The two poems of Homer, the *Iliad* and the *Odyssey*, were acknowledged as the greatest works of Greek literature; any educated Roman was expected to know them well and look to them for moral examples.
- The specific words he quotes – 'he was gentle as a father' – are spoken in the *Odyssey* (2.47) by Telemachus, Odysseus' son. At this point Telemachus is referring to the way in which Odysseus, the king of Ithaca, used to treat the other noble men of the island. Pliny therefore compares himself to a king who treats his nobles well.

We can also learn from the letter about the cultured entertainment which Pliny values. Zosimus is highly valued for his skill as a reciter of comedies and other forms of literary performance, as well as for being a gifted musician.

We could reflect too on the presentation of ill-health and its treatment in this letter. Zosimus has already been sent to Egypt for medical attention – a country with a centuries-old tradition of medicine – and this seems to have worked. Now Pliny wishes to send him to southern France. This time, however, there is no tailored medical care on offer, beyond the fresh country air and local milk, which have a restorative reputation. Zosimus is to be sent on a restful retreat in nature to help his health, something which many doctors today would still recommend.

FIGURE 3.50
A statue of Odysseus.

Letter 9.6

In this letter Pliny writes to Calvisius Rufus, an equestrian friend from his home town of Comum, about his disdain for the chariot races, and in particular their fanatical supporters. Pliny seems to come across as quite snobbish in this letter, but he does make some important points about supporters being obsessed about their favoured team winning, rather than actually enjoying the quality of the spectacle – something that would seem to apply equally to many football supporters today.

It is hard not to find Pliny very self-satisfied in this letter. He is disdainful of the behaviour of spectators at the chariot races, and at the start draws a contrast between his own focus on his books and the deranged behaviour of the supporters at the races. This contrast is brought sharply back into view at the end, where he even admits to feelings of superiority over so many of his fellow Romans. The language he uses indicates his scorn and contempt, with words and phrases such as 'pointless', 'tedious', 'low enjoyment', 'wasting' and 'idlest of pursuits'. By contrast, he talks of his own 'utmost delight' at being able to devote his time to literature. Clearly, Pliny intends to place himself far above the crowd by using these words.

Study questions

1 Why do you think that Pliny was happy to publish a letter in which he is so critical of a popular obsession such as chariot racing?
2 Do you feel any sympathy for the views Pliny puts forward here?
3 What impressions do you form of Pliny from all six letters? To what extent would you say that he is wise, or self-satisfied, or arrogant, or humane or inhumane? Would you agree that the letters suggest that he is a complex character?

TOPIC REVIEW

You should be able to:

1. Describe:
   - the key details of Pliny's life and world
   - an outline of each of the six prescribed letters
   - the main characters in each of the letters.

2. Explain:
   - the impression we receive of Pliny and his world from his letters
   - how Pliny uses language to further his ideas
   - what the letters can tell us about Roman city life.

PRACTICE QUESTIONS

Source A: Pliny, *Letter*, 5.19

Some years ago, while narrating vigorously and keenly, he began to spit blood, and for this reason was sent by me to Egypt; after a long absence abroad he has recently returned, restored to health. Then, while he was putting too much strain on his voice over several days, he was reminded of his old infirmity by a fit of coughing, and again spat up blood.

For which reason, I decided to send him to your estate which you own at Forum Iulii. For I have often heard you mentioning that there both the air is healthy and the milk is most suitable for this kind of recovery. Therefore, I ask you to write to your household that your estate and house be thrown open for him, even that they cover all expenses, if need be. But the outlay will be modest. For he is so thrifty and abstemious, that he abstains not only from luxuries but also what's necessary for good health by his self-denial. I shall give as much to him for the journey as is enough for him to reach your estate.

1. Who is Pliny talking about in this letter, and what is his relationship to him? [2]
2. To what extent do Roman authors idealise life in the country? Use the source as a starting point, as well as the other Roman literature you have studied. [8]

3.7 Experiencing Roman City Life

TOPIC OVERVIEW

How the authors depict aspects of Roman city life and the attitudes of Romans regarding them, including:

- The dangers of city life
- Life in the city for rich and poor
- Leisure and entertainment
- Food and dinner parties

The prescribed sources for this topic are:

- Horace, *Satires*, 2.2, 2.6, 2.8
- Juvenal, Satire, 3.190–322
- Petronius, *Satyricon: Dinner with Trimalchio*, 29–33; 37–38; 49–50
- Pliny, *Letters*, 1.9, 2.6, 3.14, 4.19, 5.19, 9.6

Don't forget that you will be given credit in the exam if you study extra sources and make relevant use of them in your answers.

This topic enables you to draw on your knowledge of what you have already studied in the culture section of this component. It is considerably shorter than the previous two topics, since you will already have covered its themes during your reading – so what follows suggests ways in which you can develop your awareness of them.

THE DANGERS OF CITY LIFE

The most obvious passage to think about here will be the prescribed lines of Juvenal. Umbricius himself lists some of the dangers in the city, including falling masonry, fires and collapsing buildings.

However, beyond this, it is important to consider what might be thought of as dangers. You might reflect that both Horace (2.6) and Pliny (1.9) reflect on the stresses the city brings them, and how much better the country seems to be for their wellbeing. Horace even comments that he is glad to be out of the city while the weather conditions bring illness and death. A similar theme seems to emerge in the fable of the town mouse and the country mouse, where a life in the city is portrayed as being fraught with danger and anxiety.

EXAM TIP

Note that this topic requires you **both** to think about how the authors depict aspects of Roman city life **and** to think about the attitudes of the Romans regarding them. Therefore, you should be alert to both – it is probably much easier to recognise the former than the latter. However, one good example of the latter can be found in Pliny, Letter 1.9. Here Pliny reflects on all the activities and responsibilities that he is engaged with on a daily basis in Rome, after which he says:

> On the day you do them, these things seem important; but the same things, if you consider that you have done these every day, seem pointless? much more so when you go to the country. For then comes reflection: How many days have I wasted on such dull things!
>
> Pliny, Letter 1.9

In these lines, Pliny gives us an insight into his attitude towards his own life as a wealthy man in Rome – he concludes that much of it is a waste of time in the grand scheme of things. From this letter, therefore, we learn **both** about the sort of business an important man in Rome would typically attend to, **and** about his attitudes towards this.

LIFE IN THE CITY FOR RICH AND POOR

There are plenty of examples that you can draw on here, including:

- Umbricius' contrast between the reaction of people to the burning of a large house and the burning of an insula.
- Umbricius' portrayal of the street scene, with a wealthy man carried comfortably in a litter, and poor men crushed as they try to make their way.
- Pliny's description of his regular duties in 1.9.
- Horace's description in 2.6 of people trying to use him to get access to the wealthy and powerful Maecenas.
- Petronius' portrayal of the excess of Trimalchio, including his lavish house, the food he serves, and the wealth of his freedmen guests.

LEISURE AND ENTERTAINMENT

Of course, a major theme here will be the description of dinner parties, which is explored further below. However, there are other ways in which leisure and entertainment feature in your prescribed reading, such as:

- Horace (2.6) and Pliny talk about using leisure time for reading, study and writing.
- Cervius' fable presumably entertained his companions.
- Pliny's reference to the baths in 3.14, his description of Zosimus' talents as an entertainer in 5.19, and his snobbish disdain for the chariot races in 9.6.

- Trimalchio's use of tricks and jokes to try to provide entertainment at his dinner party.

FOOD AND DINNER PARTIES

This is one of the main themes of three of our sources: Pliny (Letter 2.6), all three of Horace's *Satires*, and the *Satyricon*; moreover, even in the Juvenal passage there is reference to the preparations for dinner.

One important idea to reflect on is: what does food symbolise in each source? Do different types of food represent different things? For example, in Satire 2.2, Horace refers to people eating peacock when chicken tastes just as good. It is no coincidence that the peacock is a bird that is known to preen and show off by raising its feathers – perhaps Horace is trying to suggest to us here something of the character of those who eat peacock, that they too are show-offs?

Secondly, we might think about how the authors play with the conventions of dinner parties, which we have learnt about in the culture section. A good example comes in Satire 2.8, when Horace lists the diners at Nasidienus' dinner party:

FIGURE 3.51

A seating plan of Nasidienus' dinner party

> I was there at the head, and next to me Viscus
> From Thurii, and below him Varius if I
> Remember correctly: then Servilius Balatro
> And Vibidius, Maecenas' shadows, whom he brought
> With him. Above our host was Nomentanus, below
> Porcius, that jester, gulping whole cakes at a time.
>
> Horace, Satire 2.8, 20–24

	MAECENAS	VIBIDIUS	BALATRO	
NOMENTANUS				VARIUS
NASIDIENUS				VISCUS
PORCIUS				FUNDANIUS

Horace is being clever here – the narrator Fundanius lists the guests in the order in which they sat, starting with himself at the top. However, there is a key point: Maecenas is the guest of honour, but next to him is not the host (Nasidienus) but his freedman Nomentanus, who has been appointed to explain the food to Maecenas. This change in the usual convention allows Horace to emphasise Nasidienus' eagerness to ensure that Maecenas understands all the food that has been prepared for him.

> ### Study questions
>
> 1 To what extent do the authors suggest that life in Rome is a danger to physical and mental well-being?
> 2 From what you have read, do you think that there was a greater gap between rich and poor in Rome than there is in our society today?
> 3 How much can we learn about Roman entertainment from the prescribed literature?
> 4 To what extent does food represent human character in the prescribed literature?

Moreover, this is not the only example in our prescribed literature of the conventional seating plan being changed: in *Satyricon*, 31, Trimalchio arrogantly has the place of honour reserved for himself. In both cases, then, the authors have changed the conventions to say something important about the host of the dinner party.

TOPIC REVIEW

You should be able to:

1. Describe:
   * the various dangers of city life that the authors portray
   * examples of the lives of the rich and the poor from the prescribed texts
   * examples of leisure and entertainment in the prescribed texts
   * examples of food and dinner parties in the prescribed texts.

2. Explain:
   * how dangerous life in a Roman city is depicted to be
   * the way in which the authors portray the differences between the lives of the rich and the poor
   * what we can learn about leisure and entertainment in the Roman city from the prescribed texts
   * what the authors tell us about the importance of food and dinner parties in Roman city life.

PRACTICE QUESTIONS

Source A: Juvenal, *Satire*, 3, lines 239–250

When duty calls, the crowd gives way as the rich man's litter,
Rushes by, right in their faces, like some vast Liburnian galley,
While he reads, writes, sleeps inside, while sped on his way:
You know how a chair with shut windows makes you drowsy!
Yet, he gets there first: as I hasten, the tide ahead obstructs me,
And the huge massed ranks that follow behind crush my kidneys;
This man sticks out his elbow, that one flails with a solid pole,
This man strikes my head with a beam, that one with a barrel.
Legs caked with mud, I'm forever trampled by mighty feet
From every side, while a soldier's hobnailed boot pierces my toe.
Do you see all the smoke that rises, to celebrate a hand-out?
There's a hundred diners each followed by his portable kitchen.

1. a. Explain what is meant by a 'hand-out' in this passage. [2]
   b. What was the significance of this hand-out for many Romans? [1]
2. In your opinion, how exaggerated are the dangers of life in Rome presented in the sources you have read? Use the source as a starting point, as well as your own knowledge. [8]

3.8 Relationships and Roman Society

The section on this topic is once again shorter than the first two, since it requires you to focus more deeply on the prescribed literature you have already examined. In looking at the relationships between these different groups in Roman society, it is important to be aware that you should reflect **both** on how the authors depict these relationships **and** on how they depict the attitudes the Romans have regarding them.

SLAVES AND MASTERS

Petronius will be one key source for this theme. There are two scenes in which a slave is threatened with a beating (in sections 30 and 49), while in section 29 one of the paintings on the wall of Trimalchio's house portrays a slave market. This gives us an insight into Roman slave markets, and it is perhaps surprising that Trimalchio wants to acknowledge his own origins as a slave in the paintings that reflect his achievements.

A further notable point comes in section 30, where we can observe the hierarchy of slaves in Trimalchio's household: the steward is his senior slave, who has the power to beat a junior slave for losing his smart clothing; the steward also claims to have a client, something not suitable for a slave. In section 51 we might focus on Encolpius' reaction to the possible whipping of the cook for not having stuffed the pig: he supports the idea that the slave should be whipped for his incompetence, showing little sympathy for him.

A similar lack of sympathy towards slaves can be seen from Pliny in Letter 3.14. We might be surprised that he approves of a severe punishment, whereby innocent and guilty slaves are killed alike, but this does give us an insight into the attitude to slaves even by those who are educated and relatively humane.

Finally, we get an interesting insight into slaves preparing the food for a dinner party in Juvenal 3.

PATRONS AND CLIENTS

We get a helpful insight into the attitude of patrons towards clients in Pliny's Letter 2.6 – and here we can also think about how food is used to denote social status. Further examples of the patron/client relationship can be seen as follows:

- The clients of Maecenas trying to get access to him in Horace 2.6, 33–39.
- The behaviour of the clients of Nasidienus and Maecenas at the dinner party in Horace 2.8.
- The fact that Trimalchio's steward himself has a client, even though he is a slave.

MEN AND WOMEN

There are relatively few examples of female characters in your reading. Indeed, Horace's three satires do not feature female characters apart from brief mentions of two divine figures, the muse of satire and Libitina, and one witch, Canidia. However, Fortunata in section 37 of the *Satyricon*, and the two Calpurnias in Pliny's Letter 4.19 are all characters of interest. It is notable that there is a great contrast between the characters of the two wives here, Calpurnia and Fortunata.

Study questions

1 What can we learn about Roman attitudes to slavery in the prescribed literature?
2 How much sympathy is there for clients in the prescribed literature?
3 Compare and contrast Fortunata and Calpurnia as Roman wives.

TOPIC REVIEW

With reference to the prescribed sources, you should be able to:

1. Describe:
   - examples of relations between slaves and masters
   - examples of relations between patrons and clients
   - examples of relations between men and women.

2. Explain:
   - what we can learn about the variety of relations between slaves and masters
   - what we can learn about the nature of relations between patrons and clients
   - what we can learn about how men and women interacted in Roman life.

PRACTICE QUESTIONS

Source A: Petronius, *Satyricon*, 31

A very excellent entrée was brought in, for now everyone was reclined except for one man, Trimalchio, for whom a place was saved at the top, in a new fashion. And then, on a large dish, an ass of Corinthian bronze with a double pannier was served up; in one basket there were white olives, in the other black. Over the ass there were two dishes on the edges of which was written the name of Trimalchio and the weight of the silver. Some little bridges soldered onto the plate were even supporting dormice sprinkled with honey and poppy seeds. There were also roasting sausages placed above a silver grill, and below the grill there were Syrian plums along with the seeds of pomegranates.

1. Why is Trimalchio's place at the table described as 'a new fashion'? [2]
2. 'Dining in the Roman world was above all about snobbery.' To what extent do you agree with this statement based on the literature you have studied? Justify your response. [15]

Further Reading for Literature and Culture 2: Roman City Life

Culture

Beard, M. (2010) *Pompeii: The Life of a Roman Town*. London: Profile Books

Beard, M. (2016) *SPQR: A History of Ancient Rome*. London: Profile Books

Beard, M. and Hopkins, K. (2011) *The Colosseum*. London: Profile Books

Berry, J. (2007) *The Complete Pompeii*. London: Thames and Hudson

Connolly, P. (1990) *Pompeii*. Oxford: Oxford University Press

Connolly, P. (2000) *The Ancient City*. Oxford: Oxford University Press

Fagan, G. (2002) *Bathing in Public in the Roman World*. Ann Arbor: University of Michigan Press

Futrell, A. (2006) *The Roman Games: Historical Sources in Translation*. Hoboken, NJ: Wiley-Blackwell

Shelton, J. (1997) *As the Romans Did: A Sourcebook in Roman Social History*. Oxford: Oxford University Press

Treggiari, S. (2001) *Roman Social History*. London: Routledge

Wallace-Hadrill, A. (2012) *Herculaneum*. London: Frances Lincoln

Literature

Braund, S. (ed.) (1992) *Roman Verse Satire*. Oxford (*Greece & Rome* New Surveys in the Classics No. 23)

Braund, S. (2013) *The Roman Satirists and their Masks*. London: Bloomsbury

Courtney, E. (2001) *A Companion to Petronius*. Oxford: Oxford University Press

Courtney, E. (2013) *A Commentary on the Satires of Juvenal*. Berkeley: California Classical Studies

Davie, J. (2011) *Horace: Satires and Epistles*. Oxford: Oxford University Press

Freudenburg, K. (ed.) (2005) *The Cambridge Companion to Roman Satire*. Cambridge: Cambridge University Press

Gibson, R. K. (2016) *Reading the Letters of Pliny the Younger: An Introduction*. Cambridge: Cambridge University Press

Rudd, N. (1998) *Themes in Roman Satire*. London: Bloomsbury

Walsh, P. G. (2009) *Pliny: Complete Letters*. Oxford: Oxford University Press

Walsh, P. G. (2009) *Petronius: Satyricon*. Oxford: Oxford University Press

What to Expect in the Exam for Roman City Life

This chapter aims to show you the types of questions you are likely to get in the written examination. It offers some advice on how to answer the questions and will help you avoid common errors.

THE EXAMINATION

This component of the GCSE examination is designed to test your knowledge, understanding and evaluation of Roman City Life. The examination is worth 90 marks and lasts 1 hour and 30 minutes. This represents 50% of the total marks for the GCSE.

There are two sections to the paper, one focusing on the 'Culture' topics and sources, the other focusing on the 'Literature' – the prescribed sections from Horace, Juvenal, Petronius and Pliny. Each section is worth 45 marks, and is therefore worth 25% of your GCSE. The question paper will consist of both short-answer and extended-response questions.

For the 'Culture' section, you will be required to respond to visual and material sources. Some of these will be the prescribed sources you have studied in class, and some of these you will not have seen before. Sources for the 'Literature' section will only be drawn from the prescribed sections of Horace, Juvenal, Petronius and Pliny that you have studied.

There are two Assessment Objectives in your GCSE in Classical Civilisation. Questions will be designed to test these areas. These Assessment Objectives are explained in the table below:

	Assessment Objective	Marks
AO1	Demonstrate knowledge and understanding of: • literature and visual/material culture from the classical world • how sources reflect their cultural contexts • possible interpretations of sources by different audiences and individuals.	50
AO2	Analyse, interpret and evaluate literature and visual/material culture from the classical world, using evidence and producing coherent and reasoned arguments.	40

For AO1 in this component, you will need to demonstrate the following:

Culture

- A good range of accurate and relevant knowledge of Roman city life, including sites and inscriptions.
- How the sites and inscriptions tell us about Roman city life.
- An understanding of the way the Romans lived: their housing, their family life, their social structure and their main forms of entertainment.
- Different interpretations that can be made about the sites and inscriptions from the Roman world, and the different conclusions that can be drawn from these.

Literature

- A good range of accurate and relevant knowledge of the prescribed texts.
- An understanding of the relevant genres, and of the historical and literary context in which the prescribed texts were written.
- Knowledge and understanding of the key themes of each text.
- An understanding of the literary styles of each of the authors.
- Different interpretations that can be drawn from the texts, and the conclusions that can be drawn from these.

For AO2 in this component, you will need to demonstrate that you can analyse, interpret and evaluate the sources you have studied, giving opinions and backing them up with evidence, for example:

Culture

- A range of reasoned opinions about Roman city life.
- Appropriate evaluation of different sources to provide reasoned ideas.

Literature

- A range of reasoned opinions about the genres, characters and themes of the prescribed sources, and about what they can tell us about Roman city life.
- Appropriate analysis of the genres, characters and themes of the prescribed sources, and of what they can tell us about Roman city life.

QUESTION TYPES

There are five types of questions that will feature in your exam. Each type will appear in both the Culture and Literature sections. With the exception of the extended-response questions (see below), all questions will be linked to a source. In the Culture section this will be a piece of material evidence such as a picture of a site or an inscription or a literary source. In the Literature section this will be a passage from one of the prescribed texts.

The question types are listed in the table below. They really fall into two categories: the first three types (knowledge and understanding, significance, and stimulus questions) are all short-answer questions. The final two types (detailed-response questions and extended-response questions) require a longer answer.

The final two types will usually be the final questions of each section. The short-answer questions can come in any order. For example, there could be a two-mark knowledge and understanding question, followed by a four-mark stimulus question, followed by a three-mark significance question.

Question type	Number of marks in each section for each question type
Knowledge and understanding questions	9
Significance questions	3
Stimulus questions	10
Detailed-response questions	8
Extended-response questions	15

Knowledge and understanding questions

There will be 9-marks' worth of knowledge and understanding questions in total (all AO1). The 9 marks will be broken down into a series of short-answer questions, typically worth 1, 2 or 3 marks. Some questions will require you to show your **knowledge** of one of the prescribed texts, or of an object or inscription from the Roman world. Other questions will require you to show **knowledge** and **also** demonstrate an **understanding** of these facts.

There will be a **source** to assist you. For literature, this will be a passage from one of your prescribed authors. For culture, it could be a prescribed source you have studied, or it could be one that you have not seen before.

For example, you might be shown the image on the right with the following questions:

Question: What furnishing is seen in this photo? What was it used for? [2]

Answer: A wooden partition [1]. It was used to separate the atrium from the tablinum in this house [1].

Knowing that this is a wooden partition is a piece of knowledge, and you can then show further understanding of this object by explaining how it was used. This answer should be brief. There is in fact no need to write full sentences if it seems that only a single word or a phrase is needed, as is the case in the first part of the answer.

The following represents a typical Literature knowledge and understanding question, together with its answer:

Source A: Juvenal, *Satire*, 3, lines 239–242

When duty calls, the crowd gives way as the rich man's litter,
Rushes by, right in their faces, like some vast Liburnian galley,
While he reads, writes, sleeps inside, while sped on his way:
You know how a chair with shut windows makes you drowsy!

Question: **(a)** What was a Liburnian galley?   [1]

                   (b) What is it being compared to here?   [1]

Answer: A Liburnian galley was a Roman warship [1], and it is being compared to a litter being carried through the streets of Rome [1].

The first part is asking for one piece of factual knowledge from the passage and the other mark is for your understanding of what it is being compared to in the passage. Remember, if you are asked to only give a certain number of facts, or make a certain number of points, you should stick to the instructions.

In this type of question, each correct fact or explanation is worth one mark. You will not be asked to evaluate ideas (e.g. whether you think that the wooden partition was a useful furnishing, or if you think that the simile of the Liburnian galley is an effective one), so do not waste time in doing so.

Significance questions

There will be one of these questions in each section. It will be split into two parts. You will be asked to give two pieces of information (2 marks AO1) and state why one or both are important or significant, or what this knowledge tells us (1 mark AO2). Look at the Literature example based on these lines from Horace's Satire 2.6:

O when shall I see you, my farm? When will I be free
To breathe the delightful forgetfulness of life's cares,
Among ancient classics, with sleep and idle hours?
When will they set before me beans, Pythagoras' kin,
And those little cabbages oiled with thick bacon-grease?

(a) Where was Horace's farm, and who had provided it for him?   [2]

(b) Suggest one way in which this farm might have been important to Horace.   [1]

The answers to part (a) are that the farm was in the Sabine Hills outside Rome [1] and that Maecenas had provided it for him [1]. For the second part, this might lead to the idea that it gave him the space and relaxation to write his best poetry for Maecenas [1] or it was a status symbol and acknowledgement of his achievements [1].

In the culture section the question might look something like this:

Source A: *Part of the garden in the House of Octavius Quartio*

Study **Source A**.

(a) Identify two key features of this garden. [2]

(b) Suggest a reason why it was important for the owner of this house to have a garden such as this. [1]

Two marks would be gained in part (a) for saying any two of: there was canal which ran the length of the garden [1], that it was decorated with statues, paintings and crossing bridges [1], that midway along the canal was a fountain [1] and that there was a small temple beyond that. You could also say that the garden was planted with rows of acanthus and fruit trees [1] and in the wall at the back was another entrance to the property [1]. Remember that you only need to make two points to get the marks – it does not help you to make more than two points.

One mark would be gained in part (b) for saying that the owner would be able to provide a beautiful view for dinner guests, or that the garden could give visitors the sense that they had left city life behind and were relaxing in the country, or that it gave the members of the household a shrine where they could worship the gods. Again, remember that you only need to make one point to gain the mark.

Stimulus questions

These questions will ask you to identify something relevant from a stimulus passage or image, and to analyse what you have recognised. Each **relevant** quotation or feature of the image that is picked out will be worth a mark, as will each piece of analysis. Therefore, these questions are each worth equal amounts of AO1 and AO2.

In the culture section, you might be given a picture of a Thracian gladiator figurine and asked:

Question: Select **two** items of Thracian equipment shown in the source, and suggest what each tells us about the combat style of the Thracian. [4]

Answer: To gain the first two marks (AO1), you might identify any two of the following items: a broad-rimmed, full-face helmet; a short sword; two thigh-length greaves.

To gain the next two marks (AO2), you might make the following suggestions:

- protected his the entire head, so clearly at risk of heavy blows to it
- implies a close-combat fighter
- implies he was at risk of being hamstrung or having leg broken by a heavier opponent.

Part (a) requires two pieces of knowledge and part (b) asks you to give your opinions of the evidence. You should be careful not simply to show an understanding of how it was used in the second part, but instead to give your own ideas based on the evidence.

In the Literature section, you will be given a passage and might be asked for your opinions on a character or for how the passage is made exciting. For example, you might be given the following passage from *Satyricon* and asked how the character of Trimalchio is portrayed, for 4 marks:

Source A: Petronius, *Satyricon*, 33

While he then dug out his teeth with a silver toothpick he said, "Friends, it was not yet agreeable to me to come into the dining room, but so that you might not be delayed any longer by my absence, I have denied myself every pleasure. You will, however, permit me to finish my game." A boy followed him with a board of terebinth wood and crystal pieces, and I noticed the most luxurious thing of all. For instead of counters of black and white he had gold and silver denarii.

You would be expected to make two points of **analysis**, giving your opinions. You might say that Trimalchio is badly-mannered and that he likes to show off how wealthy he is. Two points of **evidence** to back this up would be the fact that he uses a toothpick at the dinner table and the fact that he uses silver and gold coins as pieces on a board game.

Look at the number of marks available. If there are three pieces of evidence and three pieces of analysis required, do not give more than this amount. You will be using up time that would be better spent in detailed-response and extended-response questions.

Detailed-response questions

You will get one of these questions in each section with one or more stimulus passages or images to prompt you. This stimulus is meant only as a starting point, and it will be clear from the question that you will need to bring in **extra information and examples**.

Four marks are awarded for your knowledge and understanding (AO1), and four marks given for your analysis, interpretation and evaluation of your facts and understanding

(AO2). These questions are marked in a different way, however; you are not given one mark for each correct opinion and each piece of evidence, but the answer as a whole is marked using a Levels of Response Grid. A Levels of Response Grid explains to examiners what answers may look like to achieve a certain number of marks. An examiner will read the whole answer and then check the grid to work out what level the answer belongs to. It is important to remember that the quality of your answer is more important than the amount you have written. The Levels of Response Grid is included in the mark schemes for exam papers.

It is also important to remember that for AO1 you will need to show knowledge and understanding of a source's context and the different ways people interpret the sources.

Remember that you can examine both sides of an argument. For example, if you are asked whether you admire the character of Umbricius in Juvenal's third Satire, there are likely to be arguments on both sides of the question. It may be that you largely admire him, but that he has some flaws, or that you largely do not admire him but that he has some redeeming features. If you do not examine both sides of an argument, you may have missed some key facts, and your answer may not show a full evaluation.

This question is not meant to be an essay. You are advised not to write an introduction that simply outlines how you will write your response, as this will not add anything to your answer and will take up valuable time. You may find you have more to say than time allows, so you might have to be disciplined in moving on. Make your key points at the start, keep to the point, and if you do choose to have a conclusion, keep it brief, as you will ideally have answered the precise wording of the question throughout your answer. It is not necessary to have a conclusion to gain full marks.

For example, on the paper you might be given one or more than one source relating to the baths, and then you might be asked the following question:

'The most important reason to go to the baths was to keep clean.' To what extent do you agree with this statement? Use the sources as a starting point and your own knowledge in your answer. [8]

In order to show that you know about the baths, you might include some of these facts:

- few people had bathing facilities at home, so most Romans went every day
- people could exercise in the palaestra first
- the tepidarium and caldarium allowed a bather to build up a sweat
- olive oil was rubbed into the body and then scraped off with a strigil
- the process finished with immersion in the cold frigidarium, which closed the pores of the skin – the whole process was very thorough
- the baths were also a social place where people could meet up with friends
- the baths were a place where wealthy Romans went to do business and to be seen.

You then need to weigh up the reasons that people went to the baths:

- the fact that there were not baths in most homes meant that people needed to use the baths
- it was vital for public health that people washed properly every day

- however, exercise and keeping fit in the palaestra might be just as important for many people
- meeting up with friends was important but that could take place elsewhere, whereas bathing could not
- wealthy Romans could also do business elsewhere, but often the baths were a very important setting for this – it might be more important for them to go to the baths for this reason than for the rest of the population.

Half the marks are awarded for AO1 and for AO2, but remember this does not necessarily mean that you should give four facts and four explanations. Examiners will read your whole response and judge how good they feel it is overall.

In Section B, on Literature, a question might ask you about the importance of a theme, or the portrayal of one particular character or episode.

Extended-response questions

This type of question is different from all the other questions in two respects: there is no stimulus passage to introduce it, and you will be given a **choice** of questions to answer (there are two extended-response questions in each section, and you must do **only one**). However, it is marked using a Levels of Response Grid in the same way as the detailed-response question.

Five marks are awarded for your knowledge and understanding (AO1), and ten marks given for your analysis, interpretation and evaluation of your facts and understanding (AO2). This means more marks are awarded for how good your argument is than for simply what you know. Therefore, you might want to spend a bit of time thinking about the structure of your answer. As for the detailed-response question, it is important to remember that for AO1 you will need to show knowledge and understanding of the literary and historical context of sources and the different ways people interpret them.

Extended-response questions will be broader than the detailed-response questions, and will draw upon material from across topics of either the Literature or the Culture sections. These questions will never, however, cover both Literature and Culture. For example, whereas you might be asked a question about the baths in a detailed-response question, as shown on p. 339, an extended-response question might ask about Roman entertainment more generally, and also ask you to draw on wider knowledge of Roman city life.

The following is an example of a possible extended-response question:

'Pliny comes across as a very impressive character in his letters.' To what extent do you agree with this statement? [15]

To answer this question you should look for evidence of Pliny's character from your prescribed letters (remember too that you can get credit for introducing material from outside the prescribed sources, so if you have read other letters you could draw on these too). You might include some of these facts:

- 1.9: he is aware of his flaws when he is busy in the city; he realises how much benefit he gets from being in the country.

- 2.6: he takes a moral line about treating freedmen well at dinner and disapproves of those who do not; he gives moral advice on this to a younger man.
- 3.14: he approves of the murder of an entire household of slaves, although he admits that Macedo was cruel and arrogant.
- 4.19: he is very grateful for the excellent character of his young wife, but also talks about how much she admires him.
- 5.19: he wants to be seen as being a master who is 'gentle as a father' and wants to look after his sick freedman Zosimus.
- 6.9: he criticises the behaviour of the crowds at the races and is thankful that he is not like that.

You then need to analyse how impressive a character Pliny is. You might draw conclusions such as:

He is impressive because:

- he is self-aware about his emotional state when in the city, and of his own character flaws – this is a sign of an impressive character
- he is also concerned that people at the top of the social ladder treat those lower down it properly and respectfully
- he wants to act as a moral example to younger Romans
- he is keen for his wife to study and learn, and treats her with respect and admiration
- he shows genuine concern for the members of his household such as Zosimus
- he would prefer to write and study than to go to the races, so he is confident enough to pursue his own interests rather than simply doing what everyone else does.

He is not impressive because:

- he admits that he gets life out of balance in Rome
- he is not prepared to give freedmen his best wine, but only to share lower quality wine with them
- his approval of the murder of all the slaves in Macedo's household, including the innocent ones, seems cruel and lacking in humanity
- his letter about his wife shows that he is vain and wrapped up in his own sense of self-importance
- his letter about those who go to the games shows someone who thinks that he is superior and looks down on other people.

Key points

The following applies to both detailed-response questions and extended-response questions:

- Your facts must be **relevant**. Do not merely state everything you know about a particular topic.
- It is a common mistake in the literature to over-narrate the plot and to retell a whole story. You should instead **summarise** the main points, or focus in detail on

one or two parts of it. This is particularly important in your extended-response answer, where five marks are available for your knowledge, but ten marks are given for your evaluation, interpretation and analysis.

- Show that you **understand** things from an ancient point of view wherever possible. For example, characters in the literature texts may have had different attitudes to slavery than we would today, or Roman baths may have seemed far more luxurious to the Romans than they would do to us today.

- Evaluation is best done throughout the response. **Keep referring back** to the title in your essay to do this. If you give all your facts, and then give all your opinions, it is easy to miss something out, or to run out of time.

- Try to find a **balance** of ideas as the question will usually require you to argue both for and against an idea.

- Sometimes a piece of evidence can be taken two ways. If so, remember to give **both interpretations** in order to show a high level of understanding.

- You will not have a lot of time to do these questions and so it is always best to present your most important arguments first in case you find yourself running out of time.

- Ultimately make your conclusion **logical**, and supported by evidence from your whole answer, not just one part of it.

Look at these two extracts attempting to answer the question:

Question: How impressive a character does Pliny seem to you from the letters you have read?

Extract 1

Pliny is an impressive character in his letters. He had an interesting life, escaping from Mount Vesuvius and becoming a rich man who had a really big villa in the country. He was also an important person, although he preferred chillaxing in his villa. He treated his slaves well but was happy for other masters to kill their slaves as a punishment. He also treated his wife well, although she was much younger than him. She really rated him as a writer, so he must have been good. He was a bit of a snob though, as he didn't like people who went to the chariot races, which were a bit like football matches today. People could get fanatical about following their chariot teams. Apart from that, Pliny was an impressive character, and he drank cheap wine if he had to.

Extract 2

Pliny is quite an impressive character but he does have flaws. It is impressive that he cares so much for his freedman's health that he is prepared to send him to France to recuperate from illness. He also wishes to be seen as 'like a father' to his household. However, against this he also approves of the execution of all the slaves in Macedo's household, even the innocent ones – this suggests someone who can be very heartless. He treats his wife well, even though she is much younger than him: it is impressive that he encourages her to read and learn and writes a letter to her aunt to say what a good wife she is. However, Pliny can come across as very self-important in the way that he talks of her reading his books, listening to his speeches and singing his music.

Notice how the first extract spends more time on presenting the facts than giving opinions, and some of the facts are irrelevant. The evaluation is not developed fully, and the final statement is not made relevant to the question. The second extract is much more concise, and is much more balanced. It argues both sides and flows smoothly from one example to another, providing a rounded view of Pliny's character.

GENERAL EXAM SKILLS

When you are sitting the examination, read the instructions carefully so that you realise which questions are compulsory and which are optional (the only option you have is which of the two extended-response questions you choose to answer). Remember that the examination will have a range of difficulty of questions; some of it is designed to be challenging, and you should not be panicked if you cannot think of an answer immediately. The following pieces of advice may seem obvious, but you should not underestimate their importance:

- The examination lasts 90 minutes and is worth 90 marks. Do not assume this means you should spend a minute per mark: in reality a lot of short questions will take less than a mark a minute and you should spend longer than a mark a minute on the longer questions.
- Both the Culture and Literature sections are worth 45 marks. Do not spend too long on whichever you choose to do first; this is especially tempting if you like the questions that have been set and feel you could say a lot.
- If you see a question that you do not know the answer to, move on quickly to another question and do not waste time thinking. Leave enough time to go back to it as during the examination you might well remember the answer.
- Stick to the question: if you are asked for facts, do not give opinions and vice versa.
- Do not try to answer a slightly different question if you wish another had been set, or if you have practised a similar one before at school.
- For detailed-response and extended-response questions, present different interpretations.
- More marks are available in the paper for opinions than knowledge or understanding. It is vital that you do not over-narrate, especially in your Literature answers.

L&C 3
War and Warfare

Introduction to War and Warfare

In this component, learners will explore war and warfare in ancient Greece and Rome, with a particular focus on the Athenian, Spartan and Roman armed forces, as well as on the works of four authors who wrote about warfare, two Greek and two Roman.

The Culture section of this component comprises a study of a variety of aspects of ancient war and warfare. It is sub-divided into the following key topics: Sparta at war in the fifth century; Athens at war in the fifth century; Roman Imperial Military Systems, Tactics and Equipment; and the Romans at war. These topics will enable you to learn about the military systems in each society, and to study four important battles and conflicts: the battle of Thermopylae, the battle of Salamis, the battle of Actium and Trajan's campaigns against the Dacians. You will be encouraged to think about the impact that war and warfare had on wider society.

In the Literature section of this component, you will read the work of four famous ancient writers: Homer, Tyrtaeus, Horace and Virgil. All four offer an insight into how war and warfare was viewed in their time. The epic poems of Homer and Virgil are set in the mythological past, while the shorter poems of Tyrtaeus and Horace refer to fighting in their own day. All present a compelling picture of the importance of war and warfare to their societies, and of how ideas of human heroism and dignity were forged through conflict.

EXAM OVERVIEW	J199/23

Your examination will require you to show knowledge and understanding of the material you have studied (AO1) and will require you to analyse and evaluate it (AO2), giving your opinions on areas such as characters in the literature or objects in the culture.

This component makes up 50% of your GCSE. In this component 50 marks will test your AO1 skills and 40 marks will test your AO2 skills.

There will be a distinct section of questions on the Culture section of this component, and a distinct section on the Literature material. Neither section will ask questions requiring knowledge of the other: for example, you will not be asked how far Virgil's *Aeneid* confirms knowledge of what you have learnt in the culture section about Roman military systems.

In both sections you will be asked to answer a series of short factual questions, based around quotations or images concerning the Culture material, or around passages from the prescribed authors. Some of these will also ask for your opinions. You will be required to write longer answers in each section, worth 8 marks and 15 marks, showing knowledge and giving opinions. There will be 45 marks' worth of questions on the Culture section, and 45 marks' worth on the Literature section. You will have a choice of longer questions worth 15 marks in each section, but all other questions will be compulsory.

Culture

4.1 Sparta at War in the Fifth Century

TOPIC OVERVIEW

- The structure of Spartan society and how this influenced the military
- Training and recruitment of the Spartan army, including the *agoge* and the *syssitia*
- The equipment, tactics and formation used in battle
- The structure, organisation and command of the army, including the role of the *perioeci* and the *helots*
- The idealisation of war and warfare in Spartan society
- The battle of Thermopylae, including:
  - key events and individuals: Xerxes; Demaratus; Leonidas; Ephialtes; Dienekes
  - the significance of the battle and how it was commemorated

The following are the prescribed sources for this topic:

- Bronze Warrior figure, Spartan, British Museum (1929,1016.6)
- Helmet of Corinthian type, dedicated to Zeus at Olympia, c. 460 BC, British Museum (1824,0407.32)
- Red figure Kylix of a Persian and a Greek fighting, the Triptolemos Painter

Don't forget that you will be given credit in the exam if you study extra sources and make relevant use of them in your answers.

This topic focuses on the nature of warfare in Sparta during the fifth century BC. At this time, the Greek world was not unified as one political state. Rather, it consisted of hundreds of independent 'city-states', which typically had small territories and just a few thousand inhabitants. Sparta became so powerful partly because it was much larger in size, controlling territory of about 3,200 square miles. In all Greek cities, large or

S & C We have no actual evidence for Sparta in the fifth century from Sparta itself, since the city was highly secretive, nor did it produce any historians or poets during this period. Indeed, the most detailed surviving source on Spartan society is Plutarch, who lived from AD 45 to 120. Those who wrote about the city often seem to have presented an idealised picture, and it is likely that by Plutarch's time such an idealised version had grown and developed even more. We should always be aware that few facts about Sparta can be known for certain.

small, it was normal for a large proportion of the citizen body, and other residents, to be conscripted to serve in the military. However, they were only mobilised for the duration of particular campaigns. There was no such thing as a 'professional' army as we have today.

THE STRUCTURE OF SPARTAN SOCIETY

To understand the success of the Spartan army, we must try to understand the sort of society that Sparta had constructed by the fifth century BC. About two centuries earlier, they had conquered and subjugated most of the other peoples in the two regions surrounding the city of Sparta – Laconia and Messenia. When Sparta conquered these new territories, the land was re-assigned to Spartan citizens in allotments. However, these were worked by native Laconians and Messenians, who were obliged to hand over a proportion or a fixed amount of their produce to their Spartan citizen masters. These native inhabitants, now enslaved as agricultural labourers, were known by the Spartans as **helots**.

The allotments of land were designed to be large enough for the Spartan citizen to live off its income. As a result, in Sparta a larger proportion of men than in other Greek cities could afford to dedicate more of their time to warfare. They were still not 'professional' soldiers as we would understand them, since they did not make a living from waging war, nor were they 'full-time' soldiers as they lived at home with their families and were called up only for the duration of a campaign. However, they did spend more time on physical exercise than Greeks elsewhere, and they ate their daily dinners in the company of men who also formed a military unit. Furthermore, they were in principle always available for war, which was not possible for all citizens in other parts of Greece.

However, the presence of the helots presented a significant danger for the Spartans, since they were greatly outnumbered by them (perhaps by a ratio of seven to one). Elsewhere in the Greek world, slaves were imported individually or in small groups from foreign parts. By contrast, the Spartans controlled communities of native Greeks who could more easily band together and rebel. (In the 460s, the helots did actually engage in a major revolt after Sparta was hit by an earthquake, and it took many years for the Spartans to suppress this rebellion.) So although the Spartans had a better army than other Greek cities, they needed to use it in part to keep down their enslaved population rather than to fight wars against other Greeks. For a long time, Sparta was able to wage successful external wars, but after the 460s they seem to have become more cautious about sending too many citizens abroad to fight for too long.

There was one other important group within Spartan society. When the Spartans conquered Laconia and Messenia, they left some communities to get on with their way of life, as long as they recognised Sparta's overall control of the region. They knew the people who lived in these communities

> **helots** a large class of enslaved native inhabitants of Messenia and Laconia who worked for their Spartan masters

FIGURE 4.1
The vale of Sparta.

perioeci a class of people who lived in scattered, less fertile parts of Spartan territory

as the **perioeci**, which meant 'those who live around'. The perioeci tended to live in the less-fertile parts of the region, and they were allowed to make their living as craftsmen and traders, as well as landowners. The Spartans permitted them to run their own communities themselves, as long as they followed Sparta in matters of war and foreign policy. Therefore, if the Spartans went to war, they would call up members of the perioeci to fight with them. Indeed, by the fifth century the perioeci were an integral part of the Spartan army.

TRAINING AND RECRUITMENT

The main source of information about Spartan education is Plutarch, so there is no way of knowing how accurately he represents the nature of a system from centuries before his time. However, in his view, Spartan education aimed to prepare each Spartan boy to be a highly trained and unquestioningly loyal citizen. This apparently started from the moment of birth. Babies were inspected by a committee of elders and, if considered deformed or too weak, they were left on a mountainside to die of exposure.

agoge the training school that all Spartan boys attended from the age of seven

At the age of seven, a Spartan boy began his training in the school for citizen boys known as the **agoge**, a word which literally meant 'rearing'. The boy was put into a pack, each led by prefects, young men in their late teens. All the boys were under constant supervision and the prefects could whip the boys for any offence. Little reading or writing was taught – only enough to train them for basic literacy. Instead, a great deal of time was spent developing physical strength and obedience. Music was also an important aspect of their education. By learning to sing and dance in choral competitions, the boys were taught the value of precise movement and teamwork.

When they reached their teens, the training became even more intensive. Boys were trained to go barefoot at all times so that they could run faster, scale heights more easily and clamber down cliffs. They had to cut their hair short and were allowed only one cloak for the whole year, whatever the weather. This of course helped foster a sense of equality amongst all boys. Food was deliberately rationed to make them used to doing without it on a military campaign if necessary, and as a result the boys were forced to steal to get more. If they were caught, they were beaten 'for stealing carelessly'. In fact, any offence was punishable by beatings. When walking in the streets, the youths were forced to stay silent and keep their eyes fixed on the ground ahead of them, in order to show respect.

krypteia a period of survival training for the strongest Spartans in their mid-to-late teens

When they were in their late teens, the strongest youths were enlisted into the **krypteia**. It is not clear exactly what this unit was designed to do, but it seems to have been a form of 'survival training' for these young Spartans, during which they were sent out into the countryside of Laconia and Messenia and given minimal rations so that they had to live off the land. Plutarch also suggests that a further purpose of the unit was to kill any helot they thought presented a danger to Sparta.

syssitia dining-clubs of about fifteen Spartan citizens, which met every evening and shared a tent together on campaign

The syssitia

In order for a young Spartan to gain full citizenship after leaving the agoge, he had to be elected into one of a number of dining-clubs, known as **syssitia** (singular: syssition).

Each syssition had about fifteen members who were expected to eat together every night. The food they shared was relatively simple fare, further encouraging equality among the men. When on campaign, the members of a syssition also shared a tent together. The syssition was a key element in the success of Spartan society, since it bred comradeship, and ensured that different generations of Spartans mixed with one another.

EQUIPMENT AND TACTICS

The fully-armed soldier in the Greek world was called a **hoplite**, from the Greek word 'hopla', meaning 'weapons'. The basic item of a Spartan hoplite's uniform was a tunic, over which a cuirass of bronze (later of linen) protected the torso. To protect his legs a hoplite wore bronze greaves (shin-guards), while leather boots were also used in battle. A helmet completed the uniform. Early in the fifth century this was made of bronze and plumed in the Corinthian style. It gave great protection to the head, but did not make vision or hearing very easy. During the fifth century, Spartans stopped wearing this type of helmet and replaced it with a very open-faced, crestless helmet. In addition, Spartan men wore their hair long to make them appear larger in stature and more frightening in battle.

> **hoplite** a heavily-armed Greek infantry soldier who fought in the phalanx

A Spartan hoplite carried three important weapons:

- **Shield** The Spartan shield was two-handled and large (up to a metre in diameter). It was made of wood and bronze and fitted onto the left forearm. It was inscribed with a capital lambda –Λ – the Greek letter L, which stood for 'Lacedaemonians', the collective name of the Spartans and the perioeci.
- **Spear** The spear was made of wood and had an iron head. It was held in the right hand.
- **Sword** If the hoplite lost his spear or fought his enemy at close quarters, he could resort to using a short iron sword, which hung on the right side of a belt around his waist.

The bronze warrior statuette shown in Figure 4.3, about 10 cm in height, was found in Sparta, and shows a heavily armed hoplite of the sixth century. There would originally have been a spear in his right hand, and so the image gives a good idea of the forward thrusting motion a hoplite would have made with his spear during battle. Notice, too, that the hoplite is wearing the Corinthian-style helmet, which would go out of fashion in the following century. It is also interesting that the hoplite is tilting back his shield so as to rest it on his shoulder as well as on his arm. This suggests that it was heavy and offered a lot of protection, but also that it needed a lot of effort to handle it.

The bronze helmet in Figure 4.4 is a good example of a fifth-century hoplite helmet in the Corinthian style. The inscription on it says that the helmet was a spoil of victory for the Argives against the Corinthians, and that the Argives dedicated it to Zeus in his sanctuary at Olympia. It was common for Greeks to dedicate weapons and armour to the gods

FIGURE 4.2
A hoplite.

to thank them for a victory, although such dedications went out of fashion shortly after this one was made.

The Spartans were masters of the **phalanx**, the standard method of fighting in the Greek world during the fifth century. The phalanx was a rectangular formation, a number of rows deep, with soldiers closely packed together in each row. In battle, most Greek phalanxes charged at each other and, when they met, a soldier would thrust at an opponent with his spear, attempting to hit an unprotected area on his body. If a hoplite in the front row fell, the man behind him would step up to take his place. Each hoplite held his shield in his left hand and so often depended on his neighbour's shield to protect his exposed right side. The phalanx was therefore a team effort and soldiers needed to maintain tight discipline. Any disruption to the front line could rip a hole in the formation, at which point the soldiers would have to turn and flee, and the battle would be lost.

The lifestyle of the Spartan citizen ensured that he was in prime physical condition if he needed to fight. The focus and intensity of the Spartans in battle is perhaps suggested by the fact that they were very unusual in the Greek world in approaching an opposing phalanx at a deliberate pace rather than at a run. Another strategy the Spartans employed was a policy of trying not to come up against an enemy too often, so that their tactics would remain a mystery and they would be more difficult to fight against.

> **phalanx** a Greek rectangular fighting formation in which men fought in massed ranks and tried to force their way through the enemy phalanx opposing them

PRESCRIBED SOURCE

Bronze Warrior Figure

Date: 6th century BC

Location: British Museum; found in Sparta

Significance: a small statuette of a Spartan warrior in armour from the 6th century

PRESCRIBED SOURCE

Bronze Helmet of Corinthian Type

Date: *c.* 460 BC

Location: British Museum; found at Olympia

Significance: a good example of a Corinthian-style helmet

FIGURE 4.3
Bronze Warrior Figure from Sparta.

FIGURE 4.4
A Corinthian-type helmet dedicated at Olympia.

THE STRUCTURE AND COMMAND OF THE ARMY

A further key feature of Spartan success was its efficient command structure. The army was led on campaign by one of the two kings who jointly ruled in Sparta. The Spartans believed that their kings were descended from Heracles, and they were also Sparta's religious leaders, so it must have been inspiring to have a king fight in battle with them. The actual divisions of the army seem to have changed during the years of the fifth century, and no source gives an entirely clear picture of how the army was divided up at any one point. However, it seems that the largest sub-division of the Spartan army was a regiment often known in Greek as a **mora**. The smallest unit of the Spartan army was the **enomotia**, which meant the 'sworn-band', it probably consisted of about forty men, similar to a modern platoon. This was a distinctive feature of the Spartan army, as other ancient Greek armies do not seem to have had units this small. It is likely that the enomotia was in some way linked to the syssition, so that two or three syssitia made up an enomotia. The enomotia was therefore probably a further way to breed comradeship. It is likely that the members of the enomotia swore the following oath:

> I shall not desert my taxiarch or the leader of my enomotia, whether he is alive or dead, and I shall not leave the battlefield unless our commanders lead us away.

From *The Oath of Plataea*

The **taxiarch** mentioned here was a senior officer who was directly responsible to the kings, who are described here as commanders. The fact that with this pledge a Spartan soldier swore not to desert the officers above him illustrates how important loyalty and discipline was to the Spartan army.

The perioeci and helots were also used on campaign. For example, at the battle of Plataea in 479, 5,000 Spartan citizens were joined by 5,000 perioeci and 35,000 helots. Perioeci were used both as hoplite fighters and as craftsmen to repair weaponry and equipment. By the end of the fifth century, when Spartan citizen manpower had declined, the perioeci even fought in the same units as Spartan citizens. Helots carried equipment and supplies, cooked and ran errands for their Spartan owners, but sometimes they also served in much greater numbers as light-armed troops, as they did at Plataea. In order to prevent helots from rebelling while on campaign, Spartan citizens always carried their spears with them in camp and kept a close guard on the weapon store.

THE IDEALISATION OF WAR AND WARFARE

Once again, we are reliant on non-Spartan sources to help us try to understand the extent to which war and warfare was idealised within Spartan society. This makes it difficult, but one thing that other Greek sources emphasise is how highly the Spartans valued a noble death in battle, not least Spartan women. One famous anecdote records that a Spartan mother sent her son off to battle with the words: 'either with your shield or on

---

mora (pl. **morai**) a name for a Spartan army regiment

enomotia a 'sworn-band', the smallest unit of the Spartan army

taxiarch a senior commander in the Spartan army

EXPLORE FURTHER

Read Thucydides' account (5.64–74) of the battle of Mantinea fought in 418 by Sparta and its allies against an army led by Argos and Athens. What can we learn about Sparta's use of the hoplite phalanx from this passage?

Study questions

1 How did the structure of Spartan society allow its army to have such an advantage over the armies of other Greek cities?

2 Can you think of other societies where a large group of people has been enslaved by a much smaller, militarily stronger group?

it,' meaning the one thing for a Spartan soldier to avoid was to return defeated, having deserted in battle and lost his shield. Rather, the son was either to return victorious carrying his shield, or with his dead body carried on it.

Moreover, Spartan women were taught to show no emotion except pride for a fallen relative. One story by the fourth-century historian Xenophon, who spent time in Sparta and so knew their society well, illustrates this. In 371, after the news of a defeat to the Thebans at the battle of Leuctra was relayed to Sparta, he reported that:

> On the following day you could see those women whose relatives had been killed going about in public looking bright and happy, while as for those whose relatives had been reported living, there were not many of them to be seen, and those who were to be seen were walking about looking gloomy and sorry for themselves.
>
> Xenophon, *Hellenika*, 6.4.16

Xenophon also gives us interesting information about those Spartans who deserted in battle. They were deprived of citizenship and referred to as **tresantes** instead – tresantes means 'tremblers' and of course implies that they were afraid. Xenophon explains how the tresantes were treated in Spartan society:

tresantes 'tremblers' – Spartans who had deserted in battle and so been deprived of citizenship

> In other cities the coward suffers nothing more than the stigma of cowardice – he goes to the same market-place as the brave man, sits with him and attends the same gymnasium if he wishes. In Sparta anyone would think it a disgrace to take a coward into his mess or be matched against him in a wrestling bout . . . [a coward] must give way to others in the street, and rise even for younger men when seated . . . he must not go about the city looking cheerful, nor must he imitate those who are without reproach; if he does, he must submit to a beating from his betters. When such disabilities are attached to cowardice, I am not surprised that Spartans prefer death to such a deprived and disgraceful existence.
>
> Xenophon, *The Constitution of the Spartans*, 9.4–6

One important point in this passage is that tresantes could be beaten – in other Greek cities, corporal punishment was reserved for slaves alone.

THE BATTLE OF THERMOPYLAE

The battle of Thermopylae, which took place in 480 BC, was the most famous battle in Spartan history, even though it ended in a defeat for the Spartans. Our main source for the battle is the historian Herodotus, who was writing in the third quarter of the fifth century. His account was based on a number of different sources, most of them spoken rather than written. By his day, the battle had entered Spartan folklore, so we might think of his account more as the version of events that the Spartans had chosen to remember and idealise.

In 480, the vast Persian Empire to the east of Greece invaded the Greek mainland with a huge force, led by their king **Xerxes**. Only a minority of Greek cities chose to stand and fight the invasion force – about thirty out of several hundred. In fact, some

KEY INDIVIDUAL

Xerxes the Persian king and leader of the invasion in 480

Greeks even encouraged the Persians to invade and worked with them when they came. As the Persians advanced into northern Greece in the summer of 480 – where they met little resistance – the Greek allies debated what to do. They decided to send an advance party to try to block the Persians in narrow pass in central Greece, where the mountains met the sea, and where it was easy for a small number of men to hold back a large army. The pass was called 'Thermopylae', literally 'hot gates' since the area contained hot springs. Herodotus tells us that this advance party consisted of about 7,000 men. The Spartans contrib-

FIGURE 4.5
A plan of the battle of Thermopylae.

uted 300 men to accompany their king, **Leonidas**; all of the 300 had to be fathers of living sons, so that, if they died, they had provided future warriors for the state.

The Greek allies reached the pass at Thermopylae before the Persians did. Herodotus tells us that it was very narrow – just wide enough for two wagons to pass between the foot of the mountains and the sea. Led by the Spartans, the Greeks rebuilt an old wall at the narrowest point of the pass, and waited. On the Persian side, king Xerxes did not know what to do, and so he summoned one of his key advisers, **Demaratus**. Remarkably, Demaratus was a former Spartan king who had been deposed, after which he had defected to the Persians. Xerxes had welcomed him as a trusted adviser on Greek affairs. Demaratus had warned Xerxes about the extraordinary courage of the Spartans when he had asked about them:

> First then, they will not under any circumstances accept terms from you which would mean slavery for Greece; secondly, they will fight you even if the rest of Greece submits. Moreover, there is no use in asking if their numbers are adequate to enable them to do this; suppose a thousand of them take the field – then that thousand will fight you, and so will any number, greater than this or less.

Herodotus, *Histories*, 7.102

Xerxes simply laughed at Demaratus when he heard this, but he was soon to learn that he was right. There was a tense stand-off for four days, while the Persian king waited in hope that the Greeks would retreat, terrified by the number of Persian forces facing them. During this time he sent a spy on horseback to survey the Greek camp. He was astonished when the spy reported back that the Spartans were readying themselves for battle by combing their hair. Demaratus explained to Xerxes that the men were preparing themselves for a glorious death in battle.

Day 1

After four days, Xerxes' patience finally gave up, and he sent in his troops. The battle continued all day, and the Persians suffered heavy losses. Even though there were so many of them they did not have the equipment or skill to match the hoplite tactics of

KEY INDIVIDUALS

Leonidas the Spartan king who led the Greek allies at Thermopylae

Demaratus a former Spartan king who had defected to the Persians

FIGURE 4.6
The site of the pass at Thermopylae today, where the sea is no longer nearby.

FIGURE 4.7
A drinking cup (kylix)
showing a Persian and
a Greek fighting.

PS

PRESCRIBED SOURCE

**Red figure Kylix of a
Persian and a Greek
fighting, the
Triptolemos Painter**

Date: *c.* 460 BC

Location: National
Museums of Scotland;
made in Attica, Greece

Significance: a painting
of an imagined scene
from the Persian Wars

KEY INDIVIDUAL

Ephialtes a local Greek
who told Xerxes about
the mountain path to the
other side of the pass at
Thermopylae

the Greeks, and the narrow space evened up the contest. Late in the day, the Persians decided to send in their elite troops – the King's Immortals – who advanced confidently. However, even they were beaten back and suffered great losses. It was at this point that the Spartans successfully employed the tactic of pretending to withdraw, thereby sucking in more of the enemy, and then turning to fight them suddenly. During the day, Xerxes sat and watched the battle and apparently three times jumped up from his chair in terror for what was happening to his army.

The scene on the inside of the Greek-style drinking cup in Figure 4.7 shows a Greek hoplite poised to kill a fallen Persian soldier. The fact that the two are both using swords may suggest that the hoplite has lost his spear and so has pulled out his sword as a secondary weapon. The scene well illustrates the difference in armour and weapons between the two. The heavily armed hoplite carries a round shield with a Pegasus motif. He towers over the Persian, who is easily recognised from his dress. He wears heavy clothing but no armour.

Day 2

The Persians fared little better on the second day of the battle. The Greeks continued to rotate their front-line troops, so allowing their men to rest, and they suffered few losses. Xerxes had no idea how to resolve the situation, but then he had a stroke of luck. A local Greek, **Ephialtes**, hoping for a huge reward, came to the King and told him of a path over the mountains that could lead his troops to the other side of the pass. That evening, Xerxes sent another band of elite troops up along the mountain path so that they could attack the Greeks from the rear and trap them in the pass. The Persian troops made easy progress. Although a division of Greek troops had been posted to defend the mountain pass, they withdrew when they heard the Persians approaching.

Day 3

As dawn broke on the third day, the Greek forces learnt from scouts returning from the hills that they were about to be surrounded. While Leonidas dismissed most of the Greek forces, it was unthinkable for the Spartans to desert a battle and so they stayed, along with 700 Thespians and 400 Thebans (these Thebans surrendered early in the final engagement), as well as an unknown number of perioeci and helots. The remaining Spartans knew that they would all die that day, but did not flinch from fighting with extraordinary bravery. We are told by Herodotus that when their spears were broken, they fought with their swords, and when these were broken they resorted to fighting with their hands and teeth. Their great courage and resolution was epitomised by one comment from a Spartan warrior called **Dienekes**. Herodotus tells the story as follows:

> Of all the Spartans and Thespians who fought so valiantly the most signal proof of courage was given by the Spartan Dienekes. It is said that before the battle he was told by a native of Trachis [*a local region of Greece*] that, when the Persians shot their arrows, there were so many of them that they hid the sun. Dienekes, however, quite unmoved by the thought of the strength of the Persian army, merely remarked: 'This is pleasant news that the stranger from Trachis brings us: if the Persians hide the sun, we shall have our battle in the shade.' He is said to have left on record other sayings too, by which he will be remembered.

Herodotus, *Histories*, 7.226

KEY INDIVIDUAL

Dienekes one of the 300 Spartans who was remembered for his brave comments before the battle began

Led by the 300 Spartans, the Greek allies again inflicted great losses on the Persians. However, once the allies were surrounded, it was only a matter of time before they were all killed.

King Leonidas was incredibly brave in the face of death. Before the Persians invaded, the Delphic Oracle had informed the Spartans that their city would either be conquered or that they would mourn the death of a king. In short, when Leonidas set out to defend the pass at Thermopylae, he believed that his death would be the necessary price for Sparta's survival. After the battle, the Persians found his body lying amongst those of the other Greeks. Persians normally showed respect to the dead of their enemies, but in his fury Xerxes ordered the body of Leonidas to be decapitated. His head was driven onto a stake, where it rotted in public.

FIGURE 4.8
The modern memorial to the Spartans at Thermopylae.

Even though the Persians won the battle, the example shown by the Spartans at Thermopylae inspired the other Greeks for the coming battles. Although the Greeks had lost this battle, they would go on to beat back the Persian invasion. Herodotus records that an inscription was set up at the spot:

> Go tell the Spartans, you who read,
> we took their orders, and here lie dead.

Herodotus, *Histories*, 7.228

This was one of a number of memorials set up to commemorate the sacrifice of the Spartans at Thermopylae. Herodotus tells us that he was able to learn the names of every one of the Spartan soldiers – as well as their fathers' names. The event was remembered in Sparta even centuries later. A Greek travel writer called Pausanias who visited the city in the early second century AD, reported that a memorial was still in place with the names of the 300 and their fathers' names.

ACTIVITY

Imagine that you are Leonidas. Write a speech that you will deliver to your men before the battle starts.

S & C

Herodotus gives a moving account of the battle of Thermopylae in his *Histories*, 7.198–233. We know that he visited Sparta, and he would have learnt there about the tradition of the battle. What can we learn about the Spartan ideal of military heroism from this account?

For comparison, you can also read an account of the battle by a later historian, Diodorus Siculus, in his *Universal History*, 11.5–11. How does his account differ?

Study questions

1 Why do you think that the Spartans remembered the battle of Thermopylae so proudly, despite the fact that it was a military defeat?
2 From what you have learnt about the Spartan army, why do you think that the Spartans were able to hold their ground against the Persians at Thermopylae for so long?

TOPIC REVIEW

You should be able to:

1. Describe:
   - the social structure of Sparta and the training of Spartan soldiers
   - the arms and armour used by Spartan hoplites, and the nature of phalanx fighting
   - the structure of the Spartan army
   - the key events and individuals involved in the battle of Thermopylae.

2. Explain:
   - the importance of the army to Spartan society
   - how Spartan education prepared boys for war
   - why the Spartan army was so successful against its enemies
   - why the battle of Thermopylae became so legendary in Sparta, even though it was a military defeat.

PRACTICE QUESTIONS

Source A: Account of the battle of Thermopylae, Herodotus, *Histories*, 7.223–224

The Greeks, who knew that the enemy were on their way round the mountain track, and that death was inevitable, put forth all their strength and fought with fury and desperation. By this time most of their spears were broken, and they were killing Persians with their swords.

1. Explain how a Spartan hoplite would use a spear and a sword in battle. [2]
2. In what ways did the Spartans show bravery at Thermopylae? Use the source as a starting point and your own knowledge in your answer. [8]

4.2 Athens at War in the Fifth Century

TOPIC OVERVIEW

- How the army and navy were paid for, recruited and trained
- The equipment, tactics and formations used in battle on land and sea
- The structure, organisation and command of the army and navy
- The impact of the Athenian military on Athenian politics and society
- The battle of Salamis, including:
  - key events and individuals: Themistocles; Xerxes; Artemisia
  - the significance of the battle and how it was commemorated

The following are the prescribed sources for this topic:

- South frieze (the Greeks fighting the Persians), Temple of Athena Nike, Acropolis Athens now in the British Museum
- Lenormant Trireme relief, Acropolis relief

Don't forget that you will be given credit in the exam if you study extra sources and make relevant use of them in your answers.

During the fifth century, Athens grew to become the most powerful Greek city, eventually controlling an empire that consisted of hundreds of other smaller Greek cities. Most of these were dotted around the Aegean Sea. The city's key strength lay in its navy, and it was this that allowed it to gain so much power, although that is not to say that it did not have a strong army. This topic will look first at the Athenian army and it will then focus on the Athenian navy – in each case, the first three bullet points in the topic overview will be treated together as a whole. It will finish with an examination of the famous Athenian-led Greek victory over the Persians in a naval battle at Salamis in 480.

THE ATHENIAN ARMY

One key difference between Athens and Sparta was the way in which the military in each city was funded. In Sparta, while individual hoplites were well-funded by income from land cultivated by helots, there was little money in the public treasury. This meant that it was difficult for the Spartan government to find funds for large endeavours needing a reserve of collective money, such as building fleets and maintaining sieges. In Athens, by contrast, for much of the fifth century the city had a large public treasury that could more easily fund significant campaigns.

As in Sparta, all adult male Athenian citizens were expected to serve in the military when required to do so (although men over the age of sixty were exempt). Those citizens wealthy enough to do so would buy their own sets of hoplite armour. As in the rest of the Greek world, the Athenians fought in the phalanx formation. The armour and weapons used by an Athenian hoplite were very similar to those used by a Spartan hoplite, although the Athenian did not of course have the distinctive 'lambda' on his shield. If a man was not wealthy enough to buy a full set of armour, then he made do with what he could. A shield and spear were the two most essential items. We have little evidence for the training given to Athenian soldiers, but they would not have had the same amount of time to dedicate to physical fitness that the Spartans had.

It is important to be aware that a large number of Athenian citizens were unable to afford any of the equipment required to serve as a hoplite in the army – estimates for the number of hoplites in the Athenian army vary from thirty to fifty per cent of the citizen population, and so somewhere between fifty and seventy per cent of citizens would have fought as light-armed troops. In a battle, a light-armed soldier might throw stones, javelins or arrows from a distance. At the other end of the economic spectrum, the very wealthiest citizens could afford to keep a horse and serve in the cavalry. A cavalryman carried one important weapon, a spear. The cavalry divisions were led by three commanders and divided into ten units based on tribe (see below). While Athens was renowned for its navy, it also had a strong land army and Athenian soldiers had a particularly strong reputation for siege craft.

There is good evidence for the command structure of the Athenian army during the fifth century. It had ten regiments, each one provided by one of the city's ten **tribes** (a tribe was a political constituency). We know the names of these tribal regiments, the areas from which they were recruited, and the fact that they were subdivided into smaller units called **lochoi** (singular, lochos) – although we do not know the size or make-up of these lochoi. Each tribe elected a general, known as a **strategos**, on an annual basis, and collectively the ten generals made the key decisions for the army, voting if necessary to resolve a disagreement. As in Sparta, the second most senior officers in the Athenian army were the taxiarchs, of which there was also one for each tribe.

Figure 4.9 shows a frieze on a temple built on the Athenian Acropolis in the 420s BC. A **frieze** is a sculptured horizontal decoration depicting a scene or a number of scenes, and this one was dedicated to Athena Nike – Athena the goddess of victory – and celebrates scenes from famous Athenian military victories. The south frieze shows hoplites fighting against Persians, some of them on horses. The Persian forces are recognisable from their thick, belted jackets, with long sleeves and tight-fitting trousers. By contrast, the Athenian soldiers are naked apart from their armour – Greek artists often depicted male subjects naked to emphasise the strength of their bodies. This frieze is usually taken to depict an Athenian victory against the Persians, most probably the battle of Marathon in 490.

tribes one of ten political constituencies in Athens. Every Athenian citizen belonged to a tribe, which made up a regiment of the Athenian army.

lochoi units of a tribal regiment in the Athenian army

strategos an elected general in the Athenian army; every tribe elected one each year

frieze a horizontal sculptured or painted decoration depicting a scene or number of scenes

FIGURE 4.9 **PS**
A scene from the
south frieze of the
Temple of Athena Nike.

PRESCRIBED SOURCE

South frieze of the Temple of Athena Nike

Date: *c.* 420 BC

Location: British Museum; originally part of the temple on the Athenian Acropolis

Significance: a frieze showing Athenian hoplites fighting Persians

---

THE ATHENIAN NAVY

The Athenians focused on developing their naval power in the late 480s as they prepared for the Persian invasion. During these years, they greatly expanded their navy so that their fleet came to number about 200 ships. This was comfortably the largest navy in the Greek world, and their decision paid off when in 480 they led their Greek allies to a stunning naval victory over the Persians in the bay of Salamis near Athens (see p. 364).

The Athenian fleet was primarily made up of triremes. A **trireme** was a long, thin ship, typically about 35 metres in length, with a bronze-plated ram extending out from its front. The ship's low centre of gravity gave it stability in the water. It was rowed by 170 men, who sat in three banks, one above the other, on either side of the ship (the name 'trireme' literally meant 'three rowers'). The lower two rows each had twenty-seven rowers on each side; the upper row had thirty-one men on each side. In addition to the rowers, there would be about thirty other men on board, including ten hoplites who served as marines, four archers, a piper who sounded time for the rowers, as well as officers such as a steersman, a quartermaster, and a trierarch (see below). As we have seen, the rowers were normally drawn from the poorer classes of society who could offer their services for pay if rowers were being hired – except in an emergency, service in the fleet was not compulsory. The Athenians usually needed more rowers than they could find from the citizen population, and so their navy often contained a significant number of slaves, as well as mercenaries from other cities.

The navy was largely paid for out of the public treasury, including pay for the rowers and the building of ships. However, this state funding was supplemented by a super-tax on the wealthiest citizens, called a **liturgy**. This required them to pay for something of great civic importance each year (the word 'liturgy' meant 'service to the public'). One of the most prestigious liturgies was payment for the upkeep of a trireme for one year, and the wealthy Athenian who paid for this liturgy was called a **trierarch**. He was responsible for repairs and replacement of anything damaged during the year, while if he

trireme a Greek warship with three banks of rowers on each side

liturgy a super-tax on the wealthiest citizens in Athens to fund important civic projects

trierarch a wealthy Athenian who captained and paid for the upkeep of a trireme for one year

FIGURE 4.10
A modern reconstruction of an Athenian trireme.

FIGURE 4.11
Rowers on a trireme.

diekplous a naval manoeuvre whereby a trireme sailed through the enemy line of ships and turned at pace to ram the side of an enemy ship

hypozomata two stretched cables that were tied from one end of a trireme to another and kept it in shape

relief (from the Latin verb 'relevo', 'to raise') a carving that projects from, and is a part of, the same background material, and has the effect of shading and being in 3D

was ambitious he might also offer bonus payments in order to attract the best quality rowers to his ship. It seems that many trierarchs relished taking on this liturgy, since it allowed them to show off their wealth and gain popularity and prestige in the city. On board, the trierarch was technically in command of the ship, although in practice he was likely to allow the more experienced steersman to make the key decisions.

Naval warfare involved two main tactics. Traditionally, a naval battle had been little more than a land battle at sea. Ships would come alongside one another and the marines on deck would try to board and take possession of the other ship, using grappling irons; the rowers simply had to manoeuvre the ships to enable this. However, during the fifth century the practice of ramming became more popular (one of the earliest records of effective ramming is at the battle of Salamis). There was one tactic at sea which needed special skill at sailing and ramming, and this was called the **diekplous**. This involved a ship sailing through a gap in the line of its enemy and then turning at speed to ram the side of an enemy ship from the rear. Ramming from this direction made it slightly easier to withdraw from the damaged enemy ship, which must have been hard to do.

Such a manoeuvre required great skill. Since the Athenians had by far the largest navy in Greece, their regular experience of fighting at sea meant that their rowers were usually experienced, fit and battle ready. Moreover, the Athenians normally factored in a few days at the start of a campaign to practise their rowing. By contrast, most other cities tended not to keep much of a regular navy, so the Athenians had a great advantage on the water, much as the Spartans did on land. There is also some evidence that the Athenians kept improving their triremes so that they gave them advantage over their opponents. For example, they introduced two great cables that stretched down the middle of the hull the whole length of the ship. These were known as the **hypozomata**, and were set at a tension that kept the ship in shape and gave it greater strength when ramming. The hypozomata were considered an important and secret Athenian invention, and it was illegal to export them from the city.

The **relief** shown in Figure 4.12 was dedicated on the Acropolis in Athens, and is one of the very few images of a trireme that has come down to us. The main piece of what

S & C

During the 1980s, a team of archaeologists tried to build a trireme based on ancient records of how they were constructed. The ship was named *Olympias*, and you can read more about it here: http://www.triremeolympias.com/home.html. With an inexperienced crew, the trireme was able to reach a speed of 9 knots (17 km per hour) and to turn through 180 degrees within a minute, in an arc no wider than two and a half ship-lengths. This experiment suggested that the accounts of trireme battles by ancient historians were believable and likely to be accurate.

EXPLORE FURTHER

Read about a naval battle between Athenian and Corinthian ships in 429 in Thucydides, 2.83–85. What can we learn about trireme naval tactics from this passage?

FIGURE 4.12
Lenormant trireme relief

PRESCRIBED SOURCE

Lenormant trireme relief

Date: *c.* 410 BC

Material: marble

Location: Acropolis Museum, Athens

Significance: one of very few images of an ancient Greek trireme

survives of the dedication shows a trireme being rowed; there are three banks of oars, with the rowers in the top bank clearly visible. Another surviving piece from the dedication fitted at the top right. This is thought to be the hero Paralos, whom the Athenians believed had invented navigation, and to whom the relief was dedicated. The ship was called the Paralos after him, and was a sacred trireme used for official state business.

Study question
We have far fewer images of ships than we do of hoplite and cavalry fighters from ancient Athens. Why do you think that land fighting was a more natural topic for Athenian artists to focus on?

THE IMPACT OF THE MILITARY ON ATHENIAN POLITICS AND SOCIETY

As we have seen, being a citizen of Athens was bound up with serving in the military. The Athenians elected their generals on an annual basis, and so the citizen body could choose who would lead them in war. We have also seen that wealthy Athenians could gain prestige in the city through serving as a trierarch.

There were other ways in which the Athenian military impacted on Athenian politics and society. In about 508, the Athenians had established a new political system, which came to be called 'democracy'. This gave extensive power to citizens to vote in the citizens' assembly and serve in the political system. For the first years of the new system, it was unclear whether it would survive, not least because the city was threatened by the

Persian Empire. The former tyrant of Athens, Hippias, was now with the Persians and hoped to be restored to power with Persian backing. In 490, the Persians launched an attack on Athenian soil, landing at Marathon on the east coast of Attica. Despite being outnumbered, the Athenians won a remarkable victory with the help of some soldiers from their allies from the city of Plataea. This was a key moment in the development of the Athenian democratic system, since the hoplites were largely drawn from the middle ranks of Athenian society. The traditionally powerful aristocrats realised that they had to depend on their hoplite force for defence, and the later thinker Aristotle commented that the Athenian common people grew in confidence as a result of this victory.

A similar effect seemed to happen ten years later, when the Athenians led the Greeks in a remarkable naval victory at Salamis (described below). During the late 480s, the Athenians had developed a policy of significantly increasing the size of their navy, believing that this was the best form of defence against the Persians. The bulk of the rowers in the Athenian fleet were drawn from the lower classes, as we have seen, and after the victory at Salamis, Athens became a naval superpower in the Greek world for the rest of the fifth century, controlling many other Greek cities. It is often thought that the victory at Salamis helped to establish Athenian democracy in its fullest form, since the Athenian state now relied upon its rowers first and foremost for its defence.

Throughout the fifth century, the topic of warfare was ever present in the Athenian consciousness, something that is clear from the ancient sources. Those who gave their lives in battle were held in great esteem: each year, a prominent Athenian made a speech in the city's main cemetery commemorating those men who had died in war during the previous twelve months. Moreover, the sons of soldiers who had fallen in battle were educated at the expense of the state and given a suit of armour upon reaching manhood. However, there are also other voices more critical of war: the comic playwright Aristophanes wrote a number of plays during the late fifth century in which objections to war and its effect on daily life are made. Perhaps the most celebrated example is his play *Lysistrata*, in which the heroine Lysistrata is an Athenian woman who tries to meet with women from other Greek cities to see if they can put a stop to the Peloponnesian War (by agreeing to a sex strike).

There are many examples of the impact of warfare on wider society and on non-combatants. One famous one comes early in the Peloponnesian War fought between Athens and Sparta, and their respective allies, between 431 and 404. In 431, the Athenians decided to bring all those who lived in the countryside around Athens inside the walls of the city, so that the Spartans would not be able to attack and kill them. This may have been a sound strategic move, but it had devastating consequences for health and hygiene in the city. As a result, a terrible plague broke out in 430 (it may have been typhus), and perhaps as many as 75,000 to 100,000 people were killed – about a quarter of the population.

EXPLORE FURTHER

You can read Thucydides' moving and terrifying description of the effects of the plague on victims at 2.47–55.

EXPLORE FURTHER

Read Herodotus' account of the battle of Salamis in *Histories*, 8.40–96.

THE BATTLE OF SALAMIS

As at Thermopylae, Herodotus is our main source for this battle. He lived for part of his life in Athens so he would have known well Athenian folklore about the victory that the city did so much to achieve. Herodotus tells how after Thermopylae the Persians marched south

**S
&
C** Three other accounts of the battle of Salamis have survived for us to read. The first comes in a tragic play, *Persians* (lines 331–461), written by Aeschylus and first performed in 472. Aeschylus probably fought in the battle, and his account is worth reading, even if it is clearly framed within a fictionalised narrative of the Persian response to their defeat. The other two come centuries later, in the *Universal History* of Diodorus Siculus (11.14–18), and in Plutarch's *Life of Themistocles* (9–16). Read these accounts. What are the differences and similarities between them? How does the style of each author differ?

FIGURE 4.13
Themistocles.

towards Athens. At the same time as the battle at Thermopylae, the Persian and Greek navies had been engaged in a series of skirmishes at the nearby Cape Artemisium. However, when the Persians broke Thermopylae, the Greek ships turned tail to defend southern Greece. The Persian navy did not pursue them, but made their way south at their own pace.

The Persian army marched south through central Greece, brutally sacking those cities that had opposed it, but sparing those that had taken the Persian side. However, the focal point of the Persian march was Athens, the city that had dared to stand up to it since 499, and had administered a humiliating defeat on the Persian army at Marathon in 490. The Persians clearly hoped for revenge. However, when they arrived at the city, they found it almost empty, with just a few people remaining on the Acropolis. What had happened to the Athenians?

The Athenian strategy

Long before the Persians had reached Thermopylae, the Athenians debated how to meet the Persian advance. After seeking advice from the oracle of Apollo at Delphi, they debated what to do. Some Athenians wanted to remain in the city, but the leading Athenian politician **Themistocles** persuaded them otherwise. He would go on to be the tactical genius who oversaw the Greek victory. The men of fighting age sailed to the nearby island of Salamis in their triremes, while most of the women, children and elderly took refuge in two allied cities, Aegina and Troezen. The Persians arrived in an empty city, looted the temples of the Acropolis and burnt them to the ground. Archaeology has revealed evidence of this burning of the city, as there is a 'burn-level' that corresponds to this exact period. The Athenians could only watch the smoke rising from nearby Salamis.

KEY INDIVIDUAL

Themistocles the Athenian leader who convinced the Athenians to abandon their city for Salamis, and who then brilliantly commanded the Greek navy in the sea battle against the Persians

Preparations for battle

The Greeks

After withdrawing from Artemisium, the Greek naval commanders brought their ships to harbour on the east side of the island of Salamis. Herodotus lists twenty-one different cities that provided ships for the Greek fleet, which he numbered at 380 in total. Athens provided by far the greatest number of ships, 200 in all. However, there was great division among the Greek commanders as to the best place to meet the Persians. Most of the cities providing ships were from the Peloponnese, and they wanted to move the Greek ships back to the south side of the isthmus, the narrow strip of land separating the Peloponnese peninsula from the rest of Greece (see map, p. ix). This way, they could support their land forces, who were planning to blockade the routes into the Peloponnese by building a wall across the isthmus. When they saw the smoke rising from Athens, some Peloponnesian ships took fright and sailed away, while the council of commanders passed a resolution to sail to defend the isthmus.

This of course did not please the Athenians, nor the other non-Peloponnesian cities, whose lands would be left undefended. Therefore, the cunning Themistocles managed to engineer it that the Greeks had little choice but to fight in the straits of Salamis. First of all, he had a private meeting with Eurybiades, the Spartan admiral of the fleet, and persuaded him to bring the commanders together again. At this meeting he put forward more arguments in favour of fighting at Salamis, in particular that the narrow waters would help them make up for the fact that they had fewer ships than the Persians, and that their ships were heavier and slower. This was a clever plan, since the narrowness of the strait meant that not all the Persian ships could enter it at the same time. Eventually, the Greek commanders agreed to stay at Salamis and join the battle there.

The Persians

Herodotus also reports the deliberations on the Persian side. The Persian navy had been drawn up in Phaleron, which was the harbour of Athens and just a short distance away from the straits between Salamis and the mainland. It is hard to tell how many ships the Persians had. Both Herodotus and Aeschylus give an original number of 1207 ships, but this must have been a wild exaggeration. Scholars offer figures ranging from about 400 to 1200.

Xerxes himself went to Phaleron to consult his naval captains about strategy. Every single one of his captains spoke in favour of fighting at Salamis except one – **Artemisia**, the queen of Halicarnassus, a Greek city on the coast of Asia Minor (many Greek cities fought on the Persian side). Artemisia had come to the throne after her husband's death. As a woman she did not need to fight, since her son was by then old enough to take her place. Nonetheless, she chose to fight for the Persians, believing that an alliance with them was in the best interests of her people.

Ironically, Herodotus portrays Artemisia as the only one of Xerxes' commanders who is 'man enough' to stand up to him and urge him not to fight, saying that he should be prepared for a more long-term and patient approach than an immediate naval action against a more skilful Greek navy. She even says the following words:

> Spare your ships and do not fight at sea: for the Greeks are as far superior to your men in naval matters as men are to women.
>
> Herodotus, *Histories*, 8.68

Xerxes listened to Artemisia's arguments respectfully and was impressed by her honesty. However, he went with the majority view and ordered his captains to engage with the Greeks in the straits of Salamis.

KEY INDIVIDUAL

Artemisia queen of the Greek city of Halicarnassus, which fought for the Persians

The battle

The Persian fleet put out to sea on the evening after the Greeks last deliberated. The Peloponnesian crews and commanders then started to panic and again planned to withdraw to the isthmus. It was at this point that Themistocles made his next decisive intervention: he ordered one of his slaves, Sicinnus, to journey in a boat across the straits to deliver a message to the Persians. He was to tell them that the Greek commanders were at each other's throats and were planning to sail away. Moreover, he was to say that Themistocles was secretly on Xerxes' side and wished to help him. Sicinnus duly delivered this message, and the Persians believed him. They moved their ships out into the bay of Salamis in order to block the entrance to the straits. When news of this was brought to the Greek commanders, they realised that they had no choice but to fight where they were. They prepared for battle the following morning.

Before the Greeks boarded their ships at dawn, Themistocles delivered a rousing speech. They then lined up according to their cities, with the Athenians on the left and the Spartans on the far right. The Persians moved into the straits towards their enemy. Initially, the Greeks rowed their ships backwards, but then an Athenian ship burst forward and rammed a Persian opponent. The battle had begun. The accounts of both Herodotus and Aeschylus are confusing and do not let us create a coherent picture of what happened. Perhaps this is itself a fitting reflection of the chaos of battle. However, it seems that the Persians had not understood the currents and that many of their ships were turned to one side, making them easy prey for the Greek rams. Fighting in a narrow channel and shallow water gave the advantage to the Greeks, just as Themistocles had foreseen. By contrast, the Persians' superior numbers worked against them: their ships crowded into one another.

FIGURE 4.14
A map showing the opposing forces in advance of the battle of Salamis.

FIGURE 4.15
A Greek ship rams a Persian ship.

Aeschylus gives a vivid picture of the battle as a bloodbath, with one Persian describing his side's losses as follows:

> The shores and reefs were crowded with our dead, and every ship that formed a part of the barbarian fleet plied its oars in disorderly flight. But, as if our men were tuna or some haul of fish, the foe kept striking and hacking them with broken oars and fragments of wrecked ships.

> Aeschylus, *Persians*, 418–426

Herodotus adds the detail that many of the Persian sailors could not swim and so drowned, whereas the Greek casualties were largely able to swim to safety. Perhaps the most dramatic moment in Herodotus' account of the battle brings Artemisia to the forefront of the action. Her ship was in danger of being rammed by an Athenian ship, and so she deliberately rammed one of her own ships to make it seem as if she had switched sides during the battle. The tactic worked – the Athenian ship backed off, while the ship rammed by Artemisia sank. This was not the only confusion that turned out to her advantage. On the shore, Xerxes' advisers reported to him that Artemisia's ship had rammed another, which they assumed to be from the Greek fleet. Hearing of her supposed bravery, and in despair at the general performance of his navy, Xerxes commented:

> My men have turned into women, my women into men.

> Herodotus, *Histories*, 8.88

Indeed, Xerxes was enraged by what he saw, even ordering the beheading of a group of Phoenician sailors who came to complain about the efforts of some of the Greek ships fighting on the Persian side.

Aftermath

The Greeks won a comprehensive victory and the surviving Persian ships withdrew. The Persian troops headed back to the north of Greece. The following year the Greeks would go on to deliver a final defeat to the Persians on land at Plataea. However, Herodotus, no doubt reflecting the Athenian opinion of his day, argued strongly that it was the Athenians who contributed most to the overall victory in the Persian wars by providing nearly half the ships for the Greek fleet, as well as the belief that victory was possible:

> One is surely right in saying that Greece was saved by the Athenians . . . whichever side they joined was sure to prevail. It was the Athenians, too, who, having chosen that Greece should live and preserve her freedom, roused to battle the other Greek states which had not yet submitted. It was the Athenians who – after the gods – drove back the Persian king.

> Herodotus, *Histories*, 7.139

Study questions

1 Why was Themistocles so important to the Greek victory at Salamis?
2 Are there examples today of politicians using religious guidance to help them make major decisions?
3 What plays, films or other works of art are there today which seek to glorify a military victory?

Just eight years after the battle, Aeschylus wrote his play *Persians*, which was performed in front of thousands of his fellow citizens in the city's largest theatre. The play emphasised the Athenian achievement as the leaders of the Greek naval force, and idealised the Athenian citizens as free men fighting against an empire who were slaves to a tyrannical king.

TOPIC REVIEW

You should be able to:

1. Describe:
   - the structure of the Athenian army
   - the structure of the Athenian navy
   - how a trireme was funded and manned
   - the key events and individuals involved in the battle of Salamis.

2. Explain:
   - how the Athenian army and navy were funded
   - the tactics involved in trireme warfare
   - how the army and navy influenced Athenian political life
   - why the victory at Salamis was so important to the Athenians.

PRACTICE QUESTIONS

Source A: *The Old Oligarch, Constitution of the Athenians*, 1.2

It is right that the poor and the ordinary people there [i.e. in Athens] should have more power than the noble and the rich, because it is the ordinary people who man the fleet and bring the city her power.

1. a. How were Athenian rowers recruited and paid for? [2]
   b. What was the significance of this for Athenian politics? [1]
2. Why do you think that the Athenian navy was so effective? Use the source as a starting point and your own knowledge in your answer. [8]

4.3 The Roman Military in the Imperial Period

This topic examines how the Roman army was organised during the time of the Roman Empire, specifically focusing on the first and early second centuries AD. At this point, the Roman Empire controlled much of Western Europe, as well as North Africa and parts of western Asia. This is one way in which the study of the army in the Roman world is very different from studying armies in fifth-century Greece, where each relatively small city-state had its own army. A second key difference, which follows on from this, is that the Roman army of the Imperial Period was fully professional in a way the earlier Greek armies never were. The Roman world, therefore, had a clear distinction between its civilians and its professional soldiers.

> **Imperial Period** the period of Roman history from 30 BC, when Rome was ruled by emperors

THE ORGANISATION OF THE ARMY

The Roman army was divided into many divisions and sub-divisions. The largest unit was the legion, and in the time of the emperors there were about thirty legions in all; legions were posted all over the empire. Each legion was given a number, although it was not as simple as 1 to 30 because during the time of the civil wars in the first century

BC there had been opposing legions with the same number. When they were brought under the control of the emperor Augustus, the numbering was not changed. This meant that a legion often had a name after it too, which might have been taken from the legion's beginnings or to commemorate a particularly fine achievement by that legion. For example, two of the legions stationed in Britain during the first century AD were II Augusta and IX Hispana; the former took its name from having been loyal to Augustus during the civil wars, while the latter was originally raised and recruited in Spain.

The structure of a legion

The legion itself was broken down into a number of different subdivisions. It is perhaps easiest to work from the smallest unit upwards, thinking about how the legionary soldier fitted into his legion.

- **The contubernium** A unit of 8 men who shared the same tent and dealt with their own mess arrangements.
- **The century** Despite the name, this was a unit of about 80 men (although the first cohort consisted of double-sized centuries of 160 men – see below).
- **The cohort** With one exception, each cohort consisted of six centuries; the exception was the first cohort of a legion, which was made up of five double-sized centuries of about 160 men each.
- **The legion** The legion was made up of ten cohorts; the first cohort containing about 800 men, while each of the other nine cohorts was made up of 480 men, a total of about 4,320. In all, therefore, the legion typically had something over 5,000 ordinary legionary soldiers.

In addition to these numbers, there were other members of the legion. Attached to each one were about 120 horsemen, who acted as scouts and dispatch riders. Other numbers were made up by those in the command structure.

contubernium a unit of eight men in a Roman legion, who shared the same tent and dealt with their own mess arrangements

century a unit of about 80 men in a Roman legion (there were some double-sized centuries of 160 men)

cohort the largest unit of a Roman legion; the first cohort of a legion had five double-centuries; cohorts two to ten each consisted of six centuries

legion the largest unit of the Roman army

FIGURE 4.16
A diagram of a legion showing its divisions of cohorts and centuries.

centurion the commander of the century in a Roman legion

primi ordines the collective name for the five centurions of the first cohort of a Roman legion

primus pilus the most senior centurion in the legion

signifer the Roman soldier responsible for the century's standard

standard a Roman war flag, the emblem of a century, a set of medallions hoisted on a pole

optio the centurion's deputy in a Roman legion

tesserarius the Roman soldier in charge of organisation of guards and communication of passwords

cornicen the horn-player in a Roman legion who sounded orders to the soldiers

legatus the commander of the Roman legion

tribunes the six senior officers in a Roman legion after the legatus

tribunus laticlavius the senior tribune of a Roman legion, of senatorial rank

tribuni angusticlavi the five tribunes of equestrian rank in a Roman legion

Command of the centuries

A century was commanded by a **centurion**. The five centurions of the first cohort, known collectively as the **primi ordines** ('those of the first rank'), were the most senior centurions. In turn, they were ranked by seniority, with the most senior known as the **primus pilus** ('the first spearman'); he was a figure of considerable importance in the whole legion. Centurions were responsible for discipline in the army and they were expected to be very tough – they could beat soldiers with a vine cane, often brutally. A centurion would dream of becoming the primus pilus, a position that was usually only open to men over fifty and which lasted for a year. After that, the centurion would retire or be promoted.

Each century had a number of other officials. The **signifer** ('standard-bearer') looked after the **standard** of the century, which was the century's military emblem. It was typically a set of medallions hoisted on a pole, and the signifer carried it into battle. In addition, he was in charge of the century's pay and savings. The **optio** was the centurion's deputy who was also responsible for training. The **tesserarius** organised the guards and communicated the passwords, while the **cornicen** was the horn-player whose main duty was to sound orders to the soldiers.

Command of the legion

The legion as a whole also had a number of senior figures. Some were drawn from the Roman upper classes – the senatorial and equestrian classes (see pages 267–268) – and they served in the army for a much shorter period of time than the regular soldiers. They were therefore really semi-professional soldiers. The **legatus** was the commander of the legion who was of senatorial rank and appointed by the emperor. He was normally a man in his mid-thirties, who had probably served some years previously as a tribunus laticlavius (see below). He would spend about three or four years commanding the legion, and then resume his civilian career, often in politics.

Below the Legatus were six **tribunes**, one of whom held a different and more senior status than the other five. He was the **tribunus laticlavius**, a young man under the age of twenty-five from the senatorial class, the highest class at Rome. He was therefore allowed to wear the broad purple senatorial stripe on his toga ('laticlavius' meant 'broad-striped'). His posting to a legion would be the first in his career, and he would usually do one tour of duty lasting two to three years and then return to Rome, where he would continue a civilian career in financial and legal administration. About ten years later, he might return to the army as a legatus.

The other five tribunes were the **tribuni angusticlavi**. They came from the equestrian class (the second highest social class at Rome), and could therefore wear the narrow purple stripe on their togas ('angusticlavi' means 'narrow-striped'). They were typically wealthy, educated men in their thirties, who served as tribunes for a few years. After that, some returned to civilian life, often in the imperial civil service, while others stayed on in the army as commanders of auxiliary regiments. The main duties of these tribunes were to act as staff officers, doing administrative work and overseeing the welfare and daily routine of the troops.

Agricola

Gnaeus Julius Agricola was born to a senatorial family in AD 40. At the age of eighteen, he was sent to the province of Britain as a tribunus laticlavius, remaining there until he was twenty-two. He then returned to Rome and held various political posts. In 70, at the age of thirty, he was sent to Britain again as the Legatus of the XX Valeria Victrix legion. His command ended in 73, and he became a provincial governor in Gaul. In 77, he was posted back to Britain again – this time as the provincial governor – and remained there until AD 83. He is unique in our records as the only man to have held three military appointments in the same province.

The other senior soldier of the legion was the **camp prefect**. He was the most senior professional soldier in the legion, who was usually a former primus pilus. He was the legatus' right-hand man, responsible for the legion's equipment and transport, much like a quartermaster today.

In addition to these senior officers was the **aquilifer**. His rank was below that of centurion but above that of optio. He was always a soldier of the first cohort, and his role was to protect the legion's **aquila** and carry it into battle. The aquila was the emblem of the legion – it was an eagle, made of gold, with outstretched wings and set on top of a pole. It was the legion's most important possession and symbolised its spirit. Soldiers had an almost religious loyalty to it, and losing it in battle was considered both a terrible disaster and a deep disgrace.

> **camp prefect** the right-hand man to the legatus of a Roman legion

> **aquilifer** the legionary soldier responsible for carrying the aquila
>
> **aquila** the emblem of the legion, an eagle made of gold set on a pole

The legionary fortress

The legionary fortress was the headquarters of the legion. Although no two legionary fortresses were exactly alike, they all shared the same common features; many were originally built in wood, but from the early second century AD they were typically built in stone. A fortress was rectangular in shape with rounded corners, and it was defended all around by a ditch and a wall, while there were towers along the perimeter wall. Each side had a fortified gate, and one of the gates on the shorter side was the main gate. From here one of the fortress' three main streets, the **via praetoria**, led to the main buildings, including the headquarters, the **principia**. At this point, the via praetoria met the main cross-street of the fortress, the **via principalis**, which itself ran from one side gate to the other. The third main street, the **via quintana**, crossed the fortress on the other side of the main buildings.

The principia was the administrative heart of the fortress. It was divided into three parts. At the front lay a large courtyard surrounded by verandas, and notices were often posted here. Beyond lay a large hall known as a **basilica**, where many members of the legion could assemble, to hear the morning report, for example, since it contained a platform for the legatus to address his men. The basilica was usually an impressive and large building – the one at Chester was 73 metres in length. Beyond the basilica lay a range of

> **via praetoria** the road from the main gate to the principia in a Roman fortress
>
> **principia** the headquarters of a Roman fortress
>
> **via principalis** the road crossing the fortress in front of the principia in a Roman fortress
>
> **via quintana** the road crossing the fortress behind the principia in a Roman fortress
>
> **basilica** the large hall used for assemblies of troops in a Roman legionary fortress

FIGURE 4.17
A signifer, a centurion and an aquilifer.

> **praetorium** the private quarters of the legatus in a Roman fortress

S & C Chester's name comes from the Latin 'castra', which meant 'camp' or 'fort'. There are very many places in England today that have the suffixes '-chester', '-cester' or '-caster', and in most cases these indicate that they were originally the site of a Roman camp. In Wales, exactly the same is true for the prefix 'caer'.

rooms where the clerks toiled over their documents and pay. The central room was the temple, where the unit's standards were kept, ranged round a statue of the reigning emperor. To one side of the basilica was the **praetorium**, the private quarters of the legatus. This was built like a high status Roman villa, and contained central heating and its own private suite of baths. The legatus was able to receive and entertain important visitors here.

The fortress had a number of other buildings. There was a hospital and workshops, while well-designed granaries kept grain cool and dry in all weather conditions. There was also a set of baths to allow the troops to stay clean and healthy, as well as to socialise. There were of course many barracks, which were split up by cohort, and then by century and contubernium. One contubernium shared two rooms in the barracks – one room was for sleeping, the other contained a hearth and was a living-room and kitchen. A centurion was given his own larger suite of rooms.

Outside the fortress was usually to be found an amphitheatre. This had to be large enough to seat the whole legion, and was used primarily for military purposes: training, assemblies and parades; at times, it could also be used for traditional gladiatorial shows.

One good example of a legionary fortress is the one at Chester, which was initially built in wood in the late AD 70s. The site of its construction was strategically significant since it was located between two areas that the Romans were seeking to subdue: Wales to the west and Brigantia (a large area of northern England) to the east. It was also built at the head of an estuary that was easy to cross, while there was good access for shipping – one of the side gates led straight to the harbour.

Early in the second century, the fortress was rebuilt in stone (by this time the legion garrisoned there was XX Valeria Victrix). Its dimensions were about 591 × 412 metres; its stone perimeter wall was 5 metres in height, with a width of 1.83 metres at the base and 1.37 metres at the top. The surrounding ditch had a width of 6 metres and a depth of 3 metres. The fortress occupied nearly 25 hectares, making it larger than any other in the province of Britain. Three of the fortress' corner towers have been located and one, the south-east tower, has survived. Six other towers have also been identified.

Many buildings have been identified, including the principia. The 73-metre long basilica had a central nave 12 metres wide. Above it was a vaulted roof and on each side columns separated it from an aisle 6 metres wide. Other buildings identified include the praetorium, the baths, the granaries, as well as workshops and barracks. The use of one oval-shaped building near the principia has yet to be properly understood. Today the via praetoria and via principalis have become part of the centre of the modern city of Chester, and are now called Bridge Street and Eastgate. Outside the walls was a very large amphitheatre, which could comfortably seat 8,000. Half of it has survived and can be visited today. It dates to the third century AD, and was built over an earlier version.

gate

corner tower

turret

rampart

ditch

via quintana

prison

workshops

hospital

parade ground

basilica

Barracks for First Cohort

gate

gate

via principalis

granaries

tribunes' houses

stables

drill hall

officers' club

via praetoria

tribune's house

main gate

camp prefect's house

Amphitheatre

FIGURE 4.18
A plan of a legionary fortress.

PRESCRIBED SOURCE

Roman Fortress at Chester

Date: first built in wood in the AD 70s; rebuilt in stone in the early 2nd century

Location: Chester, England

Significance: the largest legionary fortress in Roman Britain

FIGURE 4.19
A reconstruction of the principia at Novae in the province of Moesia in the Balkans. The room shown in cut-away is the temple.

FIGURE 4.20
Auxiliary cavalryman.

ala a cohort of Roman cavalry, theoretically 512 strong

turma a Roman cavalry squadron of 32 horsemen

praefectus the commander of a Roman naval fleet

navarch the captain of a squadron of Roman naval ships

Auxiliary troops

The auxiliary troops were formed into smaller regiments separate from the legions. Their infantry units were typically 480-strong, but there were some of nearly double-size at 800. They were also called cohorts, and a cohort of 480 was divided into six centuries. All the auxiliary units were commanded by Roman citizens of equestrian rank. They lived in their own forts separate from the legionaries.

Perhaps the most important type of auxiliary unit was the **ala**, a cohort of cavalry. These were 512 strong, and divided up into squadrons of 32 horsemen each; this squadron was known as a **turma**. Each ala had a flag and each turma a standard. A third type of auxiliary cohort was mixed with both infantry and cavalry. Members of the cavalry could also serve as the bodyguard of the legatus.

The auxiliaries played a very important role in the Roman army. Some cohorts offered skills that the legionary army did not have in abundance – horsemen, archers, slingers etc. However, the infantry cohorts often bore the brunt of the fighting in a battle – they were sent in first since it was felt better to lose auxiliary soldiers than the Roman citizens fighting in the legions. Despite this, the numbers fighting as auxiliaries remained strong, no doubt because the men could win Roman citizenship for themselves and their children by serving well.

The Roman navy

During the time of the emperors, the Romans faced little threat from any enemy with strong naval power, and so the Roman navy played a less important front-line role than the army did in conquest and defence of the empire. Nonetheless, the emperor Augustus had learnt from his own victory in the civil wars (particularly at the battle of Actium; see p. 385) that it was important to maintain a strong navy. Just as he did with the army, he established permanent professional naval forces, as well as three large naval bases for the fleet: one was at Forum Iulii (modern Fréjus) on the Mediterranean coast of Gaul, and this controlled the coasts of Gaul and Spain; one was at Misenum on the Bay of Naples, which covered the south-west Mediterranean; the third was at Ravenna and this protected the Adriatic coast and the sea crossing to the eastern provinces of the empire. One key responsibility of the navy was to suppress piracy.

Since the fleets were largely drawn from the ranks of non-citizens in the eastern empire, they were given the same status as auxiliary units. A fleet was commanded by a **praefectus**, who would be a man of the senatorial class. Individual ships were captained by trierarchs, while squadrons of ships were led by **navarchs**. The marines who worked alongside the sailors were organised into their own centuries and commanded by centurions and optios. The main duties of the navy were as follows:

- to transport land troops
- to support land campaigns

- to protect coastal settlements
- to suppress piracy and support merchant shipping
- to repel any barbarian incursions into Roman waters.

EQUIPMENT AND TACTICS

The Roman army

Roman military equipment changed over the centuries, and varied in different parts of the empire, and so any detailed analysis of the equipment used by a Roman legionary should be flexible to reflect this. Nonetheless, the following are the core items of equipment in any era, which the soldier wore over a tunic that reached down to the knees:

- **Helmet** From the middle of the first century AD, these were typically made of iron on the inside with bronze plating on the outside; they had cheek and neck guards. A helmet could also have a crest holder – a crest of horse-hair or feathers could be used to indicate the unit a soldier belonged to or his rank.
- **Plate armour** The most common type is known by scholars as lorica segmentata; made predominantly of iron, it covered the chest and shoulders. Both the chest and the shoulder units consisted of overlapping metal strips attached on the inside by leather strips and on the outside by hinges, which made it flexible enough for the soldier to move around. The two units were held together by hooks.
- **The sporran** This was like an apron of leather thongs hanging off the belt (as is often worn with a kilt today). It gave the waist area extra protection but was also decorative.
- **Shield** The shield was rectangular and curved. It was made from three sheets of wood glued together, which was then encased in leather; the front of the shield also had a linen covering. Its rim was normally reinforced with bronze. The handgrip was reinforced by an iron or bronze boss. The front of the

FIGURE 4.21
Three Roman soldiers: to the left a centurion, to the right two legionary soldiers.

FIGURE 4.22
Bronze statuette of a legionary.

shield could have a painted design, which perhaps denoted the soldier's unit.

- **Sword** The legionary's sword was known as a gladius. It was a key weapon with a blade between 45 and 50 cm long. The soldier used it to thrust at short range. He carried it in a scabbard on the right side of the body.
- **Dagger**: The dagger was between 20 and 25 cm long, and was attached to the belt. It could be used in battle or for cutting generally. It went out of use during the second century.
- **Spear** This was typically about 2 m long; it was constructed with a long wooden shaft and then an iron head, which was typically between 65 and 75 cm long. A well-thrown spear could pierce the shield or armour; even if it did not kill the enemy, it was then very difficult to remove since the iron often bent upon impact, so the tactic was to kill or disarm as many enemy soldiers as possible at the start of the battle. A legionary often had a second, shorter spear.
- **Leather sandals** Many examples of these have been discovered. They were heavy sandals with several layers of sole and held together with hobnails. Leather thongs could wrap half-way up the shin and could be stuffed with wool or fur for reinforcement or warmth.

The small bronze statuette shown in Figure 4.22 (height 11.43 cm) dates to the second century AD and gives us an idea of the equipment of a typical Roman legionary. Visible is: his tunic, over which are the lorica segmentata and a sporran; his strapped sandals; his crested helmet.

PRESCRIBED SOURCE

Bronze statuette of a legionary

Date: 2nd century AD

Location: British Museum

Significance: a statuette illustrating the equipment of a legionary soldier

---

EXPLORE FURTHER

1. The most complete legionary shield was found in Syria. It has been rebuilt and is on display at the Yale University Art Gallery. Find out more here: http://artgallery.yale.edu/collections/objects/5959.
2. The Roman emperor Caligula's real name was Gaius Julius Caesar Germanicus. However, he was given the nickname Caligula, which means 'Little Boot' after the Latin word for a soldier's sandal, 'caliga'. Find out how he came to be given this nickname.

Battle tactics

The Romans had a great variety of battle tactics honed over centuries. Generally speaking, once a battle had started the legionary would throw his spear first to kill or disable opposing soldiers, after this would advance to close combat using his sword and shield. When they needed to, legionaries could use more sophisticated formations during battle. The most famous is the **testudo**, or 'tortoise', whereby a group of soldiers in formation would place their shields over their heads, except for the front row, which would bring them to head height. They would then move forward with strong protection against enemy artillery fire.

The Romans are particularly famous for their artillery, including the following two devices, which were particularly potent in siege warfare:

- **The ballista** This functioned like a crossbow and fired iron darts to great accuracy.
- **The onager** A catapult that fired rocks and large stones at the enemy.

To break down the walls of a city, a battering ram on wheels was often used; to try to breach the walls, siege towers were brought forward.

FIGURE 4.23
Image of a testudo from Trajan's column.

Naval warfare

During the third to first centuries BC, the Romans had copied the ship construction of those they fought against at sea – in particular, the Carthaginians and the Greeks. As well

FIGURE 4.24
Drawings of a quadrireme (top) and a quinquereme (below).

> **testudo** a group of Roman soldiers advance in formation with shields over their heads
>
> **ballista** a Roman crossbow that fired iron darts
>
> **onager** a Roman catapult that fired rocks and large stones at the enemy

as using triremes, both these peoples had designed heavier ships with more rowers; the most common were the quadrireme and the quinquereme. The quadrireme had two banks of rowers with two men to an oar, while the quinquereme had three banks of rowers, the top two with two men to an oar, and the lowest with one man to an oar. It is thought that the quinquereme had 300 men on board, 270 of them rowers: 58 two-man oars on the upper level, 54 two-man oars on the middle level, and 46 one-man oars on the lowest level. We also hear of other types of ship, including the 'hexareme', which was often used as a flagship, as well as lighter ships known as **liburnae**, which were swift in the water and were therefore useful for scouting.

liburnae swift Roman military ships which were used for scouting

Battle tactics for these ships were very similar to those used by the Greeks of the fifth century, based around ramming and boarding. However, after the battle of Actium in 31 BC, the empire faced little naval threat and the navy was generally used to support land troops. Therefore, lighter ships came back into fashion and at this time the trireme was the most common type of ship in the Roman fleet.

RECRUITMENT AND TRAINING

The army

A legionary soldier had to be a Roman citizen (although in the eastern empire, where there were fewer citizens, citizenship was sometimes granted upon enrolment). An applicant, usually a young man, might bring a letter of recommendation, and he would appear before an examining board of experienced officers. Vegetius, an author who writes about the Roman army in the fourth century AD, makes the following recommendations for what to look for:

> A young recruit should keep his eyes watchful and his head upright. He should be broad-chested, with muscly shoulders and strong arms, and his fingers should be on the longer side. He should have a flat stomach and a lean bottom. His calves and feet should not be flabby, but rather full of tough sinews.
>
> Vegetius, *About Military Matters*, 1.6–7

Vegetius goes on to comment that interviewers should find out about the trade practised by the applicant – carpenters, butchers, smiths and hunters are named as the most suitable kinds. Along with this interview there often came a period of probation, during which the applicant underwent a careful medical examination. If he was finally accepted into the army, he was given some money to pay for his journey to the legionary fortress, the headquarters of the legion. Upon arriving he took the military oath, which he had to renew at the beginning of each year thereafter. He was then dispatched to do a period of training.

ACTIVITY

Imagine that you have just spent your first few weeks as a Roman soldier in training. Write a letter home to your family outlining all that you have experienced since you applied to join the army.

The new legionary would need tough and extensive training before he was ready to serve in the army full-time. He would learn first to march, since regular soldiers were expected to be able to complete a route march of around 20 miles in five hours. Marching drill was therefore a key part of training; it helped develop good discipline (armies today still use it for the same purpose), and even a fully trained legionary had to drill once per day. In addition, the trainee built up his fitness and skills set by practising swimming, riding, running and jumping, the latter three wearing heavy packs.

The recruit then moved on to weapons training. He would be armed with a wicker shield and wooden sword, each of double weight, and taught to attack a head-high wooden stake. He learnt to thrust with his short stabbing sword, which would inflict more damage on his enemy than the longer slashing sword – an upward thrust would strike into his enemy's vitals. The recruit was also given a wooden javelin which he hurled at the stake, while another training exercise was learning to jump onto and off either side of a horse in full armour. He might also learn to defend himself with his shield, as well as to use it as an offensive weapon to punch an opponent. A final key element in the training was to learn how to construct a camp, a vital task for an army needing to protect itself in hostile territory.

Auxiliaries

Auxiliary soldiers were normally recruited from non-citizens within the empire, although there are records of recruitment from foreign peoples. Therefore, auxiliary soldiers were mainly recruited in the provinces, and service provided a good prospect of employment – upon retirement an auxiliary would be given citizenship. Like the legionaries, they were expected to serve for twenty-five years. It seems that they underwent a similar level of training as the legionaries, since they had similar fighting capabilities.

Some auxiliary soldiers were recruited for their particular capabilities. The auxiliaries provided the backbone of the cavalry squadrons, while certain regions were known for certain skills; for example, archers were often recruited from Syria.

The navy

The Roman fleets were organised very similarly to the auxiliary units of the army. Recruits tended to be non-citizens from parts of the empire with a strong maritime tradition, such as Greece, Phoenicia and Egypt. Sailors were required to serve for twenty-six years and were given Roman citizenship upon honourable discharge, as well as a sizeable cash payment. There is no evidence that slave labour was used, despite the popular belief that the Roman navy relied on 'galley slaves'.

Training for the fleet must have been very standard – learning to row to time and change pace, and learning to follow instructions and engage in naval manoeuvres. Most importantly, a new recruit had to build the required body strength, and the best way to do this would have been to row as much as possible.

PAYMENT

When Augustus became the first Roman emperor in the late first century BC, he created a fully professional, standing army for the first time. This meant that the state paid the salaries of all those working for the army and navy. At this time, the entire Roman army numbered about 300,000. The emperor was the commander-in-chief of all the armed forces, and it was he who appointed senior officers, decided where and when soldiers should fight, and against whom. He also claimed all victories as his own, even if he had not been present.

This was clearly a huge expense for the Roman treasury. In the time of Augustus, the legionary soldier was paid 225 denarii per annum, although in the late first century AD the emperor Domitian raised this to 300 denarii. If a soldier was promoted, he would get a pay rise – a centurion was paid much more than a legionary. However, before pay was handed out a number of deductions were made – the legionary was expected to pay for his own food, clothing and equipment, and would also probably pay into a pension scheme, which guaranteed him a proper burial when he died. Therefore, a soldier's 'take home pay' was much less than the figure given above. Upon completing his service, if he was given an honourable discharge, he was given a lump sum of 3,000 denarii or an allocation of land, although the latter was later phased out.

Auxiliaries and sailors were paid much less – perhaps about a third of the legionary's rate. In their case, however, there was a great incentive to serve and eventually receive an honourable discharge, as this would bring them – and their children – the coveted Roman citizenship.

Study questions

1 How does the command structure of the Roman army compare to the command structure of a modern army today?
2 Why do you think that Roman legionary fortresses were so important and successful in supporting the work of the legion?
3 What are the requirements for new recruits into the army today?

TOPIC REVIEW

You should be able to:

1. Describe:
   - the structure of a Roman legion
   - the plan and main buildings of a Roman legionary fortress
   - how Roman soldiers were recruited, trained and paid
   - the equipment, weapons and tactics used by Roman soldiers and sailors.

2. Explain:
   - how the recruitment and training process produced the soldiers Rome required
   - how the command structure enabled the Roman army to be successful
   - how a Roman legionary fortress was designed to meet the needs of the legion
   - why serving in the army may have been an attractive career for a Roman.

PRACTICE QUESTIONS

Source A: *A Roman centurion*

1. Give **one** important duty of a centurion. [1]
2. Name **three** pieces of protective armour shown here, and explain why each was effective. [6]

4.4 The Romans at War

- The battle of Actium, including:
  - key events and individuals: Octavian; Marcus Agrippa; Mark Antony; Cleopatra
  - the significance of the battle and how the Romans commemorated it

- Trajan's campaign against the Dacians, including:
  - reasons for the war
  - presentation of warfare in the material sources
  - the image of Trajan as emperor
  - the pursuit of military glory
  - victims of warfare

The following are the prescribed sources for this topic:

- Mark Antony Legionary denarius, Obv: galley with banners, Rev: eagle between two standards, likely minted in Patrae 32 BC (example BMC 197, RSC 33, Sear 356)
- Relief commemorating the battle of Actium, Vatican Museum
- Trajan's Column, Rome
- Arch of Trajan, Benevento

Don't forget that you will be given credit in the exam if you study extra sources and make relevant use of them in your answers.

This topic examines two important military campaigns in Roman history. First it focuses on the battle of Actium in 31 BC, the result of which enabled Octavian to become the most powerful man in the Roman world and to become the first Roman emperor, under the name Augustus. The topic then moves to the campaigns of the emperor Trajan against the Dacians in the early second century AD, which illustrate how important it was for the emperor to be successful in war.

THE BATTLE OF ACTIUM

The context

From 91 BC, the Roman world had been convulsed in a series of civil wars. Powerful generals, with soldiers personally loyal to them, vied with each other to win power in Rome. As well as fighting against each other, these men came to challenge the status quo of the traditional Roman system of government, the Republic, which allowed a relatively small number of aristocratic families to keep the main offices of state to themselves. These generals – successful men who had proved themselves in combat – often seemed to want to reform the Republic. Ultimately, however, the civil wars brought the entire system to an end.

The most famous of these generals was Julius Caesar, a remarkable leader who ruled the Roman Empire as dictator between 49 and 44 BC. When he was assassinated in 44, two men closely associated with him aimed to continue his legacy. One was Mark Antony, Caesar's closest ally who had campaigned alongside him as a general; the other was Gaius Octavianus, Caesar's great-nephew who was named as Caesar's adopted son and heir in his will. In 44 Octavian (as he is commonly known) was just 18 years old.

In the year after Caesar's death, the two men joined forces to defeat the conspirators who had organised the assassination. They then set about dividing up the rule of the Roman world between them and one other, Lepidus. However, Lepidus was soon marginalised, and by the mid-30s BC the Roman world had been divided into east and west – with Octavian based in Rome and in charge of the west, and Antony based in Egypt and in control of the east.

Egypt at this stage was a 'client-state' of Rome. This meant that it was not formally part of the empire, but that it needed to follow Rome's lead, acting as a junior ally. Egypt's great attraction to Rome was its fertility, which made it a huge source of grain. The queen of Egypt at this time was Cleopatra, who has gone down as one of the most colourful and remarkable female rulers in history. Egypt had already become embroiled in Rome's civil wars in the early 40s BC, and when Julius Caesar campaigned in the east in 48, he started an affair with the queen. She soon bore him a son, Caesarion, and came to live with him in Rome. After Caesar's assassination in 44, she returned to Egypt.

In 41, Cleopatra was summoned to Asia Minor to meet Antony, now Rome's commander in the east. This was the beginning of one of the most famous love affairs in history, immortalised by Shakespeare in his play *Antony and Cleopatra*. After the two fell in love, Cleopatra bore him twins. However, politics intervened and in 40 Antony was required to return to Italy to seal his pact with Octavian; as part of their alliance, Antony agreed to marry Octavian's sister, Octavia, who bore him two daughters. None the less, in 37 Antony headed east again and renewed his affair with Cleopatra, who bore him another son. Antony now lived permanently with Cleopatra and in 32 he formally divorced Octavia.

There had long been tensions between Antony and Octavian, but this was the moment at which everything came to a head. It was not hard for Octavian to portray Antony as

FIGURE 4.25
Cleopatra.

FIGURE 4.26
A denarius of
Mark Antony.

KEY INDIVIDUAL

Marcus Agrippa the commander of Octavian's fleet at Actium

someone who had broken his ties with the Roman world and was under the spell of a foreign queen. He obtained and read out a copy of Antony's will, which he claimed named Cleopatra as his heir and main beneficiary (it is unclear how honest Octavian was being in his presentation of the will). At this point, many of Antony's soldiers deserted. Octavian declared war on Cleopatra and Egypt, cleverly portraying it as a war against a foreign rival rather than yet another round in Rome's civil wars.

However, Antony marshalled the rest of his troops to prepare for a showdown. The coin shown in Figure 4.26, called a denarius, was issued to his soldiers in the winter of 32/31 BC and probably minted at his headquarters in Patrae, Greece. Such coins were of a lower silver content than the norm, with copper having been added to the alloy, and so they look like money minted out of necessity for the use of Antony's troops in a time of difficulty.

The reverse of the coin simply shows the legionary eagle flanked by two standards of the type carried by the signifer of a century. The coin is dedicated to the sixth legion, which was fighting for Antony. On the obverse, there is a galley with banners at the prow of the ship. The writing stands for 'Antonius augur' – an augur was a senior priest at Rome, an office that Antony had held. The lower writing stands for 'Triumvir Rei Publicae Constituendae' – 'One of three men for the constituting of the Republic'; this was a reference to his joint rule with Octavian and Lepidus after the death of Julius Caesar – Antony is clearly trying to portray himself as someone who wishes to protect the Republic rather than destroy it.

The battle

Both sides prepared for war. In the east, Antony mobilised all the Roman client states, and gathered his forces at Ephesus in Asia Minor with a total of about 100,000 infantry, 12,000 cavalry and hundreds of warships. In the autumn of 32, they moved to Greece where Antony set up a winter headquarters at Patrae. However, his troops and ships were largely based around the Ambracian Gulf on the west coast – in particular at Actium, the southern promontory at the entrance to the gulf (see map, page ix). Octavian moved his ships and men over to the north-west of Greece, and the two sides spent the winter skirmishing. Octavian had a force of around 80,000 infantry, 12,000 cavalry and about 260 ships. Octavian's fleet was commanded by his close friend and ally **Marcus Agrippa**, who a few years before had gained a reputation as an outstanding admiral by master-minding the defeat of a large pirate fleet that was threatening Rome.

As the spring and summer of 31 wore on, Octavian's forces took the initiative. Agrippa managed to blockade the supply lines of Antony's forces by capturing key locations further south in Greece, including Patrae. Moreover, he also captured the island of Leukas close to the mouth of the Ambracian Gulf, which allowed him to set up a naval blockade at the mouth itself. Antony and Cleopatra were by now with their forces, which were suffering starvation and disease; many deserted. Antony was left with two choices: to abandon the fleet and withdraw his troops to the east of Greece to fight another day, or to try to break out of the blockade by meeting Octavian in battle at sea. Cleopatra urged the latter option, hoping to be able to withdraw back to Egypt to regroup. Antony agreed to fight at sea, and hoped that he would then score a decisive victory over Octavian and secure the west coast of Greece for himself. In preparation for battle, Antony and Cleopatra ordered their war chests of treasure to be loaded on, as well as masts and sails – this was an unusual move for a naval battle, when ships tried to be as light as possible.

The battle itself took place on 2nd September. There is some contradiction in the sources as to the number of ships on each side. Octavian's fleet probably had about 250 ships, consisting of quinqueremes, triremes, liburnae and a few hexaremes. It is harder to put a number on Antony's fleet. One Roman historian gives 500, although this was probably the total number of ships under Antony's command. In the battle, it is more likely that he had about 230, of which 60 were Egyptian ships commanded by Cleopatra. As well as quinqueremes, there seem to have been many heavier ships in his fleet, including hexaremes and even larger ones. Antony's fleet was therefore slower and more vulnerable to ramming. In addition, it was undermanned because of illness and desertions. However, his stronger ships had an advantage when fighting at close quarters.

Antony's fleet moved out into the sea early in the morning, with Cleopatra's fleet of sixty ships remaining behind the main line; Antony himself was commanding on the right. Octavian also commanded his fleet on the right, with Agrippa on the left facing Antony. Octavian ordered his wings to spread out in a crescent formation, from where some ships made to ram Antony's wings. Antony did not wait but engaged in battle. It lasted for a long time without decisive progress; Agrippa moved his ships further north, trying to outflank Antony, and therefore thinned his centre.

By now it was late morning, and the daily breeze from the north-west was starting to blow strongly. Cleopatra's ships had not yet joined the battle; but seeing the centre of Octavian's line thinned, she ordered her ships to raise their masts and sails and to charge through the enemy lines, not stopping to fight. They did so with ease, pulling clear and sailing south. This may not have been Antony's plan, but when he saw this he moved from his own flagship (a 'ten') to a quinquereme, and ordered the rest of his fleet to disengage and follow Cleopatra. Why did he do this? This is one of the great questions of Roman history. Perhaps he simply could not bear to be parted from the woman he loved so much. However, few of his men saw his signal or were in a position to do anything about it. Antony sailed south with some other ships and caught up with Cleopatra. The rest of his fleet fought on manfully through the afternoon, but the survivors eventually withdrew back to Actium, the battle lost. Antony's remaining land troops surrendered to Octavian, who showed them mercy and incorporated many into his own army. The game was nearly up for Antony and Cleopatra.

Aftermath

After his victory, Octavian spent the winter in Greece before sailing to Egypt the next year to finish off Antony. As a result of so many desertions, Antony was beaten again in Alexandria. He heard a false rumour that Cleopatra had been captured and killed, and so he tried to take his own life. Yet his death took days and he died in Cleopatra's arms. Cleopatra then offered Octavian an alliance. When he refused, she pleaded for the life of

FIGURE 4.27
Battleplan of Actium.

EXPLORE FURTHER

Read the accounts of the battle by Plutarch (*Life of Antony*, 60–68) and Cassius Dio (*History of Rome*, 50.11–34). How do the two accounts differ?

EXPLORE FURTHER

Read the poetic accounts of Actium by Horace (*Ode*, 1.37) and Virgil (*Aeneid*, 8.671–713). To what extent does each seem to be propaganda on behalf of Augustus?

Study questions

1 What other naval battles have had a decisive effect on a nation's history? How have they been marked and commemorated?
2 Why do you think that Shakespeare found the story of Antony and Cleopatra such good material for a play?

FIGURE 4.28
A sixteenth-century painting of Cleopatra killing herself with a snake.

Caesarion, but it was already too late – Octavian had had him killed. Cleopatra knew that she would be paraded through Rome as a captive, and so she killed herself. One source claims that she did this by having a poisonous snake bite her, although she may simply have taken poison.

Octavian was now master of the whole Roman world. He soon took the title 'princeps' – 'the first citizen' – and changed his name to Augustus. Later Romans and modern historians have regarded him as the first Roman emperor, and the battle of Actium as the day on which the Roman Republic finally died. Augustus himself portrayed Actium as a great moment of liberation for the Roman people. He had a new town built near the battle site, and called it Nicopolis – Greek for 'Victory City'. Nearby a huge monument was set up overlooking the sea, which was decorated with thirty-six battering rams of captured ships. Back in Rome, a number of other monuments to the battle were set up, while two famous poets loyal to Augustus – Virgil and Horace – celebrated the victory in their poetry. Horace (see p. 424) wrote an ode in which he focused on Cleopatra, describing her as a 'fatale monstrum' – a 'deathly monster'. In his *Aeneid* (see p. 429), the poet Virgil gives a vivid description of the battle.

The relief shown in Figure 4.29 was created as part of a monument celebrating Octavian's victory at Actium. It was set up in the town of Praeneste (modern Palestrina) near Rome. The relief seems to show one of Octavian's ships – perhaps the hexareme used as his flagship – with a small tower on deck. It is notable that a crocodile is depicted on the side of the ship. This seems to be a clear reference to Egypt, and perhaps therefore an attempt by Octavian's propagandists to portray the victory at Actium as one against a foreign foe, Cleopatra. This conveniently airbrushes out the fact that the victory at Actium was the final major engagement of a bloody civil war in which Roman had fought against Roman.

PRESCRIBED SOURCE

Relief commemorating the battle of Actium

Date: late 1st century BC

Location: found at Praeneste, near Rome; now in the Vatican Museums

Significance: a relief that seems to celebrate Octavian's naval victory over Antony

FIGURE 4.29
Relief commemorating the victory at Actium. **PS**

TRAJAN'S CAMPAIGN AGAINST THE DACIANS

Trajan

Marcus Ulpius Traianus (known in English as **Trajan**) was Roman emperor from AD 98 until his death in 117. He was not born in Rome but in Italica, a town in the Roman province of Hispania Baetica, an area corresponding to the southern Spanish region of Andalusia today. Although Trajan was born into a high-ranking Roman family and his father served as a consul, it was still remarkable that he progressed to become the most powerful man in the Roman world. Indeed, he was the first Roman emperor born outside Italy.

Trajan made his name as an officer in the Roman army, serving initially as a military tribune. Among his postings at this time was one in Syria during 76–77, while his father was the governor. In about 87 he became the legatus of the Legion VII Gemina in Spain, and in 89 he helped put down a rebellion against the emperor Domitian. In 91, Trajan was made consul for the year. Around this time, he also married Pompeia Plotina, a noble woman to whom he remained married for the rest of his life.

The emperor Domitian was popular with the army, but unpopular with the Roman upper classes. When he was assassinated in 96, he was replaced by the elderly and childless Nerva, who was himself unpopular with the army. In 97, Nerva therefore adopted Trajan as his co-emperor and successor, understanding that Trajan had the respect of the army. It was vital for an emperor to have the support of the army in order to survive. When Nerva died in January of the following year, Trajan became the sole ruler of the Roman world.

Trajan is remembered as one of the best Roman emperors. In fact, after his death every new emperor was welcomed by the senate with the wish that he be 'luckier than Augustus and better than Trajan'. Militarily, his reign is remembered for two great wars of conquest; in Dacia between 101 and 106 (see below), and in Parthia (an area equivalent to modern Iran) between 113 and 116. In these years, the Roman Empire reached the largest extent in its entire history. The conquest of Parthia proved to be short-lived, but Dacia was fully incorporated as a province of the Roman Empire. As emperor, Trajan took a great interest in his soldiers, and is on record as describing them as 'my excellent and most loyal fellow-soldiers'. He formed two new legions, and when he was on campaign he marched on foot at the head of his men.

Trajan was also highly respected as emperor in civilian life. He treated the senate and upper classes with respect, and instigated many impressive building projects, including a new forum and grand new baths in Rome, a canal to prevent the river Tiber in Rome from flooding, a new harbour at Ostia (Rome's port), and a new highway in the south of Italy, the via Traiani (see map on page viii). Trajan was also seen to be a generous emperor to the Roman poor. He extended the corn dole, the system by which the poorest Romans received a state handout of corn, while he also developed a state-funded welfare programme that helped orphaned and poor children throughout Italy. The scheme was initially funded by the booty won during the Dacian wars, indicating the importance of military conquest for the prosperity of life within the empire.

FIGURE 4.30
The emperor Trajan.

The Dacian wars

During the reign of Augustus, the northern frontiers of the Roman Empire had largely been set along two rivers, the Rhine and the Danube. During the first century AD, the barbarian peoples across the Rhine had proved to be the greater danger, but during the reign of Domitian (81–96) the peoples across the Danube became more hostile. In order to divide these peoples, Domitian chose to make a peace with the Dacians, a people based about half-way along the Danube, in a region today corresponding to western Romania. However, the Dacians had themselves not always been on good terms with the Romans. Indeed, they had raided the Roman province of Moesia to the south twice in living memory, once in 69 and then again in 85/86. When the Romans ventured into Dacia in 87, the barbarian people won a clear victory, led by their new and charismatic king **Decebalus**.

KEY INDIVIDUAL

Decebalus the leader of the Dacians

The following year, however, the Romans did win a victory on Dacian soil, and it was after this that the two sides made a peace agreement. Dacia was established as a client-state of Rome, and Decebalus was given a crown to symbolise Roman support for his rule. He was also lent Roman military engineers and given an annual grant to strengthen the outer borders of his region. By the time of Domitian's death, the focus of Roman military defence had moved from the Rhine to the Danube. Whereas earlier there had been eight legions on the Rhine and six on the Danube, those figures were reversed by 96.

When Trajan became emperor in 98, he first inspected the entire northern frontier from west to east. He then returned to Rome to win over the upper classes, and it was only in 101 that he launched his first military campaign – against the Dacians. There is a shortage of written evidence as to his motives, but it is clear that the 'official' Roman account – in the written sources and on Trajan's column (described below) – put the war down to the need for frontier security. By this line of reasoning, Trajan was unimpressed with the generous terms given to Decebalus, and particularly with the annual payments being made to him. Moreover, Decebalus was believed to be ignoring the peace terms and seeking to expand his power so that he posed an increasing threat to Rome. He was apparently building alliances with northern peoples, giving refuge to runaway slaves from the Roman Empire, and even recruiting Roman soldiers into his army.

Modern scholars have sought to suggest other reasons for the attack on Dacia in 101, which could be seen either as alternatives or as additions to the official version. One motivation may have been that morale in the legions on the Danube was dangerously low at this time because they still resented the assassination of Domitian. A war would focus their minds and a victory would seal their loyalty to Trajan. Another very plausible reason is that Trajan himself wanted and needed to make his mark as emperor, and that his inspection of the northern frontier when he came to power was an attempt to look for the best place to launch a successful campaign. Another incentive for the war may have been that the outer reaches of Dacia had gold-mines, which would provide ample riches for the Empire.

In the early summer of 101, Trajan launched his first campaign, crossing the Danube and engaging the Dacians in a major battle at Tapae. The Romans won, but there were heavy casualties on both sides. The following year the Romans pursued Decebalus further into Dacian territory close to his capital at Sarmizegethusa and forced him to submit. He was forced to surrender his war-machines, to give back deserters (most of them soldiers or technical experts), to demolish forts and to withdraw from captured territory. Trajan left garrisons behind and returned to Rome in triumph, where he was granted the title Dacicus ('the conqueror of Dacia').

Decebalus should now have been reduced to the role of loyal client-king again, but the Roman sources suggest that he began to break the terms of his surrender and to build an alliance against the Romans. Trajan was left with no choice but to go back to war, this time in order to reduce Dacia to a full province of the Empire. This he did between 105 and 106, first building a huge bridge across the Danube by which his army could cross. After a hard-fought campaign, the Romans emerged victorious. Decebalus was about to be captured when he committed suicide. Dacia became a Roman province and Trajan founded new cities there. It would remain a Roman province for more than 150 years.

Back in Rome, Trajan celebrated his victories with a **triumph**. During the imperial period, this saw an emperor (or member of his family) celebrating a military victory by leading his troops through the city of Rome, with the spoils of war on display and the captive forced to march in chains in the procession.

> **triumph** a grand procession through the streets of Rome to celebrate a military victory

The material sources

We have no detailed written source about Trajan's campaigns in Dacia, although some historians do make reference to it. Therefore, the largest body of evidence comes from the monuments built to commemorate both the victories and Trajan's achievements more generally. It is quite clear that Trajan saw the Dacian conquest as his key military triumph, and wished to promote his achievement in the eyes of the Roman people. Two of your prescribed sources reflect this – Trajan's Column and the Arch of Trajan at Beneventum.

As other emperors had done, Trajan instigated a large building project in the centre of Rome both to improve the city's infrastructure and to commemorate his reign. This project included a new forum with impressive public buildings, the world's first shopping centre ('Trajan's Markets'), two new libraries and Trajan's Column. The whole project was funded by the spoils of the Dacian conquest, and the column sought to give a record of Trajan's victory there.

The column still stands in the centre of Rome today and is one of the ancient city's best known landmarks. However, its original context has all but disappeared. As Figure 4.33 shows, it was originally surrounded on three sides. To the south was the Basilica Ulpia, a multi-purpose building where Romans might do business or where legal cases might be heard. To the east and west were two libraries, one with Greek texts, the other with Latin texts. Their location is significant. Trajan is known to have written his own account of the Dacian Wars, and this was no doubt a major work in the Latin library. Many scholars think that the column is an attempt to record Trajan's written account in art. It is also likely that these buildings had windows on different storeys that gave visitors views of different parts of the column, so they acted as viewing points.

The monument itself consisted of three parts: a large marble pedestal at the base, the marble column, and a bronze statue of Trajan on the top. The statue disappeared centuries ago, probably after an earthquake. (In 1588 Pope Sixtus V had a statue of St Peter

FIGURE 4.31
Trajan's Column on one side of a denarius minted in AD 114.

FIGURE 4.32
Trajan's Column.

PRESCRIBED SOURCE

Trajan's Column

Date: completed in AD 113

Material: marble

Location: central Rome

Significance: a major architectural column in the centre of Rome presenting Trajan's conquests against the Dacians

FIGURE 4.33
Plan of the location of Trajan's Column.

FIGURE 4.34
Scene showing Victory writing on a shield, from Trajan's Column.

placed there instead, and this remains today.) The pedestal is about 5 metres in height and became Trajan's tomb. The actual column is about 30 metres in height. It was made from nineteen marble drums and has a diameter of 3.7 metres. On the outside, the frieze depicting the Dacian wars is nearly 200 metres long and winds around the column twenty-three times. Inside the column there is a spiral staircase of 185 steps, which leads to a viewing platform at the top.

The frieze is divided into two halves. The lower half depicts the campaigns of 101–102, the upper half the campaigns of 105–106. The two narratives are separated by a personification of Victory writing on a shield. This was a celebration of the Roman victory in the first campaign. In the 1890s the German historian Conrad Cichorius had plates drawn of every scene on the column. His scheme divided the column into 155 scenes, which he numbered in Roman numerals. This scheme is still used today to refer to the different scenes on the column. The scenes are notable for the relative lack of depictions of fighting or the violence of warfare, and there are no scenes which depict violence towards Dacian women and children. There is much more emphasis on the orderliness of the army, and soldiers are often depicted building camps and forts or enacting ceremonies. The column, therefore, should be seen as propaganda presenting Roman power and rule rather than as an accurate record of the nature of the warfare. Three types of set scenes reappear on the column:

- Trajan addressing his troops
- Trajan presiding over a sacrifice
- The army setting out on campaign.

In addition, certain specific events from the wars are portrayed. These include the first crossing of the Danube by the Roman army, the Dacian surrender of 102, a sacrifice made at the bridge over the Danube at the start of the second war, and the suicide of Decebalus. In scene 147 his head is displayed to the Roman troops. The presentation of Trajan himself on the column is significant. He appears between 57 and 60 times (three portraits are unidentifiable). He is shown in military armour in about half of these images, although always helmetless so that his head is visible. When he is in the company of officers or advisors he is usually set in the middle of the scene, and slightly taller than the others. He is seen presiding over a sacrifice on six occasions, showing him to be a pious follower of the gods.

The column offers a portrayal of the victims of warfare, which shows the Romans as enlightened conquerors. For example, in scene 30, Dacian women holding their children are shown pleading to Roman soldiers for mercy. The Romans do not kill them but have them taken away to a ship (one particularly aristocratic woman in this scene may be the sister of Decebalus). In scene 146, boys are seen with captive Dacian soldiers, and they may be the sons of Decebalus. Perhaps the most intriguing portrayal of non-combatants, however, is in the so-called 'torture scene' in scene 45. Here, captured Roman soldiers are shown naked and being tortured by Dacian women. The scene is in great contrast to the way in which the Romans treat prisoners of war on the column, and is thought to be a way of promoting Roman civilisation over the barbarism of foreign peoples.

Beneventum was a relatively unremarkable town in southern Italy, and so we might ask why such an impressive ceremonial arch was built there. The answer lies in the fact that the town was the starting point of an important new highway commissioned by Trajan, which would connect Rome to the port of Brundisium in the south-east of Italy.

FIGURE 4.35
Two scenes from Trajan's Column. To the left, soldiers are engaged in construction, to the right they are tying up Dacian prisoners. Trajan is at the top of the left-hand scene.

FIGURE 4.36
The 'torture scene' on
Trajan's Column.

FIGURE 4.37
The Arch of Trajan at
Benevento.

PRESCRIBED SOURCE

Arch of Trajan, Benevento

Date: completed in AD 114

Material: limestone and marble

Location: Benevento (known to the Romans as Beneventum), Italy

Significance: a major triumphal arch set up to commemorate Trajan's achievements as emperor.

Via Appia The traditional highway from Rome to Brundisium.

Via Traiana A new highway from Beneventum to Brundisium, which offered a faster journey than the southern section of the Via Appia.

Brundisium was important to the Romans since it was traditionally the port from which Roman legions sailed to campaign in the east. For centuries, the main highway south from Rome to Brundisium had been the **Via Appia**. Trajan's new route peeled off from the Via Appia at Beneventum and offered a shorter route to Brundisium. It was opened in 109 and known as the **Via Traiana** ('Trajan's Road'). The arch was dedicated by the Senate in 114 to celebrate the opening of the new highway and to commemorate Trajan's rule.

The arch is one of the best preserved triumphal arches in the Roman world. It is built in limestone and covered with marble blocks, on which are reliefs depicting scenes from the reign of Trajan. There was also originally a four-horse chariot with a statue of Trajan riding in it. As a whole, the artwork on the arch may therefore be taken as an attempt to present Trajan's character and achievements as emperor. Scenes depicted include the emperor founding cities and reorganising the corn supply. There are also sacrifices, most notably on the inside of the arch, where Trajan presides over a sacrifice commemorating the opening of the Via Traiana. In another key scene on the inside of the arch, Trajan is seen to hand out money to poor children. Nearby, a personification of Victory crowns Trajan with a laurel wreath, and the emperor is depicted in full military uniform.

This personification of Victory seems to link directly to one of the key scenes on the outside of the arch which portrays the Dacian conquest. This takes the form of a continuous frieze running around the arch at a level just above the top of the central passageway. This is believed to show the triumph held by Trajan in Rome in 107. It portrays a procession that is just reaching the **Capitoline Hill** in Rome, the political and ceremonial heart of the city. The frieze depicts 107 figures: soldiers carrying the spoils of war, chariots carrying chained prisoners, bulls being led to sacrifice, and at the rear Trajan himself is seen riding in a triumphal chariot. Once again, therefore, we see Trajan portraying his victories in Dacia as one of the central achievements of his reign, and using military glory to promote an image of a great conqueror.

> **Capitoline Hill** One of the seven original hills of Rome, it was the political and ceremonial heart of the city.

> **S & C** One of the new towns founded by the Romans in Dacia was called Civitas Tropaensium, where today there is the town of Adamklissi. In 109, a large memorial to the Roman victory in Dacia was set up there, Tropaeum Traiani ('Trajan's Trophy'), and it contained fifty-four separate metopes, sculpted scenes of the Roman campaigns. Most of these metopes are now in the site Museum and are therefore referred to as the Adamklissi Metopes. Find out about these metopes – what can we learn about the campaign from them?

TOPIC REVIEW

You should be able to:

1. Describe:
   - the key events of the battle of Actium
   - the key individuals involved in the battle of Actium
   - the key events of Trajan's campaign against the Dacians
   - an outline of the decoration on Trajan's Column and the Arch of Trajan.

2. Explain:
   - why the battle of Actium came to be fought
   - why the battle of Actium was so important in Roman history
   - what Trajan's Column and the Arch of Trajan can tell us about Roman war and warfare
   - how Trajan is portrayed in these monuments.

PRACTICE QUESTIONS

Source A: *Relief commemorating Actium*

1. Look at this image.
   a. State **two** ways in which this can be identified as a Roman warship. [2]
   b. How did this image seek to glorify Octavian's victory at Actium? [2]
2. 'To the Romans, military discipline was the most important element of a successful army.' To what extent do you agree with this statement? [15]

Literature

4.5 Homer

Literary context

- The genre and author of your set text
- Its composition and aims
- Narrative and descriptive techniques, including:
  - speeches
  - similies and imagery
  - epithets
  - use of emotive language
  - the role of the divine

Characterisation

- The actions of the characters in your selections
- The traits of each of the main characters and how these are depicted
- Interactions and relationships between characters
- The depiction of:
  - leaders and soldiers
  - comrades and enemies
  - non-combatants
  - women

Themes

- Glory, honour and shame
- Comradeship
- Freedom
- Hubris and arrogance
- Love and patriotism
- The horror and glorification of warfare
- Fear and courage
- Family and ancestors
- Military and civilian victims of war

Heroes and Warfare

- How the content of your selections reflects its political or cultural context, including:
  - details of the historical context
  - what constitutes a 'hero'
  - attitudes towards war and warfare
- The possible responses to the text from different audiences

The prescribed source for this topic is:

- Homer, *Iliad*, 5.84–469; 6.118–529; 22.21–409; 24.468–620

Don't forget that you will be given credit in the exam if you study extra sources and make relevant use of them in your answers.

This section will introduce you to the Homeric poems in general, and then move to examine your prescribed passages of Homer's *Iliad*. Throughout, you should keep referring to the topic boxes at the start of the chapter to think about how your prescribed literature includes the themes mentioned.

LITERARY CONTEXT

The *Iliad* and the *Odyssey*, attributed to Homer, are the earliest surviving works of literature from the ancient Greek world, and many would say that they remain its greatest literary achievement. There is no doubt that later Greeks looked to the poems as a deep source of wisdom, inspiration, and entertainment. However, we immediately confront a problem: we have no idea who 'Homer' was, if he ever existed, and (if he did exist) if he composed either or both of the poems. This is often called the **Homeric question**.

We do know that the Homeric poems were probably first written down at some point between 750 and 650 BC, soon after the Greeks had developed a written script (the same one that remains in use today). Since the Greeks had not used writing in the centuries before this, their culture at this time was what is called an **oral culture**. This means that it relied on the spoken word rather than the written word. Anthropologists who have studied oral cultures have noticed some common features in them. Above all, their people have to develop great powers of memory as they do not have books to refer back to. Moreover, in such cultures, song, dance and poetry all become very important, since they make the recording and remembering of stories and information much easier.

All cultures throughout history found ways to tell stories. In our society, we might engage with a story by reading a book, watching television, seeing a film or going to

> ### KEY INDIVIDUAL
>
> **Homer** the name given to the poet who was thought to have composed the *Iliad* and the *Odyssey*

> **Homeric question** the debate about the authorship of the *Iliad* and the *Odyssey* and about the identity of Homer
>
> **oral culture** a society where people rely on word of mouth rather than writing

---

PRESCRIBED SOURCE

Homer, *Iliad*, 5.84–469; 6.118–529; 22.21–409; 24.468–620

Date: probably between 750 and 650 BC

Author: attributed to Homer

Genre: epic poetry

Significance: selections that show aspects of ancient Greek warfare as follows:

- 5.84–469: the prowess and achievements in battle of the Greek warrior Diomedes – 6.118–529: a contrast between events on the battlefield and life inside the walls of Troy
- 22.21–409: Achilles kills Hector and mistreats his corpse – 24.468–620: Priam visits the tent of Achilles to beg for the return of Hector's body for burial

Read it here: OCR source booklet

bard a public storyteller who recited vast amounts of poetry to the accompaniment of the lyre, often during banquets

the theatre. None of these options were of course available to the Greeks who lived before the eighth century BC. Yet one form of entertainment was particularly prominent then – public storytelling by a professional storyteller. In those times, such a public storyteller, known as a **bard**, would recite to an audience very long poems to the accompaniment of a lyre, a musical instrument like a small harp (we might also, therefore, talk of the bard 'singing' his tale). This was the way myths and tales were passed on, and developed and improved over generations. It was also the way people were entertained for centuries.

The *Iliad* and the *Odyssey* centre on events surrounding the Trojan War, a treasure trove of remarkable, wonderful and moving stories. No one believes that the Trojan War happened exactly as described in these poems. However, it is likely that the poems emerged out of the experience of a war or series of wars. The most likely time for such wars was around the twelfth century BC, when we know that the Bronze Age civilisation in the eastern Mediterranean collapsed spectacularly. Many cities were burnt to the ground, and the population declined significantly. Bards presumably started singing about these wars as they were happening. As time went on and the generations passed, the stories were changed by other bards who developed their own interpretations and emphases. Their focus was not on producing factual accounts of the past, but on producing stories with examples of great heroism and nobility.

FIGURE 4.38
This ivory lyre was used by Greek bards in the thirteenth century BC.

When the Greeks started using a written script during the eighth century BC, they had the means to set down these stories for the first time. It is at this point that the figure of Homer emerges. The most common school of thought believes that he was a bard who was literate enough to write down his poems, or who at least dictated them to scribes to write down. In fact, little is known about Homer – he is really a figure of mystery. The best-known tales about him are that he was blind and that he came from the eastern Aegean, possibly the island of Chios. Amongst scholars, there remain wide differences of opinion over his identity. Some think that the two poems were composed by different people, others that 'Homer' is really a term for a group of bards.

We are unlikely ever to be able to answer this Homeric question fully, but what is clear is the huge influence that the poems had on subsequent Greek culture and literature – a huge number of the poetic verses cited by later Greek writers are from Homer, and many Greek writers and artists turned to the Homeric poems for inspiration. Indeed, their influence reaches far beyond the Greek world, since they have inspired countless writers and artists ever since: the *Aeneid* by the first-century BC Roman poet Virgil, which you will also be reading, is a notable example. It is for this reason that Homer – whoever he may have been – is regarded as the father of Western literature.

FIGURE 4.39
Although later Greeks did not know what Homer looked like, they created images of him such as this one.

Oral poetry

Although the *Iliad* was written down, it still bears the hallmarks of oral poetry – that is, poetry recited by heart without reference to a written version. Of course, it is much easier to remember poetry than it is prose since poetry has a rhythm and metre (think how lines from a catchy song can easily stay in your head). The Homeric poems were composed in a specific poetic metre, the **hexameter**, which had six 'feet', or metrical units, to each line. Greeks used a word to describe the hexameter line or hexameter poetry – 'epos', originally meaning 'word' or 'utterance'. We therefore call it **epic poetry**.

However, the *Iliad* contains more than 15,000 lines, and so we might ask how a bard was able to remember such an extraordinary amount. Part of the answer is that the poem has a number of repetitive elements typical of oral poetry – in fact, about a third of the lines of the poem are repeated wholly or in part. Moreover, it seems that each poet would develop his own version each time he presented it – he could use the repetitive elements as a starting point, and then insert his own lines around them, or use lines with which he was already familiar. The repetitive elements therefore acted as building blocks for each poet to work from, and allowed him to improvise each time he gave a performance (a comparison could be made with the way in which improvisation is a key feature of jazz music today).

An example of a repetitive element in the *Iliad* is the **epithet**. An epithet is an adjective or adjectival phrase that is repeatedly used to describe a character. When you read the poem, you will notice that the goddess Athena is often referred to as 'bright-eyed' or 'golden-haired', while Diomedes is frequently 'of the loud war-cry', and Hector 'of the gleaming helm'. These phrases neatly made up metrical units and so allowed the poet to fill up part of a line with ease. While each epithet tells us something important about the character being described, it is not always relevant to the exact situation of the poem. Two contrasting examples can be found early in your prescribed literature if we focus on the epithet 'Diomedes of the loud war-cry'.

In the first example, after Diomedes has wounded the goddess Aphrodite at the end of Book 5, section 297–351, the narrative reads as follows:

> Over her Diomedes of the loud war-cry raised a great shout of triumph: "Daughter of Zeus, leave battle and strife to others. Isn't it enough that you snare feeble women? Rejoin the fight and you'll learn to shudder at the name of war!"
>
> Homer, Iliad, 5.347–351

Clearly, in this instance the epithet is entirely appropriate to the situation, since Diomedes is shouting triumphantly at Aphrodite on the battlefield.

However, consider the follow example from Book 6, where Diomedes meets an opponent, Glaucus, on the battlefield and learns that he has old family ties with him:

> Diomedes of the loud war-cry rejoiced at these words. Planting his spear in the fertile earth, he spoke to the Lycian general courteously: "You are, then, a friend of long-standing to my father's house."
>
> Homer, Iliad, 6.212–215

Here Diomedes' polite speech does not match with him being 'of the loud war-cry'. The poet has used the epithet to fill up a line and to remind us of Diomedes' general character; however, perhaps this also makes his polite conversation with Glaucus even more surprising and remarkable.

MODERN PARALLEL

Our use of the word 'epic' to mean 'incredible' or 'remarkable' comes from the fact that most epic poems recount tales of great heroism and bravery.

---

hexameter a poetic metre that has six units to a line

epic poetry poetry focusing on great deeds, composed in hexameter verse

epithet an adjectival word or phrase regularly added to a name to denote a personal or physical quality

---

Study questions

1 How are jazz musicians and rap musicians able to improvise when they perform?
2 Do you think that this adds to an artist's performance?

EXPLORE FURTHER

For a long time it was doubted that it was humanly possible to recite such a long poem that had not been written down, especially since each line had to fit the same metre. However, in the 1930s an American scholar called Milman Parry studied poets in Bosnia, where there was a low level of literacy and long poems were still recited by heart. One illiterate poet was able to recite a 12,000-line poem, proving that what had been done in Greek times was indeed possible. What is also interesting about this survey is that Parry noted that each performance was different, even if the storyteller believed that he had produced an exact repetition of an earlier performance. This therefore illustrated that improvisation was a key feature of oral poetry.

There are other examples in the *Iliad* of repetitive poetry besides epithets. Sometimes entire lines are repeated, while there are also longer repeated sections for situations such as making a prayer to a god or a feasting scene. Therefore, when you read the poem, do not be surprised to see this repetition – and remember that it is evidence of the remarkable way in which it came to be composed.

PLOT STRUCTURE

The Trojan War story was well known in ancient times. It tells of a war at Troy in Asia Minor (see map, pp. viii–ix) between the Greeks and the Trojans over Helen, the wife of King Menelaus of Sparta, and by reputation the most beautiful woman in the world. Helen had been kidnapped by a Trojan prince, Paris, who brought her back to his home city as his wife. In outrage, the Greek chieftains prepared a huge armada of ships to sail to Troy and retrieve her. The ensuing war lasted for ten years, and the Greeks finally won thanks to the trickery of one of their leaders, Odysseus. He came up with the famous idea of ambushing the Trojans by concealing Greek soldiers inside a wooden horse and presenting it to them as a peace offering. The Trojans pulled the horse inside their city and began wild celebrations at what they thought was victory at last. That night, however, the soldiers climbed out of the horse and opened the gates for their comrades, who had returned in secret. The Greeks overran the city, set it on fire, and either killed the Trojans or took them away as slaves.

However, the *Iliad* does not tell this whole story, or indeed anything like it. Instead, it focuses on one short period during the final year of the war; at times, the poet makes mention of other parts of the story, but for the most part he relies on the fact that his audience already knows it well. The poem is divided into twenty-four 'books' – although the word 'book' here really corresponds to what we would understand as a 'chapter', and the name comes from the fact that each book equated to the length of a papyrus scroll, on which it was written down. The whole action of the poem takes place over a fifty-day period. Of this, twenty-two days pass in Book 1; the action of Book 2 through to Book 22 happens over a period of just five days, while twenty-three more days pass during the final two books. Such a short span of time gives the work great intensity.

Plot summary: the anger of Achilles

The central theme of the poem is the anger of the greatest Greek warrior, Achilles. In **Book 1**, Achilles gets into a great quarrel with Agamemnon, the overall commander of the Greek forces. As a result, Agamemnon takes from Achilles a slave girl he has won in battle, Briseis. This is a great dishonour – the concept of honour is very important to Homeric heroes, and it is gained by the award of trophies captured in war, both people and rich possessions (see p. 405). Enraged by his treatment, Achilles refuses to fight for the Greeks any more, and also withdraws his own people, the Myrmidons, from the fight. Moreover, Achilles' mother, the sea goddess Thetis, who is also angered by her son's treatment, travels to Zeus and persuades him to allow the Trojans to get the upper hand so that the Greeks will realise how much they value Achilles. Zeus agrees to allow this, although he says that he cannot alter the fact that Troy is fated to fall to the Greeks.

Books 2 to 7 cover the first day's fighting after this quarrel. Within the poem, these books serve to introduce the main characters and to give the context against which the anger of Achilles will play itself out. In your two prescribed books from this part of the poem, you will read first in **Book 5** about the exploits of a great Greek warrior, Diomedes, as well as about the involvement of the gods in the battle; the focus then shifts in **Book 6** to within the walls of Troy when Hector, the greatest Trojan warrior and the oldest son of Troy's King Priam, returns from battle and meets his mother Hecabe and his wife Andromache, as well as Helen and Paris. At the end of this day's fighting, there follows a day-long truce while each side buries its dead – a theme that will become very important.

Book 8 describes the second day's fighting after the quarrel, and it is at this stage that Zeus actively enables the Trojans to gain the upper hand by forbidding the gods to take part – until now they have been taking sides and balancing out the contest. The Greeks are now alarmed by the fact that the Trojans are camping out on the plain. In **Book 9**, the same evening, Agamemnon concedes that he has made a terrible mistake by insulting Achilles and sends other eminent Greeks to offer him a sincere apology – together with a fabulous collection of prizes and the return of Briseis. However, Achilles will have none of it. He argues that honour is not something that can be valued inconsistently. Despite listening to powerful arguments urging him to return to the fighting, he remains stubborn and even threatens to go home to Greece. At this point we see Achilles unable to let his anger go, something that will have terrible consequences in the coming days.

Book 10 recounts a daring spying mission during the same night into the Trojan camp by two Greek warriors, Odysseus and Diomedes. The action of the third day's fighting takes place between Books 11 and 17. In **Book 11**, the leading Greeks, Agamemnon, Odysseus and Diomedes, are all wounded, while Ajax is forced to retreat. The following book sees the Trojans breach the wall of the Greek camp. In **Books 13** and **14**, the action slows down as Zeus is tricked by Hera into taking his eye off events – the queen of the gods seduces her husband. He falls asleep and so Poseidon helps the Greeks. In **Book 15**, Zeus wakes up and restores the Trojan fortunes – not only have the Trojans breached the wall, but they are now actively threatening the Greek ships, which they intend to burn, so trapping the Greeks without a supply line.

Book 16 is one of the pivotal books of the poem: Patroclus, Achilles' closest friend and one who had also stayed out of the fighting, begs Achilles to let him rejoin battle wearing Achilles' armour; he believes (correctly) that the Trojans are so scared of Achilles that if they believe he is back in battle, they will be intimidated and retreat. Achilles relents but warns Patroclus not to get carried away; he should only drive the Trojans back from the Greek camp and not try to go as far as the walls of Troy. Achilles also sends the Myrmidons back into battle and urges them to fight bravely. Initially, the plan works and Patroclus has great success in driving back the Trojans, including killing a noble Trojan, Sarpedon, a son of Zeus. However, Patroclus becomes overconfident and advances to the walls of Troy where he is killed by Hector; as he lies dying, he prophesies that Achilles will avenge him.

In **Book 17** there is a fierce fight over the body of Patroclus, which the Trojans want to win so that they can keep his armour (which is of course really Achilles' armour) as a

trophy, and then ransom back the body. They manage to strip the armour but eventually the Greeks recapture the body. **Book 18** is set back in the Greek camp, where news is brought to Achilles of Patroclus' death. He is distraught and becomes fixated on taking revenge on Hector, transferring the anger he felt towards Agamemnon onto the Trojan hero. Although he knows that he is fated to die soon after Hector does, he plans to return to the battle to avenge his dear friend. His mother arranges for the blacksmith god Hephaistos to make new armour for him, including a magnificent shield, which is described in detail. In **Book 19**, Achilles and Agamemnon make up their quarrel and the Greeks prepare themselves for battle once more, and then in **Book 20** Zeus allows the gods to rejoin the fighting, and the battle starts; Achilles and Hector inspire their troops, but Hector is warned by Apollo to stay clear of Achilles. The fighting continues in **Book 21**, with the gods coming into sharp focus. Achilles is merciless in his killing.

FIGURE 4.40
A scene from an earlier stage in the war, where Achilles tends Patroclus' wounds.

Book 22 is another central book in the poem, and sees the final showdown between Achilles and Hector. The other Trojans have now retreated inside the walls of Troy but Hector is left outside. From the walls, his mother and father beg him not to fight against Achilles, but he does not listen to them. However, when Achilles comes closer, Hector becomes scared and takes flight; he is chased round the walls of the city three times; eventually, however, he chooses to stop and fight after the goddess Athena tricks him by disguising herself as his brother who has come to help him. He turns and faces Achilles but soon realises that he has been tricked and his time has come. He begs Achilles to return his body for a proper burial – it was believed that without burial a person's spirit could not travel to the underworld and was in limbo forever. Achilles refuses to do this; he kills Hector, strips his armour and ties his naked body to his chariot, dragging it away to the Greek camp. His anger has led him to ignore all the norms of human behaviour, which are sacred even in a time of war.

In **Book 23**, Achilles holds funeral games for Patroclus. There is a great contrast between the way he treats his friend in death and the treatment given to Hector, whose body is left unburied outside Achilles' tent. **Book 24** begins with Achilles a picture of unresolved grief – his revenge over Hector has brought him no closure; each day, he drags Hector's corpse around the funeral mound to Patroclus. However, most of the gods are horrified by this behaviour, and Apollo protects Hector's corpse from any disfigurement or decay. They send Thetis to tell Achilles to cease from his outrageous behaviour and to accept a ransom for the body of Hector. Zeus then sends Iris, the goddess of the rainbow, to tell Priam to prepare to go to the Greek camp with a fabulous ransom for his son's body.

He is escorted there in secret by the god Hermes, and led to Achilles' tent. He enters and begs Achilles for his son's body back. He asks him to think of his own father, Peleus, who will not now see his son again since Achilles is fated to die soon. Priam even kisses Achilles' hands. Achilles reacts with amazement and compassion to Priam's request, and agrees to return Hector's body, and the two enemies weep together: Priam for Hector and Achilles for Patroclus. They are united in experiencing the tragedy of war and of human life. Achilles has returned to being fully human again; his anger has been resolved as he accepts his forthcoming death and abides by the rules of human decency. He returns the body and agrees to a truce of eleven days to give Priam time to bury and remember Hector. The poem ends with Priam's return to Troy with the body, and the lamentations of the Trojans who see him arrive with it.

The Homeric hero

Even this short outline of the poem forces us to confront how Homeric heroes understood their world and their place in it. A Homeric hero is ultimately preoccupied with two related concepts: his honour and his glory. In Greek, these two words were represented by the words **time** (pronounced 'tim-air') and **kleos**. Closely related to these was the concept of 'shame' or 'respect', as represented by the word **aidos**.

- **time** (honour) Homeric heroes win honour by being awarded highly valued possessions as trophies of excellence: for example, such a trophy could be an enemy's armour, treasure from a conquered city, cattle, or human trophies who serve as slaves having been captured in war.

> **time** the honour a Homeric warrior hopes to win

- **aidos** (shame/respect) Closely linked to the concept of time is the idea that the people around you show you great respect and choose to give you the trophies of honour – in Greek, the word for such respect was **aidos**. This is often translated as 'shame' but may equally be thought of as showing humility and respect in the face of the honoured person. In Achilles' case, he had been awarded Briseis as a trophy of war by the army, who had showed aidos towards him. Agamemnon's removal of this prize was therefore a great dishonour.

> **aidos** the shame or respectful modesty a Homeric character feels towards someone who has great time

- **kleos** (glory) The most basic meaning of kleos was 'what people hear said about you' – we might think of it as 'glorious reputation'. To have great honour means that you will be well spoken of and that your memory will live on long after you

> **kleos** the glorious reputation a Homeric warrior hopes to win

Study questions

1 How is the word 'hero' used in our society today?
2 How would you define a hero?

S & C Our world has a modern set of 'rules of war', which are governed by the Geneva Conventions. Find out about these conventions – would you add or change any of their main rules? Do you think that there are any noticeable 'rules of war' in the sections of the *Iliad* that you read?

Achaeans, Argives, Danaans all Homeric terms for the Greeks

KEY INDIVIDUAL

Diomedes one of the greatest Greek warriors, often referred to as the son of Tydeus

aristeia a scene in an epic poem in which a great warrior fights with exceptional courage

have died. This is the way in which a Homeric hero can achieve a form of immortality.

One of the key related themes of the *Iliad* is how a Homeric hero treats the corpse of a conquered enemy. A victorious fighter will try to strip the armour from a man he has killed in battle, and keep it as a trophy. He will also seek to take away the body so that he can ransom it back to the dead man's family for burial. Both Greeks and Trojans believed that a body needed burial in order to reach the underworld, and so denying a man a burial was a terrible thing to do, and one of which the gods generally disapprove.

One other point might be made about the heroic warfare depicted in the *Iliad*. It focuses largely on high-status heroes rather than the soldiers fighting in the ranks. Indeed, there is almost no focus on the common soldier in the poem, and the interest is on the fights between the high-status heroes who lead their men into battle, and who try to defend their people and comrades, and in so doing to win time and kleos.

Greeks and Trojans

In your text, you will notice that the Greeks are often referred to by one of three other names – the **Achaeans**, the **Argives** or the **Danaans**. In fact, these are the only terms that Homer uses for the Greeks, although your translation often refers to them as Greeks instead.

Moreover, even though the Trojans are perceived to be foreigners, they have the same language, customs and gods as the Greeks. This made it much easier for Homer to portray both sides in the conflict, and for the two sides to engage with each other during the poem.

BOOK 5.84–469

The action of Book 5 is largely centred on the great prowess and achievements in battle of the Greek warrior Diomedes. Although not as great a fighter as Achilles, Diomedes is one of the Greeks' finest and it is he who leads the attack against the Trojans in Achilles' absence. The focus on Diomedes in battle begins in Book 4, after Agamemnon insults him about his lack of effort in battle and compares him unfavourably with his father Tydeus. Slighted, Diomedes sets out to prove Agamemnon wrong; there follows the first major battle sequence in the *Iliad*. It is also the poem's first example of a focus on one particular warrior's achievements in battle; such a sequence is commonly known as an **aristeia**, from the Greek word 'aristos' which meant 'best' – an aristeia portrays a great warrior's best moments in battle.

Diomedes is given special strength at the start of Book 5 by the goddess Athena, who wants him to stand out among all the Greeks. We see him rampaging across the battlefield bringing death and destruction, and it is worth focusing for a moment on one short scene:

Astynous and General Hyperion he killed, striking one above the nipple with a throw of his bronze-tipped spear, the other with his long sword on the collarbone, shearing the shoulder from the neck and spine. Leaving them lying there, he chased down Abas and Polyidus, sons of old Eurydamas, interpreter of dreams. They came not back again, whom great Diomedes slew, for their father to tell their dreams. Then he pursued Xanthus and Thoön, Phaenops' dear sons: an old man too weighed down with age to get himself fresh heirs. Diomedes killed both, leaving their sorrowing father to weep when they failed to return, and his surviving kin to inherit.

Homer, *Iliad*, 5.144–158

In this scene, the poet tries to give very short biographical details about the men Diomedes slaughters. In the cases of Astynous and Hyperion, it is simply the way in which each one dies. For the brothers Abas and Polyidus, we hear of their father Eurydamas, and the poet reflects for a moment on a typical scene from their family life that will happen no more: Eurydamas, an interpreter of dreams, will no longer be able to use his skill for the benefit of his sons. The same theme of fatherhood is seen in the deaths of Xanthus and Thoön; in this instance, it is the age of Phaenops that is emphasised, as he is now too old to have more children. We are left with the image of an old man weeping at the loss of his beloved sons.

These few lines are indicative of the skill of the poet. They portray the mayhem and violence of the battlefield, but also the tragedy surrounding the deaths of some of the men. It would be much less interesting if we knew nothing about them and if Homer simply gave us a list of names of those Diomedes killed – by adding these short biographical details the poet adds great richness to the narrative. We might also note that a key theme in these lines is that of bereaved fathers, something that will come to the fore during the final book of the poem.

Two examples of the *Iliad*'s influence today

The contemporary poet Alice Oswald in 2011 published a poem called *Memorial*. She developed Homer's idea of saying a little about each man who died, and her poem focuses on the more than 200 men who are named as having died fighting at Troy in the *Iliad*. Her poem starts simply by listing the names of the dead, like a war memorial does. Oswald then tries to bring out poetically all that we know from Homer about the dead. The narrative is interspersed with direct translations of some of Homer's similes. Her poem is meant as a tribute to each individual soldier, and so tries to highlight the poignancy of each death.

A second example of how the *Iliad* has been interpreted in modern times is given in the book *Achilles in Vietnam* by Jonathan Shay. Dr Shay is an American psychiatrist who found that reading the *Iliad* in therapy groups with traumatised veterans of the Vietnam War was helpful to their recovery; the veterans found that they could identify with many of the themes and characters in the poem, and with the terrible situations in which they found themselves. In *Achilles in Vietnam*, Shay describes how he used the *Iliad* to work with these veterans.

Why do you think it might be that the *Iliad* continues to have such influence today, nearly three thousand years after its composition?

PS

Interpreting similes

One special feature of the *Iliad* is the number of beautiful similes which the poet uses. Your own selection from Book 5 begins with one example:

> As for Diomedes, none could have said which army Greek or Trojan he fought for, since he stormed over the plain like a raging winter torrent that sweeps away the dykes in its swift flood. Close-built embankments and the walls of fertile vineyards fail to hold its onset driven by Zeus' storm and before it the proud works of men all tumble to ruin: so the dense ranks of the Trojans were routed by Tydeus' son, giving way to him despite their numbers.
>
> Homer, *Iliad*, 5.85–94

Homer often draws on the natural world as a source of similes. Here, the poet uses the image of a torrential, overwhelming flood which destroys everything in its path to try to capture the carnage caused by Diomedes' fighting. The warrior is also seen to be elevated above the level of human beings ('none could have said which army Greek or Trojan he fought for'), while he manages to kill vast numbers of men on his own.

In an exam, it is important to explain why a simile is powerful and effective. In this case, the simile presents an image that it is easy for us to conjure up: flood-waters that overrun all before them. Rather than simply giving us facts about the number of men Diomedes killed, the simile allows us to create an image of just how devastating and overwhelming his fighting is. The use of such a simile also has another effect, which is to act as a 'pause button' on action that is happening at breakneck speed: we are allowed to step back from the events of the battle for a moment, and to reflect on them more deeply.

Pandarus and Aeneas

The focus of the episode you first read in Book 5 is the contest between Diomedes on one side, and the Trojan warriors Pandarus and Aeneas on the other:

KEY INDIVIDUAL

Aeneas a Trojan warrior who is the son of the goddess Aphrodite

KEY INDIVIDUAL

Pandarus a Trojan warrior who is an expert archer

- **Aeneas** became associated in later times with leading surviving Trojans away from the city after its defeat, and bringing them to Italy as settlers – he therefore becomes the main character in Virgil's *Aeneid*, which you will read about on pp. 429–439. However, in the *Iliad*, Aeneas is just one of a number of impressive Trojan warriors, although in his case he receives special protection from his mother, the goddess Aphrodite.

- **Pandarus** is an expert archer who has already made his mark in Book 4; in Book 3 a truce had been agreed between the two sides while Menelaus and Paris fought a duel between themselves to decide the outcome of the war. Menelaus wins, but the gods supporting the Trojans refuse to accept the result, and Athena in disguise persuades Pandarus to break the truce by firing an arrow at Menelaus, which he does, wounding the Greek commander.

In the action in Book 5, Pandarus has once again had success as an archer, managing to wound Diomedes. Unaware of this, Aeneas comes to him and urges him to shoot an arrow at Diomedes; Pandarus reflects that he has already done so, and has not managed to halt the Greek's progress – he concludes (correctly) that a god is helping him. At this point, the poet allows Pandarus to give us some more biographical detail about himself, specifically the reason that he fights with a bow in the absence of horses and a chariot.

This biographical information will make the death of Pandarus more moving, since we know something about his homeland. Aeneas suggests that Pandarus jump into his chariot and they attack Diomedes together, and it is worth reflecting here on the use of chariots in Homeric poetry: the chariot is not a weapon of war to give warriors speed in battle in the way that a horse might – in fact, it only serves the purpose of delivering fighters to the thick of battle; some commentators have even referred to Homer's chariots as glorified taxis.

The involvement of the gods

Athena has already been active supporting Diomedes in Book 5. After the death of Pandarus, the role of the gods in the battle comes into sharper focus; first Aphrodite protects Aeneas from being killed by Diomedes; then Diomedes himself goes after Aphrodite and manages to wound her. She returns to Mt Olympus upset, and is comforted by her mother Dione while other gods also make comments about the situation. Then Apollo intervenes in the battle, rescuing Aeneas and warning off Diomedes, then calling upon Ares to join him in battle. To a modern reader, the involvement of the gods in battle may seem strange, and so we should reflect for a moment on this key aspect of the *Iliad*.

FIGURE 4.41
Two Homeric warriors fighting.

On one level, the gods come across to mortals as powerful, awe-inspiring and at times terrifying. However, they have very human flaws and also take sides in the battle. Apollo, Ares and Aphrodite side with the Trojans, while Athena, Hera and Poseidon side with the Greeks. Zeus, the father of the gods, tries to stay above the fray – although he does of course agree to Thetis' request to help the Trojans. To us, it may seem like cheating to rely on a god's help in battle, but the Greeks did not see it this way: they thought that only great heroes were supported by the gods, and so it was a measure of heroic status to have a god support you.

Moreover, it is interesting to observe the gods relating to each other on Mount Olympus, as we do in lines 352–430. Here they behave like any other family – both supporting and annoying each other. Dione tries to comfort her upset daughter Aphrodite, but afterwards Hera and Athena – who of course support the other side in the war – try to provoke Zeus with mockery of the situation:

> Bright-eyed Athena was the first to speak: "Father Zeus, I hope you won't be angry at what I say. It seems your Cyprian daughter has been at work luring some Greek girl to chase after those Trojans she loves so deeply, and while fondling this girl and her golden brooch, scratched her own delicate hand."

> Homer, *Iliad*, 5.418–425

The joke here is on Aphrodite. Athena pretends that she cannot imagine the goddess of love fighting in battle, so assumes that she must have been encouraging a Greek woman to chase after one of the Trojans Aphrodite is so fond of; in so doing, she must have scratched her hand on the woman's golden brooch as she stroked her. Zeus' only reaction is to smile at the joke and tell Aphrodite that she does not belong in battle.

This episode illustrates something very important about Homer's gods. While they have human qualities and human frailties, in one crucial way they are very unlike human beings: they cannot die. Therefore, their difficulties seem trivial in comparison with human lives. For example, Aphrodite's wound is minor, especially compared to wounds of mortals on the battlefield; neither does she face the possibility of death. However, this also means that the gods cannot display great nobility or heroism by putting their lives on the line in the way that mortals can. The easy, deathless lives of the immortals therefore serve to highlight the risks that mortals must take in battle – as a result, the mortals are far more impressive characters who can face the possibility of death with courage and nobility. This is a key point about the characterisation of the gods in the *Iliad*.

BOOK 6.118–529

At the end of Book 5, Diomedes even manages to wound the war-god Ares with the help of Athena. Although Zeus has promised Thetis that he would let the Trojans have the ascendancy, at this point it is the Greeks led by Diomedes who are having the best of it. Therefore Helenus, a son of Priam with prophetic powers, advises his brother Hector to return to the city of Troy and order the women to make offerings to Athena so that she might hold back Diomedes from conquering the city. Hector agrees to do so, and for most of the rest of the book the action takes place inside the walls of Troy.

Diomedes and Glaucus

Before that, however, the focus switches to the battlefield and a meeting between Diomedes and Glaucus, a fighter on the Trojan side from the region of Lycia to the south of Troy. When they first meet, Diomedes asks Glaucus his name and his ancestry, something which might seem strange to us. However, it fits well with the theme of time and kleos – a warrior wants to win significant victories and so it is important to know who he is up against so that he can add to his reputation if he wins (we might think today of the way in which prize-fighters in boxing will speak up about their record before a fight).

Diomedes has been so impressed by Glaucus' fighting that he suspects that he may be a god. He has learnt now not to take on gods (despite having wounded Ares) and uses a myth involving Dionysus to back up his point. In reply, Glaucus also uses a myth – that of Bellerophon – to explain his family lineage and to trace it back to Greece. The two realise that their families have a tradition of 'guest-friendship', in Greek known as **xenia**, a formal relationship between two noble families which carried sacred importance. Diomedes then greets him warmly and suggests they behave as follows:

xenia in Homer, hospitality given unconditionally to a traveller, involving the giving of any help needed; known as 'guest-friendship'

Let us avoid each other's spear in the battle, there are plenty more Trojans and their worthy allies for me to slay, if a god lets my feet overtake them, and many Greeks for you to kill, if you can.

Homer, *Iliad*, 6.226–229

It might surprise us that Diomedes is prepared not to fight an enemy, and even more that he acknowledges that Glaucus will have the chance to kill many of his fellow Greeks. However, many wars have stories of friends on either side of the conflict who try to avoid fighting one another, and so Homer here acknowledges how complex warfare can be.

Inside the walls of Troy

One of the remarkable features of the *Iliad* is that the poet is able to portray both sides of the war – Greeks and Trojans – in a sympathetic light. This is often not the case with war literature, or even with war films in our modern world. In some ways, it is much easier for a writer to create a plot where the 'good guys' take on the 'bad guys' and the reader or viewer has a clear preference for one side over the other. The *Iliad* resists this, something which contributes to its greatness as a poem – it is able to portray sympathetic characters on both sides of the conflict. It is often said that the poet uses great **pathos**, a literary term that describes an appeal to a reader's emotions by inviting them to feel pity and sadness.

This is especially the case in Book 6 when we see Hector withdraw into the walls of Troy. It could be argued that Hector is the most impressive character in the entire poem: while he fights for his time and kleos as the Greek heroes do, he is also defending his city and its people from defeat, which will bring them death or slavery. In Book 6, therefore, we meet him not just as a warrior, but also as a son, a husband, a brother and a father. We are introduced to his mother Hecabe, his wife Andromache and his sister-in-law Helen. This allows the poet to explore and portray the experience of female non-combatants in the war, and the pain that they must endure as they watch on helplessly. At times, the events of the book are almost unbearably moving.

Each of the three women tries to keep Hector away from the battle. First, he meets his mother; he refuses a cup of wine – such is his determination to stay focused for fighting

FIGURE 4.42
Diomedes and Glaucus exchange armour.

> **pathos** literally 'suffering' in Greek, an appeal to the reader's emotions by inviting them to feel pity and sadness

Study question

The episode between Glaucus and Diomedes contains some of the most famous lines in Homer, spoken by Glaucus:

> Like the generations of leaves are those of men. The wind blows and one year's leaves are scattered on the ground, but the trees bud and fresh leaves open when spring comes again. So a generation of men is born as another passes away.
>
> Homer, *Iliad*, 6.146–149

Why do you think that people find this simile so moving? What idea is it putting across?

– and instructs her to make an offering to Athena. He then moves to Paris' home, where he finds his brother with Helen (in Book 3, Paris has been rescued from a duel with Menelaus and brought back into Troy by Aphrodite). Paris is handling his weapons while Helen and her womenfolk are weaving – the comparison portrays Paris as a coward most at home in the company of women, a great contrast to Hector. Hector criticises him for staying out of the fight, a criticism Paris accepts as he agrees to ready himself for battle again. Helen then speaks, full of self-loathing at her situation – she is the cause of the war and all its suffering. It is hard not to pity her. She then invites Hector to sit down and talk with her, an offer he refuses so that he can return to the battle.

Next comes one of the most celebrated scenes in the poem, the meeting of Hector and Andromache at the Scaean gates, the main gates of the city. Andromache runs up to her husband; behind her is a nurse carrying their baby son Astyanax. Andromache begs him to stay out of the fighting; she lists the family members she has already lost in the war, most notably her father and seven brothers. Her plea culminates in the following words:

Hector you are parent, brother, husband to me. Take pity on me now, and stay here on the battlements, don't make your son an orphan, your wife a widow.

Homer, *Iliad*, 6.429–432

Hector rejects her plea, explaining that he must return to the battle for the sake of his kleos and his people. Yet he acknowledges that he knows deep down that Troy will fall sooner rather than later. What he fears most when this moment comes is not the fate of his people, or his parents, but for Andromache as she is hauled off into humiliating slavery. He concludes his speech with these words:

May I be dead, and the earth piled above me, before I hear your cries as they drag you away.

Homer, *Iliad*, 6.464–465

The scene is not yet over. Hector stretches out his arms to take his son, but the baby is terrified by his father in full armour and, in particular, by his helmet (remember that a common epithet of Hector is 'of the gleaming helm'), and so he withdraws crying into his nurse's chest. His parents laugh gently at the reaction; Hector removes his helmet and takes his son, moving him lightly up and down in his arms. Beneath the armour of the great warrior emerges the tender and loving father. This paradox between tenderness and ferocity is further brought out in Hector's next speech, where he prays that his son will grow up to be a greater warrior than he is, and bring joy to his mother's heart through his performance in battle.

Having said these words, Hector then returns Astyanax to his mother:

With this he placed the child in his dear wife's arms, and she took him to her fragrant breast, smiling through her tears. Her husband was touched with pity at this, and stroked her with his hand, saying: "Andromache, dear wife, don't grieve for me too deeply yet. None will send me to Hades before my time: though no man, noble or humble, once born can escape his fate."

Homer, *Iliad*, 6.464–465

Study questions

1 Why do you think that this scene has remained so famous?
2 In what ways does it still speak to us in our world today?

ACTIVITY

Create a drawing or painting of one of the scenes the poet describes in Book 6.

With this, he tells her to return home while he himself heads back out to war with Paris. This is the last time that Andromache will see Hector alive, something she seems to know instinctively – she returns straight home, where she and her maids mourn for Hector as if he is already dead.

BOOK 22.21–409

Your final two selections of reading come from near the end of the poem. Book 22 describes the death of Hector at the hands of Achilles, and its aftermath. In Book 5 you have read about warfare out on the battlefield and in Book 6 you have read about the situation inside the walls of Troy. Book 22 unites the two, as Hector and Achilles fight on the battlefield while Hector's parents and fellow Trojans look on from the walls of Troy. Once again the poet uses pathos as both Priam and Hecabe appeal to Hector not to stay and fight against Achilles, whom he cannot beat. Hector debates what to do, and he resolves to stand and fight; but when Achilles approaches, he takes fright and runs. Achilles chases him three times around the walls of Troy.

FIGURE 4.43
Hector, Andromache and Astyanax. Astyanax reaches out to touch his father's helmet.

The gods and fate

The poem presents a world in which every mortal has their fated time of death. The concept of **fate** – meaning those events that are destined to happen and cannot be changed – stands apart from the gods. It is not the Olympian gods who decide a person's fate, but three other goddesses, known collectively as the Fates, who spin out the length of a life when someone is born. However, Zeus does have a role as overseer of fate – he has to ensure that what is fated comes to pass, however much it may sadden him.

He is certainly saddened by the impending fate of Hector as he is chased around the walls by Achilles. He even wonders aloud to the other gods if he should try to save him. Athena replies to say that this would not win the support of the other gods, and she implies that it would be wrong for him to do so. Zeus agrees, and Athena heads off to assist Achilles. A few lines later, as the chase continues, Zeus dramatically weighs up the lives of the two men in his golden scales:

> When they reached The Springs for the fourth time, the Father raised his golden scales, and set the deaths of Achilles and horse-taming Hector in the balance, and lifted it on high. Down sank Hector's lot towards Hades, and Phoebus Apollo left his side, while bright-eyed Athena came to Achilles.
>
> Homer, *Iliad*, 22.208–214

> **fate** a set of future events that are destined to happen and cannot be changed

Here, Zeus is seen as the god who upholds fate no matter the situation. As the fight unfolds, the modern reader might be surprised or unimpressed that Achilles needs the assistance and trickery of Athena (who disguises herself as Hector's brother Deiphobus) to make Hector stand and fight him. We might think that a great hero should be able to win unaided. However, it is important to state once more that in the Greek mind the support of a god indicated just what a great hero you were – from this perspective, a victory for Achilles without the help of the gods would be less impressive.

The death of Hector

Before their duel, Hector offers Achilles a pact that the victor will not mistreat the dead body of the loser, but will return it for burial. Once again, it is essential to understand how important this idea is in the Homeric world – to be unburied after death is worse than to die itself, since the spirit can never find peace. Yet Achilles will have none of it, such is his rage towards Hector and what he has done: he says that there can be no treaties between lions and men, or between wolves and lambs.

When Hector realises Athena's trick, and that he is doomed, he accepts his fate, but says:

> But let me not die without a fight, without true glory, without some deed that men unborn may hear.
>
> Homer, *Iliad*, 22.304–305

Hector remains noble to the last, and hopes that his death will add to his kleos. However, he is no match for Achilles, who drives his spear through his enemy's throat, but does not cut the windpipe so that Hector can still just speak before he dies. He begs again for Achilles to return his body to his parents so that he can receive a decent burial. Achilles' reply is chilling:

> Don't speak of my parents, dog. I wish the fury and the pain in me could drive me to carve and eat you raw for what you did, as surely as this is true: no living man will keep the dogs from gnawing at your skull.
>
> Homer, *Iliad*, 22.345–348

FIGURE 4.44
Achilles prepares to drag the body of Hector behind his chariot.

This is the height of Achilles' rage, and his anger seems to have robbed him of all sense of humanity. He continues like this after killing Hector, piercing holes in his dead foe's ankles and dragging him back to the Greek camp behind his chariot. From the walls of Troy, the people grieve as if the city were on fire – which it soon will be, given that they know the prophecy that Troy will fall after the death of Hector. Soon afterwards, Andromache hears the cries and runs from her home to the walls, where she sees Hector's body being dragged away. She faints at the sight.

BOOK 24.468–620

During Book 23 the Greeks hold funeral games for Patroclus, honouring his memory and giving him a good burial. The contrast with the treatment of Hector's body is stark. At the start of Book 24, the poet describes Achilles' behaviour towards Hector's corpse: he can get no peace or resolution from having killed him, and continues to weep for Patroclus; from time to time, he gets up, climbs into his chariot, and drags Hector's body around the funeral mound that has been raised for his beloved friend.

However, most of the Olympian gods are outraged by Achilles' behaviour. Apollo protects the corpse, while Zeus orders that a resolution be found – Thetis must persuade Achilles to accept a ransom from Priam for Hector's body. Thetis manages to do this, while the messenger goddess Iris travels to Priam to tell him to prepare a ransom and to travel to the Greek camp with it. Despite the misgivings of Hecabe, he agrees to do so. Priam arrives at the tent of Achilles with the aid of the god Hermes who comes to him in disguise as a Myrmidon attendant of Achilles, and guides him through the Greek camp unseen. Here is another example of a god enhancing the status of a mortal by giving him help. Although Priam is an old man who does not fight in the war, he is still worthy of a god's support.

Achilles and Priam

The meeting between the two men is another remarkable scene in the poem (lines 468–620). It starts with silent action as Achilles sits in his tent after finishing dinner, attended by two friends:

> Great Priam slipped in unobserved, and reaching Achilles, clasped his knees, and kissed his hands, the fearful, man killing hands that had slaughtered so many of his sons. Achilles was astonished at the sight of godlike Priam, as were his friends. They stared at each other, astounded.
>
> Homer, *Iliad*, 24.477–483

Priam is able to kiss the hands of the man who has killed not just Hector but many other sons of his too. The aged king then appeals for the return of the body with one poignant request – he asks Achilles to think of his own father, Peleus, who is an old man back home in Greece. Achilles is fated to die soon, and so he will never see his father again – Priam appeals to their shared experience and the appeal reminds him that his own father will soon be bereaved in the same way that Priam is. The two men then weep,

Study questions

1 How does the poet create pathos through the speeches of Priam and Hecabe at the start of Book 22?

2 Why do you think that Achilles behaves in this way? Do you think that his anger against Hector is reasonable or understandable given what he has suffered in the war?

PS

Priam for Hector and Achilles for Patroclus. Achilles at this moment is much softened and deeply changed from the moment when he took such savage revenge on Hector.

In reply, Achilles is able to acknowledge how much Priam has suffered. He asks the old man to sit with him, then reflects on how much suffering human life can bring – the two men, although enemies in the war, share the human experience of suffering. Priam replies that he cannot sit until he can see Hector's body and know that he will have it back. Achilles has to hold back anger, and at this point we see that his savage side is lurking just below the surface and that he is straining to hold it in. This theme re-emerges a few lines later, when Achilles leaves the tent to organise the return of the body:

> Achilles then summoned two servant-girls and ordered them to
> wash and anoint the body, first carrying it to a place where Priam
> could not see his son, lest his grief at the sight provoke his anger
> and Achilles be angered in reply, and kill him in defiance of Zeus'
> command.
>
> Homer, *Iliad*, 24.582–586

Achilles shows great self-awareness here: he knows that his anger could explode, and yet he takes all precautions to prevent this from happening. The body is prepared, and he returns it to Priam. Achilles then invites the old man to eat with him, reminding him that all must eat, no matter their pain. He tells the story of Niobe to illustrate this: Niobe had boasted of being more fertile than Leto, the mother of Apollo and Artemis. As a result, Niobe had lost all ten of her children, but even she started eating again after nine days of mourning (the exact length of time that had elapsed since the death of Hector). It is also significant that in the story of Niobe the gods bury dead mortals, since they had urged Achilles to release Hector's body for burial at the start of Book 24.

The two men sit down to eat together. Achilles will go on to release the body and offer Priam eleven days' truce so that he can bury Hector and commemorate him suitably. Achilles' anger, which began at the start of the poem, is finally resolved; he has accepted death – that of Patroclus, and his own, soon to come.

FIGURE 4.45
Priam kisses the hand of Achilles.

TOPIC REVIEW

You should be able to:

1. Describe:
   - oral poetry and epic poetry
   - the overall storyline of the *Iliad*
   - the storylines of your prescribed sections of Books 5, 6, 22 and 24
   - the roles played by the main characters, including the gods, Diomedes, Hector, Andromache, Achilles and Priam.

2. Explain:
   - how the Homeric poems are thought to have been composed
   - the requirements of a Homeric hero
   - the key themes of the *Iliad*, especially heroism and the pathos of war
   - how the key characters are portrayed and how sympathetic you find them.

PRACTICE QUESTIONS

Source A: Homer, *Iliad*, 6.297–311

At the shrine of Athena on the Acropolis, lovely Theano flung open the doors. She, whom Troy had appointed priestess of Athena, was daughter to Cisseus, and wife to Antenor, the horse-tamer. They lifted their hands to Athena, with ecstatic cries, while lovely Theano took the robe, laid it on golden-haired Athena's knees, then prayed to the daughter of Zeus. "Lady Athena, fairest of goddesses, protectress of the city, shatter Diomedes' spear. Topple him headlong before the Scaean Gate, and we will sacrifice in your shrine twelve yearling heifers, unused to the goad. Take pity on the city, the Trojan women and their little ones." So Theano prayed, but Pallas Athena denied the prayer.

1. What sort of a phrase is 'golden-haired'? Why does the *Iliad* contain so many of these phrases? [2]

2. How important is it for characters in the *Iliad* to treat the gods with respect? Use this passage as a starting point, and use your own knowledge in the answer. [8]

4.6 Tyrtaeus

Literary context

- The genre and author of your set text
- Its composition and aims

- Narrative and descriptive techniques, including:
  - similes and imagery
  - use of emotive language

Characterisation

- The actions of the characters in your selections
- The traits of each of the main characters and how these are depicted
- Interactions and relationships between characters

- The depiction of:
  - leaders and soldiers
  - comrades and enemies
  - non-combatants
  - women

Themes

- Glory, honour and shame
- Comradeship
- Freedom
- Love and patriotism

- The horror and glorification of warfare
- Fear and courage
- Family and ancestors
- Military and civilian victims of war

Heroes and warfare

- How the content of your selections reflects its political or cultural context, including:
  - details of the historical context
  - what constitutes a 'hero'

  - attitudes towards war and warfare
- The possible responses to the text from different audiences

The prescribed source for this topic is:

- Tyrtaeus, Fragment 10 – *The Fallen Warrior*

Don't forget that you will be given credit in the exam if you study extra sources and make relevant use of them in your answers.

This topic will examine Tyrtaeus, starting with what we know about his life and the times in which he lived. It will then move on to focus on one of the most famous fragments of his poetry, the 'Fallen Warrior' poem. As with your other authors, you should refer to the topic boxes at the start of the chapter to think about how this poem includes many of the themes mentioned there.

BIOGRAPHY

Although Tyrtaeus was composing poems in the same era that the *Iliad* was first written down, he presents a very different type of war poetry. He was a Spartan writing poetry for other Spartans, urging them on in a war they were fighting against their Messenian neighbours. Whereas the *Iliad* is set in the legendary past, Tyrtaeus is writing about men and fighting of his own day. It is therefore very important to understand the historical context in which he is writing.

We have read on page 349 that by the seventh century BC the Spartans had conquered part of the region of Messenia to the west of Laconia, and that at this time the majority of the Messenian population were enslaved as helots to toil on what were now Spartan lands. At some point during the seventh century, the Messenian helots rose up against their enslaved status, and fought a brutal war against their Spartan masters. The Spartans eventually managed to put down the rebellion, but only after years of hard fighting.

It is thought that Tyrtaeus was composing poetry during the years of this war. Regrettably, only fragments of his work have survived – about 250 lines in all. Apart from what we can glean from his poetry, we know very little about his life, although he may have been a Spartan commander during the war. His poems encourage Spartan warriors to put their lives on the line for their city, and emphasise the glory associated with dying for the city in the front line of battle. The focus of his poetry is very different from that of the *Iliad*, since rather than recounting the deeds of great heroes as they duel on the battlefield, Tyrtaeus emphasises the courage needed by Spartan citizen-soldiers to be victorious in battle. Therefore, it is the brave but nameless soldier who is the hero of Tyrtaeus' poetry.

PRESCRIBED SOURCE

Tyrtaeus, Fragment 10 – *The Fallen Warrior*

Date: mid-7th century BC

Location: Sparta

Genre: elegiac poetry

Significance: a poem urging young Spartan warriors to fight bravely

Read it here: OCR source booklet

Tyrtaeus' poetry came to epitomise Sparta's warrior ideal. Indeed, later Spartans regarded him as their national poet and for centuries his poems were used to inspire Spartan soldiers. Plutarch, a biographer writing in the second century AD (long after Sparta had ceased to be a power), reports a story in which the famous Spartan king Leonidas (see p. 355) comments on the importance of his poetry to Spartan society:

> There is a story that when the Leonidas of ancient times was asked his impression of Tyrtaeus' quality as a poet, he replied: "A good one for firing the spirits of the young." For the poems filled them with such excitement that they stopped caring for themselves in battle.

Plutarch, *Cleomenes*, 2

GENRE AND COMPOSITION

elegy a genre of poetry that can focus on a number of topics, and where lines have an alternating metre of hexameter followed by pentameter

pentameter a poetic metre with five units to a line

Tyrtaeus' poetry belongs to a genre known as **elegy**. Today, an elegy is a lament for the dead, but it had a much wider meaning in Greek times – such a poem could reflect on one or more of any number of topics, including war, politics, religion, love and friendship. An elegy was composed with an alternating metre – a hexameter line followed by a **pentameter** (five-foot line). Like the *Iliad*, it was designed to be listened to by an audience rather than read by an individual. It could, therefore, be performed on public occasions such as religious festivals or military events, or at private social gatherings. It was either sung or spoken, to the accompaniment of a musical instrument called an aulos, a reed instrument similar to an oboe.

THE FALLEN WARRIOR POEM

EXPLORE FURTHER

You can read all of the fragments of Tyrtaeus' poetry by searching online at www.perseus.tufts.edu or by reading them in M L West's *Greek Lyric Poetry* (see reading list on p. 440).

This poem may actually have been two separate poems, something which is acknowledged in your translation by dividing it into two paragraphs. Each paragraph makes clear what is and is not the ideal for a Spartan warrior. The first paragraph begins with a statement of what a Spartan warrior should be proud to do – fight and die in the front line of battle. The poem then shifts its focus abruptly to the opposite, giving an example of what life would be like for a defeated Spartan warrior. He is described as wandering as a beggar with his entire family, having brought shame on his ancestors; moreover, he is a curse to those he meets. Following on from this image, the poem returns to the theme of the opening line: what is good is to put your life on the line in battle, and to give your life for Sparta if the city requires it.

The second paragraph begins with the poet making a direct appeal to the young men who will fight for Sparta. Again, the message is to be brave and not to fear death in battle. A strong contrast is made with an old man fighting in battle – the message is that the young men should not desert and leave old men to do the fighting; it is the duty of the young men to fight in the front line, and it is, therefore, shameful for an old man to be exposed and to die in battle. One way of reading this poem is as a warning to young men about what will happen to their city if they do not do their duty – old men will be forced to take their place in the front line and to die horribly. The younger men are, therefore, encouraged to take

Language and imagery

Tyrtaeus presents a very powerful image of such an old man dying:

> For it is of course shameful for an older man fallen among fighters at the front to lie ahead of the young men, his head already white and beard grey, gasping his stalwart spirit out into the dust, clutching his bloody genitals in his own hands – a shameful thing in one's eyes, a sight to cause outrage – his naked skin exposed.
>
> Tyrtaeus, Fragment 10, lines 21–27

We might focus on the language and imagery the poet has used here. The word 'shameful' appears twice, a concept further emphasised by the phrase 'a sight to cause outrage'. There are two senses in which this event would be thought shameful: first of all, it would be shameful for the young warriors who have allowed this to happen; beyond this, it would also be shameful for the wider Spartan community, since it is not producing the sort of brave young men who are prepared to put their lives on the line in battle.

It is not hard for us to conjure up the image, since he communicates it so graphically. The old man's appearance and character are described – his white hair and grey beard, as well as his 'stalwart spirit'; however, the image of an eminent old man is then contrasted with his situation – he is metaphorically 'gasping his stalwart spirit out into the dust', and literally 'clutching his bloody genitals in his own hands'. In this image, he has been killed in battle and stripped of his armour; the reference to his genitals may also suggest that his body has been mutilated. It is a horrifying image of an old man who has died in battle.

S & C

The First World War produced some remarkable poets, who reflect different perspectives on the warfare. Read two patriotic poems by British poets: *The Soldier* by Rupert Brooke and *In Flanders Fields* by John McCrae. How do they compare to the fragment of Tyrtaeus that you have read?

their place ahead of the older men, to spare them the greatest danger, and to stand their ground to keep them out of danger. The Spartans revered the elderly and gave them a special place of honour in their society, and so this message is especially powerful.

What might be most surprising to us in the lines that follow is that Tyrtaeus says that such a death is fitting for a young man – the poet is not horrified by the nature of the death itself but by the fact that it is an old man who is suffering it. He therefore concludes the poem by once again encouraging the young men to stand firm in the front line. It is striking in these final lines that he describes a fallen young warrior as 'beautiful', a great contrast from the degraded image of the fallen older man.

Study questions

1 Do you think it is better and nobler for young men to fall in battle instead of older men?
2 Do you think that it is possible for a soldier who has fallen in battle to look beautiful?

ACTIVITY

In class, imagine that you are a group of Spartans who are to listen to the first public performance of this poem by Tyrtaeus. Choose one person to recite the poem, and another to give musical accompaniment (perhaps with an oboe), while the rest of the class are members of the audience. Act out the scene – how do the members of the audience respond to what they hear?

TOPIC REVIEW

You should be able to:

1. Describe:
   - the historical context in which Tyrtaeus was writing
   - the importance of Tyrtaeus' poetry for later Spartans
   - the nature of elegiac poetry
   - an outline of the *Fallen Warrior* poem.

2. Explain:
   - how Tyrtaeus' historical context influenced his poetry
   - the nature of the heroism that the poem encourages
   - the importance of the concept of shame in the poem
   - the way that young and old Spartans are contrasted in the poem.

PRACTICE QUESTIONS

Source A: Tyrtaeus, Fragment 10, Lines 1–8

To die is noble when a good man falls among fighters at the front while he defends his fatherland. To leave behind his city and its fertile fields and go begging is the most wretched thing of all, wandering with his dear mother, his elderly father, his tiny children and wedded wife; for he will be hated by the people around him wherever he goes, overcome by need and grim poverty.

1. Which is the 'fatherland' referred to in this poem?   [1]
2. What points do you think Tyrtaeus is making in this passage? Use **two** phrases and suggest what
they tell us about his message.   [4]

4.7 Horace

Literary context

- The genre and author of your text
- Its composition and aims
- Narrative and descriptive techniques, including:
  - speeches
  - similes and imagery
  - use of emotive language
  - the role of the divine

Characterisation

- The actions of the characters in your selections
- The traits of each of the main characters and how these are depicted
- Interactions and relationships between characters
- The depiction of:
  - leaders and soldiers
  - comrades and enemies
  - non-combatants
  - women

Themes

- Glory, honour and shame
- Comradeship
- Freedom
- Hubris and arrogance
- Love and patriotism
- The horror and glorification of warfare
- Fear and courage
- Family and ancestors
- Military and civilian victims of war

Heroes and warfare

- How the content of your selections reflects its political or cultural context, including:
  - details of the historical context
  - what constitutes a 'hero'
  - attitudes towards war and warfare
- The possible responses to the text from different audiences

The prescribed source for this topic is

- Horace, *Odes* 3.2

Don't forget that you will be given credit in the exam if you study extra sources and make relevant use of them in your answers.

This topic will examine Horace, starting with his life story and how it influenced his poetry. It will then move on to examining Ode 3.2, a poem that contains one of the most famous lines of Latin poetry. As with your other authors, you should refer to the topic boxes at the start of the chapter to think about how this poem includes many of the themes mentioned there.

KEY INDIVIDUALS

Octavian/Augustus (63 BC–AD 14) a leading Roman aristocrat who was Julius Caesar's adopted heir. In 30 BC he became the sole ruler of the entire Roman world, and is regarded as the first Roman emperor

Maecenas (c. 64–8 BC) a close adviser to Octavian/ Augustus who was appointed his patron of the arts. He welcomed Horace into his circle of poets, and became his mentor and close friend

BIOGRAPHY

Horace had a remarkable life; he was born the son of a freedman in the small town of Venusia in southern Italy, and yet he grew up to become one of the leading poets in the Roman world. He lived during very troubled times, which have been described in some detail (see pp. 295–296). When Julius Caesar was murdered in 44 BC, one of his leading assassins, Brutus, fled to Greece to try to raise an army there. Horace was studying in Athens at the time and he signed up for Brutus' army, fighting in the assassins' final defeat at Philippi in 42 BC – however, despite fighting on the losing side he survived to live another day. Soon afterwards he returned to Rome, taking advantage of a general amnesty given by Caesar's adopted heir, **Octavian**, to those who had fought against him.

In 38 BC Horace was introduced to **Maecenas**, a close adviser to Octavian who was responsible for influencing public opinion in his favour. To do this, he aimed to nurture poets who would write poetry sympathetic to Octavian and his regime. Horace had already started writing poetry, and was welcomed into Maecenas' circle of poets; this was a huge break for him in his writing career, and indeed in the whole direction of his life.

Horace may have been present at the battle of Actium in 31 BC (see p. 385). When Octavian's victory brought an end to decades of civil wars and left him as the sole ruler of the Roman world, Horace found himself writing poetry for the most powerful man in the known world – the first Roman emperor, who was now referred to as **Augustus**. Horace, therefore, had to be suitably patriotic and praising of his emperor.

THE ODES

Horace published his first three books of odes in 23 BC (a fourth book was published in about 13 BC), and he wrote 103 such poems in all. He consciously looked to the ancient Greek world for his models, and his odes imitate the style of the **lyric poetry** written by a number of Greek poets of the seventh and sixth centuries BC; they had composed personal poems to be sung to the lyre for an audience. However, while Horace drew their inspiration from their style of poetry – and particularly the metres they commonly employed – it is unlikely that he wrote his poems to be sung to musical accompaniment as they did. Instead, he had them published just as a poet might today, although he may have given some recitals himself when they were first published.

His odes focus on any number of themes relevant to his life: some reflect on aspects of his personal life such as love, friendship and social occasions, while others focus on

lyric poetry personal poetry originally performed to the lyre for an audience war, politics and religion – we have already seen on p. 388 that he composed a poem to celebrate Octavian's victory at Actium.

ODE 3.2

stanza a verse of poetry with a set metre repeated throughout the poem

This ode focuses on war, politics and statesmanship. The poem is divided into eight stanzas of four lines each (a **stanza** is a type of verse in a poem – it has a set metre, which is repeated in every verse of the poem), and these can be divided up thematically as follows:

- **Stanzas 1–4** Young Romans from the highest social classes should undergo tough military training so that they can fight bravely and successfully against Rome's enemies, and so that they are prepared to fight to the death rather than desert in battle.
- **Stanzas 5–6** The courage that such a soldier learns in the army will also be needed in civilian life in Rome. Some exceptional men are examples of this, and such a man does not derive his sense of importance from political status but from his own conduct. This sort of man will be given a place amongst the gods after his death.
- **Stanzas 7–8** Not all Romans can be as great as this, but other men can still serve the Roman state by being loyal and discreet. Those who do not show these qualities are sure to be punished by the gods.

Clearly, one major theme of the poem, therefore, is that the qualities learnt in military life can be transferred across to civilian life, and this suggests how important the army was felt to be for the development of character.

The opening stanza introduces this theme. We know that Augustus established a tough training programme for teenage boys aged 15–18 who came from the top two Roman social classes – the senators and equestrians – so that they were ready to serve in the army as tribunes (see p. 372). Horace therefore opens his poem by approving of this, and then moves on to hope that such a highly trained young man will fight successfully against the Parthians, one of Rome's great enemies. The **Parthian Empire** lay to the east of the Roman Empire and was centred on what is now Iran. In 53 BC, the Romans had suffered

FIGURE 4.46
A statue of Horace in Venusia today.

Parthian Empire an Empire lying to the east of the Roman Empire, centred on what is now Iran

---

PRESCRIBED SOURCE

Horace, *Ode 3.2*

Date: published in 23 BC

Author: Horace (65–8 BC)

Genre: lyric poetry

Significance: a poem reflecting on how military training should prepare aristocratic young Romans both for life on campaign and for later civilian life

Read it here: OCR source booklet

EXPLORE FURTHER

You can read about the Roman defeat to the Parthians at Carrhae in Plutarch's *Life of Crassus*, Chapters 24 and 25.

PS

a crushing defeat to the Parthians at Carrhae. However, during the 20s BC, Augustus negotiated a reasonable settlement, which ended in a formal peace being signed in 20 BC.

In stanzas 2 and 3, Horace then imagines a scene from a war in which such a young officer would fight. The poem views the war from the perspective of a young woman and her mother, who is the wife of the local ruler hostile to Rome. The young woman watches from the walls of her city in terror and speaks as follows:

> "Alas, don't let my royal bridegroom unskilled in war
> provoke the lion that's dangerous to touch,
> whom blood-stained anger sends raging
> swiftly through the midst of slaughter."

Horace, Ode 3.2, lines 9–12

How might this stanza be thought powerful? First of all, we hear from one of the victims of the Roman army in her own words, a young woman who will not herself fight but must watch instead. The terror she feels at the uneven match-up between her beloved and a highly trained Roman soldier gives the impression that even Rome's enemies recognise that Roman soldiers are far better than their own. There is also great pathos at the prospect that the young woman's fiancé will die before their wedding day. Furthermore, in her speech she uses a **metaphor** to describe the ferocity of the young Roman. She does not refer to him as a person but simply as a lion dangerous to touch, an image easy for the reader to form vividly. We might also notice in the stanza two allusions to the *Iliad*, with which Horace would have been very familiar. Lion imagery to describe fighters is common in Homer, while the idea of a non-combatant watching her beloved fighting from the walls of her city echoes the scene at the start of *Iliad*, Book 22.

The fourth stanza starts with one of the most famous lines from Roman poetry – in Latin it reads: 'dulce et decorum est pro patria mori'. It is very similar to the first line of Tyrtaeus' 'Fallen Warrior' poem, and some commentators think that Horace may have been consciously imitating it. Moreover, the idea of death in battle being 'sweet' ties closely in with Tyrtaeus' description of such a death as 'beautiful' later in the same poem. In the rest of the stanza, Horace emphasises that death comes to all of us – even to those who flee from battle; they will end up, shamefully, wounded from behind rather than in front. In these lines, Horace uses **personification**, whereby something non-human is given human characteristics to make it more vivid, by suggesting that death literally pursues the fleeing soldier.

The fifth stanza moves the focus from military to civilian life. The key theme is found in the word 'Virtue', and Horace uses a second personification to emphasise this – Virtue is personified both here and in the next stanza. This virtue, which suggests a combination of courage and good character, may have been learnt in the army but should be applied to all areas of life. The man who shows this virtue does not take his sense of self-worth from worldly successes, for example by winning an election (the reference to 'axes' indicates that the poem is talking about senior politicians, since their symbol of power was the **fasces**, a bundle of rods with an axe-head emerging from the top). Such a man is not driven by a need to please the mass of the common people, but instead his character remains constant. Many commentators think that Horace is here referring to the emperor Augustus, and signalling that he is the great man who can show such virtue.

metaphor a figure of speech in which a word or phrase is used to describe something that it cannot literally be

personification a figure of speech by which something non-human is given human characteristics

fasces a bundle of rods with an axe-head, which were the symbol of the authority of a senior Roman magistrate

This interpretation makes even more sense when we examine the sixth stanza, which continues with the theme of virtue. The poet claims that the virtuous man will journey to the heavens on wings, where he will be given a place among the gods. The Romans believed that only the greatest heroes were worthy of becoming divine after death, but Emperors were often included in this category. Once again, this suggests that Horace is describing the emperor Augustus. A great contrast is made with the common people, who do not have the character to ascend to the gods after death.

In the final two stanzas, the poem changes direction once again. These stanzas focus on the quality of keeping a discreet silence – those who transgress this principle will eventually be punished for their indiscretion. Silence is presented as a sacred duty, not least by the mention of 'those secret **rites of Ceres**'. This is a reference to an ancient Greek religious cult, the Eleusinian Mysteries, which centred on the worship of the goddess of the harvest, Demeter (known to the Romans as Ceres) at Eleusis near Athens. Those who became initiated into the cult took part in its secret rites (religious practices) and were promised a blissful life after death. However, they had to swear to keep the secrets of the cult and were not allowed to divulge what took place during the rites. Those who transgressed this faced the death penalty. Interestingly for our poem, the emperor Augustus himself became an initiate of the Mysteries, and was reportedly well known for his discretion.

In these stanzas Horace says that he will avoid the company of the indiscreet man, and thereby seems to encourage his readers to do the same. He concludes by saying that even if Jupiter sometimes punishes the innocent with the guilty, the guilty never manage to get away with their crimes, even if it takes time for punishment to catch up with them. The point here is that it is best to avoid the company of indiscreet people since Jupiter is likely to bring them to ruin at some point – perhaps by a house falling in or by drowning at sea – and, since Jupiter sometimes allows the innocent to suffer with the guilty, it is advisable to keep out of the way of such people so as not to share their fate. In the final stanza, Horace uses a third personification – this time of Punishment. One could compare the way in which death and punishment both catch up with people who do not live up to Roman ideals in stanzas 4 and 8 respectively.

The last two stanzas are something of a mystery, and seem to represent somewhat of an anti-climax from the previous two. There is no clear way to interpret them, but perhaps one point is that most Romans, even educated ones, cannot aspire to the greatness of Augustus. However, they can serve the Roman state well, and this will involve loyalty and discretion. One way of reading this is to relate it to the growing imperial civil service that Augustus had established. Educated Romans working in this bureaucracy would have needed to keep secrets and to be loyal. There is another way to read this, which is to relate it more directly to Horace himself. By the time of this poem, Horace is no doubt living and working within the Emperor's circle; these final stanzas could therefore be read as the poet talking about himself and his own loyalty to the Emperor – he understands how to behave and who to avoid.

In just thirty-two lines Horace covers a great deal of ground, with a variety of images and themes. The courage learnt by the upper-class soldier will stand him in good stead for his civilian service to the Roman state, a state that looks to the example of the emperor Augustus as its ultimate role model.

S & C The line 'dulce et decorum est pro patria mori' was famously used by the First World War poet Wilfred Owen in his poem entitled: *Dulce et Decorum Est*. Read this poem yourself. Why does Owen describe Horace's line as 'the old Lie'? How is the tone of Owen's poem different from that of Horace?

---

rites of Ceres an ancient Greek religious cult, also known as the Eleusinian Mysteries, in which members were sworn to secrecy

---

ACTIVITY

Imagine that you are asked to present the moral messages of this poem in a school assembly. Write an assembly that includes and explains the examples and morals that Horace puts forward.

Study question

How effectively does Horace use imagery in this poem?

EXAM TIP

Explaining personification

In this poem, personification is used of three concepts: death, virtue and punishment. If you comment on personifications such as these, try not to say simply 'this is effective because Horace uses a personification'. Rather, explain why you think that the personification is effective. For example, you might say that virtue is such a powerful and important quality in the poem that Horace personifies it in order to present it as something that has a way of behaving and a character all of its own.

TOPIC REVIEW

You should be able to:

1. Describe:
   - the historical context in which Horace wrote his odes
   - the outline of *Ode 3.2*
   - the three different stages of *Ode 3.2*.

2. Explain:
   - the key themes of the poem, particularly bravery and cowardice
   - the importance of the emperor Augustus in the poem
   - the literary techniques used in the poem to make it powerful.

PRACTICE QUESTIONS

Source A: Horace, *Ode 3.2*, lines 25–32

And there's a sure reward for loyal silence:
I'll forbid the man who divulges the secret
rites of Ceres, to be under the same
roof as me, or to untie with me

the fragile boat: neglected Jupiter often
includes the innocent with the guilty,
but slow-footed Punishment rarely
gives up on the wicked man, despite his start.

1. a. What is Horace referring to by the words 'the rites of Ceres'? [2]
   b. What is the significance of this reference in the context of this poem. [1]
2. How does Horace convey the personal qualities expected of a well-trained Roman soldier?
   Make **two** points and support your points with reference to Source A. [4]

4.8 Virgil

TOPIC OVERVIEW

Literary context

- The genre and author of your text
- Its composition and aims
- Narrative and descriptive techniques, including:
  - speeches
  - similes and imagery
  - epithets
  - use of emotive language
  - the role of the divine

Characterisation

- The actions of the characters in your selections
- The traits of each of the main characters and how these are depicted
- Interactions and relationships between characters
- The depiction of:
  - leaders and soldiers
  - comrades and enemies
  - non-combatants
  - women

Themes

- Glory, honour and shame
- Comradeship
- Freedom
- Hubris and arrogance
- Love and patriotism
- The horror and glorification of warfare
- Fear and courage
- Family and ancestors
- Military and civilian victims of war

Heroes and warfare

- How the content of your selections reflects its political or cultural context, including:
  - details of the historical context
  - what constitutes a 'hero'
  - attitudes towards war and warfare
- The possible responses to the text from different audiences

The prescribed source for this topic is:

- Virgil, *Aeneid*, Book 2.268–end

Don't forget that you will be given credit in the exam if you study extra sources and make relevant use of them in your answers.

This topic will examine Virgil and his *Aeneid*, starting with what we know about his life and the context of his famous poem the *Aeneid*. It will then move on to focus on *Aeneid*, 2.268 to the end. As with your other authors, you should refer to the topic boxes at the start of the chapter to think about how this poem includes many of the themes mentioned there.

BIOGRAPHY

Since Roman times, Virgil's *Aeneid* has been acknowledged as the greatest work of Latin literature; indeed, for Romans, Virgil held the pre-eminent status that Shakespeare holds for English speakers today. As with all our authors, we must start by finding out something about his life and times.

Publius Virgilius Maro was born near Mantua in northern Italy in 70 BC to a land-owning family. He was therefore able to receive a good education, which culminated with his moving to study in Rome as a young man. In his early 30s, he published his first set of poems, the *Eclogues*, which focused on life in the countryside. At around this time he came to the attention of Maecenas, whom we have read about on p. 424; like Horace, Virgil was welcomed into Maecenas' circle of poets who wrote poetry supportive of Octavian (Virgil and Horace became very close friends – so close, in fact, that in *Ode 1.3* Horace refers to Virgil as 'the other half of my soul').

When Octavian took sole command of the Roman world after the battle of Actium and adopted the name Augustus, he invited Virgil to compose a great poem in praise of his new regime – a national poem for Rome and its empire. Virgil duly spent the remaining years of his life writing the *Aeneid*, which was almost complete when he died in 19 BC. Tradition has it that on his deathbed he asked that the manuscript be burnt, but Augustus forbade this and so the poem survived; indeed, there are still a few lines that are only half-finished – probably evidence that Virgil had not quite completed his task.

FIGURE 4.47
Virgil holds a volume of the *Aeneid*. He is flanked by the muses of history and tragedy, Clio and Melpomene.

LITERARY CONTEXT

Virgil chose to set his great poem in the world of the Trojan War. To understand why he did this, it is important to appreciate the enormous influence that Greek literature had on the Roman world.

Before the third century BC, the Romans had almost no literary tradition – for centuries, Rome had been an agricultural community and its people had developed little love of writing. It was only when the Romans came into contact with the Greek world in the third and second centuries BC that they began to develop their own literature, inspired by the many great Greek writers whom they could now read. Roman poetry therefore came to be heavily influenced by earlier Greek models – something symbolised by the fact that the Romans had no native word that simply meant 'poet', and so borrowed the Greek 'poeta'. It is also worth noting that this is the period in which the Romans started to merge their own native gods with the Greek gods and their accompanying mythology (e.g. the Roman god Mercury became associated with Hermes, the Roman goddess Minerva became associated with Athena, etc.).

The *Iliad* and the *Odyssey* came to be recognised as pre-eminent classics by educated Romans, just as they long had been in the Greek world. We have already met the figure of Aeneas in Book 5 of the *Iliad* – a leading Trojan warrior and the son of the goddess Aphrodite. Later in the poem (20.300–308), Poseidon says that Aeneas is destined to survive the sack of Troy, and also that he and his descendants are fated to rule over the Trojans for generations. Later Greek writers who wanted to continue the saga of Troy therefore wrote of Aeneas' wanderings after the war, and one tradition brought him to Italy. As Romans came to admire Greek civilisation more and more, they became especially interested in this tradition; the idea grew that the Trojans led to Italy by Aeneas were the ancestors of the Romans – indeed, the founder and first king of Rome, Romulus, was said to have been descended from Aeneas himself.

It was this tradition that Virgil worked with. He chose to make Aeneas the central character of his new poem, which was therefore called the *Aeneid*. One appeal of this was that it placed Rome's ancestors in the heroic age of the Trojan War – Romans too could link themselves to that world of admirable and noble fighters. Although Rome's ancestors were the losers of the war, Virgil portrays the sack of Troy as an act of trickery and deceit on the Greeks' behalf – since the Greeks had won through low tactics, the Trojans could keep a sense of the moral high ground. Moreover, Virgil worked with the Homeric tradition that Aeneas was fated to rule over the Trojans by making the hero's journey to Italy an act of destiny, in which he would establish a new race of people who would go on to found the greatest city on earth. Crucially, in the *Aeneid* Aeneas' son Ascanius marries Lavinia, the daughter of a local Italian king, and so Romulus could be said to be descended both from the Trojans and from native Italians – Virgil's tale wove the two peoples together.

Another advantage of Virgil's method was that his poem could seek to emulate the two greatest poems of Greek literature. Virgil chose to write his poem in hexameter so that he could model himself on Homer as closely as possible, thus creating a Roman epic poem, which he hoped would win comparable status in the Roman world. His imitation of Homer takes many forms, not least his use of epithets and of extraordinarily powerful similes. The gods of the *Aeneid* play a similar role to the gods in the *Iliad*, with Venus (the Roman name for Aphrodite) in particular supporting her son Aeneas, while Juno (Hera) opposes the Trojans at every move. As in the *Iliad*, Jupiter (Zeus) must arbitrate between feuding gods and oversee the workings of fate. However, although Virgil seeks to imitate many of the forms of oral poetry, we should remember that his own poem was written down to be read, and he is said to have taken a painstaking amount of time over each and every line.

AN AUGUSTAN EPIC

Although the *Aeneid* is set in the heroic past, Virgil cleverly manages to establish many links and allusions to the Roman world of his own day. Indeed, one of his key aims is to create a national epic that would speak to his fellow Romans who now ruled the world under the command of Augustus. In addition to allusions, the poem contains three direct prophecies of Rome's future. In Book 1 Jupiter unrolls the scroll of fate and speaks to Venus of the future of Rome; he says that he will allow the Romans to have a limitless empire, one which will be well ruled and at peace under Augustus (lines 257–296). In Book 6 Aeneas travels to the underworld, where his dead father Anchises shows him a parade of great Romans of the future, and Augustus himself is given a prominent place as a glorious conqueror (lines 791–807). Finally, in Book 8 Aeneas is given a new shield (just as Achilles is in the *Iliad*), on which are depicted scenes from later Roman history; in pride of place at its centre is a portrayal of the battle of Actium (lines 675–713, which have already been mentioned on p. 388).

Part of the success of the *Aeneid*, then, is that it can look back to the heroic past as well as speaking about the Roman world of Virgil's day. However, the poet is not blindly patriotic; a key theme of his poem is that creating a Roman Empire will involve great sacrifice and no little tragedy; Aeneas himself suffers greatly, losing amongst others his wife Creusa during the fall of Troy, and being forced by the gods to desert Dido, the woman he loves. Indeed, such is the suffering in the poem that commentators have often wondered just how enthusiastic Virgil felt about Rome's rule of the world, and whether he believed that so much sacrifice was really worthwhile. The poet certainly manages to create great pathos amongst a variety of different characters, some of them in opposition to Aeneas, and the poem allows for no straightforward interpretation. As with the *Iliad*, this is one of its greatest strengths and fascinations.

HEROISM AND PIETAS

We have read about the culture of heroism in the *Iliad*, where warriors were concerned to win time and kleos. In the *Aeneid*, Virgil presents a new type of heroism. It is important to remember that his heroes (and Aeneas in particular) must set an example to Roman readers as to the qualities needed to succeed in ruling the world. In the *Aeneid*, therefore, heroism is not defined simply by one's achievements in battle (although fighting bravely is a key attribute of a hero) but by one's character and temperament in all situations.

> **pietas** the most important heroic quality in the *Aeneid*, a Roman virtue that means 'sense of duty', and applies to a man's duty towards his family, his city and his gods

The most important quality that Aeneas is required to show is **pietas**. This Latin word is hard to translate directly into English (the word 'piety' does not capture it properly), but it might be defined as 'sense of duty', with the understanding that the duty is to your family, to your city and to your gods. Pietas, then, required a Roman to show a sense of responsibility: to his family, for whom he was a role model and provider; to his city and its people, whom he had a patriotic duty to lead or support; and to his gods, whom he was obliged to worship and honour appropriately.

Often, pietas involves great personal sacrifice, since duty must be put before personal desire or happiness. The most famous example of this in the *Aeneid* comes in Book 4, when Aeneas is required to abandon Dido, the queen of Carthage and the woman he loves. The god Mercury comes to tell him that Jupiter commands him to leave Carthage, since he has a duty to found a new race of people in Italy; at this moment, Aeneas must follow the will of the gods, so that he can fulfil his duty to his Trojan people, and also to his young son Ascanius (also called Iulus) who will succeed him. He must therefore put the requirements of pietas before his own interests; Dido is so distraught that, tragically, she takes her own life. It is no wonder that, early in the poem, the founding of the Roman race is described as an enormous struggle.

However, in many ways pietas is an admirable quality, and one episode in Book 2 has provided the most enduring image of this. When Aeneas finally accepts that he must abandon the city of Troy, which is now beyond help after the Greek attack, it is a sign from the heavens which has convinced him. He instructs his elderly father Anchises to climb onto his shoulders so that he can carry him out of the city:

> "Come then, dear father, clasp my neck: I will
> carry you on my shoulders: that task won't weigh on me.
> Whatever may happen, it will be for us both, the same shared risk,
> and the same salvation. Let little Iulus come with me,
> and let my wife follow our footsteps at a distance.
> [. . .]
> You, father, take the sacred objects, and our country's gods,
> in your hands . . ."

Virgil, Aeneid, 2.707–711; 717

Here we have a symbolic moment of pietas in action: Aeneas is following the signs of the gods and providing help to his aged father – the man who is actually the head of his family. Anchises himself holds onto the city's holiest images of its gods, which will be brought all the way to Italy and given a new home there. The future of the Trojan race is symbolised in the figure of Iulus, at this time just a small boy who holds his father's hand. Sadly, however, Aeneas' wife Creusa will not survive the escape.

THE CONTEXT OF BOOK 2

The *Aeneid* is divided into twelve books (these books are somewhat longer than the books of the *Iliad*), and thematically the poem is divided into two halves. The first six books describe the sack of Troy and Aeneas' wanderings thereafter; at the start of Book 7 he arrives at the shores of central Italy, and the last six books focus on the alliances he makes and wars he must fight to establish his people there. It is often said that the first half of the poem is modelled on the *Odyssey*, in which Odysseus must endure many hardships and adventures before arriving home from Troy, and the second half is closer in spirit to the *Iliad*, as we read of the wars between Aeneas and hostile Italian peoples.

Your prescribed reading in Book 2 is therefore located during Aeneas' travels. The action of the poem begins in Book 1 with the Trojan survivors of the destruction of Troy shipwrecked on the shore of North Africa. They find themselves near Carthage, a new city still being built under the watchful eye of its queen, Dido, who is herself a refugee from her own native city of Tyre in Phoenicia (a region roughly corresponding to modern Lebanon). It is Juno who has caused the shipwreck – she remains as implacably opposed to the Trojans as she is during the *Iliad* (as Hera); an additional concern of hers in the *Aeneid* is that Dido's Carthaginians are her favourite people, and she does not want to see a rival city emerge in Italy. Aeneas and the other Trojans who have survived the storm are welcomed by Dido, and invited to stay with her as honoured guests. Book

PRESCRIBED SOURCE

Virgil, *Aeneid*, Book 2.268–end

Date: 19 BC

Author: Virgil (70–19 BC)

Genre: epic poetry

Significance: an account of the night that the Greeks finally sacked and conquered Troy

Read it here: OCR source booklet

S & C Artistic representations of Aeneas fleeing from Troy have survived from Roman times, and it has continued to inspire artists ever since, most notably the seventeenth-century Italian sculptor Bernini. Research his sculpture of this scene shown in Figure 4.48, and how art scholars have interpreted it.

1 ends with a banquet in their honour, during which Venus stirs Dido's heart and she begins to fall in love with Aeneas. She asks him to tell them about the day that Troy was finally conquered.

Book 2 opens with Aeneas starting to speak. He opens by saying that he has been given an impossible task, since no words could ever capture the horrors he has seen or the sufferings that his people have endured; still, he promises to do his best. His narrative picks up the story of the Trojan war soon after the *Iliad* finishes; by now Achilles has been killed too. Before line 268, Aeneas' narrative focuses on the arrival of a huge wooden horse on the shore near the city and the disappearance of the Greek army. The Trojans are unsure what to make of it, and want to believe that it is a peace offering from the Greeks who have conceded defeat and sailed away. A Trojan priest, Laocoon, frantically warns them not to trust the Greeks, claiming that the horse is a trick. At this moment, another man appears: Sinon is his name, and he claims to be a Greek deserter; in fact, he is a Greek spy who deceives the Trojans into believing that the horse is a gift to Athena, which they should take into the city and give a place of honour. After he finishes speaking, a terrible event occurs – two huge snakes appear from the sea and make for Laocoon and his two young sons, suffocating them to death.

The Trojans interpret this to mean that they should avoid following Laocoon's advice, and instead honour the horse as Sinon suggests, and so they drag it into the city.

FIGURE 4.48
This sculpture of Aeneas leaving Troy with Anchises and Ascanius was created by the seventeenth-century Italian artist Bernini.

Study question
Virgil could have chosen to tell the story of the sack of Troy in his own words. Why do you think that he decided instead to have Aeneas retell his own experiences in the first person? How might this make the story more moving and more powerful?

EXPLORE FURTHER
To give you a fuller context for lines 268 to the end of Book 2, try to read the opening 267 lines of the book.

FIGURE 4.49
The journey of Aeneas.

Unknown to them, however, some of the greatest Greek warriors are hidden in its hollow belly – Laocoon was right after all. That night, the Trojans celebrate wildly and then sleep, believing that they have seen off the Greeks at last. As they slumber, the Greek fleet sails back from a nearby island where it has lain hidden. The warriors in the horse climb out and head for the gates, where they kill the guards and open the city to the rest of the Greek army. The scene is set for the final night of the war.

BOOK 2.268–END

Three visions

Your prescribed reading begins with Aeneas telling of a terrifying dream that he has in his sleep that night. This is the first of three important visions that Aeneas will have in the book, and which advise him how to respond to the events around him.

FIGURE 4.50
This Roman sculpture shows Laocoon and his sons being killed by the serpents.

Vision 1 (lines 270–297): Hector

In one of the most famous scenes from the *Aeneid*, the dead Hector appears to Aeneas, his body defiled by its treatment at the hands of Achilles:

> See, in dream, before my eyes, Hector seemed to stand there,
> saddest of all and pouring out great tears,
> torn by the chariot, as once he was, black with bloody dust,
> and his swollen feet pierced by the thongs.
> . . . His beard was ragged,
> his hair matted with blood, bearing those many wounds he received
> dragged around the walls of his city.
>
> Virgil, *Aeneid*, 2.270 273; 277–279

It is a vivid and terrible image, made more poignant by Hector's tears – perhaps they are shed both for his own fate and for the impending fate of his city. Aeneas initially gives a confused response, welcoming Hector as if Troy's saviour has returned just in time. There is great irony in his description of Hector as 'Light of the Troad, surest hope of the Trojans', since Hector can offer no light and no hope. Aeneas' confusion here is symbolic of his struggle throughout the book – he is torn between staying and fighting for Troy, or giving up hope and abandoning the city.

Hector soon sets Aeneas straight: Troy is finished, and Aeneas must flee the city. Moreover, he outlines to Aeneas a new mission: he is to take Troy's holiest religious icons and travel over the seas, after which he will establish a new city. This is a highly symbolic moment in the poem: Hector, the greatest Trojan warrior in the *Iliad*, hands over the leadership of the Trojans to Aeneas and is seen to give him permission to leave their beloved city behind.

Vision 2 (lines 567–623): Venus

After his vision of Hector, Aeneas wakes up and prepares himself to leave his house and gather fellow Trojans to fight – thereby ignoring Hector's advice. He admits that it may be of little use, but fury drives him into battle:

> Frantically I seize weapons: not because there is much use
> for weapons, but my spirit burns to gather men for battle
> and race to the citadel with my friends: madness and anger
> hurl my mind headlong, and I think it beautiful to die fighting.

Virgil, Aeneid, 2.314–317

These are noble sentiments, but they will indeed be useless; Hector's words have made no impact yet. Aeneas has some success in battle, and at one point he and his comrades put on the armour of some Greeks they have killed. They then head towards Priam's palace, where the worst horrors of the night are playing themselves out. On their way they see Cassandra, the priestess daughter of Priam, dragged from a temple of Minerva (the Roman name for Athena). Aeneas is keen to emphasise that as he fights for his city, he gives everything to the cause:

> Ashes of Ilium, death flames of my people, be witness
> that, at your ruin, I did not evade the Danaan weapons,
> nor the risks, and, if it had been my fate to die,
> I earned it with my sword.

Virgil, Aeneid, 2.431–434

We should remember that Aeneas is telling this story to Dido and her guests at a banquet in Carthage, and he will want to emphasise that he did not abandon his city willingly.

Aeneas' account of the deaths of Polites and Priam in the palace is one of the most moving and tragic episodes in the *Aeneid*. Aeneas watches, perched high above, after which he catches sight of Helen. For a moment, all his fury is transferred onto her, and he resolves to kill her. It is at this moment that he receives his second vision: his mother Venus appears before him. She tells him to control his anger and think instead of his duty to his family, whom she is even now protecting from Greek soldiers. Moreover, she explains that the destruction of Troy is ultimately the work of the gods:

> You do not hate the face of the Spartan daughter of Tyndareus,
> nor is Paris to blame: the ruthlessness of the gods, of the gods,
> brought down this power, and toppled Troy from its heights.

Virgil, Aeneid, 2.601–603

After this, Venus alters his sight so that he can see the gods in action in the sack of the city: Neptune, Juno, Minerva and Jupiter are all giving help to the Greeks. Venus sets Aeneas back with his family so that he can protect them. This scene is particularly important since it reinforces to Aeneas what Hector has already said to him – Troy is destined to fall, and there is nothing he can do about it. Aeneas must accept this and follow a new destiny.

Vision 3 (lines 771–794): Creusa

When Aeneas finds himself back home, his father Anchises refuses to leave the city; he is an old man and would prefer death to the life of an exile. Aeneas – showing great pietas – refuses to leave his father behind, and so prepares to return to battle. But his wife Creusa begs him not to leave the family behind. At this moment, the gods intervene once more, sending two omens. First, Ascanius' hair catches fire, although the flame does him no harm. Anchises believes that this is a sign from the gods, and asks Jupiter to confirm it with another; soon afterwards, a shooting star passes through the sky and he is convinced, believing that it is destined for the whole family to leave Troy. It is at this moment that Aeneas lifts his father onto his shoulders, and takes Ascanius by the hand, as we have read on p. 433.

The family make a terrifying escape from the city, with Creusa hanging a little behind them in order to spread the group. It is only when Aeneas reaches the holy mound of Ceres outside the city that he realises that she is no longer with them. In despair, he once again heads back into the city to look for her. He sees his own house in flames as he wanders through the city, and even dares to call out Creusa's name. At this moment, Aeneas receives his third vision of the night: his wife has been killed and her ghost appears to him. She explains that her death is fated by the gods, and that Aeneas must move on without her; she predicts his future:

> Yours is long exile, you must plough
> a vast reach of sea: and you will come to Hesperia's land,
> where Lydian Tiber flows in gentle course among the farmers'
> rich fields. There, happiness, kingship and a royal wife
> will be yours.
>
> Virgil, *Aeneid*, 2.780–784

Hesperia is another name for Italy, while the Tiber is the river which flows through Rome (it is called Lydian since it was believed that some settlers in central Italy came from Lydia in Asia Minor). Aeneas has been given a little more information of the destiny that awaits him. He tries to embrace Creusa, but his hands can only reach through her shadow.

Together, these visions set Aeneas up for his difficult, painful but ultimately triumphant mission after the sack of Troy. They also represent a clever literary device by Virgil, since they allow him to portray his hero in an impressive light, despite his being on the losing side of the war. Indeed, one difficulty for Virgil with his characterisation of Aeneas was how to portray him as a refugee from Troy with his dignity intact. By creating these visions, the hero is seen to have fought as bravely as possible, but to have bowed to the inevitable. He cannot therefore be blamed for abandoning his city – it is the gods' will both that Troy should fall and that Aeneas should survive the night.

Pathos and the horror of war

One of the features of this book is its pathos in portraying the horrors of war. The vision of the dead Hector is an outstanding example of this, as is the tragedy at the end of the book as

Aeneas is widowed. One other profoundly moving episode comes with the death of Priam (lines 526–558). By a great irony, he is heartlessly killed by Pyrrhus, the son of Achilles. Pyrrhus first slaughters Polites, one of Priam's sons, in front of his father's eyes. Priam tells Pyrrhus that he is unworthy of his father, a man who had respected a suppliant's rights. The king tries to fight back but is too old and feeble to do so. In reply, Pyrrhus is heartless:

> Pyrrhus spoke to him: "Then you can be messenger, carry
> the news to my father, to Peleus's son: remember to tell him
> of degenerate Pyrrhus, and of my sad actions:
> now die."

Virgil, *Aeneid*, 2.547–550

Pyrrhus drags the old king to the altar and puts a sword through him. The character of Pyrrhus here embodies the behaviour of the Greeks in Book 2 – they are brutal villains who inspire little sympathy. By contrast, the Trojans are presented as honourable characters and victims of savagery.

Imagery

Another striking feature of the book is the imagery used by Virgil. One prominent image is that of fire representing destruction. Moreover, a number of similes, all of them drawn from the natural world, are woven into the narrative to give mood and context to Aeneas' terrible tale. They can be summarised as follows:

- **The shepherd** (304–309) Aeneas' view of the burning of Troy from his rooftop is compared to a shepherd watching from a peak as fire or a flood attacks his crops (compare the simile at lines 5.85–94 of the *Iliad* mentioned on page 408).
- **The wolves** (355–358) Aeneas and his young companions who head into the city for battle are compared to hungry wolves, desperate to feed their young.
- **The snake (1)** (379–381) Androgeos, a Greek, realises that he has come upon a band of Trojans and recoils in fright like a snake.
- **The winds** (416–419) When Aeneas' Trojan band is attacked from all sides by Greeks, the repeated onslaught of Greek attacks is compared to winds clashing with one another.
- **The snake (2)** (471–475) A second snake simile is used to describe Pyrrhus as he arrives in Priam's palace: he is like a snake with a forked tongue that has fed on poisonous herbs.
- **The river** (496–499) The Greeks bursting into Priam's palace are likened to a river bursting its banks.
- **The doves** (515–516) Hecuba and her daughters seek refuge in the palace like doves trying to find shelter from a storm.
- **The ash tree** (627–631) The sack of Troy is compared to foresters cutting down an ancient ash tree; when it is about to fall it groans in an almost human way.

Just as Homer does, Virgil uses these similes to allow the reader to step back from the fast-paced action for a moment, and to bring to mind an image of what is happening.

ACTIVITY

Choose one or more of the similes on this page, and create a drawing or painting to illustrate the image that you think Virgil is trying to portray.

Pathos

If you comment on a literary device such as pathos, remember to explain why it is effective – what emotions might the author be trying to bring out in the reader in lines rich in pathos?

TOPIC REVIEW

With reference to Virgil, *Aeneid*, 2.268–end, you should be able to:

1. Describe:
   - the historical context in which Virgil wrote the *Aeneid*
   - the storyline in this prescription, including the context in which Aeneas narrates it
   - the roles played by the main characters, including Aeneas, Hector, Creusa, Priam and Pyrrhus
   - examples of imagery used by Virgil.

2. Explain:
   - how the politics of Virgil's time influenced the themes of the *Aeneid*
   - the nature of Aeneas' destiny, and the importance of pietas
   - how warfare is depicted, including examples of heroism and of its innocent victims
   - how Virgil's use of imagery lends power to his narrative.

PRACTICE QUESTIONS

Source A: Virgil, *Aeneid*, 2.518–525

And when she saw Priam himself dressed in youthful armour
she cried: "What mad thought, poor husband, urges you
to fasten on these weapons? Where do you run?
The hour demands no such help, nor defences such as these,
not if my own Hector were here himself. Here, I beg you,
this altar will protect us all or we'll die together."
So she spoke and drew the old man towards her,
and set him down on the sacred steps.

1. Give **three** ways that Virgil creates sympathy for Priam and Hecuba in these lines. Support your points with reference to the passage. [6]

2. 'Pathos is an essential part of ancient war poetry.' Based on the texts you have read, to what extent do you agree with this statement? You should refer to at least **two** texts. [15]

Further Reading for Literature and Culture 2: War and Warfare

Culture

Breeze, David (2016) *The Roman* Army. London: Bloomsbury

Cartledge, Paul (2013) *Thermopylae, the Battle that Changed the World*. London: Pan

Connolly, Peter (2016) *Greece and Rome at* War. Barnsley: Frontline

Lange, Carsten (2011) 'The Battle of Actium: a Reconsideration', *Classical Quarterly* 61(2): 608–623

Lepper, Frank and Sheppard Frere (1988) *Trajan's Column*. Stroud: Sutton

Morrison, J. S., Coates, J. F. and Rankov, N. B. (2000) *The Athenian* Trireme. Cambridge: Cambridge University Press

Strauss, Barry (2005) *The Battle of Salamis*. London: Simon & Schuster

van Wees, Hans (2004) *Greek Warfare: Myths and Realities*. London: Bloomsbury

Literature

Camps, W. A. (1979) *An Introduction to Virgil's Aeneid*. Oxford: Oxford University Press

Jenkyns, R. (2013) *Classical Epic: Homer and Virgil*. London: Bloomsbury

Owen, E. T. (1994) *The Story of the Iliad*. London: Bloomsbury

Powell, Barry B. (2007) *Homer*. London: Blackwell Introductions to the Ancient World

Silk, M. (2010) *Homer: The Iliad*. Cambridge: Cambridge University Press

West, David (2002) *Horace Odes III: dulce periculum*. Oxford: Oxford University Press

West, M. L. (2008) *Greek Lyric Poetry*. Oxford: Oxford University Press

Williams, R. D. (2009) *The Aeneid*. London: Bloomsbury

What to Expect in the Exam for War and Warfare

This chapter aims to show you the types of questions you are likely to get in the written examination. It offers some advice on how to answer the questions and will help you avoid common errors.

THE EXAMINATION

This component of the GCSE examination is designed to test your knowledge, understanding and evaluation of War and Warfare. The examination is worth 90 marks and lasts 1 hour and 30 minutes. This represents 50% of the total marks for the GCSE.

There are two sections to the paper, one focusing on the 'Culture' topics and sources, the other focusing on the 'Literature' – the prescribed sections from Homer, Tyrtaeus, Horace and Virgil. Each section is worth 45 marks, and is therefore worth 25% of your GCSE. The question paper will consist of both short-answer and extended-response questions.

For the 'Culture' section, you will be required to respond to visual and material sources. Some of these will be the prescribed sources you have studied in class, and some of these you will not have seen before. Sources for the 'Literature' section will only be drawn from the prescribed sections of Homer, Tyrtaeus, Horace and Virgil that you have studied.

There are two Assessment Objectives in your GCSE in Classical Civilisation. Questions will be designed to test these areas. The Assessment Objectives are explained in the table below:

	Assessment Objective	Marks
AO1	Demonstrate knowledge and understanding of: • literature and visual/material culture from the classical world • how sources reflect their cultural contexts • possible interpretations of sources by different audiences and individuals.	50
AO2	Analyse, interpret and evaluate literature and visual/material culture from the classical world, using evidence and producing coherent and reasoned arguments.	40

For AO1 in this component, you will need to demonstrate the following:

Culture

- A good range of accurate and relevant knowledge of war and warfare, including how it is presented in material culture.
- What the material culture tells us about ancient war and warfare.
- An understanding of the way different peoples from Greece and Rome fought: the Spartans, the Athenians and the Romans.
- Different interpretations that can be made about material culture representing Greek and Roman warfare, and the different conclusions that can be drawn from it.

Literature

- A good range of accurate and relevant knowledge of the prescribed texts.
- An understanding of the relevant genres, and of the historical and literary context in which the prescribed texts were written.
- Knowledge and understanding of the key themes of each text.
- An understanding of the literary styles of each of the authors.
- Different interpretations that can be drawn from the texts, and the conclusions that can be drawn from these.

For AO2 in this component, you will need to demonstrate that you can analyse, interpret and evaluate the sources you have studied, giving opinions and backing them up with evidence, for example:

Culture

- A range of reasoned opinions about ancient war and warfare.
- Appropriate evaluation of different sources to provide reasoned ideas.

Literature

- A range of reasoned opinions about the genres, characters and themes of the prescribed sources, and about what they can tell us about ancient war and warfare.
- Appropriate analysis of the genres, characters and themes of the prescribed sources, and of what they can tell us about ancient war and warfare.

QUESTION TYPES

There are five types of questions that will feature in your exam. Each type will appear in both the Culture and Literature sections. With the exception of the extended-response questions (see below), all questions will be linked to a source. In the Culture section this will be a piece of material evidence, such as a picture of a site or a work of art, or a literary source. In the Literature section this will be a passage from one of the prescribed texts.

The question types are listed in the table below. They really fall into two categories: the first three types (knowledge and understanding, significance, and stimulus questions) are all short-answer questions. The final two types (detailed-response questions and extended-response questions) require a longer answer.

The final two types will usually be the final questions of each section. The short-answer questions can come in any order. For example, there could be a two-mark knowledge and understanding question, followed by a four-mark stimulus question, followed by a three-mark significance question.

Question type	Number of marks in each section for each question type
Knowledge and understanding questions	9
Significance questions	3
Stimulus questions	10
Detailed-response questions	8
Extended-response questions	15

Knowledge and understanding questions

There will be 9-marks' worth of knowledge and understanding questions in total (all AO1). The 9 marks will be broken down into a series of short-answer questions, typically worth 1, 2 or 3 marks.

Some questions will require you to show your **knowledge** of one of the prescribed texts, or of an object or site from the ancient world. Other questions will require you to show **knowledge** and **also** demonstrate an **understanding** of these facts.

There will be a **source** to assist you. For Literature, this will be a passage from one of your prescribed authors. For Culture, it could be a prescribed source you have studied, or it could be one that you have not seen before.

For example, you might be shown the image of a trireme on the right with the following questions:

Question: (a) How did a trireme get its name? [1]

(b) How did the design of a trireme make it an effective warship? [1]

Answer: (a) It was named after its three banks of rowers [1].

(b) The three banks of rowers gave the ship great power and ability to turn or ram into another ship at speed [1].

Knowing that a trireme has three banks of rowers is a piece of knowledge, and you can then show further understanding of it by explaining how this design made it effective in battle. This answer should be brief. There is in fact no need to write full sentences if it seems that only a single word or a phrase is needed, as is the case in the first part of the answer.

The following represents a typical Literature knowledge and understanding question, together with its answer:

Source A: Virgil, *Aeneid*, 2.270–273

> See, in dream, before my eyes, Hector seemed to stand there,
> saddest of all and pouring out great tears,
> torn by the chariot, as once he was, black with bloody dust,
> and his swollen feet pierced by the thongs.

Question: (a) Who killed Hector? [1]

(b) Why are Hector's feet described as swollen and pierced by thongs? [2]

Answer: Achilles [1]. Hector's feet were swollen because after Achilles killed him, he pierced his feet [1] to tie him to his chariot and drag him away [1].

The first part is asking for one piece of factual knowledge. The second part then asks for a combination of knowledge and understanding. Remember, if you are asked to only give a certain number of facts, or make a certain number of points, you should stick to the instructions.

In this type of question, each correct fact or explanation is worth one mark. You will not be asked to evaluate ideas (e.g. whether you think that a trireme was as well designed as it might have been, or if you approve of Achilles' behaviour), so do not waste time in doing so.

Significance questions

There will be one of these questions in each section. It will be split into two parts. You will be asked to give two pieces of information (2 marks AO1) and state why one or both are important or significant, or what this knowledge tells us (1 mark AO2). Look at the Literature example based on these lines from Homer's *Iliad*:

Source A: Homer, *Iliad*, 22.331–336

> "While you were despoiling Patroclus, no doubt, in your folly, you thought yourself quite safe, Hector, and forgot all about me in my absence. Far from him, by the hollow ships, was a mightier man, who should have been his helper but stayed behind, and that was I, who now have brought you low. The dogs and carrion birds will tear apart your flesh, but him the Achaeans will bury."

(a) Why did Achilles stay by the hollow ships and why does he regret not going into battle with Patroclus? [2]

(b) Why might the Greeks have disapproved of Achilles' decision to remain out of the fighting? [1]

The answers to part (a) are that Hector stripped Patroclus of the armour he was wearing [1] and that Achilles had refused to fight for the Greeks at this point [1]. For the second part, you could explain that the Greeks expected warriors to show courage in battle and to fight for their people [1].

In the Culture section the question might look something like this:

Look at the outline plan of a Roman legionary fortress.

(a) Identify two ceremonial items on display in the temple of the basilica.　[2]

(b) Choose one of these items: why was it important to a typical legionary soldier?　[1]

In part (a) you could say that there was a statue of the emperor [1] and that the legion's standards were also on display there [1].

One mark would be gained in part (b) for saying either that the statue of the emperor would be inspiring for a soldier, or that a standard gave a soldier a sense of pride and loyalty to his century. Remember that you only need to make one point to gain the mark.

Stimulus questions

These questions will ask you to identify something relevant from a stimulus passage or image, and to analyse what you have recognised. Each **relevant** quotation or feature of the image that is picked out will be worth a mark, as will each piece of analysis. Therefore, these questions are each worth equal amounts of AO1 and AO2.

In the Culture section, you might be shown an image of the relief commemorating the battle of Actium (right) and then be asked:

Question:　Identify two features of this image, and suggest what each might tell us about Roman naval warfare.　[4]

Answers:　To gain the first two marks (AO1), you might identify any two of the following features:

- it shows a warship with two banks of oars
- you can see a row of small round shields arranged along the length of the ship
- this one has a crocodile emblem on the prow
- soldiers are standing along the ship and it appears packed
- the soldiers are armed with spears and shields.

To gain the next two marks (AO2), you might make any two of the following suggestions:

- The multiple banks of oars must have made the ship fast
- The upper parts of the ship were protected by the banks of shields
- The crocodile shows that ships had important emblems or symbols on them
- the ships carried large amounts of soldiers
- these soldiers must have boarded other ships, or protected against being boarded as they are dressed for close combat.

In the Literature section, you will be given a passage and might be asked for your opinions on a character or for how the passage is made exciting. For example, you might be given the following passage from Tyrtaeus' Fragment 10 and the question below:

Source A: Tyrtaeus, *Fragment 10*, lines 15–27

Do not run away abandoning your elders – agèd men, whose limbs are no longer nimble. For it is of course shameful for an older man fallen among fighters at the front to lie ahead of the young men, his head already white and beard grey, gasping his stalwart spirit out into the dust, clutching his bloody genitals in his own hands – a shameful thing in one's eyes, a sight to cause indignation – his naked skin exposed.

What point do you think Tyrtaeus is making in this passage? Use **two** phrases from the passage and suggest what they tell us about his message.   [4]

You would be expected to select two phrases and analyse how they communicate Tyrtaeus' message. You might choose the phrase 'his head already white and beard grey' and say that Tyrtaeus is emphasising the old age of the soldier who should not have to be fighting in the front line. You might say that the phrase 'clutching his bloody genitals in his own hands' emphasises the horror and indignity that an old man must suffer when dying in war.

Look at the number of marks available. If there are two pieces of evidence (e.g. choosing two phrases) and two pieces of analysis required, do not give more than this amount. You will be using up time that would be better spent in detailed-response and extended-response questions.

Detailed-response questions

You will get one of these questions in each section with one or more source to prompt you. This source is meant only as a starting point, and it will be clear from the question that you will need to bring in **extra information and examples**.

Four marks are awarded for your knowledge and understanding (AO1), and four marks given for your analysis, interpretation and evaluation of your facts and understanding (AO2). These questions are marked in a different way, however; you are not given one mark for each correct opinion and each piece of evidence, but the answer as a whole is marked using a Levels of Response Grid. A Levels of Response Grid explains to examiners what answers may look like to achieve a certain number of marks. An examiner will read the whole answer and then check the grid to work out what level the answer belongs to. It is important to remember that the quality of your answer is more important than the amount you have written. The Levels of Response Grid is included in the mark schemes for exam papers.

It is also important to remember that for AO1 you will need to show knowledge and understanding of a source's context and the different ways people interpret the sources. Remember that you can examine both sides of an argument. For example, if you are asked whether you admire the character of Diomedes in the *Iliad*, there are likely to be arguments on both sides of the question. It may be that you largely admire him, but that he has some flaws, or that you largely do not admire him but that he has some redeeming features. If you do not examine both sides of an argument, you may have missed some key facts, and your answer may not show a full evaluation.

This question is not meant to be an essay. You are advised not to write an introduction that simply outlines how you will write your response, as this will not add anything to your answer and will take up valuable time. You may find you have more to say than time allows, so you might have to be disciplined in moving on. Make your key points at the start, keep to the point, and if you do choose to have a conclusion, keep it brief, as you will ideally have answered the precise wording of the question throughout your answer. It is not necessary to have a conclusion to gain full marks.

For example, on the paper you might be given the following quotation:

Source A: Vegetius, *About Military Matters*, 1.6–7

A young recruit should keep his eyes watchful and his head upright. He should be broad-chested, with muscly shoulders and strong arms, and his fingers should be on the longer side. He should have a flat stomach and a lean bottom. His calves and feet should not be flabby, but rather full of tough sinews.

You might then be asked the question:

How well did the training of a Roman legionary soldier prepare him for life in the Roman army? Use the source as a starting point and your own knowledge in your answer. [8]

In order to show that you know about the training of a soldier, you might include some of these facts:

- recruits had to be physically strong and alert
- they were trained to do drill route marches
- they also practised swimming, jumping, running and riding
- there was offensive weapons training with a wooden sword and javelin
- there was defensive training with a wicker shield
- recruits were also taught to build a camp.

You then need to weigh up how well this training prepared him for life in the Roman army:

- soldiers needed to be physically strong to fight well, build camps etc.
- drilling instilled discipline and teamwork, which was vital for military efficiency
- route marches prepared him for marching through a province at speed, particularly at a time of war
- activities such as riding and swimming developed other skills, which could come in useful in times of war or peace
- being able to use both offensive and defensive weapons efficiently was vital to success in battle
- building a camp quickly would enable the legion to move around a province and house itself efficiently.

Half the marks are awarded for AO1 and for AO2, but remember this does not necessarily mean that you should give four facts and four explanations. Examiners will read your whole response and judge how good they feel it is overall.

In Section B, on Literature, a question might ask you about the importance of a theme, or the portrayal of one particular character or episode.

Extended-response questions

This type of question is different from all the other questions in two respects: there is no stimulus passage to introduce it, and you will be given a **choice** of questions to answer (there are two extended-response questions in each section, and you must do **only one**). However, it is marked using a Levels of Response Grid in the same way as the detailed-response question.

Five marks are awarded for your knowledge and understanding (AO1), and ten marks given for your analysis, interpretation and evaluation of your facts and understanding (AO2). This means more marks are awarded for how good your argument is than for simply what you know. Therefore, you might want to spend a bit of time thinking about the structure of your answer. As for the detailed-response question, it is important to remember that for AO1 you will need to show knowledge and understanding of the literary and historical context of sources and the different ways people interpret them.

Extended-response questions will be broader than the detailed response questions, and will draw upon material from across topics of either the Literature or the Culture sections. However, these questions will never cover both Literature and Culture. For example, whereas you might be asked a question about the training of a legionary soldier in a detailed-response question, as shown on p. 447, an extended-response question might ask about life in the Roman army more generally, or even ask you to compare the Roman army with the armies of Athens or Sparta.

The following is an example of a possible extended-response Literature question:

> 'The willingness to die bravely in battle was the most important quality of an ancient soldier.' Based on the literary sources you have read, to what extent do you agree with this statement? [15]

There is a great deal of evidence you could draw on from your four sources to answer this question, and you are unlikely to be able to use all of it (remember too that you can get credit for introducing material from outside the prescribed sources, so if you have read ancient authors' accounts of war, you could draw on these too). You might include some of these facts:

- *Iliad*: Hector dies bravely, but wishes rather to save Troy.
- *Iliad*: Diomedes and Glaucus put the importance of xenia above risking their lives fighting one another.
- *Iliad*: the women of Book 6 try to keep Hector back from the fighting.
- *Iliad*: Priam and Hecuba beg Hector not to fight Achilles in Book 22.
- *Fragment 10*: a young man dying in the front line is described as 'beautiful', and it is shameful to be defeated or to let an old man die instead.

- *Ode 3.2*: dying for one's country is sweet and fitting, but the poem also hopes that the young Roman will defeat the Parthians in battle.
- *Aeneid*: Aeneas says that it is beautiful to die in battle.
- *Aeneid*: Aeneas is persuaded to leave Troy and lead the surviving Trojans instead.
- *Aeneid*: the elderly Priam wants to fight, but is persuaded by Hecuba to wait beside the altar instead.

You then need to analyse whether the willingness to die in battle really was the most important quality for an ancient soldier. You might draw conclusions such as:

It was the most important quality because:

- In the *Iliad*, when Hector knows he is doomed, he chooses to die bravely in order to win a glorious reputation.
- Achilles remembers Patroclus most for the brave way he died in battle.
- There are many examples in Book 5 of warriors dying bravely, and this is sometimes the only times they are mentioned in the poem.
- In Fragment 10, the success of an army and therefore of Sparta itself depends on young soldiers putting their lives on the line.
- Horace's description of a brave death in battle as 'sweet and fitting' shows that it was vital to the success of the Roman army against enemies such as the Parthians.
- Despite being in a hopeless situation, Aeneas is prepared to put his life at risk because he believes it is the right thing to do.

It is not the most important quality because:

- The meeting of Diomedes and Glaucus shows that family ties can sometimes be more important than risking your life.
- Hecuba, Andromache and Helen would all prefer Hector to stay within the walls and not risk his life in Book 6, as would Priam and Hecuba in Book 22.
- Hector would have preferred to have been good enough to defeat Achilles than to die bravely in battle at his hands.
- Horace suggests that the Roman army was a training for civilian life where other qualities, such as virtue and tact, would be the most important.
- Aeneas' duty to lead the Trojan people and their household gods to another land is seen as more important than dying bravely in battle.
- Priam is encouraged to seek refuge at the altars of the gods than to die fighting.

Key points

The following applies to both detailed-response questions and extended-response questions:

- Your facts must be **relevant**. Do not merely state everything you know about a particular topic.

- It is a common mistake in the literature to over-narrate the plot and to retell a whole story. You should instead **summarise** the main points, or focus in detail on one or two parts of it. This is particularly important in your extended-response answer, where five marks are available for your knowledge, but 10 marks are given for your evaluation, interpretation and analysis.

- Show that you **understand** things from an ancient point of view wherever possible. For example, characters in the literature texts may have had different attitudes to slavery than we would today, or Roman baths may have seemed far more luxurious to the Romans than they would do to us today.

- Evaluation is best done throughout the response. **Keep referring back** to the title in your essay to do this. If you give all your facts, and then give all your opinions, it is easy to miss something out, or to run out of time.

- Try to find a **balance** of ideas as the question will usually require you to argue both for and against an idea.

- Sometimes a piece of evidence can be taken two ways. If so, remember to give **both interpretations** in order to show a high level of understanding.

- You will not have a lot of time to do these questions and so it is always best to give your most important arguments first in case you find yourself running out of time.

- Ultimately make your conclusion **logical**, and supported by evidence from your whole answer, not just one part of it.

Look at these two extracts attempting to answer the question above:

Extract 1

It is very important to be willing to die bravely in battle. In the *Iliad*, Hector dies bravely in battle even though he could have stayed in Troy with his wife. His wife and mother do not want him to fight and offer him some wine instead, but Greek women didn't understand how important it was to be brave. Loads of fighters die bravely when fighting Diomedes so it must have been important to do this. However, Achilles is a wimp and stays out of the fighting, and so does Paris. Tyrtaeus says that Spartans must be prepared to die in battle or else old men will die instead and people will be homeless. Horace also says that it is good to die in battle, although Roman soldiers could be really scary if you were up against them and you hadn't had enough training. But in the *Aeneid* Aeneas does not think it is important to die in battle and wants to escape from Troy instead.

Extract 2

I believe that the willingness to die in battle was an important quality for an ancient soldier, but not the most important. It is certainly important for Hector to die bravely when he knew that his time had come, but he clearly would have preferred to have been a better fighter so that he would be a match for Achilles. In this case, the most important quality was to be a great fighter. Moreover, the fact that in both Book 6 and Book 22 members of Hector's family urge him not to fight outside the walls suggests that to them it was more important for him to be alive to look after them than to die bravely. Similarly, in the *Aeneid*, it is clearly an important quality to be willing to die in battle – Aeneas describes such a death as 'beautiful' – but ultimately it is made clear to him in a series of three visions of Hector, Venus and Creusa that his duty to lead the Trojans to a new land is more important.

Notice how the first extract spends more time on presenting the facts than giving opinions, and some of the facts are irrelevant. The evaluation is not developed fully, and the final statement is not made relevant to the question. The second extract is much more concise, and is much more balanced, and it focuses on the issue of whether the willingness to die in battle was the **most** important quality. It flows smoothly from one example to another, providing a rounded view of the answer to the question.

GENERAL EXAM SKILLS

When you are sitting the examination, read the instructions carefully so that you realise which questions are compulsory and which are optional (the only option you have is which of the two extended response questions you choose to answer). Remember that the examination will have a range of difficulty of questions; some of it is designed to be challenging, and you should not be panicked if you cannot think of an answer immediately. The following pieces of advice may seem obvious, but you should not underestimate their importance:

- The examination lasts 90 minutes and is worth 90 marks. Don't assume this means you should spend a minute per mark: in reality a lot of short questions will take less than a mark a minute and you should spend longer than a mark a minute on the longer questions.
- Both the Culture and Literature sections are worth 45 marks. Do not spend too long on whichever you choose to do first; this is especially tempting if you like the questions that have been set and feel you could say a lot.
- If you see a question that you do not know the answer to, move on quickly to another question and don't waste time thinking. Leave enough time to go back to it as during the examination you might well remember the answer.
- Stick to the question: if you are asked for facts, do not give opinions and vice versa.
- Do not try to answer a slightly different question if you wish another had been set, or if you have practised a similar one before at school.
- For detailed-response and extended-response questions, present different interpretations.
- More marks are available in the paper for opinions than knowledge or understanding. It is vital that you do not over-narrate, especially in your Literature answers.

GLOSSARY

Component-specific glossaries can be found on the companion website.

Achaeans Homeric term for the Greeks

acropolis the highest point of a Greek city, usually reserved for religious buildings

Actium port on the west coast of Greece, it is now called Preveza

aegis the breastplate or shield of Athena that contained an image of a gorgon in the centre

agoge the training school that all Spartan boys attended from the age of seven

aidos the shame or respectful modesty a Homeric character feels towards someone who has great timē

ala a cohort of Roman cavalry, theoretically 512 strong

Altis the sacred area in the centre of Olympia that contained religious buildings

Amazons a mythical race of women from Asia Minor

Amazonomachy mythic battle between the Greeks and Amazons

amphora (pl. **amphorae**) a clay storage jar, often containing wine or olive oil, with two carrying handles

Anthesteria a Greek festival to Dionysus and the dead held over three days in late January or early February

anthropomorphism giving human form or attributes to something that is otherwise not human

aphorism a short saying that communicates a common truth

apobates in Greek means *dismounter*. A chariot race in which the rider would dismount and remount his chariot during the race

apodyterium changing room in a baths complex

aquila the emblem of the legion, an eagle made of gold set on a pole

aquilifer the legionary soldier responsible for carrying the aquila

Argives Homeric term for the Greeks

aristeia a scene in an epic poem in which a great warrior fights with exceptional courage

Asia Minor the western two thirds of modern Turkey

atrium the main room of the Roman domus, where the family received friends and clients

Attica the region around Athens in south-eastern Greece

augur a person who reads the flight of birds to predict the outcome of future events

Augustales Roman public officials connected to preserving the honour of the emperor, largely drawn from the ranks of freedmen

Bacchanalia a Roman festival in honour of Bacchus

ballista a Roman crossbow that fired iron darts

bard a public storyteller who recited vast amounts of poetry to the accompaniment of the lyre, often during banquets

basilica the large hall used for assemblies of troops in a Roman legionary fortress

blood sacrifice the killing of an animal as offering to a god

caduceus a traveller's staff most closely associated with the god Hermes (Mercury)

caldarium the hot room in a baths complex

camp prefect the assistant to the legatus of a Roman legion

Capitoline Hill one of the seven original hills of Rome, it was the political and ceremonial heart of the city

carceres the starting cages for the chariots – there were twelve in all

cella (Greek: **naos**) meant *small room* in Latin and was the room of the temple that contained the cult statue

cena the Roman word for a dinner

centaur a mythical creature with the upper body of a man and lower body of a horse

Centauromachy mythical battle between the Centaurs and Lapiths

centurion the commander of the century in a Roman legion

century a unit of about 80 men in a Roman legion (there were some double-sized centuries of 160 men)

Cerealia a major festival in honour of Ceres held in Rome every year between 12th and 19th April

chamber tomb a tomb, dug from rock, in which a body or bodies would be buried in a chamber

chiton a large, loose-fitting, woollen tunic worn in ancient Greece

choregos *chorus director*? the financial backer of a set of plays at the City Dionysia in Athens

chthonic relating to the gods that were connected with the earth and the underworld

cist grave a grave in the form of a stone-lined pit, dug into the earth, and covered up

client a Roman who would attach himself to a wealthier patron in order to boost his income and business opportunities

cloisonné the soldering of a wire onto metal and then putting glass or gemstones in the soldered pattern

cohort the largest unit of a Roman legion; the first cohort of a legion had five double-centuries; cohorts two to ten each consisted of six centuries;

colonnade an open-air covered walkway supported by columns

consul the most important public official in Rome after the emperor; two consuls were elected annually

contubernium a unit of eight men in a Roman legion who shared the same tent and dealt with their own mess arrangements

corbelling a technique used to span a gap between two walls by placing increasingly larger blocks of stone on each other, thereby creating a vaulted roof

cornicen the horn-player in a Roman legion who sounded orders to the soldiers

cornucopia a horn shell that contained an endless supply of food and drink

cultrarius an official at a Roman sacrifice who slit the throat of the sacrificial animal

curse tablet a tablet on which someone wrote a prayer to the gods asking them to put a curse on an enemy

Danaans Homeric term for the Greeks

diadem a crown often associated with gods or kings

diekplous a naval manoeuvre whereby a trireme sailed through the enemy line of ships and turned at pace to ram the side of an enemy ship

dithyramb a choral dance in honour of the god Dionysus

domus a large Roman private house in a city or town

Doric frieze a continuous strip of stone or marble divided into square spaces called metopes

dramatic irony when a character does not know the full significance of what is happening or being said, but the readers do

dromos a passageway leading to the tholos tomb

ekphora the funeral procession in ancient Greece

elegy a genre of poetry that can focus on a number of topics, and where lines have an alternating metre of hexameter followed by pentameter

Eleutherae a town on the northern border of Attica

enomotia a 'sworn-band', the smallest unit of the Spartan army

epic poetry poetry focusing on great deeds, composed in hexameter verse

Epicureanism a philosophy of life that encouraged people to live for simple pleasures and to reduce anxieties as much as possible

epithet an adjectival word or phrase regularly added to a name to denote a personal or physical quality

eponymous archon an Athenian magistrate elected for one year (eponymous meaning that the civil year was named after him)

equites members of the second social class in Rome; an equestrian had to own property worth at least 400,000 sesterces

Etruscans the exact origins of the Etruscans are not known, although it is believed that they inhabited Italy from at least the 9th/8th century BC. By the time Rome was founded they were well established in Italy

exclamation a figure of speech in which a writer seems to exclaim words aloud

fasces a bundle of rods with an axe-head, which were the symbol of the authority of a senior Roman magistrate

fate a set of future events that are destined to happen and cannot be changed

figurine a small statue of a person, god or animal

formula (pl. **formulae**) a section of an epic poem, longer than an epithet, that is regularly used to describe a person, place or object

fresco a painting originally done on damp plaster in which the colours become fixed as the plaster dries

frieze a horizontal sculptured or painted decoration depicting a scene or number of scenes

frigidarium the cold room in a baths complex

funeral club a social club set up to support the less wealthy members of Roman society

funerary mask a mask made by placing wax on the deceased's face to take their image. When it was dry it was taken off and sorted in the family shrine

Gaul a Roman province to the west of the Alps encompassing much of modern day France and northern Italy

Genesia a Greek festival to dead ancestors celebrated in late September

genre a category of literature, examples of which might include epic, tragedy, comedy, history and satire

gilding the covering of a surface in a thin layer of gold

grammaticus a teacher for secondary-aged children in the Roman world

granulation dropping molten metal onto an object to give a spotted effect

Great Panathenaia an Athenian festival to Athena that took place every four years and contained more athletic and literary competitions than the annual Panathenaia

haruspex (pl. **haruspices**) a Roman priest who read omens from entrails

hecatomb the sacrifice in honour of a god of at least 100 bulls during large festivals

Hellenes a collective name for the Greeks, a group of peoples who shared the same social and religious customs and language

helots a large class of enslaved native inhabitants of Messenia and Laconia who worked the land for their Spartan masters

hequetai the nobles in Mycenae; they were probably also important troops in the army

hexameter a poetic metre that has six units to a line

hiereia (pl. **hiereiai**) 'one who sacrifices to a god', a Greek priestess

hiereus (pl. **hiereis**) 'one who sacrifices to a god', a Greek priest

hind a deer

Hispania a Roman province covering the area of Spain

Homeric question the debate about the authorship of the *Iliad* and the *Odyssey* and about the identity of Homer

hoplite a heavily-armed Greek infantry soldier who fought in the phalanx

hydra a many-headed serpent monster

hypocaust underfloor heating system

hypozomata two stretched cables that were tied from one end of a trireme to another and kept it in shape

iconography the symbols attached to a particular character when represented in an image

Imperial Period the period of Roman history from 30 BC, when Rome was ruled by emperors

impluvium the pool in the centre of the atrium of a Roman domus that gathered rainwater

infamis literally 'shameful' or 'disgraceful', the very low legal status given to a number of groups in the Roman world, including gladiators, charioteers, actors and prostitutes

inlay a technique where one metal is put on top of another on an object

insula (pl. **insulae**) the Roman name for a block of flats

Ionic frieze an unbroken strip of marble that goes all the way around a temple

irony a way of expressing what you mean by using language that normally suggests the opposite

Kerameikos an area of Athens which included the main burial ground outside the city

kleos the glorious reputation a Homeric warrior hopes to win

kōmos meaning *revel*. A party that took place in the streets in honour of the god Dionysus

krater a large bowl used for mixing wine and water

krypteia a period of survival training for the strongest Spartans in their mid-to-late teens

kylix (pl. **kylixes**) a drinking cup

lament a passionate expression of grief or sorrow

Lapiths a mythical race of men based in Thessaly, northern Greece

lararium a small shrine to the household gods (Lares) that was found in Roman homes

Lares the Roman family's household gods, representing the spirits of the family ancestors

lawagetas the leader of the people in Mycenae, who was also probably the leader of the army

legatus the commander of the Roman legion

legion the largest unit of the Roman army

libation a drink offering poured in honour of the gods

Liburnian galley a Roman warship

liburnae swift Roman military ships which were used for scouting

linchpin (pl. **linchpins**) a fastener used to stop a wheel from coming off its axis

litter a portable taxi carried by slaves in the Roman world

litterator a teacher for primary-aged children in the Roman world

liturgy a super-tax on the wealthiest citizens in Athens to fund important civic projects

lituus staff used by a Roman augur

lochoi units of a tribal regiment in the Athenian army

Lupercal the cave in the Palatine Hill of Rome where the Lupercalia took place

Luperci a priest of Lupercus

Lupercus a Roman god of fertility and purification

lot the random drawing of a name from a pot

lyre a small Greek harp consisting of a sound box with two curved arms connected by a crossbar from which strings are attached

lyric poetry personal poetry originally performed to the lyre for an audience

maenads female followers of Dionysus

magistrate an elected politician in Rome

Magna Graecia 'Great Greece', the term used to describe the region of southern Italy and Sicily where there were many independent Greek cities

Manes meaning 'the deified ancestors', these were the spirits of the dead in the Roman world

mantis (pl. **manteis**) a Greek soothsayer who read entrails of animals or bird signs to predict the outcome of future events

megaron the central hall in a Mycenaean palace, used for banquets, worship and meetings

metae the set of three turning posts located at each end of the spina

metaphor a figure of speech in which a word or phrase is used to describe something that it cannot literally be

metope (pl. **metopes**) square decorative spaces that ran around a Doric temple and could contain sculpture

Minoan civilisation a civilisation based on Crete that influenced neighbouring areas. It lasted from around 3500 BC until around 1400 BC, overlapping in both time and area with the Mycenaean civilisation

mola salsa a mix of salt and flour made by the Vestal Virgins in Rome and sprinkled on the heads of sacrificial victims

mora (pl. **morai**) a name for a Spartan army regiment

mulsum a type of Roman wine sweetened by honey

muse (pl. **muses**) nine sister goddesses who presided over various arts

Mycenaean a civilisation that was powerful from around 1600 BC to 1150 BC, named after the city of Mycenae in southern Greece

navarch the captain of a squadron of Roman naval ships

nemesis the concept of a downfall or undoing after overconfidence or arrogance

noble a member of the upper class in Rome

nostos the desire to return to your homeland

oculus a circular opening at the top of a dome

onager a Roman catapult that fired rocks and large stones at the enemy

opisthodomos the rear room in a temple that contained the city or town's treasures.

optio the centurion's deputy in a Roman legion

oracle an utterance, often ambiguous or obscure, given by a priest or priestess said to be speaking the words of a god

oral culture a society where people rely on word of mouth rather than writing

oral poem a poem that is composed and told without the aid of writing

oral tradition the passing on of information by word of mouth rather than the written word

orchestra in a Roman theatre, the semi-circular area in front of a stage normally reserved for VIP seating

palaestra exercise-ground

Pallas a Giant who fought against the gods, not to be confused with Evander's son, also called Pallas, or with Athena when called Pallas Athena

Panathenaia an annual Athenian festival celebrating Athena's birthday

Panathenaic amphora (pl. **Panathenaic amphorae**) storage jars containing olive oil given as prizes at the Great Panathenaia

pantheon the term given to the gods when we speak of them collectively, not to be confused with the Pantheon in Rome, which was a temple build by the Romans and dedicated to all the gods

parody an exaggerated and comic imitation of the style of a particular writer or genre

Parthenon the temple to Athena built on the Athenian Acropolis

Parthian Empire an empire lying to the east of the Roman Empire, centred on what is now Iran

paterfamilias the male head of a Roman family

pathos literally 'suffering' in Greek, an appeal to the reader's emotions by inviting them to feel pity and sadness

patron a Roman who gives financial or other such support to a client in return for work and favours

patronage the provision of help and support

pax deorum the peace of the gods

pediment triangular area at the top of each end of a temple, which could contain sculpture

pentameter a poetic metre with five units to a line

peplos (pl. **peploi**) a Greek dress

perioeci a class of people who lived in scattered, less fertile parts of Spartan territory

peristyle a colonnaded garden within a Roman domus

personification a figure of speech by which something non-human is given human characteristics

phalanx a Greek rectangular fighting formation in which men fought in massed ranks and tried to force their way through the enemy phalanx opposing them

pietas the most important heroic quality in the *Aeneid*, a Roman virtue that means 'sense of duty', and applies to a man's duty towards his family, his city and his gods

Pisa a town near Olympia in the Greek Peloponnese

pithos (pl. **pithoi**) a large clay storage jar

plebs the lowest social class of Romans, making up the majority of the Roman population

pollution when a person has done something to make them impure in the eyes of the gods

polytheism the belief in many gods

pompe a grand procession

pontifex (pl. **pontifices**) a Roman priest in charge of protecting temples, regulating religious law and overseeing the religious calendar

Pontifex Maximus the head of the pontiffs, greatest pontiff

popa an official at a Roman sacrifice who struck the sacrificial animal with a wooden rod

praefectus the commander of a Roman naval fleet

praetor the second highest category of public official in Rome, responsible for the law courts and imperial administration

praetorium the private quarters of the legatus in a Roman fortress

primi ordines the collective name for the five centurions of the first cohort of a Roman legion

primus pilus the most senior centurion in the Roman legion

principia the headquarters of a Roman fortress

prothesis during the preparation of the body in the Greek world, the deceased would be laid out for two days to receive mourners

public Penates sacred objects dedicated to the city

pyre a funeral mound made of wood on which to cremate a body

pyxis a box, often with a lid, to hold cosmetics or possibly jewellery

relief (from the Latin verb 'relevo', 'to raise') a carving that projects from, and is a part of, the same background material, and has the effect of shading and being in 3D

repoussé a technique where a design is hammered onto an object from the inside of it

rhapsode (pl. **rhapsodes**) someone who recites epic poetry at a festival competition

rhetor a teacher for tertiary-aged boys in the Roman world

rhyton (pl. **rhyta**) a vessel, either in the shape of a cone or animal head, probably for pouring liquid, and made from either pottery or metal

rites of Ceres an ancient Greek religious cult, also known as the Eleusinian Mysteries, in which members were sworn to secrecy

rotunda a round Roman building, especially one with a dome

sanctuary an area of holy land dedicated to a god or gods that contained the temple and altar

sarcophagus (pl. **sarcophagi**) a stone coffin, especially one bearing sculpture and inscriptions

sally port a gap in the outer wall through which defenders could rush out to surprise attackers

satire a genre of writing that aims to show up hypocrisy, pretence or other character flaws through the use of humour

satyrs in myth, half man, half goat attendants of Dionysus, known for their promiscuous nature

scaenae frons the back wall of a stage set in a Roman theatre, usually two or three storeys tall and with elaborate decoration

seer a person who is reputed to be able to see the future

semi-engaged column a supporting column that is embedded in a wall, half protruding from it

senators members of the highest social class in Rome; a senator had to own property worth at least one million sesterces

shaft grave a grave in which a deep shaft was dug and a space created at the bottom for a body, often re-used for later burials

signifer the Roman soldier responsible for the century's standard

simile a figure of speech whereby one thing is compared to another thing of a different kind in order to make a description more vivid

spina the thin dividing bank down the middle of a Roman stadium's racing track.

standard a Roman war flag, the emblem of a century, a set of medallions hoisted on a pole

stanza a verse of poetry with a set metre repeated throughout the poem

stele (pl. **stelai**) stone slabs, often with patterns or images carved on them, most commonly used as tombstones

stilus a pen-like implement used to write on wax tablets

stock character a character in a work of literature or drama who is easily recognisable as a particular type of person from certain behaviour traits

strategos an elected general in the Athenian army; every tribe elected one each year

strigil a curved scraper used to remove oil and dirt from the body

suppliant a person who begs for something from someone in a position of authority

syssitia dining-clubs of about fifteen Spartan citizens, which each met every evening and shared a tent together on campaign. Each man had to contribute food to the mess

tablinum a reception room in a Roman domus, often used as the master's study

Taenarus the traditional entrance to the underworld in the south of the Peloponnese

taxiarch a senior commander in the Spartan army

tepidarium the warm room in a baths complex

tesserarius the Roman soldier in charge of organisation of guards and communication of passwords

testudo a group of Roman soldiers advancing in formation with shields over their heads

Thebes an ancient city in Greece that is the focus of many mythological stories

Theoric Fund a supply of money that was used to pay for the poor to attend the theatre in ancient Athens

Thessaly a region in central Greece

tholos tomb a large domed tomb in the shape of an igloo, roughly circular in its floor space, also known as a beehive tomb

thyrsus a staff associated with the god Dionysus, which was tipped with a pine cone; it could also be intertwined with ivy

Tiber the main river running through Rome

time the honour a Homeric warrior hopes to win

topos (pl. **topoi**) a poetic scene that occurs regularly, which is made up of a series of standard elements

tresantes 'tremblers' – Spartans who had deserted in battle and so been deprived of citizenship

tribes one of ten political constituencies in Athens. Every Athenian citizen belonged to a tribe, which made up a regiment of the Athenian army

tribunes the six senior officers in a Roman legion after the legatus

tribuni angusticlavi the five tribunes of equestrian rank in a Roman legion

tribunus laticlavius the senior tribune of a Roman legion, of senatorial rank

triclinium a dining room in a Roman domus

trierarch wealthy Athenian who captained and paid for the upkeep of a trireme for one year

trireme a Greek warship with three banks of rowers on each side

triumph a grand procession through the streets of Rome to celebrate a military victory

tumulus a raised mound of earth under which bodies were buried

turma a Roman cavalry squadron of 32 horsemen

Vestal (pl. **Vestals**) female priest in charge of the cult of the goddess Vesta

via praetoria the road from the main gate to the principia in a Roman fortress

via principalis the road crossing the camp in front of the principia in a Roman fortress

via quintana the road crossing the camp behind the principia in a Roman fortress

vomitoria the staircases of the amphitheatre, via which people could pour out of the stadium in great numbers

votive an offering to the gods

Vulcanalia a festival held in Rome each year on the 23rd of August in honour of the god Vulcan

wanax the Mycenaean word for a chieftain or king

xenia In Homer, hospitality given unconditionally to a traveller, involving the giving of any help needed; known as 'guest-friendship'

SOURCES OF QUOTATIONS

*Numbers in **bold** refer to page numbers.*

Thematic Study (Myth and Religion)

19 'Muse, tell . . .' Virgil, *Aeneid*, 1.8–11, trans. A. S. Kline; **20** ''I am Demeter . . .' *Homeric Hymn to Demeter*, lines 267–277; 292–315; 399–406, trans. OCR; **22** 'Heracles, Zeus' . . .' *Homeric Hymn* 15, lines 1–3, trans. OCR; **25** 'The Nemean . . .' Hesiod, *Theogony*, 327, trans. H. G. Evelyn-White, *Hesiod: The Homeric Hymns and Homerica* (Cambridge, MA: Harvard University Press, 1914); **25** 'The grisly- minded . . .' Hesiod, *Theogony*, 313, trans. H. G. Evelyn-White; **26** 'Some say . . .' Diodorus Siculus, *Library of History* 4.12.13, trans. C. H. Oldfather, *Diodorus Siculus: Library of History*, vol. 2 (Cambridge, MA: Harvard University Press, 1946), p. 385; **26** 'Heracles shot . . .' Pseudo-Apollodorus, *Bibliotheca*, 2.5.4, trans. J. G. Frazer, *Apollodorus: The Library* (Cambridge, MA: Harvard University Press, 1921); **28** 'Now it . . .' Diodorus Siculus, *Library of History*, 4.13.2, trans. C. H. Oldfather, p. 386; **28** 'Heracles was . . .' Pseudo-Apollodorus, *Bibliotheca*, 2.90, trans. J. G. Frazer; **30** 'He [Eurystheus] . . .' Homer, *Odyssey*, 11.623–626, trans. E. V. Rieu, *Homer: The Odyssey* (London: Penguin, 1991), p. 156; **31** 'Not long . . .' Pseudo-Apollodorus, *Bibliotheca*, 2.7.3, trans. J. G. Frazer; **35** 'Arcadians have . . .' Virgil, *Aeneid*, 8.53–56, trans. A. S. Kline; **35** 'Now look . . .' Virgil, *Aeneid*, 8.193–199, trans. A. S. Kline; **36** 'Now at . . .' Virgil, *Aeneid*, 8.200–204, trans. A. S. Kline; **36** 'At this . . .' Virgil, *Aeneid*, 8.219–224, trans. A. S. Kline; **36** 'Hot with . . .' Virgil, *Aeneid*, 8.230–233, trans. A. S. Kline; **37** 'he threw . . .' Virgil, *Aeneid*, 8.256–262, trans. A. S. Kline; **37** 'By chance . . .' Virgil, *Aeneid*, 8.104–107, trans. A. S. Kline; **37** 'all the . . .' Virgil, *Aeneid*, 8.106–108, trans. A. S. Kline; **38** 'Because of . . .' Virgil, *Aeneid*, 8.268–279, trans. A. S. Kline; **39** 'Theseus having . . .' Ovid, *Metamorphoses*, 8.548–549, trans. A. S. Kline; **39** 'I will . . .' Ovid, *Metamorphoses*, 9.5–7, trans. A. S. Kline; **40** 'Nevertheless he . . .' Ovid, *Metamorphoses*, 9.98–102, trans. A. S. Kline; **40** 'shooting the . . .' Ovid, *Metamorphoses*, 9.127–130, trans. A. S. Kline; **41** 'Nessus trapped . . .' Ovid, *Metamorphoses*, 9.130–132, trans. A. S. Kline; **44** 'Let all . . .' *Homeric Hymn to Demeter*, 270–271, 301–304, trans. J. Cashford, *The Homeric Hymns* (London: Penguin, 2003), p16–18; **50** 'As you . . .' Pausanias, *Description of Greece*, 1.24.5, trans. W. H. S. Jones (Cambridge, MA: Harvard University Press, 1918), p. 123; **50–51** 'In his . . .' Pseudo- Apollodorus, *Bibliotheca*, 3.14.1, trans. J. G. Frazer; **51** 'The statue . . .' Pausanias, *Description of Greece*, 1.24.5–7, trans. W. H. S. Jones; **52** 'Some say . . .' Pausanias, *Description of Greece*, 5.13.8– 11, trans. W. H. S. Jones; **54** 'The god . . .' Pausanias, *Description of Greece*, 5.11.13, trans. W. H. S. Jones; **57–58** 'Since they . . .' Livy, *The Early History of Rome*, 1.7, trans. OCR; **63** 'It has . . .' Cassius Dio, *Roman History*, 53.27.2, trans. Earnest Cary (Cambridge, MA: Harvard University Press, 1917) p.264; **66** 'And now here . . .' Aeschylus, *Seven Against Thebes*, 271–279, trans. Herbert Weir Smyth, *Aeschylus: Persians. Seven against Thebes. Suppliants. Prometheus Bound* (Cambridge, MA: Harvard University Press, 1914); **70** 'Some of . . .' Plutarch, *Life of Theseus*, 6.5, trans. Bernadotte Perrin, *Plutarch Lives*, Vol. I (Cambridge, MA: Harvard University Press, 1914), p. 15; **71** 'he might . . .' Plutarch, *Life of Theseus*, 9.1, trans. Bernadotte Perrin, p. 19–20; **72** 'He is . . .' Pausanias, *Description of Greece*, 1.39.3, trans. W. H. S. Jones; **73** 'Poseidon did . . .' Pseudo-Apollodorus, *Library*, 3.1, trans. J. G. Frazer; **74–75** 'The Athenians . . .' Plutarch, *Life of Theseus*, 35.5–36.2, trans. Bernadotte Perrin, p. 84–85; **77** 'I do . . .' Livy, *The Early History of Rome*, 1, trans. OCR; **77** 'Besides, my . . .' Livy, *The Early History of Rome*, 1, trans. OCR; **77** 'This indulgence . . .' Livy, *The*

Early History of Rome, 1, trans. OCR; **77** 'Anchises, most . . .' *Homeric Hymn to Aphrodite*, 192–201, trans. J. Cashford, p. 93; **80** 'From this point . . .' Livy, *The Early History of Rome*, 1.1, trans. OCR; 'Remus was the . . .' Livy, *The Early History of Rome*, 1.7, trans. OCR; **88** 'The reason . . .' Pausanias, *Description of Greece*, 1.38, trans. W. H. S. Jones; **92** 'This place . . .' Dionysius of Halicarnassus, *Roman Antiquities*, 1.32, trans. Earnest Cary (Cambridge, MA: Harvard University Press, 1937), p. 105; **93** 'Why, you . . .' Ovid, *Fasti*, 23.267–474, trans. A. S. Kline; **94** 'many women . . .' Plutarch, *Life of Caesar*, 61.3, trans. Bernadotte Perrin, *Plutarch Lives*, Vol. VII (Cambridge, MA: Harvard University Press, 1919), p. 585; **96** 'Meanwhile the . . .' Macrobius, *Saturnalia, 1.24.22–23*, trans. Beard, North, Price, *Religions of Rome: A Sourcebook*, Vol. 2, (Cambridge: Cambridge University Press, 1997), p.124; **98** 'Meanwhile the head . . .', trans. Beard, North, Price; 'This place the Romans . . .' Dionysius of Halicarnassus, *Roman Antiquities*, trans. Earnest Cary; **100** 'When Pirithous . . .' Plutarch, *Life of Theseus*, 30.3, trans. Bernadotte Perrin, *Plutarch Lives*, Vol. I; **104** 'Of the . . .' Pausanias, *Description of Greece*, 8.41.7, trans. W. H. S. Jones; **107** 'At the . . .' Augustus, *Res Gestae Divi Augusti*, 1–3, trans. Thomas Bushnell, http://classics.mit.edu/Augustus/deeds.html; **108** 'After putting . . .' Augustus, *Res Gestae Divi Augusti*, 34, trans. Thomas Bushnell; **110** 'After I . . .' Augustus, *Res Gestae Divi Augusti*, 12, trans. Thomas Bushnell; **119** 'The next . . .' Pliny, *Letters*, 7, trans. H. Walker, http://www.vroma.org/~hwalker/Pliny/Pliny07–27-E.html; **121** 'Their shades . . .' Ovid, *Fasti*, 2.535–539, trans. A. S. Kline; **122** 'He who . . .' Ovid, *Fasti*, 5.431–444, trans. A. S. Kline; **123** 'From Bovillae, . . .' Suetonius, *Life of Augustus* 100, trans. Robert Graves, *Suetonius: The Twelve Caesars* (London: Penguin, 1965); **125** 'She made . . .' *Homeric Hymn to Demeter*, 2.305–309, trans. OCR; **125** 'By means . . .' *Homeric Hymn to Demeter*, 2.310–313, trans. OCR; **126** 'I begin . . .' *Homeric Hymn to Demeter*, 2.1–3, trans. OCR; **126** 'Roses and . . .' *Homeric Hymn to Demeter*, 2.7–9, trans. OCR; **126** 'From its . . .' *Homeric Hymn to Demeter*, 2.10–13, trans. OCR; **126** 'He seized . . .' *Homeric Hymn to Demeter*, 2.20, trans. OCR; **126** 'So long . . .' *Homeric Hymn to Demeter*, 2.33–39, trans. OCR; **127** 'A sharp . . .' *Homeric Hymn to Demeter*, 2.33–39, trans. OCR; **127** 'A more . . .' *Homeric Hymn to Demeter*, 2.90–95, trans. OCR; **128** 'She (Demeter) . . .' *Homeric Hymn to Demeter*, 2.305–313, trans. OCR; **128** 'Dark-haired Hades . . .' *Homeric Hymn to Demeter*, 2.305–313, trans. OCR; **128** 'Keep the . . .' *Homeric Hymn to Demeter*, 2.361–369, trans. OCR; **129** 'Child, you . . .' *Homeric Hymn to Demeter*, 2.394–402, trans. OCR; **130** 'To the . . .' Apollodorus, *Argonautica*, 4.898–900, trans. E. V. Rieu (Penguin, 1975); **130** 'Hymen, called . . .' Ovid, *Metamorphoses*, 10.4–7, trans. A. S. Kline; **131** 'When Thracian . . .' Ovid, *Metamorphoses*, 10.11–16, trans. A. S. Kline; **131** 'O gods . . .' Ovid, *Metamorphoses*, 10.18, 32–35, trans. A. S. Kline; **131** 'The bloodless . . .' Ovid, *Metamorphoses*, 10.41–46, trans. A. S. Kline; **132** 'The poet . . .' Ovid, *Metamorphoses*, 10.50–51, trans. A. S. Kline; **132** 'Dying a . . .' Ovid, *Metamorphoses*, 10.60–62, trans. A. S. Kline.

Literature & Culture 1 (The Homeric World)

168 'At his . . .' Homer, *Iliad*, 16.131–44, trans. A. S. Kline; **177** '2 tripod . . .' inscription of Linear B tablet from Palace of Pylos, trans. Michael Ventris (1952), https://linearbknossosmycenae.files. wordpress.com/2015/03/linear-b-tablet-pylos-641–1952-translation- drawing-by-michael-ventris-1952.jpg; **200** 'I am . . .' Homer, *Odyssey*, 9.383–384, trans. A. S. Kline; **202** 'Keep it . . .' Homer, *Odyssey*, 19.486–489, trans. A. S. Kline; **202–203** 'So they . . .' Homer, *Odyssey*, 21.404–411, trans. A. S. Kline; **204** 'Old woman . . .' Homer, *Odyssey*, 19.383–384, trans. A. S. Kline; **204** 'The row . . .' Homer, *Odyssey*, 22.468–472, trans. A. S. Kline; **205** 'The point . . .' Homer, *Odyssey*, 22.16–21, trans. A. S. Kline; **206** 'Devoid of . . .' Homer, *Odyssey*, 9.287–298, trans. A. S. Kline; **207** 'There a . . .' Homer, *Odyssey*, 9.187–190, trans. A. S. Kline; **208** 'These women . . .' Homer, *Odyssey*, 22.462–464, trans. A. S. Kline; **209** 'Good sir . . .' Homer, *Odyssey*, 9.269–271, trans. A. S. Kline; **210** 'But the . . .' Homer, *Odyssey*, 19.332–334, trans. A. S. Kline; **212** 'But though . . .' Homer, *Odyssey*, 19.209–212, trans. A. S. Kline; **212** 'Once ashore . . .' Homer, *Odyssey*, 10.103–106, trans. A. S. Kline; **214** '. . . lopped off . . .' Homer, *Odyssey*, 22.477, trans. A. S. Kline; **215** 'If he . . .' Homer, *Odyssey*, 9.532–535, trans. A. S. Kline; **217** 'When Circe . . .' Homer, *Odyssey*, 10.293–298, trans. A. S. Kline; **219** 'I sacked . . .' Homer, *Odyssey*, 9.40–42, trans. A. S. Kline; **219** 'Where do . . .' Homer, *Odyssey*, 9.252–255, trans. A. S. Kline; **221** 'They groaned . . .' Homer, *Odyssey*, 10.201–202, trans. A. S. Kline; **222** 'Yet despite . . .' Homer, *Odyssey*, 22.236–258, trans. A. S. Kline; **225** 'It's not . . .' Homer, *Odyssey*, 21.251–255, trans. A. S. Kline; **225** 'Remember how . . .' Homer, *Odyssey*, 10.435–437, trans. A. S. Kline; **226** 'My fine . . .' Homer, *Odyssey*, 9.447–448, trans. A. S. Kline; **227** 'why would . . .' Homer, *Odyssey*, 9.351–352, trans. A. S. Kline; **227** 'It is . . .' Homer, *Odyssey*, 21.312–313, trans. A. S. Kline; **229** 'It was . . .' Homer, *Odyssey*, 21.343–345, trans. A. S. Kline. **231** '"Those were his . . .' Homer, *Odyssey*, 10.438–448, trans. A. S. Kline.

Literature & Culture 2 (Roman City Life)

247 'Two of . . .' Cicero, To Atticus 14.9, trans. Jo-Ann Shelton, *As the Romans Did* (Oxford: Oxford University Press, 1997) p. 64; **248** 'We were accompanying . . .' Aulus Gellius, *Attic Nights*, 15.1, trans. J. Renshaw **259** 'Thalamus, his . . .' CIL IV 933, trans. Cooley and Cooley, *Pompeii: A Sourcebook* (London: Routledge, 2004), p. 116; **260** 'Whoever has . . .' CIL IV 8562, trans. Cooley and Cooley, p. 171; **260** 'What do . . .' Martial, *Epigrams*, 9.68, trans. Jo-Ann Shelton, p. 105; **261** 'My slave . . .' CGL III, pp. 645–647, trans. Jo-Ann Shelton, p. 109; **263** 'The student . . .' Cicero, *About the Orator*, 1.17–18, trans. Jo-Ann Shelton, p. 119; **264** 'Let water . . .' CIL IV 7698a–c, trans. Cooley and Cooley, p. 74; **265** 'My slave . . .' CGL III, pp. 645–647, trans. Jo-Ann Shelton; **267** 'On your . . .' Plautus, *The Pot of Gold*, 507ff., trans. Jo-Ann Shelton, p. 127; **269** 'I have . . .' CIL XV 7194, trans. Jo-Ann Shelton, p. 177; **270** 'Ceratus, freedman . . .' CIL IV 910, trans. Cooley and Cooley, p. 116; **271** 'Naevoleia Tyche . . .' CIL X 1030, trans. Cooley and Cooley, p. 152; **273** 'Ceratus, freedman . . .' CIL IV 910, trans. Cooley and Cooley, p. 116; **277** 'The gladiatorial . . .' CIL IV 1189, trans. Cooley and Cooley, p. 52; **284** 'I call . . .' ILS 8753, trans. Jo-Ann Shelton, p. 344; **285** 'Marcus Holconius . . .' CIL X 833, 834, trans. Cooley and Cooley, p. 67; **297** 'What stops . . .' Horace, *Satires*, 1.1.24–5, trans. J. Renshaw; **298** 'Ofellus judges . . .' Horace, *Satires*, 2.2.53– 55, trans. A. S. Kline; **301** 'His words . . .' Horace, *Satires*, 2.6.95–103, trans. A. S. Kline, p. 81; **302** 'I'm not . . .' Horace, *Satires*, 2.6.18–19, trans. A. S. Kline; **306** '. . . then in . . .' Horace, *Satires*, 2.8.14–15, trans. A. S. Kline; **307** 'It's not . . .' Juvenal, *Satires*, 1.30–31, trans. J. Renshaw; **309** 'The place . . .' Juvenal, *Satires* 3.197–199, trans. A. S. Kline; **314** 'Trimalchio clicked . . .' Petronius, *Satyricon*, 27, trans. J. Renshaw; **315** 'Trimalchio himself . . .' Petronius, *Satyricon*, 29, trans. OCR; **316** 'More wine . . .' Petronius, *Satyricon*, 38, trans. OCR; **318** 'You'll credit it . . .' Horace, *Satires* 2.2.112–128, trans. OCR; **322** 'What a . . .' Pliny, Letter 1.9, trans. OCR; **325** 'Some years . . .' Pliny, Letter 5.19, trans. OCR; **327** 'On the . . .' Pliny, Letter 1.9, trans. OCR; **328** 'I was . . .' Horace, *Satire* 2.8, 20–24, trans. OCR, **329** 'When duty . . .' Juvenal, *Satire* 3.239–250, trans. OCR.

Literature & Culture 3 (War and Warfare)

353 'I shall . . .' From *The Oath of Plataea*, trans. Tod II, GHI 204, lines 25–28; **354** 'On the . . .' Xenophon, *Hellenika*, 6.4.16, trans. Rex Warner, *A History of My Times* (Harmondsworth: Penguin, 1966); **354** 'In other . . .' Xenophon, *The Constitution of the Spartans*, 9.4–6, trans. J. M. Moore, *Aristotle and Xenophon on Democracy and Oligarchy* (Berkeley, CA: University of California Press, 2010); **355** 'First then . . .' Herodotus, *Histories*, 7.102, trans. Aubrey de Sélincourt, *Herodotus: The Histories* (London: Penguin, 1996), p. 404; **357** 'Of all . . .' Herodotus, *Histories*, 7.226, trans. Aubrey de Sélincourt, p. 445; **357** 'Go tell . . .' Herodotus, *Histories*, 7.228, trans. Aubrey de Sélincourt, p. 446; **368** 'Spare your . . .' Herodotus, *Histories*, 8.68, trans. Aubrey de Sélincourt, p. 470; **368** 'The shores . . .' Aeschylus, *Persians*, 418–426, trans. Herbert Weir Smyth (London: Heinemann, 1963); **368** 'My men . . .' Herodotus, *Histories*, 8.88, trans. Aubrey de Sélincourt, p. 477; **368** 'One is . . .' Herodotus, *Histories*, 7.139, trans. Aubrey de Sélincourt, p. 415; **380** 'A young . . .' Vegetius, *About Military Matters*, 1.6–7, trans. J. Renshaw; **401** 'Over her . . .' Homer, *Iliad*, 5.347–351, trans. A. S. Kline; **401** 'Diomedes, of . . .' Homer, *Iliad*, 6.212–215, trans. A. S. Kline; **407**

'Astynous and . . .' Homer, *Iliad*, 5.144–158, trans. A. S. Kline; **408** 'As for . . .' Homer, *Iliad*, 5.85–94, trans. A. S. Kline; **409** 'Bright-eyed Athena . . .' Homer, *Iliad*, 5.418–425, trans. A. S. Kline; **411** 'Let us . . .' Homer, *Iliad*, 6.226–229, trans. A. S. Kline; **411** 'Like the . . .' Homer, *Iliad*, 6.146–149, trans. A. S. Kline; **412** 'Hector you . . .' Homer, *Iliad*, 6.429– 432, trans. A. S. Kline; **412** 'May I . . .' Homer, *Iliad*, 6.464–465, trans. A. S. Kline; **412** 'With this . . .' Homer, *Iliad*, 6.464–465, trans. A. S. Kline; **413** 'When they . . .' Homer, *Iliad*, 22.208–214, trans. A. S. Kline; **414** 'But let . . .' Homer, *Iliad*, 22.304–305, trans. A. S. Kline; **414** 'Don't speak . . .' Homer, *Iliad*, 22.345–348, trans. A. S. Kline; **415** 'Great Priam . . .' Homer, *Iliad*, 24.477–483, trans. A. S. Kline; **416** 'Achilles then . . .' Homer, *Iliad*, 24.582–586, trans. A. S. Kline; **417** 'At the shrine . . .' Homer, *Iliad*, 6.297–311, trans. A. S. Kline; **420** 'There is . . .' Plutarch, *Cleomenes*, 2, trans. Richard J. A. Talbert, *On Sparta* (Harmondsworth: Penguin, 1988), p. 99; **421** 'For it . . .' Tyrtaeus, Fragment 10, lines 21–27, trans. OCR; **426** 'Alas, don't . . .' Horace, *Ode 3.2*, lines 9–12, trans. OCR; **433** 'Come then . . .' Virgil, *Aeneid*, 2.707–711; 717, trans. A. S. Kline; **435** 'See, in . . .' Virgil, *Aeneid*, 2.270–273;277–9, trans. A. S. Kline; **436** 'Frantically I . . .' Virgil, *Aeneid*, 2.314–317, trans. A. S. Kline; **436** 'Ashes of . . .' Virgil, *Aeneid*, 2.431–434, trans. A. S. Kline; **436** 'You do . . .' Virgil, *Aeneid*, 2.601–603, trans. A. S. Kline; **437** 'Yours is . . .' Virgil, *Aeneid*, 2.780–784, trans. A. S. Kline; **438** 'Pyrrhus spoke . . .' Virgil, *Aeneid*, 2.547–550, trans. A. S. Kline; **439** 'And when . . .' Virgil, *Aeneid*, 2.518–525, trans. A. S. Kline.

SOURCES OF ILLUSTRATIONS

Forget/Wikimedia; **2.29** Zde/Wikimedia; **2.30** Zde/Wikimedia; **2.31** Schuppi/Wikimedia; **2.32** Sailko/Wikimedia; **2.33** Zde/Wikimedia; **2.34** Zde/Wikimedia; **2.35** Zde/Wikimedia; **2.36a** Zde/Wikimedia; **2.36b** Zde/Wikimedia; **2.36c** Zde/Wikimedia; **2.37** Zde/Wikimedia; **2.38** Xuan Che/Wikimedia; **2.39** Bloomsbury Academic; **2.40** michael clarke stuff/Wikimedia; **2.41** Bloomsbury Academic; **2.42** Zde/Wikimedia; **2.43** Xuan Che/Wikimedia; **2.44** Hay Kranen/ Wikimedia; **2.45** Yorck Project/Wikimedia; **2.46** DEA/S. VANNINI/Getty images; **2.47** DEA/G. DAGLI ORTI/Contributor/Getty images; **2.48** Print Collector/Contributor/Getty images; **2.49** Print Collector/Contributor/Getty images; **3.1** James Renshaw; **3.2** akg images/Peter Connolly; **3.3** Bloomsbury Academic; **3.4** Bloomsbury Academic; **3.5** James Renshaw; **3.6** James Renshaw; **3.7** After S. Nappo (2008); **3.8** James Renshaw; **3.9** James Renshaw; **3.10** After S. Nappo (2008); **3.11** Alastair Thorley; **3.12** Alastair Thorley; **3.13** INTERFOTO/History/Alamy; **3.14** Bettmann/ Contributor/Getty images; **3.15** WolfgangRieger/Wikimedia; **3.16** Print Collector/Contributor/ Getty images; **3.17** Bloomsbury Academic; **3.18** Yann Forget/Wikimedia; **3.19** Walters Art Museum (purchase with funds provided by the S. & A. P. Fund, 1969); **3.20** Pascal Radigue/ Wikimedia; **3.21** James Renshaw; **3.22** DEA/G.DAGLIORTI/Getty images; **3.23** Mentnafunangann/ Wikimedia; **3.24** akg images/Peter Connolly; **3.25** James Renshaw; **3.26** DEA/G. DAGLI ORTI/ Getty images; **3.27** akg images/Peter Connolly; **3.28** G.dallorto/Wikimedia; **3.29** akg images/Peter Connolly; **3.30** Pascal Radigue/Wikimedia; **3.31** Leemage/Contributor/Getty images; **3.32** James Renshaw; **3.33** De Agostini Picture Library/Contributor/Getty images; **3.34** Jebulon/Wikimedia; **3.35** Ad Meskens/Wikimedia; **3.36** James Renshaw; **3.37** Alice Wright; **3.38** After J. Deiss (1985); **3.39** Alastair Thorley; **3.40** Alice Wright; **3.41** Adam Eastland/Alamy Stock Photo; **3.42** James Renshaw; **3.43** Jebulon/Wikimedia; **3.44** James Renshaw; **3.45** DEA/G. DAGLI ORTI/ Contributor/Getty images; **3.46** James Renshaw; **3.47** Yann Forget/Wikimedia; **3.48** DEA PICTURE LIBRARY/Contributor/Getty images; **3.49** Wolfgang Sauber/Wikimedia; **3.50** Sailko/ Wikimedia; **3.51** Bloomsbury Academic; **source p. 335** James Renshaw; **source p. 337** Alastair Thorley; **4.1** Spyros Tragas; **4.2** Image from *The Spartan Army* by Nicholas Sekunda © Osprey Publishing, part of Bloomsbury Publishing Plc; **4.3** Trustees of the British Museum; **4.4** James Renshaw; **4.5** Image from *Thermopylae 480 BC* by Nic Fields © Osprey Publishing, part of Bloomsbury Publishing Plc; **4.6** James Renshaw; **4.7** Alonso de Mendoza/Wikimedia; **4.8** James Renshaw; **4.9** James Renshaw; **4.10** Athina Mitropoulos; **4.11** Image from *Salamis 480 BC* by William Shepherd © Osprey Publishing, part of Bloomsbury Publishing Plc; **4.12** Athina Mitropoulos; **4.13** James Renshaw; **4.14** Image from *Salamis 480 BC* by William Shepherd © Osprey Publishing, part of Bloomsbury Publishing Plc; **4.15** Image from *Salamis 480 BC* by William Shepherd © Osprey Publishing, part of Bloomsbury Publishing Plc; **4.16** akg-images/Peter Connolly; **4.17** Image from *The Roman Army from Caesar* to Trajan by Michael Simkins © Osprey Publishing, part of Bloomsbury Publishing Plc; **4.18** OCR; **4.19** Image from *Roman Legionary Fortresses 27 BC–AD 378* by Duncan B. Campbell © Osprey Publishing, part of Bloomsbury Publishing Plc; **4.20** Image from *The Roman Army from Caesar* to Trajan by Michael Simkins © Osprey Publishing, part of Bloomsbury Publishing Plc; **4.21** Image from *The Roman Army from Caesar* to Trajan by Michael Simkins © Osprey Publishing, part of Bloomsbury Publishing Plc; **4.22** Trustees of the British Museum; **4.23** Conrad Cichorius, 1896; **4.24** Image from *Roman Warships* by Raffaele D'Amato © Osprey Publishing, part of Bloomsbury Publishing Plc; **source p. 383** Image from *Roman Centurions 31 BC – AD 500* by Raffaele D'Amato © Osprey Publishing, part of Bloomsbury Publishing Plc; **4.25** 360b/Shutterstock.com; **4.26** CNG/Wikimedia; **4.27** Image from *Actium 31 BC* by Si Sheppard © Osprey Publishing, part of Bloomsbury Publishing Plc; **4.28** De Agostini/A. Dagli Orti/Getty images; **4.29** DEA PICTURE LIBRARY/Contributor/ Getty images; **4.30** Carole Raddato/Wikimedia; **4.31** CNG/Wikimedia; **4.32** James White; **4.33** Bloomsbury Academic; **4.34** Conrad Cichorius, 1896; **4.35** James White; **4.36** Joe Mabel/ Wikimedia; **4.37** Decan/Wikimedia; **4.38** James Renshaw; **4.39** Hay Kranen/Wikimedia; **4.40** Miguel Hermoso Cuesta/Wikimedia; **4.41** Digital image courtesy of the Getty's Open Content Program; **4.42** Jastrow/Wikimedia; **4.43** Jastrow/Wikimedia; **4.44** Digital image courtesy of the Getty's Open Content Program; **4.45** DEA/G. DAGLI ORTI/Contributor/Getty images; **4.46** Alice Wright; **4.47** Youssefbensaad; **4.48** wjarek/shutterstock.com; **4.49** Bloomsbury Academic; **4.50** Zoran Karapancev/shutterstock.com.

INDEX

Page numbers in **bold** refer to figures.